THE ROMANOVS

OTHER WORKS BY WILLIAM GERHARDI

Novels

FUTILITY
THE POLYGLOTS
JAZZ AND JASPER
PENDING HEAVEN
RESURRECTION
OF MORTAL LOVE
MY WIFE'S THE LEAST OF IT

Short Stories

A BAD END
THE VANITY BAG
PRETTY CREATURES

Drama

DONNA QUIXOTE OR PERFECTLY SCANDALOUS

Criticism and Biography

ANTON CHEHOV

Autobiography

MEMOIRS OF A POLYGLOT
RESURRECTION

Collaborations

THE MEMOIRS OF SATAN
  (*With Brian Lunn*)
THE CASANOVA FABLE
  (*With Hugh Kingsmill*)
MEET YOURSELF:
CHARACTER STUDIES THROUGH SELF-ANALYSIS
  (*With Prince Leopold Loewenstein*)

THE
ROMANOVS

EVOCATION OF THE PAST AS
A MIRROR FOR THE PRESENT

by William Gerhardi

O.B.E., B.LITT., M.A. (OXON.)

NEW YORK · G. P. PUTNAM'S SONS

Designed by Robert Josephy

TO

PATRICIA

IN UNDYING AFFECTION, GRATITUDE

AND REGARD

CONTENTS

BOOK THREE

BOOK FOUR

AN HISTORICAL CREDO

THE historian, a dealer in astonishing facts, is, when capable of astonishment, astonished at some mass accomplishment of endurance. The Pyramids! The Roman roads! The Forth Bridge! A confession of a brittle imagination incapable of stretching sufficiently to conceive even of that which has clearly proved itself to be possible.

But he is not astonished at the absolutely incredible: why the individual human being, who is the focal point, the spearhead of sensibility, the residence of consciousness—*that's* where it hurts, where the damage is done—should, complacently, rank last in the hierarchy of human values.

❧

If he thinks at all in terms of human happiness, our insensate historian is prepared to sacrifice the suffering unit for the greatest happiness of the greatest number—a phrase coined by Jeremy Bentham, and which is used to excuse the actual unhappiness of large numbers on the ground that they are contributing to the hypothetical happiness of the rest. If the historian has a tear to spare, it is not for the suffering unit, but again for an abstraction. He is appalled at mere numbers—two million dead! Two million don't feel anything.

❧

Why does the "serious" historian write like this:

The rapid development of commerce and agriculture imperatively required an outlet to the sea, this necessitating a bold expansionist policy which drew heavily on the available man-power, large numbers, variously estimated between one and two hundred thousand, falling in the first unsuccessful assault undertaken with a view to strengthening the position of the left flank of General A's Army Corps, in the campaign which preluded the incorporation of the Dnieper basin?

❧

It is easy to understand why statesmen and generals in the rough and tumble of danger should assign lasting consequences to their own decisions, while regarding the maiming, blinding and killing of the individual involved in the result as of a passing nature.

What is more difficult to assimilate is why historians, who have the advantage of a perspective of years and calm reflection in which to envisage the ravages caused by wars promoted in pursuance of policies which cancel themselves out, should echo the generals and statesmen.

∾

This is frightening. It is a cog come loose in the human consciousness. It is man having taken leave of his senses on the most crucial point of life. Not indeed the man of battle in the heat of excitement—you might expect that—but reflective man, *homo multarum literarum,* the sage, the *savant,* the historian, the academician, the longhead, the *esprit fort,* man at his leisure reclining in his chair before his large desk in a well-appointed library of cumulative knowledge, and taking stock of the world.

∾

Divinity, entire and indivisible, descends into each individual whole and unsplit as if he alone had being: each of the Many is indeed the One. (A *dimmed* One; yet differentiated only in degree and variety of dimness.) But the historian's is a wholesale business; he deals in great numbers of people: that is to say, deals in unrealities. When the poet garners "emotion recollected in tranquillity," the historian is merely unable to recollect other people's emotion.

History as we know it is, therefore, always history of the unreal, of the unfeeling, of the phantasmic—indeed, of the insane. It acquires value only in satire; humanity only in indignation; sanity only in recognition of the criminal lunacy of a state of affairs which, in deference to unfeeling and ever-receding abstractions, always sends the suffering unit packing.

∾

The truism that the individual cannot be considered because his name is legion has never been anything but an excuse for sacrificing him in his legions. Again—for whom?

∾

On the rare occasions on which our insouciant historian does feel anything for the individual, it is only for the individual who has killed in great numbers. Unhappy Frederick toying with the truly terrible idea

of suicide! Poor Napoleon on St. Helena! What that dear man must
have suffered!

∽

The only pity which stirs pity in most people is self-pity. Napoleon,
who slaughtered some ten million men on the battlefields and reduced
by three inches the whole subsequent stature of Frenchmen, is sincerely
sorry for himself. That seems to get everybody.

The grueling humiliation and disappointment suffered in love, through
the fault of Napoleon, by some undersized republican of today gets
nobody.

∽

"What," Lytton Strachey asks, "are the qualities that make a historian?"
And he answers his question: "Obviously these three—a capacity for
absorbing facts, a capacity for stating them, and a point of view. The
two latter are connected, but not necessarily inseparable. The late Profes-
sor Samuel Gardiner, for instance, could absorb facts, and he could state
them; but he had no point of view; and the result is that his book on
the most exciting period of English history resembles nothing so much
as a very large heap of sawdust."

∽

The incomplete academic person adheres to the pedantic tradition that
a point of view is unscholarly. "To understand everything is to pardon
everything" might pass as his point of view, if he could be credited with
anything half so human.

∽

But if moral judgment in relation to the individual is regrettable,
history is but a sorry compilation of facts if it is not also, *by implication,*
a moral indictment of the crime against the individual. Morality was
never meant for man, who suffers individually, but for systems and institutions, which would not suffer from improvement.

∽

History must be *morally* accurate—accurate in the relation of what
has been done to what has been suffered. Otherwise it is no more human
history than a timetable is a book, and might just as well have been
compiled by a dispassionate observer from Mars or some human moron
or monster.

∽

History must at last convince of the uselessness of insensate mass movements riding roughshod, now as ever, over anonymous suffering and claiming priority in the name of some newly clothed abstraction. If it does not teach that, it does not teach anything.

∽

But the stiff-jointed historian does not unbend himself to assign the individual man's case even a place in his tome.

Instead, he writes weightily of political necessities, strategic reasons, politico-economic causes. That sounds important and scholarly.

∽

Europe has not redeemed its past, and thus has not conquered it. Historians have made light of the crime against the individual, have slurred over that which it should have been their duty to expose and lash with their wit. History as we know it has always bowed down before the successful and let bygones be bygones.

∽

Under the disguise of abstaining from judgment, the scholar has merely echoed the bias of the time, so perpetuating the glory of the tyrant, usurper and bully, to give heart to bullies as yet unborn.

Nor need he have raved and screamed. Through the wise economy of his art, by husbanding his natural humor and irony, applying emotional restraint in situations which engage the emotions, he could have thrown into relief the suffering of the individual; while, by seeing the result of treaties in perspective, instead of through the eyes of their authors, he could have given us what is in truth history—human life in perspective.

∽

This is where the films (if the men who make them could be credited with sufficient sense to perceive the "human interest" for which they are alleged to be seeking) could do a great deal to correct these insidious human mistakes. Instead of blithering tinselly romances, how much more interesting to see historic figures in real situations!

What was interesting in *Marie Walewska* was not Greta Garbo as Walewska, or Napoleon's love for her, but seeing Napoleon as it were in the flesh. Taking the Tsars—or any other human landmarks—the film could give us genuine human history in perspective, the grandest cavalcade, on the one hand, and the most poignant theme, on the other: the truly historic way we sacrifice the suffering unit for the sake of distant and unfeeling abstractions. Treasures of history lie buried and untapped: single films revealing long vistas of compressed human drama seen in perspective; trilogies enhancing the same effect. But "the industry" can think only of tinsel romances!

∽

What irritates is the bloated solemnity of the ordinary history as it treats of farcical happenings. If you ask me: can princes and governments behave quite as idiotically as, for example, Kaiser Franz and Frederick William III in the present volume? I answer that they do, as a matter of consistent practice, today as ever, behave idiotically, and in no other way idiotically than as King Frederick William and Kaiser Franz and Napoleon and Alexander.

But you would never think so on reading a historian, who uses the same language about these past imbecilities as contemporary statesmen about their present ones.

∽

Such all-too-ready approbation of the current delusions of the past hardly merits the respect which might be felt for one elevated above human passion and error, a lighthouse for the coming generations. The apologist of the past is the one ready, we feel, to step himself into the ranks of contemporary chicanery and bias and play his part of advantage, not enlightened by knowledge of past facts and the wiser inferences to be drawn therefrom.

∽

It is a terrible inheritance—our imbecile past—pointlessly cruel, abjectly sordid. But it has been conventionalized and made respectable by historians over-eager to enter into the spirit of the times so as to show off their scholarship. We have allowed them to dress and prepare it for us, and have swallowed our past, just as they have served it up to us, over-cooked, over-seasoned with pleasant spices, great big chunks of untruth floating in the sauce of hypocrisy; and though we have decimated it we have not digested it. And our present world malady is no other than historical indigestion.

∽

History is neither exact nor unfeeling enough to be a science. The scientific historian divested of feeling might, if he cares so to employ his time, prove the resurgence and prosperity of races and nations in certain, say, uncomfortable circumstances; and from this deduce that we should not only disregard the pain occasioned to the individual by poison gas, aerial bombardment or a bayonet in the intestines, but positively seek fresh opportunities to plunge the suffering unit into conditions of privation, nay, partial extermination by fire and water, with a view to developing stamina in the distant descendants surviving such salutary ordeals and breeding a hardy maritime race, with inestimable benefits to accrue in the following century from trade with the Levant.

If so—what? Our scientific historian (and we do not lack such amphibians) will prove—what? That he is, like Herbert Spencer, gifted with an extraordinary faculty for building general ideas round insignificant facts.

∾

What the historian knows is but a fraction of what he cannot in any circumstances know. History can be completely, if insignificantly, accurate. But to inflict such authenticity on the eager student of human affairs is like taking advantage of a trusting child to acquaint it with the timetables of forty years ago of the London and South Eastern Railway— accurate to a fault!

∾

Being human, history is an art. It communicates to the reader the effect of recorded events upon the not wholly insensitive retina of the writer.

∾

But if history is an art, it must have artistic form; which is the natural fusion of subject and expression. What is wrong with most history? Precisely this—defective artistic form.

∾

It is notorious that mankind, considered as a chain of generations, has proved itself incapable of learning the lessons of history because the new generation cannot feel the emotions of revulsion experienced by a previous generation, and so blithely commits the same errors, only to feel in due course the same revulsion and disappointment; which, again, it cannot communicate to the rising generation.

∾

As with life, so with history. Were our memories such that we could retain all the lessons of history, the total effect would correspond to a moral conclusion which would necessarily change the course of subsequent history. But we learn nothing because history as it is written mimics the shortcomings of experience. It rounds off each successive period and starts cheerily on the next, oblivious of the salutary effect of historical perspective, which reveals that the fortunes of war and the rise and fall of nations when seen in quick movement are like a run of red and black on the roulette, of no abiding interest to man, who would do well to turn his face away from such futile hazards.

❧

In other words, the non-artistic historian leaves it to the reader to do all the work. And if the net effect left on the student of history is one of rapid evaporation, it is no concern of the historian. "It's all there between the covers," he says in effect. "I have compiled the facts; you'll find them there. If it is more than your memory can carry, it is also more than my own could have retained. Hence do as I have done: shut off one compartment of your mind as you open another. You have my book for reference. It has an index." And that is all *he* cares.

❧

Such history today is like a modern flat that has not been wired for electricity. It has no points to plug a light in—consequently no glow which should remain in the mind long after the reader has put down the book. The ideal history should be so "wired" that one lamp lights up another—till they all glow cozily in the mind.

❧

How often one hears it said, "Whenever I hear of a new book I open an old one."

The absurdity of such a boast becomes apparent when one reads in old books of the same self-satisfied claim being made in the days of Proust, Chekhov, Tolstoy, Thackeray, Pushkin, Wordsworth, Goethe, Fielding, Cervantes.

A better case can be made in the sphere of action. When the air is thick with dictators, strife, politics and contention, it is illuminating to read of old times, old despots, old wars, old peacemaking.

❧

While art constantly renews the spirit, action rooted in collective self-approbation merely repeats itself.

Whether men kill for the glory of ancient Rome or the Third Reich, it is always the same kind of glory, the same kind of killing, the same kind of men, and the same kind of lies.

All Caesars are alike as peas, treading the same donkey-round of power and ambition with not a new idea in their skulls.

∽

In these days when the dictators, in pursuance of what they think is a philosophy, and new at that, assume autocratic power, not indeed by "divine right," but by virtue of an "ideology" which, though itself devoid of any thought, yet devours the one ideology meriting the name—to wit, the legal integrity of the individual—it is interesting to follow the careers and personalities of the autocrats and self-upholders by "divine right"— the Tsars, Emperors and Empresses of Russia, to see what *they* made of it and what their subjects made of *them*.

For the past puts a fine edge on our own days. It tells us more of the present than the present can tell us.

∽

Events, recent or ancient, are all equally past for us, and should be sifted and interposed in the manner making them most present to us.

Figures of history must be loosened from their umbilical cords which tie them, each to his period. They must be free to move and meet their fellows across the illusions of centuries.

It is therefore meet that we present them not in order of time, but of interest. History should weave a tapestry of interest.

∽

If we leave a preliminary period till we have dealt with a crowded epoch following on its heels, the initial stage will be more interesting by reason of our foreknowledge of the important consequences of its modest beginnings.

If, for example, we had known of the impending German-Soviet non-aggression pact at the time of the Anglo-Franco-Russian talks in Moscow our interest in the said talks would have been more illuminating.

∽

History, in other words, should be "telescoped" by the historian himself. Since all these things, *all* of them, belong to the past, why should we narrate history in single file? Why suppress relevant facts lying ahead in order of time and tell things as though we had only just learned of them as they percolate to us through the Late News column in the *Evening Standard*?

History fails to carry its point unless it is brought home into the present —a stranger entering our parlor.

◇

Cumulative historical interest is best achieved by building up the narrative on the principle that we want to know more of what we know a little, but do not want to know anything of what we know nothing.

Why?

Man, to maintain his self-esteem, must feel he is complete. New information springs a leak in his hull, and he hastens to repair the damage. That of which he is not aware cannot enter the enclosure of his preconceptions. Whatever knowledge or presumption there be gathered inside him is hermetically enclosed in that which lies outside his ken. Be he ever so ignorant, he is not sensible of aught but what he thinks he knows; and whatever fills him constitutes his sense of intellectual completeness.

The complete man may sometimes be a fool. Even so, he will be a complete fool.

◇

Initial interest, then, can be kindled by advance information of that which is to come. When more is at hand the reader, from motives of discomfort arising from incompletion, will be tempted by the little he already knows to complete his information.

◇

History, being for the writer a method of associative presentation, is, for the reader, a pursuit of recognition. The reader's emotion should be expressed in a recognitory: "Ah!"

By implication, history can be a running commentary on the events now developing before our eyes. In the mirror of the past the perceptive reader should be able to see the face of the present.

◇

In a sense, history does repeat itself, and precisely because, sooner or later, if he waits long enough, it provides every politician with the event which justifies his prediction.

The Liberal, who advocated letting Germany off lightly after the last war in order to encourage a democratic government in Germany, points the accusing finger at the French, who marched into the Ruhr and thus gave birth to Nazi Germany, and says: "There! I told you so—Hitler!" The Diehards, who would have kept a Franco-British garrison on the

Rhine for the term of this planet's natural life, point to the same belligerent phenomenon and say: "There! What did I tell you—Hitler!"

◇

The same with tariffs, which are, alternately, a cog in the wheels of trade and the cause of prosperity, and, whichever view you take, will in turn bear out your warning and confirm your prophecy.

And in this sense, since we ignore it when it proves us wrong but bide our time till it proves us right, history is encouraged to repeat itself. Each faction but deduces from it its own prejudice, and it is this alternate current that makes history go round.

◇

To transfer, by implication, the past, intact, into our times, provides for deliberate composition on the part of the writer dealing with a mass of intractable material without, however, curtailing the liberty of the reader, who is left to draw his own conclusions.

There should be a disinclination on the part of the writer to draw some one definite conclusion—necessarily narrow and arbitrary—and he should be content with a broad composite effect of irony, of incredulity, of deep wonderment, a sorrowful perplexity, an unfocused longing that life should either change or cease.

Once the broad total effect of a history has been gauged, the writer sets to work as in any other work of art—a poem, a novel, a play—to arrive at the desired cumulative effect. Art being the most effective statement of a perceived truth.

◇

It is obvious that a narrative covering a thousand years of history cannot, on the balance of suffering *versus* achievement, whether considered individually or collectively, produce a very heartening effect, except as a result of much artificial expurgation or through a naturally defective memory.

Ours is a new, a nascent mood. History, said always to repeat itself, has been playing out its variations on familiar themes too long; and this old Europe is a little weary. It is not clear to us what the new mood is. All we know is that we can't stand any more of the old. For my part, having familiarized myself in four languages with the last one thousand years of European history, and being confronted daily by more history in the making, I feel like addressing a note of warning to the present rulers of the world: Now, now! Kind I am, patient I am. I still have faith. But do not push me too far. . . .

⌒

Such associative presentation of the past, with a retarded design becoming increasingly apparent, must in some manner be akin to work on a tapestry. But in its cumulative reiteration of the essential absurdity, of the repetitive foibles and cruelties of history, it resembles nothing so much as that matchless description by Proust of those long-necked sinuous phrases of Chopin, so free and flexible and tactile, which begin by essaying their steps outside and out of reach of their starting place, wide of the mark at which one might have hoped that they would attain their consummation, and that whirl away on their truant's flight of fantasy merely to return with more deliberation, a recoil more premeditated, with more precision, like some crystal bowl which will ring till you could scream, as they beat against your heart.

WILLIAM GERHARDI.

Rossetti House,
  Hallam Street,
    *London, W.*1.
August, 1939.

THE ROMANOV DYNASTY

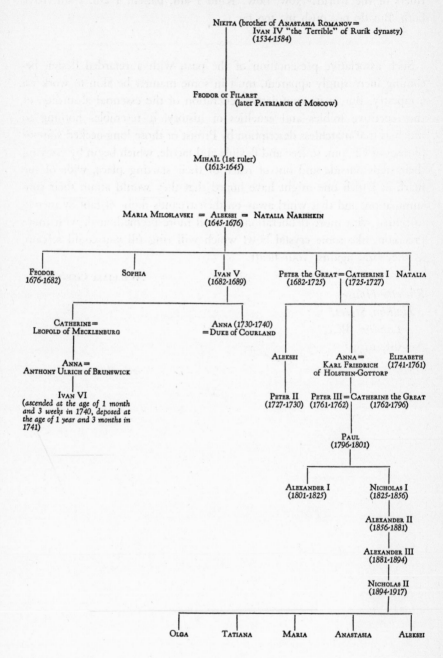

BOOK ONE

AFTER THE ABDICATION

I. NICHOLAS COMES HOME

EVEN before the white and gold imperial train had come to a stand-still in the station at Tsarskoye Selo, most of the courtiers and officers composing His Majesty's suite had gained the platform and taken to their heels, scattering in all directions.

Haste, indeed, was not to be despised in the gathering shadows of Petrograd, ill-disposed to the lackeys of a sovereign it had deposed with an enthusiasm far more wholehearted than it had ever been capable of exhibiting at the spectacle of him at the helm, even upon that day in 1914 when, as he appeared on the balcony of the Winter Palace, the people thronging the immense cobbled square below had sunk on their knees and burst into that musically most satisfying of national anthems: "God Save the Tsar."

"Down with Nicholas Romanov!" was the 1917 version of patriotism, even more symbolic of Russian national unity than the opening words of the anthem invoking the Deity to preserve the life of their sovereign. They had at last had enough of him. For a Russian emperor was not, as the King of England is, a perpetual expression of national self-approbation—the Nation, in fact, wearing royal purple to pat itself the more agreeably on the back. The English political genius, evolving the maxim that the throne is greater than the man, makes the sovereign feel he is a tenant who occupies it by courtesy of a people expecting that the civilities and good will must be mutual. And the longer he occupies it, the greater the marvel at his patience, fortitude and endurance in a position recognized on every side as being all but untenable.

The Russian national anthem, like the English, exhorts that the tsar should reign to the glory of his people. It exhorts also, parallel with the English requirement that God should confound the king's enemies, that the tsar should reign to the terror of foes. But there is no "long may he reign."

Which, perhaps, is not surprising when the tsar is king, president, prime minister, archbishop, judge, chief of police rolled into one, and persists in being all these things till God Himself grows bored with him and calls him away. "May it be soon," is almost a mental reservation of the Russian national anthem.

The Romanov genius indeed has never been political, having in the space of three hundred years evolved nothing more constitutional than absolute monarchy tempered by assassination. Nicholas was pushed not merely off the throne, but out of life. Alexander II was blown up in his carriage. Alexander I, after playing every variation on the theme of Self-Upholder of All the Russias, faked his own death, took a staff— and went, feeling that the farther he got, the better. The mad Paul, and the queer Peter before him, were both assisted out of life almost as soon as they had, after years of trying apprenticeship, climbed impatiently to the throne. And great Catherine, after reigning illegally for a third of a century, suddenly, as if struck by the enormity of her conduct, fell on the floor in a fit of apoplexy. Peter the Great, monstrously cruel and callous, died a natural death groaning and yelling in agony. And his grandfather, the gentle Mihaïl, the first of the Romanovs, who enjoyed a long and quiet reign, died, we are told, of melancholy.

The first and the last of the Romanovs bore a remarkable likeness in feature and character, the last tsar developing in his days of captivity a blankness of mind, a resignation, surpassing the melancholy of the founder of his house and which a Bolshevik guard describes unkindly as "Nikolai Romanov's almost imbecile indifference to his surroundings." Already in the middle of his reign, Nicholas II was in the habit of confiding in men who he thought envied him his destiny that only his promise to his father to do his duty had kept him from throwing up his job of being tsar. "I have all my life," he confessed, "only done what I was told it was my duty to do. I did not want to be emperor; but they told me it was my duty to ascend the throne, and I ascended the throne. They told me it was my duty to marry, and I married. Then it was my duty to go to war, and I went to war. Afterwards I was told it was my duty to make peace, and I made peace."

At last other men, whom it had been his duty to suppress, told him the country demanded his abdication; and, under pressure of events, he complied, adding in his manifesto that he had become convinced the salvation of Russia necessitated his retirement from the helm. Then, having formally relinquished his supreme command at the front, he now returned from headquarters to the bosom of his family. The ex-Tsar Nicholas II, the last of his dynasty, stepped out of an all but empty train, his glittering staff, once so precipitantly obeisant, having for the most part dispersed with astonishing alacrity and left him alone on the station platform.

The Tsar walked calmly to the car which awaited him and took his seat as though he assumed that he was not less the emperor for having surrendered his sovereignty on demand. For Nicholas II had been trained for the job, and he had not been trained for anything else. Man and boy he had been at that grind since he was weaned. After twenty-three years of wondering hourly in what circumstances he might explode, being Emperor of Russia had become a habit he could not shed overnight. And that he had complied with the request to vacate the throne of his ancestors had satisfied him that all was well now; that, having paid the price of his liberty, nobody could in reason demand anything more of him.

There by the side of him in the car was Prince Dolgorukov, a general-in-attendance to whom he had hitherto shown very little favor but who now, alone of the brilliant suite, accompanied his master to the Palace guarded by the hostile troops gone over to the Revolution. Some of the others, however, percolated through a little later.

When the car was at the gate, a dilatory soldier with a red badge on his cap and no shoulder straps kept them waiting till he was persuaded to go to fetch the keys. He sulkily opened the gate and as the car drove in he demonstratively abstained from saluting. But the Tsar, as the car swung past into the courtyard, returned the absent salute as though he could not do otherwise than assume that the guard had presented arms.

II. MEEK-EYED NICHOLAS LAYS DOWN THE BURDEN

IN a moment he would be with his wife. Perhaps he would have to face the music? For the Empress Alexandra, having been born as an inconspicuous German princess, laid great store by Russian absolutism and had always urged her husband Nicky to be a Peter the Great and never surrender a tittle of his autocratic powers. Her last message had been: "Concessions are necessary." But he had surrendered all his prerogatives at one go.

Events had followed each other like a quick-motion film. Enjoying till a week ago the position of absolute autocrat, but warned and pulled simultaneously in all directions, Nicholas II, a target for every party in the State, including factions in the family, was in reality the most helpless and befuddled man in Russia. Having left with his Minister of the Interior a signed manifesto ordering the dissolution of the Duma, to be put in force at the Minister's discretion, the Tsar had proceeded with profound relief to Headquarters at the Front, where he felt happiest and safest in the bosom of his loyal army.

He had appointed himself Supreme Commander in Chief of the Russian Armies, against the advice of General Brusilov, who doubted whether the Tsar's total lack of military talent, supported by a stubborn but vacillating will, fitted him for the post.

But Nicholas saw it from a different angle. The Front was the safest place for any Tsar of Russia, soldiers being notoriously patriotic, monarchical and absolutist to the last degree. There had been schisms in the High Command. Grand dukes had taken sides. Decisions had to be taken for and against this or that general or grand duke being appointed the new Commander in Chief; and it occurred to Nicholas II that to appoint himself was indeed the happiest solution. In relieving him of the necessity to weigh rival claims, it made the least demands on his brain power. "My brain," he notes in his diary, "is resting here. No Ministers. No troublesome questions demanding thought."

In Petrograd everyone had been getting at him. But here, at General Headquarters in Moghilëv, he could lead a healthy routine existence, take his daily walks and drives. There was nothing so safe for a tsar as going to war. He was shielded all round from the bombs of urban revolutionaries by the entire strength of his armies, reinforced by those of the enemy.

The Russian newspapers depicted the Tsar as never abating his vigil. While his lowly subjects snored luxuriously in trench and dugout, while commanders and generals sprawled in deep sleep on feather beds, a light in one window burned steadfastly through the night: the Tsar was working.

Indeed, everything was going quite well. The war had settled into a steady routine. Ministers could not get at him. His uncles had been told to mind their own business. All went on tolerably smoothly. At any rate he had gained a breathing space. And he was therefore a little annoyed when, soon afterwards, the President of the Duma, Rodzianko, telegraphed as follows:

There is anarchy in the Capital. The Government is paralyzed. It is necessary immediately to entrust with the formation of the Government a person who enjoys the confidence of the country. Any delay is fatal.

He was irritated when Rodzianko, who should have accepted the snub of being imperially ignored, followed his initial importunity with another and a worse next day:

The situation is growing worse. Measures must be adopted immediately, because tomorrow will be too late. The last hour is come, when the fate of the Fatherland and the dynasty is being decided.

"The Tsar remarked to his Headquarter's staff: "This fat-bellied Rodzianko has written me some nonsense to which I will not even reply."
The Emperor completed the routine of his duties. He dined as usual, sitting long over his drinks and avoiding any discussion which savored of "shop"; and after dinner he liquidated this matter, still pending, with a telegram to General Khavalov in Petrograd:

I command you to suppress from tomorrow all disorders on the streets of the capital, which cannot be permitted when the Fatherland is carrying on a difficult war with Germany.

NICHOLAS.

The Minister of the Interior, Protopopov, having dissolved the Duma with the document previously signed by the Emperor, took flight and next day presented himself before the Duma members, who had ignored the order of dissolution, to seek protection for himself from the mob hot on his trail. All the garrison had now gone over to the Revolution; and the Grand Duke Nicholas, the Tsar's uncle, together with several other grand dukes, all telegraphed to him the melancholy but certain fact that his authority was gone and that the Duma alone exercised a precarious and declining control over the capital, where anarchy was reigning.

Even the frail, thin-lipped Empress, who had steadfastly urged her darling husband Nicky to emulate the drastic brutality of the founder of St. Petersburg and resist all demands for a constitution, now telegraphed feebly that the Palace at Tsarskoye Selo, with her children and herself, was surrounded by hostile red troops, and urged that "concessions are necessary."

The Tsar, who in the past had weakly resented his wife's admonitions to stand firm when he had been in the mood to compromise, now took a strong line and refused all concessions. He telegraphed that he was well, was returning to Petrograd, adding: "lovely weather." He left Headquarters for Petrograd, having instructed General Russki to march on the capital and quell the Revolution.

General Russki's army, on approaching Petrograd, joined in with the revolutionaries, and the Tsar's own train was stopped on the way and was turned off to Pskov. Whereupon the Emperor dispatched the following telegram:

HIS IMPERIAL MAJESTY THE EMPEROR TO PRESIDENT OF THE DUMA, RODZI-ANKO, QUOTE WILL NOW MAKE THE NECESSARY CONCESSIONS UNQUOTE NICHOLAS.

He received the following reply:

FROM PRESIDENT OF THE DUMA, RODZIANKO, TO HIS IMPERIAL MAJESTY THE EMPEROR QUOTE IT IS TOO LATE UNQUOTE RODZIANKO.

Two days later, by which time the Revolution had swept over the entire country and the idea of having any emperor at all became repugnant to the people, who felt in no wise indebted to the Crown for having brought about the Revolution, Nicholas abdicated in the following terms:

We Nikolai the Second Aleksandrovitch, by the will of God, Sovereign-Emperor, Self-Upholder of All the Russias, Tsar of Poland, Grand Duke of Finland, etc., etc., to all our faithful subjects:

In agreement with the State Duma we have deemed it good to abdicate the crown and lay down the supreme power. Not wishing to be separated from our beloved son, we leave our heritage to our brother, His Imperial Highness the Grand Duke Mihaïl Aleksandrovitch.—NICHOLAS.

There were references to the country's overwhelming struggle with a cruel enemy, a struggle which, the Tsar stated, could only be overcome by a united nation, while he, it seemed, stood in the way. The ceremony of abdication took place in the imperial train at a siding at Pskov. One of the two members of the Duma who delivered the ultimatum was overcome by the pathos of the Tsar's abdication. The other, Gutchkov, whom the Emperor disliked, made a long formal speech, stipulating somewhat sternly that the Duma required the Emperor to abdicate in favor of his son, with the Tsar's brother, the Grand Duke Michael, as regent. Nicholas listened politely to the triumphant speech of his life-long enemy and at the end of it stated quietly that he had already made up his mind to abdicate for himself and his son as well in favor of his brother Michael.

Gutchkov, now abashed by this double gesture and moved by the display of parental tenderness, agreed on his own authority and that of his colleague. But there are those who say that in making this decision the Tsar had sealed his own doom and that of his family. The country was still in the mood for a boy emperor with a fairly enlightened uncle for regent. But when the manifesto naming the Grand Duke Michael as imperial successor was brought back by Gutchkov and his colleague to Petrograd, the Duma could muster no enthusiasm for another adult wearing the Russian crown. The Grand Duke Michael himself declined the honor, unless elected by the Constituent Assembly when the war was over.

After the abdication the Emperor returned to Headquarters to take leave of his generals. He seemed in no hurry to return to Petrograd. If we recall the bearing in similar circumstances of Charles I of England and Louis XVI of France, we see that a monarch stepping down from his throne cannot immediately get used to the glaring disparity between the position he now occupies in the estimation of his late subjects and that which he maintains in the eyes of God as whose anointed representative he continues to regard himself. At Headquarters the Tsar went for his usual motor ride and performed his customary constitutional. He still occupied his comfortable quarters. At last it was arranged that he should take leave of the vast Headquarters' staff at a brief ceremony to take place the day before his inevitable return to Petrograd, where he was to lead the life of a private citizen. The brilliant staffs, a little uneasy at the rapid spread of events, assembled in the big hall, awaiting the appearance of their emperor. He appeared. There was a curious expression on his face, a strange flicker of a smile: half grin, half stare. His mouth seemed strangely twisted. It was as if he were conscious at once of the pathos and the foolishness of his position. But he spoke firmly and, in the well-worn words of a retiring manager, he thanked them for their loyal co-operation and expressed the hope that the good cause they all had at heart would not suffer materially by his taking a back seat. He stressed the necessity for the war to continue and he urged his successors to prosecute it with vigor till complete victory was achieved.

III. MOTHER AND SON

THEN he was driven to the station, where he entrained. He was informed that the train of his mother, the Dowager Empress Maria

Feodorovna, bound for Kiev, was due in, and some minutes later he left his train and entered his mother's. Maria Feodorovna, a sister of Queen Alexandra, had in her time frequently urged her son (who because of his diminutive stature compared with that of his giant father, Alexander III, seemed to her unequal to the task of ruling Russia without his mother) to be firm when her son showed signs of wanting to be conciliatory, and to be conciliatory when he wished to show he could be firm. Now she cast eyes at him, eyes full of woe, saying only too eloquently that if *only* he had listened to her, things would not have come to such a pass. For an hour they were closeted in the private saloon of the empress-mother and no one knows what was said by meek-eyed Nicholas or by his Danish mother who had reared him for the Russian throne.

When their tête-à-tête was interrupted at last, the intruders observed an embarrassing scene. The empress-mother was sobbing bitterly, weeping freely and without restraint; and her son sat silently with averted gaze fixed guiltily at the carpet.

Mother and son lunched together. In the first years of his reign they had exchanged frequent letters and each had praised in turn, now the financial, now the social, now the imperial, administration of "dear Papa," whose foresight and perspicacity had raised the State to a pitch of security it had not enjoyed before. And now—how it would have grieved poor dear Papa!—as they were finshing their meal, there it lay all about them in fragments, like a costly china clock her dear Nicky had once inadvertently brushed off the mantelpiece with his sleeve. That the empress-mother who had—or thought she had—ably assisted the work of her late husband, the broad, bearded giant, Alexander III, in securing firmly the foundations of the empire, did not openly reproach her son with the machinations of his wife, did not detract from the implication in her eyes, all the more pointed for what she left unsaid. When Maria Feodorovna's train went past the stationary train of the Emperor, he looked at her for the last time through the window.

They never saw each other again. She was speeding towards Kiev. He was going back to Petrograd to face the music.

IV. NICHOLAS BROUGHT BACK BY THE PEOPLE

WHEN the Emperor's train moved out of the station, his late Chief of Staff, now Commander in Chief of the Russian Armies, General

Alekseiev, raised his hand to the salute. But when the last coaches containing the representatives of the Revolution, who, unknown to the Emperor, had installed themselves in the rear of his train by way of emphasizing that he was their captive, passed level with the Commander in Chief, he took off his cap and bowed low to his new masters.

The Emperor was speeding towards the capital, still an emperor, he thought, in name at least, and a free man; but the Red guards in the rear of his train were dispatching telegram after telegram from every stop. The telegrams were addressed to various revolutionary bodies in Petrograd, and they were all in the sense that they, the Red guards in the back coach of his train, were bringing him back to Petrograd and no mistake. Yes, him, Nicholas Romanov, now sitting at dinner in the front imperial coach, no doubt fortifying his drooping spirits with alcohol. They were bringing him right back to the capital, now.

The Emperor, from long habit, also sent telegrams. But his telegrams seemed neither to arrive nor did he seem to receive replies; neither did his train appear to follow the accustomed route. It pulled up unexpectedly at odd stations, when the Red guards in his rear palavered excitedly with Red guards on the platform. Oh, yes, they were taking him back all right! There he was, in the front coach; that was him all right, Nicholas Romanov. There was no mistake about that.

In front was another imperial train, full of his brilliant suite, all uneasily putting their heads together as to what awaited them on arrival; and when, as already described, the imperial train pulled up at the station of Tsarskoye Selo it really looked as though the Emperor had arrived alone. There was no sign of a suite. They seemed to have dispersed before the train had come to a standstill. The Emperor, as stated, drove to the Palace, and after a long delay and some chicanery at the gate was admitted into his home.

V. HUSBAND AND WIFE

THERE the Empress, who had nervously waited for him all day, advanced to greet her husband, that poor little Nicky whom she had always urged to be firm. The long days of restraint, of the necessity of putting on a good face, the habit of a lifetime to appear calm and dignified on all occasions, assisted by a temperament essentially cool and self-possessed, now gave way under stress of emotion. The Emperor and Empress, who had reigned together for twenty-three years since almost the day on which they were married, fell into each other's arms and he cried like a baby.

When, having exhausted the pathos of his humiliation, he recovered his pride, he said to his bewildered wife: "If the *whole* of Russia now entreated me on *bended knee* to resume the crown—I would not do it."

The children were laid up with measles. The Palace was under the surveillance of the soldiers and sailors of the Petrograd Soviet. From being the Autocrat of All the Russias and receiving officials who came to take his orders, Nicholas, in the space of a few days, had been transformed into a "late emperor" who received officials in order to hear from them what he was not permitted to do.

The girls had been told by their mother of the change in their daddy's status, and the little boy's Swiss tutor had been instructed by the Empress to break the news to her son, who hitherto had rather liked the idea that one day he himself would be emperor. He was told that his august father would never go back to the Army.

The boy asked: "Why?"

Gilliard, the tutor, replied lamely that the reason, no doubt, was that his father did not want, things being as they were, to be Commander in Chief any more.

"What? But why?" asked Aleksei.

"He is very tired. There has been a lot of trouble lately," said the tutor.

The boy said he had heard there had been trouble and that they had even stopped his daddy's train. "But won't Papa be tsar again afterwards?" he asked.

The tutor said he doubted it. In fact, he was sure he wouldn't.

"But who's going to be tsar, then?"

"I don't know. Perhaps nobody now."

This answer seemed to perplex Aleksei. "But if there isn't a tsar, who's going to govern Russia?"

VI. UNDER PROTECTIVE ARREST

THE imperial family, placed under protective arrest in the Palace at Tsarskoye Selo, did not at first notice any appreciable difference in their routine of life, which had always been conditioned by isolation. They had spent all their lives under protective arrest of their own choosing. The choice being broadly between death or a life like death, the Emperor complied with rules and regulations issued for his conduct with the unquestioning obedience of a private in his army. He had always liked the simple life. Now he could hack wood in the snow to his heart's content; then, glowing with health after the strenuous exercise in the open, rejoin the family circle for tea, read aloud to them—in short, do what he liked, always provided he did not do what he shouldn't. No ministers now—"no troublesome questions demanding thought."

The girls and the boy did not take the restrictions as literally as their father. They would advance a yard farther than the limit set them, converse with the guard. Aleksei, barely twelve, and brought up by his German mother to be a future Peter the Great, however unpromising the material on his father's side, would defy the soldiers or scowl at them angrily, to the delight of his older sisters.

The Empress took her new position badly indeed. She was *humiliated.* She would not deign to notice the officers of the revolutionary guard. Sprung from one of the most trifling principalities in Germany, Hesse-Darmstadt, oh! she was proud! Her mother had been a daughter of Queen Victoria and she had spent some little time at the English Court. Even as a girl, whatever she did always turned out unlucky; and when she left her native Darmstadt for Russia, a woman had shouted after her as the train drew out: *"Pechvogel, nimm dein Pech mit!"* ("Bird of ill omen, take your ill luck with you!") A Lutheran by birth, an Orthodox by conversion, she had thrown herself with a vehemence unnatural in a native into the worship of local shrines in the land of her adoption, and the calendar of Russian saints had no mysteries for her. And who indeed has not heard about Rasputin and his sway over the Tsaritsa? Empress Alexandra was the cause of Nicholas's unpopularity, as surely as Marie Antoinette had been the cause of Louis XVI's downfall.

Kerenski, on one of his regular calls of inquiry at the Palace, conveyed to her a message from Queen Mary received through official channels. The Queen inquired anxiously after the health of the Empress. Kerenski, after making his bow, put it thus: "The Queen of England inquires after the health of the former Empress."

Alexandra colored deeply with vexation at the word "former," but replied after a pause:

"I'm well. . . . I sleep better now, my nerves are better, but I have headaches."

Late one night they woke up the ex-Tsar to tell him that a company of workers had come from Petrograd to Tsarskoye to make sure with their own eyes that Nicholas Romanov had not bolted abroad but was still safely under lock and key. They noisily demanded to see him. The Emperor dressed hurriedly and went out to them into the long cold corridor where the crowd of workmen faced him in silence. They looked at him as if they could not believe that this mild, inoffensive little man with the blue eyes was indeed Nicholas the Bloody. They looked at him, and he looked back, for a full ten minutes without saying a word; and then they turned and went away. The Tsar went back to bed.

VII. THE BOY WHO WOULD NEVER BE TSAR GOES ON WITH HIS LESSONS IN RUSSIAN HISTORY

ANOTHER day Aleksei questioned Kerenski. "You are a lawyer," he said. "Tell me: had my father any legal right to abdicate for me, too—to sign away my right to the succession?"

Kerenski quibbled. "Legally, perhaps not. Parentally, yes. But what does it matter? The decision was the Nation's."

The Tsarevitch's life in other respects was not apparently affected by the change in the status of his father. His tutor continued with his studies. The Tsarevitch was forging ahead with his study of Russian history, and this meant that he was inevitably being acquainted more and more with his father's predecessors. For three hundred years these predecessors had belonged to the House of Romanov, and for seven hundred years before that they were of the House of Rurik. And now, for the first time, the business had passed out of the family into the hands of one Alexander Kerenski.

The ex-Tsarevitch was making good progress.

His father, coming up to see his son seated at his lessons, would look over the boy's shoulder, now and then dip into a page of Russian history. And it would touch associations, strike home. This tsar or that would look back at him from the picture: patient Tsar Aleksei with silent reproach; Peter the Great with his mouth screwed up in ferocious contempt under those awful cat's whiskers. Sometimes the boy asked embarrassing questions: would any of them have *minded* if they had known? Would Tsar Mihaïl, who had founded the dynasty, have minded it coming to an end at the close of a bare three centuries? Would Catherine the Great, who had—so the book stated—extended the work begun by Peter the Great and placed the throne on an unassailable foundation: would *she* have minded? What would grandpapa have said? And great-grandpapa, the noble-minded Alexander II who had given his life to liberate the serfs?

And when in the bleak, silent evenings, after his wife and children had gone up to bed, Nicholas, to wear off his restlessness, paced up and down the half-lit halls and picture galleries, arrogant ancestors looked down at him moodily from their heavy frames. The tsaritsas looked wistful and the tsars nodded ironic assent. *"You* would," said their lips, "you *would!...*" Gorgeously epauletted, his great-grandfather and namesake, Nicholas I, stared icily at him, replete in poise and pose, as though disputing anew the claim of his contemporary, George IV of England, to the coveted distinction of being the first gentleman of Europe.

But, then, was that so surprising? Nicholas I, whose one ambition in life had been to mount the throne! "I have three sons," his mother was wont to say. "Alexander is an idealist and he is charming. Constantine is hot-tempered and out of all control, but he can be sweet and he is really good at heart, though insanely cruel when roused. As for my third son, Nicholas, he has but one ambition in life, a single overmastering passion—to *reign*."

And, true to the divining of a mother's heart, the report of Alexander's death had scarcely reached the capital, and Constantine, away in far-off Warsaw, had not yet been heard from, when Nicholas, with a yelp and a laugh, fairly leaped onto the vacant throne.

No, if there was any one among the faces on the wall to wring his heart, it was the gentle, ineffable Alexander I, who, if he had but reaped where Peter and Catherine had sown, had yet carried Russian grand monarchy to a peak of glory it had never known either before or since. He, without any doubt, was Russia's *Roi-Soleil*. He, the most elegant, as he was also the most brilliant and versatile of them all. Had he not shone in the drawing rooms and council chambers of Europe and, driving Napoleon out of Moscow, ridden into Paris at the head of his cuirassiers? He was the Emperor Charming. And, besides, his fame covered the longest stretch of Romanov history. His childhood fell far back into his grandmother's reign, the brilliant, affable Catherine, who adored him; and his closing years are shrouded in mystery and do not seem to tail off till the last but two of Romanovs sat precariously on a shaking throne.

Yes: *he* might have minded. But, then, Alexander who had himself so often played with the idea of abdication and a peaceful hamlet in Switzerland, and had finally staged his own death to vanish without trace...perhaps he would have understood....

CHAPTER II

ALEXANDER'S BACKGROUND

I. HISTORY AN ART?

LYTTON STRACHEY said that history was presumably an art. "What else is it? It is certainly not a science."

I hope not. Goethe, too, was of opinion—and it would be difficult to find anything on which Goethe had not expressed an opinion—that history yielded more of her secrets to the congenial intuition of the artist than to the over-diffident approach of the scientist. The drawing of inferences was safer in the hands of the artist, to whom psychology is second nature, than if entrusted to the scientific mind inclined to over-stress in the cause of veracity the importance of sifting facts: again, better served by the drawing of inferences than by the sifting of facts.

True.

Queen Victoria objected to Gladstone addressing her as if she were not a woman but a public meeting. And this ill-starred dynasty shall be treated here as a family exposed to the indignity of living in glass houses and, in sheer befuddlement, throwing stones; a family deserving, despite their faults and crimes, some of the ordinary sympathy due to the least of human beings. They are, so considered, human voices speaking out of silent portraits and the gathering torrent of accumulating facts.

Whatever a writer may make of the history of a dynasty, one thing is certain: it is not a book of short stories. It is a single story with a gathering purpose. A river with many tributaries flowing into the main stream and down the common waterway of Time.

We have seen the last emperor, Nicholas II, approaching the rapids. Before we follow his frail canoe drifting over the treacherous waterfall ahead, we must go back a little and observe the great river with its earlier tributaries higher up the stream.

If the early Romanovs are dismissed as having skirmished the ground for Peter; and if Peter is seen as the carpenter of Greater Russia; if, then, Peter's daughter, the dissolute but splendid Elizabeth, is regarded as the first to live in the new "Versailles" style compatible with Peter's work of hacking out a window into Europe; if, further, Catherine the

16

Great is seen as completing Peter's work and enlarging on Elizabeth's splendor, then Alexander can be seen in full perspective: as the heir of the grand monarchy and the noblest Romanov of them all.

But—make no mistake about it—the most interesting thing about Alexander I is precisely that he was not great, not strong, not even remarkable. He did not accomplish anything. But suddenly fate accomplished everything for him. He is the most charming sovereign who ever mounted the Russian throne. It may be that he is the most charming sovereign who ever ascended any throne.

Napoleon said that it would be difficult to be more intelligent than Alexander. The story of his duel with Napoleon is certainly the most astounding chapter in Russian history.

But what of Peter the Great? It is impossible to ignore that Peter's duel with Charles XII, in the previous century, is the most amazing chapter in Russian history. The writer can freely say so because he can take no credit for history which obviously is not his invention, the writer being concerned with two things only: selection and effect.

Peter, a tough, ruthless man who, in the space of a few years, transformed Russia from medieval Muscovy into a great power, has nothing of the fascination of Alexander, who transformed nothing but who was dropped and lifted on the wings of fate from tears and despair to the summit of earthly glory, only to be gently laid down again; after which he gathered his mantle about him and went his way.

II. THE POWER OF SUGGESTION

IF the truth must be told, neither Peter nor Catherine are styled "the Great" except outside their own country. In Russia the title has never caught on. It has been said that Peter the First was called Peter the Great by none other than Peter himself. This is inaccurate. Returning to his new capital, St. Petersburg, after the signing of the long-pending treaty with Sweden, his ambition moderately satisfied, Peter had put it to one of his senators as a good idea that henceforward he might be styled, for the greater glory of them all, Father of the Fatherland, Emperor of All Russia, and—well, if they liked—Peter the Great. Before that he was only known as Tsar. "His zarish majesty" they addressed him on his visit to London.

The suggestion, coming from an autocrat of uncertain temper six foot eight in his socks and habitually carrying a big stick with him which he brought down there and then on the shoulders of offending subjects; a sovereign who put people to the torture through his interest in the working of mechanical devices and who had chopped off heads with his own hands—the suggestion that he be known as Peter the Great met with instant acclamation from his Senate.

He is entitled to the pleasure; for though, considered soberly, he was only great in driving force, he is a great landmark in Russian history, the division between old and modern Russia. And he is probably the greatest beast who ever wore a crown. In a competition of human bestiality, to include not only Nero, Caligula, Tiberius, Genghis Khan and Ivan the Terrible, but any monster of the rank and file, Peter the Great would be well in for winning the palm. He was the least un-balanced of them all. But, besides being calculatingly cruel, he was also callous, prepared to inflict the utmost pain on others without satisfying either his anger, vindictiveness, or even his sadism: merely because other men's extremity meant nothing to his imagination and less to his sensi-bility. Suffering other than his own roused no note in him at all. And he had not a touch of chivalry in his heart. He was mean. When a Swedish commander who had been defending a fortress against Peter, at last, after days of gallant resistance, surrendered his garrison and came before his conqueror, Peter struck him across the mouth for having stuck out so long against him.

No, Alexander shall be our trump card. It is easy and it is profitable to relate both his forebears and successors to Alexander I, since, in some uncanny way, he includes them all. The more closely you look at him, the more he eludes you, and the more fascinating he grows. From the first to the last, all the Romanovs who had occupied the Russian throne are mirrored in the soul of Alexander. Mihaïl, the founder of the new dynasty, died of acute melancholia after a long reign. Alexander towards the end of his rule lapsed into uncontrollable melancholy and, as will appear in due course, ended his days as a wanderer. The second Romanov, Aleksei, was kind, broad-minded and level-headed—qualities all to be found in Alexander I. He performed six hundred prostrations each day. Alexander, in the end, developed a similar piety and contracted house-maid's knee. Peter the Great was brutal, willful, and quite fantastically promiscuous. Alexander could be all these things—when he was not being the opposite. He even proved himself cruel beyond all expectation during an abortive rebellion in the Semënovski Regiment. He ordered, against the earnest pleas of his generals, that the men found guilty of insubordination be flogged to death. When he heard that part of his sentence (which would have caused the death of the offenders) had been remitted, he flew into a rage and ordered the balance to be carried out. When a scheme of his for settling soldiers on the land met with some resistance at the hands of the people (for whose benefit he had conceived the plan) he said that he would cover the road between Petersburg and Moscow with corpses to carry out a scheme which so appealed to his humanitarian instincts. And he was not being cynical.

Catherine II was brilliant, clever, charming and immoral. Alexander, her grandson, was all these things, too. If Napoleon did say that it would have been difficult to be more intelligent than Alexander, he more than once changed his mind on that score. The point about Alexander is that no single opinion of him can be entertained for any length of time since he is sure to reveal the opposite trait before you have finished with him. He is the despair of his biographers; and, frankly, he fascinates me.

III. THE EMPEROR CHARMING

BUT if Alexander were a grand monarch in the French sense he would be neither interesting in the Russian sense nor indeed representative as a pattern of Russian monarchy. Alexander, when we consider him as a whole, strikes us as singularly futile. He was the first to defeat Napoleon and the first to enter Paris. But if this should sound as though he were superior to Napoleon in military genius, the reader's mind must be promptly disabused. Alexander was utterly useless as a military commander. He trembled in his shoes at the approach of Napoleon's Grand Army and hid himself in Petersburg while Napoleon advanced on Moscow. But, as the tide turned, Alexander displayed unexpected courage in galloping in front of his troops. Yet he invariably lost the battle since he could neither see nor hear well and was devoid of every trace of military talent.

If the four emperors who succeeded Alexander I on the throne of Russia are, in contrast to him, colorful nonentities, even then it would be idle to deny that Alexander I shares with them a measure of mediocrity. He was no eagle. Even his brilliance, if examined more scrupulously, looked more than it really was. Only against such dullards as Kaiser Franz of Austria and King Frederick William of Prussia—in turn his friends, companions, allies, foes, pals, enemies and friends again—did it seem as though Alexander was brilliant. He was tall, elegant, handsome, and adored by women. He had a moist, tender look in his eyes which made every woman succumb to him at sight. He was fond of saying that he was "not an emperor but a happy accident." By sheer force of circumstances he had been pushed into a glittering position. Europe called him "the Agamemnon of Kings." And, though he was shy by nature, the universal adulation which surrounded him at the peak of his career made him bold. He said things as they struck him without taking thought; he conversed easily, in fluent French, which he spoke even better than his native tongue, and since he was worldly and excessively charming he also passed off as brilliant.

The last of the Romanovs, the unlucky Nicholas II, was a mystic, and grew more mystical and resigned the more hopelessly he became entangled in the web of State. So, indeed, in the end, did Alexander. He combined the mysticism of Nicholas II with the religious mania of Nicholas's German consort. He even had his Rasputin of the day. In short, it would be difficult to say what Alexander was not. He combined in his person all the qualities of his dynasty. If you superimpose all the Romanovs one upon the other you obtain a composite moral portrait—which is no other than Alexander I. I should even be inclined to think that if you superimposed all the Romanov monarchs one upon the other you would get approximately the features and stature of Alexander I.

Several circumstances combine to account for Alexander's charm. He was good-looking. But not extremely so. He was fair, slender, graceful in his movements, and he had a youngish, clear-skinned, blue-eyed, innocent face. He was lucid, and he was educated. At least, so far as the education of sovereigns went in those days, Alexander's training at the hands of his Swiss tutor, Laharpe, was above the average. He was well-grounded in the humanities, and brilliant at languages; whereas his predecessors and successors were brought up in the belief that an acquaintance with strategy and military discipline was all that behove a sovereign and a gentleman. It is ironic to reflect that the best educated of Russian sovereigns, Nicholas II, was also the most ill-fated; who, though well-grounded, among other things, in economics, owes his fame to having brought the ship of State aground.

Alexander was twenty-four when he came to the throne.

Catherine, who disliked her son Paul, "adored" her eldest grandson, Alexander. She meant him to succeed her, over the head of his father. But she was afraid of being too explicit during her lifetime, and she thought it better policy to keep them guessing. The chancellor, Panin, a powerful man in the State, had been Paul's tutor, and it was assumed that he would defend his late pupil's rights to the succession. Catherine feared Panin. He was one of the pillars of what the gentry in the land regarded as legitimacy. They stood behind him; he was therefore a force to be reckoned with. What Panin said was regarded by the nobility throughout the country as legal. That did not prevent his engineering two palace revolutions which deprived two legal sovereigns of their throne.

Catherine knew that, in helping to depose Peter III, Panin did not mean her to become an empress in her own right, but merely wanted her to be appointed regent during her son's minority. For a third of her reign she was intermittently apprehensive of Panin's party, who might require her to give way to Paul when her son came of age. For the rest of her reign—she reigned for a third of a century—she felt that in Panin's eyes she was, as the years went by, encroaching on what should have been by traditional right her son's reign.

And Paul felt so, too, and felt it more bitterly as he passed out of his twenties into his thirties, then into his forties. To realize the irregularity of the legal position one would have to imagine our own Queen Mary succeeding King George V over the head of her son Edward VIII, who was kept guessing in the position of Prince of Wales, whether he would succeed the Queen at all, or whether she would eventually pass on the crown of England to his son instead.

Catherine died suddenly from a fit of apoplexy on November 17, 1796, and Paul at once proclaimed himself emperor. He rightly felt there was not a moment to lose. He was staying at his own place in Gatchina, where he amused himself in training troops, when the news reached him. He drove to the Winter Palace without sparing the horses. A sealed letter from Catherine, proclaiming her successor, was to be opened by the Chancellor and read solemnly in Paul's own presence and that of the entire court.

Paul snatched the letter from the hand of the Chancellor, broke it open and read it to himself. The contents did not, it is inferred, meet with his approval, because he tore it into small fragments and threw them on the fire. There was a moment of consternation. Then the Chancellor proclaimed, out of his own intuition: "His Imperial Majesty the Emperor Paul has deigned this day to ascend the throne of All the Russias."

IV. USURPATION BY PRECEDENT

BUT four years later the same Chancellor Panin, deemed to be an authority on legality and legitimacy, the Panin who had been Paul's tutor and was considered to be his stanchest supporter, the same Panin who had thirty-seven years before apprenticed his hand in deposing his pupil's father, Peter III, now initiated Paul's forcible removal in favor of his young son—the man of charm—Alexander.

Would it, then, be correct to say that Catherine had no right whatever to the Russian throne? It would not. Peter the Great, by murdering his own legitimate son and heir, Aleksei; by marrying a second time a Lithuanian servant girl without divorcing his first wife; by arrogating to himself the right of appointing his successor, but failing specifically to do so; by suggesting to the Senate that they should choose the most suitable candidate among themselves to succeed him as tsar if he died in a Turkish prison; and by dying at home with the words: "Give it all back to ——" and breathing his last without forming a name with his lips—Peter the Great, by all this, made such chaos of precedent and set such a precedent for chaos, that Catherine had as much right as, and no less right than, anyone else in the running for the throne.

If we go back thirty-seven years, we find that Peter the Great, though originally co-sovereign with his half-witted half-brother, the Tsar Ivan, had really no right to discriminate in favor of his own kith and kin, still less to nominate (however tentatively) his second wife, Catherine I, for the succession, Ivan being the elder. Ivan was an idiot—and dead at that. But Ivan had daughters, granddaughters, and finally, a great-grand-son—also Ivan, and also an idiot.

But would that have mattered so much in a sovereign of Russia? Besides, we only have Catherine's word for it. She liked to think Ivan was weak-minded because he was a living reproach while she sat on his throne. For Ivan was, by that time, the only Romanov extant—that is to say, the only Romanov who really *was* a Romanov beyond mere conjecture. Paul's parenthood, on both sides, was wrapped in mystery. If Catherine II was his mother, it is practically certain that Peter III was not his father. (Which would debar him from having one drop of Romanov blood.) If, on the other hand, he was the child of the unmarried Empress Elizabeth, the younger daughter of Peter the Great, by a favorite, then he would still be of the blood Romanov on his mother's side. In either case, he would be a bastard.

Catherine detested her supposed son Paul, whereas the Empress Elizabeth worshiped him. The day he was born the Empress sent for the baby and did not return him to Catherine till two weeks later. A rumor spread that the unmarried Elizabeth, to conceal the birth of a baby by a favorite (no wonder the baby Paul was a favorite!) and at the same time to ensure the succession for her own flesh and blood, substituted her child for Catherine's.

Catherine, married to the heir-apparent, the Tsarevitch Peter (later Peter III), who was impotent, took a lover, the handsome Saltikov, largely at the veiled suggestion of Elizabeth's ladies in waiting, who conveyed to Catherine that it was her Majesty's opinion that, one way or another, it was absolutely incumbent on her to produce an heir to the throne.

Even after Elizabeth had returned the baby, she would never allow Catherine to have him for more than two hours and took him away for weeks on end, much to Catherine's relief. Solomon would have quickly decided who was Paul's real mother.

Therefore the issue whether Alexander I and the subsequent tsars were Romanovs at all hangs on that. But, as Peter the Great was only of the third generation of Romanovs and, but for an earlier connection by marriage with the former dynasty of the Ruriks, the Romanovs were nobodies, the issue of whether the Russian emperors since Peter III were Romanovs or *not* Romanovs need rob nobody of his sleep. They *called* themselves Romanovs, and that should be good enough for the reader. Alexander I called himself a happy accident—and that is better still.

The fact remains that the illustrious Catherine II, a German, having deposed her husband, Peter III, reigned as though in her own right, and continued to do so; while a genuine Romanov, Ivan, whom she preferred to regard as weak-minded, by her orders languished in a fortress. Proclaimed emperor while still a suckling, deposed while a babe by Elizabeth, he was later confined to a damp cell in the Schlüsselburg fortress on Lake Ladoga, where he was kept a close prisoner till he grew to manhood and was shot by order during a pretended plot to effect his escape.

He, then, is the last of the known Romanovs, as distinct from the Romanovs by surmise.

V. ALL USURPERS

BUT if we go further back than that, we are impelled to ask: was the Romanov choice in 1613 a valid one? Better families than the Romanovs, whose link with the Ruriks was merely a connection by marriage, were surely available. First and foremost the Dolgorukis—a family of direct Rurik descent. Yuri Dolgoruki, the founder of Suzdal, the ancient precursor of Moscow, had himself been a Rurik. His nickname, "Dolgoruki" —"the long-handed," had clung to him. He was in the habit of helping himself to more than his share. He had gone to Kiev and depleted it of its treasure, which he brought back to his own Suzdal. (So perhaps this early cupidity ought to rule out his descendants?)

But not even the Ruriks themselves were all legitimately descended in an unbroken line from Rurik, the founder of the ancient dynasty. The Tartar invasion had for two hundred years played havoc with the thrones of the great princes. For three hundred years Genghis Khan's descendants held the great princes of the House of Rurik in vassalage to the Golden Horde. They deposed and replaced them at will. Anyone who undertook to squeeze sufficient tribute out of a stricken population was their man. There was an infusion of Tartar blood in some cases, the reigning Khan, as a special favor, sometimes giving away his own daughters in marriage to a worthy vassal.

Was it even certain that the Rurik line remained unbroken? Brother fought brother and took away his throne. But sometimes it was a brother-in-law; at other times a connection even more obscure. And, finally, what right, if we pursue legitimacy to its logical conclusion, had the original Ruriks, invaders from Scandinavia, to assume full sovereignty over the townships? They had been asked to give protection against bellicose neighbors; that was all. No hereditary rights were stipulated in return. Like Novgorod and Pskov, which remained for a long time stubbornly republican, the other townships, too, showed no desire for a monarchical order. The republican constitution was the oldest known in Russia. Allowing for the historic invitation at the hands of a local delegation itself— "Come and rule over us"—was that valid for the entire land these Norseman warriors overran?

It will be seen that the precedent for Russian legitimacy is an almost unbroken line of illegal usurpations. Here and there a father is succeeded by his elder son and, once in a hundred years, by a grandson. Usurpation is the rule and precedent; legitimacy the unprecedented exception.

But need this so astonish us? If we examine closely the history of most kingships by divine right in other lands we shall find substantially the same unprecedented state of affairs posing as precedent for legitimate succession. If with Catherine the Great we face a double-barreled usurpation, posed against the cumulative effect of usurpations running through Russian history, it merely strikes one as a rather charming *coup de main* by a delightful German hailing from Stettin in Pomerania, clever enough to don the cap of Monomachus and enjoy it, too!

It is ironic to reflect that Alexander III, the grandson of Nicholas I, begged his son Nicholas II to continue the good work his great-grandfather had initiated in setting the principle of primogeniture firmly on its feet. At long last they had managed to maintain it unbroken for a second generation, twice in succession handing on the throne from father to son. Just think of it! "Now remember," Alexander III enjoined his son, "that when I pass the scepter to you on my death, you are not to let it pass out of your hands except to your eldest son on your death. Remember: no brothers! No women! No uncles! Always the eldest son. Is that clear?"

"Yes, papa."

"Promise me."

"Yes, papa."

Alexander III was not to know that his son was to prove himself unable to carry the happy precedent beyond his own reign, which unhappily mopped up the line.

Nor do these firm believers in the principle of primogeniture appreciate the corollary that, but for the violation of their cherished principle in the past, *they* would not have been tsars with heirs-apparent to instruct in the sacred principle of primogeniture. Catherine's right is based on less casuistry and a more honest lust for power. It follows the principle implicitly laid down by Peter I, which bears out the Russian proverb: Who gets up quick and grasps the stick, *he's* the corporal all to lick!

Catherine cherished the ambition to set up her two elder grandsons, Alexander and Constantine (named accordingly), on the thrones of Petersburg and Constantinople. Nicholas, Paul's third son, who leaped onto the throne over the head of Constantine, was born in the closing years of Catherine's reign, which had lasted a third of a century. That Catherine did not like her assumed son, Paul, she made no secret of; but that she did not want him to succeed her was a wish she did not broadcast, rightly assuming that, so long as Paul and his satellites had hopes of his eventual elevation to the throne, they would not plot against her but abide in good hope.

That Catherine had communicated her wishes to Alexander we gather from his guarded answer to her letter. Her own letter he was careful to destroy. His letter the reigning Empress was careless to leave behind. His ingratiating answer suggests that he has understood her well and understood that she wishes him to be discreet. "Never," he writes in reply, "shall I be able to express my gratitude for the confidence with which Your Majesty has condescended to honor me and the gracious kindness with which you have written with your own hand a commentary elucidating the other papers. . . . I can never repay, even with my blood, all that you have deigned to do for me. These documents clearly confirm all the reflections which Your Majesty has been so gracious as to communicate to me, and which, if I may venture an opinion, could not be more just. Once more assuring Your Imperial Majesty of my most deep and lively gratitude, I take the liberty to remain, with profound reverence and inviolable attachment, Your Imperial Majesty's very humble and very obedient servant and grandson, ALEXANDER."

There is always something faintly ridiculous in the devotion to the throne on the part of a prospective occupier.

Who was this woman who excited such "profound reverence" in her grandson, who had "condescended to honor him," a future tsar, by writing "with her own hand"? Who was this illustrious grandmother whose fame and name and power so awed the youth whom she adored that he "took the liberty" and felt *presumptuous* even "to remain, with profound reverence and inviolable attachment, Her Imperial Majesty's very humble and very obedient servant and grandson"?

She was, if we go back some sixty-five years, a daughter of Prince Christian August von Anhalt-Zerbst. Of all the mediatized princes of Germany it would be difficult to find a prince more minute, more insignificant, than Catherine's father, who succeeded with his brother to the principality of Anhalt-Zerbst. The principle of primogeniture having been waived in Zerbst, the State had for generations been divided and subdivided between all the sons of every son. When the last ruling prince died, his plot of land was so microscopic that with the best will in the world Anhalt-Zerbst could no longer be divided, and Catherine's father and his elder brother "reigned" together. Even so, they had their "court" with their Chamberlain and Master of the Horse, who, appropriately, was master of *one* horse.

From Anhalt-Zerbst hails the most illustrious Empress of Russia.

CHAPTER III

CATHERINE'S CHILDHOOD

I. THE RUSSIAN JOURNEY

ON A cold day in January 1774, a bright girl of fourteen, accompanied by her father and mother, set off from the tiny principality of Zerbst, of which her father was co-ruler, on her way through Berlin to St. Petersburg and Moscow.

Her father indeed was not to accompany them any farther than Stettin, where she was born. A most explicit stipulation to that effect was contained in the letter received from St. Petersburg, which stated: "At the same time our incomparable Monarch has expressly commanded me to inform Your Highness that His Highness, the Prince, your husband, shall in no circumstances take part in the journey. Her Majesty has very weighty reasons for desiring this."

One can picture the two Pomeranian parents—he, owlish, near-sighted, bespectacled and fifty-three; she just turned thirty and still game—puzzling over this sentence when dinner was over, and their fourteen-year-old daughter Figgy, the mainspring of this cryptic communication, had been told to run away and play. And indeed I can find no elucidation to this specific objection on the part of the Empress Elizabeth of Russia, unless it is that she deemed one German parent enough for a start. The ill-fame of her predecessors, the two Annas, who had imported German stewards into Russia, with the consequence that the Russian nobility had staged a palace revolution which had placed portly Elizabeth herself on the throne, was perhaps too fresh in Russian memory to risk provoking the native aristocracy with the importation of any more Germans than absolutely necessary to provide a bride for the heir to the Russian throne. Hence the invitation strictly confined to mother and child.

But Elizabeth was too devoted a daughter of Peter the Great to neglect his ruling that the future emperors of Russia were to be provided with consorts from the extensive breeding stables scattered through the forty-odd mediatized principalities of Germany. Elizabeth herself, though already in her teens a dissolute wench, was technically unmarried; and she had two years earlier designated as her heir-apparent her elder sister's boy,

27

Karl Peter Ulrich, whose mother had been the eldest daughter of Peter the Great, but whose father had merely been the Duke of Holstein-Gottorp.

Both parents of the boy were dead. His mother died soon after bringing him into the world. His father followed his wife, whom he loved, eleven years later. Karl Peter Ulrich was later to become Emperor Peter III of Russia—an exalted position he was to enjoy for a bare six months before being murdered by his consort Catherine's satellites who had placed her on his throne. The girl of fourteen they called Figgy at home, now setting out on her visit to the Russia she was never again to leave, is the future Catherine II—sometimes called Catherine the Great.

She was eighteen months younger than Karl Peter Ulrich. On a visit to Hamburg at the age of eleven she met him, and he took a great dislike to her. At that time he was unaware that, two years hence, they would take him, much against his will, to Russia, change his religion and turn him into a tsarevitch, the heir-apparent to the throne of his maternal grandfather, Peter the Great. And still less could the boy foresee that, a year after that, they would send out this awful girl Figgy he so disliked at Hamburg and make her his wife. That they should then, together, endure the most agonizingly boring eighteen years of gilded captivity under the tutelage of his exacting and suspicious Aunt Elizabeth, before he succeeded her for six months on the throne, to be overthrown by his wife, this same girl Figgy, and then brutally murdered by her men after a struggle for life with his assailants lasting twenty minutes, was a fate mercifully hidden from his boyish eyes.

It is a tradition with Russian historians to vilify Karl Peter Ulrich so as to smooth the transfer of the crown to his consort, Catherine II. After all, Catherine, after disposing of Karl Peter Ulrich, *alias* Peter III, reigned gloriously for a third of a century, while Peter III reigned six months without specially distinguishing himself except by his drunken bouts and by preferring his Holsteiners to his Russians. You cannot do much in six months. Imperial drunkenness was not a characteristic peculiarly his own. His Aunt Elizabeth, his immediate predecessor on the throne, drank intermittently and only made brief appearances in public, punctuated by sudden exits when she darted behind a screen or out of a room to fortify her failing spirits with another...and yet another.

Her mother, Catherine I, the peasant girl, whose real name was Martha Skavronski, and whom Peter the Great married without divorcing his first wife, drank like a fish. She got drunk at frequent intervals while she was Peter's mistress and later his consort. When, after Peter had screamed his last, she was proclaimed Empress and Self-Upholder of All the Russias, she ceased to uphold sobriety altogether. She handed the government of the empire to her original lover, Prince Menshikov, the hot-pieman, out of whose hands Peter had first obtained her; and abandoned herself to deep, fathomless drinking. It occurred to her that now as autocrat she could do exactly as she liked, which was to drink herself into a progressive state of unconsciousness; and that as she drank deeply the fact of her being Empress of Russia appeared to her more incredible, like a wonderful dream she could never quite believe while she was sober, but which, as she swooned on the floor, she dreamed anew in her sleep. Human beings are said to be incapable of prolonged ecstasy: their nerves cannot endure too much happiness. Two years later she was dead.

And what of Peter the Great, Peter III's grandfather, who drank uninterruptedly all through the winter season, as a bear hibernates between autumn and spring, drank disgustingly and behaved twice as obnoxiously as when he was sober: which was bad enough?

But, bleat the Russian historians, it would never have done for Peter III to remain tsar—he drank.

When Figgy met him as a boy in Hamburg, she did not care for him because even then, she says, he drank a great deal of beer. He was at the time the Duke of Holstein-Gottorp, a ward of his uncle, the Prince Bishop of Luebeck, who ruled the duchy during his nephew's minority. Karl Peter Ulrich was greatly bullied and pestered by tutors who watched his every step and supervised even his leisure. For the boy was a great asset in the Holstein-Gottorp family. Though Holstein-Gottorp was insignificant, Karl Peter Ulrich was not. Potentially, he could claim the succession to two great realms—Russia and Sweden. He wanted neither. He only wanted his little Holstein-Gottorp, and even when he was made Grand Duke of Russia and heir to the throne he still wanted nothing better than to be allowed to return to Holstein-Gottorp. And when his wife dethroned him and he was kept a prisoner at Ropsha, he wrote her a piteous letter, telling her she could reign instead of him and that he wished her joy of it: only would she please let him get back to Holstein-Gottorp; that was all he asked. But they also took his life.

II. HOLSTEIN-GOTTORP

THE story of Holstein-Gottorp is an amazing tangle, which I have found profitable and amusing to unravel. It demonstrates the fortuitous manner in which tiny princelings are turned unexpectedly into grand monarchs of vast foreign empires because, though nothing more tricky is asked of kings and emperors than to provide male issue to ensure the direct succession of their own illustrious line, they have rarely been able anywhere to keep up the good work for more than three generations.

And so the last authentic Romanov (the rest are guesswork) is a Holstein-Gottorp on his father's side. And his wife and successor, the great Catherine, is a Holstein-Gottorp, too—on her mother's side.

The question is upon us, the pressing, all-important question which will not brook evasion or delay: who—and what—are the Holstein-Gottorps?

In 1448 an old German family, the Counts of Oldenburg, were offered the throne of Denmark. Twelve years later the burghers of Schleswig and of Holstein elected to be ruled by the Danish crown. But in 1544 the King, Christian III, decided to share Schleswig and Holstein with his two brothers, Johann and Adolph. He was fond of his brothers and generously divided up the provinces in such a way as to give them the major part of Schleswig-Holstein, contenting himself with the minor portion.

That started all the trouble. And if Hitler has his eye on that territory, it is not yet ended. Doubtless he will demand its "return" into the Reich.

When Duke Johann died, his portion was divided between the new King and Duke Adolph, with the result that most of Schleswig-Holstein was now ruled by Duke Adolph and his descendants of the cadet branch of the house of Oldenburg. They went by the name of Gottorp—the name of their chief castle and residence. In the years which followed the two branches had occasional tiffs, but their relations were tolerably peaceful.

During the Thirty Years' War, King Christian IV of Denmark took up arms to protect the German Protestants against Emperor Ferdinand II of Habsburg, but suffered defeat, and all his own German states fell a prey to Wallenstein. Duke Frederick III of Gottorp, on the other hand, decided to leave his royal relative of Copenhagen in the lurch rather than risk incurring the graver displeasure of the German Emperor in Vienna, with whom in 1627 he hastened to conclude a separate peace, throwing his fortresses open to the Emperor's troops.

The King, angered by the disloyalty of his kinsman, punished the Duke by invading the Gottorp part of Schleswig-Holstein—the big part —and annexing it to his own (small) part of Schleswig-Holstein. But by the terms of the treaty forced on the King by the Emperor, the King was obliged to return to the Duke the big part of Schleswig-Holstein he had annexed and in addition to surrender to the Duke some of his own (small) part of Schleswig-Holstein, the cadet branch now holding sway over four-fifths of the territory.

Tension increased and never again abated between the two courts, the two branches of the Oldenburg family—the royal branch of Copenhagen, and the ducal branch of Gottorp. When, in 1654, the Duke married his daughter Eleanor to Charles X, King of Sweden, all love between the two Oldenburg branches ceased for good and all. The Swedish king made use of his victory over the Danish king to secure for the Duke some more territory at the expense of the royal branch of the Oldenburgs. The cadet branch, convinced that the senior branch cherished no greater ambition than to revenge itself and retrieve the lost Holstein territories, allied itself with the crown of Sweden, which bound the younger Gottorp branch of the house of Oldenburg irretrievably to the hereditary foe of Denmark. When in 1698 Duke Frederick IV married Hedwig Sophie, the sister of Charles XII of Sweden, the ties of blood and interest which bound the Dukes of Holstein-Gottorp to Stockholm by their combined antipathy for the royal house of Copenhagen were cemented fourfold. The wall which towered between the two branches of the blood of Oldenburg could no longer be scaled.

III. MORE HOLSTEIN-GOTTORP

THEN the wind changed. The Duke and his adventurous brother-in-law, Charles XII, hit it off together. The Duke threw himself with unbounded enthusiasm into Charles XII's wars against Denmark, Russia and Poland, with the result that by 1702, four years after his marriage to the Swedish king's sister, an enemy bullet had ended the Duke's life.

But he had a son who became the new duke at the age of two, and who was to be the father of Karl Peter Ulrich—eventually Peter III of Russia. The fate of the Holstein-Gottorps, seen in perspective, demonstrates how fortune may arise out of misfortune and misfortune follow on the heels of fortune. The two-year-old duke had an uncle, his father's brother, for regent, whose regency ended in complete disaster for the House of Holstein-Gottorp. When the luck turned against Sweden, the Regent tried to make it up with the King of Denmark, appealing to their common kinship. They were both, after all, of the House of Oldenburg, he urged; and the Danish king was about to lend a sympathetic ear. A fleeting Swedish victory made the Regent pause. For an interval he flirted with both kings, with the result that the King of Denmark, convinced of the Regent's perfidy, overran the whole of Holstein-Gottorp. And the Duke, attaining his majority, found that he was the Duke of Holstein-Gottorp without any Holstein-Gottorp. A landless pauper, the young man became a traveler and adventurer. When the Russian troops, who were fighting the Swedes and were allies of Denmark, came to Holstein, a remark dropped by Menshikov in his cups reached the young Duke, Karl Frederick (for that was his name). It was that the only way he could mend his fortunes was to marry Peter the Great's elder daughter. As Russia and Denmark were allies, Russia as the senior partner would see to it that Holstein-Gottorp was restored to him.

The Duke sent a representative to St. Petersburg to solicit for the hand of the Tsar's eldest daughter, Anna—a suggestion which Peter the Great repulsed with scorn. A Duke of Holstein-Gottorp with no land to call his own seemed to Peter a poor match for the Tsar of Russia's eldest daughter. Moreover, the perfidious record of the Holstein-Gottorps did not appeal to Peter, who found that other people's treacheries were the cause of serious miscalculation when he launched his own. The Gottorp envoy returned empty-handed.

Duke Karl Frederick settled down to lick his wounds. His tender devotion, indeed his hero-worship, for his uncle, Charles XII of Sweden, and the hope that as the son of the late Hedwig Sophie, eldest sister of Charles XII, he might succeed his uncle on the throne of Sweden, convinced the Duke that a family alliance with Sweden's arch-enemy, Russia, would not after all have been to his advantage.

But when, after the murder of Charles XII, Karl Frederick's aunt, Ulrike Elenore, the younger sister of Charles, pushed herself onto the throne in the place of her nephew, Karl Frederick began to look round for someone strong enough to stand up for his hereditary rights.

And again his eye fell on the victorious Tsar. Peter the Great, at that time again at war with Sweden, now thought better of the project. If he married Karl Frederick to his daughter Anna and then took up his cause he could count on dividing Swedish loyalty and putting up his own prospective son-in-law as King of Sweden—at once a puppet monarch and an eligible husband for his eldest daughter. Peter replied to the pretender to the Swedish crown in terms so flattering that Karl Frederick hurried in person to St. Petersburg in order, as he said, to expedite the realization of his political ambitions.

He was disappointed. In the peace treaty soon afterwards concluded between Russia and Sweden at Nystadt, the Duke of Holstein-Gottorp was not mentioned by a single syllable. And the Tsar, who no longer needed the Duke, kept him dangling for a whole three years without favoring him with an answer, one way or the other, about the Grand Duchess Anna. There were, Peter clearly thought, better fish in Europe's waters than Karl Frederick of Holstein-Gottorp. Peter had had in view for one of his two daughters—probably Elizabeth—the boy king, Louis XV of France, and having been snubbed in that quarter, was himself all the more inclined to feel the ignominy of having to content himself with an all but landless minor German duke who would never be King of Sweden anyway. A mere Gottorp for the eldest daughter of a tsar who had just "suggested" to his senate that they proclaim him "Father of the Fatherland," "Peter the Great" and "Emperor and Autocrat of All the Russias"! It didn't sound right.

So he tarried with his answer. And—unexpected to himself—the young Duke had fallen in love with Anna; and she, too, moved by his tender persistence, had begun to love him. The Duke had a thick skin, but a tender heart. Impervious to imperial rebuffs, he hung on; and, at last, two months before the Tsar died, he had agreed to the engagement of the couple.

Peter died early in 1725, and was succeeded by his wife, Catherine I, the plebeian mother of Anna and Elizabeth. Anna was her favorite, and she thought the Duke a nice young man who would make a devoted husband for her elder daughter, also so nice; and she expedited their marriage, which took place on the first of June, 1725, in St. Petersburg.

He had sought to satisfy his royal ambitions, but found love instead. Anna was beautiful and good. But his marriage into the House of Romanov had not furthered his two objects of wresting the crown of Sweden from his usurper aunt, Ulrike Elenore, and of getting the Danish king to restore to him his Gottorp territories in Schleswig. Such restoration as took place even before the Duke had journeyed to Petersburg was confined to his share of Holstein and was due to the intervention not of the Romanov but the Habsburg emperor, who had ordained that the Duke's territories within the Holy Roman Empire of the German Nation were to be restored to him forthwith. But the Danish king sat tight on the Gottorp part of Schleswig, from which nothing in the world seemed able to dislodge him.

Catherine I died of drink in 1727, two years after her husband, Peter the Great. The scramble for the throne which ensued convinced the Duke of Holstein-Gottorp that he had little else to hope from his Russian con-nections, and three months after the death of his mother-in-law he retired with his dear wife Anna to his piece of Holstein where, a year later, she died after giving birth to their son, Karl Peter Ulrich, the future Peter III of Russia.

IV. HOLSTEIN-GOTTORP: THE SEQUEL

THE Duke, who loved her tenderly, survived Anna by eleven years. He refused to consider marrying again and rejected the hand of an English princess of the House of Hanover: he could not forget his Anna. When the Duke breathed his last in 1739, his son, Karl Peter Ulrich, was eleven years old. Where fate had so stubbornly withheld a crown from the father, who had fought doggedly for his Swedish right of succession, it offered two crowns to the son, who wanted none. Karl Peter Ulrich was called Karl after his father, Karl Frederick; Peter after his maternal grand-father, Peter the Great; and Ulrich after his great-aunt, Ulrike Elenore, the Queen of Sweden, despite her usurpation of his father's crown and evidently with hopes of a kinder future.

His Russian mother's sister, Elizabeth, had scarcely secured her seat upon her father's throne before she sent for her nephew, Karl Peter Ulrich, who had reached the age of fourteen, and declared him her heir and successor. Elizabeth, twice snubbed by the house of Capet, at the time when her father, Peter the Great, had wanted to marry her to the boy Louis XV, and again when her mother had schemed to marry her to the Duke of Orleans, had decided to remain unmarried. Her pride had been wounded. The reason implied in the Bourbons' refusal to consider her as a suitable consort for the grandson of the *Roi-Soleil,* or even a mere prince of the blood, was, as all Europe knew, her mother's low birth. Her mother, the drunken Catherine I, as already stated, had been a Lithu-anian peasant girl, actually a serf, who had passed through several hands till Peter the Great had made her his mistress, then married her and crowned her as his consort, and after his death left her the imperial throne. Elizabeth, the younger daughter of Peter and Catherine I, in-herited her parents' most pronounced characteristics—the love of the bottle which both parents shared in abundance, and a passionate lust of the flesh which particularly distinguished her father. It occurred to Elizabeth that by remaining unmarried she could the better satisfy her natural promiscuity. Also she must have observed that her cousin Anna Ivanovna (daughter of the idiot Tsar Ivan, her father's half-brother) who had reigned, among other claimants, in the interval elapsing between the death of Catherine I and her own accession, had been specially chosen by the Russian aristocracy who wielded the power, on account of her single station, Anna Ivanovna's husband, a duke of Courland, having happily expired before. For all these reasons Elizabeth remained technically a virgin; in practice the reverse. But now that she was seated firmly on her father's throne she desired to be succeeded by the blood of Peter. The idiot Tsar Ivan's progeny, whom she had forcibly displaced, was still extant and always a menace. And Elizabeth felt that she could not do better than choose her dead sister Anna Petrovovna's boy, Karl Peter Ulrich, who had their father Peter's blood in his veins, Gottorp though he was and hopelessly German on his paternal side. She sent for him at Kiel, where he was; and the boy, much against his will, was brought to Petersburg, made to change his religion from Lutheran to Greek Orthodox and was created a Russian Grand Duke and Tsarevitch.

A few weeks later an embassy arrived in St. Petersburg from Stockholm to offer Karl Peter Ulrich, who had cashed in on the "Peter" side, the chance to exploit the "Ulrich" side, too, and become the heir-apparent to the throne of Sweden, on the heels of King Frederick I, a man rapidly tottering to the grave. The offer, though sensational, was not unnatural. The boy's father had after all been the son of Charles XII's eldest sister, Hedwig Sophie, and Karl Peter Ulrich was accordingly in the line of the Swedish succession.

Here, then, was this fourteen-year-old lad who, in addition to Romanov blood, had in his veins the ancient blood of the Wasas. And what he had of old Oldenburg blood and of Gottorp acquisitiveness in respect of Holstein-Gottorp we shall see in due course.

The Swedes were wily. They knew quite well that Karl Peter Ulrich, having embraced the Greek faith, was not eligible for the throne of Sweden where only a Lutheran was acceptable. But by offering Elizabeth's nephew a scepter he could no longer accept they thought they would bribe her into concluding a favorable peace with Sweden. They hoped that Elizabeth would make the gesture of returning Finland, which Russia had again seized from Sweden in a war raging intermittently ever since the time of Peter the Great.

But Elizabeth and her counselors were no less wily than the Swedes. They saw through their intentions. What the Swedes had in mind was no longer a secret to the Russian "College of Foreign Affairs." After accepting from the Empress's hands the return of Finland, in consideration for an offer her nephew would be unable to accept, they would proceed to carry out their scheme at home. This was to reunite the three Scandinavian countries, no longer able singly to withstand the growing power of Russia, under one scepter which, on the death of the present King of Sweden, was to go to the Crown Prince of Denmark, who would rule them all. Being very much at Russia's mercy, the Swedes were afraid to pursue this idea without first placating the Empress Elizabeth by giving her nephew the first (inevitable) refusal of the succession to the crown of Sweden, and by so doing demonstrating, as they thought, their brotherly intentions towards Russia.

But Elizabeth saw through that, too. She did not want a reunited Scandinavian kingdom—for obvious reasons. And she saw the advantage of a grateful relative on the neighboring throne—also for obvious reasons. While, therefore, declining the offer for her nephew on grounds of his recent conversion to the Orthodox faith, she accepted the offered position of Crown Prince of Sweden on behalf of Karl Peter Ulrich's next of kin, the Prince Bishop of Luebeck.

This Prince Bishop of Luebeck was administering Holstein-Gottorp during Karl Peter Ulrich's minority; as the Prince Bishop's father had administered Schleswig-Holstein-Gottorp during Karl Peter Ulrich's father's minority. (He was the one who had whittled away the whole of the Gottorp territory, reducing his nephew the Duke into a supplicant at Peter the Great's court.)

The Swedes were abashed. The idea of one reunited Scandinavian kingdom under the scepter of the future Danish king had taken hold of public imagination. It was a precursor of the "Anschluss." The idea had quickly gained ground and the people no doubt repeated the Scandinavian equivalent of *"Ein Volk! Ein Reich! Ein Führer!"* And nobody —positively nobody—wanted the Prince Bishop of Luebeck.

But they wanted their Finland back: and it was Finland *and* the Prince Bishop of Luebeck for their future King of Sweden, and no "Anschluss" —or it was no Finland and no peace for Sweden.

The Swedish embassy then reluctantly took their leave and returned to Stockholm, from where they set out to Holstein-Gottorp for the Prince Bishop of Luebeck. He, too, could boast of the ancient blood of the Wasas running in his veins. This meant that his sister, who was Figgy's mother, could also boast of the ancient blood of the Wasas running in *her* veins; and so, by infinite transference, could Figgy, who in due course, deposing her husband Karl Peter Ulrich (Peter III), became Empress Catherine the Great of Russia, with not a drop of Romanov blood, but with the blood of the Wasas and, as seems probable, Hohenzollerns, and in liberal measure the Holstein-Gottorps, coursing through her system.

For not only Karl Peter Ulrich, not only the Prince Bishop of Luebeck, but Catherine's mother, too, were all Holstein-Gottorps, springing from the cadet branch of that old German family, Oldenburg, which, in the middle of the fifteenth century, had been invited to occupy the throne at Copenhagen.

V. THE PRINCE BISHOP OF LUEBECK SAILS

WHEN the Swedish embassy arrived in Holstein-Gottorp they found that the Prince Bishop of Luebeck was staying with his mother and brothers and sisters at Hamburg. So the ambassadors with their numerous retinue proceeded to Hamburg to fetch the Prince Bishop, who, by the terms of the peace treaty concluded between Sweden and Russia, had officially become Crown Prince of Sweden. The Prince Bishop's mother and numerous relatives, which included his sister, Figgy's mother, and Figgy herself, assembled on the last day on which the new Crown Prince was to take leave of his family and be conveyed across the North Sea in the custody of the Swedish envoys and senators who had come to fetch him. They were all gathered on the terrace overlooking the sea, and away in the distance, barely visible with the naked eye, was the Swedish ship moored and awaiting the man who was taking protracted leave of his relatives.

The parting was long and tender. All the Holstein-Gottorps extant seemed to have arrived for the occasion. When the Prince Bishop of Luebeck had embraced the last and least Holstein-Gottorp of the ancient blood of Oldenburg he rejoined the Swedish envoys with their retinue, who were waiting for him some distance away on the shore. Here, at last, after three hundred years, the cadet branch of the Oldenburgs had caught up with the senior branch. Nay: they had gone one better. They had produced a future King of Sweden, whereas the elder branch could only boast of producing kings of Denmark.

They looked on, this bunch of Holstein-Gottorps; they stood and looked out in the failing light. And there was the Prince Bishop of Luebeck going away with the foreign envoys, turning round now and then to wave to them, then going on, advancing against the wind which ruffled his hair, waving again and going away into the gathering desolation. The wind which blew along the shore raised sand into his face, and the Prince Bishop with the band of foreign envoys surrounding him in their flowing capes was going away, no longer waving now, but going away with them. In the dim distance the ship which was to take him away was no longer visible. The Prince Bishop of Luebeck also could no longer be discerned by his family, whom indeed he never saw again.

VI. THE EMPRESS ELIZABETH'S INVITATION TO RUSSIA

SIX months later, on the first of January, 1744, the all-important letter from the Empress Elizabeth arrived in Zerbst. Signed by Count Brümmer, Master of the Russian Horse, the imperial letter read:

At the emphatic and particular command of Her Imperial Majesty, I have to inform you, Madame, that the sublime Empress desires Your Highness, accompanied by the Princess, Your eldest daughter, to travel to our country as soon as possible and set out without loss of time to wherever our Imperial Court may be at that time. Your Highness is too percipient not to realize the reason of the great impatience of Her Majesty to see you here, together with the Princess, Your daughter, of whom rumor tells us so much that is charming. There are situations when the world speaks with no other than the voice of God Himself.

This letter had arrived while the family sat at their evening meal. It was addressed to Catherine's mother but was enclosed in a large packet of letters addressed to Catherine's father. The parents read it together in an atmosphere of hushed silence, in the belief, common to parents, that any significant news which particularly concerns their child must be kept from it. They looked like two conspirators, and Figgy (as she was called at home) had no difficulty in catching sight of the crucial sentence "...accompanied by the Princess, Your eldest daughter, to travel to our country."

The response was the reverse of conventional. In stories depicting similar situations it is the heartless parents who urge a sobbing daughter to sacrifice her own feelings for the glory of the family. In this case, both father and mother were against accepting the imperial invitation, and it was the fourteen-year-old Figgy who was urging them to accept because she did so awfully want to be an empress. The parents pleaded danger— a remote country, unsettled conditions, a precedent, almost a tradition, for violently displacing and replacing Russian sovereigns and heirs-apparent. Only recently the Empress Elizabeth had herself ascended the throne by first pulling down the infant Tsar Ivan, consigning him and his parents to perpetual exile within Russia. Surely Figgy did not want to risk *that?*

Figgy was prepared to risk everything for a crown. When she was still younger her relatives had often speculated on her future. Somebody had even suggested that she might marry her second cousin, Karl Peter Ulrich. Their grandfathers had been brothers on the Holstein-Gottorp side. And they were nearly the same age. But Figgy's mother had said that, as Karl Peter Ulrich's claims to a crown either in Sweden or Russia were sure to be contested by others nearer at hand, he would have to marry the daughter of some powerful king or emperor who would be able to back his claims effectively, whereas Figgy was far too small a fry to help anybody.

But all this was changed now. Though the parents were not too sure that it was safe for their Figgy to marry the heir to the Russian throne, they could not resist voicing their amazement that, within a year or so, here was a third member of the House of Holstein-Gottorp reaching out towards the purple. It was all too good to be true. And there was, that first evening, after the parents had closeted themselves in, a great running to and fro in the house.

Herr Bolhagen, for one, was excited. He was all for it. Herr Bolhagen was a sort of old retainer who made up for his lack of specific success in life by offering advice at large. When Figgy was only seven or eight Herr Bolhagen had read out to them a paragraph in a newspaper concerning the forthcoming marriage of a second cousin of Figgy's, the Princess Augusta of Saxe-Gotha, with the soon-to-die Frederick, Prince of Wales, son of George II of England. "Do you know," he said, "this Princess is by no means as carefully educated as ours, and yet she is now destined to be Queen of England. Who knows what ours may yet become?"

It was Herr Bolhagen who had first planted the idea of a crown in Figgy's head. This Bolhagen had been an assistant of Figgy's father. Then he became an adviser, and finally his confidential friend. Catherine's mother did not care for Bolhagen. She was extravagant, whereas her husband was thrifty, in which habit Bolhagen encouraged the old prince. Catherine's mother often fell out with Bolhagen, who reproached her for her extravagance, while she reproached him with not liking her.

A Baroness von Printzen confessed her astonishment at Figgy's advancement. "She was born, grew up, and was educated under my eyes;

I watched over her school years and progress; I helped her with her packing before she left for Russia. She confided in me so much that I think I knew her better than anyone else knew her. Yet I would never have believed it possible that she should have achieved such fame. In her adolescence I noticed about her a cold, deliberate, calculating intelligence as far removed from anything noble or outstanding as it was from vice, capriciousness, and frivolity. In a word, I regarded her as an average girl, and you can well imagine my surprise when I heard of her unusual destiny."

VII. FREDERICK THE GREAT—CATHERINE'S FATHER?

ON the heels of Count Brümmer's letter from St. Petersburg there arrived for Figgy's mother a letter from Frederick the Great from Berlin.

The high respect which I entertain for you, Madame, and for everything which concerns your person, obliges me to inform you what is really involved in this journey. And the confidence which I repose in your estimable qualities emboldens me to hope that you, Madame, will handle correctly what I have to tell you concerning a matter the success of which depends upon the greatest secrecy. In this confidence, therefore, Madame, I will no longer withhold from you that, on account of the respect I entertain for you, Madame, and for the Princess, your amiable daughter, I wished to secure for her an unusually good fortune, and the idea had occurred to me that a possibility might exist of seeing her united with her second cousin, the present Russian Grand Duke....I beg of you to rest assured, Madame, that I will not cease to endeavor to be useful in the matter in question...."

Frederick the Great, as we know, modeled his French on Voltaire. With due allowance for the polite mannerisms of the age, it still seems singular that a man intimate enough to have planted in no unfruitful way his own seed in the womb of a dearly loved woman should be madame'ing her all along the lines of his letter. It echoes that little tune of insipid gallantry:

> *Ich küsse Ihre Hand, Madame.*
> "*I kiss your little hand, Madame.*"

On the other hand, it is no mean act, and certainly more than many another playboy would have done for the young bud grown of his unreflecting seed, and most affecting in that knave of genius, that Frederick the Great should have taken the trouble to insure for the illegitimate offspring of his youthful loins no less a position than that of the future Empress of All the Russias.

For that Frederick the Great, and not Christian August von Anhalt-Zerbst, was Figgy's real father, is almost certain—though, in the natural secrecy which pervades these things, not *quite* certain.

Minute investigation of the kind undertaken by George Moore, who proved that Wagner and Mathilde Wesendonck (contrary to the accepted view of modern scholarship, which had reversed the popular belief of a liaison between the composer and his hostess), *did* have sexual intercourse after all and *in spite of all* in the summerhouse at the far end of the lawn —proof of such sniggering meticulousness I am unable to provide. Such evidence as is advanced chiefly by German historians is circumstantial, hardly conclusive enough to hang a man on in an English court of law which, after hearing the case, would decide that the charge was not proven. Were I to sit on such a jury, I, too, could come to no other decision, remembering that the accused is entitled to the benefit of the doubt. But since Frederick and the wife of Christian August von Anhalt-Zerbst and Catherine II have all been dead a long time and have nothing to lose and everything to gain in interest for posterity by a relationship of illustrious illegitimacy, I must confess that, with nothing involved, I am inclined to think that, on the face of it, it is almost certain that Frederick II and not Prince Christian August of Anhalt-Zerbst was Catherine's progenitor.

There is a resemblance in their faces. In the portrait showing Catherine at the age of eleven she looks like the offspring of Frederick II. Even in later portraits she has the beaming eyes and receding forehead of that Potsdam knave. When Frederick was fifteen he experienced the agonies and ecstasies of first love. He fell in love with Countess Anna Orzelska, the natural daughter—the mistress, too—of Frederick Augustus I of Saxony, who thought that her being his *natural* daughter loosened their relation sufficiently to allow of a further spurt of loose morals. After Anna Orzelska, who broke him in, Frederick had a tender relationship with the Princess Johanna Elizabeth von Holstein-Gottorp. She was the daughter of the uncle and administrator of the Duke Karl Frederick who married the eldest daughter of Peter the Great as a direct result of his uncle's administration depriving him of all his lands and income. Johanna Elizabeth was no other than Figgy's mother. And her brother, the Prince Bishop of Luebeck, the administrator's son, whose career we have traced up to his departure for Stockholm to take up his duties as Swedish Crown Prince, had been Karl Peter Ulrich's uncle and administrator. So that, on the Holstein side, Catherine the Great springs from the uncle-administrator side, whereas her husband and second cousin, Karl Peter Ulrich, is the scion of reigning elder brothers. Figgy's mother was nine months younger than Frederick the Great. She was married at fifteen to the thirty-seven-year-old Prince Christian August von Zerbst, then a major general in the Prussian service and Commandant of the fortress of Stettin, where Figgy was born.

Catherine herself nowhere admits that she was the daughter of Frederick the Great. She tells us that while her mother was gay her father was of a retiring disposition: which in itself is no evidence; or perhaps evidence to the contrary, in suggesting that the older husband in retiring took his girl wife with him. But soon after Catherine had ascended the Russian throne, her attitude to Frederick underwent an abrupt and dramatic change. It was just after—this is the contention—Frederick had revealed to her in profound secrecy that he was her father.

That Catherine did not proclaim the news from the throne is not surprising. Gratified though she might be to know that she had sprung from the loins of the King of Prussia instead of the mere Prince Anhalt-Zerbst, in reality the reverse was preferable. Better be a Zerbst than add a reputation of illegitimacy to a position she was already occupying illegally. *Whatever* would the Russians think? Not only had she no right to reign, but no right even to have been born! When Catherine was a Russian Grand Duchess and the wife of the heir to the throne, Prince Christian August of Anhalt-Zerbst died and Catherine went into mourning. A lady in waiting of the Empress Elizabeth reprimanded the Grand Duchess in the name of the Empress for wearing mourning so long for a man who was no king. "Your father was no king," the lady in waiting repeated with some pertinacity, till Catherine was at last moved to make a reply: "I *know* he was no king. But he was my father."

Retrospectively, Catherine may have felt some satisfaction in learning that though the dead man was not her father, her father was a king.

What is the evidence for it? There is—as they say in divorce cases— evidence of opportunity. There is evidence of mutual desire, both Fred-

erick and Catherine's mother being what is called "fast." There is evidence
of mutual attraction. She had beauty and wit. Married to a man more
than twice her age whom she did not love, Johanna did not find it easy to
resist the advances of the young heir to the Prussian throne, nine months
her senior. She soon became Frederick's friend. While the unloved husband carried out his duties as Commandant of Stettin, his young wife
made frequent visits to his family at Zerbst. She was so keen on spending
all her time in the neighboring pleasure castle of Dornburg and stayed
there so long that many people believed that the future Empress Catherine II was born there. That is not true, since Catherine was born on
May 2, 1729, at Stettin in Pomerania, her mother having taken the precaution of going there for her confinement. However, exactly nine months
earlier, the future Frederick the Great had paid his beautiful friend a
long visit at Dornburg. He had come, he said, to be soothed. His relations with his impossible father had preyed on his nerves.

There is no official document to testify that the process of soothing had
living consequences. That the husband knew or suspected who was the
real father of their first-born is not certain. But it is evident that this insignificant prince, anxious to advance in Prussian service, was a wily man.
Immediately on his accession to the throne of Prussia, Frederick the
Great promoted Christian August of Anhalt-Zerbst to the rank of
General of Infantry, and soon afterwards to be Governor of Stettin, and
already in the following year General Field Marshal. Christian August's
military services hardly deserved such recognition. During both years of
his rapid promotion he was on the sick list. Frederick II was well-known
to confine his awards to men of indisputable merit. Neither could the
promotions be explained on the ground that Christian August was a ruling prince. It was, in fact, the other way round. Only after his promotion
to the rank of General Field Marshal was Christian August invited by
his elder brother, Johann Ludwig, to share with him the rule over the
tiny principality of Zerbst.

As already shown, it was Frederick the Great who had arranged for
Catherine's marriage with the future Peter III, though he was keen on
offering the hand of one of his sisters. It is suggested that he chose Figgy
because she was even nearer to him than his sisters, and because he
thought that it would be easier to marry off his royal sisters than a girl
so obscure as Figgy. But chiefly, it is thought that the King expected
consequences favorable to Prussia to follow from the marriage on which

he had set his heart, and that a bright girl like Figgy was more likely to hold up her end in Russia than either of his two unmarried sisters. That Figgy showed promise of intelligence Frederick knew from personal observation. She had spent by far the greater part of her childhood and adolescence in Berlin and had been brought up at his own court. He could see with his own eyes that she had in fact inherited something of his own spirit and alertness.

A Russian Grand Duchess, brought up in Prussia and owing her fortune to its king, was not likely to betray ingratitude. But so long as the Empress Elizabeth, the Grand Duke Peter and Catherine's mother were alive, Frederick knew that nothing would be served by revealing the secret. Elizabeth, not too certain of her own legitimacy (Peter the Great took her mother without divorcing his first wife) would have been furious at having a bastard thrust upon her. Karl Peter Ulrich, though a fervent admirer of Frederick the Great, would scarcely have been pleased at the discovery that his wife, who shamed him with her infidelities, was herself conceived in sin.

For Catherine in her promiscuity was indeed walking in the steps of her presumed father, who had been a gay lad in his youth. Only after the fall of Peter III and the death of Catherine's mother in Paris (where she had finished by swinging a loose leg), did Frederick at last disclose to Catherine the secret of her parentage. Catherine, who, to offset the unpopularity of her deposed husband's preference for Prussia, had in her first manifesto of July 9 declared Frederick II as Russia's greatest enemy, abruptly swung round and began to see him as her greatest friend.

Already by July 30, the Prussian Ambassador at St. Petersburg was reassuring his royal master that the Empress of Russia would respect the peace treaty her deposed husband had concluded with Prussia and that the Russian troops which had occupied the Prussian provinces would be withdrawn forthwith. It was stated that the description in Catherine's manifesto of Frederick as the greatest enemy of Russia was attributable to an error in translation. Catherine subsequently neglected her one surviving brother, for whom while she was still a Russian Grand Duchess she had planned to do so much. And this brother suddenly conceived a bitter hatred for Frederick the Great, it being assumed that the cause of his hatred was his sudden discovery of Frederick's early betrayal of his father. Such are the reasons advanced by German historians in support of the view that Catherine was Frederick's natural daughter.

VIII. UNCLE GEORGE

IT had cost Frederick a pretty penny to square all the important people in Russia, including the priests and bishops who, after they had been squared, decided that the marriage of second cousins was in accordance with the tenets of the Greek Church. The King, anxious lest the fruits of his labor and money be wasted, wrote again. "According to all that I have heard from Petersburg in the meantime, the business in question, Madame, is so far advanced that we can hope it will be ripe for words, assuming that meanwhile the secret is well kept and that you, Madame, decide to make haste and accelerate your departure for Moscow in order, Madame, not to lose these favorable moments."

Count Brümmer at St. Petersburg was of like opinion. "I take the liberty," he wrote a second time, "of most humbly beseeching Your Highness to set out on your journey as quickly as ever possible, without losing a moment." He wished to say that there was a tide in the affairs of men which, taken at the flood, led on to fortune. Omitted, all his days were spent in shallows and in miseries. But he lacked Shakespeare's golden tongue, and he put it less felicitously—thus: "You know, Madame, one must strike while the iron is hot and there are favorable moments which one may not allow to pass without the risk of losing them forever."

Never was this more true than of Catherine. She was impatient; her mother was not. The Empress Elizabeth invited them to Russia on the pretext of affording them the opportunity of thanking her for all she had done for her sister's husband's family. She had performed three good deeds in about one year: appointed Karl Peter Ulrich her successor; appointed the Prince Bishop of Luebeck successor to the Swedish throne; and selected Figgy as a wife for Karl Peter Ulrich. Could her devotion to the Holstein-Gottorp family go further? Catherine's mother was officially required to travel to Russia to express her gratitude to the Empress (*a*) as a first-cousin-once-removed of Karl Peter Ulrich; (*b*) as a sister of the Prince Bishop of Luebeck; (*c*) as the mother of Figgy.

And—not unnaturally—she was not keen. She would far rather have married Figgy off to her own favorite brother, George, who was in love with his niece. This Uncle George was a constant visitor at the house of his sister. Nobody appreciated him quite so much, he said, as this particular sister. And indeed she must have appreciated him quite amazingly well to wish to marry her young daughter to him. Uncle George was then twenty-five, and as Figgy already by the age of eleven looked remark-

ably developed and mature, with a leering smirk of a hardened cor-
ruptress of youth on her rather unpleasant mouth, it is hardly to be
wondered at that Uncle George was unsettled by her premature charms
at fourteen.

When her mother was out or wrote letters—which she did incessantly
and with gusto—Uncle George went into Figgy's room and spent hours
with her, till the governess, Babet Cardel, began to complain. When they
all went to Hamburg and the governess was left behind, Uncle George
never left Figgy's side. But as they were approaching Brunswick he grew
moody and, in reply to her questions, answered that at Brunswick they
must be discreet on pain of being misunderstood. Brunswick was full of
idle gossipers; it would never do, he said, his being seen talking intimately
to her at Brunswick.

And, indeed, at Brunswick Uncle George kept away from his niece.
During the day he was melancholy, reflective, *distrait*. He blew great
sighs and shook his head as if wondering at and deploring his own tragic
obsession. In her mother's room in the evening he drew Figgy to the window and complained of the intolerable restraint imposed on his passion.
Figgy understood nothing. What restraint? Had she perhaps been un-
restrained in her behavior, treated him without the respect due to an uncle
ten years her senior?

"Ah!" he groaned. "You understand nothing!" His greatest misery, the
most cruel misfortune with which fate had seen fit to punish him, was
to make him Figgy's uncle.

Again she understood nothing. Was she then an inadequate niece?

He seized his head in both hands and groaned. "You understand
nothing! nothing!" he shouted. She asked him what she had done to make
him angry with her; and he replied, mystifying her still more: "Nothing.
Nothing whatever. But the trouble is I'm too fond of you."

Figgy paused for thought; she came to the conclusion that the right
answer was to thank her uncle for his friendship.

He grew angry and shouted rudely: "Oh, you're a child with whom
one cannot talk anyhow!"

She excused herself and begged him to tell her very simply and quietly
the cause of his trouble, and he agreed on condition that she had enough
friendship for him to comfort him in *his* way.

She assured him positively on this point; and he said: "Then promise
to marry me."

It struck her like a bolt of lightning. Love she did not understand, and she said, as if reproaching him, that she hadn't thought him capable of such a thing. She loved him, she said, as a brother of her mother. He looked at her sulkily as if to say: "Confound the lot of you!" He was glum, as she said: "You're joking. You are my uncle. My parents would not wish it."

"And you also would not," he answered tartly.

After this Uncle George sulked for weeks till Figgy's mother, who loved her brother more than her daughter, persuaded her to accept her uncle so as to make him happy.

Figgy then agreed—one day, but not yet—to marry her Uncle George. He had been sulking for weeks, walking about with a cloud on his face. Learning of his niece's decision, his face cleared and he abandoned himself to the full force of his passion, which was vehement. Uncle George lay in wait for opportunities to kiss her. When these were absent or frustrated he was meditative and *distrait,* lapsing into prolonged melancholia. She tried to wake him up, but Uncle George only sighed and groaned. At the name of Henry of Prussia, with whom Figgy had danced the minuet at Berlin, Uncle George flew into a murderous mood of jealousy. Then again he grew strangely quiet, and sometimes he cried.

They parted at Brunswick, Uncle George forcing a vow from his niece never, never, but *never* to forget him; which she did not find difficult to give him. Completely satisfied, he left like a lamb, and Figgy and her mother returned to Zerbst; where, on January 1, the fateful letter inviting them to Moscow reached the family. And the parents locked themselves in after dinner, and a great running to and fro began in the house.

IX. VISIT TO FREDERICK THE GREAT

FIGGY at once said, yes, she was all for going and being a future Empress of Russia. But her mother looked at her with large-eyed alarm, and said in a voice in which there was a note of reproach:

"But what of poor Uncle George?"

Figgy, weighing a crown against an uncle, had no hesitation in deciding for the crown. Her uncle already bored her considerably; a crown held incalculable romance.

And so, at last, they set off, breaking the first stage of their journey to Russia at Berlin in order to register their respect before King Frederick, who had—or claimed he had—engineered it all from a sheer abundance of human kindness.

When father, mother and daughter arrived in Berlin, Figgy's mother showed a suspicious reluctance to produce her daughter at the Prussian Court; and Frederick displayed a corresponding insistence, in the end superior to the mother's resistance, on having her appear. It is difficult to avoid the suspicion that Catherine at fourteen resembled her natural father so strikingly that her mother shrank from blatantly parading a fifteen-year-old sin before the assembled Court of Prussia. She dreaded lest others, seeing Frederick and Figgy side by side, draw the natural inference. Her persistent evasions, her insincere excuses for not producing her daughter, even after she had agreed to bring her, are indeed very odd. When commanded by the King to come to court with her daughter, the Princess of Anhalt-Zerbst at the last moment reported that Figgy was ill. The King, perhaps thinking his ex-mistress had scruples on account of the Queen, waited two days to allow for the girl's recovery from an illness in which he did not believe, and then commanded the Princess of Zerbst to dine with the Queen and be absolutely certain to bring Figgy. That there should be no mistake about it he got the Queen herself personally to request the princess to bring her daughter to dine with them.

The princess appeared—without Figgy. The King remarked sourly that he failed to see her daughter. The mother's answer was that Figgy was still ill. Frederick said he knew perfectly well it wasn't true. The mother spoke with a coy obstinacy, as though requesting the King to accept her obstinacy shrouded in protective coyness which concealed the secret shared between them. A secret he should respect, without dwelling ungallantly on the too-transparent excuses she owed him as a king. Figgy, she said, was not dressed.

Frederick, on the other hand, was reluctant to allow a woman to defy his royal command on the strength of a fifteen-year-old romance. Yet equally reluctant to parade his power, which would have lessened his self-respect, he merely transferred the onus of being tiresome from himself onto his ex-mistress. He would wait, he said, with the dinner until tomorrow, if necessary, to give Figgy ample time to get dressed.

Cornered, the princess took a moment to rally her wits. Figgy, she said, had no court dress.

The King, who had arranged for her daughter's ceremonious visit to a foreign court, could not be expected to believe this either. Instead of saying to the mother: "In that case you are a bigger fool than I took you for," Frederick, however, accepted the excuse as valid, but only in so far as the obstacle could be overcome with resources lying ready to the head of the House of Hohenzollern. One of his sisters was to send Figgy a court dress at once, while they postponed dinner by an hour. Beaten at her own game, the mother realized that, when all was said, a father who had taken the trouble to arrange such a good *partie* for his natural daughter could hardly be denied the satisfaction of looking her over and wishing her Godspeed. So she sent word to Figgy to dress and come.

Figgy appeared. She had extremely good manners. She had the manners peculiarly suited to a future empress destined to endure eighteen years of irksome apprenticeship to a female autocrat of uncertain temper, before she stepped into her shoes. Figgy's manners were those of a woman conscious of a superiority she chooses to hold in abeyance, provided others are doubly conscious of her superiority—and the abeyance. Those are exquisite manners never failing to elicit a charmed response in inferiors, who exclaim: "How simple! *And* how gracious!" But they are manners which madden men of intellectual stature a cut or two above Figgy's. They are not mollified by an artificial simplicity without charm which she lets off on them in the belief that they must share the high opinion she entertains of her own brilliance, in which they cannot truthfully concur. And they are exasperated by her deceptive accessibility to ideas, resembling those invisible inward-curving shop windows which deceive the eye, but in reality divide the pedestrian from the goods on show as surely as the more conventional plate glass.

The Princess of Zerbst had noticed in Figgy a tendency to pride which, though seemly in the daughter of a king, was unseemly in a bastard. It could be excused on both counts by Figgy's total ignorance of either fact, but was not to be countenanced for the same reason. Her mother had, since Figgy's infancy, tried to correct this trait by requiring her daughter to kiss the skirt of the grand ladies who came to visit them at Zerbst or Stettin. And it may be this early habit of submission which so admirably balanced modesty and pride in Catherine who, in the years of her apprenticeship to a capricious and exacting empress, adapted herself by a stress of modesty and humility. When, eighteen years later, she had herself stepped into Elizabeth's shoes, Figgy made the most of a modesty which came easily to her through a long habit contracted in childhood and at the court of the Empress—a modesty which she knew served the better to set off all her inherent graciousness thus thrown attractively into relief. For when others far and wide refer to you as "her gracious majesty" there is little need indeed to draw attention to what is obvious to all. The effect is enhanced by looking as nearly a human being as is compatible with being a goddess.

Frederick the Great at thirty-two beheld the not unauspicious human effect of which he had been the propulsive cause at seventeen. "She was," says a contemporary, "from a child extremely well-mannered. She was tall and well-developed, and though not beautiful, the cast of her features was pleasing, an impression greatly enhanced by her habitual friendliness and graciousness. Her education had been entirely in the hands of her mother, who took care to check in her the slightest expression of pride, a quality to which she was a little prone."

The King of Prussia, through whose hands all the letters from Russia had passed, explained to her parents the circumstances responsible for the choice of their Figgy. There were, he said, two rival parties at the Russian Court. The first, that of Count Bestushev, wished to marry the Grand Duke to a Saxon princess, while the other sought a French alliance. The French Ambassador to Russia, the Marquis de la Chétardie, would himself have proposed a daughter of Louis XV—one of those poor over-regimented princesses who watched their father dexterously slice off the top of his egg at breakfast before he departed to the hunt and they, with a sigh, to their lessons.

But the Empress Elizabeth would not hear of it. If she herself had not been thought good enough for Louis XV, then obviously *his* daughter was not good enough for one who would one day be Emperor of Russia. Figgy was hit upon as a "compromise solution."

The Queen's brother approached Figgy and said: "At the masquerade at the Opera House this evening, you, Madame, will be at the table of the King." When Catherine told her mother this, the latter remarked: "That's queer! I am invited to the table of the Queen!" The Prince of Anhalt-Zerbst was given a separate table, at which he was to do the honors.

It was as though Frederick had said to the mother: "I shall spare you the ordeal." Perhaps he also wished to spare her husband.

That evening, at the appropriate hour, an elderly lady in waiting led Figgy to the banqueting hall where the Queen's brother met her and took her hand. He piloted her skillfully through the throng of guests till she was at the very head of the table. When Figgy saw that Frederick the Great was her neighbor she had a shy impulse to withdraw. But the King told her to stay, and conversed with her during the whole evening. He talked a great deal and said many amiable and polite things in his Voltaire-modeled French.

Thirty-five years later, writing from Petersburg in the eighteenth year of her reign, Catherine says in a letter to Frederick that to her constant regret she had "only seen him and heard him converse at an age when, though capable of respect, one was not capable of understanding."

At last the dinner ended and they left Berlin. Near Stettin Prince Christian August of Anhalt-Zerbst, whom the Empress Elizabeth positively did not wish to come to Russia, took tender leave of Figgy. It was the last time she ever saw him and she cried bitterly.

X. GOOD-BY TO ALL THAT

FURNISHED with a document containing her husband's meticulous advice—his contribution to Figgy's brilliant future—entitled *Pro Memoria To Accompany My Consort on Her Journey,* mother and daughter continued their travels through Prussia and Courland...and all these things were left behind....The escort was but small, comprising a chamberlain, a maid of honor, a couple of servants, and a cook. Before Figgy stretched the unknown future; behind lay her childhood, her past from which she reconstructed images of what was to come. As she sat in the chaise beside her mother she was entirely made up of the memories she carried with her of her fourteen years of life. After she had crossed the frontier she wiped out, with a vengeance, her fourteen years in Germany, plunging with excitement, with exultation, into the mysteries of Russian life, never to look back.

What was there to look back on? There had been Stettin, where her father had been commandant, and later governor. Catherine's mother would have preferred a residence in Berlin to anywhere else. Her father thought otherwise. There had been journeys to Zerbst, to Hamburg to see grandmamma. There had been a visit to the German opera. She remembered an actress in blue velvet embroidered with gold. She had a white handkerchief in her hand and when Figgy saw that she was drying her eyes with it she began to cry and howled so loudly that she had to be sent home.

About that time she was handed over to a French émigrée, Madeleine Cardel, a woman who, because she was charming, was not considered by Figgy's mother to be very sincere. Figgy had the vice of never doing anything until she had been told to three times; and then only if bawled at. Madeleine Cardel soon gave place to her less charming if more plausible sister, Babet, who taught Figgy to read, bribing her, when all other expedients failed, with sweets, which, incidentally, ruined the child's teeth. But she still could not spell. She never learned to. If Babet did not give in to her, Figgy yelled so loud that she had to be put to bed in her parents' room. Or she pretended to be asleep so that Babet would go, and when she was alone seated herself astride her pillow and galloped in her bed till her strength left her.

When she was four years old Figgy saw King Frederick William, the father of the future Frederick the Great. The King was reputed to be very stingy. Figgy asked her mother: "Why is the King's coat so short? Surely he's rich enough to afford a long one." "What's that? What's that?" said the King; and they had to tell him. He laughed—unconvincingly.

Figgy, as she grew up, did not think herself attractive and bestowed little care on her clothes. She did not know whether she was really ugly as a child. But she was told so often that she was, that she formed a theory that she had better apply herself to being virtuous and even learned. They taught her to despise coquetry. She did not know what they meant by the word, but thought it was something very dreadful.

What else was there in her fourteen years of life she was carrying away with her to an unknown land and destiny? There were relatives, of course, and they had given tone and color to her days. There had been an aunt, an eccentric. That aunt had had an accident at the age of ten. Her wig had caught fire and her face had been badly burned. The skin was all withered and shriveled up and she looked horrible. However, she felt that beauty was only skin deep, and she obstinately desired a husband. Obstinately she made advances to each eligible German prince in turn; but they took one look at her and negatived her proposal. From this series of inner personal humiliations she transferred her attention to the outer world. She kept in her room an astonishing variety of birds, maimed birds, incomplete birds. A thrush with only one foot; a lark with a broken wing; a one-eyed goldfinch; a hen whose head had been substantially pecked away by a cock whose tail-feathers had been torn out by a cat; a lopsided, crippled nightingale; a parrot without legs who lay on his belly. All these she tended. It did not occur to her to put them out of their misery. One day Figgy, left alone in this aunt's room, rather thoughtlessly opened the window, and out flew such of the birds as could fly. The girl was alarmed; she shut the window and ran away. When her aunt returned she found that only her worst patients remained. She guessed what had happened and forbade her niece ever to enter her room again.

When Figgy was older she asked the pastor who instructed her in holy scripture which of the Christian Churches was the oldest. He said the Greek Church, and volunteered his own personal opinion that its teachings most nearly corresponded with those of the apostles. From that time Figgy developed a great interest in the Greek Church, and was curious to know more about it.—And twenty years later she was the head of that Church.

Another time she asked the same pastor what had been before the world began. He replied: "Chaos." She asked him what chaos was; and found his attempts to define it inadequate.

Figgy probed into another mystery which the Herr Pastor positively refused to explain to her. She asked: what was circumcision?

And now she was entering a dominion of the Empress of Russia, Courland, and in the sky was a terrible comet. It was 1744. Catherine had never seen a comet before and it frightened her.

On February 1, she wrote to her father from Libau: "Recently I have been a little troubled with the stomach-ache. It was principally my own fault because I drank all the beer I could get on the way. Dear Mamma has put a stop to this, and now I am quite better again."

BOOK TWO

BOOK TWO

CHAPTER IV

IN THE DAYS OF THE
EMPRESS ELIZABETH

I. TO ST. PETERSBURG

WHEN they arrived at Mitau, the commander of the Russian troops in Courland had himself announced to them. Next morning he accompanied them on their way to Riga, where they were met by the chamberlain. He presented letters from Her Majesty congratulating them on their arrival on Russian soil and conferring dignities and privileges upon them. The vice-governor, followed by a train of State coaches with courtiers and servants, drove out to welcome them before they reached Riga. They alighted from their modest German traveling coach—the best that Anhalt-Zerbst could provide—and transferred their valuable persons to the more gorgeous vehicle belonging to the reigning daughter of Peter the Great. As they drove over the ice to the other side of the river the cannons of the fortress boomed in salute.

Entering the suite prepared for them in Riga, they saw two magnificent sable skins lined with gold brocade, two sable collars, and a beautiful rug intended to cover them in the sledge—all presents from the Empress.

Among the people who called on them was a general entrusted with guarding in a near-by castle the Princess Regent, Anna Leopoldovna, her husband, Prince Anton Ulrich of Brunswick, and their son, the baby Tsar Ivan, whose throne the present Empress Elizabeth had usurped two years previously. Elizabeth had intended to deport them to Germany, but changed her mind as they reached Riga.

From Riga they traveled in sledges, and Figgy was hugely amused at the acrobatic feats the Russian courtiers enjoined her to perform with her legs in adapting herself to this, to her, new mode of travel. They sped through Baltic towns conquered by Peter the Great, with buildings which still bore marks of the bombardment, though half a century had elapsed. Lying back in their sledge, the horses galloping all the way, two days later, to the thunder of cannon, they crossed the Neva and presently pulled up at the Winter Palace. Figgy looked out on St. Petersburg.

The Court was at the time in Moscow, but such of the courtiers and ladies as had been ordered to await their arrival were drawn up on the stairs as Figgy and her mother alighted.

From Petersburg the mother writes to her husband: "Figgy endures the fatigue better than I, but we are both of us well, thank God, may He guide and direct us further."

To Frederick II she writes: "Add to that the strain of the Russian winter, the long journey, and the change of air. Really, I need an iron constitution to keep up my strength. My daughter is more lucky. Her youth fortifies her health. Like the young soldiers who scorn danger because they are not aware of it, she revels in the splendors by which she is surrounded."

The ladies in waiting at Petersburg proposed that Figgy should arrange her hair as they wore theirs. It was a fashion started by the mother of the baby Tsar Ivan, the Princess Regent, Anna Leopoldovna, now a prisoner near Riga. The hair was combed flat with a stiff little lock over the ears and a few hairs fastened down with glue to the cheek. A broad ribbon was wrapped round the head and the ends allowed to flop down to the waist. Flowers were stuck in the knots and loops and hung down with the beau-catchers glued down to the cheeks.

"Last Friday," says the court circular, "Her Highness, the Princess Anhalt-Zerbst and Her Highness, the Princess, her daughter, arrived here and were received in the Winter Palace by the high court personages of both sexes remaining there, while the cannon thundered from the Fortress and the Admiralty. On the following day and yesterday Their Highnesses deigned to take a drive in the city."

Two days later they started for Moscow.

The sledge in which Catherine and her mother were traveling struck in turning against a house, whereupon an iron hook fell out of the hood on the mother's head. She insisted that she was all but dead; but Catherine deprecated her mother's insistence by saying there was nothing to be seen, not even a bruise. The Princess of Anhalt-Zerbst describes the incident at length in a letter home. "The impact on the sledge loosened an iron bar which held the framework of the cover and kept it open; and this bar pulled with it another that supported the curtain to screen us from the sun. Both struck me on the head. I thought I was injured, but I was not. My fur had broken the full force of the blow; otherwise, no doubt, my head, neck and arms would have been smashed to pieces."

It was a point her husband had not foreseen in his *Pro Memoria To*

Accompany My Consort on Her Journey, and it puzzled him greatly. Had he not said that Russia was an incalculable land?

II. MOSCOW

THEY traveled day and night, and at the end of the third day they found themselves in Vsesviatskoye. The Empress had sent a chamberlain to meet them and convey greetings. He said that Her Majesty desired them to cross Moscow in the night. The Palace was the other side of the city. While they waited to start they all dressed up. Figgy wore a close-fitting gown without hoopskirts, of rose-colored moiré and silver. As they left, an official whom Catherine's mother had known at the Russian Embassy in Berlin threw a note into the sledge which she read eagerly. It contained brief character sketches of all the most important people at the court and the degree of favor in which they stood.

Towards eight o'clock in the evening they arrived at the Annenhof Palace.

They were met on the great staircase by the Adjutant General of the Empress. Assembled behind him stood the entire Court. He gave his hand to Catherine's mother and led them to the suites prepared for them. While they were taking off their furs and caps, silently into the room came the Grand Duke, whom they instantly recognized as Karl Peter Ulrich. He embraced them warmly. The suspense of the last hour, he said, had been absolutely unbearable. He would have harnessed himself to their sledge could it have hastened their progress.

Towards ten o'clock came Count Lestocq, the confidential friend and physician of the Empress, an expatriate Frenchman who had plotted for the *coup d'état* which had placed Elizabeth upon the throne of the baby Tsar Ivan. He imparted congratulations on behalf of the Empress and bade Their Highnesses follow him to Her Majesty's apartments. "The sooner, the better," the Empress had added.

The Grand Duke thereupon gave his hand to the Princess of Anhalt-Zerbst, and the Prince of Hessen took Figgy's. As they went through the antechamber, the Court was presented to them. The Russians scrutinized the newly arrived Germans from top to toe.

After they had passed through an array of apartments, they were led into the audience chamber of the Empress, there to await the august presence.

On the threshold of the state bedchamber Her Imperial Majesty came several paces to meet them. She scarcely gave the Princess of Zerbst time to take off her gloves before she embraced her tenderly. Whatever may be said on the score of Elizabeth's beauty, there can be but one opinion concerning her general appearance. She was tall and, though very stout, not offensively so. Her dress was of shining silver taffeta trimmed with gold lace. She wore a tall black feather in her hair. Diamonds glittered in her headdress. An enormous crinoline camouflaged her bulk. She was now thirty-five.

In her young years this daughter of Peter the Great must have been extremely good-looking. The Duke of Liria, an ambassador at the court of Elizabeth's predecessor, the Empress Anna, depicts her as follows:

"The Princess Elizabeth, daughter of Peter I, is the most beautiful woman that I have ever seen in my life. The color of her face, the light in her eyes, the perfect beauty of all her limbs, the whiteness of her hands and neck, her tall slimness—all in her amazes and bewitches you. She is tall and exceptionally lively, dances excellently and sits marvelously well on her horse. In intercourse she is adroit, clever, and displays a partiality for fame."

As she grew older, though her stature of course did not diminish, her slenderness went. Her torso was like a barrel of beer. For, indeed, she knew not frugality.

Kissing Her Majesty's hand, the Princess of Zerbst opened in German-French: "I have come to lay at Your Majesty's feet sentiments of the deepest gratitude for the gracious favors which Your generosity has lavished upon my house." For, in addition to making Karl Peter Ulrich her heir, and Figgy his consort, and the Prince Bishop of Luebeck heir-apparent to the throne of Sweden, the Empress was allowing Figgy's mother's mother a pension of £2,000 per annum, and had sent Figgy's mother her own portrait set in diamonds. "And of which," the princess went on, "new manifestations are vouchsafed to me at every step I take in the realm of Your Majesty. I have no virtue other than that of the profound gratitude which constrains me to dare beg of Your Majesty the honor of your protection for myself, my family, and my eldest daughter in especial, whom Your Majesty has graciously permitted to accompany me to your Court."

Her Imperial Majesty replied in Russian-French: "All I have done for you is but little to what I would like to do for my sister's family. My blood is not more dear to me than yours. My attitude will not change and my friendship must speak for itself."

After these exchanges of civilities the mother presented her daughter, whom the Empress embraced in the same tender manner. She then bade them enter her state bedchamber and had a sofa moved up and asked them to be seated. The conversation grew so animated that neither of them could recall a word of it. "Meanwhile," Figgy's mother records, "Her Majesty momentarily retired, to give a command as I thought. But afterwards I learned that she was so moved by my resemblance to my poor dead cousin that she could not refrain from tears and it was on that account that she withdrew. After a short interval she returned from her closet."

If the truth must be known, Her Imperial Majesty retired, as she was forced to do at brief intervals, to have another ... and yet another, without which stimulant she could not remain coherent.

After a few minutes' conversation she dismissed them, saying that they were probably tired out by the journey, and retired behind a screen— to have another.... The Grand Duke, who had meanwhile conversed with his girl cousin, now escorted them back to their apartments, where they had supper. During the meal the Empress came to the door without their seeing her, to look on.

The next day was the birthday of the Grand Duke, a day of pomp and circumstance. The Empress emerged from her dressing room in full regalia. Her dress was embroidered in silver and her hair, neck, and corsage were smothered with jewels. She was followed by the Grand Master of the Hunt, her lover and favorite, Aleksei Razumovski. He was one of the handsomest men Figgy had ever seen in her life. He carried on a golden plate the insignia of the Order of St. Catherine. Figgy stood, she says, somewhat nearer to the door than her mother, and the Empress accordingly first bestowed the Order of St. Catherine on her, and then on her mother, after which she kissed them both.

But the mother, in writing home, gives the opposite version:

"We were led to Her Majesty's apartment, where she commanded two Gentlemen of the Bedchamber to bring the Order of St. Catherine, with which she graciously invested us, throwing the ribbon over me first, and my daughter afterwards. The ladies von Vorontsov and Tchoglokov assisted us with the ribbon and pinned on the stars."

Catherine and her mother often differ in their accounts. While Catherine's inaccuracy is probably due to the lapse of time, her mother's version, who writes home there and then, is distorted by her vanity and the wish to impress the folks at home by exaggerating her effects. Though

Catherine, in recording her memories after the lapse of many years, often errs in details and sometimes prevaricates deliberately out of policy, her memory has sifted her material and she generally records, in her slapdash fashion, what is characteristic and essential. The mother piles it on everywhere and always says that they cannot make enough of her.

She goes on: "Her Majesty then took us to the Grand Duke and, presenting us to him, said that she trusted these new knights of the Order of St. Catherine would give pleasure to her dear nephew. He was delighted, for, as the Empress told me, he had desired the Order for us but had not dared to ask."

After Mass the Empress told them with the gravity of one imparting a State secret that she was preparing for Communion and would go to confession on that same day and on the following day would partake of the Holy Supper. She wore a long-sleeved dress of black velvet with all the Russian Orders: the Order of St. Andrew as a scarf, the Order of St. Alexander on her bosom, and the Order of St. Catherine on her backside.

III. BETROTHAL

THREE months after her arrival in Moscow Figgy fell ill, with what today would seem to be appendicitis. She was energetically bled, against her mother's most emphatic protests, and—curiously—she recovered. While she was bled the Empress held her in her arms and desired the mother not to interfere. The mother during a subsequent bleeding was locked out. Each time Figgy was bled the Empress presented her with diamond brooches, earrings, clasps; and the mother in her letter home always mentions the probable price: "Worth about twenty thousand roubles...must have cost at least three or four thousand roubles." Even the wound caused by the bleeding was bound up with a diamond brooch "worth thirty thousand roubles."

Figgy recovered, feeling that she was in clover, and began to overspend her allowance of £3,000 a year and contract heavy debts, which provoked the generous Empress into a fit of indignation. She herself as a princess, an emperor's daughter, she said, received nothing like £3,000 and managed to live within her allowance. Figgy's excuse was that it all went in presents, chiefly to her mother to keep her jealous nature pacified. Catherine, reviewing in mature years her extravagance, justifies it on the ground that she had a "contempt for riches" which she had "never otherwise regarded than as a means of obtaining the things which give one pleasure."

Next the Grand Duke had the smallpox, and when she saw him again in St. Petersburg she had a shock: he was so disfigured by the pockmarks that she could not recognize him. But pockmarks or no pockmarks, the Empress had decided that they were destined for each other.

Catherine had the right instinct for propitiating the Empress. During the fast Her Majesty sent word to Catherine that she would like it very much if the Princess Sophie would observe it. Catherine replied that Her Majesty had anticipated her; she had already intended to ask her permission to do so. The chamberlain reported that this had pleased Her Majesty very much.

Next they proceeded to change Catherine's religion. Catherine knew exactly what she wanted. She had no doubt that she had made a good exchange in coming to Russia. The Grand Duke preferred to be a German, an attitude which was not popular at court or in the country. Catherine wanted to be more Russian than the Russians—to capture the country and the love of everybody—and that as quickly as possible. The Prince of Zerbst had in his *Pro Memoria* laid stress that any change of religion should come gradually and should not be forced. But to Catherine it could not come quickly enough. The Empress and the Grand Duke wished a Russian bishop to visit Catherine and speak to her quietly in the hope of winning her over gradually to the Orthodox faith. But she said she was already won over. The Grand Duke, himself a convert, had argued that the change over was not as drastic as it seemed and that he had at last been convinced by reason. Catherine said she was already convinced. The Grand Duke tried to make her see that the heavenly could not be separated from the earthly crown. Catherine said: *Of course!* She saw it—or anything else they required her to see. The Russian bishop, prompted by the Empress, inquired gently whether the Grand Duchess brought up in the Lutheran faith had any objections to make or spiritual doubts to utter.—None! No doubts at all and no objections whatever!

The Empress then formally requested Prince Christian August of Anhalt-Zerbst for his consent to his daughter's change of religion and her marriage to the Grand Duke. Catherine, too, was told to write to him at Zerbst, which she did in the following eupeptic terms:

"As I am able to perceive almost no difference between the Greek and the Lutheran faiths, I have resolved (after an examination of the gracious instructions of Your Highness), to change my religion, and I will send you at the earliest opportunity my confession of faith. I flatter myself with the hope that Your Highness will not be dissatisfied with it."

In his answer her father writes: "In that case I give you then herewith my paternal blessing and consent, with the admonition that you put your faith and trust in no one but the Threefold God and in His Word, and that you test yourself well by my Instructions, and strive with diligence to reflect on what will bring you Eternal Happiness."

To the Empress, Prince Christian August replied in such terms of flowery humility as only the soul of a German pedant is capable:

"The extreme Grace and Favor with which Your Imperial Majesty has deigned to honor my daughter and your devoted servant, Princess Sophie Auguste Friedrike, is an act of Providence, for which, besides thanking my God and Your Imperial Majesty, I remain most obediently and humbly beholden; at your gracious command, however, and with the most fervent joy I give most respectfully herewith, through Your Imperial Majesty and His Imperial Highness, the Grand Duke, my paternal blessing and consent to the marriage with Grand Ducal Imperial Highness."

To the Grand Duke the Prince of Zerbst delivered himself of an even more tortuous communication:

"My paternal blessing and consent I have already most dutifully and unreservedly declared to Her Imperial Majesty and hereby also to Your Imperial Highness I do the same."

Oddly this communication filled the Grand Duke with unbounded, inconceivable joy. Catherine's mother writes to her husband:

"Since he could have no doubt of your consent, I hardly thought it possible that your letter could have moved him to such transports of gratitude.... Your letter was kissed a thousand times, and if all the good and kind wishes of your future son-in-law are fulfilled, you will be happy in time and in eternity."

Figgy learned her confession in Russian by heart, like a parrot. From the bishop who taught her she acquired a Ukrainian accent. The Grand Duke advised her to drop it, remarking that the Ukrainian accent would make people laugh. But when the day came she recited her confession with gusto and an ardor which brought tears to the eyes of the Empress, who was inclined to be lachrymose. Her Majesty presented Figgy with a clasp of diamonds "valued," her mother wrote home, "at 150,000 roubles."

"For this last day," the mother writes again, "I still had precedence over my daughter....Scarcely had we undressed when in came Her Imperial Majesty. The Gracious Monarch came to inform herself how her children felt after the fatigue of the day. She gave me the ring which my daughter was to exchange with the Grand Duke. These rings are miniature masterpieces. The two may easily have cost 50,000 ducats."

That evening the Court moved from the Annenhof Palace to the Kremlin. Next morning the Empress sent Figgy a diamond bracelet set with two miniatures of herself and her husband-to-be. The Grand Duke sent a watch and a gorgeous fan. When she was dressed, her mother took her to the Empress, where they found the Grand Duke waiting. Her Imperial Majesty departed with a great retinue and walked to the Cathedral where Figgy was affianced to the Grand Duke by the Bishop of Novgorod, who had heard her confession the day before.

Commenting on her daughter's appearance at the betrothal, the princess writes: "She was a little pale; the elegant costume enhanced her costomary paleness, and I can say" (which means a better-looking mother is generously forcing herself to make the most of it) "I can say I thought her beautiful."

A portrait of Catherine painted about that time exhibits her looking like a rather sheepish Mona Lisa who had trafficked for strange webs with eastern merchants and wasn't born yesterday, and whose strained expression seemed to say that if she wasn't beautiful it was not for want of trying.

That same evening the princess writes home to Zerbst: "Count Lestocq brought my daughter a watch set with large diamonds valued at 15,000 roubles and a fan set with diamonds in exquisite taste worth about 8,000 roubles."

In another letter the mother, writing to the father, concludes with the significant words: "The thing is done!"

IV. THE GRAND DUCHESS

IN the church, immediately after the betrothal, Figgy received the rank of "Grand Duchess" with the title of "Imperial Highness." Her real name had been Sophie Auguste Friedrike; and at home they called her Fike (Figgy). But, though Sophie was a perfectly good Russian name, the Empress did not like it. The idiot Tsar Ivan's sister, who had all but climbed onto the throne when Peter was a lad, was a Sophie of evil memory. Elizabeth's plebeian mother, Martha, had been given the name of Catherine and later reigned as Catherine I. So the Empress decided that Figgy also was to take the name of Catherine. (And, indeed, she was to reign as Catherine II.) And not only Figgy, but Figgy's father was provided with a new name—Aleksei. This was in order to furnish the new Grand Duchess with a Russian-sounding patronymic; for neither Christian nor August were acceptable to the Russian ear. And so Figgy ceased to be Princess Sophie Auguste Friedrike von Anhalt-Zerbst and became the Grand Duchess Ekaterina Alekseievna.

When the Procurator General of the Senate received the order to draw up the ukase for the title which, according to prescribed custom, she had granted Catherine, he asked whether the word *naslednitza* (meaning successor) should be added. The Empress said no.

On the strength of this one peremptorily rejected suggestion, the Procurator General spent the rest of his life claiming advancement. But Catherine says she regarded it as nothing more than what it was; namely, the action of a courtier. Good intentions count for nothing. And barren service rendered out of calculation (so thinks the sovereign who has been lifted to the throne on other shoulders) merits no reward.

Following the day of her betrothal Catherine had precedence over her mother—a circumstance which galled her mother, who was very vain. She writes: "We were informed that Her Majesty awaited us, and went to her. The Grand Duke gave me his hand; my daughter followed alone. When we had entered Her Majesty's presence I yielded for the first time precedence to my daughter."

Catherine says she avoided scoring over her mother as well as she could. Now her hand was kissed also. The mother writes to her husband at Zerbst, placing, in her usual vein, the best possible construction on a situation adverse to her personal dignity: "Well, Ekaterina Alekseievna, whose first steps on the ladder of fame have been reported to you, lays at your feet her filial obedience, which her sweet nature will certainly never allow her to forget. She adapts herself very readily to her new position, though as often as she is obliged to pass in front of me, she cannot restrain a blush."

Very soon she was reproaching her daughter violently because she said that she gave her favor to her mother's enemies. But Catherine, though she propitiated her mother, knew that her mother was growing unpopular with the Empress, while she herself was definitely in favor. She resolved to keep to her three resolutions:

(1) to please the Grand Duke.
(2) to please the Empress.
(3) to please the Nation.

She does not mention her mother.

At first she pleased all three; but finally she pleased only the nation because that was, she knew, the abiding way of pleasing herself.

V. THE WEDDING

EIGHTEEN months after her arrival in Russia Catherine was married. She was sixteen, her husband seventeen. On the night before the wedding, Catherine made all her ladies in waiting sleep in her bedroom. She had beds for the whole company made up on the floor. "Before we went to sleep," she recalls, "we held an argument regarding the differences between the sexes. Most of us, I think, were still entirely innocent; so far as I was concerned I can vouch that, despite my sixteen years, I had no idea what the difference was. More, I promised my maidens to ask my mother about it next day. The next day I really did ask my mother, and was well scolded for my pains."

Next morning at six Catherine was called into the bedroom of the Empress, who herself supervised her dressing and flew into a rage with Catherine's hairdresser for curling her front hair with irons. She went out in a rage. But what was odd indeed was that the hairdresser proved obstinate and would not, for artistic reasons, obey Her Majesty's command to have the hair flat. He appealed to the ladies in waiting, who ran to and fro between the Empress and the hairdresser. Finally, the Empress got bored and told them she didn't care what he did to Catherine's hair.

The Empress recovered her interest a little later and herself set the crown of a grand duchess upon Catherine's black hair. Elizabeth was great on jewels and told Catherine to put on all her own jewels and if that wasn't enough to borrow as many of the Empress's jewels as she had room for on her person.

Lord Hyndford, the English Ambassador, wrote in his dispatch to the Foreign Secretary in Whitehall: "The procession was the most magnificent that has been seen in this country and far surpassed anything of the kind I have seen anywhere."

The best man holding the wedding crown over the head of the Grand

Duke was none other than that good Holsteiner of our acquaintance, the Crown Prince of Sweden, *alias* the Prince Bishop of Luebeck. Catherine's wedding crown was held by the man whom the Empress considered to be the first man in the universe, her own lover and favorite, the Grand Master of the Hunt and the best-looking man in the empire, Aleksei Razumovski.

During the sermon a lady in waiting whispered in the ear of the Grand Duke that he should on no account turn his head while standing before the priest, as that meant he would be the first to die. The Grand Duke (who did die first as the result of the ambition of his betrothed now kneeling by his side) laughed it off as nonsense and repeated to Catherine what the lady in waiting had said, much to the lady's annoyance, so that she reproached him: which reproaches the Grand Duke— it was his habit—likewise repeated word for word to Catherine.

After the wedding they sat down to a banquet in the gallery of the Winter Palace. A canopy had been raised under which sat the Empress with the Grand Duke on her right and with Catherine on her left. One step lower and next to the Grand Duke sat Catherine's mother. And facing her, but level with the other three, sat her brother, the Crown Prince of Sweden, ex-Prince Bishop of Luebeck. Out of the four diners three were of the House of Holstein-Gottorp, the cadet branch of the Oldenburgs.

VI. THE RUMPUS

THE princess writes to her husband in her way of facile overstatement: "The Grand Duchess commends herself to you but has no leisure to write, since she is so newly married that she and her husband can hardly bear to be parted from one another for even a quarter of an hour."

Catherine's mother, not much over thirty herself and overshadowed by her chit of a daughter, soon tired of her position of poor relative owing eternal thanks to a female benefactor of a jealous and vacillating temper. She began to divert herself by satirical comment in congenial company, which included her old friend the Marquis de la Chétardie. Before Elizabeth ascended the throne, Monsieur de la Chétardie, the French Ambassador to Russia, had closely associated himself with Elizabeth's interests. He often visited her, and only Count Lestocq, her physician, was present at their interviews. Chétardie, by virtue of his friendship with Lestocq, knew of the coming palace revolution which was to elevate

Elizabeth to the throne. But his plans miscarried; Lestocq double-crossed him at the last minute, and Chétardie, who, as Ambassador, had already been recalled, departed from the capital a few days after the Empress's accession, laden with gifts, but not otherwise adequately recompensed.

When the French Court sent him back to Russia in a private capacity, it occurred to him that he still had in his pocket his credentials as Minister of the second rank, of which he made ample use. Things had changed a lot during his absence. The Empress had made the discovery that the devotion he had shown to her cause when Princess, did not in the least coincide with the wider interests of herself as Empress. This annoyed Chétardie; and he did not spare her in his letters to his government. He ran on in much the same vein to Catherine's mother, an old acquaintance. She laughed with him, then took her turn and added acid observations of her own, which he quoted in his letters home. They had a most agreeable time together. The Princess of Anhalt-Zerbst was famous for her wit, which had once, not less than her beauty, charmed the young Frederick. She had a gift for the pointed phrase. Monsieur de la Chétardie quoted her in the sense: *"That's* the material I have to deal with!" or "Try and do something for France in these conditions!"

But Chancellor Bestushev, less brilliant but more shrewd than they, had the marquis's letters intercepted and deciphered, and then laid all before the Empress. Monsieur de la Chétardie was arrested and banished from the country, and the Empress fell into a terrible rage with Catherine's mother. After *all* she had done for them! It just showed!

The Princess of Anhalt-Zerbst sought an audience of Her Majesty, and both women remained a long time closeted together. When they emerged they both appeared bright red. The Empress had been inarticulate with rage. Had not the princess arrived in Russia to lay her thanks, as she had said herself, at the feet of the Empress for all she had done for the House of Holstein-Gottorp? She had made her cousin a Tsarevitch; her daughter a Grand Duchess; her brother a Swedish Crown Prince. She had given her mother a pension; showered gifts on them all. . . . And then *that!*

The Empress, after walking up and down heftily, retired behind a screen to refresh herself, and then emerged indicating to the princess that if it was her wish to return to her own country she, for her part, would not detain her further in Russia.

The princess, with her wonderful gift of placing the best construction on a situation in which she herself figures to a disadvantage, writes to her husband: "Our parting was full of pathos: I found it hard in the extreme to take leave of Her Imperial Majesty, who for her part did me the honor to exhibit an emotion so profound that the courtiers who witnessed it were almost as deeply moved as we were. Many, many times we said farewell, till at last this most gracious ruler, with tears and repeated expressions of tenderness and regard, came as far as the staircase to see me off."

But a dispatch of the English Ambassador, Lord Hyndford, reads: "When she said farewell, she fell at the feet of the Empress and begged with tears in her eyes to be forgiven if she had in word or deed offended Her Majesty. The Empress replied that it was too late now to talk in this way, and that it would have been better for her if she had always been so humble."

VII. VIRORUM OBSCURORUM

THE Empress Elizabeth was popular, not because she was any better than her predecessors, but because she was anti-German. Whereas Anna Ivanovna, just before her, had lorded it over the Russian people with the aid of a German favorite, Bühren, who bullied the Russians as to the manner born, Elizabeth ruled through native bullies coated with a veneer of French polish. She was closer to the people than either Anna Ivanovna or Anna Leopoldovna. Her mother, Catherine I, was the type of Austrian maidservant imported into England. Not to mention the blood of Peter, Elizabeth had all the failings inherent in "the broad Russian nature." She drank like a fish, and every evening got so tight that she could not wait for her maids to unlace her, but ripped her clothes off herself, careless of the damage she did to them. She went on pilgrimages, kept fasts, was as superstitious as a peasant, loved finery. When she died her dresses, despite the rippings, numbered fifteen thousand. She was, with her love of precious stones, just the typical Russian merchant's wife, with no more taste than they. She had a whole room decorated with amber; which gives her measure.

Voltaire, whom Elizabeth paid a big sum to write a flattering biography of her father, Peter the Great, extended the flattery in consideration for money due but, alas! always sadly in arrears, to Elizabeth herself, whom he compared with her royal namesake of England—much to the Russian lady's advantage. The Empress was her father's daughter both as regards the pleasures of the table and of the bed. In men her tastes were liberal and unexacting, though her present lover, Aleksei Razumovski, was superlatively handsome. When she was as yet a princess she chanced to see in the street a good-looking man of the people. There and then she took him home, enrolled him in her service and made him her lover. He remained with her till she ascended the throne. Two days after her accession she appointed him a gentleman of the bedchamber, made him a landed proprietor and spent all her time in his vigorous society.

A groom of the imperial stables walked at the head of her state coach, holding the reins. The Russian for reins is *vozje*. From this word he obtained his surname—Vozjinski—previously, like all serfs, having only a Christian name. During Elizabeth's reign he too became a gentleman of the bedchamber and was also rewarded with money and estates.

Another, Yermolai Skartsov, was the son of a coachman. He became a servant of the Princess Elizabeth, and when the latter ascended the throne she made him a gentleman of the bedchamber.

The newly married couple saw little of the Empress, even when, as at Moscow, they all visited her antechamber at six o'clock each evening. Except on Sundays and holidays, she never left her own apartments. At the hour of the antechamber she mostly slept. This was natural because she stayed awake all night with her drinking companions. She often had supper at two o'clock in the morning, went to bed at sunrise, dined at five in the evening, and slept when she felt like it.

On the other hand, Catherine and the Grand Duke were required to lead a model existence: they dined punctually at twelve, had supper at six and went to bed at ten. The Grand Duke often visited her room in the course of the evening, but to no special purpose, for he far preferred to play quietly by himself with his dolls. He was then seventeen years old.

In the room adjoining his apartments, the Empress had installed a mechanical table of which she was especially proud. She often had her meals at this contrivance in the congenial company of her drinking friends, who were mostly serving-wenches, songsters and grooms. The Grand Duke, who had a highly developed sense of fun, thought it would be rather a good idea to see what actually happened in this room, so he bored some holes in the dividing door. But then, in the generosity of his heart, it did not seem to him sufficient that he should enjoy this free spectacle alone; he wanted others to share the fun. Catherine warned him this might lead to unpleasant consequences. She agreed herself to peep, but only once. What she saw was handsome Count Razumovski dining with the Empress in his dressing gown. The very next day the Empress found out what was happening; it annoyed her to be spied upon when dining with her lovers; and she pitched into the Grand Duke like a fishwife. Nothing could have angered her more than that he should have actually made holes in her door. The indignity of finding herself under observation by her seventeen-year-old nephew, just as she was letting herself go with her gentlemen of the bedchamber!

But to Catherine she said nothing at all. A lady in waiting whispered in Catherine's ear that the Empress knew that Catherine had advised against boring the holes in the door and was grateful for such...consideration.

VIII. SEVERITY AND REMORSE

ELIZABETH'S vanity was colossal. She seriously considered herself to be the most beautiful woman in the world. The smallest doubt in this respect sent her into a quivering rage. A false rumor maliciously attributing to a lady in waiting the remark that she herself was better-looking than the Empress was high treason to Elizabeth. An exceptionally beautiful woman, a mistress of the robes, Natalia Lapukhina, was by Elizabeth's orders whipped in public and had a part of her tongue clipped off by the public executioner because she had given tongue to her superior beauty by appearing at court in a pink dress—a color which Elizabeth reserved for herself.

Elizabeth was regarded as—and in some ways was—humane, even soft-hearted, having abolished the death penalty and restricted torture. Her reign, she decreed, should mark the beginning of an epoch humane and benevolent. There was to be no more impaling—torture should not go beyond breaking on the wheel. Her counselors thought her mildness a mistaken policy likely to result in an increase of treasonable activity. But she held out against them. No excessive punishment, she said, had ever proved successful as a deterrent.

Nevertheless, the Empress was not strong enough to grant justice to the innocent; she would have feared their resentment, and for that reason no one, guilty or innocent, who was once arrested was set free during her reign, except at the price of banishment. When she turned against her personal physician and confidant, Lestocq, she appointed his enemies to try him. She gave his house to one of his judges. Though the investigations revealed nothing against him, the sentence was: "Unsparing punishment with the knout, banishment for life to Siberia, confiscation of all movable and immovable property."

Yet the Empress, who could be hard, usually suffered from acute compunction when her victims had passed into a life beyond recall. When she heard of the death of Princess Anna Leopoldovna of Brunswick, who died in Kholmogori of a fever following the last of her incessant confinements, the Empress wept a great deal. Anna Leopoldovna had been Elizabeth's immediate predecessor who ruled as regent for her little son Ivan, great-grandson of the idiot Tsar Ivan, Peter's half-brother. Married to the Prince of Brunswick, who revolted her whole being, yet was the cause of her chronic confinements, Princess Anna lived only with and for her friend, Julia Mengden, from whom she was inseparable. But Elizabeth, in usurping the little boy's throne, exiled the family from one distant place to another and always so as to separate Anna from Julia. Now, over the coffin of poor Anna, Elizabeth shed bitter tears, without, however, troubling to improve the lot of her surviving family, who lived in dire need and unhealthy captivity.

Instead she ordered that the body should be brought to Petersburg for a solemn burial. The corpse arrived and was interred with imperial pomp and circumstance in the Alexander Nevski Cathedral. The Empress took part in the ceremony and Catherine accompanied her in her carriage. Elizabeth wept all through the service, shedding sincere copious tears. Princess Anna Leopoldovna was buried in the church between her grandmother, Tsaritsa Praskovia Feodorovna, wife of the idiot Tsar Ivan, and the latter's daughter, her mother, the Duchess of Mecklenburg, whom Peter openly seduced each time he passed through Mecklenburg.

IX. LIFE AT COURT

HOW life at court in the eighteenth century—and indeed in the nineteenth, twentieth, or any other century—shows up human limitations for enjoyment is suggested by this entry from the *Journal of the Court Quartermasters,* 1745:

August 22. At 10 o'clock in the morning the Gentlemen of the Court and the Ambassadors met together in the apartments of His Imperial Highness and extended their congratulations to His Imperial Highness. At noon Their Imperial Highnesses deigned to proceed by carriage from the Summer Palace to the Winter Palace, where Her Imperial Majesty condescended to receive them.—Her Imperial Majesty deigned to leave the Summer Palace and arrive at the Winter Palace at the beginning of the ninth hour. After the arrival of Her Imperial Majesty the ball began.

Another entry suggests the confines of liberty and license to which the Self-Upholder of All the Russias may carry her autocratic will:

January 6. Her Imperial Majesty has graciously condescended on this day not to leave her private apartments.

Life in a palace ... what does one do and what can one do in a palace? For one thing, one can ... read. Catherine liked to read and her boy husband read too. But what did he read? Stories of robbers. The Edgar Wallaces of his day. But what did she read? A Swedish envoy she had known in her childhood wagered that she had not read one book since she came out to Russia. He was right. She asked him what he would advise her to read. He suggested: Plutarch's *Lives; The Life of Cicero;* and *The Causes of the Greatness and Decline of the Roman Republic* by Montesquieu. She ordered the books to be brought to her; then read a few pages of *The Life of Cicero* in German. It seemed heavy going. She hopefully transferred her attentions to *The Causes of the Greatness and Decline of the Roman Republic.* She found herself falling asleep. Hastily she demanded the third book. It was not to be found.

The Grand Duke now began to take lessons on the violin from the musician Wilde—whether an ancestor of our Oscar I know not; and do not propose to delve into extensive research on this important point. He was very enthusiastic about music and often gave concerts in his rooms. He had a good ear but did not know a note; in spite of that he insisted on playing solo in all the concerts merely by ear. Professional musicians not unnaturally encouraged him, while Catherine endured in silence. She had no special aptitude or even liking for music, and she liked her husband's fiddling least of all. Nor was she accustomed to hearing praise of her own voice, the only exception being a certain lute-maker who reassured her and declared before others that her voice was a perfect contralto. Things like these she remembered and they made up her life.

She was more lonely than when she first arrived in Russia. The Empress grew more and more critical. The Grand Duke also seemed to care less for her companionship. Yet there were times when there seemed some sympathy: always when he was in trouble. He was timid, not very strong in the head; he possessed intuition, but no judgment. Very secretive when it suited him, he was at the same time extremely indiscreet.

The young couple lived as though in a glass house. The Empress removed all the courtiers who showed any liking for them and replaced them with others who reported to her every word they said. Catherine once called a lackey of whom she and the Grand Duke were both very fond to say a few words to him. Next day he sent her word that he had been sentenced to exile. Catherine ran to the Grand Duke and together they went through the vestibule, where they found him dissolved in tears. The Grand Duke was troubled because this young lackey seemed to have great loyalty for them both. They took an affectionate leave of him and all three of them cried.

Catherine was not even permitted to write home to her mother. Instructions issued by the Chancellor Count Bestushev for persons attached to the service of the Grand Duchess contained the injunction: "To avert the possibility of secret and undesirable correspondence, Her Imperial Highness can always command the College of Foreign Affairs to compose her letters for her and bring them to her for signature."

The Grand Duke, too, was separated from everyone who was even suspected of loyalty to him, and since he no longer had anyone to whom he could pour out his heart, he turned to Catherine. He often went to her room. She was the only person to whom he could talk without having his least word twisted and distorted to a false significance. She did her best to be kind to him, though he often bored her by the length of his visits, by the way he never sat down, so that she was obliged to pace about the room at his side. He took long strides and walked so fast that she had a job to keep up with him. As for his detailed descriptions of military matters, she could not keep up with them at all. He talked endlessly of these things, and once he had started it was impossible to get him to stop. She did her best to hide her boredom, because she knew that it was his only amusement and that he did not realize what a bore he was. Golf had not yet been invented.

Year succeeded year, but, despite discreet inquiries from the Empress conveyed through ladies in waiting, Catherine was unable to report any sign of a coming heir. She was indeed unable to report any progress in the Grand Duke's attitude to her, which remained that of a playmate making do with a female playmate who, though she took little interest in his dolls dressed up as soldiers, might be expected to show an interest in them as dolls. The Empress rarely, if ever, addressed the Grand Duchess herself, but made a point of transmitting her injunctions, usually accompanied by expressions of displeasure, through a favorite lady in waiting. Catherine received such injunctions, which were conveyed in a hectoring tone, in reverent silence and with a deep curtsy, as coming from Her Majesty.

No, there was no sign of an heir; and indeed there was nothing to indicate that the Grand Duke was capable of showing any interest in that direction. Yet the Empress's hopes had been lively. When, on the wedding night, the Empress had escorted the youthful married couple to their apartment, the ladies undressed the Grand Duchess and conducted her to bed, where she remained awaiting her husband for two hours till her women came in and reported with glee that the Grand Duke refused to come to bed till he had had his supper. After His Imperial Highness had eaten to his satisfaction, he came to bed. In bed he suddenly said how tickled his servant would be to see them together. He then fell asleep and snored till next morning. Catherine lay sleepless. The bed was uncomfortable, the night very close. The bed had no curtains, but was opulently upholstered in red velvet embroidered in silver. The next morning a lady in waiting tried to question the young married couple. But her hopes proved deceptive. And their hopes continued to prove deceptive for the next nine years.

X. RUSSIAN VERSAILLES

IN 1752 Elizabeth set the task before the famous Italian architect Rastrelli: "Transform Tsarskoye Selo into a Russian Versailles."

He proceeded to transform it.

At the beginning of the eighteenth century, when Russia, in the Northern War, occupied the banks of the Finnish Gulf and the Neva, St. Petersburg began to be built. Peter the Great gave away the environs of the new capital to his favorites. To Menshikov, the ex-pieman, and now Governor General of the conquered territory, he gave an old Swedish estate called Saritshof. But in 1710, undeterred by having given it to Menshikov and under the impression that, as the owner of all the Russias and all the Russians, he had it still, the Tsar gave it away to his mistress, Catherine, who in the following year became his wife and consort. Saritshof took its new name and began to be known as Tsarskoye Selo, which means Tsar's Village. Catherine put up in a little wooden house which had remained from the time of the Swedes. But between 1718 and 1724 a German architect, Braunstein, had erected a stone mansion of sixteen rooms. A year later Peter died and Catherine succeeded him on the throne as Catherine I. The mansion was called a palace. It was a two-storied house of moderate size. The upper story displayed some attempt at luxury: Catherine's bedroom and ballroom were hung with French tapestries.

When Catherine I died, Tsarskoye Selo with all its environs, villages and peasants, who had been forcibly transplanted thither from central Russia, passed to her younger daughter, Elizabeth. Princess Elizabeth resided there while she lived away from the throne, which was occupied successively by the unfortunate Aleksei's son, Peter II, and the progeny of the idiot Tsar Ivan, the two Annas. When, in 1741, Elizabeth was proclaimed Empress, it occurred to her that her mother's stone mansion was not compatible with her new position as "Self-Upholder of All the Russias," which called for a palace of the utmost magnificence.

A Russian architect was set to work, but he died, and his project was completed by his pupil. Elizabeth ordained that no expense was to be spared from the public treasury. She set the architect a double problem. On the one hand, the new palace was to be palatial in its proportions. On the other hand, the small mansion was to remain and form its nucleus. The palace was completed in accordance with her wishes—without, however, satisfying the Empress.

It was then that the Italian Rastrelli was called in to realize Elizabeth's ambitions. Russia by that time was already a great power. She meddled in Europe and her weight was felt in the European arena. The ambassadors of other great powers—England, France, Austria—attended the balls and festivities organized at the various palaces in Petersburg and on the outskirts of the capital. Elizabeth's idea was to underline the power and greatness of the Russian monarchy. Bartolomeo Rastrelli, having been told by the Empress that she required a number of palaces for the purpose of impressing foreign dignitaries, had set to work and produced a number of outsize palaces and churches in baroque. There was nothing Russian about them, except that parts of the interiors were executed by Russian masters who excelled in the carving of wood, stone and ivory. Though the architect was Italian, the builder was a Russian— by name, Kvasov. Together they built the Summer Palace (which occupied the site of the present Engineering Castle), the Anitchkov Palace, the Winter Palace, the Vorontsov Palace, the Smolni Monastery, and others.

But the palace at Tsarskoye Selo, called after the first occupant of the "stone mansion," the Catherine Palace, received Rastrelli's most concentrated attention. The stone mansion still formed its nucleus but was made higher and brought forward to stand out from the rest. Figures, pillars and every kind of baroque decoration were plastered around the windows and doorways. Gilded cupolas and statues carved in wood added to its fanciful appearance. Vast quantities of gold were used in gilding. A whole army of serfs numbering 40,000 men worked day and night. Whole regiments of soldiers and sailors assisted. Nearly all the laborers worked without pay. In the few cases where the work was rewarded no money was paid: the skilled laborers received payment in kind, such as peas, curds, bread, salt, and so on. Another party of peasants and soldiers laid out the huge park with its pleasure pavilion, called "Hermitage," at one end, and a hunting castle, "Mon Bej," at the other.

The palace impressed every foreigner who set eyes on it. At least, since visitors were conducted round with that objective in view, they were too polite to remain passive. According to Rastrelli's own definition, the palace was being built "for the glory of All the Russias." "The palace," as Elizabeth wrote in her ukase, "is to serve the purpose of receptions of foreign ministers and of functions taking place on festive days—functions which by their grandeur should be worthy of our imperial dignity."

And indeed she made the most of her new accommodation the moment it was completed. Russian grandees and foreign ambassadors were invited to Tsarskoye Selo to marvel at the general resplendence. The court journal records on August 26, 1745: "By the all-highest command of Her Imperial Majesty, the English Ambassador, who arrived soon after 11 o'clock in the morning, was shown round the new apartments in the upper story and was conveyed across the lake in a canoe to visit the gallery, and then the 'Hermitage,' where luncheon was served."

But the gilded palace could not blind the foreigners to the abject condition of the serfs. A French traveler visiting Tsarskoye Selo records in his diary: "In Russia there are two kinds of people—the nobles and the peasants. The nobles who have all, and the peasants who have nothing. The always-toiling peasants, and the all-devouring nobles."

The Catherine Palace remained the chief summer residence of all the subsequent sovereigns. The English architect Charles Cameron altered it inside and out. The great staircase was transferred to the center. The cupola on the southern part of the palace was removed, but the original "stone mansion" of Catherine I still formed the nucleus, though it was now so hidden that it was difficult to point it out. In the seventies of the eighteenth century two wings were added—one as a chapel, the other as the residence of Catherine's favorite, Zubov. The gilding and the wooden statues did not withstand the ravages of time. The statues were removed. The decorations in stucco lost most of their gilt. Some of the rooms were redecorated in the classical style.

All through the nineteenth century this palace was the favorite residence of all the empresses, but no alterations were made. Each succeeding tsar seemed to choose a different set of rooms for his own apartments. A part of Elizabeth's personal rooms was altered for Alexander I and his mother, Maria Feodorovna. The ground floor of Zubov's wing was redecorated for Alexander II, who preferred the wing to the rest of the palace. And the last tsar, Nicholas II, chose a set of rooms which most nearly conformed to his idea of bourgeois drabness.

Balls, masquerades, hunts and other recreations were daily events at the court of Elizabeth, who preferred amusements to affairs of State. Scantily educated and unaccustomed to work, the Empress was glad to delegate her duties to others. Ministers rarely had the opportunity of speaking to her on State matters. Count Panin, who was a minister during three reigns, comments on Elizabeth's time: "This epoch deserves special mention—all was being sacrificed at that time to hangers-on of all kinds and to every sort of extraneous adventure, business of State being entirely neglected." Elizabeth augmented the splendors initiated by her predecessor, Anna Ivanovna. She organized festivities designed to astonish the foreign ambassadors with the wealth and luxury of the Russian Court. The guests entered the palace by the great staircase which was purposely built at one end of the palace; so that before they could reach the tsaritsa they had to pass through a succession of brilliant ballrooms.

There were masked balls every Tuesday. The women were dressed as men, and the men as women. Only the Empress looked well in men's clothes; all the others looked atrocious. The men, dressed in crinolines, shambled about like bears and collided with their delicate cavaliers. On one occasion a M. Sievers, a frightful colossus in a gigantic hoop skirt, was dancing a polonaise with Catherine. Inadvertently he tripped up a Countess Hendrikov, who, in falling, knocked Catherine over, who found herself buried under M. Sievers' crinoline. There they all lay, entangled in one another's long skirts and dying of laughter. They had to be lifted, since none could rise without causing the others to fall.

Elizabeth loved her palaces and traveled from one to another, usually taking the Grand Duke and Duchess with her. Sometimes they went on horseback, and the ambassadors of England and Austria rode with them from Peterhof to Oranienbaum. The Austrian Ambassador, with the assistance of the Russian chancellor, Bestushev, had made Lord Hyndford, the English Ambassador, into a complete drunkard. "Otherwise," writes Catherine, "he was a very intelligent man, as the English usually are, though they are all strange people. He was," she adds, "a Scotchman."

The palaces were hastily built and were not very safe. From time to time they had to be propped up to prevent floors from collapsing. On one occasion the Empress took her family to stay with her favorite, Aleksei Razumovski, at his country seat. The annex in which Catherine and the Grand Duke were put up collapsed during the night. They were all but killed. Catherine was carried out by a soldier while the staircase was rapidly giving way.

The Empress, lodged in the main building, inquired of Catherine whether she was hurt. Her Majesty was greatly displeased when Catherine said "Yes." Their host, Count Razumovski, with whom Elizabeth was in love and who loved her too, hearing of what had occurred, drank himself blind and threatened to shoot himself to wipe out the disgrace. He evidently possessed something of the honor of Japanese generals who commit hara-kiri to save their faces.

The Empress, to whom one hair of Aleksei Razumovski's head was worth more than the combined lives of Catherine, the Grand Duke and the rest of their suite, was in a dreadful state of apprehension lest her lover really lay hands on himself. She frowned on Catherine's admission, called them all cowards, and said they were making a mountain out of a molehill. She begged her favorite to do nothing so foolish as to endanger his life. If he killed himself she would never forgive herself— or the others; and she would probably take her own life. But he, lying dead drunk on the floor of a shed, groaning and gnashing his teeth, swore to heaven that as the host he could wipe out the shame of having endangered the lives of Their Highnesses only with his own blood.

Elizabeth at last got men to disarm him and took him away with her to one of her own palaces in the neighborhood. He sobered down and, gradually responding to her cajoleries, her coaxings and entreaties, promised to spare his life for the sake of the Empress. But she never forgot this day of suspense, never got over her apprehension and tribulation. And from that day she began to hate the Grand Duke and Grand Duchess.

Elizabeth was like that; her reactions were highly personal. She went to war with Frederick the Great because she heard he had said rude things about her. The result was the Seven Years' War, which Russia entered in alliance with Austria and France. The war, which started off badly for Russia, chiefly because the Grand Duke, who admired Frederick the Great, communicated to him secret information which stultified the plans of the Russian command, ended, after the discovery of the treachery (for which the Grand Duke was severely reproached), with a smashing victory for the Russian Army, which occupied Berlin.

CHAPTER V

THE EMPEROR BUFFOON

I. ELIZABETH'S FUNERAL

ELIZABETH had been intermittently ill. But for fear that the Grand
Duke or Catherine or both might attempt a palace revolution to hasten
their succession, she pledged her maids of honor to secrecy. At the same
time she resented that Catherine, who was not supposed to know of her
illness, had failed to inquire after Her Majesty's health. When Catherine
did so inquire, the Empress resented both the breach of confidence on
the part of her ladies in waiting and Catherine's effrontery in thus considering herself to be in the know.

In short, the Empress was getting increasingly difficult. But even
more than Catherine she now disliked her nephew and successor, the
Grand Duke, whom once she adored. It had been her habit every night
when he came to bid her good night and kissed her hand, to kiss his
hand in return—an empress returning obeisance to the man who will
be emperor when she, forgotten, will be rotting in her grave. But after
the discovery that her heir had been approached by certain officers
with a view to hastening her demise, she abruptly ceased this charming
practice. "I'm damned," she expressed herself trenchantly, "if I'll kiss
his damned hand any more."

The Grand Duke had not himself participated in any plot. He had
merely listened, though not without pleasure, to overtures being made
to him by a group of officers who approached him through a cryptic
representative disguised as a huntsman during a hunt. The Grand Duke
had neither concurred in their plans nor rejected them in principle.
His aunt was approaching her twentieth year on the throne. It seemed
to the Grand Duke a long time. But beyond pious hopes for her early
demise in the course of nature, the Grand Duke had expressed no wish
to accelerate the normal process by artificial means. Nor did the conventional idea of a palace revolution appeal to him. He was content to
await his turn.

When the Empress cautioned him through a lady in waiting, bidding
him remember that he might find himself in custody with ex-Tsar Ivan

VI, the Grand Duke burst into tears. He was a sovereign Holstein prince. He had not asked to be brought to Russia. No one had the right to deprive him of his liberty.

There were too many intrigues in other directions for him to risk alienating his aunt more than she was already alienated. The Grand Duke was at that time in command of the famous Preobrazhenski Regiment; and he wanted to make friends with his officers. The Empress was dying. The Shuvalovs, the Razumovskis, the Panins were all intriguing with and without Catherine in favor of Paul, even in favor of poor Ivan—and most of all in their own favor. The Grand Duke was not popular. He had a sense of humor unintelligible to all except himself. He was a little weak in the head, but not noticeably so against a dynastic background. Elizabeth, though never sober herself, was saddened to see him perpetually drunk. Her favorite, Razumovski, hated him. Panin disapproved of his barrack-room manners. The Guards objected to his preferring his Holsteiners to good Russians. The ladies resented his inviting non-ladies to the same dinner parties as themselves. The clergy abhorred him for his unorthodox contempt for the Orthodox Church.

On Christmas Day of 1761 the Empress Elizabeth died. Peter and Catherine, with mixed feelings, stood at her deathbed. When the three accredited physicians declared that the Empress was indubitably dead, the doors of the antechamber were thrown open: the Senators, the high dignitaries of State, and the Court all entered. Everybody sobbed.

Peter bade Catherine stay by the deathbed, rightly fearing that she might be up to all sorts of tricks. He gave her a warning look, and himself briskly and joyfully departed to attend the State Council which was to proclaim him Emperor.

They had scarcely dressed the body of Elizabeth and laid it in the canopied bedstead when Catherine was informed that supper would be served in the gallery, and that no mourning was to be worn. In the adjoining death-chamber the windows had been opened and the gospel was being read.

When Catherine entered the royal chapel all were assembled to take the oath. Instead of the Requiem, a Te Deum was sung. Karl Peter Ulrich was visibly overjoyed at his accession. He made faces and uttered facetious remarks. He skipped about and leaped like a harlequin, yet exacted the last particle of deference due to his new dignity. Catherine, now an empress, merely looked on, while the others took the oath of allegiance.

After leaving the chapel Catherine went to her room, and wept. Whether she was relieved to know that the Empress who had chivied her for eighteen years was now stone-dead, or grieved that she would never come to life again, was something she herself could not even tell.

She went in to supper. The table had been set for 150 persons, and the gallery was full of spectators. There were not enough seats to go round, and many guests ran hither and thither around the table. A courtier, who knew his business, talked loudly of his great joy in the accession of the new Emperor. Many of the ladies, like Catherine, had been crying.

While they were supping, the doctors had set to work on the departed Empress, preparatory to embalming her. Couriers with pardons in their pockets had been dispatched in all directions to recall Biron, Münnich, Lestocq and the Lapukhins to Petersburg. Gudovitch was on his way to Berlin bearing to Frederick the Great the welcome news that his "fan," the Grand Duke, *alias* Karl Peter Ulrich of Holstein-Gottorp, was at last Emperor Peter III.

Then the new Empress visited Count Aleksei Razumovski in his own apartments in the palace, where he lay stricken with grief for his departed mistress—mistress in both senses of the word. He tried to fall at Catherine's feet, but she intercepted his attempt and embraced him. They cried in each other's arms, hardly able to say a word.

The Emperor had given orders that the room which was separated from his wife's by an antechamber and was occupied by a courtier should be prepared for him, and that his mistress, Elizaveta Romanovna Vorontsov, was to live in his room next to Catherine's. That evening the new Emperor attended a Christmas party, which gave him a taste for imbibing costless hospitality. From morning till night he paid visits to all the important people, who prepared great banquets for him. A sneezing cold kept the new Empress away from these drinking bouts.

Peter III, who had waited his turn nineteen years, was now enjoying his position of supreme overlord. Everyone was his subject and must obey his every whim. He invited droves of women to dine with him; but only to quarrel with them. He made no other demands on them: which was precisely what started the quarrels. He engaged in disputes about trifles and when worsted in argument locked up his opponents in the guard room. Though this practice seems more reasonable than putting them to torture and death in the style of his predecessors, his moderation provoked the most savage resentment. Because he was quick and fluent, they all thought that he had consummate intelligence. Because he wrote easily, he wrote a great deal and did nothing.

The body of the Empress lay in state for ten days in an open coffin surrounded by the entire regalia and the whole bag of tricks. The general public were admitted to have a peep at defunct, as distinct from functioning, royalty. They saw the daughter of Peter the Great in a cloth-of-silver robe with lace sleeves. A great Imperial crown of gold was on her head, inscribed on the lower band: "Elizaveta Petrovovna, Most Pious Self-Upholder, Sovereign and Empress, born December 18, 1709, ascended the throne November 25, 1741, died December 25, 1761." The coffin stood upon a lofty dais under a canopy of cloth-of-gold with hangings of ermine flowing to the ground. In the background blazed the Imperial coat of arms: the double-headed eagle of Byzantium.

Outside stood a state coach surmounted with the Imperial crown, awaiting the new Emperor. The people, conscious of the other crown adorning the dead brow of Elizabeth, murmured: "How dare he drive out with the crown? He has been neither crowned nor anointed. Too early is he taking on himself to drive out with the crown."

On January 25, 1762, the coffin was carried with great pomp and solemnity over the ice to the other side of the Neva to be interned in the Cathedral of St. Peter and St. Paul in the fortress. The Emperor himself, and his Empress Catherine behind him, then the Skavronskis (Catherine I's plebeian family), behind them the Narishkins (Peter the Great's mother's descendants), then all the others according to their rank followed the coffin on foot from the Winter Palace to the church.

That day the Emperor was in particularly high spirits. During the funeral procession he permitted himself the following little jest. He lagged far behind the coffin, allowing it to get a long start, when suddenly he ran to catch up with it. The elderly chamberlains who bore the train of his black robe of state could not keep pace with him and finally had to let go of it. As the train bellied out with the wind His new Majesty leaped for joy and repeated the performance over and over again.

II. PETER III'S START-OFF

OUTSIDE the Winter Palace, then as now at this season, blew an icy wind; with treason, with civil commotion in its wings. Inside the warm Palace they listened to the roaring of the wind, and, conceivably, thought of Siberia, exile, revolution, death. The monarchy still lacked that sense of stability which it was later to enjoy almost up to its final collapse under Nicholas II.

Peter III's very first action as Tsar was to make peace with his hero, Frederick the Great. He ordered the Russian Army to evacuate, unconditionally, all the Prussian territory that it had conquered in the course of an unusually successful war.

Moreover, he related to his assembled court as a very great joke the fact that, while still only Grand Duke, he had, in conjunction with Volkov, the Chief Secretary of the Privy Council, made a special point of communicating all the Russian Army's most secret orders to Frederick the Great, who, as head of the opposing force, had, not unreasonably, profited by the information. It struck him as excruciatingly funny that this leakage of the plans of the Russian Army should have made things a lot more difficult for them. When Volkov heard his master gaily retailing the story of this treason he nearly had a fit. But the Tsar went merrily on. He had a queer sense of humor; nothing appealed to him more than to watch the result of his indiscretions as reflected in the discomfiture of others.

His loyalties, owing to his being a German-Danish prince, reared for the Swedish throne and occupying the Russian, were mixed. And it delighted him that he was not, like other men, constrained by circumstances and upbringing to behave "in single strictness." He had never asked for anything but his Holstein heritage; and if they, contrary to his wishes, had placed him in a grotesque situation, well, he who rejoiced in the grotesque was autocrat enough to do that which afforded him the most pleasure—to play the clown.

After he had signed the peace treaty with Frederick II, in which he yielded everything that had been won by Russian valor, there was no end to his delight and rejoicing. One celebration followed another. At a great banquet he proposed three toasts, each of which was drunk to the thunder of cannon. The first to the health of the Imperial Family; the second to the health of the King of Prussia; and the third to the Peace in general.

When his Empress drank the first of these toasts, she remained seated. Peter sent an officer to ask her why she did not stand up. Catherine replied that since she presumed the Imperial Family to consist of her husband, her son, and herself, she had not imagined that it would be His Majesty's pleasure she should rise. In answer to this the Tsar ordered his messenger to go back and tell the Empress she was a fool not to realize that their uncles, the princes of Holstein-Gottorp, also belonged to the Imperial Family. And lest there should be any chance of his message being watered-down in transit, he shouted "You poor fool!" across the dinner table so that all the guests could hear him. Catherine began to cry, and to hide her mortification turned to a courtier who stood behind her chair and implored him to engage her in conversation. The courtier began to chatter. As he left the banquet, an order was handed to him that he was to proceed forthwith to his country estate, and to stay there till pardoned.

The dishonorable peace with Prussia and the projected war with Denmark over Schleswig-Holstein completed the unpopularity of Peter III. This Danish war became an insane obsession with him. From his point of view nothing could be more natural. Here, surely, after all these vicissitudes the cadet branch of the Oldenburgs had thrown up a man who had not to solicit foreign assistance at the court of a Russian emperor, but one who actually *was* himself the Emperor of Russia. Not to invoke the whole of his armed forces in the cause of getting even with the senior branch of the Oldenburgs, who, as Kings of Denmark, had lorded it over the cadet branch of the family and still sat on the Gottorp portion of Schleswig, was surely to miss the whole significance of his succession to a foreign throne.

But the Russians did not see it like that. What was Holstein to them? And why a war with Denmark, who threatened no Russian interests?

Frederick II tried by letter to persuade him to defer it, but Peter III had set his heart on the project and would not hear of abandoning it. The English Ambassador, Keith, prophesied that public feeling for the Emperor would soon be passing from contempt into hatred.

The Tsar's buffooneries were of a kind less calculated to amuse an audience—what need had the Tsar of an audience?—than their author. Their chief merit to himself was that he, Karl Peter Ulrich of Holstein-Gottorp, as a result of his new position in the world of men, was now so exalted and powerful a personage that he could afford to treat everything and everybody with contempt—including his position. As for the quality of his humor, it was of a kind which contained quib within quib, irony within irony, and therefore could not be shared except with himself.

One day when the Tsar was returning with Razumovski from the parade ground, he saw his favorite Negro fighting with the common hangman. Peter was amused; then suddenly his mood changed. He looked grave and said: "Narcisse has put himself outside the pale." Razumovski could not make out why his master should take this line, but Peter cried: "Blockhead, can't you see the point? I can't possibly keep in my suite a man who has demeaned himself by fighting the common hangman. He is disgraced—to eternity!" Razumovski then tumbled to it. Not all was lost yet. The Negro's honor might yet be restored by passing him beneath the flag of the regiment. The Emperor jumped at it. He called Narcisse, told him to pass under the flag, and then, as if doubtful whether this was quite sufficient, ordered that he be scratched by the lancehead of the flag, so that his own blood might wash out the stain on his honor. The Tsar himself conducted the whole of this improvised ritual with a serious mien.

III. PRINCESS DASHKOV

AFTER this the plot, as they say, thickens. Russian historians tend to take the view of the participants in the *coup d'état,* who naturally vilify Peter III's character to justify their own actions. But nothing more than a certain puerility, which is not unusual in persons placed in unnaturally elevated positions, can be discovered even by Catherine herself against her husband, whose character in real truth was mild and inoffensive. During his six months' reign he condemned no one to death. He recalled all the people who had been languishing in exile. Münnich, Biron, the pretty lady in waiting who had part of her tongue clipped by the Empress Elizabeth, her husband—all came back to Petersburg. The Emperor had sent out his orders for their recall almost before the body of Elizabeth had had time to stiffen. The charge against Peter III that he was hand in glove with Frederick the Great against Russia's interests was after all aimed merely at an expression of foreign policy—a reorientation foreshadowing a general reshuffle in allies and enemies. Catherine, who affected to share the indignation of the Russian aristocracy against Peter III, and who turned this indignation to her own account, followed in his footsteps after she had disposed of him.

A girl of eighteen plays a certain part—according to herself, the chief part; according to Catherine, a negligible part—in the events which ended in the deposition of Peter III and the accession of his consort, Catherine, to the throne of Russia. This girl, already married, was Princess Dashkov. She is a well-defined type of womanhood who, because she is so wholeheartedly her own heroine, succeeds in impressing posterity. That type does not usually impress her contemporaries, who are in touch with other, more realistically minded, participants who, however, do not write their memoirs. It is the female idealist who writes her memoirs with herself as a romantic figure living for some public ideal with which she identifies herself while stressing the shortcomings of others, who secures the ear of posterity. The type is not exclusively Russian, though Marie Bashkirtsev is another striking example. Had Marie Bashkirtsev lived in Russia at the time of the Revolution, instead of living abroad at a time when nothing interesting happened in Russia, we would have read in her famous memoirs how she had by her intrepid will compelled a timorous Lenin and a reluctant Trotsky to push on with the Revolution, instead of, as she makes out, proving to have been the inspiration and solace of all creative talent in music, letters and the pictorial arts of Western Europe. I could cite more than one contemporary example of this type of woman in our own country; but the laws of libel forbid my being specific. That type, however, has an unrivaled chance of her claims being taken seriously if she hails from a country, like Russia, whose conditions are obscure to Western readers, who are therefore strongly disposed to accept the memoirist at her own worth.

"I very much wish," Katharine Wilmot, an Irish girl who went to stay with Princess Dashkov, by then an old woman, writes to her friends in Ireland, "that you could see the princess herself. Everything about her —dress, language, everything—is original; whatever she does, she is entirely unlike anyone else. It is not merely that I have never seen such a creature, I have never heard of one. She helps the masons to build walls, helps cut the paths, goes to milk the cows, composes music, writes articles for the Press, talks out loud in church to correct the priest if he makes a mistake in the prayers, understands the theater perfectly and corrects her serf-actors when they are out in their parts; she is a doctor, an apothecary, a surgeon, a farrier, a carpenter, a magistrate, a lawyer; in short, she hourly practices every species of incongruity, and carries on a correspondence with her brother, who holds one of the foremost posts in the empire, with poets, with literary men, with Jews, with her son, and with all her relations. Her conversation. charming in its simplicity, sometimes borders upon childlike naïveté. Without stopping to think she babbles at once French, Italian, Russian, and English, mingling these in every sentence."

It is abundantly clear from this naïve description what kind of a woman Princess Dashkov was even in her youth. She is the woman who wants to "belong." A woman with an ardent emotionalism who would identify herself with any exciting cause, and, failing a larger issue, would with the same ardor born of sudden conviction throw herself into any broil, be it only a by-election or a meeting of shareholders, or even a mothers' meeting at the vicarage. She passionately wants to be part of the ferment of creation, and it is not surprising that she is herself more or less continually in a ferment. She longs to work, to give herself, to be used. Subordinates are impressed by her vitality; collaborators, into whom she pitches continually, consider her what she is—a blooming nuisance.

From the first time the young girl met Catherine she loved her passionately, "adored her" as schoolgirls adore their elder companions. She bombarded her with poems in which she expressed her unqualified adoration and a desire to do or die. Catherine, who at the time was still a Grand Duchess, replies: "Such verse, such prose! And you are but seventeen! So great a talent must be fostered. It may be that I am not impartial; the gratification I feel at your having chosen me as the subject for your poem may have clouded my judgment. Even so, though you may call it pride if you will, I repeat that it is long since I have read stanzas so correct and so poetical."

On the other hand, Princess Dashkov felt as genuine an aversion for the Grand Duke, though he was her godfather and her elder sister's lover. Her dislike of him was apparent to Peter, who remarked: "Permit me to hope that you will at least bestow upon our person no less attention than upon that of the Grand Duchess."

A little later he took the young princess to one side, and said: "Never forget that it is safer to deal with simple honest people like your sister and myself than with the clever people, who squeeze the best out of you and then throw you away like a sucked orange."

But the Grand Duke, who always had his foul pipe in his mouth, who drank night and day with his Holsteiners till he fell under the table and was carried to bed, was hardly her young girl's dream of a romantic hero. Catherine, on the other hand, with her poise and veneer of culture, affected the youthful Princess Dashkov as worthy of emulation. The young girl cultivated a habit of speaking to the Grand Duke—even when he was Emperor—in a manner just hovering on the brink of insolence, which he excused because she was very pretty and young and he very drunk and good-natured. He liked to provoke her by pretending to a violence of views which he neither felt nor exercised but which made the girl boil with an indignation she could hardly conceal. So he would observe—probably thinking of the lovers of his wife—that a certain officer, as a warning to others, ought to have his head cut off for his liaison with a niece of the Empress. Princess Dashkov hotly protested at the inhumanity of inflicting the death penalty for so trivial a crime.

The Grand Duke sneered at her, saying: "You're only a child. Anyone can see that by the way you talk. Grown-up persons know that there's nothing like a weak line on capital punishment to encourage every sort of treason and violence."

"Your Highness," she replied, "is only trying to frighten us. Except for one or two of the oldest generals, all of us who have the honor to be sitting at your table belong to a generation which has never seen the death penalty in operation in Russia."

"Which proves just nothing at all," he said. "Look at the way things are as a consequence! I repeat, you are a child and too young to express any opinion."

Nobody spoke. At last the young princess plucked up courage: "I am," she said, "more than willing to admit I don't follow your reasoning. But I do know this: it's a very good job that your aunt is still on the throne of Russia; and likely to stay there for years!"

All eyes were turned upon the bold young woman. The Grand Duke did not answer in words; he put out his tongue. A trick to which he often resorted instead of a verbal reply, especially when he was in church.

But now her godmother Elizabeth, on whose lap she had sat as a child, was in her grave, and the Grand Duke was Autocrat and Emperor. Princess Dashkov's elder sister, Elizaveta Romanovna Vorontsov, was Peter's mistress; and he vaguely hinted that one day he would emulate his grandfather and namesake, Peter the Great, put his wife away in a convent, marry his mistress and proclaim her Empress.

Such a project seemed most improper to Princess Dashkov, even though she and her sister sprang from the plebeian strain of that very mistress of Peter the Great whom he proclaimed his consort and who succeeded him on the throne.

Peter III resented Princess Dashkov's rebellious attitude when all her family professed devotion to him. Pointing to her sister: "There may easily come a time," he warned, "when Romanovna" (he called his mistress by her patronymic only, which was his way of being funny) "will be in *that woman's* place"—indicating Catherine.

Princess Dashkov made a show of not understanding, and hurriedly took her place at the Tsar's favorite game of *campis.*

When Peter III was in danger of losing this game, he always cheated. The result was that he then always won. The first game won in this way, he suggested another. Princess Dashkov refused. The Tsar would not take no for an answer, so that at length the young woman, taking advantage of her position as *enfant terrible,* told him straight out that she could not afford to play with somebody who always won; if he would be like other people and not cheat, that would be another story. At which the Tsar put out his tongue at her, and made faces. Princess Dashkov, with a low curtsy, withdrew.

Peter III had a passion for military uniforms. As Princess Dashkov passed through the long succession of rooms at the Winter Palace, it seemed to her that everywhere were courtiers dressed up in brand-new uniforms. She noticed the ancient, effete and cadaverous Prince Troubetskoy, arrayed in military dress for the first time in his life, in terrific top-boots with long spurs as if about to rush into battle. When Elizabeth had lain dying, he, too, had taken to his bed until he knew which way the cat was going to jump. When he had heard that it had jumped the right way, he at once got up, armed himself from top to toe, and turned up at court.

Peter's taste for making everybody look like a soldier was handed down to his son, the mad Paul, and from him to all his successors. Even the languid Panin, who affected the style of an old-world courtier, was, for services rendered to the Tsarevitch's education, promoted to the rank of general in the infantry. The idea was that Panin would be delighted; but when he showed up in his new outfit, it was so clear that he was unhappy that even Peter saw that it would never do, and permitted him to transfer to the corresponding civilian grade.

But it took the Tsar a long time to get over it. It worried him. "You know," he used to say, "I can't make it out! I always thought Panin such a sensible fellow!"

IV. THE PLOT

CATHERINE contradicts herself with a grand disregard for details. She asserts that she had no ambitions to assume the crown and merely yielded for the sake of the fatherland in response to pressing demands. On the other hand, she pours scorn on Princess Dashkov's claim to the lion's share in the plotting and says everything had been thought out and done by Catherine herself long before Princess Dashkov ever came on the scene.

Princess Dashkov's share, according to Catherine, was more dangerous than useful. Princess Dashkov, Catherine comments a little bitterly after the event, wished to take all the honors because she was acquainted with a few of the leaders. But on account of her family connections and her age, which at the time of the *coup d'état* was only eighteen, she inspired no confidence in any of the conspirators. Her sister, they all knew, was Peter's mistress. Her father did not like his youngest daughter, Princess Dashkov, and was a man renowned for his feat of acrobatics in favoring the winning side. "To be sure," Catherine writes just after the *coup d'état* had come off, "she always said that it was all her doing. But the conspirators had been in touch with me for six months before she even knew their names. Of course, she is very clever, but besides being very vain she is extremely muddle-headed and nobody really liked her. Only the indiscreet confided in her, and then only trivialities."

But what seemed to gall Catherine's pride most of all was that a courtier, Shuvalov, "the basest and most infamous human being that could be imagined," she calls him, had written to her literary god, Voltaire, that an eighteen-year-old woman had changed the government of Russia.

"Please," Catherine writes to her ex-lover, Count Poniatovski, "please disabuse this great author! We had to conceal from the princess the channels through which the others communicated with me five months before she knew anything at all. Even during the last four weeks she was told as little as possible."

This request to Poniatovski to put Voltaire right as to the authorship of the plot which turned Catherine from a consort about to be locked up for life in a convent into an Autocrat of All the Russias, is contained in a letter which opens with the words: "I am sending Count Keyserling at once to Poland to make you king after the death of the present king. In the event he should have no success for you I desire that Prince Adam Czartoriski shall be king." She adds an injunction to her ex-lover, whom in fact she is buying off with the probable throne of his own country in order that he should not come bothering her, now that she is already steeped in happiness with her new lover, Gregori Orlov: "The minds of all are still excited. I beg you not to come here and add still more to this excitement."

Catherine's statement to Poniatovski, "My accession to the throne had been under preparation for six months," does not quite tally with her more formal account of her conduct which preceded the *coup d'état,* in which she says herself: "Catherine's attitude towards the nation has always been irreproachable." She stresses her flawless conception of her duties by resorting to three synonyms: "She has never," she writes, *"wanted, wished,* or *desired* anything but the success of this nation, and her whole life will be employed in the sole purpose of furthering the welfare and happiness of the Russian people."

Princess Dashkov's account of the heroic part she played in placing her friend Catherine on the throne takes the form of a very stilted dialogue, which speaks for itself and confirms one's suspicion that her literary claims are no better founded than her other claims in the world of action.

"For God's sake trust me!" cries Princess Dashkov (according to her own memoirs). "I will show you that I merit your confidence. If you have any definite plan, use me, dispose of me, I am at your service."

Catherine bursts into tears and, pressing her friend's hand to her heart, says: "I assure you that I have no plan whatever. I can do nothing. All that is left me is to await with fortitude the course of events. I submit myself to the will of God, and repose all my hopes in Him alone."

"In that case your friends must act for you," exclaims Princess Dashkov. "For my part, I feel that I am animated with sufficient strength and vigor to carry everyone along with me; and believe me, there is no sacrifice which would deter me."

"For God's sake," Catherine interrupts, "do not expose yourself to peril in the vain hope of resisting the inevitable. If you destroy yourself for my sake, you will but add eternal regret to my unhappy lot!"

"All that I can say," replies Princess Dashkov, looking fervently into the eyes of her adored friend, "is that I will take no step which could possibly involve or endanger you. Whatever betide, let it fall on me and crush me! If in my blind devotion to you I end my life on the scaffold, a like fate shall never befall you."

Catherine would have protested, but Princess Dashkov, interrupting

her, takes her hand, presses it to her lips, and, saying that she is afraid
to continue the conversation, asks leave to withdraw. Deeply touched,
they remain for some minutes in each other's arms, then the princess
cautiously goes out, leaving Catherine in great agitation.

Catherine's agitation may have been due to a reflection that if Princess
Dashkov was ready to lose her own life on the scaffold, her reassurance
that Catherine would never be its victim could not, in retrospect, carry
much weight. If, while alive, Princess Dashkov could not be trusted
with sufficient discretion, dead, she could hardly prevent Catherine from
sharing her fate.

Meanwhile the Emperor was not entirely oblivious of opposition and
plots hatched behind his back. Rightly divining that the focus of activity
directed against him was his wife Catherine, he ordered a courtier,
Prince Bariatinski, to arrest the Empress in her room. Bariatinski was
startled at this command, but did not hesitate to carry it out. In the
waiting room he met Prince George of Holstein, the same Uncle George
who had wanted Figgy to marry him. Bariatinski confided in Prince
George, who at once went to see his nephew, the Emperor, threw himself
at his feet and at last induced him to withdraw the order.

Princess Dashkov told Catherine that there was not a moment to
lose. Time for action had come. But Catherine only wondered how
much of the plans already under way could be entrusted to Princess
Dashkov, who "wanted to be in on everything." The moving spirits
behind the conspiracy were the Orlov brothers and a Lieutenant Passek.
The plot was that after Peter III returned from the country he should
be arrested in his apartment and declared incompetent to reign. Catherine
had come to the conclusion that he was really not quite right in his
mind. She was assisted in that opinion by Peter's intention to arrest her
before she arrested him. What made her hesitate was that not all were
united in this opinion. Panin, for example, was in favor of declaring the
twelve-year-old boy Paul tsar, while appointing Catherine regent. Razumovski, the late empress's favorite, could not come to a conclusion one
way or the other.

These men, declared the fiery Princess Dashkov, were spineless. Catherine decided that the various groups, which did not know of one
another's activities on her behalf, should now be brought together. The
arrest, three days before the time set for the *coup d'état,* of Lieutenant
Passek made it necessary to advance the action. Panin and the Hetman
of the Ukraine thought it was too early. But the brothers Orlov, of whom

Gregori was Catherine's lover, sent a coach to Aleksei Orlov, who was at Peterhof, to bring the Empress to the capital.

Princess Dashkov says this was her doing. She had already ordered a man's dress for herself; she did not see herself playing the part of a woman in the decisive events in which she was to play the leading role. The tailor, however, failed her. To avoid arousing suspicion, she dismissed her maid and went to bed. But half an hour later she heard a knock at the door. The youngest Orlov had arrived to receive his instructions from Princess Dashkov. His brother wished to know whether it was not too soon to disturb the Empress.

Princess Dashkov says she was beside herself, and poured reproaches upon him and all his brothers: "Good God! As though it were a question of *disturbing* the Empress!" she shouted. "Better bring her unconscious, fainting, to Petersburg than expose her to capitivity or death with us. Tell your brothers that someone must be sent immediately to Peterhof."

If Princess Dashkov had really been the originator and most active participant in the plot, as she claims to have been, she would surely, givin her energy and impatience, have been in Peterhof herself and waking up the Empress. So far, however, her role was strangely passive. To make up for her inactivity, she records great spiritual agitation and tribulations. Agonizing hours of solitude and suspense! She trembled for her Catherine. She saw her pale, drawn, imprisoned, being dragged to the scaffold, and "all through my fault!" Distracted with anxiety, she waited for news from Peterhof. At four o'clock it came: the Empress had gone to Petersburg.

V. THE *COUP D'ÉTAT*

ALEKSEI ORLOV crept in the night to the pavilion at Peterhof where Catherine was calmly asleep and not even aware of what was happening. Catherine did not know Aleksei Orlov by sight, but she trusted her instinct. When he told her that Passek had been arrested and that there was no more time to lose, she rose and set off in the carriage he had procured for her. Orlov sat on the box impersonating a coachman. He urged the horses so hard that they broke down before they got to Petersburg, and the Empress had to walk with her maid. Presently they passed a tumbrel. Orlov commandeered it, and Catherine made her entry into her capital in the same inglorious conveyance as Marie Antoinette was to make her tragic exit in.

She was received on her arrival in Petersburg by Gregori Orlov, her lover, and Prince Bariatinski, who had saved her from arrest by appealing to her Uncle George. She was conducted to the barracks of the Izmailovski Regiment, where everything seemed unexpectedly quiet. Only twelve men were present and a noncommissioned officer. The soldiers knew all about it, but remained in the barracks. They were told, to stir up their rather lethargic interest, that Peter III had tried that night to kill her and her son—an intention of which Peter himself, who was away in Oranienbaum, was unaware. Soldiers are simple souls. They came out into the square and hailed her as Autocrat and Empress. With shouts and uproar, they escorted her from their own regiment to the Semënovski Regiment. Enthusiasm gathered force as they marched, the soldiers in front and behind, the Empress in the carriage. The people joined in the jubilation, dancing and shouting for joy. Thus escorted, she drove to the Kazan Cathedral, where the Cavalry Guards made their appearance, then the Grenadiers of the Preobrazhenski Regiment, all acclaiming her with enthusiasm. After them came the artillery. The people pushed forward, complaining that the officers were holding them back. The leading noblemen gathered together in the cathedral. The Archbishop, surrounded by clergy, received the new Sovereign with holy water.

The Empress was certainly cashing in on the Emperor's unpopularity. Amid shouts of huge crowds who ran at the side of the troops they reached the Winter Palace, where the Synod, the Senate, and all the high dignitaries were assembled. The manifesto and the oath were drawn up and everyone recognized her as the new Sovereign.

Princess Dashkov quite obviously did not take part in any of these exciting events. She has nothing to say about them, and she is not the woman to omit them had she taken part.

When, after "terrific efforts," as Princess Dashkov says, she succeeded in reaching Catherine at the Winter Palace, they rushed into each other's arms, and could only say: "Well, thank God for that!" Then Catherine told her how she had fled from Peterhof. They embraced yet again. "Never," writes Princess Dashkov, "has a mortal been happier than I at that moment!"

After they had kissed each other to their heart's content, Princess Dashkov noticed that the Empress was wearing the Catherine and not the Andrew ribbon. She ran at once to Panin, snatched off his ribbon, put it on the Empress, and put the Catherine ribbon and star in her pocket.

The Empress then said she would place herself at the head of her troops and march back to Peterhof. She told a captain to take off his uniform and there and then put it on herself. While Catherine was presiding over a scratch Council of State, the sentries at the doors admitted a young officer with a slim waist and a swagger like a principal boy in a pantomime. It was Princess Dashkov. She certainly was not going to miss her chance now to make up for her passive role at the opening. She went up to Catherine, saluted, and reported that the guard was very inefficient, that they would perhaps admit Peter III himself if he suddenly made his appearance. The guard was immediately reinforced. While the Empress was dictating a manifesto, the Council decided to march with four regiments of the Guards, a regiment of Cuirassiers, and four regiments of Infantry to Peterhof and take the Emperor into custody. Meanwhile Count Vorontsov, the father of Princess Dashkov and her sister, "Romanovna," had arrived from Peter to remonstrate with the Empress for her flight and demand her reasons. When he had earnestly pressed his master's cause, he withdrew; and was at once set on by all the others and tipped to turn his coat. This he proceeded forthwith to do, the while easing his conscience by writing a letter to the Emperor to report on the success of his mission.

Next came Prince Troubetskoy, the ancient who had shammed illness while Elizabeth was dying and then appeared booted and spurred before the new Emperor. With him was a field marshal. Both had been sent to stem the revolt in their own regiment by the effective expedient of killing the Empress. But they had arrived too late. The regiments had already gone over to Catherine. Making the best of a bad job, the pair of them flung themselves at her feet. They took the oath and went away.

VI. GREGORI ORLOV

WHEN the Empress had retired to her apartment, her lover, Gregori Orlov, came in, fell at her feet and said: "Here I behold you Autocrat and Empress! My country is freed from its chains. It will be happy under your rule. I have done my duty. I have served you, my fatherland and myself. I have but one boon to crave of you: permit me to retire to my estate. I was born an honest man. Court life might corrupt me. I am young. Your favor will expose me to envy. I am independent. I shall be happy in retreat, sustained by the glory of having given you to my country."

Gregori Orlov was the eldest of the three brothers who were the leading spirits of the conspiracy, but his underlining his performance even before Catherine had praised him is just about as pleasing as if an actor had come forward to take the curtain before any applause had been forthcoming. It reminds one of the unfortunate habit of literary agents to underline their services to their clients, who might otherwise have felt under some obligation, in words like these: "We are pleased to have been able to secure this offer for you."

But Catherine was already deeply in love with the handsome Gregori Orlov. He was young and good-looking, while she was thirty-four; and in those days women aged more rapidly. His stressing his wish—wholly insincere, since he was the most ambitious of men and really wanted to marry her and become Emperor—to retire from her orbit had, despite its crudity, the desired effect on shrewd Catherine hopelessly blinded by love.

"No, no," she, the autocrat, pleaded with him, in the accents of a weak woman terrified at the prospect of losing her latest and best lover, to whom she clung with the tenacity of an ardent body and a hungry heart.

She even pleaded with Princess Dashkov, who forced her way in at this point, swaggering in her cavalry officer's uniform with one spur high up on her riding boot. "Princess," Catherine pleaded, *"please* dissuade him. He threatens to leave us, and even leave the army!" Catherine advanced plausible arguments. Her own reputation would suffer if it got about that he, to whom she owed everything, had retired in disgrace. They would charge her with ingratitude. Worse, they might consider his part in the *coup d'état* not so vital as they had been led to believe.

The latter argument seemed to carry weight with Gregori Orlov; and he rallied, as though in response to the former. Princess Dashkov, who could desire nothing better than Orlov's retirement, remained dumb during the entire scene. The young woman was quite incapable of any insincerity. She considered herself the mainspring of the whole movement. She had some grounds for her illusion, because many officers who were sympathetically disposed to Catherine but had no means of getting in touch with the Empress had turned to Princess Dashkov instead. But the princess did not know that the rebellion had consisted of several groups who, until the last minute, were not aware that the others were in the know, and that the threads of the plot had lain in the hands of the Orlov brothers.

"But the whole thing, I confess to you," Catherine writes to her ex-lover Poniatovski, "happened under my direction."

Catherine considered herself doubly indebted to Orlov because she was in love with him and wished to retain him for herself. So she exercised her authority to induce him to stay when he, who had placed her on the throne, only wished to place himself next to her and snatch the orb and scepter for himself. He was at the time only a captain in the artillery. She hung over him the ribbon of the Order of St. Alexander and bestowed on him the chamberlain's key which carried with it the rank of major general; at which action he unexpectedly burst into tears.

VII. THE MARCH ON PETERHOF

THE new Empress issued a ukase, dated June 28, 1762, at ten o'clock in the evening: "Gentlemen and Senators: I now go with the army to secure and maintain the throne, and I leave, with the utmost confidence, the Fatherland, the people, and my son, in your protection as my highest administrative authority. CATHERINE."

This ukase, though it makes little sense, produced the intended impression: Catherine, on the assumption that she could not leave in their hands something to which she had no right, must be allowed to have a right to these things. Catherine donned a Guard's officer's uniform—having appointed herself a colonel of the Guards—and set off on horseback at the head of the regiments. Princess Dashkov, who hitherto had not been able to display much activity, now saw her chance. Similarly clad in a cavalry officer's uniform, she galloped up to her beloved sovereign and rode by her side. Thus two women in men's uniform, one thirty-four, the other eighteen, led all these masses of armed men on the march to Peterhof. Their object was to fetch the Emperor and demonstrate that he was definitely their prisoner.

The Emperor, hearing that his wife had left Peterhof without his permission, suspected some trick. Leaving Oranienbaum, he drove to the palace at Peterhof and began to look for her everywhere, even under the bed. He questioned closely such of his company as had remained there, but could come to no decision. All counseled different courses of action. He chose the most ineffective. He walked up and down in the garden, and then voted for dinner.

Later he went back to Oranienbaum. From the utmost inactivity he suddenly sprang into excessive activity. The Emperor was rushing from Oranienbaum to Peterhof, and from Peterhof to Oranienbaum. When he was at Oranienbaum it seemed to him that in remaining at the more obscure of the imperial seaside residences he was leaving open the more prominent palace at Peterhof, consigning himself to obscurity, while Catherine, one after the other, occupied all the traditional seats of pomp and majesty.

But as he got to Peterhof, the news of the approaching regiments coming to take him prisoner convinced the Emperor that he had better get back to obscure Oranienbaum to consider where he might flee to next. He heard that there were two regiments about ten miles away, and he sent for them to come to his defense, only to learn that they had gone over to the Empress.

The old field marshal, Münnich, whom he had recalled from his exile, now advised him to go to the army or take a ship and go to the naval fortress of Kronstadt. The Emperor was surrounded by no less than thirty women, including his mistress, Princess Dashkov's elder sister, and most of them advised him against going anywhere. He listened to them all and decided to send a general to Kronstadt. This general was disarmed when he arrived there by an admiral who had been sent by Catherine.

Peter waited until evening. Still without news, he decided, with all the ladies and the remainder of his court, to board a galley and two yachts and to go to Kronstadt. By one o'clock in the morning they approached the fortress. The Emperor demanded admittance, but an officer on the bastion threatened to fire. They landed, and the Emperor, followed by the thirty ladies, was seen to run forward. Next minute they were seen running back to the galley and yachts.

Peter lost his nerve and ordered their return to Oranienbaum. The thirty ladies were afraid of seasickness, and Peter was afraid of everything. Though, apart from Petersburg, the whole of Russia was still loyal to him, the Emperor threw up the sponge. It was a calm moonlight night. The Tsar hid himself in the cabin with his mistress, while Münnich and Gudovitch sat on deck brooding gloomily. There was no saving people against their will, they said.

At four o'clock in the morning they reached Oranienbaum, where he disembarked and went to bed. Next morning he sat down to write to the Empress.

In the meantime, in Petersburg, crowds, armed with sticks and stones, gathered on the shore of the Finnish Gulf, determined to prevent the Emperor from landing.

VIII. WOMEN ON HORSEBACK

CATHERINE and Princess Dashkov at the head of the Guards made the first halt at a hostelry by the name of Krasni Kabatschok. The soldiers lay down on the road. The officers, and a number of townsmen who had followed the troops from curiosity, and everyone who could find room in the house entered the hostel.

Never had there been a day so pregnant with excitement. The success of the adventure was being taken for granted. But no one could be quite certain how it would end since Peter's whereabouts were unknown. Catherine, keyed up with excitement, bandied jokes with her followers, called across the room to this one and that one from sheer excess of high spirits. She had intermittent moments of abstraction when she wondered how it would all end.

They had posted sentries outside the room and, not taking off their uniforms, had resolved to get a little sleep, not having slept at all the last few nights. Catherine, from excessive exhaustion, could not go to sleep but kept very still out of consideration for Princess Dashkov, who lay by her side. But when the Empress accidentally turned her head, she saw that the great blue eyes of Princess Dashkov were open and gazing into hers. Both broke into a laugh.

The two fiery steeds were saddled anew and Catherine and Princess Dashkov, bursting with energy and high spirits, set off at the head of their troops. They marched all night. Although the conspiracy was inspired more by vanity and ambition than by any patriotic feeling, it is yet engaging to contemplate a *coup d'état* executed by a handsome intelligent woman of thirty-four, assisted by young men in love with her, accompanied by an eighteen-year-old beauty on horseback in the uniform of a dashing hussar, with a drawn saber in her hand.

Then a succession of Peter's envoys trickled in, bearing letters from him. First he requested to be allowed to go back to Holstein with his mistress "Romanovna." Next he offered to abdicate, and stipulated only that his life be spared. Yet he still had about fifteen hundred Holsteiners, over a hundred cannon, and several Russian divisions. One of the envoys flung himself at the feet of the Empress, saying: "Do you regard me as a man of honor?"

Catherine, whose impulse was to say, "How do I know?" replied: "Yes."

"Very well, I give you my word, if you will let me go, I will bring Peter to you all by myself."

Catherine sent him back with a letter in which she accepted the Emperor's abdication. But the document to which he put his hand is couched in such humiliating and, indeed, watertight terms as to make it far more probable that it was drafted by herself and that he was made to copy it under duress.

In the short time of my reign [it reads] *as Self-Upholder of All the Russias I have realized only too well the strain and burden of a task to which my powers are not equal. Neither as Self-Upholder nor in any other capacity am I fit to rule over the Russian Empire. I was, however, percipient enough to observe that the results of my incapacity were endangering the safety of the realm and threatening inevitably to involve me in lasting contumely. I have therefore taken counsel with myself and hereby solemnly declare, without malice and of my own free will, not to the Russian Empire alone, but to all the world, that I renounce the sovereignty of this realm for the term of my natural life. So long as I live I will never reign over the Empire of All the Russias either as Self-Upholder or in any other way, and pledge myself never, either alone or in association, to endeavor to regain the throne. This I swear on my oath and without equivocation before God and the whole world. This entire instrument of abdication I have written and signed with my own hand. The 29th Day of June in the year 1762.*

PETER.

Catherine's troops immediately occupied Peterhof. Orlov, who had ridden on to reconnoiter, had found no one there. The Holsteiners, who were devoted to Peter, were ready to die for him. But he told them to put up no resistance.

He called for a horse, but, changing his mind, ordered a carriage; and in company with "Romanovna" and Gudovitch was driven off to make his surrender. At the Peterhof Palace he was conducted secretly to an obscure room. Gudovitch, who behaved throughout with the greatest dignity, was arrested; as was "Romanovna."

After Peter had been given a meal he was taken to Ropsha in the custody of Aleksei Orlov, Passek, Prince Bariatinski, and others. He chose Ropsha himself: it had been his own property when Grand Duke. It was a remote, and, as Catherine herself describes it, "a very agreeable place, not far from Petersburg."

That very evening, in a letter to Poniatovski, Catherine finds it necessary to justify her choice of the prisoner's escort. The men who, a few days later, were to murder Peter, are described as "selected for their pacific qualities." She concludes that the Emperor has been sent to Ropsha until "suitable and decent quarters are prepared for him at Schlüsselburg." Schlüsselburg was the ice-bound fortress in which the baby Tsar Ivan was murdered later in Catherine's reign when he had attained to full manhood.

The Emperor's escort consisted of a hundred men drawn from various regiments of the Guards. They had orders, according to Catherine, to make life as pleasant as possible for the deposed monarch, and to provide everything he might wish for his entertainment. It was the intention, after transferring him to Schlüsselburg, to allow him in time to depart for Holstein with his favorites. He had never wanted to leave Holstein, and the only thing that had reconciled him to the idea of becoming Emperor of Russia was that it would enable him to go to war with Denmark in order to wrest from her that portion of Schleswig which, he considered, had been unlawfully withheld from his father.

While Peter III was being conveyed to Ropsha, where he arrived the same evening and, after dinner, retired to bed, the soldiers at Peterhof became restive because they imagined that a precarious peace was being patched up between Catherine and her husband, a peace which would expose them all to the Emperor's vengeance. To reassure them, Catherine made the round of the troops on foot.

After the Emperor's departure, Catherine was advised to return without delay to the capital. Uncertain whether the weary soldiers would obey her orders, she inquired, tentatively, at what hour it would be convenient for them to start. They replied: "Ten o'clock at night. But you must accompany us."

So she started with them, with Princess Dashkov again prancing at her side. Halfway towards Petersburg Catherine withdrew into a country house, where, wholly dressed, she threw herself upon a bed. An officer took off her boots. She slept two hours and a half, and the march was resumed. She rode again at the head of the Preobrazhenski Regiment.

A regiment of Hussars went ahead; then came her escort from the
Cavalry Guards; immediately in front of her went her guard. Following
were the regiments of the Guards in the order of seniority, and behind
them three field regiments.

Amid a chorus of rejoicing she entered the capital and rode to the
Summer Palace where the Court, the Synod and her son Paul awaited
her. He stepped forward to greet her. She dismounted and kissed him.
So great was the crowd that she had to be carried into the palace. All
were cheering. In the church a Te Deum was sung to the salute of
cannons. The mob, like all mobs who have nothing to gain from such
reversals, rejoiced louder than anybody. Now that all had passed off
well, all took a pleasure in exaggerating the grievous dangers they had
escaped. Peter, they said, had proposed to abolish the Guards and replace
them with his hated Holsteiners. He had plotted to overthrow the Orthodox Church and make them all Lutherans. He had aspired to marry
"Romanovna" and kill Catherine or, at least, lock her up in a nunnery.
Now these grave perils had all been averted.

IX. PRINCESS DASHKOV'S JEALOUSY

IT was all over, except for the excitement of comparing experiences.
That evening Princess Dashkov, entering the Empress's apartments, came
upon Gregori Orlov. He was lying at full length on a sofa in Catherine's
boudoir. He did not get up, saying that he had hurt his foot. He was
opening a large envelope. Princess Dashkov knew all about such en-
velopes: she had seen them in the hands of her uncle, the Vice-Chan-
cellor, and she knew that they were used only for the most important
documents of State.

"What are you doing with that?" she cried.

"The Empress's orders."

"Impossible! You have no authority," flared out the princess, once
again a stickler for legality.

News came that the soldiers had found their way into the cellars, and
were busily swigging priceless Hungarian wine out of their helmets, mistaking it for mead. Orlov never moved. Princess Dashkov went down to
the cellar, and in her thin girlish treble took them severely to task.
Emptying her purse, she told them her means were below her intentions,
but that they could all have free drinks at government expense another
day.

In Catherine's boudoir Orlov was still lying on the sofa. The table had been laid for three. The Empress bade her sit down with them; but, seeing her face, inquired what the matter was.

"Nothing. I am weary with sleeplessness and emotion."

Catherine, who wanted the princess to be civil to Orlov, told her that despite her urgent wishes he had insisted upon retirement; and she implored her to persuade him to change his mind, saying, "If he leaves the army, I shall be charged with the basest of ingratitude towards him." But Princess Dashkov, mortified by her discovery, responded coldly that she was sure Her Majesty did not lack ways and means to reward him without forcing him to do violence to his own convictions.

"And it was only then," she adds significantly, "that the dreadful truth struck me like lightning: yes! there was *une liaison* between them!"

Princess Dashkov never admits that she is jealous of Orlov. She but deplored, she says, his *influence* over the Empress. Nor did she like "the tone" between them. And what was more, her dream of "exclusive confidence, romantic friendship, all-powerful influence" faded at her shocking discovery. How bright had been her hopes, and how soon defeated! ...

She meditated sadly on what Peter had said on the subject of oranges: how, after squeezing, one was flung aside. How true! And how soon! Orlov and Catherine, doubly united by ties of love and interest, were chatting away, exchanging impressions, each interrupting and amplifying the other. Princess Dashkov, unwilling to be outdone, talked as much as the others, but her heart was heavy. Catherine related how Gregori's brother Aleksei had come into her room at six o'clock in the morning and said very calmly: "It is time for you to get up. All is ready." She had asked for news. He told her that Passek had been arrested. She dressed quickly and even omitted her toilet, while he awaited her in the carriage. Crossing the gardens she lost her way and wasted an hour. Some passers-by on the road saw and recognized her. They regarded her curiously, wondering perhaps why she looked so distraught. Only her maid was with her, and one servant, who ran hither and thither looking for the carriage.

She went on to relate her emotions when, on arriving at the barracks of the Izmailovski Regiment, she found only twelve men there, with a noncommissioned officer and a drummer boy. The drummer at once beat the alarm. Within three minutes the officers and the soldiers came out to her, embracing her, kissing her feet, her hands, her dress, and crying that she was their savior. Two of them dragged a faintly recalcitrant priest before her. He was easily won over. He held out his cross, and all recited the oath of allegiance. She was bidden to enter her state carriage. The Hetman also got in and sat beside her. The priest with the cross walked in front of the open carriage. They proceeded thus to the Semënovski Barracks, where the cheering soldiers came out to meet them. In the midst of the these two regiments she drove to the Kazan Cathedral.

Gregori Orlov took up the tale. The grenadiers, he said, of the Preobrazhenski Regiment, the first regiment of the Guards, met them close by the cathedral. Looking ashamed of themselves, they apologized for being the last to arrive, saying their officers had restrained them. As earnest of their good intentions they brought four of these officers with them, under arrest. Having explained themselves and stressed their zeal to serve her, they then fell in immediately behind the Empress's carriage. As senior regiment in the Guards it seemed to them that this was the obvious place for them. But the men of the Izmailovski Regiment waxed sarcastic, and jeered: "Last comers fall in last!" It seemed for a moment as though the Preobrazhenski Guards were going to dispute the point with their bayonets. But they calmed down and, loudly blaming their officers, fell in quietly in front of the state carriage. Now that everyone had gone over to the Empress, the officers of the Preobrazhenski Regiment were pleased enough to do so, too. Perhaps it was the memory that their regiment was the very first unit to be created by Peter the Great, while he was still a boy, which accounted for their comparative loyalty to his grandson. But loyalty had its limits.

X. POOR UNCLE GEORGE

PRINCESS DASHKOV had not witnessed these early and most decisive events and listened mournfully as Orlov recalled the details for her benefit, and the Empress followed his recital with lovelorn eyes. Then, he went on, came the Cavalry Guards, shouting and weeping for joy, celebrating the liberation of the Fatherland. There was a special reason for their high spirits.

Catherine sighed. She knew. And she was sorry. Peter III had appointed her Uncle George of Holstein-Gottorp colonel of the Cavalry Guards. This was the same Uncle George who had been so in love with his niece nineteen years before, and who had since come to seek his fortune at the court of his exalted nephew-by-marriage and dear niece. Now, though adored by his family in Holstein, Uncle George was hated by his regiment, who also hated his nephew, but not Catherine who had long since become more Russian than the Russians. Mindful of the safety of Uncle George, who might show his zeal by appearing at the head of his regiment, Catherine had dispatched secret messengers to warn him to stay at home. She owed him some gratitude, after all, for having persuaded her husband only three days before to cancel his order for her arrest. And it would have been the wrong moment altogether to parade her German uncle just as all these Russian soldiers were shouting in joy and gratitude that she, Catherine, had freed them from the German yoke.

But though—or because—Uncle George of Holstein on Catherine's advice had stayed at home, he suffered more than if he had appeared at the head of his regiment. The Cavalry Guards, interpreting his absence as a sign of defection, sent a detachment to his home to arrest him. They broke in, smashed everything they could lay hands on and manhandled poor Uncle George.

XI. CATHERINE DECORATES PRINCESS DASHKOV

AFTER this supper with Catherine and her lover, where she felt an unwelcome third, Princess Dashkov went away to see her father, her uncle, and most of all, to have a look at her baby girl. Her father's house was full of soldiers, stationed there partly for his protection, and partly because her sister "Romanovna" had been brought home. Princess Dashkov dismissed half the guard. Wearing a uniform made her feel she was an officer who could give orders to other officers.

She galloped back to the Winter Palace, but Catherine received her with disapproval. The officer of the guard had already complained to Orlov. The Empress reproved the princess for taking too much upon herself; and also rebuked her for speaking French before the soldiers. The princess, "to change the subject," she says, produced from her pocket the ribbon and the order she had put there the day before and handed them back to Catherine.

"Not so fast, not so fast," said the Empress. "I had to reprove you for your impetuosity—you had no authority to dismiss the sentries; but I also wish to reward you for the services you have rendered to me." And with this she flung around the princess's shoulders the very ribbon of the Order of St. Catherine which Princess Dashkov had just handed back to her, and pinned the star on her breast.

Looking sorrowfully with her great blue eyes at the object of her love, Princess Dashkov shook her head and spoke reproachfully: "Your Majesty must pardon me for what I have to say: but the time is at hand when truth must be forever a stranger to you. Before that time, I must beg you to take back this order. I cannot, as a decoration, value it adequately. Were it a recompense, however great it might be, it could not recompense *my* services. For they are not for sale."

The Empress embraced her. "But surely," said she, "friendship too has its claims? Am I now to be deprived even of these?"

Princess Dashkov, again as pleased as Punch, kissed Catherine's hand, and galloped back home to display herself to the baby. "Fancy me in a uniform!" she writes fifty years later when she was sixty-eight, "looking like a boy of fifteen with one spur on a high boot and the scarlet Catherine ribbon over my shoulder!"

Catherine showed them Peter's letters. He wrote, in one, of his abdication; in another, of the persons he would wish to retain about him. He gave a list of all the things he required to make life supportable, not forgetting a store of Burgundy and his tobacco. He asked further for a violin, a Bible and various novels, adding that he meant to become a philosopher.

Catherine, who had scarcely slept from early Friday morning until the evening of Sunday, then went to bed. At midnight, just as she had fallen asleep, Passek came into her room and woke her, saying: "The men are horribly drunk. A tipsy hussar had spread the rumor that thirty thousand Prussians are coming to capture you. An armed mob is at the palace gates and they say that they will not go home until they hear from your own lips that you are safe. They won't listen to their leaders, not even the Orlovs."

So up Catherine got again, and drove out to speak to the troops and the people. She told them that all was well and that they must go home to bed, and allow her to do likewise. She explained to them that she had only just lain down after three very strenuous days, and bade them in future do what their officers ordered them. They told her of the alarm that had been raised of the coming of those blasted Prussians, and expressed their willingness immediately to die for her. She said: "Good. Thank you. But now go to bed." So they wished her good night and went away like lambs, turning back every now and then to send a maudlin gaze after her departing carriage.

CHAPTER VI

THE MURDER OF PETER III

I. PETER'S LETTERS

WHETHER Peter was as comfortable at Ropsha as Catherine is anxious to assure Poniatovski may best be gathered from three letters Peter wrote to her from his captivity.

Madame [he writes in French], *I beg Your Majesty to rest assured on my account and have the goodness to order that the sentries be removed from the second room, because the room I occupy is so tiny that I can scarce move about in it, and because, as you know, I always run up and down in my room and if I can't I fear my legs will swell. I implore you furthermore to order that the officers do not remain in the same room when I have necessities: it is impossible for me. Finally, I beg Your Majesty not to treat me like a great criminal; I am not aware I have ever offended you. I commend myself to your generous consideration and entreat you at least to permit me to go to Germany with such persons as I have named. God will certainly reward you and I am*

Your devoted servant,

PETER.

P.S.—Your Majesty may rest assured that I will do nothing to imperil the security either of yourself or of your reign.

Catherine reassures herself that her deposed husband had everything he wanted, except his freedom. He had asked for his mistress, his dog, his Negro and his violin. But in order, as Catherine explained, to avoid a scandal and prevent increasing the excitement of his guards she had only sent him the last three. "Romanovna" had been sent back to her father, where her young sister, Princess Dashkov, kept an eye on her.

Peter again wrote to his wife, that Figgy of old with whom for eighteen years he had endured a life amounting to gilded exile under the despotic supervision of the Empress Elizabeth. He wrote, again in French:

YOUR MAJESTY,

If you do not wish to murder outright a human being who is already sufficiently wretched, have pity on me and grant me my only comfort, Elizaveta Romanovna. You will thus perform the most merciful deed of your reign. For the rest, if Your Majesty would but visit me for a few moments, my highest aspirations would be fulfilled.

Your very devoted servant,

PETER.

He received no reply, and he wrote once more, this time in Russian:

YOUR MAJESTY,

I beseech you to permit me, who have fulfilled your wishes in all respects, to go abroad with those for whom I have already petitioned Your Majesty, and I trust in your generosity not to leave me without hope.

Faithful servant,

PETER.

Whether Catherine had connived at what happened a week afterwards at Ropsha it is impossible to say with certainty. That after the deed she did her best to exonerate the assassins is no proof of her guilt. She could not have done anything else without associating herself with the murder in the eyes of all Russia; without flagrant ingratitude to them to whom she owed her new position; or indeed without exposing herself to the vengeance of their friends. Catherine had to go very cautiously. "I am under great compulsion," she writes to Poniatovski. "I cannot tell you all, but it is true." Worry, natural enough in his predicament, had caused the Emperor to have a diarrhea which lasted for four days. That is her version. On the fourth day he drank a great deal. He was seized with a haemorrhoidal colic and fever. He lingered thus for a couple of days; then sank and, defying all remedies, died in the very effort of asking for a Lutheran pastor.

This is Catherine's story conveyed to Poniatovski in Poland, who was to pass on this legend to the rest of Europe.

II. ALEKSEI ORLOV'S LETTERS

ALEKSEI ORLOV'S three letters to Catherine throw a strange light on the occurrence. The letters, written by a strong man in his cups, betray, in a kind of half-sober, half-drunken mixture of sincerity and guile, the uncertain assumption that the course they were pursuing in desiring the death of the Emperor would meet with Catherine's tacit consent, so long as they decently clothed the deed in a convention which would relieve her from the ugly role of accessory before the fact.

Little mother, gracious Sovereign [Aleksei writes from Ropsha on July 2, 1762—that is, on the third day after their arrival], *health we wish you for uncounted years. As this letter leaves us, we and the whole command are well, but our monster has become very sick of an attack of colic which has unexpectedly seized him. And I fear that he might happen to die tonight, and fear still more he might recover. I fear the first, because he babbles pure nonsense and that is no joke, and the other because he is really dangerous for us all because he often talks as if he had his former power.*

Following your imperial orders, I have paid the soldiers for half a year; also the noncommissioned officers, with the exception of the Captain of the Guard, Potemkin, who is serving without pay. Many of the soldiers spoke with tears of your graciousness; they had never deserved so much of you, to be rewarded after so short a time. Herewith I am sending you a list of the whole command that is at present here; but a thousand roubles were lacking, little Mother, so I have added them in ducats. There was much laughter here among the grenadiers because of the ducats they received from me; many complained because they had never before seen any, and gave them back because they thought they were worthless. Tchertkov, who was dispatched to Your Majesty, has not yet returned and therefore I have been delayed with my report. This, however, I am writing on Tuesday, at the middle of the 9th hour.

Till death, your faithful servant,
ALEKSEI ORLOV.

The second letter is undated. The third letter, informing Catherine of the death of Peter III, is dated July 6. Catherine's failure to intervene in what she must have clearly inferred from Aleksei Orlov's two previous letters was happening at Ropsha barely a few miles away from Petersburg—to wit, an attempt to poison her husband—indicates an attitude of "non-resistance to evil."

Such an attitude, calculated to contribute to her own future safety, must have commended itself to Catherine; and she remained aloof. Moscow and the far-flung Russian provinces had not yet accepted the deposition of the grandson of Peter III as a historic fact. The usurpation of the Romanov throne and the crown of Monomachus by a German woman hailing from

Stettin still seemed to them a trifle singular. Catherine, aware of the facility, indeed, the agility, with which palace revolutions and palace counter-revolutions are accomplished overnight in Russia, could never feel absolutely safe in the enormous Winter Palace while the legitimate Tsar of Russia was extant, even though fettered in a fortress cell. Aleksei Orlov's initial letter seems to hint at a policy of "Safety First," which, he assumes, the Empress is too prudent to forego for the sheer luxury of having a conscience.

And indeed Catherine's mild pangs of conscience, transparent in occasional attempts at self-justification, are those of a woman who might conceivably blame herself for having done nothing to prevent this dark deed, but who was blameless of initiative or even of tacit consent.

In his second letter, Aleksei Orlov, reporting progress, mingles hope with apprehension lest Catherine and Russia regard these their latest activities as perhaps not being in the best of taste.

Our little Mother, gracious Sovereign, I know not how I shall begin, for I fear the anger of Your Majesty, lest you deign to believe dreadful things about us and whether we were not the cause of the death of your rascal—and also all Russia and our law; but now the valet Maslov who was assigned to him has fallen ill, and he himself is so sick that I do not believe that he will live till evening, and he is already almost unconscious, of which the whole command here is aware and is praying to God to be rid of him as soon as may be; and this fellow Maslov and the officer who was dispatched to you can inform Your Majesty in what condition he now is, if you deign to doubt my word. This wrote
Your faithful servant,

The signature on this letter was torn off, but the writing is that of Aleksei Orlov.

In the third letter the note of alarm and even remorse colors the news. The date is July 6, 1762.

Little Mother, merciful Empress! How shall I tell, how describe what has happened? You will not believe your faithful servant, but before God I speak the truth. Little Mother! I am ready to die, but I do not myself know how the mischief came to pass. We are lost if you have not mercy on us. Little Mother, he tarries no longer on this earth. But no one would have believed it, and how could we have thought of laying hands upon the Emperor! But, Sovereign, the mischief has happened! He fell into a quar-

rel at table with Prince Feodor; we could not separate them and already
he was no more. We ourselves could not remember what we had done,
but we are all guilty to the very last one and deserving of death. Have
mercy upon us, if only for my brother's sake! I have made my confes-
sion, and there is nothing left hidden. Pardon, or else command quickly
that an end be made! I do not wish to see the light; we have angered
you and consigned our souls to eternal perdition.

III. REGICIDE

ALEKSEI ORLOV'S elder brother, Gregori, toyed with the idea of becoming the husband of Catherine. Poniatovski remarks in his memoirs:
"I was soon superseded by Gregori Orlov. For a few months this was
hidden from me, but by degrees her letters grew noticeably less warm."
On April 11, 1762, ten weeks before she ascended her husband's throne,
Catherine gave birth to a son who became Count Aleksei Gregorievitch
Bobrinski, whose father was Gregori Orlov. Gregori, already a father
and expecting to become a husband, thought his own hands had better
be kept clean by delegating the indispensable murder of Peter III to his
brother Aleksei.

Aleksei Orlov combined the strength of a Hercules with the stature of
a Goliath. So careless and confident of immunity was Aleksei that he
acquired without any real need a number of witnesses in the shape of
accomplices. He was sure that nothing would happen to him, but he
thought that a number of associates would diffuse the deed in the eyes
of others. His companions accordingly included his cousin Gregori Orlov,
the younger Prince Bariatinski, a certain Teplov, the actor Volkov, a
boon companion of the Orlovs, and a government messenger. They were
joined on their arrival at the little Castle Ropsha, a few hours' ride from
Petersburg, by the older Prince Bariatinski, a gentleman sergeant in the
Guards, Engelhardt, and two guardsmen.

The poisoned burgundy with which they hoped to kill the Emperor
did not act because Peter III, after drinking it, guessed their intention
and quickly took some warm milk, which made him vomit. The officers
then decided, after retiring for a short consultation, to throttle the Emperor. Aleksei Orlov was the first to lay his hands on the Tsar. But as
Peter sprang up, scratched his face and called out with tears in his voice:
"What have I done to you?" Orlov was for a moment distraught with

drunken compunction. His arms sank and he abandoned his victim to the fists of his accomplices.

They first tried to stifle him with pillows. This, they argued among themselves, while the Tsar all alone struggled with many, would leave no incriminating marks. But in the fury of despair the Emperor had gained such unbelievable strength that, realizing it was impossible to kill him in this way, they once again pulled him out of bed, threw him into an armchair and from there on to the floor, where for some time he continued to struggle for his life with all these men setting singly and severally upon him. At intervals, when he could draw breath, he reasoned with them, assured them quickly, brokenly, that he meant no harm to anyone, only wanted one thing, to be allowed to return to Holstein, that was all. But when he understood that they were absolutely implacable, and meant to destroy him, he screamed, screamed fearfully. No one had ever heard such a terrible haunting scream.

For twenty minutes he had struggled with his assailants. At last he had no strength left; no chance of help remained except his voice. The government messenger, who did not take part in the murder and was merely an involuntary witness, and another man who was in the adjoining room, declared that they had never heard such a cry as this despairing yell for help which came from the breast of the Emperor whom drunken men were slowly and inefficiently destroying. "No!" he cried. "No! ... You mustn't!" As most of them were drunk he thought he might somehow deflect their intentions, which were not wholly concerted. One of the Bariatinskis, more sober than the rest, then took three table napkins, made a noose of them and put it around the throat of the man of thirty-five who, twenty years before, as Karl Peter Ulrich, had unwillingly come to Russia when he would rather have stayed in Holstein or availed himself of his right to the Swedish crown. The others held his hands and feet and knelt on his chest, stepped on his stomach. Englehardt pulled at the noose with such force that the grandson of Peter the Great at last gave up the ghost.

His newly Imperial wife received the intelligence with remarkable indifference. Catherine believed in political necessities, and she did not believe in God. "On the seventh day after We, Catherine the Second, had by the Will of God ascended the throne of All the Russias," she diffused to the world at large in a manifesto, "We received intelligence that the former Emperor, Peter the Third, had fallen sick of a severe colic, in conjunction with one of the haemorrhoidal attacks to which he was subject. Mindful, therefore, of Our Christian charity and the sacred commandment which makes it incumbent upon us to cherish the life of our neighbor, We instructed that all that was needful to ward off the dangerous consequences of this attack be at once dispatched to him, together with all possible medical aid. Nevertheless, to Our deepest sorrow and distress, We yesterday evening received the further information that, by the Will of the Most High God, the former Emperor had given up his soul to his Maker."

BOOK THREE

CHAPTER VII

CATHERINE AND HER FAVORITES

I. "ARRIVED"

CATHERINE, who publicly lamented that her husband had died from a haemorrhoidal colic, rewarded handsomely the men said to have caused the said colic. There is no evidence that she sent anyone to intervene. Though in her manifesto she says she did everything to save the Emperor, she in fact did nothing. In her letter to Poniatovski she writes: "I feared the guards might have poisoned him. I therefore had the body opened, and it was then clearly demonstrated that there was no trace of poison. The stomach was healthy, but an inflammation of the bowels and an apoplexy had carried him off. His heart was unusually small and quite shrunken."

It is for medical men to tell us whether intense fear may not have been the cause of this shrinking. The doctors might also enlighten us as to whether the inflammation of the intestines may not have been caused by the assassins jumping on him. As for the "fit of apoplexy which had carried him off," it would not be unnatural after what they had been doing to him. It is also interesting to know that Catherine herself thirty-four years later died of a fit of apoplexy.

Patriotic historians, eager to glorify Catherine's reign, have consistently vilified Peter III in an attempt to justify Catherine's action. Much capital is made of his German predilections, his pranks, his tempers and his consequent unsuitability to occupy the orthodox throne. I think myself he was quite a likable fellow. His methods were more original than Catherine's, who, when she found herself powerless to eradicate a deep-rooted Russian vice, such as bribery, was content to leave it alone. Peter III was more humorous. Knowing it to be futile to stamp out bribery in Russia, he, though himself devoid of any trace of vindictiveness, punished his ministers by depriving them of one-half of their bribes, pocketing the fine, and forever after twitting them in front of the whole court.

He had not Catherine's faculty for covering infamy with a veneer of virtue. But, this trait apart, Catherine was a woman of infinite charm.

What makes her career peculiarly attractive is that she had no more right to the throne of Russia than you or I. She was a fairly clever woman, by no means a genius, but well above the average. A pleasant woman and of a cheerful disposition, such a one as, given the means, might make a success as a London hostess. Given the opportunity of more than middling intelligence and a throne, it is surprising what one can do.

There is nothing remarkable in keeping up an exalted position; what is remarkable is getting there. It is a remarkable feat of Hitler's, for example, that with all his initial disadvantages, all the obstacles strewn in his way, he should have advanced in a few years to become the master of Germany. Having got there, nothing else is remarkable. Men and women in commanding positions find themselves in a state of perpetual adulation which brings out the genius latent in all men. There is all the difference in the world between being your own boss and adapting your intelligence to please a boss. The average mind, released from the cramped conditions to which even ministers of State are subject in the presence of autocrats, acquires a new lease of life, a spring-board quality, a daring encouraged by fawning satellites, a tendency to apothegm, paradox and mental somersault. Catherine, released at last from the cramped conditions which for eighteen years she had endured at the hands of the Empress Elizabeth, now at last was able, merely with her average cheerful intelligence, to give an impression of unbelievable brilliance.

Catherine prided herself on her popularity with the Army, but the soldiers soon began to show that they were not immune from pangs of conscience. In Moscow especially, there were murmurs among the garrison and the population, who resented that an insignificant German princess should with the assistance of her lovers and satellites have deposed the grandson of Peter the Great. The soldiers grumbled that the Guards should be allowed to dispose of the throne as they liked. Most of the guardsmen had been led into the movement by a small minority. After the pleasure of novelty had evaporated, each man felt nothing but remorse. The sailors, who had not been consulted, openly reproached the Guards in the taverns with having sold their Tsar for a mug of beer. They began to pity the dead emperor.

Catherine felt that her exalted position depended on the good will of every soldier who, each time he set eyes on her, was bound to say to himself: "This is the work of my hands." She began, and never ceased, to propitiate the Army. She rewarded most handsomely the assassins of her husband. Sergeant Engelhardt, who had pulled the noose, rose rapidly in rank and died as a lieutenant general and Governor of Viborg.

Two private soldiers were banished instead of rewarded. But this was not to punish them for their complicity but for their lamentable indiscretion. They had not been able to hold their tongues and were even inclined to brag of the part they took in the murder. They were promoted to officer rank and given money. But under some pretext they were conveyed into the interior of Russia and discreetly murdered on the way.

II. "WHATEVER IS, IS RIGHT"

AND so Catherine settled down to the glamorous and exciting role of Empress and Autocrat of All the Russias. One must remember her childhood as the daughter of a minor princeling in Germany, the daughter of an insignificant princess with illustrious connections, but essentially the poor relation. One must recall her eighteen years of sustained deference to the incalculable and unapproachable Empress Elizabeth, who had not concealed her intermittent regret at having conferred so exalted and coveted a rank and position on a girl by no means deserving of such honors, a young woman not specially distinguished for either beauty or virtue, birth or brains, and showing a dangerous disposition for intrigue. One must remember those inhibitions, tears, humiliations, daily reprimands conveyed in the name of the Empress by an insolent and malicious lady in waiting and meekly received with a low curtsy, to realize the pleasure experienced by the new sovereign, who suddenly found herself in a position to command high and low, to dispense favors and privileges to all her friends.

Her power and freedom were, of course, conditioned by her ability to curry favor with those to whom she owed her elevation. Realizing her dependence, as her husband had never realized his, on the privileged classes in Russia, Catherine, fired by the liberal ideas of the French Encyclopedists and what she called her "republican" sentiments, still further "emancipated" the privileged classes at the expense of their peasants. For the peasants, who in the Russia of old had enjoyed a modicum of rights, had been progressively sacrificed for the benefit of the landowners, till they became serfs. When Catherine spoke of emancipating the classes and providing them with a liberal, "republican" form of government under her own autocratic rule, she did not think of the peasants as a class because they were by then almost beyond the pale of humanity. To ingratiate herself further with the landowners, who were the only people who really mattered, she increased their powers to an extent unknown before. Under Catherine it became legal for a landowner to punish his serfs even with death. Peasants could now be sold apart from the land. Advertisements appeared in which people offered two maidservants for a retriever.

Yet Catherine was sincerely shocked by the treatment accorded to American Negro slaves. She considered herself an enlightened ruler, free of all hypocrisy and cant, owing her modernity of outlook chiefly to her literary master, Voltaire. "I can assure you," she writes to him two years after her accession, "that I have since 1746 been under the greatest obligation to you. Before then I had only liked romances, but since your works accidentally fell into my hands I have read nothing but them. I have lost all taste for other books which were not equally well-written and improving."

In a list of books for a library which Catherine drew up we read: "No. 1. Voltaire's Works, not excluding the least of them, since they teach one to avoid dull books, and dull books are the worst books of all."

In her letters Catherine admits repeatedly the influence of Voltaire: "He is my master, or, more precisely, it is his works which have formed my mind and my spirit."

She orders several hundred copies of his works: "... I intend that they shall be a model, studied, and learned by heart."

But when Voltaire proposed paying a visit to St. Petersburg, Catherine, while professing herself delighted, repeatedly put him off.

His physical aspect had little appeal for her, and she had heard from Frederick the Great that Voltaire was mean, avaricious and tiresome. In short, she preferred corresponding with him from a distance; an imposition on the energy of the great man, who indulged in it only for the pecuniary advantages he aspired to extract from her on that nearer acquaintance to which the lengthy correspondence, which bored him considerably, was, he hoped, but a necessary if irksome preliminary.

Men of action and women of the world do not readily understand that intellectual intercourse with eminent men of thought is not for the latter the self-sufficient and self-repaying pleasure it is to them. It does not occur to them that an exchange of thought with themselves is, on account of the quality of their thoughts, more interesting to themselves than to the master whose medium they employ without contriving to engage his interest. Voltaire, poor exploited soul, was inevitably impelled to seek a *quid pro quo* in what Catherine had to dispense in her capacity of empress, not of thinker.

As an empress she had nothing to dispense to one who was not her idea of a lover, to which class she confined her gifts in serfs and land, in gold and jewels, rank, titles, decorations and position. She had developed very early, and for long after her marriage had languished a virgin. Now that she was losing whatever moderate looks she once possessed, she valued love and passion almost above a crown (which she possessed and therefore could not miss). Whereas the men who professed to be in love with her, and whose protestations she must needs believe, were in love (and in her heart of hearts she knew it) with her imperial crown.

"There is nothing so bad as to have a child for a husband," she confides in a woman correspondent many years after her accession. "I know what this involves, and I am a woman who believes that it is always the man's fault if he is not beloved. Gladly would I have loved my husband if it had been at all possible; and he so kind as to desire it."

Is there compunction here? Compunction for occupying the throne of her murdered husband? Is it natural female prudery which tries to justify to her own shocked moral sense the long row of lovers, as she passes in review before her mind's eye Saltikov, Poniatovski, Orlov, Vasiltchikov, Novosiltsov, Potemkin, Lanskoy, Yermolov, Korsakov, Zoritch, Zavodovski, Mamonov, Zubov, and a whole phalanx of obscure but no less virile stalwarts?

"From the time I was fifteen till my thirty-third year, I never really had any opportunity to talk to women," she again justifies herself. "I was permitted to have only serving-maids about me. If I desired conversation I was obliged to go into a room in which there were only men. It is, therefore, half due to habit, half to a partiality thus formed that I really understand how to carry on a conversation only with the opposite sex."

Versailles, corrupt in its own absolute style, regarded with shocked amazement the debauchery of the Russian Court polluted with the new-fangled philosophical liberalism imported from the political sewers of France. The French Court regarded the "Semiramis of the North" as a disgrace to religion, the monarchy and her sex. They might have condoned a latitude of principle in one or two departments: laxity in all three was, they felt painfully, a breach of good taste.

Yet her having all these lovers is in character. It may have retrospectively shocked Queen Victoria. It did shock Maria Theresa, who called Catherine a harlot. But, one feels, it was in Catherine's case "right." She loved, she suffered, but she hung on tenaciously to her crown. When a friend who had known Catherine as a girl in Germany wrote from Hamburg of an old flame of hers, Prince Henry of Prussia, with whom Catherine had danced minuets in Berlin and might easily have married, Catherine's reply indicates that she has no cause, widow though she is, to regret being Empress of Russia rather than the Princess Henry of Prussia.

"I beg Your Gracious Majesty's permission to relate," runs the letter, "that I had the honor about two years previously of meeting Prince Henry. He deigned to visit me and spoke with me some two hours. He referred to Your Majesty with such lively interest, with so great an admiration, that I could not refrain from reflecting that had he but had the good fortune to be united with the charming Princess Sophie, he would scarcely have been guilty of the awful deeds which darken his reputation today. But Pope asserts 'Whatever is, is right.' "

To this Catherine answered: "The conversation which you tell me you had with Prince Henry, and the interest which he takes in his old acquaintance, has naturally given me much pleasure. It is by no means the first time I have heard it spoken of, but I agree with Pope that many things which are, are right. I do not regret, therefore, that the *contredanses* had no further consequences."

Nor did she regret not having married her Uncle George, who had once desired so ardently to be united in marriage with his seductive, overdeveloped niece of fourteen; but who, on finding that his nephew and niece had become emperor and empress, had come out to Russia to see what he could get. His late nephew, Karl Peter Ulrich, had finally promised him the Duchy of Courland. The very day on which Catherine overthrew her husband the deed of transfer was to be formally sealed: Uncle George of Holstein was to be proclaimed the new Duke of Courland. But Uncle George, whose passion had so perplexed young Figgy in Germany, was a definite liability in Russia. She did not give him Courland, but returned it to the restituted political exile, Biron, who had held the duchy long ago, in the days of Anna Ivanovna.

III. RUSSIA AND EUROPE

THE correspondent of Diderot and Voltaire, the idol of the Encyclopedists, "Notre-Dame de Pétersbourg," Catherine concluded herself the most enlightened and liberal-minded woman in the world. The French Revolution reversed her republican sympathies; and she became, reluctantly, an authoritarian. "I am kind," she declared, "generally sweet-tempered. I dislike tortures and hangings. Unfortunately my position compels me to assert my will with severity, whenever I am obliged to assert it at all."

In love she was less happy. Though she usually got what she wanted, she did not get it as or when she wanted it. Had she been a Khan of Tartary, who delights in employing a large and varied assortment of slave girls without bothering to inquire whether they have feelings of reciprocity or indeed any feelings at all, Catherine in her supreme position would have had the time of her life. But, being a woman, she wanted to be wooed for her own sake, not for what she was able to dispense as empress; and, gifted with an unusually clear-sighted faculty, she found it difficult, though she tried hard, to convince herself that her lovers' passion, noticeably cooler than their zeal for self-advancement, was disinterested.

Nor, as a clever woman, could she overlook quite so easily as a clever man in the case of a woman pretty though silly, the deplorable absence of brains in her men. Catherine's was the age of literary innocence. It must be remembered that at that time not much had been done in the literary line even in the neighboring Germany. France and England had already reached their highest literary levels. Russia's was not to come till Alexander's closing and Nicholas's opening reign. To be sure, there were geniuses abroad—there was Voltaire. There was, had she had brains enough to know it, a homebred genius, von Visin, the first real satirist to appear in Russia. Another—Kniazhnin. But they did not look like gods; whereas Gregori Orlov approached the male ideal in this respect, and, though not the world's greatest wit, combined an assurance of manner with a native shrewdness which a clever empress need not find displeasing.

The greatest love of her life was Potemkin. It lasted from the time when he forced himself on her attention till the day he died. The career of a favorite in those days was the highest peak of manly ambition. In the eighteenth century a clever and ambitious man in Russia did not have the scope he might have today in capitalist countries. It had never occurred to anyone then that a great fortune might be made in commerce. To be sure, even then there were merchants in Russia who did themselves well, but they were almost a nation apart. They did not mix with the gentry till the end of the nineteenth century saw them taking a hand in the rise of industry and finances, in which foreigners took the lead. Then the Russian merchants began to invest their money in industrial undertakings and later came to the fore, marrying their daughters off to the gentry.

In order to explain Orlov and Potemkin, a digression is necessary here into the causes which make Russians so delightfully, almost idiotically, unself-conscious. Of all nations Russia is perhaps the most homogeneous. Half a generation is sufficient in Russia to turn a villager into a courtier. The Russian is pliable and adaptable beyond anything known in western or central Europe. For one thing, the Russian is too hidebound to notice the impression he produces in any foreign society; for another, in his comparatively unspoiled virgin nature he is conscious, not of his own shortcomings, but of what, seen by him objectively, appears as a quaintly comic, if often graceful, affectation in everything which isn't Russian. Therefore, if a Russian makes a fool of himself abroad, he thinks the laugh is on foreign customs and habits which, for his own part, he cannot seriously accept as valid.

A further cause which mitigates Russian self-consciousness abroad is the Russian's aptitude for improving on what he borrows from other nations. They take only that which suits them and without sacrificing Russian feeling. Witness Tchaikovsky improving on Italian and German romanticism by a liberal infusion of Slavonic melancholy, with a novel effect of Russian straightforwardness and a devastating sincerity over something about which he is painfully unable to make up his mind. Russia, largely due to her size, her potential resources, and the victories of her armies abroad all through the eighteenth century, which made other nations court her as an ally, had developed in international affairs the insolent outlook which characterizes the powerful newcomer. This attitude was reinforced by a veneer of culture which, while reassuring the Russian aristocracy that they were as good as Western Europeans, whose languages they spoke as to the manner born, prevented them by the very thinness of the veneer from knowing that they were not. France was the country which attracted them most, since in the eighteenth century France was still the Mecca of elegance; while England had the same remote curiosity for Russians as the United States later acquired for Englishmen, as a vigorous nation notorious for its energy in undertaking pioneering work in countries one might, if one were sufficiently curious, trace on the map; a nation famous for daring exploits chiefly of a nautical character, but lying aside, off the main track of interest.

The German-speaking peoples, though their thoroughness, cleanliness and godliness were recognized, always provoked a certain ill-disguised contempt in the Russians, probably caused by a resentment that a people so ingloriously cautious, temperate and industrious as the Germans who settled in Russia should be getting the better of the Russian "broad nature" which did not count the cost when it filled its pockets, in a way which was no foreigner's business.

IV. CATHERINE'S "LOVE ME FOR MYSELF"

POTEMKIN'S versatility was a good example of how rapidly assimilated facts may be passed off for knowledge. His natural laziness that had resulted in his early expulsion from Moscow University (which, when he became the favorite, heaped every academic honor on his head) took the form of acute aversion from the printed word. The loss of an eye, said to have been caused by Gregori Orlov in a fit of rising jealousy throwing a chair at him, completed his disinclination for bookish knowledge. What he knew he picked up in arguments with others. He was a great lover of argument, which he merely used as a means of weaving provisional theories around the points made by opponents, whom he interrupted at every step in order to expose their fallacy before they developed their arguments.

This practice strengthened both his self-confidence and his illusion that every proposition advanced was equally worthless. Turning the tables on his opponents, whom he contradicted in mid-sentence (on the principle of sound swordsmanship, which teaches early interception of a stroke from the opponent), had become a habit. Though it did not acquaint him with the deeper side of knowledge, it placed at the disposal of his memory a vast array of superficial facts which delighted Catherine, similarly equipped, and proved invaluable in the task of controlling others, who, if he knew a little about a lot, themselves knew only a lot about a little.

The eighteenth century in Russia was the age of favorites. Had Potemkin been born in the nineteenth century in England, his ambition would have been to become an industrialist in Birmingham or a manufacturer in Manchester. In the twentieth century he would have become a newspaper magnate, or fixed his eye on the B.B.C. But, confined to an age and land where all wealth, power and position were vested in the hands of one amiable woman, his ambition took the form of getting round her by a sustained, ridiculous, almost Charlie Chaplinesque protestation of passionate love. A passion which nothing could cool and which was driving him to the grave.

The Empress, chagrined by the tepid, half-hearted performances of lovers she had endowed with gifts, honors and benefits, was willing to hope that here at last was a genuinely fiery temperament whose passion for her as a woman, if all she heard were true, nothing could quench. She was touched; interested; she lent a willing ear to his entreaties to hearken to him or to kill him outright.

His success is testified by this letter of his to the Empress and Catherine's answer. "Do not wonder," he writes cunningly soon after their liaison had begun, "that I am disturbed about our love. Besides your countless benefits to me, you have enclosed me in your heart. I wish to stand there higher than all the others!" What he really means is that he wants to get higher honors than all the others, dig himself in more deeply into her heart, make his position more secure, impregnable, if he can. Her love was the sea bed in which he cast his anchor. Afterwards, when tired of incessant demands on his vitality—she was seven years older than he—he would go away, allegedly on State business, but always with the cord held taut and an occasional tug at the anchor to make sure it was still embedded deeply in her heart.

She, on her side, needed his physical presence partly because with the years she was growing more prurient, yet could not get the same satisfaction from other men while in love with him; partly because she yearned for tangible proof that, though aging, she still attracted him; that he was not, like the others, "just out for what he could get." To him, her love was a symbol of his own growing power—"What I say, goes!" He was intoxicated by the scope of possibilities open to a man like himself who had a knack of telling others what he wanted done, and getting it done by threats and coaxing, to which he added an endearing eccentricity which left everybody guessing at what he really thought. He built new towns, ports, harbors, fleets, raised armies, waged wars, won victories, formulated new laws, annexed the Crimea; and all without effort, without the terrible ravages in men, the tortures and cruelties of Peter the Great. In particular he was kind to the common soldier. He delayed assaults on fortified towns because he could not bear the idea of sacrificing lives. Gradually he took everything into his hands and ran the whole country from the coach in which he traveled. Catherine besought him to come home; he must come back, whatever happened to the war. He must attack at whatever cost and come home to her; delay was fatal. Man's love is a thing apart; 'tis woman's whole existence; and Catherine's interest in State affairs was just something she could share with her lover. When he sulked and did not reply to her *billets-doux,* she could always think of an excuse for writing to him without betraying too much of her heart: "Have you made arrangements for the reception of the Emperor of Austria?"

Catherine writes to Potemkin even when he is in Petersburg. She informs him incessantly of the state of her health and inquires about his with a wealth of sound advice. We learn from her letters to him that she frequently has diarrhea. And I suppose that when one is the Empress of All the Russias even imperial diarrhea is not without its interest. She tells him of her colds, perspirations, soaking handkerchiefs; she spares no details of her afflictions.

In this she betrays the error of a woman in love who thinks that a man in love is as incapable of disgust as she is herself at any unsavory details affecting his own health. Catherine was an intelligent woman, but intelligence does not feed on air but on experience. And if experience is lacking in one or more particulars, one's intelligence remains uninformed in respect of these particulars. As a Grand Duchess on whom her husband had made no demands, as an Empress before whom men competed to ingratiate themselves with a view to promoting their own careers, Catherine was without experience as to the things which do not enhance a man's desire for a woman, however much they might increase his sympathy. Potemkin, like Orlov before him, was not sensually aroused by Catherine's medical confidences. To be sure, she attracted them as a woman when arrayed in her imperial glory. Each favorite loved her in exactly the same way. For when we speak of loving a person "for herself" we really mean loving the combined effect which she and life together have wrought into the personality that bears her name.

It was not, however, in Catherine's nature to understand how she affected men. That a man who attracted her desired her stripped of all trappings of pomp, power and glory, reduced in fact to the very opposite of what she seemed, no longer a symbol but her intrinsic self, a daughter of Eve, a woman in the nude desirable not for the benefits she bestows but the passions she arouses, was to her the sweetest, to them the dreariest, of illusions.

Since all her lovers knew it well, they were loath to disappoint her by telling her the truth, which would have mortally offended her. And yet it need not have offended her if she had understood the nature of the love she inspired in men. Her charm, intelligence, her grace, to say nothing of the glamour inseparable from her position, caused men to fall in love with her person. Once they loved her, they received as sympathetically her accounts of her health, as affected in turn by indigestion, diarrhea, bad breath, bad teeth, and so on, as she received their own accounts cataloguing periodical indisposition. The difference was merely that, whereas a man's illnesses seem to endear him to a woman who loves him without making him any less desirable as a lover, a woman's illnesses also endear her to the man who loves her, without, however, making her any more desirable sensually. Catherine forgot that before her lovers could give her that tangible proof which she incessantly demanded of them to reassure her that they still desired her, they must, to sustain the performance, be suitably inflamed in their imagination, which was not assisted by her intimate accounts of perspiration, constipation, floating kidney, flying dandruff, running colds, and so on. These things perhaps interested the favorites from the point of view that they were, at the time, the sole recipients of this intimate information on the part of Her Gracious Majesty. They sympathized, within reason, with her afflictions because they loved the Empress as a human being. But—and this was a point they could not convey to her in a way to make her see it—they found it progressively difficult to sustain an ardent interest in Her Imperial Majesty's body as a body, when it was no longer young, resilient or healthy.

That her three principal lovers, Poniatovski, Orlov and Potemkin, all resorted to the same expedient—periodical absences—suggests that the job of favorite was not a bed of roses. That they did so on the principle that absence makes the heart grow fonder is borne out by their going away when their continued attendances on Her Majesty's pleasure became too irksome for them, on the one hand, and too unproductive of results to further their ambitions, on the other. Catherine's heart in absence did invariably grow fonder, while the favorites enjoyed their repose without always gaining their point.

V. POTEMKIN VERSUS ORLOV

POTEMKIN had reproached Catherine with being promiscuous—a generally accepted view—and she repudiates this charge in a letter. "You will deign to admit," she writes, "that there were not fifteen, but a mere third of that number. The first, not of my own will, and the fourth, taken in my unhappiness, can hardly be counted. As for the other three, you must not judge harshly. For, as God is my judge, I did not take them out of looseness, which is alien to my nature. If in my youth Fate had given me a husband whom I could have loved, I should have remained forever true to him. It is my misfortune, rather than my fault, that my heart is of the kind which must love or perish. One hour without love is an agony to me! We are told that by ascribing virtue to ourselves as though love was rooted in sheer kindness of heart we affect to cover our infirmities and vices. Well I know it! But such a craving of the heart is itself an infirmity and a vice rather than a virtue. It is, however, needless for me to continue to you in this strain, since if you have followed my thoughts you would love me and not wish to go away with the army for fear that in your absence I might master this vice of the heart and forget you. But then I could hardly commit so great a stupidity! Should you wish to link me eternally to yourself, then show me as much friendship as love—and love even more than friendship, and keep faith!"

Catherine had not said good-by to passion on the death of Potemkin. But it was true that he was only the third *serious* lover. The first, the handsome Saltikov, was provided for reasons of State, to produce a son and heir, since Peter III was either entirely impotent or impotent in respect of his wife. Catherine disliked Saltikov for his boastfulness and indiscretion. Her attitude to him was erratic—the attitude of a woman provoked by a lover whom she had partly begun to desire, but whose bounce and assurance annoyed her. She would send him away abroad, and then urgently require his return. He was finally disgraced. The punishment, having regard to his importance, being merely exile to Paris as Russian Ambassador.

A year later a young Polish prince with strikingly beautiful eyes, but hopelessly shortsighted, found his way to the Russian Court, and he was loved six years, almost to the time the Empress Elizabeth died. His name was Poniatovski, whom later Catherine rewarded with the throne of Poland.

But, like all Catherine's lovers, he required to take time off for re-
cuperation; which he did in 1758, and stayed away three years, during
which Catherine, though she still loved him, inclined her ear to the
persistent protestations of Gregori Orlov, a mere captain of artillery but
a handsome Russian type. Catherine's letters to Poniatovski grew cooler,
the intervals longer. From a lover Poniatovski had become a friend, a
confidant, a father-confessor.

Gregori Orlov, who occupied apartments on the floor beneath the
Empress's, had installed himself for a long stay. Extremely handsome,
masterful, fiery-tempered, for many years he was the uncrowned tsar.
Everyone expected that it would not be long before he got his own way
and induced Catherine to marry him; then he would be emperor, or at
the very least prince consort. But, though Catherine had made him a
prince of the Holy Roman Empire (by courtesy of the Emperor of Austria) she was chary of abolishing the restraining difference between them
which made him not only her lover but also her subject. Orlov therefore
began a war of attrition calculated to wear down Catherine's nerves,
which took the form of removing himself from her presence on the plea
of attending the Congress of Foxshani. "He," Catherine writes of Orlov
to his successor-but-one, Potemkin, "*he* might have stayed forever, if he
had not grown tired! I learned this on the very day of his departure from
Tsarskoye Selo for the Congress and simply drew from this the conclusion that with this knowledge I could have no more confidence. This
thought cruelly tormented me and forced me from desperation to make
a choice at random."

The choice—a brainless if good-looking youth, Alexander Vasiltchikov
—was not merely a way of filling a gap, but an attempt to show Orlov
that two could play at that game. It achieved the desired effect: it brought
back Orlov. He was seriously disturbed at the rumor that his power was
on the wane, had indeed evaporated. Quick as lightning, he was at her
side. But Catherine, convinced that Orlov loved in her not the woman
but the empress, determined, though it broke her heart, to stay firm. Vasiltchikov bored her unspeakably. He was so very young and stupid, he had
neither character nor conversation and was useless except in a physical
sense in which he displayed a commendable zeal rather than prowess. He
tried so hard, poor boy, it touched her heart, and she rewarded him with
some if not all the appurtenances of his office. He occupied a suite of
rooms in the palace. She longed for her Orlov, but she not only resented,
she even feared, his lust for power, much more formidable than his lust

for her body, which would have been so much more reassuring. "Throughout this time," she writes, "I have suffered more than I can tell, and never more than when others were happy. Every act of tenderness I witnessed on the part of others made me weep, and I believe I have never wept so bitterly since I was born as in this past year. At first I thought I would grow accustomed to it, but the longer it lasted the worse it was, for the other party would sulk for months at a time, and I confess that I was happier when he was angry and left me to myself. It was his occasional tenderness which still evoked my tears."

Orlov, who had stooped through the good offices of his brother Aleksei to resort to murder in order to remove Peter III, might, married to her, resort to the same expedient to proclaim himself tsar. And Catherine, though it would have been so much easier, so much sweeter, to deceive herself, to be weak, to give in to him, remained firm. Orlov was told to vacate his suite of rooms in the palace. The English Ambassador reported home that the Favorite's position was on the wane and was regarded in circles close to the court as all but finished.

When Orlov understood that he had lost the day, his rage gave way to a good-natured humor—which had been the quality that Catherine loved in him. One day, passing Potemkin on the great staircase of the Winter Palace, Orlov, instead of scowling at his rival, gave him a smile. Potemkin stopped and inquired politely of Orlov: how were things with the Empress? "Unchanged," answered Orlov. "You're going up, I'm coming down; for the rest, the Empress stays where she was."

Potemkin employed a slightly different technique with Catherine than did Orlov. He did not pester her to marry him, and thus she did marry him in the end, but so cryptically that no one but the priest, who had been sworn to secrecy, knew of it. Potemkin therefore derived no kudos from the marriage bond, except that it reassured him, on the one hand, of Catherine's sentimental attachment to him and, on the other, released him, as his health gave way, from the irksome duties of a lover, for which he substituted the more salutary, though unusual, conjugal task of selecting at his own discretion more virile substitutes, without relaxing his emotional grip on the woman who adored him.

He did not, like Orlov, plead affairs of State when he wanted a breathing space. He was seized at intervals with sudden powerful impulses for prayer and meditation and betook himself on pilgrimages to distant monasteries. Every now and then, when Catherine showed herself obstinate in affairs, he would feel the call of religion. At any moment he might cast off the yoke of government, abandon his life of luxury, throw all his privileges to the wind and take Holy Orders. Catherine was terrified whenever he set out on a pilgrimage lest he send her word that he had become a monk.

He had frequent lapses of melancholia, half real, half simulated. He delighted in playing the fool, indulged in eccentricity, appearing at receptions organized by municipal authorities in his honor, unshaved and wearing a dressing gown with only a short jacket beneath it, so that he was bare from the hips down except for the folds of his dressing gown which flopped about him as he walked. He would travel like that in his coach, emerging in the same attire, unshaven and unwashed, to attend parties, receptions and banquets. Yet beautiful women adored him and he had amorous relations with all his nieces, whose careers at court he promoted.

Catherine loved him more than all her previous or later lovers. She found him witty and brilliant. Though he looked not unlike Charlie Chaplin and with his one eye resembled, and indeed was called, "the Cyclop," she addressed him as her beautiful prince, her hero, "Cossack ...giaour!" She was obviously mad about him. The son of an obscure army officer of no achievement or distinction, he became in the space of a few years a prince of the Holy Roman Empire. A palace was built for him in the capital. Country estates and money were showered upon him. Appointments and commands rained down upon him. Nothing was too good for him. At Christmas, at Easter, on New Year's Day, on his birthday, his nameday, he received large gifts of money.

One Easter Catherine varied the habit and sent him a present instead. He sulked and would not speak to her for weeks, till she sent him the cash, too. She covered him with jewels. She had solicited the sovereigns of nearly all the countries of Europe to bestow upon him their highest decorations. He could boast of possessing them all ... but one.

VI. POTEMKIN AND THE GARTER

ONE decoration still failed him: the Garter. England at that time was in a serious predicament. Her North American colony had rebelled against the authority of the sovereign. Lord North was at a loss to know what to do. George III conceived the idea of an alliance with Russia that should require Catherine to send an Expeditionary Force to America to quell the rebellion.

A student of Anglo-Russian political relations of the period, Soloveit-chik, traces the progress of these negotiations, which bear a curious resemblance to the Moscow "talks" of 1939. The English Ambassador at St. Petersburg was instructed to approach Potemkin, who, while not excluding all hope of success, dragged out negotiations almost indefinitely on the plea that foreign affairs were not—though, of course, he exercised a certain influence—his direct concern. He counseled perseverance, advised Sir James Harris (afterwards Lord Malmesbury) to wait, or have a word with the Chancellor Panin, who controlled foreign policy and must be reckoned with, since he represented a powerful group gathered round the Grand Duke Paul, the heir to the throne. Even the Empress herself avoided cutting in on Panin's policy.

The Ambassador sounded Panin, who shook his head disgruntledly. English colonies in North America, whether threatened or not, internally or externally, were not, he said, a Russian interest. The Ambassador pleaded that, in associating herself with the King of England against his rebellious American subjects, the Empress would be upholding the principles of legitimacy and authority against the new-fangled republican ideas which, if not checked, might overrun the world. But Panin still shook his head. Russia had nothing to seek from England, he said. An alliance with England would be against her true interests.

Harris, pressed by Lord Stormont, the Foreign Secretary, to expedite by all possible means the dispatch of Russian Cossacks to America, requested Potemkin to secure an audience for himself with Her Majesty. Potemkin sighed; that was not easy, he said. Her Majesty avoided the granting of audiences to foreign ambassadors for fear of ruffling Panin, who might imagine that she was pursuing a foreign policy of her own behind his back. Panin, he warned, was a very powerful man in the State. Even the Empress was afraid of him. The Grand Duke Paul had long since come of age. Panin had been his tutor, and was regarded as the natural sponsor of his rights. Panin had originally joined in deposing Peter III, not in favor of Catherine, but of Paul. His idea at the time had been to declare Paul emperor and invite Catherine to rule the country as regent during her son's minority. Now that Paul was not only grown up, but approaching middle age, many people might consider that his mother was reigning illegally in his stead. Panin, regarded throughout the whole country as an authority on legality, might, if crossed, decide to make his voice heard. Catherine in that event would have to step down from the throne, and she regarded the prospect of a dowager-empress-ship with misgiving bordering on horror.

Potemkin, who began to invite Sir James Harris to stay with him at his country residences, where nobody, he said, could overhear them, hinted at these difficulties. But, he added, not all was lost yet. He might be able to win the Empress over to his own ideas, provided he could be sure that he himself felt strongly enough on the point pressed by the English Ambassador to overcome the Empress's objection, by sheer eloquence sprung from inward conviction. Patience, he urged, infinite patience was needed—*among other things*. Potemkin would sigh and look meaningly at Sir James.

Harris, who really showed unbelievable patience and pertinacity, wrote home that he was slowly but steadily gaining ground. The Foreign Office in London urged him to press forward his demand to the point of dangling before the Russians some unspecified British territory to be ceded in return for Russian military aid, being, however careful not to commit his Government to any specific pledge which might later have to be honored. Harris wrote back that he had to go slowly, but had now made sufficient progress to be able to consider the Favorite, Prince Potemkin, as united with him by ties of personal friendship. From now on he refers in his dispatches home to the Favorite as "my friend," and reports a growing intimacy springing up between them. He had even proved successful at last in persuading his friend to obtain for him an audience with the Empress in order to try his own eloquence upon her; the audience had been fixed two months ahead.

The Cabinet at home was growing impatient, but there was nothing for it but to wait for the day appointed for the audience. The day arrived and the English Ambassador delivered himself of an eloquent harangue in French designed to win the Empress over to George III's cause in America, an address he had rehearsed for two months. Her Majesty, Harris reports, listened with amiable graciousness. She assured him that her heart warmed towards England, many of whose institutions she admired. But in pursuing a foreign policy she was guided by a single ideal—to serve Russia's interests, and the Chancellor Panin assured her that the safety of English possessions in North America was not a Russian interest.

Harris sought out his new friend, who listened with apathy to what he appeared to regard as a foregone conclusion. He, Harris, had even mentioned the possible cession of colonial territory to Russia. Potemkin hummed as though to himself. What could Russia do with colonies? They were too far. Harris assured him he had used all the eloquence on the Empress of which he was capable. "You should have used your eloquence on me instead," Potemkin murmured gloomily. Harris stared at him. Potemkin stared back, it seemed, meaningly. What did he want? Money? Skillfully Harris led the conversation on to money. Potemkin did not seem especially interested. He responded with pious good will. Came vague promises, counsels of patience, of the need to step warily, to go slowly. Downing Street was losing patience with Harris and was about to recall him.

And then, one morning, light came to the English Ambassador. He had it! Off he rushed to see his friend. Cautiously he tried his new key in the lock—it turned. The door opened.

Overjoyed, he drove back to the Embassy and sat down to write his dispatch. Now he knew what would do it—the Garter! There was not the slightest doubt he had hit, he wrote, on the most eloquent argument of all. The Favorite had given him to understand in no uncertain terms that it could not fail to make him use his influence with the Empress, who was devoted to him and accepted his advice against an army of Panins. The Favorite was in possession of all the highest orders of every nation represented at the Imperial Court—except the English. He had everything the heart of man could desire—wealth, power, women, rank, honors, palaces and country estates. His melancholia, his repeated declarations that he wished to renounce this life and become a monk, sprang from satiety with the world. His friend had in fact often confessed to him that his melancholia was caused by his cruel misfortune in having nothing left in this world to desire, since he was overloaded with everything. But he, Harris, had discovered a chink in his armor. There was one thing which he did not have and in fact greatly desired, one thing he was not and greatly wanted to be—a Knight of the Most Noble Order of the Garter. Nothing less than the Garter would have any effect, save that of rubbing him up the wrong way. But if the King could see his way to conferring the Garter on the Favorite, he, Harris, was absolutely confident that the Empress would be won over to their cause and a Russian army would embark forthwith for the New Hemisphere to subdue the American rebels.

The Ambassador then awaited a reply from Whitehall. It came in due course. King George III was shocked at the idea that such a suggestion should ever have come from one who was his ambassador, and desired that he should be severely reprimanded for making it and recalled from his post.

And so, no Russian army landing in America, the United States came into being; when they could have been saved for the "Greater British Commonwealth of Nations" at the price of a garter.

CHAPTER VIII

CATHERINE CARRIES ON

I. LUXURY AND SORDIDNESS

WHEN Catherine began her reign she met with a certain amount of opposition from old senators, who gave as the reason for the continuance of a costly and cumbersome procedure the fact that it had been thus before. There would arise a heated argument in the Senate. If the Empress was losing ground, the Procurator General would leave his place, come over to Catherine and say, in an ingratiating manner, turning the while a threatening eye at the senators: "Tell me, Your Majesty, *exactly* how you wish it done, and it will be carried out *exactly* as you wish it."

Catherine lived in pomp and luxury, rebuilding her palaces to the still greater glory of the Fatherland. The favorite of the day occupied a wing in whichever palace the Empress was in residence. At Tsarskoye Selo there was the Hermitage, which contained mechanical tables designed to appear out of the floor fully laden with delicacies and when required vanish out of sight. The contrivance by which this eighteenth-century "mechanism" was set in motion was of the crudest, the tables being lowered on ropes by a forest of human hands concealed in the cellar. But it was considered the high-water mark of mechanical invention and was shown with patriotic pride to distinguished visitors to Russia. The tables, ready-set and laden with wine and dishes, appeared and vanished on demand. But while the royal guests and courtiers sat round at supper, in the cellar beneath, habitually flooded, a whole regiment of men stood up to the waist in water. The ropes frequently broke and the "mechanical tables" fell down and crushed the men gathered below to operate them.

This sharp contrast of luxury with wretchedness was to be seen everywhere. Pomp and sordidness lived side by side. The ballrooms in the palaces rivaled Versailles, but lacked the rudiments of ventilation. The palaces were lit only by tallow candles. Hygiene was unknown. Drainage was nonexistent. There were no lavatories, but the servants as required brought into the bedrooms little wooden commodes upholstered in velvet. These were carried out on to the staircase where they awaited removal.

The "nobility" of the rank and file lived even a more ramshackle and primitive existence. "Moscow I do not like at all," Catherine notes, "but I have no preference for Petersburg. I must discipline myself and be guided merely by public welfare and always speak my mind. Moscow is the city of idleness. Its unwieldy shape and size is mainly responsible. I will make it a rule when I am there never to send for anyone, since you can never know till next day whether the person you want is able to come. In order to pay a visit you spend all day in your carriage; thus the whole day is wasted. The nobles who live there certainly enjoy themselves, and that is not surprising. From their early years they adopt the tone and manner of idle luxury. They grow soft and spineless, spend all their time in driving in a coach-and-six and behold around them only sordidness—enough to depress the keenest spirit. Besides, there never was a people with so many objects of fanaticism before their eyes: miracle-working saints at every step, churches, priests, cloisters and monasteries, bigots, vagabonds, thieves, useless servants in all the houses—and *such* houses! what dirt in the houses, which occupy a great deal of space and have miry bogs for courtyards. Speaking generally, every person of consequence in that city has not merely a house but something of a small country estate surrounding it."

Men of the type of Potemkin were addicted to luxury and sordidness and took a special delight in combining the two. When Potemkin went to war he had an underground residence built for himself in the front line and furnished like a palace. There were ballrooms complete with orchestra, whole suites of opulent rooms. While he waited for military operations to begin, he amused himself to the sound of guitars with a harem of concubines, intermittently relapsing into fits of melancholia. He had a secretary called Popoff, with whom he would shut himself in for days on end, refusing admission to generals and ministers of State. He ended by relegating everything to Popoff, including the planning of campaigns and the direction of military operations. While the high command and special messengers sent by the Empress awaited for days the privilege of an interview with the Favorite, at intervals they could hear Potemkin's raucous voice shouting for his secretary permanently seated in an anteroom within earshot of "The Prince" who, between lapses of acute melancholia, languishing half-naked in his dressing gown, unshaven and unwashed, bawled intermittently: "Popoff! ... Popoff! ..."

II. PUBLIC EXPENDITURE

WHETHER through his own or Popoff's genius, Potemkin won all his campaigns. He was the virtual dictator of Russia—always allowing for the overriding competence of Panin's judgment. Overbearing with equals, Potemkin was indulgent with subordinates. A young man annoyed Catherine's secretary, Bezborodko, who threatened to complain to the Empress. The young man appealed to a relative of Potemkin and was told to report that evening to the Favorite. "And tell him," Potemkin had added, "to be bold and daring with me."

Bezborodko was also there, and they began to play cards. "My dear fellow," Potemkin addressed the young suppliant, "I'm stuck. Please tell me: how do I go on now?"

"Play as best you can, but don't pester me!" said the young man.

"My dear chap," rejoined Potemkin, "what an angry fellow you are. One has only got to say one word to you and—there!—you're all in a temper!"

Bezborodko drew his own conclusions from this conversation, deciding that if the young man could talk like that to Potemkin, it might be risky to complain of him to Catherine.

There was a certain roguish humanity about Potemkin which endeared him to Catherine. She respected his astonishing versatility, his competence in getting things done. "It has always been easy to lead me," she says. "For to be able to do that it was only necessary to have better and more worthy ideas than my own. Then I was as docile as a lamb."

The stories of the cardboard cities he built to impress her on her travels through Russia are slight exaggerations. What is true is that as the Empress proceeded down the Volga he had whole populations of peasants decked out in new bright clothes and flocks of picked cattle transferred to the banks of the river where the imperial barge passed by; and they were mostly the same peasants and flocks she had already passed by at the bend of the river, quickly transferred ahead by a short cut across country. The same fairs and merry-go-rounds were set up anew, to give an impression of a gay, idyllically happy and prosperous population welcoming their Sovereign.

In contrast to the luxury of the Russian Favorite, who could command magnificent shows and displays, it is painful to find that Sir

James Harris, the English Ambassador, was kept so short of funds by the home government that he could not afford to entertain. When, at long last, he ventured to give a banquet at the English Embassy, he had to borrow a dinner service from his French colleague. One is reminded of superbly monocled Sir Austen Chamberlain at the League of Nations Palace in Geneva, in the midst of diplomatic representatives of beggared South American and Balkan States driving up in their newest and most luxurious limousines, himself alighting from an ancient car with rattling windows, a door nearly coming off its hinges and the handle as you turn it probably remaining in your hand. In a similar vehicle, Sir George Buchanan, Ambassador of Great Britain, perambulated the quayside of St. Petersburg. A potent reminder of a rich country keeping count of public expenditure in an attempt to balance its budget.

III. CATHERINE GOES LOOSE

CATHERINE was struck dumb by the death of Potemkin, who died suddenly on his travels in Moldavia, stopping his coach to be lifted out and laid down on the grass at the roadside. She was seized with compunction. She had, shortly before his end, taken a new favorite—Zubov; and this time she had turned the tables on Potemkin. Hitherto, it was he whom she cajoled to return to her from the wars which he waged as a relaxation from her incessant demands on his vitality. Hitherto, he had himself provided her with suitable young men who, while answering the purpose for which they were designated, remained his obedient subordinates, never questioning the supremacy of his influence over the Empress.

But this youth Zubov was acquired in Potemkin's absence on Catherine's own initiative, and he was presuming to claim his rights as a full-fledged favorite and rival of Potemkin, wheedling favors, exerting influence. . . . The news of it brought Potemkin back like a shot, as indeed Gregori Orlov had been brought back many years earlier at the news of Potemkin's good luck. Now it was Potemkin's turn to plead with the Empress. He threatened, he entreated, he cajoled, he finally gave a fabulous banquet and ball in his Tavrida palace in honor of the Empress. He was eaten up with rage, jealousy and envy. He believed himself again in love with the toothless, aged Empress. He was no chicken himself, and he deprecated Catherine's passion for a mere youth like Zubov—all without creating any impression on the Empress. Zubov stayed, and Potemkin was sent away to the wars.

Now that he was dead, the Empress was inconsolable. But now that he was no more, how could it have profited Potemkin if she renounced her darling Zubov, to whom, on the contrary, she turned for consolation, which he did not withhold from her? Nay, he even condoled with her. The dead man, he allowed, had his qualities.

Though a comparison with so respectable a monarch as Queen Victoria may appear startling, the parallel in one particular is sufficiently close to allow of it. After all, Potemkin had been as precious to Catherine as the Prince Consort to the Queen. They had been secretly married; thus, in a way, he, too, was a Prince Consort. When, after the death of Prince Albert, Queen Victoria for a time retired from public view and only resumed her public life under protest at the instigation of the Cabinet, who deemed it wrong that just because she had lost her husband she should knock off work, she wrote: "That my people should want to see a *poor, lonely, suffering* widow draped in deepest mourning *expose* herself to the public gaze, is something *I* shall *never* understand!!"

Catherine's grief took a more desperate turn. She had always considered herself hitherto as being, essentially, a one-man woman. She had in her letters to Potemkin reduced the number of her lovers from fifteen to five, and she had explained again and again that, since feeling was the only thing that counted with her, the five could be reduced to three, of which the first two had themselves deserted her, and that, anyway, they were but a prelude to the one great love of her life, himself.

Now that her darling was gone, a feeling of despair overtook her. Good-by to chastity! Let everything rip! No more curbing self-restraint. No further concession to *feeling*. Lust had meant nothing to her without feeling. Now that all feeling had been taken from her by an unkind Providence, very well, then, let the flesh have its way!

It was after the Favorite's death that Catherine acquired the greatest number of lovers. Birds of passage they were; here one day, gone the next. There were exceptions, of course; some men, like Zubov, who "continued to give every satisfaction," lingered on. As time went on she began to divorce lust from every vestige of feeling, considering it—to give it a philosophical term—"a thing-in-itself." Like her late mother-in-law, the much lamented Empress Elizabeth, Catherine in her choice of lovers was not prejudiced by rank or social position. Prowess was everything. A lady in waiting with a Scottish name, Countess Bruce, née Rumiantsev ("To whom," Catherine writes in her dedication, "I can speak freely without fear of consequences") was appointed *"essayeuse,"* her task being to sieve suitable applicants and recommend such of them as had passed the test.

A huge sergeant major in the Grenadiers passed the test with flying colors and confirmed the Empress's opinion that, when all was said, simple folk were best. Simple people employed simple remedies, beyond the ken of an Orlov with all his common sense and mother-wit, beyond Potemkin with all his verbal brilliance. The sergeant major did not resort to any psychological expedient to augment the Empress's longing for his society by devising flimsy excuses for absence sorely needed for recupera-tion. His method was homely. He placed a fresh young village wench in the room next to that occupied by the Empress. Roused to excitement by the kind of girl who awoke the old red Adam in him, the sergeant major, without losing a moment, dashed across into the room of the aging Empress, who not only failed to excite any normal passion in him but dangerously intimidated him by her august Majesty. Not a moment too soon, he transferred all the lust aroused in him by her Majesty's fresh if humble subject, from the said humble subject to the austere if aging person of the Empress; with perfectly satisfactory results, to judge by the sergeant major's rapid promotion in rank and advancement at court, with pleasing consequences to his family who, from being peasants in one generation, became nobles in the next.

IV. RUSSIAN NOBILITY

THIS frequently encountered word "noble" needs some explanation. Every person in Russia who achieved the rank of colonel or the corre-sponding grade in the civil services—particularly if he owned some land —automatically became a noble. That is to say, if he was not a noble already, because his father or grandfather had in the ordinary course of service reached the same inevitable rank—which they were bound to do if they served long enough. The Russian word for noble—*dvoryanin*, deriving from *dvor* ("yard")—does not signify nobility but the posses-sion of a foothold of one's own—a yard filled with serfs. As government service in the time of Catherine offered almost the only occupation for any man who could remotely read or write, all so-called literate people were technically "nobles." All their children and their children's children, and so forth, were nobles, too, from birth.

Since Peter abolished the old Russian order—which had its boyars rep-resenting descendants of the more prominent families who had at one time or another clung around the court and occupied responsible positions in the Army—everybody, unless he was a peasant (in which case his status was about equal to that of an American Negro slave), was a noble. Later a new class was defined, of villagers living in market towns, and still later a class above villagers and below "nobles," called citizens, whose fathers had not yet risen to the rank of colonel or the corresponding grade in the civil service. It is therefore well to remember that the rank of a Russian "noble" corresponds to that of gentry in other countries —and that is putting it high. It is necessary to bear this in mind throughout Russian history, since the continuous use of "noble" brings to mind in the English reader a peculiarly exalted type of grandee enjoying the wealth and position of an Essex or Southampton in the reign of Queen Elizabeth—a rank defined in Germany, in contra-distinction to every "von" who likewise styles himself and his family "nobles," as *"der Hohe Adel."*

Such a *"Hoher Adel"* still existed in Russia. They were the products of old families, like the Princes Dolgoruki, Troubetskoy, Golitsin, and the like, of a lineage more ancient than the relatively new Romanovs, having sprung conjointly with or from the first dynasty of Russian rulers, the Ruriks. In addition to these, the *"Hoher Adel"* was, since Peter the Great, often recruited from obscure newcomers without regard to their origin and raised overnight to the highest peak through favoritism resting on an amorous basis.

Compared with this (in the German sense) "high nobility," the rank and file of Russian nobility which English readers are apt to confuse with the former, were as though men enjoying the hereditary position of, let us say, a Lord Derby, or the rapidly acquired positions of, say, the first Duke of Marlborough or Wellington, were indistinguishable from a British colonel in Poona (who, by the Russian standard, would belong to that vast heterogeneous provincial population officially registered as "nobles").

Therefore, when mention is made in books dealing with Russian history of "nobles," the reader must correct his first impression of a country, apart from peasants, populated almost entirely by families enjoying the standard of living and wealth of the Dukes of Norfolk and Westminster, but should instead imagine the Russian towns as swarming with the kind of army officer and civil servant who go out to India to serve the British Raj. If the reader further compares the native population of India with that of Russian peasants, the picture will be tolerably accurate.

V. PUGATCHÒV

CATHERINE'S reign counts for one of the most glorious in Russia; and by dedicating a magnificent monument to Peter the Great, bearing the simple inscription: "To Peter I from Catherine II" it is as if she herself invites comparison and suggests she has completed what he began. She extended the frontiers of Russia, strengthened the Army, codified the laws. But the peasants—that is, the immeasurably largest portion of the population—sank to the lowest level of slavery during her so-called enlightened reign. A huge revolt broke out, gathering force like a forest fire. It was nothing less than a revolution of the serfs and dispossessed classes. A Cossack brigand by the name of Pugatchòv started the movement by posing as Tsar Peter III miraculously escaped from the attempted murder by Catherine's favorites and now trying to regain his lawful throne. The movement spread rapidly, not so much because many believed Pugatchòv's story as because general discontent was ripe for revolt. The oppression of the people was like a prolonged draught leaving every living impulse parched and inflammable: the first spark set the whole depressed population aflame, and the soldiers went over to them where they could with the same facile enthusiasm as when they had gone over to Catherine.

The outbreak nearly cost Catherine her throne, but the big battalions got the better of the rebels, and the movement was finally suppressed with great cruelty. Pugatchòv, betrayed by his people, was taken prisoner. The general before whom he appeared tore out a handful of the rebel's beard. What outraged the generals of the old school was that a simple common Cossack should have posed as His Imperial Majesty Emperor Peter III, who, in death, no longer inspired the contempt which had led to his untimely assassination. Pugatchòv was placed in a cage and carted round all the principal towns.

As he came into view, the people thronging the Red Square for his execution caught sight of him standing in the moving cart, turning round and bowing incessantly to right and left, as though paying homage to the crowds he was passing, the while wailing aloud: "Forgive me, Orthodox folk, if I have done you any harm: forgive my soul before God!"

Catherine had ordered that the execution be carried out as painlessly as possible. Before Pugatchòv had mounted the platform the executioners vehemently threw themselves upon him and began to tear his coat off his back. At the same moment the ax flashed in the air: off flew his head.

Only then did they cut off his legs and arms and exhibit them to the people, in confirmation of the sentence passed upon him.

VI. CATHERINE GIVES UP SOCIAL HOPE

CATHERINE found the job of self-upholding all the virile Russians a congenial one. When Potemkin died she consoled herself with young Zubov, whom she had acquired shortly before Potemkin's death. Zubov, a good-looking youngster, came up jeeringly to a hideous visitor to the palace, by name Tchertkov—"Well, my beauty——"

Tchertkov scowled and snapped back: "I, my dear sir, have never stooped to make a career with my body."

Catherine, who was in the room playing cards, remarked as she tossed them casually to the youths seated around her: "You are all of you much too young to remember Tchertkov in his prime, and looking at him now no one could have credited him with any looks. But I can assure you that there was a time, before he wore himself out, when Tchertkov was quite presentable, and, I can tell you—he was pretty good."

Having solved the problem of satisfying her desires, Catherine discovered that her own happy nature was not general. Other people not being as reasonable as she was, there was no helping them against their will. Though she had earlier introduced some sweeping reforms, she soon realized that if she was to remain on the throne she could not tackle the problem of liberating the serfs. The French Revolution and a feeling of hopelessness which, in Russia, will lay hold of the most sanguine temperament, had long made her hang her head. It is not therefore quite just, or, if just, not quite kind, to reproach her for her reactionary views, to sigh over her as one who had begun so hopefully and ended so hopelessly. She gives vent to her feeling in words showing some indignation with prevailing conditions she is powerless to eradicate.

"Moscow," she returns to the attack, "that city which all so love, where all is sloth and indolence! They would gladly pass all their days there, driving about in a broken-down gilded coach-and-six, concealing from the masses by such shows the true worthlessness of their masters. It is far from unusual to see a richly dressed lady in an ornate carriage drawn by six horses with greasy trappings, drive out from a great courtyard piled high with filth and dung; while the house that surrounds the courtyard is a mere barrack of rotting timbers. Unkempt lackeys in handsome livery shame her by their odious manners. For the most part both men and women grow soft in this former capital. So great is the squalor in which all live, that even genius itself would pale and die in such surroundings. They have no law but their own whims and fancies, and so they do not keep the Law themselves, and when they administer it, administer it badly. Never having learned how to command, they are reduced to becoming tyrants. There is nowhere in the world so favorable a breeding ground for despots as this Russia. From their cradles the children grow accustomed to it, seeing with what savagery their parents treat the servants. No house but has its pillory, whipping-post, dungeons and such horrors with which to torment for the least fault those who by accident of birth belong to that unhappy class which cannot even rattle its fetters without committing the deadliest crime. Scarce anyone dares to say that these are also humans; and were even *I* to say as much, I should risk stoning for my opinion. What was I not forced to suffer from obstinacy and prejudice when these matters were discussed by the Law Commission! And then the high-born rabble, whose numbers were far larger than I had thought because I judged by the enlightened few who surrounded me, began to suspect such discussions might result in some amelioration of the condition of the people. Almost all were inspired only by prejudice or self-interest. I do not believe there were a score of them who had even for one moment entertained the least sense of our common humanity or thought there could ever be any other estate for the servant class than that of the most abject serfdom."

Serfdom was in those days the currency in which the nobles counted their wealth; they counted it in so many "souls." And when I say "nobles," it must be understood that everybody in Russia who was not a serf was *ipso facto* a "noble," the number of nobles in Russia being until the Revolution approximately equal to the entire electorate of France. This circumstance accounts for the mystery which seems to perplex the French, who wonder how it is that every Russian refugee in France describes himself as a noble. The reason being that he is not a peasant, and that the peasants have remained in Russia.

CHAPTER IX

PRINCESS DASHKOV BRIDGES FIVE REIGNS

I. A PLEBEIAN ARISTOCRAT

PRINCESS DASHKOV, who was considered at home and abroad as a blue-blooded aristocrat of the purest dye, really owes her destiny to her plebeian blood. Peter the Great's second wife, who succeeded him as Empress Catherine I and was the mother of Elizabeth, had been a Lithuanian peasant girl—by name, Martha Skavronski. She had two brothers, Carl and Theodore, two uncouth peasants who were tucked away during Peter the Great's reign in Tsarskoye Selo; and although Peter, to please his wife, made them counts a year before he died, they were not seen about, being illiterate and too common to be displayed with advantage even by so democratic a tsar as Peter the Great.

The truth of it was that Peter loved his wife, who had enough mother-wit to adapt herself to the pioneering days of the new court. But Peter was a little ashamed of his new brothers-in-law, who had none of the redeeming grace of their sister, who owed her advantage to early training in domestic service in the family of a Lutheran pastor. He did not feel it was fair to his wife, who had already had to contend with a lot of criticism since he had married her, and more since he had made her his consort, to have to show the Court what ungainly and primitive brothers she had.

When Peter died and his consort began to reign in her own right as Catherine I, she produced her two brothers, Carl and Theodore, and her sister Christina, whom nobody had seen, and pushed them forward. Christina, already married to a Lithuanian peasant called Simon Heinrich, was lost for the royal market. So the best Catherine I could do for her peasant sister was to make her peasant husband a count and change his name from Heinrich to Hendrikov. (Two hundred years later, a descendant, Countess Hendrikova, was the loyal lady in waiting during the final eclipse of the Romanov dynasty in 1918.) Carl, the eldest peasant brother, had a daughter who was married off to one Roman Vorontsov. Their daughter was Princess Dashkov. This makes her a granddaughter of our illiterate Lithuanian peasant. As for her father, Count Roman Vorontsov, it is not that Princess Dashkov's plebeian mother was married off to the aristocrat, Vorontsov, but that the obscure Vorontsov owes his new dignity and title to having married the daughter of the peasant Carl, brother of the housemaid-empress.

It is not therefore surprising that, since her mother was a cousin of the Empress Elizabeth, Princess Dashkov should consider herself well connected at Court, even though herself an offspring of the poor relations of a humble upstart. Elizabeth, who had had Peter the Great for a father to offset the plebeian origin of her mother, could afford not to ignore the children of her mother's poor relations. Princess Dashkov was accordingly her godchild.

Twenty years after her accession Catherine II traveled to Finland to see the new King of Sweden (a brother of her uncle, the late Prince Bishop of Luebeck, whom she had as a girl seen off at Hamburg as he embarked with the Swedish envoys to take up his duties of Crown Prince in a new land). Catherine took with her to Finland her favorite of the day, Lanskoy, who disliked Princess Dashkov and kept making annoying inquiries why in the news published under the auspices of the Academy, of which she was the President, her name was the only one mentioned of all who accompanied the Empress. Princess Dashkov said she had nothing to do with it, that the Court news was not written by herself and she couldn't accept any responsibility. But Lanskoy kept on sulking and complaining till she lost her temper.

"You ought to know," she said at last, "that, though it is naturally always an honor and a pleasure for me to dine with the Empress, you can't really expect me to be overwhelmed about it, not to the extent of getting the papers to make special mention of it. I'm so used to all that sort of thing. As a baby I was in the habit of sitting on the Empress Elizabeth's knee; as a mere child I sat at her table. It's so much second nature that it would be absurd for me to brag about it."

This made Lanskoy lose his temper, but Princess Dashkov, seeing that others were listening to them, began to declaim at the top of her voice so that his reply could not be heard. "Monsieur," said she, "people whose whole existence has been devoted to furthering the public weal may be neither especially powerful nor especially happy, but they have at least earned the right to be treated with common civility. They quietly," she raised her voice to a shout, "go their ways and outlive those meteors of an hour which blaze and fall, leaving no trace behind."

The great doors were flung open and in came the Empress; the conversation ending abruptly.

II. *CHAGRIN D'AMOUR*

I WANT here to touch on the salient points of Princess Dashkov's life because it affords the rare opportunity of spanning the gulf between Elizabeth and Alexander, since Princess Dashkov was a little girl in the days of Elizabeth, grew up to admire Catherine, took part in the *coup d'état* which overthrew Peter III, outlived Paul, and lived well into the reign of Alexander I, becoming an emblem of a vanished age, almost a *revenant* from the spacious days of Great Catherine, romantic in retrospect, when the age of Alexander, mellow to us, appeared so fresh and brazenly modern to itself.

The story of Princess Dashkov, who was so prominently associated with Catherine's reign, is, curiously, the story of a young woman who aged very rapidly and lived away from the Court in proud, self-imposed retirement after her strenuous days at the age of eighteen. Catherine's supposed ingratitude aged Princess Dashkov, who, after her husband's death, requested permission to go abroad for the sake of her children's health.

"I deeply regret," answered the Empress, "that a cause so distressing obliges you to depart. But, naturally, princess, you are a free agent, and must make such arrangements as best please you."

Princess Dashkov never permitted the opportunity to pass of making the Empress feel guilty of ingratitude. The day after Peter's murder Princess Dashkov was saying to Catherine in the hearing of the entire Court: "Yes, Your Majesty, this death has come too quickly: too soon for your fame; and for mine." And, as she proceeded through the drawing room, she observed in a still louder voice before them all, that, no doubt, Aleksei Orlov would henceforth spare her the moral embarrassment of his acquaintance.

For over five-and-twenty years they were sworn enemies.

Abroad the princess's naturally high spirits revived. In Paris she was fêted and made friends with all the men of letters except Rousseau, whom she ignored because of what she called his hypocritical humility and affected originality. She spent whole evenings with Diderot, discussing everything under the sun, advancing her own opinions and being, she says, much too interested in them to listen to his. She demonstrated to him, successfully she claims, that serfdom was not half so bad as it was made out to be. She made him contradict himself a thousand times. In the end poor Diderot (she says) got into such a state that he told her he agreed with absolutely everything she said.

In Paris Princess Dashkov cashed in on her fame as the leading spirit of the *coup d'état* which had placed Catherine on the throne. Madame Necker, the mother of Madame de Staël and wife of Louis XV's famous Minister of Finance, came to see her. So did Madame Geoffrin, whose salon was frequented by the leading philosophers of the day. But, though Princess Dashkov was only twenty-seven, she looked forty. Catherine's ingratitude, she said, was rapidly killing her.

In London she encountered Paoli and considered his Italian grimaces incompatible with greatness. In Geneva she visited Voltaire and was amused to see him lose his temper over a game of draughts. He, too, made extraordinary faces.

But intellectual encounters meant little enough for one who was, essentially, an emotional woman. Since she lost her husband, men ceased to matter in her life. No man except her husband had ever engaged her emotional interest. She had been in love with Catherine, and their estrangement had meant to Princess Dashkov not only the ruin of her youthful ambitions, but the estrangement of lovers, the ruin of a *grande passion*.

But when she left Geneva and went to Spa she found the substitute which filled her vacant heart. She met a Mrs. Hamilton, a Scottish authoress, with whom instantly she fell in love. She had no doubt that, after Catherine, Mrs. Hamilton was her most romantic encounter in life. She threw herself, with all the vehemence of a love-starved creature, on Mrs. Hamilton. When at last she tore herself away from Spa and went back to Moscow her days and nights were dedicated to an unending correspondence with the Scottish authoress. In Moscow Princess Dashkov put up at the house of her sister, Madame Polianski, who was no other than the celebrated "Romanovna," for whom Peter III had clamored in vain before they killed him and who had since married a Monsieur Polianski. Had Peter III had his own way, Madame Polianski would have been Empress of Russia.

Catherine, to make up for her earlier neglect, sent Princess Dashkov £6,000 to buy a country estate. Princess Dashkov made another attempt to attach herself to the life at Court, but she could not get on with anyone except Potemkin. She rubbed everyone up the wrong way by insisting on her own virtue and impeccability. The Empress suffered Princess Dashkov's importunities with good grace. Only once she retorted, with a gentle smile: "Dear princess, your reputation is better established than that of the whole calendar of saints." Princess Dashkov did not perceive the irony and accepted the remark as showing a real if tardy recognition of her virtues.

Unable to regain her intimate relationship with the Empress, deprived of Mrs. Hamilton, Princess Dashkov looked round for someone upon whom she could lavish her attentions. And she discovered her son. For want of anything better to do, she began to be deeply absorbed in his education. A passionate admirer of English institutions, Princess Dashkov made up her mind to take her son—not to London, or to Oxford or Cambridge, but to—Edinburgh. Mrs. Hamilton lived in Edinburgh, and that may have had something to do with her choice. Besides, it was only too plain to her, she adds, that she would not be missed at the Winter Palace!

In Edinburgh she wanted her son, who was only fourteen, to complete his studies in two years and a half, to comprise Logic and the Philosophy of Reasoning; Experimental Physics; Chemistry; Philosophy and Natural History; Natural Law; International Law; Public and Private Law in its Applications to the Legal Systems of European Nations; Ethics; Politics; Latin; English; German; French; Literature, classical, medieval and modern of all nations; Mathematics; Civil and Military Architecture; History, ancient, medieval and modern; Political Institutions; and the Science of Fortification.

Her son was set upon by tutors; all this information was crammed into him, forced down his throat like food into a Strasbourg goose. He took his B.A. But he never did anything and died young.

Princess Dashkov went to Ireland, was lionized by Dublin society, composed Russian church music which, as a matter of "Muscovite" curiosity, was sung in the Chapel of Magdalen, and "entered," she says, "into negotiations with David Garrick for the stage performance of my musical works." Princess Dashkov was now very famous. Her quick-change-artist trick twenty years before when, after Catherine had already gained the day, the princess appeared in the uniform of a hussar and pranced by her sovereign's side, had become a myth of feminine daring. Abroad her adroitness had been distorted into a fable of Amazon heroism: here was the woman who, at eighteen, had single-handed, etc. Even Frederick the Great, impressed by the legend of her unparalleled exploits in placing his natural daughter on the Russian throne, invited Princess Dashkov to a military review at Potsdam. He made a point of not inviting women, and Princess Dashkov, in her peaked cap, appreciated the compliment paid her by that knave of genius, who evidently and very properly, she thought, regarded her as a man.

In Holland, Catherine's ex-lover, Gregori Orlov, now a married man and out of favor, called on her and made improper proposals for her son to try his luck with the Empress in the hope of displacing the present favorite, Potemkin. Princess Dashkov flared up. She recognized no favorites, she shouted. How dare he say such things in the presence of her son, a mere boy of seventeen! And how dare he insult the Empress, whom her son had been taught to respect?

Gregori Orlov shrugged his shoulders. The boy's golden youth was a clear asset where the silver-haired Empress was concerned. He was good-looking enough to oust that one-eyed monster Potemkin—*God!* how ugly he was!—who had embedded himself, as he seemed to imagine, for good. *However* did he manage it? "Princess, tell me," Orlov pressed his hand to his heart and looked into Princess Dashkov's blue eyes with a soulful, essentially Russian sincerity: "tell me, I implore you in the name of all that is holy: *however* can she put up with this ugly duckling?"

"I forbid you, prince" (Russian aristocrats "prince" and "princess" each other liberally) "I forbid you, prince," she flared up once more, "to discuss this topic before my son—or in fact at all! I recognize no favorites, I tell you!"

A pity, said Orlov. The boy might go far under his auspices. It would be a sheer pleasure to ditch that ugly Cyclop.

At which suggestion Princess Dashkov, prospectively jealous of the Empress in getting hold of her son after jilting the mother, and equally jealous of her son in gaining the favor of the Empress where she herself had so lamentably failed, now properly blew up in the air, so that even Gregori Orlov was at last conscious of a *faux pas*.

Moral indignation was indeed her normal state. When, to propitiate the princess, Catherine appointed her President of the Academy of Science, the reply was a sharply worded letter declining the honor. Princess Dashkov was so pleased with her answer that at midnight she drove with her letter to Potemkin, insisted on waking him and reading him her letter to the Empress. The Favorite took the letter, yawned, and tore it up. When he saw that she was speechless with rage he said, amid more yawns, "Here's pen and paper. Write it again, if you want to. Only it's all rubbish! You're silly to decline the position she offers you. As President of the Academy you would be in constant touch with the Empress. This Academy is a pet idea of hers. She can talk of nothing else. She's bored to tears with the fools who surround her. It's a great honor, I tell you."

Princess Dashkov instantly accepted.

The succeeding years she spent in intermittent rage: with Potemkin for having designs on her son as an understudy favorite to take his place under his orders and so relieve him of the more irksome part of his duties; with her son for marrying secretly and contracting a "mésalliance," as she puts it; with Field Marshal Rumiantsev for interceding on behalf of her son; with the Empress for suppressing a play of Kniazhnin's.

To Potemkin she said she would take her son abroad if he had any designs on him for the Empress. To Rumiantsev she wrote that if she had been endowed with such remarkable eloquence as the count's, she would have used it to show the superiority of good breeding over bad. To her son she wrote that his father before marrying her had craved his mother's permission to do so, though her mother-in-law had done no more to deserve to have a friend in her son than she had herself. To the Empress, who told her that Kniazhnin's inflammatory tragedy directed against her regime ought to have been burned by the hand of the common hangman, Princess Dashkov replied: "Whether it is burned by the hand of the common hangman or not is no business of mine. *I* shall not have to blush for it. But for *God's* sake, Madame, before you resolve to embark on a course so opposed to your true character, *read* the whole play!"

At the next Court, Princess Dashkov resolved to tender her resignation unless the Empress made a point of sending for her to her dressing room. A courtier patronizingly assured her that it was all right: the Empress had forgiven her. *That,* Princess Dashkov says, she really could not stand. Suppressing the indignation which was almost choking her, she said as loudly as her voice would carry and for all to hear, including the Empress, who that moment came out of her inner apartments: "I have no cause to expect the displeasure of Her Majesty, to whom I have dedicated my youth and indeed my life. My conscience is clear. I have never done anything but my duty. It would, of course, distress me if the Empress entertained unjust feelings towards me. Even so, I should not be astonished. I have lived too long and seen too much to be surprised by injustice and misfortune."

The Empress, who could not live an hour without love and had just emerged from the satisfying embraces of her young favorite, Zubov, was in too beatific a mood to resent Princess Dashkov's words, since she also knew that the princess's bitterness was rooted in unrequited love. After all, Catherine was never without a lover, whereas poor Princess Dashkov still lived on her memories of 1762, when she had pranced by Catherine's side at the head of the army, or shared a bed with her on the road. The Empress felt sorry for her and tried again to explain, very patiently, precisely why she had objected to Kniazhnin's tragedy.

But Princess Dashkov, still unreconciled to the Empress's preference for male society, interrupted Her Majesty: "A gray cat has run between us, Madam: you and I shall never again get to rights!"

She notes that Petersburg was becoming utterly repugnant to her: she was absolutely *sick* of the place. Never had she felt more completely solitary and superfluous in these surroundings which were stifling her very soul and growing every day more distasteful and unendurable.

So strong was this feeling of positive nausea that she had determined to leave everything—the Court—the capital—her two Academies—her Empress, whom in spite of all she had loved long and passionately and perhaps still loved, but who had not treated her, she said, as her better self would have prompted her.

Catherine, and indeed the whole Court, by now had had their fill of Princess Dashkov. When the princess gave her reasons for resigning her post and came to take her leave of Her Majesty, she expected the Empress to plead with her to stay. She was greatly astonished when the Empress instead cut short her recital of the weighty motives which had made it morally impossible for her to remain at her post and merely said in a dry restrained voice but looking absolutely furious: "I wish you a pleasant journey."

Princess Dashkov could have been struck dead with a feather. Here was gratitude for you! And after all she had done for the Empress!

"All was black, hopeless," she writes. "I was so racked, so utterly worn out, so wasted with suffering, that I was visited with the idea of suicide."

Next day Her Majesty sent her an unpaid tailor's bill, expressing her surprise that the princess should leave the capital without settling her debts. The credit, it transpired, had been run up not by the princess but by her son-in-law; and *this,* said Princess Dashkov, was positively the last straw: she really *was* leaving now. Nothing would make her stay, not if the Empress implored her with tears in her eyes to reconsider her decision.

It was indeed Zubov, who disliked the princess, who had produced the tailor's bill. It just showed you. The pettiness of men! She and Catherine without bothering about tailors' bills could have run the empire quite well between them, and what there was of love to go round she and Catherine could have spent on each other. How mean were men!

Princess Dashkov, then, utterly crushed, speechless with humiliation, left for her country estate. There she gave vent to her suppressed energy. She began to build houses, lay out parks. That is to say, she interfered with her architect, her gardeners and the other experts, reversing the truism that if you want to see a job well done you should get others more competent than yourself to do it. One day as she was bursting with rustic energy the Marshal of the Nobility suddenly arrived, looking embarrassed.

"Now what is the matter with you, you gloomy man?" she asked with mock sternness. "Is idleness driving you melancholy?"

"Haven't you heard?" he asked. "The Empress is dead."

Princess Dashkov's daughter gave a shriek and rushed to her mother's assistance, thinking that she would faint. "No, no, don't worry about me," said her mother; "I am all right—though, I confess, it would be sheer happiness," she added, "for me to die at this moment!"

With these words she fell into convulsions—and fainted.

III. PAUL

CATHERINE was no more. She had reigned thirty-four years and was preparing to reign another thirty-four years when, bang! down she went with a stroke of apoplexy.

Peter III had leaped with joy when his Aunt Elizabeth breathed her last. Paul's delight was nothing to Peter's, because, whereas Peter endured nineteen years of his aunt's exacting but not unbenevolent tutelage, Paul waited thirty-four years for his right to mount the throne which should have been his on his father's death.

Besides, Catherine hated the sight of her *soi-disant* son, and Paul revered the memory of his *soi-disant* father, Peter III, who, whatever doubts may be entertained on the score of Paul's mother, almost certainly was not Paul's father. Had Paul known that Peter III had only awaited the opportunity of confining Catherine into a nunnery, to repudiate his alleged parenthood in respect of Paul and to strike him off the succession, Paul might not have revered Peter's memory. Catherine also hoped to deprive Paul of the scepter and left a document naming Alexander I, Paul's eldest son, as her successor: which document Paul tore into little bits and, throwing the little bits into the fire, stepped onto the throne while his alleged mother lay stiff and helpless in the adjoining room.

The subsequent emperors of Russia—to wit, Alexander I, his brother Nicholas I, his son Alexander II, his son Alexander III, and his son Nicholas II—who smoothed the line of succession after so many up-heavals and female reigns conducted by favorites, were all the proud descendants of Paul, that 100 per cent illegitimate Paul whom neither his alleged mother nor his indignantly repudiating father wanted to reign, and who not only had no visible right to the throne but no claim to an established father and mother.

With the death of Elizabeth's nephew, Peter III, the Romanov line seems to end, unless we assume one of two alternatives, neither of them proven, to have taken place. Elizabeth, though she had numerous lovers and some illegitimate children, was unmarried. Catherine II was notori-ously unfaithful to Peter III, while he was believed to be impotent and had no children even by his mistresses.

When a boy was born to Catherine, the Empress Elizabeth took him as soon as he was weaned and is believed to have substituted him for a child of her own to whom she had given birth about the same time in great secrecy, being to all official purposes a virgin. Elizabeth would only allow Catherine to have the baby Paul two hours and then take him away for two weeks. She adored him—and no one else adored him.

That child whom she brought up, later known as the Emperor Paul, the "Mad Paul," could only be a Romanov on the theory of his being the Empress Elizabeth's illegitimate child. He could not be a Romanov if the first, perhaps more plausible, theory that he was the child of Catherine by her lover Saltikov is accepted, as it generally is.

Catherine herself, during the years she was married to Peter III, then still a Grand Duke, refers contemptuously to his flirtation with the Princess of Courland and says that she "knew it would not go beyond languishing glances on account of the idiosyncrasies of that gentleman, which had not changed, though five whole years had elapsed since we were married."

On another occasion she speaks of the Empress Elizabeth, who had regarded her very sharply that evening, taking a lady in waiting, Madame Tchoglokov, aside and talking to her a long time; then the said lady in waiting coming to inform her that Her Majesty was very indignant with her because after four years of marriage she still had no children; the fault must lie with her; apparently she had a secret infirmity of which nothing was known. The Empress would therefore send a midwife to examine Catherine.

The Grand Duke felt indignant because, Catherine says, "he felt that the fault was not all on my side; or else he felt offended on his own account."

Another lady in waiting thought the Empress was unreasonable: "How can it be your fault that you have no children if you are still a virgin? The Empress must surely know it, and Madame Tchoglokov is an innocent to come and talk such nonsense. Her Majesty should blame her nephew, or blame herself for marrying him off so early."

To her personal friend, Sir Charles Hanbury-Williams, Catherine writes of the bad treatment she was enduring at the hands of the Empress Elizabeth: "Madame Kruse told me that the Empress had already twice inquired whether I was up. A moment later she herself entered my room and told me with an angry look to follow her. She stopped in a room where we could be neither seen nor heard (incidentally, during the two years that I had been in Russia this was the first time that she had spoken to me without others being present). She began to abuse me for all she was worth and inquired whether I was acting on the instructions of my mother. I was playing into the hands of the King of Prussia! All my plots and treacheries were known to her. Yes, all was out! It was my fault that my marriage was still barren (in a case where the woman cannot be to blame). She was not responsible if I did not love the Grand Duke; she had not married me against my will. She said a thousand dreadful things—half of which I have forgotten. I saw the moment approaching when she would strike me. Fortunately the Grand Duke came in, and she abruptly changed the subject so that he noticed nothing. I don't know what she might have done to me: she really looked like a living fury. Again and again I tried to put in a word. But every time I opened my mouth, she shouted: 'Hold your tongue! I know you have no answer.'"

Writing to Potemkin many years later, Catherine confesses: "When Marie Tchoglokov realized that after nine years of marriage things were no better than they had been before, while she herself was always taken to task by the late Empress for what was obviously beyond her control, she came to the conclusion that the only thing to do was to propose to both parties that they should each select a substitute according to personal predilection. For the one party, the choice fell on the widow Grooth, who is now married to Lieutenant General Miller of the Cavalry; for the other, on Sergei Saltikov, who was chosen chiefly on account of his obvious predilection and on the insistence of his mother, who was convinced of the dire necessity of it all. After two years had elapsed S.S. was sent away as ambassador, because he behaved indiscreetly and Marie Tchoglokov could no longer have him at the Great Court."

Finally, in a confidential explanation addressed to Sir Charles Hanbury-Williams, Catherine hints at what really did happen. "Saltikov, for seven years an aspirant and rival of another, and during six months decidedly in the running, induced Tchoglokov to agree to one of two alterations: either the Grand Duke was to be compelled to seek medical assistance, or else they were to embark on an altogether different course of action."

At this point the husband of Madame Tchloglokov, who was constantly keeping his wife in an "interesting condition" and through whose good offices another lady in waiting was also "expecting," conceived the idea of putting his exceptional services to a national use by providing an heir to the throne. He began to make studied and persistent advances to Catherine. But, as Catherine did not favor him, and his wife, moreover, was jealous, the plan was altered. Madame Tchoglokov pressed forward Saltikov's claims and "employed," Catherine writes, "all possible arts of persuasion to seduce me."

At the same time Catherine's husband was not neglected. "At last the *boundless innocence,*" she writes, "of the Grand Duke compelled them to seek somewhere a mate for him. The choice fell on the widow of a painter by the name of Grooth."

Catherine, a little humiliated by her husband's complete lack of interest in herself as a woman, stresses the deformities of the women in whom the Grand Duke took some interest. She even ascribes this trait to the whole Holstein clan. Speaking of the Duchess of Courland, for whom the Grand Duke had shown a decided partiality, she says: "She was small, and not only abjectly developed but actually hunchbacked. This defect, however, would scarcely appear as such in the eyes of a prince of the house of Holstein-Gottorp. For they have never been known to be discouraged by a physical deformity. Quite on the contrary. For instance, the late King of Sweden, my uncle on my mother's side, would never have a mistress who was not hunchbacked, or one-eyed, or at least crippled." A new side light on the Prince Bishop of Luebeck!

Of Princess Dashkov's sister, "Romanovna," to whom Peter III was so attached, Catherine writes: "The elder, Maria Romanovna Vorontsov, promised to be pretty; the younger ("Romanovna") had no trace of it. On the contrary, she was even then very ugly. The pockmarks with which she was later visited disfigured her in a way in which she is painfully familiar to us today. Both sisters were endowed with a dark olive skin, which did not render them any more beautiful. They later discovered a remedy in applying various artificial colors in order to lighten their complexions." Ekaterina Romanovna—Princess Dashkov by marriage—was the youngest and prettiest of the three sisters.

It is just possible that Paul, who was as ugly and misshapen as an abortion, was the son of Peter III and the widow Grooth, said to be deformed. Paul, somebody stated, could not possibly claim to be Peter III's son—except for the accident that he looked like him. Moreover, Paul was a hunchback, which seems to support the theory—nowhere advanced, however—that Paul was by Peter out of Widow Grooth. That Peter wanted to repudiate Paul may be explained in two ways. Either he did not consider a product of his own loins out of Widow Grooth worthy to follow himself on the throne, or he had well-grounded suspicions that Paul was not his son but a substitute of Catherine's or, for that matter, the Empress Elizabeth's.

Which takes us back to Catherine and Saltikov—and, alternatively, to the Empress Elizabeth and Tchoglokov. There is no evidence, in any case, that the widow Grooth was brought to bed with a child. But Catherine makes no secret that Saltikov's advances had consequences. Madame Tchoglokov's persuasion on the instruction of the Empress, "combined with the good looks and talents of the object of her recommendations, would," says Catherine, "have met with less resistance with any woman other than myself. It is perfectly true that I was endowed with uncommon intuition and an exemplary innocence."

"I became pregnant," she says, "and had a miscarriage in July, 1753."

At this stage we may perhaps credit the theory that the Empress Elizabeth, though now forty-three, decided to take a hand at producing an heir for her lamentable nephew. Two years after Catherine's marriage to the Grand Duke, the Empress, chagrined by persistent lack of results, had commanded her Chancellor to instruct Madame Tchoglokov on her appointment to be governess to the imperial young pair to speed up matters. "Since Her Imperial Highness," runs the injunction, "has been selected as the august consort of Our dear nephew, His Imperial Highness the Grand Duke and Successor to the Throne, and has been raised to her present rank of Imperial Highness solely in the fervent hope and sincere expectation that through her insight, intuition, virtue and good will, she would win the true love of His Imperial Highness and conquer his heart, that thereby the long-wished-for Heir to the Empire, the offspring of Our Imperial House might be conceived, which, however, cannot be expected to take place save on the basis of sincere mutual love and complete marital confidence and attachment; We therefore cherish the most gracious hope that Her Imperial Highness, remembering how her own happiness and personal welfare must depend on it, may ponder well on this most important expectation and on her part most diligently strive to leave nothing possible undone in the cause of such fulfillment.

"You, however (meaning their governess), We command most forcibly to impress most emphatically, most deliberately at every opportunity upon Her Imperial Highness the Grand Duchess this Our desire so important to Us and the entire Fatherland."

Surely the Empress had not failed to make her meaning clear. If words could do it Catherine should have been brought to bed with quintuplets. But words proved vain.

Well, the young generation had scandalously failed. It was up to her as an illustrious representative of the old to see what she could do, though, at forty-three, it was no laughing matter. The Empress Elizabeth had in her day been brought to bed with not a few illegitimate brats, notably Princess Tarakanov, on whom Aleksei Orlov played such a dastardly trick in the course of Catherine's reign. Fearing that Princess Tarakanov, of the Blood Imperial, might one day show some disposition to contest Catherine's claim to occupy the Russian throne, Aleksei Orlov got to work. Having done in Peter III, he was not going to stop at a mere princess of the blood who had not been openly acknowledged as her daughter by the pious God-fearing Elizabeth, even though everybody knew it. Aleksei Orlov, a dashing fellow, made love to Princess Taraka-nov. She fell in love with him and trusted him, and he, taking advantage of her trust, took her to the Peter-and-Paul fortress, as though to show her round, point out a few sights of historic interest, and then locked her up for life. She died there of consumption—an arrangement in which Catherine, for State reasons, presumably concurred. Aleksei Orlov for his services in safeguarding the throne was made a count. His elder brother, Gregori, for more intimate services, had been made a prince.

But the Empress Elizabeth, though a dissolute woman, was too pious and fearful of tradition openly to push any of her bastards onto the orthodox throne. She was shy about her confinements and expressly forbade her women of the bedchamber to speak of her "illness" even to Catherine and the Grand Duke; which did not prevent her resenting their "negligence" (she called it) in making appropriate inquiries about her health. Moreover, the Empress was so stout and wore such loose robes that no one was specially aware of her condition. When the pains came she let it be known that she was suffering from acute indigestion—which she may well have been as a result of her confinements, or even independently, for she was a cormorant eater. When the Empress while on her travels was overtaken by one of these attacks of indigestion, the carriage in which she sat was driven at foot-pace and stood still every few moments. Catherine and the Grand Duke followed in theirs, and the whole train of courtiers in their coaches behind, the horses champing their bits and proving very restive on account of this method of progress.

Coincident on the Empress Elizabeth's idea that she should try to do her part in ensuring an unbroken succession to the blood of Peter, Monsieur Tchoglokov was visited with the happy idea of falling in love with Her Majesty. He first confided in Monsieur Saltikov, then in Catherine. They encouraged him to go ahead.

He met apparently with an excellent reception at the hands of the Sublime Monarch. Monsieur Tchoglokov was a man of extremely limited intelligence and rather common appearance, but of overwhelming vanity. He owed his position at court to his wife's being a descendant of Christina—that sister of Catherine I, who along with her brothers was deemed too common to appear at court, till the death of Peter the Great brought them out into the great world. Monsieur Tchoglokov was flattered at the idea of becoming the progenitor of a dynasty all but come to grief, giving the Romanov line that little spurt it needed to acquire a new lease of life.

We possess no direct evidence that the Empress Elizabeth, again brought to bed with indigestion, here gave birth to a son. That Catherine's son by Sergei Saltikov was secretly taken away by Elizabeth, who substituted her own whom she officially declared to be the son of her nephew Peter and his wife Catherine and to whom she gave the name Paul, is a view held by some historians. It is a theory which receives some force from the incredible love bestowed by the Empress Elizabeth on the baby Paul, whom, by contrast, his alleged mother Catherine neglected and acutely disliked during the whole of her life. Elizabeth, we already know, took him away from Catherine the day he was weaned and kept him for weeks at a time in her room, allowing no one to see him, not excluding his alleged mother, who asked for nothing better. Also Paul's character tallies with the asinine haughtiness of Monsieur Tchoglokov. Like father, like son. The Empress's forty-three years may account for the dreadful bundle of hunchbacked humanity with a receding, almost animal brow and half-closed eyes (more like an Australian aboriginal than a normal European: which is what Paul looks like). It may be the Lithuanian ancestry of Elizabeth's mother, Catherine I, to which Paul is a throwback, coming out unexpectedly, rendered comic by a twist of ruffled dignity in his features, the absurd haughtiness of the upstart Monsieur Tchoglokov. Paul, it is ironic to reflect, was the haughtiest megalomaniac who ever mounted the Russian throne. And if he did have Peter III's eyes, Peter III had the eyes of his grandfather, Peter the Great, and Elizabeth was, after all, the latter's daughter. May this not tally with Paul's being Elizabeth's son, and explain that any resemblance he may have borne to Peter III was that of first cousins?

All went well between the Empress and Monsieur Tchoglokov. The flirtation progressed and during a ball she was seen to give him languid glances. But when her indigestion was upon her, suddenly she began to hate him, calling him publicly at dinner a fathead and a traitor, which he took so to heart that he fell ill with the jaundice. The Empress sent him away—an attitude not unnatural in a woman of her unimpeachable position and violent, secretive temper to a man who had served his purpose. Moreover, at a certain physiological stage of pregnancy women are possessed of acute disgust for the male.

Poor Tchoglokov, who had so hoped to be a favorite, fell ill, and the doctors declared that he had been treated like a man whom one desires to kill. The work—an attempt to poison him—was attributed to a rival and very powerful faction at the court of Elizabeth—the Shuvalovs, who resented Tchoglokov's ambition. Three weeks later he was dead.

At this time Catherine records that she herself is pregnant. And on the 20th of September, 1754, she was delivered. "Three weeks later," she writes, "Saltikov was sent to Sweden with this intelligence. It distressed me greatly, since it exposed me to the malicious gossip of the entire world. In December orders were dispatched to him to travel on to Hamburg, but I made such determined protests to the Chancellor that S. returned here before the courier got to Stockholm. After a great deal of noise, innumerable complaints and a lot of heated argument we decided that in his own interests S. had better leave again. After that, less from predilection than from self-will, I pursued my original course and bent all my will power, all my energies, strained every nerve for the single purpose of overcoming every obstacle that stood in the way of his return. I succeeded against all expectations. Yet I expected no bliss from his return; the difficult character of this gentleman amply precluded that."

In the absence of positive evidence to the contrary, it is best to assume the conventional (outside imperial Russia) theory that Paul was the son of Catherine II and Monsieur Sergei Saltikov. And who might be Sergei Saltikov? A chamberlain of the Grand Duke Peter, a young man married to a Mademoiselle Balk, who so aroused the interest of Monsieur Saltikov while swinging high up in the air that he was moved to propose marriage to her. Catherine also aroused his interest while swinging. Monsieur Saltikov was susceptible to the charm of the female leg: result, the Emperor Paul.

But if Paul and his descendants cannot, except by courtesy, really call themselves Romanovs, there is a peculiar Nemesis in the idiot Tsar Ivan's (whose consort had been one Praskovia Saltikov) thus asserting himself to the end, if only through his wife's line, but to the bitter end, against the blood of Peter.

IV. PAUL EXILES PRINCESS DASHKOV

SOON after the accession of Paul, Princess Dashkov was discharged from her post as president of the two academies. Insolent to the last, she testified to the Emperor her gratitude for relieving her of a task which had become too heavy for her strength.

In Moscow a message reached her from Paul. She must return at once to her country estate and there ponder deeply on the year 1762.

Princess Dashkov replied, characteristically, that she never ceased to think of that year, yet she would obey the Tsar's will and dwell on that fateful year which had left her neither stings of conscience nor remorse.

When Catherine died, Paul ordered his father's body to be exhumed and to be buried conjointly and side by side with his mother. Paul hated his mother, who was perhaps not his mother at all, but he honored the memory of his father who was almost certainly not his father. Princess Dashkov's brother thought that after Paul had rehabilitated his father's memory his anger against the surviving conspirators of 1762 would die down. But Princess Dashkov thought that she was called again by destiny to play a historic part, this time a martyr's. She received a great deal of moral satisfaction from the inconvenience—hardly more—she suffered from Paul, who felt he really ought to do something against the people who had robbed his alleged father of his scepter and his life. "Examining my past life," she pounds herself on the chest, "I am not without inner consolation, conscious within myself of sufficient strength of character, steeled as I am by many calamities, to feel certain that, once again, I shall find strength to endure my new Calvary!"

Paul was afraid to tackle Aleksei Orlov, so he issued orders that Princess Dashkov should proceed to her son's country estate in the Novgorod Province; which, when her offense is weighed, is not a very cruel deprivation. Paul knew that Princess Dashkov was his bitter enemy, but all he wanted was to feel reasonably sure that she was out of the way and not plotting to overthrow him; which she might well be thinking of doing if allowed to remain in the vicinity of Petersburg or Moscow.

This command caused another outburst of righteousness in the indefatigable princess. "The consciousness of complete innocence and the feeling of supreme indignation," she writes to her relatives, "serve to give me courage to endure my trials so long as his growing malice does not touch you all. Of one thing you may all rest assured, that *no circumstances whatsoever* will compel me to do or say anything to demean myself."

From her son's distant estate in the Novgorod Province, where in mid-winter she found living conditions uncomfortably primitive, Princess Dashkov, who took her daughter and a staff of servants with her, soon appealed, but as it were on *their* behalf, to Paul's consort, the Empress Maria Feodorovna, a Württemberg princess by birth, "in the name of religion and humanity to save all my people from this cruel exile."

The Emperor Paul flew into a rage. Pen, ink and paper, he commanded, should be taken from Princess Dashkov. "It is not easy," he said, his eyes flashing dangerously, "to turn *me* off the throne!" (He did not know *how* easy; his reign, after awaiting his turn for twenty-four years, lasted but four years and four months. And, like his alleged father, he too was assassinated, and in a sufficiently similar manner.) It is said that Paul's consort, Maria Feodorovna, and his mistress, Madame Nelidov (the two women were friends) got his youngest boy, the Grand Duke Michael, to beg his father to pardon Princess Dashkov. Whereupon Paul, feeling good, took up a pen and wrote: "Princess Ekaterina Romanovna, since you wish to return to your Kaluga estate, I hereby grant you permission to do so. I remain well disposed to you.—PAUL."

A second courier with the pardon overtook the first with the injunction to deprive Princess Dashkov of pen and paper; thus she was even spared the knowledge of her sovereign's displeasure. Yet she still regarded herself as a martyr to righteousness.

Paul, moreover, suddenly took a great fancy to her son, showered all kinds of favors upon him and made him the present of an estate. The dutiful son asked whether, instead of an estate, the Emperor would permit his mother to live where she liked. Paul agreed to that also, on condition that she was never to be found in any town while he was there; which seems reasonable.

Paul was greatly attached to young Dashkov, till he heard that Dashkov had told somebody that a certain man whom the Emperor was trying for misappropriation of public funds was, in his opinion, innocent. The same evening young Dashkov received a note from the Emperor: "Since you meddle in matters which are no concern of yours, I have dismissed you from your duties.—PAUL."

When news came of the Emperor's assassination Princess Dashkov heaved a deep sigh of relief. Her martyrdom was over! The monster was dead. "How many, many times," she adds with her usual self-centeredness, "have I rendered thanks to heaven that Paul exiled me! By so doing he saved me from the degrading necessity of appearing at the court of such a sovereign!...Thank God! Thank God!"

V. THE MURDER OF THE EMPEROR PAUL

THE study of kings and queens, emperors and empresses, fascinates us, not because we like to read of men and women in high places, but because our common human nature is intrigued to know what it feels like for ordinary human beings to be placed in grotesquely artificial situations. Classical literature tells us about gods, whom we can only imagine if we think of them as men and women. In the case of kings and queens, it is our own human nature elevated to the status of divinity which arouses our curiosity. It appeals to the megalomania latent in all of us—a bacillus kept harmless by the give-and-take of social obligations, the amiability early instilled into us which makes us "good mixers." Royalty in a democratic age will of necessity develop the habit of "good mixers"; which explains their popularity. The man-in-the-street, however eager to mix with the crowd, would hardly be called a good mixer unless he brought to the common stock some distinction that it was an advantage to mix; which in the case of royal persons mixing with commoners is not their commonalty but their royalty. "Just like ourselves," says Mrs. Brown after shaking hands with the King and Queen; which she would not say if she were shaking hands with Mr. and Mrs. Smith, who really are exactly like themselves.

A circuitous approach to the proudest and worst mixer among monarchs, who yet, if he guessed all his life, could not have told who were his father and mother! Paul was the complete megalomaniac and military martinet. Having all his life been kept down by Catherine and reached the age of forty-two when he seized the scepter, Paul began to reign with a vengeance. He had a great eye for effect, and at his entry into a crowded room he sent covert glances right and left to observe the effect of his entry: and the effect was abject. As a Grand Duke, and married to a Württemberg princess, Paul, at his mother's instigation, traveled to Europe, and Marie Antoinette recalls, without comment, that the King and she were visited at Versailles by the "Prince and Princess du Nord"—the name the young couple assumed on their travels in Europe, which made as little impression on Paul as Paul upon Europe. As Louis XVI, Marie Antoinette and the future Emperor Paul sat at table together, they could never have guessed what their fate was to be.

Paul began by refusing to fight the French Republic. Two years later he became an enemy of Bonaparte. He had been elected, no one quite knew why, as the Grand Master of the Order of the Knights of Malta—an office he took very seriously; and Bonaparte's sudden occupation of Malta annoyed him. As a child he had read a book about the Order and it had fascinated him. Malta, having regard to his position, was, he considered, under his special protection. Henceforward he considered himself to be at war with France. But it had come to his ears that Bonaparte had said something agreeable to his vanity, and Paul turned overnight from an enemy of Bonaparte into a fervent friend and ally.

As an ally of France he was automatically the enemy of Britain. In the first place, he aimed at depriving England of her German possessions. Next he embarked on a joint campaign with Napoleon directed against India. This plan was not original, but merely the renewal of a project envisaged some time before but shelved by Catherine and considered eminently feasible by Napoleon. An army of 35,000 French infantry supported by light cavalry was to proceed from Ulm down the Danube into the Black Sea, to be conveyed by a Russian fleet to Taganrog, thence down the Volga to Astrakhan, where the French force was to be joined by Russian troops consisting mainly of cavalry and supported with heavy artillery, to be conveyed across the Caspian Sea to Astrabad, Persia being also invited to share in the conquest of India. According to Paul's arrangement with Napoleon, Masséna was to be appointed generalissimo over the combined French and Russian forces. A few days before his murder Paul had given orders that the 10,000 Cossacks originally agreed upon were to be increased to 50,000.

Paul was murdered on March 23, 1801. The British Press received the news of his strangling with undisguised pleasure, thereby enabling Napoleon to exploit the legend that the British Ambassador had had a hand in the murder. Lord Whitworth, the Ambassador, had a love affair with a Madame Gerebsov, a sister of the Zubovs; and he accordingly frequented her house, rightly considering the British Embassy to be ill adapted for amatory uses. It was in her house that, till the day of the murder, the conspirators met; and it was there, it was urged, that the plot was conceived. Hence the suspicion, which Napoleon adroitly exploited, that the British Ambassador was not innocent of the crime from which his government had everything to gain.

In actual fact, the British Ambassador had no hand in the business. His mistress supplied him with information which he did not discourage. He supplied her with money—his own, and, quite conceivably, some from the Secret Service Fund—to which very likely she also did not object. He may have heard of a projected plot to depose the Emperor. Since the Emperor was rapidly growing insane and dangerous to England, the news may not have displeased Lord Whitworth, who doubtless kept the Foreign Office informed of the latest developments. But he did not take part in the plot, for the reason that it is not customary for British ambassadors to take a hand in assassinations. It is also quite useless for a political faction desiring to depose their sovereign to invite the participation of an ambassador of a foreign power. He is not likely to compromise his government by wielding a weapon. Even were he to bribe the actual conspirators, all men in key positions, it is hardly likely that men playing for high stakes would be tempted by the meager sum which a British ambassador could produce out of his own pocket. If he applied to the home government, he would, in due course, receive an answer forwarding a memorandum from the Deputy Director, Finance Branch, FA 494/63/LN9, that a rebellion directed against the life of the Emperor of Russia, however desirable in principle, was, in his view, clearly no ground for imposing the charge on the Treasury.

No, the murder was the unassisted work of the Russian aristocracy, who suffered from Paul's interruption of Russia's trade with England, which controlled the whole of Russia's foreign commerce. Great Britain alone of all countries bought Russian agricultural products, which constituted the chief if not the only source of revenue of Russian landowners. The throne was "occupative" rather than hereditary, to judge by so many precedents, and they judged that in the four years Paul had sat on it he had occupied it too long.

false!

In the last years of his life he had behaved so oddly that even Napoleon later confessed that Paul must have been mad. The Russian Emperor had caused an invitation to be printed in the court circular under date of December 30, 1800, in which he formally invited all the rulers of Europe to St. Petersburg in order to decide in open combat, supported by their ministers (Pitt, Thugut, Talleyrand, etc.) all international differences.

To Napoleon, who in due course caused some ten million deaths on the battlefields, this seemed stark lunacy. It might perhaps be more sound to say that this was one of few points on which the Emperor Paul showed a luminous sanity.

Thiers remarks that, concurrently with Russia, on the throne of England, too, there sat a madman, to wit, George III, that year and for many years to come; but, thanks to the free constitution of the land, he remained on the throne without any harm to the country and without it ever occurring to a single soul to deprive him of his life.

In freezing cold ?!...

Not so in Russia. At the beginning of the year 1801, Panin arranged a meeting with Paul's eldest son, the young Grand Duke Alexander (later Alexander I) at a seaside resort. In the water, well out of hearing of everyone, Panin disclosed to Alexander that a plot was afoot to put an end to the reign of Paul, who he thought was mad. No violence was to be done to him. He was to be invited to retire from the helm to one of his palaces suitably converted into a Self-Upholder's mental home.

Alexander concurred. Panin, who had once been Paul's tutor and whom everyone regarded as his stanchest supporter, had at last despaired of the folly of Paul's foreign policy. And if Panin had turned against the Emperor, then it was high time indeed to depose him. This was how Alexander felt about it.

Rumors of a plot had been reaching Paul for some time. He had a palace built for himself which was virtually a fortress. It had a moat and drawbridge heavily guarded and, within its thick walls, Paul thought himself secure. One day he buttonholed Panin: what was all this talk that reached him about a conspiracy? Was there any truth in it?

Panin's answer was adroit. *"Of course,"* he said, with a broad smile, *"of course,* there's a conspiracy! Everybody's in it. I'm a conspirator myself—in order to find out who are the real conspirators." When Paul asked him for a list, Panin produced one, warning him that it would surprise him. Paul's own consort, the Empress Maria Feodorovna, and his son and heir, Alexander, headed the list.

Paul hummed to himself; then said: "In that case arrest them and exile them to Siberia."

Panin requested the Emperor to put it in writing and showed the order to Alexander.

It was then that Panin secured Alexander's adhesion. Paul had on and off warned his son that unless he bucked up he would deprive him of his right to the succession and hand on the crown to a Holstein relative. Paul had reintroduced all the military paraphernalia, powdered wigs and and other wearisome impedimenta long discarded by Potemkin, and he was crazy about discipline. He ordered a regiment to march all the way to Siberia because he found them slovenly. They set off but were at last overtaken by a messenger who ordered their return. Once when Alexander, a mere boy, had fallen down on his knees to entreat his father to pardon a friend, Paul had kicked his son in the face. Alexander could not forget this. Yes, he thought, it might well be true that his father was mad and growing madder every day, in which case common safety demanded that he be removed from the throne.

The Mihailovski Palace, an impregnable fortress, was guarded on the fateful night of March 23 by the third battalion of the Semënovski Regiment. But the regiment was itself in league with the conspirators. Count Pahlen, Military Governor of St. Petersburg, and General Bennigsen, each headed the two groups. Prince Peter Volkonski, Prince Yashvill, Prince Platon and Prince Nicholas Zubov, Prince Alexander Golitsin and Count Ouvarov, all belonging to the Guards, completed the gang. The Guards once more assumed the leading role they had played in the palace revolutions which had planted Catherine I, Anna Ivanovna, Elizabeth and Catherine II on the throne of their respective predecessors.

The impregnability and remoteness of the Mihailovski Palace, in which Paul felt so safe, was an asset to the conspirators, who had removed the previous guard and posted their own: they had the Emperor all to themselves, far from the madding crowd! It was just as though Goering, Goebbels, Ribbentrop, Hess and Himmler had all privately agreed to do away with Hitler. Hitler, having made himself unpopular with everybody, everywhere, had decided to give up Berchtesgaden and remove himself to a solitary mountain fortress which could only be reached by a drawbridge on passing the parole. Goering, Goebbels, Ribbentrop, Himmler and Hess, having on their own accepted authority replaced the guard on duty, all set out together for the said impregnable fastness, from where no one can hear you if you scream till you are blue in the face. They cross the drawbridge by giving the agreed parole and find their way to the Führer's bedroom, where they proceed at leisure to terminate his existence.

I don't suggest that any of the Führer's loyal lieutenants would for a moment stoop to such tactics. I merely want to point out how easy it was in a country like Russia, where palace revolutions were almost a tradition, for the chief lieutenants of the autocrat to unite and, on the principle that unity is strength, to give practical expression to a well-worn tenet.

Though Pahlen, Bennigsen and the Zubovs were the chief culprits, they had the tacit consent of the entire Russian aristocracy, who seldom neglected the acknowledged method of tempering as the need arose the absolute rule of the monarch with a discreet assassination. The higher strata of Russian society were well aware of the manifesto in which Peter III had expressly excluded the bastard Paul from the succession on the ground that the latter and his issue possessed no legal or even natural rights to the Romanov diadem. In forcibly removing Paul, the men in key positions were fortified by the knowledge that they were in a sense acting as the legal executors of Peter III. That they were replacing the bastard by the bastard's son was too fine a point for a pack of hotheads and firebrands to see or argue about. Paul must go. And he went—in this manner.

The insanely proud Emperor's private apartments were on the first floor. He had gone to bed, suspecting nothing. But in his first sleep the sound of hearty laughter from tough men in their cups made him start up in bed.

Pahlen, the principal author of this plot, was at the foot of the palace stairs in order to play the part of the Emperor's savior in case he succeeded in escaping from the blows of his murderers. Bennigsen with his pack marched in first. A Frenchman, Count d'Allonville, who visited the place soon after the murder, speaks of the old palace servant who showed him the cupboard where Paul hid himself behind his flags; the screen above which the head of General Bennigsen, leader of the gang, appeared. Bennigsen said to the other assassins, who seemed frightened because they could not see the Emperor anywhere: "There he is! If you hesitate, I'll butcher you all!"

Having dragged Paul out of the cupboard, the conspirators, most of whom were drunk, flung themselves upon him, struck at his head and pressed with their swords, with their fists, with their boots, and finally strangled him with a scarf. When the dead body seemed to stir for a moment, one of the murderers jumped on the belly with both feet "to drive out his soul." The old palace servants could not show Count d'Allonville the camp bed upon which, after having been beaten by the officers and finished off by one of the surgeons, who cut the arteries of his neck, Paul was thrown bleeding.

The Empress Dowager, said the old servant (and one of her women of the bedchamber confirmed it), had this bed taken away with its blood-stained sheets and carried with her wherever she resided. The two sentries who followed Maria Feodorovna everywhere were the two hussars who were wounded as the conspirators forced the door of her late husband's bedroom.

When Pahlen came in to report to the Grand Duke Alexander, who was awaiting the news in the Winter Palace, he saw Alexander and his wife huddled together sobbing and trembling.

"Is it done?" Alexander asked Pahlen nervously.

"It is done," answered Pahlen.

Paul's consort, the Empress Maria Feodorovna, was running up and down the corridors of the palace screaming, "I'm the Empress, I'm the Empress!" She thought she was another Catherine the Great. And indeed she had the precedents of Catherine I, the two Annas, Elizabeth, and Catherine II to confirm her in her illusion that this was indeed a woman's kingdom. Alexander, trembling and staggering, scarcely able to walk, was told to pull himself together and make a speech to the Guards; who, as he appeared among them, shouted:

"Long live the Emperor Alexander!"

VI. PRINCESS DASHKOV IN OLD AGE

AND Princess Dashkov, who as a child had sat on the Empress Elizabeth's knee, and had played *campis* with Peter, snuggled close to Catherine beneath the same bedsheets, and flaunted her integrity in Paul's face, now passed into the reign of Alexander I. He was the fifth sovereign to reign within the span of her life; she was indeed to last another decade, to die at sixty-six in the year Alexander and Napoleon met at Erfurt.

Princess Dashkov, having reached the pinnacle of "the grand old woman," was critical of the younger generation surrounding Alexander. In her opinion, loudly expressed, they were all either Jacobins or martinets, and equally detestable. Nearly half a century now divided her from that fateful year in which, by prancing in hussar uniform at the side of her Empress, she created abroad the legend of having been the author of the famous *coup d'état* which had placed Catherine on the throne. The myth which had originated abroad had all these years been gathering volume like a snowball, and now rolled back into Russia, where the rising generations clamored to be presented to the legendary woman upon whom they looked with the same hero-worshiping eyes as once did her uninformed contemporaries abroad.

Old Princess Dashkov was being lionized in Alexandrine drawing rooms in Petersburg and Moscow. She was the one heroic link with the age of Great Catherine. She pulled up young girls over their manners and fashions. Mothers revered her and pointed her out to their young as an historical personage: Catherine the Great's bosom friend who had shared all the Empress's confidences.

Princess Dashkov enjoyed her new lease of fame, but she considered the young generation as feeble and decadent. Only one presence—not perhaps unnaturally—attracted her. She was the young Empress Elizabeth, the new Tsar's consort, a daughter of the Margrave of Baden, whom Alexander was made to marry at the age of sixteen while Catherine was still on the throne. This princess, imported from Germany, had to pass the scrutiny of two previous princesses, likewise uprooted from Germanic soil and acclimatized in Russia, before she in turn became an imperial consort. Alexander's mother, from Württemberg, was an imperious, bad-tempered woman, who was held in check while Catherine sat on the throne. And now, after a mere four years and three months of being the first lady in the land, Maria Feodorovna was relegated to the position of a dowager, and young Elizabeth had stepped into the shoes of her mother-in-law. This young woman from Baden was, like Anna Leopoldovna, who loved her Julia Mengden more than she could love a man, a woman's woman; and it may be guessed that this suited our Princess Dashkov down to the ground.

But Princess Dashkov preferred Moscow to Petersburg. In the former capital away from the red granite banks of the Neva where the young court held its sway, the glittering old fogeys of her own generation had retired together, supporting one another's illusions that they were still at the head of affairs. Her arch-enemy, Aleksei Orlov, a raw and terrible old man, who had a daughter growing up whom he loved tenderly, sought reconciliation with the princess who, since his murder of Peter III forty-two years before, had sworn never to speak to him. For the sake of his daughter Annushka, whom he supposed in need of cultural advice, he ventured to call on Princess Dashkov, who, consigning the murder to history, let bygones be bygones. Having crippled her son, if not killed him, with education, Princess Dashkov enjoyed a reputation for culture, and Orlov commended his dear Annushka to his ex-enemy's beneficial attention.

Thereupon, to celebrate the reconciliation, he gave one of those legendary parties which remind one of the Golden Horde. The house and the lighted gardens were full of serfs dressed up in silk for the occasion and put to the service of art and entertainment. His own lovely daughter Annushka was made to dance Russian and Gypsy dances with a shawl and a tambourine, while her enraptured father beat time. She danced with such charm, such natural grace and simplicity that her movements seemed her language, and her father bade his daughter after each dance run and kiss Princess Dashkov's hand, who took her tenderly to her bosom and called her "this angel ... this tender angel who has brought us together...."

Tears trickled down the cheeks of the hard, terrible old man who, many years after his murder of Peter III, had driven round Petersburg parading the crown of his victim. He had amassed a huge fortune. Catherine, in her gratitude, had turned over to him the confiscated wealth of the monasteries. Orlov lived in fabulously luxurious retirement, breeding a new race of thoroughbreds called after his name and inspiring a fearsome respect in his neighbors. Even Paul during his short reign was afraid to touch him; was nevertheless dispatched without Orlov's assistance. And now Count Aleksei Orlov's last wish on earth—reconciliation with the old princess and her promise to guide the social steps of his daughter—had been granted him as well. The stern old man, reassured on his tender side, suffered not a trace of remorse or compunction in his hard heart. But his daughter, his sweet and graceful Annushka, grew up to a life of prayer and pious sacrifice in the hope that she might herself atone for her father's sin and save his soul from eternal perdition.

Aleksei Orlov owed his position to two outstanding events: the individual murder of Peter III; and the mass murder of Turkish sailors when, at Cheshme Bay, he burned the whole Turkish fleet. Princess Dashkov, prepared to honor him for the latter act, despised him for the former. He, feared by all the rest, had felt the sting of her contempt of forty-two years' standing, and was now washing it away in wine. When, after a fabulous feast in her honor, which must have cost Orlov a fortune, Princess Dashkov got up to take leave, the count, standing in the hall of his palace, bowing and kissing her hand, thanked her profusely for honoring his poor house.

But, though Princess Dashkov called Aleksei Orlov's young daughter "this tender angel," she could not take to her as she had taken to Catherine, to Mrs. Hamilton, to Alexander's young consort Elizabeth, and now to Mrs. Hamilton's niece, Mary Wilmot. This Mary Wilmot, soft, credulous and clinging, had come out to stay with the old princess in Russia as a substitute for her aunt, who had shown her the passionate letters written to her by Princess Dashkov, but could herself no longer keep up with them. Mary Wilmot, who had never been out of her native Ireland, readily absorbed the whole legend of Princess Dashkov's exploits, and joined her in the year 1803, just as Alexander I was entering on the second year of his reign.

A short old lady, dressed in a mannish, tight-fitting coat of dark cloth reaching down to her heels and suggestive of a general's uniform, came forward to meet her. She wore a peaked hat. A large star (the very same which Catherine had conferred on her in 1762) was pinned to her side over the broad Catherine ribbon flung over her shoulder. There was something military in the bearing and appearance of this small old lady, as though she thought she was still the dashing officer of Catherine's days. Wrapped around her neck was an incredibly shabby old scarf. This, she explained on a later occasion, was a holy relic she always kept about her person. One damp evening, twenty years earlier, while out for a stroll with Mrs. Hamilton, the Scottish authoress had insisted on taking it off her own neck and tying it round Princess Dashkov's. It was a pledge of love, a living token from her friend. Mary Wilmot was another. Mary thought the old lady looked like a very benevolent witch.

Princess Dashkov fell in love at first sight with Mrs. Hamilton's soft willowy Irish niece who, from the word "go," was all over her, snuggling up to her, clinging to her like a young vine to a gnarled old tree. From the first day they were to each other "my Russian mother" and "my Irish daughter." They couldn't make enough fuss over each other. Mary thought she had struck oil. As for the old lady, who had named her village Hamiltonovo after Mrs. Hamilton, she now completely lost her head over Mary. How she loved her! She could not do enough for Mary. She took her to all the balls in Moscow, presented her to the two Empresses, ordered her maids to sing for Mary's entertainment, each day filled her room with flowers. In the evenings the old lady carefully brought in an album—her holy of holies—containing the letters of Catherine, which she and Mary, with heads close together, read with bated breath.

Two years later, at the suggestion of Mary, Princess Dashkov invited Mary's sister, Katherine, to stay with her. Now Katherine was a very different kettle of fish. Whereas Mary, who was uncritical of her benefactors, was unconscious of the sufferings of their serfs, Kate, frankly cynical of her hosts, was sensitive of the discomfiture of their subordinates. Katherine, who had lived and circulated freely in Paris, wielded a fluent and incisive pen joined to a detached and ironical source of outlook. "Russia," she says, "is like a girl of twelve—wild and awkward—who has been dressed up in a fashionable Parisian hat. We are living here in the fourteenth or fifteenth century." It is interesting that, whereas cynical Kate was shocked by serfdom, amiable Mary was not. Kate, emancipated by her sojourn in the France of the First Consulate, was disconcerted by the pitiful cringing, the shameless servility, of the lesser ranks of Russian nobility in respect of their betters. In this she percipiently discerned the Nemesis of Russian serfdom, a two-edged sword. She saw so-called nobles standing for hours on end, hat in hand, at the door, shifting from foot to foot, till appropriately dismissed with a nod by the more powerful grandee on whom they had called socially to register their respect.

Unlike receptive Mary, our detached Kate was not impressed by overobvious Russian standards of dignity. "I feel," she writes in a letter home in 1806, "that I have been floating all this time among the shades and spirits of Catherine's Court. Moscow is the imperial political Elysium of Russia. All the personages of power and authority in the reigns of Catherine and Paul, long since superannuated by Alexander, retire into the lazy luxury of this superb Asiatic town, keeping up an *ideal* consequence awarded by courtesy, for all effective influence and power have long since passed to another generation; yet the grand chamberlain of the Empress Catherine, Prince Golitsin, is plastered all over with orders and decorations under the added burden of which his ninety years bend double to the ground; still, as in the palace of Catherine, a diamond key hangs from his skeleton, which is dressed in an embroidered kaftan, and he still majestically receives the homage of his brother shades who once shared with him the honors of the State.

"By his side is another gaudy *revenant,* Count Osterman, once the grand chancellor; he is bedecked with glittering baubles and ribands, red, blue, and striped; four-score years are piled upon his head, but still his gibbering skeleton rattles in his coach and eight, with outriders; still he dines with *heiduks* standing behind his chair, and exacts the same etiquette from courtesy which was once awarded him by right."

Among the shades she saw, too, Count Aleksei Orlov.

"The hand that strangled Peter III is covered with its recompense of brilliants, amidst which the portrait of the Empress stands out conspicuously; Catherine smiles from it in everlasting gratitude."

She speaks of having seen in lucrative retirement one of Catherine's favorites, Korsakov, "who might have been taken for a veritable vision of diamonds"; of Prince Bariatinski and other figures from a vanished world, "from which they have retained the habit of court gossip about important nonentities, haughtiness, vanity, and the empty ostentation which make up their joy and their sorrow.

"And yet the open grave yawns at their tottering feet, menacing to consign their brocaded existence to earthly oblivion. All these old grandees are surrounded by wives, daughters, and granddaughters, dressed up to the nines, and sitting in gilded apartments, in slave-owner fashion making their maids dance for their amusement and incessantly regaling one on jam. There is something French in their appearance, and, being brought up by Frenchwomen, they speak that language well and dress in the latest Parisian fashion. But there is very little real politeness in these ladies; their education is entirely superficial, and there is not a trace here of the charming lightness of French society. When Moscow ladies have eyed you from head to foot and kissed you five or six times (though twice, one would think, would be ample), have assured you of their undying devotion, told you to your face that you are absolutely bewitching, asked you the price of everything you are wearing, and babbled about the coming ball at the Assembly of the Nobility, their répertoire is at an end."

In 1807, having acquired all her "copy," Katherine joyfully set sail for home. She did so with the full approval of Princess Dashkov, who found Kate lacking on the side of feeling. "Not very loving," was her verdict. Mary, who wanted a husband, but knew full well that to detract her attention for this purpose from "her Russian mother" would be more than her stay in Russia was worth, decided to follow suit. She was detained by a calamity which befell Princess Dashkov, whose son died suddenly. The mother had still not forgiven him for having married without her permission, and, what aggravated his offense, contracted a *mésalliance*. For fourteen years she had kept up that grudge against him. She had refused to see him, though she could not refrain from writing to him in a didactic tone, and, despite the entreaties of relatives and even of her own dear Mary that she should make it up, Princess Dashkov would not receive his wife. Now that he was dead, she sent for her daughter-in-law and fell sobbing into her arms. She was reconciled, she says, forever to his widow over the coffin of the man whom they had both so wildly loved!

One consolation remained—Mary Wilmot, "her Irish daughter" who, however, soon renewed her wish to leave "her Russian mother." She had nothing specially to do in Ireland; her relatives played an insignificant part in her life; but Princess Dashkov's love was smothering her, was indeed getting too much even for soft and clinging Mary. She began to suffer from claustrophobia. Though Russia had immensely developed her power of the soul, she could not call her soul her own. She understood what Catherine II, what her aunt Mary Hamilton, and her sister Kate had realized before: that a little of a Princess Dashkov goes a very long way.

Princess Dashkov, frightened of her isolation, wanted to go with her to Ireland, there, she said, to end her existence. Mary persuaded her against it and promised to come back to her. To spare her, Mary set off secretly, but, detained in Petersburg by police measures taken against the British because of the Treaty of Tilsit, which had reversed Russia's allies and enemies, she decided to return for some months to Moscow. She wrote she was coming back.

In her joy and relief at the news Princess Dashkov ordered the release of five of her peasants who were in prison for debt, and bade them celebrate at once a thanksgiving service for her.

But Mary, in the face of all the rising hope her return had implied for the old lady, would not stay. As soon as passport formalities had been complied with, she announced her departure for England and Ireland.

The day came. Princess Dashkov, heartbroken at the impending separation, had gone to bed to face the ordeal in the morning. During the night Mary slipped quietly into her room. The old princess, who had been weeping the whole day, had fallen asleep from exhaustion. "The expression of her face," Mary records, "was serene as a child's. I softly kissed her and went away."

They never saw each other again.

"What am I to say to you, my beloved child, not to grieve you?" the princess writes two years later. "I am sad, very sad, tears flow down from my eyes, and I cannot get used to our separation. I have built a few bridges. I have planted a few hundred trees, I am told successfully; all that distracts me for a minute, but my sadness returns."

One almost hears an echo of *Mein irisch Kind, wo weilest du?*

She writes four days later: "And how changed all is here since you left! The theater is boarded up, there has not been one performance, the pianos are mute, and even the maids do not sing. But why am I telling you this? You are surrounded by your own people, you are happy, contented...."

She writes for the last time a week later and ends in English: "God bless you!" Two months later Princess Ekaterina Romanovna Dashkov was dead.

But before her death she could not help noting down, with incorrigible self-righteousness:

"With an honest heart and pure intentions I have had to endure a great many calamities; I should have been crushed beneath them if my conscience had not been clear ... now I look forward without fear and without anxiety to my approaching dissolution."

BOOK FOUR

CHAPTER X

HOW TSARS ARE MADE

I. LOVE AT THE PALACE

ALEXANDER had begun his reign auspiciously enough. Amiable,
liberally predisposed, he had set out to improve the internal conditions
of the country. These are at all times, as students of the present and
scholars dealing with the past both know, susceptible to improvement.
He applied himself in the first instance to education—hitherto conspicuous by its dearth. Everywhere he set up schools and universities, and
proclaimed himself—to everyone's satisfaction, not least his own—a progressive monarch. He formed a committee—"The Committee of Public
Safety," they styled themselves—of his closest friends, young men sharing
his ideals, and together they evolved a plan. That plan was in fact nothing
less than the Covenant of the League of Nations. It defined the aggressor
approximately in the words of Comrade Litvinov. And, likewise, they
believed in collective security and considered that peace in Europe was
"indivisible."

They were, these young men, a very fine set of chaps, by no means
to be sneered at either for their intellectual powers or the eminent
reasonableness and sanctity of their ideas.

But—as they were told by their elders—the world was not ripe *as yet*
to settle its collective quarrels by collective arbitration. Nicholas II, a
hundred years later, had a go at it—at The Hague. And President Wilson, later still—at Geneva. The world seems never ripe "as yet" for
settling anything except by generally unsettling everybody.

The leading light of this committee of young idealists was Prince
Adam Czartoriski, as handsome as he was brilliant, as rich as he was
noble. His family had been in the running for the Polish crown, and
we remember how Catherine II on the day she mounted the Russian
throne had written to her ex-lover Poniatovski: "I am sending Count
Keyserling at once to Poland to make you king after the death of the
present King. In case he should have no success for you I desire that
Prince Adam shall be king."

Catherine's wish to make her former lover Poniatovski a king was carried out two years later. But an Adam Czartoriski was always in the running for the elective throne of Poland. The present young man was indeed more than the Tsar's bosom friend. Alexander carried friendship a stage further by sealing a triangular bond of tenderness between Czartoriski, himself, and his consort Elizabeth.

The Empress Elizabeth extended the design for living by squaring the triangle with a lady in waiting. Alexander, having the most to give and the least to gain, was the first to desert; and Czartoriski the next. Married since he was sixteen, attacked from his early days by that essentially Russian malady of being "dissatisfied with his surroundings and seeking a meaning in life," Alexander was in need of a woman who could make him a home—a woman preferably unlike his wife Elizabeth, because Elizabeth was too much like himself.

He found such a woman in Madame Narishkin. A Pole by birth, delightfully animating in her very placidity, she was so much more suitable to him than the German Elizabeth, placid in her very animation. Marie Narishkin was what he wanted—a tonic.

She was, to him, more than visually beautiful. She engaged his emotions; she responded in her slumbrous gleaming whiteness, her dark hair and brows, her physical resilience, to some fundamental need in him capable of being satisfied completely only by a woman of her type. And while his need of her was real, her need of him was not rooted in anything more fundamental than the glamour of his imperial majesty.

The carrier of majesty, himself, bored her a little when she was alone with him. This boredom gave her a listless and distracted air as though her soul were full of sad and beautiful thoughts. Physically not her ideal, he seemed to her at his best in a brilliant assembly of courtiers and ladies in tiaras when she, outdistancing all the others by the exquisite simplicity of her dress and coiffure, drew envied looks as she entered a ballroom: "This is her!"

Meanwhile, the Empress Elizabeth, who confided copiously in her mother, the Margravin of Baden, wrote:

"Have I told you, my dear Mamma, that this creature had the impudence to tell me of her pregnancy, which was so little noticeable that it might otherwise quite easily have escaped me? Such a piece of brazen crudity takes a great deal to believe! It happened at a ball, and few knew about the scandal at the time. I spoke a few words to her—just as I might to anyone else—and asked after her health. She answered that she was not very well—*'comme je crois que je suis grosse.'* Don't you think, my dear Mamma, that that was brazen impertinence on her part? She knew quite well, of course, that I was not unaware *why* she was pregnant."

Elizabeth's mamma shared her daughter's indignation. But the "creature," a Princess Tchetvertinski by birth and married to a descendant of the mother of Peter the Great, did not care a rap for a margrave's daughter who, though she carried the title of Empress of Russia, exercised not the slightest influence on an autocrat quite absurdly pliable in the hands of the creature Marie Narishkin, and not least because she never talked to him about politics or affairs of State.

II. MEN OF POLAND

AND Czartoriski, in cooling off in his rather artificial passion for the Empress, was animated very much by the same considerations. Czartoriski, like all Poles, had a single passion—Poland. Other countries, too, have their patriots, perhaps not wanting in energy with which to protest their devotion. But a Pole cannot talk of his country without facial contortions, eyes darting fire, ears glowing scarlet, angry strides, a knock on his chest and a challenge to a duel for alleged insult to Poland if you presume to withstand his excitement. The Pole speaks of Poland in the accents of a wincing neurotic speaking of a dearly loved wife who, even while he speaks, lo! has again been ravished in the room adjoining.

For that is the singular thing about Poland. On the map of Europe one day—off the next. Back overnight, split, cut, chewed, swallowed and spewed again like Jonah from the belly of the whale. Poland and Russia; Poland and Austria; Poland and Prussia: how much useless blood has been poured through the centuries in the cause of dividing and collecting chunks of Poland. No wonder they love their Poland with the inflamed and morbid love of a husband whose wife every man is after. By anticipating other lands with an electoral monarchy in the midst of a medieval Europe of grab-and-take, men of Poland, fired by a noble idea, placed the Polish crown within the reach of any crafty foreign monarch quick to seize it, unleashing in the wake unceasing corruption, rebellion, vexation, conspiracy and chicanery, foreign and homemade.

At the moment in question, while Czartoriski was Alexander's Minister for Foreign Affairs, there was no Poland, Alexander's grandmother

Catherine, called the Great, having divided it between Russia, Prussia and Austria. Czartoriski was all for restoring Poland under their joint scheme of national self-determination—for the clever young men had discovered that principle, also—and the scheme was receiving Alexander's sympathetic consideration.

Elizabeth found herself deprived of her lean and somber Polish lover who, despite his sovereign's encouragement, had not been able to stay put. Plunged into a well of loneliness, the Empress abandoned herself to an orgy of tenderness with a lady in waiting, Countess Golovin. A frenzied correspondence ensued in which she assured her angel that she lived only for the next hour when she would see her again:

"Sunday, at 9 o'clock in the evening: ah! that 30th! What ages before there will be another like it! God! What sensations the mere recollection of those delicious moments brings back to me! Will you ever understand how dear to me is the date on which I gave myself to you?"

No comments are available from Countess Golovin. Her daughter, Countess Fredro, points out in her memoirs that Alexander's behavior in encouraging Prince Adam Czartoriski to seduce Elizabeth was in bad taste. She says, unconvincingly, that Czartoriski did not want to love the Empress, but that, in his fight to overcome his passion for her, he had the misfortune to sweep her off her feet.

III. BACK TO THE OLD BOYS

The turkey ran pas'
With a flag on its mas'
And cried: "Wha-at's the mattah?"

EVERYONE asked: "What's the matter with the Emperor?" Czartoriski relates that at his coronation in Moscow Alexander was an abject sight. There was no sign of his rejoicing in the ancient ceremony, of taking pride in attaining the position which had placed him, a young man of twenty-three, at the helm of the State. He was melancholy, sighed, cried and, though at that early stage he did not yet believe in God, prayed a great deal. Here, at the seat of the ancient shrines, the older history of his country unfolded itself before him; and he, brought up by a Swiss revolutionary, felt a stranger in the midst of the ancient Muscovite ceremonial, felt astonished when they placed the cap of Monomachus on his head. Later he was wont to say that he was not an emperor but a happy accident.

At the coronation he felt it had all been an accident, and an extremely unhappy one, that he should be sitting here, a parricide, on his father's throne. But his father, having regard to the circumstances of his birth, was surely the initial mistake, tragic and sinister; and though he, Alexander, had not acquiesced in his murder, had in fact expressly insisted that the Emperor Paul should be removed without bodily harm, the plot, ending in murder, implicated him morally by making him an accomplice before the fact. And what was worse, like his grandmother Catherine before him, he saw himself compelled to reward the murderers; so that his high-principled tutor Laharpe had written to him from Switzerland to remonstrate, to tell him that abroad he was quickly drawing upon himself all the opprobrium for the murder.

The official version of Paul's death was "apoplexy." Quite a traditional imperial disease in Russia, was the comment abroad.

But it was easy to criticize from afar. He, Alexander, had found himself in a precarious situation. He had been exposed to the wrath of his father, as Panin had made quite clear to him. On the other hand, having once decided to act against his father, no half-measures would have sufficed. The gang of officers who undertook to remove Paul were determined, dangerous fellows. They had half-promised him not to injure his father; but, as Pahlen had remarked, "you couldn't make an omelette without breaking eggs"; and Paul's resistance had to be reckoned with. Their attitude was not that of people meticulously obeying his orders: they must have a free hand in the dangerous job they were to do for the sake of them all; and if he, Alexander, was not with them, well, then he was against them and might have to be scrapped along with Paul.

So Alexander could not have really insisted on his own conditions; he had merely hoped for the best, that was all. And now he could not get it out of his head that he was reigning prematurely as a result of having plotted to murder his father. This obstinate feeling of remorse dogged him all his life. He had the unstable temperament of a Hamlet compelled to endure the conscience pangs of a Macbeth. And seated in the Kremlin on the ancient throne of the Muscovite tsars, he recoiled from the long roll of treachery and murder which had preceded his own crime, and wished that life had vouchsafed him a better fate than to hold this golden orb and the bejeweled scepter and bear the weight of these rich robes when his heart itself was so heavily weighed down with guilt.

Of course, if one took it philosophically and was not over-sensitive, as he was, one had to recognize that there had been violence all along, even more so in the days of the Ruriks. The ancient autocrats of Russia had been displaced from their thrones by their brothers. In the middle period they were assisted out of life by courtiers. In modern times the incentive came from the people. There seemed no alternative to a life in the purple but that of no life at all. Ivan the Terrible killed his eldest son. Peter the Great killed his. But it was something new to kill your father. Well, Alexander, indirectly, had done so.

This Moscow was so pregnant with cruel memories, even more so than Petersburg. Like Catherine, he did not know which capital he hated more. In Moscow reposed the bodies of the ancient tsars and great princes of medieval Russia. The Peter-and-Paul fortress in Petersburg contained the coffins from Peter the Great onwards. Alexander, who longed to confess his guilt, to unburden his soul, had no one before whom he could lay his case, since the whole of Russia, military and ecclesiastic, regarded Paul's forcible decease as a good riddance. This longing to make a clean breast of it, to confess, to take public baths, to cleanse body and soul of intermittent abominations, is an impulse native to Russia. Ivan the Terrible, in a confession before the Abbot Kuzma, called himself, with eupeptic abandon, "a stinking hound, steeped in drunkenness, whoremongery, adultery, murder and bloodshed, assault, robbery, theft and every other kind of abomination and shameful corruption." Wholehearted as this confession is, it is yet an understatement. Ivan the Terrible's cruelty is only comparable with that of Peter the Great, whose guilt is the heavier because he was sane.

A contemporary of Queen Elizabeth, whom he wanted to marry, Ivan the Terrible is the last but one link in the chain of the ancient dynasty, the Ruriks, and the first link of the new—the Romanovs. His wife was the daughter of an obscure provincial landowner—by name, Romanov. When the Rurik dynasty fizzled out with the monster's weak-minded son, Feodor, they fell back, after an interim of civil strife, on a relative of the consort of Ivan the Terrible—to wit, the son of her nephew, a lad of sixteen, Mihaïl Romanov, the first of his line.

The last Romanov, the luckless Nicholas II, who in 1913 celebrated the tercentenary of his house, was loath to surrender an inch of his unconditional power. Confident of his divine right to rule singlehanded over the nation bequeathed to him by his forefathers, he was troubled neither by doubt nor uncertainty, except in one respect: wondering by the hour and the minute in what circumstances he might blow up. The monarchy, he could not insist enough, was a sacred trust passed on to him undiluted by popular franchise, from his forebears—who as a matter of explicit fact had been elected to occupy the ancient throne of the Ruriks on conditions amounting to a limited monarchy.

The former dynasty of Rurik had come to an end after seven centuries and a half of rule of alternate severity and benevolence. It had been a dynasty boasting Norseman descent.

A dynasty does not acquire proper distinction till a later link in the chain "makes history," and, in the cause of blowing his own trumpet, stresses the distance which he has traveled from his upstart forebear. Conjointly, the upstart founder gains glory from the prolongation of his line, though he owes it all to such accidental concatenations of capacity and fecundity in generations as yet unmated and unborn as are quite beyond his foresight or his control. "I'm a descendant of Rurik," says in effect the great-grandson Vladimir. "I hope," we may legitimately imagine Rurik as saying to himself as he charges his old friend Oleg to see to it that his infant son Igor succeeds him and so in time founds a dynasty, "I hope that one day I may be ancient." He succeeded. But he had not the satisfaction of knowing it.

Of course, we know nothing of Rurik's Scandinavian antecedents. For all we know he may have been "very well born." Coming south with his brothers in A.D. 862, from somewhere in Scandinavia, Rurik, the founder of the dynasty, had been profusely welcomed by the natives of Russia, who had bowed down to the ground and said: "Our land is large and abundant, but there is no order within. Come and reign over us." Rurik, Sineus, and Truvor were brothers. The latter two died.

According to another version, Rurik, Sineus, Truvor were not three brothers, as accepted by Russian history. There was but one man— Rurik, "sineus truvor" being Scandinavian for "his troops," the Russian delegation mistaking the message *"Rurik sineus Truvor"* (Rurik with his troops) for Rurik and his brothers of the names of Sineus and Truvor. There are no such names in Swedish; whereas Rurik is a genuine Swedish name.

Rurik lingered and roamed about in the North and found his way to Novgorod. Askold and Dir went south to Kiev. They were subordinates, and had broken loose and advanced without orders, on the principle of each man for himself. The land seemed to them big enough for that. And indeed, a hundred and fifty million acres of "black earth," and south of these as much again of ordinary arable earth was enough for more than one Norseman in search of gain and adventure.

Rurik, with his loyal lieutenant, Oleg, gained a firm foothold and eliminated Askold and Dir from their settlements in the south. When Rurik died, Oleg, a skillful warrior, did not act in his own interests, as he might well have been expected to do, but continued the conquest of the Khazars in the name of Rurik's infant son, Igor, who, when he grew up, came to a bad end. Proceeding against a tribe of tree-worshipers called *drevlyani,* Igor lost the day. He was tied to two sapling trees and in this manner torn asunder by the worshipers of the tree. The Drevlyan chief, Malu, then cut off Igor's head and converted the skull into a drinking cup, which was engraved with the words, "Thou camest to take what was another's, and coming, didst lose what was thine own."

IV. RUSSIA'S FIRST SAINT

IGOR'S wife, Olga, had been a remarkable woman who had skirmished the ground for introducing Christianity into the heathen land. She had been to Byzantium and had returned greatly impressed by the advantages of religion. But it was her grandson, Vladimir, who felt the time had come to replace the heathen gods by a more reputable faith so as not to be looked down on by his more progressive neighbors.

The whole course of Russian, even world history, may be said to have changed because Vladimir I was—yes—a snob. It happened in 988 (A.D., of course). Nothing in Russia—nothing at least that may be termed "Russia"—took place before Christ. The very name Russia derives from *russy,* meaning russet—the color of the Vikings' hair, by which the natives designated the Norseman conquerors who penetrated into the land and became its rulers. But let that rip. I may—or may not—return to it in due course. The trouble about narrating the story of what happened within three hundred million square miles over a thousand years is that at every step you are torn in different directions by the sheer power of conflicting associations. History, once you let yourself into it, is so confoundedly interesting.

Yes—a snob. The dynasty had not been going long—a bare one hundred years and a bit. Vladimir was the fourth of his line, being the great-grandson of Rurik, who had come south from Scandinavia and secured the succession of his line for seven centuries and a half, without —the shame of it!—being aware of it. Vladimir's mother had been a beautiful slave girl in the service of his grandmother Olga, who, with admirable disregard for convention, had married her son to her hand-maiden: the result being Vladimir, who owed his good looks to his mother, and his snobbishness to his knowledge that in addition to the blood of a slave there coursed through his veins the blood of Vikings. Vladimir had a smiling genial nature and was called affectionately "Vladimir Fair-Sun." His affectionate nature found expression in numer-ous wives, who spoiled him because he was so handsome. But not con-tent with the love of his lawful wives, he had 800 concubines. It may be that his yearning for love being satisfied as soon as it arose, in those reflective moments which follow repletion he felt that life was not all that it might be. What was lacking? Ah! the deference of his neighbors. He discovered that, other things being equal, it was nicer to be looked up to than to be looked down upon. What was it that made the rulers of the neighboring states so haughty in their relations with him? In-quiries showed plainly that they despised a prince and a people who worshiped idols.

Very well, then, away with the idols! He would adopt a modern faith, because one must march with the times. Vladimir accordingly sent for exponents of the more representative religions—Roman, Jewish, Greek and Moslem—and listened sympathetically to the learned men who, with the aid of interpreters, expounded the advantages of their particular brands of godliness.

He chose the Moslem faith as most suited to his deeply rooted habits. The Hebrew, Greek and Roman systems, he decided, demanded more self-denial in the matter of fasting and other abstentions than he, for his part, was prepared to exercise. So Vladimir adopted the Koran, and not for himself alone but for his entire people, and that meant for their descendants, for the whole of Russia, for all time.

Had he stuck to his decision, the vast continent of Russia would later have joined the Moslem warriors, Arab and Turk; and Islam would have overrun the world, with what results, baleful or beneficent, who can tell? But at the last he was deflected from his purpose by a snobbish motive.

The joint emperors of the East, Constantine and Basil, sovereigns of Byzantium, offspring of a far more ancient and illustrious house than the Ruriks were in 980, offered him the hand of their sister, Anna, on condition that he adopt for himself and his country the Greek faith. They also, finding themselves at the time in a precarious situation, stipulated for military aid. It may be assumed that the Emperors of Byzantium would not seek a matrimonial alliance with an uncouth barbarian for the sheer pleasure of his company, still less for the honor of uniting their family with his own; and indeed their sister shrank at the prospect of marrying this genial savage, already joined in matrimony with a small army of wives. The imperial brothers therefore stipulated that Vladimir first rid himself of his wives—as well as concubines. They thought he might jib at the concubines. No. He got rid of the whole lot at one go. He had had enough of them all, anyway, he explained. But still Anna tarried—more so than before.

Then Vladimir's patience gave out. His sunny countenance clouded. He felt they had tricked him. Eight hundred and thirty years later Napoleon also waited moodily for the hand of the Emperor Alexander's sister, likewise called Anna, and tarried with the ratification of their joint agreement over Poland till his pride at the prospect of being the brother-in-law of the Russian Tsar was appeased. Now Vladimir, convinced that they had acted in bad faith, attacked the Byzantine Army till the brothers sued for peace, and Anna was delivered to him. She had sacrificed herself, she said, for Byzantium. It was hard on her. She had paid the penalty for her brothers' incompetence.

Now that he had her, a genuine princess of Byzantium, Vladimir's pride knew no bounds. He smashed up the wooden idols and images, and at the point of the sword drove his people into the rivers to be baptized. This is how Russia became a Christian Greek Orthodox country. Snobbishness had determined Russia's Church. As for Vladimir, they went on to call him affectionately, "Vladimir Fair-Sun"—or, perhaps, more accurately: "Bright Little Sunshine." Posterity calls him Saint. The 800 concubines were forgotten and forgiven. Vladimir became Saint Vladimir. He died in the odor of sanctity in the year 1015, and was canonized in 1257.

V. WHO WAS WHO IN ANCIENT RUSSIA

THE Orthodox (in Russian *pravoslavnaya*) Church literally means "the right-glorious" Church. The word Slav likewise is derived from "glory" —*slava*—and not "slave," as is popularly supposed by people whose ignorance of the Russian language leads them to jump to a conclusion which their common sense should have told them was surely improbable. For it is not given to races to vilify themselves in their own tongues, while it is common for all peoples to give themselves glorious names. Which also explains why nationalities sound so glorious in their own language and so abject in a foreign tongue. What could sound more proud, fitting, and integral than "an Englishman," or more remote and absurd than "ein Engländer"—which, for the comic flavor it suggests, might be a Laplander? Readers with a knowledge of tongues can test the truth of it for themselves. Suffice it to say here that in Russian, perhaps more so than in other languages, all foreign nationalities have a ridiculous sound. *Anglitchanin, amerikanets, nemets, franzooz*—these do not sound like designations of nationals belonging to great civilized countries, each proud of its history and artistic heritage immortalized in a world-famous literature; they sound like nicknames assigned to some comic subhuman tribes of dwarfs dwelling somewhere off the map and not remarkable for anything but their alien antics; while the Russian for a Russian—*russki tchelovèk*—suggests, in the original, something central, natural, forceful, good, sincere and inalienable, pertaining to the major inhabitants of the globe, who are, indeed, the salt of the earth. Man has not yet learned modesty in the mass; and in A.D. 980, whither we have followed *homo sapiens* in Russia, he had not as yet learned anything; though he was soon to begin to make rapid strides in collective virtue till baleful influences again retarded him.

Yaroslav, who reigned between 1015 and 1054, was the son of Vladimir. From being Prince of Novgorod he made himself Great Prince of Kiev. There were no tsars in Russia till Ivan the Terrible half a millennium later assumed the title. "Grand Duke" is a mistranslation for Great Prince. There never was a Grand Duke in Russia, either in ancient or modern times. When, since the days of Peter the Great, the tsars began to style themselves emperors, relatives of the imperial family began to be called "great princes"—a designation formerly reserved for the reigning sovereign. When the great princes traveled abroad, the Germans accurately translated "great prince" as *"Grossfürst";* but the French, incurably inaccurate in anything which is not French, translated "great prince" as *"grand duc";* and the English, with their readiness to read exotic grandiloquence into anything that is not English, retained "duke" for "prince," adding a mistranslation of their own—"grand" for "great." Finally, the Russians themselves, who greedily accept foreign misconceptions about themselves in the naïve belief that the error adds to their quality, stuck to the "grand duke," despite the fact that there never were any dukes, plain, great or grand in Holy Russia (except, of course, the German Oldenburgs and Mecklenburgs).

Anyway, Yaroslav was the first to style himself "Great Prince of Kiev." He was a humane and far more civilized ruler than most of those who followed him in the next seven hundred years or so. He compiled a code of crimes, called *Russkaya Pravada* ("Russian Right"—or "Truth") which tabulated punishments, as follows: The death of a noble cost 80 lbs. of silver; the death of an ordinary man was assessed at 40 lbs.; and the death of a woman, noble or otherwise, was squared with 20 lbs. No capital punishment was known in the State; but dissatisfied plaintiffs were not debarred from taking the law into their own hands, provided that in the exercise of their murderous craving for justice they paid strictly according to tariff. Yaroslav had four daughters who married well—respectively, the Prince of Norway, the Kings of Poland and Hungary, and Henry I of France.

Another enlightened great prince of the Rurik dynasty, Vladimir Monomachus, benign and glorious, began his reign in 1113—that is to say, exactly 500 years before the first Romanov donned the "cap of Monomachus" with which all the sovereigns of Russia were traditionally crowned. This, then, was the prince whose sable cap served as a crown during five hundred years for the great princes and tsars of the Ruriks; and for another three hundred years after that for the Romanov emperors; Nicholas II, who celebrated the tercentenary of the Romanov reign in 1913 being the last to don that cap.

Vladimir Monomachus was married to an Englishwoman—namely, to Gytha, the daughter of Harold, the last Saxon king of England. He accordingly strongly disapproved of the upstart usurper, William the Conqueror, who, moreover, was begotten on a village girl by a marauding freebooter. Who was he to displace Gytha's father? Though Vladimir Monomachus could not overlook the patent fact that Harold was an elected king—nothing against him, of course; but Gytha must understand that it was not the same as being a direct descendant of the Viking Rurik, being able to boast, even now, three hundred years and more of an unbroken succession.

Harold may have been an elected king, but, as one proceeds to delve into the growing chaos of Russian history, one fails to see, progressively, why one who is elected for what he is, is any less a king than one who inflicts himself with his whole unwanted issue into the bargain. Moreover, primogeniture was unknown in old Russia. The father split his

State between all his sons; and on his death some one son rose against the others, killed them, and annexed their lands. Boldened by success, he proceeded against cousins and uncles. Yet when he had collected and united all their lands, he did not profit by his experience but divided all the territory he had amassed among his own many sons.

So the mischief went on, accumulating blood, grievances and injustices. A powerful father nearly always had a weakling son, who in turn produced a strong heir, the spit of his grandfather. And nearly always it was the younger who succeeded, more often from the cadet branch. But they were still of the blood of Rurik. Before the Tartar invasion there were 64 principalities, ruled over by 293 independent princes, between whom there were no less than 83 civil wars in the course of the next two and a half centuries. When the Tartars came they solved the succession by a comprehensive test. It was no longer the direct line, or power, or capacity that mattered. The question was settled by whoever paid them most. The sum raised determined a man's title to the land, his own and another's. The succession got somewhat obscured, a brother-in-law, or the brother-in-law of a man who was not even a brother-in-law getting the crown in lieu of a Rurik, thanks to a knack in squeezing the peasants for the benefit of the Golden Horde. No one can tell for certain—though historians assume to surmise—that despite deflection here and there it was still the line of Rurik. The Tartar invasion crippled Russia for two hundred and forty years. Had it not been for the Greek Church, Western Europe would not have been so indifferent to Russia's lonely plight, and might have helped her to shake off the yoke of the Golden Horde.

VI. THE TARTARS

THE Tartars were incomparable horsemen who lived on mare's milk and horseflesh, which made them into a mobile unit whose motor power also, so to speak, provided them with supplies. When needing a tonic, they opened their horses' veins and drank some of the blood to refresh themselves, always careful not to increase unduly the strength of the fighting arm at the expense of propulsion. They were thus independent of their base. They burned and sacked Moscow. But they were not city men. They developed a fiscal system which, while absolving them from the responsibility of government, filled their treasury. The Great Khan remained at the headquarters of the Golden Horde in North Asia, whither the Russian princes journeyed when he sent for them, to commend or rebuke them, to promote or displace them, and more often to behead them. The original method of appointing Tartar tax collectors did not yield good results, peasants and landlords uniting together to conceal their sources of revenue. Even occasional acts of frightfulness, such as wholesale raiding and massacre of towns and villages, only in the end dried up the supply of revenue at source. The new method was as simple as it was brilliant. The Great Khan sent for the most covetous and crafty Russian he could find and authorized him to tax boyars and peasants at will, fixing the amount of the tribute due to the Golden Horde. And what Tartar could not do, the native produced with ease, squeezing the population to an extent which only native knowledge and ingenuity was capable of achieving—ostensibly in the name of the cruel Tartar, in real fact to enrich himself even more than the Golden Horde.

The Tartar yoke left its mark upon Russia which, before the invasion, had been making remarkable progress as a free-and-easygoing community. The habit of bowing to the strong, of doing obeisance, engraved itself on the character of the nation and was not to be shaken off for long after the Tartars had been chased out of Russia.

The Tartars went as suddenly as they had come. They came as a result of one accident; they went as the result of another. The son of Genghis Khan, forced out of the steppes of northern Asia by stronger neighbors, broke into European Russia and carried terror into Russian towns. After two centuries of Tartar domination over Russia, Timur, the Khan of a rival Tartar tribe, by destroying the Golden Horde, made it possible for Russia to throw off the Tartar yoke.

The final battle was among the most comic in military history. Ivan III, a descendant of crafty vassals of the Golden Horde, who had enriched themselves while collecting tribute for their Tartar suzerain, took the plunge. The Golden Horde, attacked by Timur, could ill spare its horsemen in Russia. The Tartar forces had never been used to garrison Russian towns. It was not a duty to which they were accustomed. The tactics of the Golden Horde had been to employ them in occasional acts of frightfulness when tribute was slow in coming. Far from resenting such acts of barbarism, the reigning Great Prince of Muscovy might even welcome such extraneous aid to taxation. It helped him, as the official tax gatherer for the Golden Horde, to collect the stipulated tribute and fill his own pockets. "You see what they are like," he might turn to his subjects. "Dare we delay payment?"

But now, for a generation or two, reports had been current that the

Golden Horde was in difficulties. Shock tactics became rare and timid. Now this, now that, town was resisting payment, was even turning upon the invader, who, here and there, had been seen to turn tail. At long last Ivan III, whom the whole country had been urging to turn out the Tartar, took his courage in both hands and assembled an army. In those days a sovereign was required to lead his own troops, and that was no small matter for a man such as the Great Prince Ivan III, who was a man of great craftiness but little courage. However, national opinion compelled him to take the fateful step. Trembling in his shoes, he set forth at the head of his army. They marched for many weeks, and at last on the far horizon they could discern the Tartars. As night fell both armies came nearer and pitched camp. At daybreak they became increasingly conscious of each other's proximity. The two armies sat there on their haunches, staring at one another as if mesmerized; then, seized suddenly with unspeakable panic, they fled simultaneously in opposite directions.

This was the end of the Tartar domination. Ivan III returned in triumph to Moscow. The bells of all the gold-domed churches boomed and pealed in deliverance. Ivan was proclaimed a hero. His success went to his head. The Emperor Frederick III of the Holy Roman Empire of the German Nation offered him the title of King, but Ivan declined. He, the reigning Great Prince of Muscovy, was not going to accept titles from the hands of a foreign monarch, however exalted. He also declined an offer, from the same source, that one of his daughters should marry a nephew of the Emperor, the Margrave Albrecht of Baden; but wanted no less than the Emperor's own son and heir. For his own part, Ivan III contracted a second marriage and took for his wife a most distinguished and accomplished lady, the niece and heiress of Constantine, the last Emperor of Byzantium. She was at the time a refugee in Italy, deprived both of wealth and the succession, since the Turk ruled and raged at Constantinople. But she brought with her to Moscow, as part of her dowry, the emblem of Byzantium, the two-headed eagle, which Ivan III adopted as the crest of his house, the arms of Muscovy, as a portentous claim to the Byzantine Empire. The two-headed eagle remained the arms of the Russian Empire till displaced by the hammer and sickle of the Soviets.

Not satisfied with his present title of Great Prince of Muscovy, but unwilling to accept a foreign one, Ivan III, who had brought under his sway all adjoining territories, proclaimed himself Hospodar of All Russia. His grandson Ivan IV, called the Terrible, was the first officially to proclaim himself Tsar.

VII. IVAN THE TERRIBLE

IVAN THE TERRIBLE, never an angel, slipped off his moorings after the death of his wife, Anastasia Romanov. He began to indulge in fantastic tortures, one of his favorite indulgences being the disemboweling of pregnant women in a manner which would not make pretty reading. Finally, the voice of the country rose in protest against his cruelties. He then, in the middle of his reign, laid down the burden, because, he said, he was offended at the reproaches of his people. One morning a long trail of wagons containing his treasures and chattels set out on the way to a distant monastery where, the Tsar said, he would end his days as a monk. A deputation of his people came to him and humbly begged him to come back, and finally he consented—*on his own terms,* he stressed—which were to torture them as much as he fancied; to which they humbly agreed.

Peter the Great admired Ivan the Terrible, who ties with him for first place as a fiend in human shape; with this difference, that Ivan impaled, roasted, racked to death, boiled, flayed alive and flung men and women to be torn and mangled by bears, out of sheer lunatic satisfaction at the thought that there was no limit to the absolute power of his will, as an illustration of which power his smallest whim called for the maximum suffering of the greatest number of men, women and children: he was fascinated and looked on with a faint inner smile of wonderment at the depravity of which he was apparently capable; whereas Peter the Great tortured people in anger and revenge because they had crossed his impetuous will and thus, in his view, deserved to go through it to the last extremity. Peter watched his victims as they were being put to the torture with a certain scientific curiosity born of his combined interest in mechanics and the anatomy of the human body.

Ivan was mad in the same way as Nero and Caligula were mad. Historians say that Ivan went mad after the death of his wife, to whom he had been sincerely devoted. But, already as a boy, he had amused himself by throwing cats and dogs from top windows in the Kremlin, and riding roughshod over crowds kneeling in the street at his approach. Novgorod and Pskov, which were independent republics, paid heavily for their resistance. He massacred nearly the whole of their populations, and while the slaughter went on he spent five days praying in a monastery. Having completed his prayers, he witnessed 27,000 victims being lingeringly and variously disintegrated in the presence of himself and his son Dmitri, whom he enjoined to rejoice with him at the spectacle rich in comedy and variety.

Other Russian historians point out that there is probably exaggeration in the actual number of Ivan's victims at Novgorod and Pskov, in substantiation quoting a Russian proverb about fear having large eyes. It is easy to understand how reports spread and multiply events, and very possibly the number is much smaller. But numbers do not determine the amount of pain which is borne and registered by the individual nervous system.

Ivan the Terrible habitually carried a long heavy staff with a knob, with which he bashed the heads of offending subjects, and a spike, with which it was his pleasure to transfix the foot of a petitioner to whom he listened with an expression of earnest meditativeness, as though devoting all his thoughts to the cause unfolded by the man before him. There was a grim sense of humor in the Tsar, who varied his manipulations of the spike, on one occasion fixing it, for support, in the elegant calf of the English envoy who brought him Queen Elizabeth's negative answer to his offer of marriage. The Tsar, with a look of absorbed interest, leaning comfortably on his staff lodged in the silk calf of the envoy, enjoined him with great kindliness to take his time in reading to him Good Queen Bess's amiable answer, or he might tire himself.

The Queen, while declining his offer of marriage, invited the Tsar when his subjects got tired of him to settle in England, where he could live comfortably, she said, "at his own expense." She sent him in return for his costly gifts of furs and jewels a cheap silver cup which produced the worst impression. His subsequent offer of marriage to the Queen's niece, Lady Mary Hastings, likewise proved fruitless. The Tsar, with his lean, ascetic face, with the long thin beard and terrible pale eyes, was not unattractive—but his reputation was. He was the first to open the Russian White Sea port to English merchant ships. But to marry Ivan IV, the Terrible—well, that was a proposition which no one was going to handle for sport for some time yet. It was a long cry from civilized Vladimir Monomachus's marriage to valiant King Harold's daughter, Gytha!

Ivan, tired of the world, played with the idea of becoming a monk, hoping perhaps to be made a saint in due course; and when he died his dead body was habited in a monk's cassock and renamed Ioan. But he has not been canonized—so far.

Peter the Great in 1725, and Ivan the Terrible in 1584, each messed up the succession of his respective dynasty—a practice usual to violent characters, dynastic storm-heads. In a fit of rage Ivan had clubbed Dmitri, his dearly loved son, with the knob of his staff so that Dmitri ceased to live, and Ivan was left with a second son, the dithering, blithering, weak-minded Feodor, to succeed him. Feodor's son, the child Dmitri, was poisoned by Feodor's brother-in-law, Boris Godunov, who calculated that in the event of the Rurik dynasty fizzling out he, as the brother-in-law and one well-versed in affairs of State, would be elected tsar; in which calculation he proved correct. Legend credits him with dying of a bad conscience. He was succeeded for a brief space by another boyar, called Shuiski; then ensued a period of confusion known as "The Troubled Times," at the end of which a grandson of an earlier brother-in-law—to wit, Ivan the Terrible's—a Romanov, was elected by the gentry and people to replace the ancient dynasty of Rurik, fizzled out, alas, alack! after seven centuries and a half with the imbecile issue of a sadistic lunatic, to which followed infanticide, usurpation and a muddy period of pretenders and false pretenders, ending in an offer of the Russian crown to Poland.

VIII. THE FIRST ROMANOV

AS a last resort, when all other hopes of settling differences had failed and the better-known boyars had been pretty well decimated in the civil war, they fished out a large-eyed zany of sixteen called Mihaïl Romanov and clapped the crown on him. His father had owed his advancement in affairs to the accident of *his* father, an obscure provincial, having been the brother of a pretty girl called Anastasia. In other words, Mihaïl's grandfather was the brother of Anastasia Romanov, whom Ivan the Terrible had picked out of two hundred virgins put up in the palace for him to choose a wife from. She was good-looking. Mihaïl owes it all to her good looks. But, as he died of melancholy, perhaps he does not owe her much, after all.

Yet Anastasia had been very pretty, a smooth, plump, dark-browed beauty, as they liked them in those days. It was then the custom when the tsar conceived the wish to marry, that all the gentry, far and near, should offer their best-looking daughters, from which assortment the young monarch selected a spouse to his taste, who then became the tsaritsa, to the profit and advancement of her relatives. The young girls were housed in the palace, in bedrooms and dormitories, and the young Tsar—in this case the crazy Ivan the Terrible, almost a boy—did the round, accompanied by his surgeon, and together inspected and tested the attractions of the shy débutantes of the day. Tsar and doctor together testing the soundness of the constitution of 200 blushing brides. Fantastic! Moving from chamber to chamber they gradually narrowed the selection till, weighing in his mind the rival charms of beauty and rude health in the finalists, the Tsar made his abiding choice.

She was Anastasia, the daughter of an obscure landowner hailing from the provinces—by name, Romanov. And that started it all—Peter, Elizabeth, Catherine, Alexander and all the rest—and was not to end but with the hapless Nicholas II. Pretty Anastasia was their one and only link with the Ruriks. But, since the issue of this union evaporated in a grandchild poisoned in infancy, there was not one drop of Rurik blood in the Romanov dynasty. They were merely connections by marriage.

Anastasia's brother, in common with the whole brood of her relatives, as was customary, did not tarry to avail himself of this piece of good fortune. Each one of them profoundly installed himself in key positions at court. Her brother's son, a shrewd man when he grew up, in due course saw his main chance in taking holy orders. He took the name of Filaret. He had the qualities of a born politician, such as in England weigh carefully whether politics or the Church offers the better chance of rapid advancement, and having decided for the Church, end up as Archbishop of Canterbury.

He, in fact, in time became Patriarch of Moscow. In the thick of the convulsions which overtook the land during the dark days of the civil war, when no one was tsar and everyone ran his own candidate, he was, however, at the Polish Court negotiating with the King of Poland for the latter's son and heir to assume the Russian crown. There was a hitch. It was not unwillingness on the part of King Sigismund to allow his son to become Tsar of Russia, but his overriding willingness to assume the Russian crown himself: to hold it in addition to his own. In later years the Russian emperors styled themselves Emperor of All the Russias, Tsar of Poland and Grand Duke of Finland. King Sigismund wanted to be King of Poland and Tsar of Russia; and while not, in principle, opposing the Russian offer to his son, he considered that, in practice, it would work out far better for all concerned if he, Sigismund, bequeathed to his son the two crowns, rather than create a situation whereby his son as Tsar of Russia would, on his father's death, be exposed to the distasteful necessity of contesting the Polish crown, already seized by another.

Filaret Romanov was weighing these alternatives in the light of his own advantage, when news came from Moscow that the boyars, to end the strife of rival claimants, had clapped the cap of Monomachus on his young son, Mihaïl. The news acerbated Filaret's relations both with King Sigismund and the King's son. Neither was willing to believe that such a turn of events could not but be agreeable to the new Tsar's father, who no longer had cause to solicit royal favor at the Polish Court.

Filaret Romanov had now but one favor to ask: to be permitted to get back, and as quickly as possible, to Moscow. Neither the King nor his son shared this view of the imperative urgency of Filaret's return. What about his offer to them? Filaret begged them to let him go. And, at last, with a twofold reluctance, they consented, without, be it clearly understood, relinquishing their claim to the throne of Russia.

Filaret, who not so long ago had congratulated himself on his perspicacity in choosing an ecclesiastical career, in which his political foresight had pushed him up to the highest place in his country's Church, now had cause to regret that he had not remained a layman. Had he not thus burned his own dynastic boats, and had he not so unnecessarily rushed off to Poland in the hope of becoming the King's right-hand man, they might easily have offered him the crown. Mihaïl would not have had anything to lose, since he, Filaret, would have handed the crown to his dear son in due course.

As it was, Filaret could not do what King Carol, for example, did with *his* Michael. But what he could do he did. He stood behind his son like a wall of granite and ruled the land for him, and he ruled with success, wisdom and moderation.

Filaret, Patriarch of Moscow, perfectly appreciated the situation. Here was his Michael, an inconspicuous youth, a dreamy-eyed lout of sixteen who was elected for want of anyone better by such boyars as had remained in Moscow and with the acclamation of the crowds, which would have acclaimed anyone else with the same heartiness. But—this was crucial—he had been elected as a constitutional monarch by the nobles and with the tacit consent of the clergy and people, after a deadlock reached by the rival claims of the more illustrious families. Very much as Mr. Baldwin was sent for to occupy the post of Prime Minister because the distinguished and brilliant Lord Balfour did not want the equally distinguished and brilliant Lord Curzon to put him in the shade. And Mr. Baldwin was chosen because his "utmost insignificance" was the outstanding quality required to end the rivalry between a man who had been Viceroy and Foreign Secretary, but not Prime Minister, and a man who had been Prime Minister and Foreign Secretary, but not Viceroy. "A man of the utmost insignificance! But not even a public figure!" Lord Curzon had wailed aloud when his superior claims had been so heartlessly overlooked in favor of obscure Stanley Baldwin. It is not recorded what utterance the Dolgorukis and Golitsins had made when balked of the crown in favor of this raw youth of a sweetly docile nature, but no Rurik blood. But Mihaïl Romanov was given to understand that families ancient and rich, as his own had been poor and obscure, would not regard him as anything but a tsar in name alone. He was to wear the ancient cap of Monomachus, but never forget by whose leave. He was to behave himself and do nothing of importance—such as declaring war, or making peace, or promulgating laws—except at their express bidding.

"Seeing the difficulties of a limited monarch," King George V of England is said to have confessed to Walter Page, Ambassador of the United States, "I thank God for being spared those of an absolute one." The first Romanov may have shared this very reasonable view of his exalted position, and he had dad to guide him. Mihaïl's son, Aleksei, who came after him, also gave intermittent signs of awareness that he reigned by the grace of God as expressed in the good will of his people. And thus it was with the third Romanov, the consumptive, well-meaning Feodor, while his young brother Ivan was too far gone in idiocy to do more than just sit on a throne with half-closed eyes.

But since Ivan's half-brother, Peter the Great, set the furious pace of ruling neither by the divine will, nor by that of the people, but by simple fear, the later Romanovs concluded that fear of God and fear of the tsar were in fact the same thing. Whatsoever they did, they considered must also be pleasing to God, who had anointed them because He trusted their judgment. And the further a tsar was removed by length of lineage from the original Romanov who was responsible at least to *some* of his people, the more jealously he guarded what he considered his inherited pleasure and privilege. And the more modern, democratic and enlightened the time into which a Romanov monarch projected his sovereignty, the more strongly he pressed his claim to be the single arbiter of the destiny of his subjects.

IX. ALEKSEI THE QUIET

MIHAÏL reigned a fourth of a century and was succeeded by his son Aleksei, who reigned a third of a century. These reigns of one-fourth and one-third of a century are curiously recurrent in Russian history. He ruled, as he was elected, as a constitutional monarch. Mihaïl and Aleksei reigned, as they say, "satisfactorily." During both reigns there were revolts and rebellions. They were liquidated with the help of the clergy, who conveyed the love and forgiveness of the Tsar on condition that the ring-leaders were handed out for punishment—a demand which the rebels invariably considered as reasonable, and handed out their leaders with a ready alacrity, thanking the Tsar for his mercy. There had been intermittent wars with Poland and Turkey—wars waged, it would seem, out of habit, in conventional defense of the faith on all sides, with alternate success and disaster. There were large bodies of Cossacks of unsettled religion on the Don and the Dnieper, Cossacks who bartered their independence, now in allegiance to the King of Poland, now to Russia's Tsar; and sometimes the Turk. They had picked up their superb horse- and swordsmanship from the Tartars. Sometimes, when the whole body was firmly and passionately converted to this or that faith, this or that sovereign, their leaders would unexpectedly turn tail, and two sections of the same body of Cossacks would be fighting each other with a passion and vehemence surpassing that with which they had fought side by side. Cossacks, who had but overnight adopted the Greek faith of the Russians, would descend on a Polish town and, in their new zeal for religion, exterminate the Catholic inhabitants, sparing neither men, women nor children, cutting down the men and whipping the women and children to shreds with their flails. All this on the ground of a deeply felt disapproval of the Catholic faith.

There is a folk song in Ukrainian which extols the virtue of a Cossack father who, in a fit of religious zeal, knifes his own wife and children because their mother had been a Catholic. The Cossack in question married her fully knowing that she was a Catholic; which did not strike him as wrong at the time. But, later, in a war between Orthodox Russians and Catholic Poles, the illogicality of his own conduct in having married a Catholic strikes the Cossack full in the face. Murder as well as charity surely must begin at home, and, with heroic consistency (argues the poet) and a long knife, the Cossack dispatches his kith and kin to bring the situation at home in line with his ideology. The song celebrates him as a great hero. Think, implies the native bard, what it must have cost him to kill his own wife and children—especially the children. (For what is a Cossack's wife to a Cossack when she is old?) Think of a father's feelings in plunging, amid tears, his own and theirs, the knife into his flesh and blood, in the name of religious consistency. And his deed— do not miss the moral significance—has a twofold action. His bad conscience at killing Polish Catholics while he has a Catholic family at home, now that he has none, is eased; and now he can take it out of Catholics abroad because he has not spared his family at home. It is a mistake to suppose that simple folk reason simply: they merely reason badly.

Such things as these went on while mild Mihaïl Feodorovitch sat piously on the throne of Muscovy; and they were the same when his son Aleksei succeeded him for a third of a century. He was cleverer than his father and even more pious. The Tsar Aleksei Mihaïlovitch prostrated himself six hundred times every day. He was called Aleksei the Quiet. He regarded himself, and he was regarded by others, as God's proconsul on earth in the domain entrusted to him. When news reached him that the people of England had descended to such a depth of ungodliness as to take the life of their own king, he was shocked to the very depths of his being. Such a scandalous thing had never been heard of before. True, Russian rulers of the previous dynasty had occasionally displaced each other, adding a touch of finality to the act by liquidating their brothers' or cousins' existence, but that was a matter in the family. Roman emperors had been assassinated by their immediate supporters, the leading patricians of the day. But that the common people should have taken it upon themselves to cut off the head of their anointed king was something unheard of.

It was—though the word was not as yet in being—it was in fact— Bolshevism! Tsar Aleksei forthwith dispatched the English Ambassador back to his own ungodly country. It was evident to him that the English people were barbarians and he wished to have no truck with them at all, least of all with the red-handed assassin-in-chief, Oliver Cromwell.

Tsar Aleksei had a large number of children, but they nearly all died as soon as they were weaned. In those days the chances of drawing breath were just about equal to the chances of drawing a lucky number in a lottery. But perhaps these *were* the lucky numbers, because, as Shakespeare says, "we came crying hither: thou know'st the first time that we smell the air we waul and cry."

"Alack! alack the day!"

Again—

"When we are born, we cry that we are come to this great stage of fools."

Aleksei had married twice. When he was young he was married off by parental authority to a wife belonging to the clan of Miloslavski, who at once obtained all the sinecures at court and exploited their position to their own advantage and the detriment of rival families. This happened every time a Russian tsar married a daughter of the gentry. Instances of a Russian tsar marrying foreign royalty were rare indeed. During seven hundred years of the previous dynasty this had happened perhaps three or four times. It had not happened at all in the Romanov dynasty, as yet, and was not to happen for two hundred years to come. Aleksei's first wife, who was to say the least *maladive,* bore him numerous offspring, of which only three survived—an epileptic son called Feodor, infirm in body but upright in spirit; a masterful daughter commanding alike in spirit and carriage, Sophia; and a second son, Ivan, so hopelessly sunk in idiocy that he could neither say a word nor sit on a chair without drooping and collapsing all in a heap, nor even keep his eyelids from closing, least of all when later he sat on a silver throne.

When Tsar Aleksei's wife of the Miloslavski clan breathed her last, he recouped himself for a choice imposed on him in his teens by selecting in his mature years a young girl of sparkling youth, health and beauty. She was a girl of an obscure family—in fact of no family, since she had been early adopted by the boyar Morozov, who was married to a Scottish woman, one Mary Hamilton. Her name was Natalia Narishkin. Marcel Proust would have pursued with singular delight, I am sure, all down the corridors of time the growing prestige of a family like Narishkin, obscure and of vulgar sound, gaining a growing distinction, to become in little more than two centuries one of the most aristocratic names in Russia, not least because it had kept clear of a title; but chiefly, of course, because it was the name of that little orphan from nowhere who was the mother of Peter the Great.

CHAPTER XI

PETER THE GREAT

page 265

I. CHILDHOOD

TSAR ALEKSEI MIHAÏLOVITCH died in 1676, leaving three-year-old Peter. I said that Peter's mother was an orphan adopted by the boyar Morozov and his wife, Mary Hamilton. Whether this statement is vitiated by the appearance of her father, Kiril Polouektovitch Narishkin, at the court of his daughter by the time she was a tsaritsa, it is difficult to say. It suggests at any rate a father willing and eager to take an active part in bringing up his grandson, a tsarevitch, after having been quick and eager to have his own daughter taken off his hands to be brought up by others. The father Narishkin is now described as a boyar—no doubt a rank conferred on him retrospectively to provide the new Tsaritsa with a more worthy father. Since no one quite knew whence he came, no one could dispute what he had been before. The Miloslavskis, now that Tsar Aleksei was safely in his grave, began to oppress the Narishkins, none of whom had in fact been promoted to any important position in the State. Peter's grandfather, Kiril Narishkin, whom Tsar Aleksei had appointed Chief Justice, was now dismissed. Peter's widowed mother was, on the pretext of there not being enough room, removed from the Kremlin to a remote palace in order to deprive her of any influence at court. She resented the suggestion and sent Peter along with his tutor to request the new Tsar's protection. Peter kissed the hand of his reigning half-brother; and Tsar Feodor, a kindly man, allowed them to stay.

The boy Peter's education was entrusted to a drunken deacon, Nikita Zotov, to whom the widowed Tsarista, upon presentation, had said: "You are a good, honest fellow. Take my young son in hand, and teach him all that is necesary." Zotov, an incurable drunkard with no partiality for education, taught young Peter to read and write of a morning, as well as the scriptures, and in the afternoon he told him stories culled from Russian history. His own knowledge was so embryonic and his method so sketchy that Peter even as a man could never spell correctly and his handwriting remained that of an urchin. The walls of his rooms when he was a child were painted to represent the main scenes from history, all the chief cities

this is true

207

of Europe, famous buildings, ships, battles, uniforms; and all this stimulated the boy's imagination. In addition to Zotov, two foreigners, Lefort and Timmermann, taught him geometry and fortification. Peter was particularly keen on the latter, which seems to have been a popular science for at least two centuries. Even in the reign of Alexander I a certain retired general, whose sons had all been killed in either defending or assaulting fortresses, passed the time of his retirement in teaching his spinster daughter the science of fortification.

When Tsar Feodor, whose health was precarious, was advised to marry again, because his first marriage had been without issue, he answered: "My father intended that my brother, the Tsarevitch Peter, should ascend the throne; I intend likewise." The Miloslavski faction succeeded in persuading Feodor to marry again, but he died the same year, having left nothing undone to produce an heir, alas, without success. His endeavor to comply with the desires of the Miloslavski faction is said to have killed the frail Tsar.

At the time of Feodor's death his idiot brother Ivan was sixteen, and Peter ten. All government ranks gathered before the palace. The Patriarch, supported by the clergy, proposed that they should elect the future tsar. Thereupon men of all ranks, including the palace servants, the deacons, tenants, the nobles in the city, the children of boyars, visitors to Moscow, the soldiers, the populace, all chose in one voice the Tsarevitch Peter to be tsar. There was no counting of heads or votes. The Patriarch put the question. A shout came in return, the general impression being that most of the people shouted in favor of Peter. The Patriarch, as though not entirely satisfied, later solicited the opinion of the more influential men among the boyars and other ranks, too; and they were all apparently of this opinion. Ivan was considered disqualified.

Peter was proclaimed tsar on the tenth of May, 1682. He was three weeks short of being ten years of age. His mother was appointed regent, and the same day everyone was made to swear allegiance to him.

II. ASSAULT ON THE KREMLIN

BUT three weeks later everything collapsed. Peter's half-sister, Sophia, a Miloslavski on her mother's side, had organized a popular revolt in favor of her brother, the idiot Ivan. Somebody shouted in the midst of the troops that the boyars had deprived the legitimate tsar, Ivan, of his scepter and given it to his younger half-brother, an offspring of Tsar

Aleksei's second marriage. Rumors were spread that Ivan had been killed and a list of the alleged murderers, satellites of Peter's mother, were distributed among the troops.

These troops were called the Streltsi—a name which recurs a great deal in connection with Peter, who later abolished them. Streltsi is merely the Russian for "shooters" and, assuming that they could shoot straight, would correspond to "sharpshooters." The Streltsi were easily roused to indignation. On the fifteenth of May, having sung the Te Deum at the Znamenski Monastery, taking with them a vessel with holy water and the ikon of the Mother of God, headed by a procession of popes and deacons, to the sound of church bells and the beating of drums, the Streltsi forced their way into the Kremlin.

They began to demand the unpopular leaders of the Narishkin faction. It was a case of "We want ———." In the first instance, they wanted Peter's uncles, his mother's ambitious brothers. Rumor had it that one of the Tsaritsa's brothers had "measured himself" for the crown. What exactly that meant is not clear. Did he in actual fact put on the cap of Monomachus, give instructions to alter it, take it in an inch and a half to conform to the size of his own head? Doubtless the Streltsi, being plain men, visualized some such concrete act. The rumor that he had measured himself for the crown having been spread by the Miloslavskis, the Narishkins had no effective means of dispelling it. There was no radio in those days, or the Narishkins could have ridiculed the suggestion in a broadcast to the nation.

The Streltsi were in no mood for argument. They demanded one after another of the adherents of the Narishkin clan. As they appeared on the ramparts they were pushed down so that they fell into the midst of the Streltsi assembled below, who caught them on their lances. Peter's mother, in response to their clamorous demands, had herself appeared on the ramparts, holding Peter and Ivan before her, displaying them with an eager, demonstrative precipitation to the Streltsi below, as one who might say: "Here they are, the two dear boys. Here is Ivan," patting him eagerly, "not dead, you see, but safe and sound and *quite* as dear to me as my own boy. Here he is. Ivan, step forward!"

The Streltsi, in the meantime, went on shouting for all the prominent men known to have espoused the Narishkin cause, and when the list was exhausted they called for their own commanders who had either shown themselves to be lukewarm or tried to moderate the ardor of their men. Peter's mother at first tried to hide some of her relatives and adherents.

Each time, however, when the alternative seemed to be her own life and that of her son, she yielded precipitately. The Streltsi were curiously reluctant to lay hands on the boy Peter or his mother. A superstitious feeling embedded deep in their natures almost confused the child Tsar and his mother with the boy Jesus and the Mother of God. Every time a boyar was pushed off the ramparts to be caught on a forest of spears far below, the Tsaritsa Mother pushed forward the boys and patted their shoulders as if to say, "We are all friends, aren't we, boys?"

Peter trembled like a leaf. Ivan looked on with an imbecile grin. The impression produced by these horrors on the ten-year-old Peter could never be effaced. It explains his fear and hatred of the Streltsi; it explains his subsequent cruelty in exterminating them, with a sort of glee of aversion rooted in this early image of horror. In exterminating them, he could no more be likely to wish to lessen their pain than a sea captain would wish to administer an anesthetic to the sharks he had caught just after they had devoured half his family.

It is interesting to note that Peter, who is famous as a conqueror, was quite a coward himself. When he was yet a babe in arms his mother in crossing an overflowing stream frightened him, who was asleep on her lap, with her sudden screams, with the result that Peter until he was fourteen was terrified of water. He was cured of his fear and became a passionate mariner.

The sight of his mother's relatives and friends being pushed off ramparts to be caught on a forest of lances below planted the seed of fear in him at the age of ten. Moreover, the narrow margin between the choice of his relatives and himself, a choice depending on the murderous plans, the intractable mood of an angry crowd storming and shouting below and climbing up to the ramparts, must have implanted in the boy Peter a precedent for being ready to face the death of others, however near and dear to him, in preference to that of himself: a readiness characteristic of him. The seed having been sown, the plant which makes the coward began to grow. We see Peter through the succeeding years developing a sharp distinction between his own and other men's sensibility. If we follow him in his unimaginable cruelties we are left hesitating between ascribing to him a callousness so coarsened that it is unaware of other men's susceptibility to pain; or a sensibility aware of the pain and rejoicing in the gulf which divides the individual from his brother man—a gulf he first appreciated when he saw his uncles being pushed off the ramparts in order that he himself might be spared.

III. IVAN AND PETER

The Streltsi, having completed their work, resolved that Ivan and Peter were to reign together and that Sophia, Ivan's elder sister, was to rule as regent. Sophia was very keen on reigning. Since there were now two tsars, she might well make a third. She had her signature annexed to all official documents. New money was minted representing the names of the two tsars on one side of the coin and her own on the other, the two boys being described as Tsars, Grand Dukes and Self-Upholders, and she herself as Tsarevna, and even Tsaritsa and Self-Upholder. She had twin silver thrones made for the boys, on which Peter sat upright looking about him with his big round eyes, and Ivan sat all in a heap with his eyes half-closed, indifferent to the world.

see about Paul's eye resembling Peter Ist!

The Streltsi received many grants, rights, honors and privileges, such as the right to elect their own deputies, as in the Soviet Army; the right in commemoration of their recent activities to erect a monument on the Red Square; testimonials with government seal commending them for the efficacy of their "purge"; and honorable transformation from sharp-shooters into a court infantry. The elected representatives carried these testimonials on their heads back to their regimental huts, where the troops met them to the pealing of bells and the beating of drums.

Sophia promoted her lover, Prince Vassili Golitsin, to the rank of Great Chancellor. This Golitsin was a man both capable and, compared with his contemporaries, cultured. It is facilely assumed that Russia's break with the Muscovite traditions and change over to modern European usages was entirely due to Peter. That is far from being the case. Had Peter never been born the change would not have been as swift and abrupt, but it would have come all the same. As far back as Ivan III there had been attempts to introduce foreign gunsmiths and artillery men to Moscow. Ivan III addressed himself to Germany, desiring that "doctors of cannon rights" be sent to him. During the reign of Peter's father, Aleksei Mihaïlovitch, there had been a steady influx of foreigners, notably Germans, into Moscow; and a whole suburb, called the German Quarter, had sprung up, populated almost exclusively by Germans who carried on their own traditions and built houses in the Hansa style.

this is True

But there had been Dutchmen, too, and an occasional Englishman. A certain Scottish soldier of fortune, Gordon, famous in Russian history as the military preceptor of Peter the Great, had come out, but had had enough of it and applied to go home. He wanted to retire from the

Russian Army and settle down in Scotland. Sophia finally let him go, but to make him come back retained his family as a pawn. In London Gordon appealed to James II, who furnished him with a stupendous document, addressed to the two joint Tsars, who were described as High and Mighty Tsars of Muscovy and Great Princes of practically every Russian town on the map. Gordon's release from the Russian service was requested and his desire to settle down at home stressed.

On his return to Moscow Gordon appeared at the Granovitaya Palata in the Kremlin before Ivan and Peter, who were seated on the twin silver thrones, and handed Sophia the letter from James II of France, England, Scotland and Ireland King, Defender of the Faith. She sent for an interpreter. He turned out to be a Dutchman who dissimulated his ignorance of English; and Sophia understood King James's message in her own way. After the Dutchman had finished translating, Sophia said kindly to Gordon: "You are an honest man. You have kept your word; here you are back with us in Moscow."

Gordon stayed on for good, and founded a Russian clan. He turned young Peter into a good soldier; and a better drunkard. In those days Russians merely drank mead; the furious pace of drinking neat spirits was set by the foreigners who lived in the German Quarter of Moscow; and young Peter took to it, and later introduced tobacco, in the belief that it was the first sign of being Westernized. Gordon was alive when William III mounted the throne of England; but whenever they drank the toast of Scotland, he gloomily raised his cup to King James, muttering, with a smack of his lips: "God bless him!"

Prince Golitsin, a man acquainted with the rudiments of foreign learning, was not averse to the infusion of new ideas. There was in Russia a sense of growing strength, a superflux of energy which only needed to be canalized for it to throw off the old sloth. Prince Golitsin was in favor of introducing new methods slowly and painlessly, without discarding such of the old essentially Russian traditions as were native and even beneficial. He and Sophia intended to do a great deal together. There was a secret understanding between them; with this difference, that Sophia intended by and by to push off her brothers and reign in her own right in collaboration with Golitsin, whom she might marry and thus enjoy equally his love and his advice in his capacity of Prince Consort; while Golitsin, fully concurring in his mistress's ideas, went further still and imagined himself by and by sitting on the throne beside her—in fact anticipating William and Mary of England. Had Peter not acted promptly as a boy of fifteen there would have been in Europe in addition to William and Mary a Vassili and Sophia.

In the meantime Peter amused himself in a village near Moscow called Preobrazhenskoye, where he formed his first regiment composed of his playmates—a regiment of which we hear so much in Russian history, the Preobrazhenski Regiment. He was now twelve years old. His brother Ivan had been married off by Sophia to one Praskovia Saltikov. At that time events with which the reader is already familiar were in the lap of time. Who was to know then that their younger daughter, Anna Ivanovna, was one day to be Empress of Russia; or that her elder sister would marry a certain Duke of Mecklenburg, and have a daughter, whose baby boy Ivan (named after his great-grandfather, the present idiot Tsar Ivan) would be deposed as a babe in arms and confined for twenty years to a damp cell in a fortress?

While Ivan was now, despite his idiocy, successfully planting the seed of his progeny, Peter played in the company of foreigners. From a citizen of Geneva, by name Lefort, twenty-three years his senior, he had picked up bits of German and Dutch. While Golitsin was considering the restoration of an old law abolished by Tsar Feodor in 1681, a law which determined promotion in the service strictly according to rules of precedence enjoyed by a forefather, Peter's mind was in fact moving in the opposite direction. His idea was to abolish what remained of the old nobility—the boyars—and to introduce in their place the Teutonic system of civil grades and appointments. The boyars resented Peter's leanings towards the ungodly ways and customs of Lutherans. They prevailed on his mother to put a stop to the young Tsar's love of drill and military exercises improper in a youth of his rank, because they could see that his infatuation with foreign ways would lead to a break with native traditions. Like Hitler, Peter had no use for sport but excelled in military training. With the help of a German lieutenant, Franz Timmermann, he had a small fortress built for himself, which he himself attacked and took by assault. He reversed all his father's articles of war, and he conscripted his brother's huntsmen and enrolled them in the ranks of his own Preobrazhenski Regiment. Soon he had so many men that he transferred the surplus to another village—the Semënovski village. Hence the famous Semënovski Regiment which Alexander I quelled so severely.

IV. SOPHIA'S PLOT

PETER seemed more interested in playing at soldiering, and later in sailing a boat across a lake, than in being tsar. He did not seem to care who was tsar so long as they left him alone at his games. Fireworks were his hobby, and many a soldier was badly hurt as a result of being forced to take part in Peter's experiments. When he was sixteen his mother married him off to a nice but dull girl, Evdokia (Eudoxia) Lapukhina. This was in 1689, when Peter was sixteen years old. The following year the unhappy Aleksei was born, whom twenty-eight years later Peter tortured to death. *He killed him but did not torture*

Sophia was against Peter's marriage. She obviously could not desire that her half-brother should early provide himself with an heir. There began a tug-of-war between Peter and Sophia. He believed that she was plotting to kill him, while she believed that he had had enough of her regency and was going to shut her up in a convent. Her lover, Golitsin, who had returned to Moscow in a triumphal progress from the Turkish campaign, in which he had been defeated (a practice which Peter himself later followed after his unsuccessful campaigns), was snubbed by the young Tsar, who refused to see him because he considered that Golitsin had disgraced himself. Golitsin felt that a struggle was imminent and took the precaution of dispatching his son to Poland, out of harm's way.

Then the struggle began. Sophia and Golitsin won the first round. She had the Streltsi on her side. The leader of the movement arrived with every intention of murdering Peter, who had fled to take refuge at the Troïtsa Monastery, galloping there during the night in his nightshirt. Ivan was still in the Kremlin.

When the arch-plotter, by name Tcheglovitov, with the assassins, galloped up to Peter's quarters in Preobrazhenski Village, and found the Tsar had left for Troïtsa Monastery, he pretended he had come to change the guard and galloped back to Sophia to consult her on their further course of action. Golitsin advised flight to Poland, but Sophia would not agree.

Soon Peter's supporters arrived at Troïtsa Monastery. After consultation with them he decided to send a ukase to Moscow summoning to Troïtsa all the boyars and foreign officers with deputies from every regiment. The Swiss Lefort and the Scotsman Gordon, Peter's wife and mother and his sister Natalia, had already joined him at Troïtsa. The decision rested with the Streltsi. To reinforce his own ukase, Peter wrote to

Ivan at Moscow, requesting his brother's permission that representatives of all the regiments should come to him.

Sophia, in the name of Ivan, issued orders forbidding any troops, on pain of death, to leave Moscow. The conflicting orders resulted in more and more troops leaving Moscow stealthily to go and join Peter at Troïtsa. When Sophia saw that she was being deserted she sent her aunt Tatiana Mihaïlovna (the late Tsar Mihaïl's daughter) and two of her own sisters as emissaries of peace. Arriving at Troïtsa, they threw themselves at Peter's feet to beseech his Christian forgiveness for an erring sister. But Peter, having heard them, began to point out why Sophia was culpable. Thereupon Aunt Tatiana remained with Peter, and the two sisters returned to Sophia to confess it was no good—their embassy had failed.

Sophia, now really frightened, appealed to the Patriarch. The old man went to Troïtsa, but Peter not only refused to listen to him but dismissed him from his post and appointed another man in his place. The Patriarch was detained at the Monastery. Sophia, now out of her wits with terror, set out in person in order to implore Peter to let bygones be bygones and to be friends once more. She set out accompanied by a number of notables and holding the Saviour's ikon in her hands all the way to the monastery. But Peter, hearing of her journey, sent a servant to intercept her and to tell her straight out that she would not be admitted and should go back at once.

Sophia insisted on being allowed to see her brother. Peter sent out one of his sternest boyars to advise her that unless she turned back she would be manhandled. The Tsarevna, in despair, returned to Moscow.

Peter wrote again to Ivan, complaining bitterly that his request that all regimental deputies should report to him had not been complied with, and in a ukase in his own name he ordered all the regiments to carry out his instructions; after which all army deputies arrived at Troïtsa in a chastened mood. Peter came out to them, accompanied by his mother, Aunt Tatiana and the Patriarch. Aunt Tatiana was a sister of Peter's father, the late Tsar Aleksei, and accordingly a daughter of the first Romanov, Tsar Mihaïl. The ease with which she deserted Sophia and went over to Peter may be due either to cowardice or to a dislike of the Miloslavski clan. "Aleksei's first wife, I *must* say, I never greatly cared for"—Aunt Tatiana may have been saying this: particularly if she had been fond of her late brother who had adored his second wife, Natalia Narishkin, who had presented him with bright-eyed Peter. Tsar Aleksei,

in his old age, had developed a taste for secular distractions and had had
a theater built for his own entertainment at his pleasure palace, where his
young wife Natalia encouraged him in this amusement frowned upon by
the pious fathers of the Church. Tsar Aleksei and his second wife were
considered gay and frivolous by the sedate boyars. Now the once gay
widow and the late monarch's sister were lending moral support to
sixteen-year-old Peter, who, in the first year of his marriage, had to face
a revolt organized by his ambitious half-sister.

Peter ordered the accusations against Tcheglovitov and his accomplices
to be read aloud, and the assembled notables pronounced the death
penalty. Peter "thanked them for their zeal," and sent one-half of the
people who had come to him back to Moscow in charge of two hundred
of his soldiers. He ordered that Tcheglovitov and his accomplices be
found and seized, but the man could not be discovered because the
Tsarevna Sophia herself had hidden him in her quarters in the Kremlin.
Peter again wrote to his brother, to complain that Ivan was sheltering
an assassin. Sophia, foreseeing the death of her accomplice, advised him
to be quick to call in a priest and make his peace with God. Peter's messenger arrived and demanded that she hand him Tcheglovitov, but Sophia
tarried in the hope of still saving him. Peter's messenger then declared
that he was empowered by the Tsar to search her apartments. At the
same time a messenger arrived from Ivan to tell Sophia that he had no
intention of quarreling with his brother on her account, least of all on
account of Tcheglovitov, and ordered her to hand him over; which, with
tears in her eyes, she did.

Tsar Ivan demanded that Tcheglovitov and his accomplices be brought
before him, in the first instance, and he questioned them about their plot
against his brother. They denied everything and blamed the Narishkins
for causing all the mischief. Ivan seemed impressed, and when they saw
that he believed them they began, warmly supported by Sophia, to entreat him to rule alone over Russia. This suggestion gave Ivan a jolt. He
shouted angrily at them that they did not apparently mind getting him
into hot water with his young brother, with whom he had had trouble
enough, thanks to them; and he had them put in irons and dispatched
forthwith to Peter at Troïtsa.

Tcheglovitov and his friends were by Peter's orders turned over to the
boyars for investigation. For four days Tcheglovitov refused to reveal
anything or to say a word which might implicate the Tsarevna Sophia.
Then they began to torture him. He was weak from hunger, having

had no food for days. A few strokes with the knout ended his resistance. He confessed everything and was prepared to set down his confession in writing if only they would first give him something to eat. Tcheglovitov and two of his accomplices were broken on the wheel. Others had their tongues cut out. Still others were banished. One of those sentenced to be broken on the wheel blamed himself loudly as he was being led to execution, enjoining the people he passed to be warned by his example.

Prince Vassili Golitsin and his son were brought to Troïtsa, but the Tsar would not see them and sentence was read to them by a boyar. Their crime was that they had, without authority from the Great Sovereigns the Tsars, included the name of the Tsarevna Sophia Alekseievna as a self-upholder on all official documents and coins of the realm, and that, anyway, they had proved of precious little use in the campaign against the Turk in the Crimea. They were deprived of their boyar rank and all their property, and banished. The old prince died in exile, but his son was pardoned in old age.

When Tcheglovitov and his accomplices were first handed over to Peter he got the Patriarch to exhort them to make a clean breast of it for the good of their souls. In this way they confessed, as they thought, their sins, as distinct from their guilt. But they handed the Patriarch a petition signed in the name of all the Streltsi in which Sophia had been humbly solicited to rule alone. Peter sent this petition on to Ivan as conclusive evidence of their sister's guilt. Peter's sentence, not excessive, was that she be invited to retire of her own free will to a convent of her own choice. The Tsarevna declined her brother's suggestion and prepared to flee to Poland. Peter, knowing the danger of such a flight, which might end in Poland espousing her cause, sent a boyar to take her by force and lock her up in the Novodevitchi Convent.

Thus ended Sophia's seven-year rule, during which period her profile was stamped on one side of the coins and her two brothers' on the other, all the three described as Great Sovereigns, Tsars, and Tsarevna (sometimes Tsaritsa) and Self-Upholders. Sophia sympathized with the infirm and the sick. Among the laws promulgated by her was one which decreed that all doctors whose patients died in their care were to be put to death.

On the seventh of September a ukase issued in the name of both brothers forbade the mention of their sister on any document of State. At last Peter deemed it safe for himself to leave the sanctuary of the Troïtsa Monastery and return to Moscow. On the outskirts he was met by all ranks, grades and dignitaries in the city and vast numbers of common people. All the way from the suburbs to the capital the Streltsi lay on the road with their heads on blocks, into each of which an ax had been stuck, and wailed loudly and piteously for foregiveness. Peter passed by with insouciance and drove straight to the cathedral. The streets were lined with his newly trained troops. Peter ordered a thanksgiving service to commemorate his escape. Before the Tsar's residence he was met by Ivan. The two brothers embraced, and the elder in eager proof of his innocence surrendered to the younger his own rights and appointed Peter sole ruler of the land.

This is a fabrication, a lie; he executed them later, but after this incident he still was powerless to chastize them.

CHAPTER XII

THE MAN WHO GOT THINGS DONE

I. PLAYING THE SUBORDINATE

IVAN retired from affairs of State and led a peaceful life, wisely avoiding impinging on his brother's interests. Ivan was more or less an idiot: his retirement was a stroke of genius. Peter preserved a curious affection for his incapable brother. Since Ivan refused to see anyone connected with the State, Peter, convinced of his loyalty and lack of ambition, showed his elder brother, who was, in name, the senior Tsar, a touching deference. It was one of Peter's favorite games to take a back seat when he knew he held the reins. Provided there was no doubt that he was one thing, he always wanted to be another. So obviously was Peter the child to whom shipbuilding was make-believe that he declined to take command, but preferred to appear in some subordinate capacity because he could get more fun out of it. He had commanded the whole court and many of the gentry to Voronej, to come and watch him launch the first ship built in a Russian dockyard.

Both Tsaritsas were there. Ivan died in 1696. But it made no difference to his family. Peter still took them about; he liked the three girls. The eldest he later married to the Duke of Mecklenburg and, as stated, seduced her each time he passed through Mecklenburg. The second, Anna, married the Duke of Courland and later became Empress of Russia. But at the launching of the first Russian ship at Voronej they were only girls. Peter's wife at the time was still his first and legitimate wife, Eudoxia, to whom his mother had betrothed him while he was still a boy and who inspired in him a profound indifference. She was there with her little boy, the Tsarevitch Aleksei, a sad waif with thoughtful eyes and long lashes, unaware of the fate which was in store for him at his father's hands. Ivan's widow, the Tsaritsa Praskovia Feodorovna, was a difficult woman. During the interminable delays which preceded the launching, she was finding fault with her daughters' foreign tutor. The daughters, Catherine and Anna, were playing with their little cousin, the Tsarevitch Aleksei, son of Peter and Eudoxia. It is interesting to anticipate their fate; and, since all history, whether late or early, is past history, it is surely legitimate to do so. The little Tsarevitch with the sad eyes, who is now playing with his cousins, girls in their teens—this little boy will never see the throne. But his son (Peter II) will reign a year or two and die, a boy of twelve. But before he reigns there will reign somebody who is not now at the launching of the ship at Voronej. There is a small peasant girl in Lithuania, who will grow up to be a nursemaid in a pastor's family; she will get engaged to a Swedish sergeant, during a siege fall into Russian hands, pass from one general to another; and with Eudoxia, who is at the wharf in Voronej, shut up in a convent, that peasant girl will be Peter's consort; and when Peter the Great dies in 1725, she will reign in his place as Catherine I. She will be followed, as we said, by the unborn son of this little boy with the sad eyes, and after him will come the younger of the two girl cousins now playing with him, the one called Anna; and then will come, not the elder, Catherine of Mecklenburg, but her daughter with the baby son Ivan.

How fantastically untidy history seems when anticipated from a given point!

Peter had been running about the ship with the ax in his hand and sweat dropping from his brow. He had 'prenticed his hand in Saardam, picking up the slang of the Dutch dockyard and being pelted with stones by urchins. Shipbuilding had become his hobby. He got things done. But if he had wanted them well done he should have got somebody more competent than himself to do them. When everything was ready for the launching, Peter, in his self-appointed capacity as *bombardier*, reported to the man whom he had appointed Admiral of the Russian Fleet. The admiral was sitting at tea with the other guests on shore, and Peter came up to him and saluted. "All ready, your Excellency!"

"Let her go, *bombardier!*" ordered the admiral.

Peter, as happy as a child, again saluted and departed to obey his orders.

When you are Tsar of Russia and have nobody but God above you, to play the subordinate is an added luxury. During triumphal processions Peter, instead of appearing at the head on a horse, or in a resplendent coach, marched some way behind the carriages among the common soldiers, as if to show that he was not among the glittering generals who took all the credit for the victory, but might be found among those others who had borne the heat and burden of the day. In his orgies he chose another man to fill the highest office of "King of Pressburg," while himself retaining a fairly humble post in the hierarchy of organized obscenity in which he indulged for long periods at a time, meanwhile completely neglecting the State. The man he appointed "King of Pressburg" was Nikita Zotov, his former tutor, a congenital drunkard of no learning, who had been himself abashed by his appointment as tutor to the Tsarevitch and fallen on his knees before the Tsaritsa Mother, thinking that there must be something wrong in her selecting him of all men. Peter's mother had been a particularly good-looking wench, adopted for her looks by a clever couple with up-to-date Western ways, with whom she had lived in the most enlightened house in Moscow and enjoyed uncommon advantages, ending unexpectedly in a marriage with a tsar: all of which had yet not prevented her from remaining what she was—a complete fool. But Zotov at all events found his second appointment more congenial than his first. "The King of Pressburg" presided over the most fantastic and idiotic rites of debauchery. Peter's inventiveness had nothing of the lustful quality of Roman orgies. Drink and ribaldry, the humor of which would not be apparent to anyone who was not rendered uncritical through inebriation, were the chief features of these mostly disgusting riots. Men were forced to drink more than their bodies could hold. This was supposed to be funny. Doors were locked. Feasting lasted for hours; and they used not to get up for their small needs.

When Peter's ex-tutor died, a new candidate for the "King of Pressburg" had to be found. Candidates were supposed to display unusual endurance in their capacity for filling themselves with alcohol, and they had also to give proof of their virility. They were placed on seatless chairs and Peter roughly examined their private parts, pinching and squeezing. This was supposed to be riotously funny. The Tsar roared at his own remarks; his satellites took care not to spoil the fun with any traitorous signs of aloofness. Peter had none of the dignity of the old tsars of Muscovy and their boyars, who sat silent with their eyes fixed on their beards to show the profundity of their thoughts. He got drunk with foreign skippers and sailors. He placed above all the others the pie-vendor Menshikov. He abolished the post of the Most Holy Patriarch. He parodied Church rituals. As he was a little afraid he might be going too far, he pretended it was the Roman, not the Greek Church he was ridiculing. He ignored what was left of the old order of precedence. He rioted in the streets. He tore off the old rigid decorous mode of dress and made Russian boyars dress like German lackeys. But, worst of all, he abolished the beard. That was the most cruel blow of all. Ivan the Terrible was ruthless enough, but at all events he was pious; he had respected the beard. "To shave the beard," Ivan the Terrible said, "is a sin that the blood of all the martyrs cannot cleanse. It is to deface the image of God."

II. PETER QUALIFIES THE SIXTH COMMANDMENT

THIS partiality for foreign ways might have ended Peter, as it ended Amanullah. When during one of his trips abroad, across Sweden, Germany and Holland, Peter got to England, he was received in London with about the same curiosity as has in our own days been displayed in regard to Amanullah, Amir of Afghanistan. Russia was a remote and barbarous land.

He got on best with King William. They got on like two Dutchmen. Peter spoke in the kind of Dutch he had picked up in the German Quarter in Moscow and in the docks of Saardam. The King made the Tsar the present of a yacht. In return, Peter gave William an uncut diamond of doubtful value. Everyone thought the Tsar of Russia was fabulously rich. As a matter of fact, his treasury was empty; he had his work cut out to raise immediate cash, which he did by selling the tobacco monopoly in Russia to Lord Carmarthen.

He asked for a woman, and an actress was provided for the Tsar, who treated her far from generously. She complained, but the Tsar's answer was that, having regard to the meager pleasure he derived from her, he considered she was adequately paid.

On the way to Deptford, the Tsar and his numerous suite put up at an inn. The food and drink they consumed in twenty-four hours would have been enough for a regiment. Yet the total bill came to less than £1. At Deptford the Tsar and his company leased the house of an English admiral. When the landlord reoccupied his cherished residence, it did not at first seem possible to him that the damage to his property had been caused by a human agency. Everything that could be torn and broken was torn and broken. Even the feather beds were ripped open. In the garden the trees were uprooted and the stout iron fence was all twisted.

Peter was in the habit of testing his strength on all suitable, but especially unsuitable, occasions. A giant, he had hands of steel. King Frederick Augustus of Poland and Peter always competed at table by tying silver spoons into knots or twisting gold plate.

When he got back to Russia, Peter learned that, taking advantage of his absence abroad, the Streltsi had risen against his authority. He quelled them mercilessly. He had special barracks put up to serve as torture chambers, and he was present at the gruesome scenes, assisting at the forcible extraction of information through torture. He ordered the boyars to chop off the heads of the condemned. Whole regiments lined up before the chopping blocks. Peter, with glee, chopped off their heads, and he forced unwilling and fastidious men to assist him.

Passing through Germany, he had in Brandenburg taken especial interest in a new device for breaking criminals on the wheel, and had expressed the wish to see it in operation. When his host, the Elector, had regretted his inability to oblige the Tsar, as at the moment there was no criminal in the prison condemned to such punishment, Peter had cheerfully suggested providing a man from his own suite.

It might be said, in extenuation, that those were raw, ferocious times. But to this it might be replied that it hurt as much to be broken on the wheel in 1670 as it would hurt you and me to be broken on the wheel in 1939. Ivan the Terrible was cruel; yet there was an insane theatricality about him that was grimly humorous. But Peter was mean in spirit. He condemned to death one Mary Hamilton, a mistress of his and a niece of the Mary Hamilton who had adopted his mother. Her crime was that she had, long after he had himself discarded her, taken a lover. He had her whipped, and as she fell on her knees before him to implore his pardon, he gave a sign to the executioner, who chopped off her head. Peter lifted it, kissed the bleeding mouth, and, holding the head by the hair, took this opportunity to give the spectators a little lecture on anatomy, with special reference to the construction of the human skull, the functions of the arteries, and so on.

Some time later Peter expounded the Ten Commandments as a basis of conduct for his subjects, writing marginal notes to elucidate their meaning. When he came to "Thou shalt not kill," he annotated: "As applying to highway robbers and such-like."

III. PETER AND CHARLES XII

PETER was not, like his rival, Charles XII, courageous. It is a mistake to think that a man is brave always. Courage, even of the same kind, is intermittent. Sometimes a man is courageous, at other times he is not. It depends on circumstances and the state of his nerves. Peter was terrified of Charles XII, at whose approach he ran, having given over the command to a certain prince of the Holy Roman Empire, who made a resplendent display before battle and ended by instant surrender.

The Tsar cursed and retreated. Peter's conventional disregard of danger is not sufficiently established, though he could endure the maximum of physical pain—in others. When he ran at Narva, in 1700, it was on the pretext of raising money for a new army. But he did not lead it. Instead of, like Hitler, bilking the Jews, who at that time had no great hold on Russian money, Peter bilked the merchants. He needed more and more money for his continuous wars. There was no plan of campaign, no rhyme or reason in it all, either on Peter's side or that of Sweden's famous king.

Charles XII thirsted for glory. To exercise his swordsmanship, he would have sheep, calves and pigs driven into the dining hall where he feasted with his fellows, and there chop off their heads with his sword, to the vociferous applause of his youthful staff. They were all very young then, and martially ambitious. Charles's Senate was against war. But he lusted for "glory."

Russia did not seem to him a country worthy of his steel; and he was only drawn on by Russian insolence. Peter, in concert with Frederick Augustus of Saxony and Poland, was supporting a revolted Lithuanian vassal of Sweden, Johann Patkul. Boiling with rage, Charles XII came down with his army. He first turned his attention to Peter, appearing suddenly under the walls of Narva. Peter, howling with fright, fled before Charles had fired a shot. Next this bareheaded boy of nineteen went after Frederick Augustus right into the heart of Poland, knocked him off his throne, put up Stanislas Lesczinski in his place—a candidate agreeable to Charles's ally, Louis XIV (and subsequently to become the father of Louis XV's mother). Not content with this, Charles chased Frederick Augustus into his native Saxony, where he raised lethal hell. This job done, he went after Patkul, broke up his army, captured him and had him twice broken on the wheel, from below up—whatever that may mean.

It took Peter eight years to get up an army on the Swedish model before he could venture to face Charles again. Peter did not, as is often believed, deliberately draw Charles XII into the interior of Russia. It was not a cunning plan to separate Charles XII from his base. Peter again retreated in sheer panic, and Charles floundered after him, till, like two drunkards who stagger at large without knowing how or where, both found themselves in July of 1709 going round and round each other somewhere in the Ukraine. The Russian Army, to Peter's astonishment, defeated the ragged remnants of the Swedish invaders at Poltava.

When the battle was all but over, Peter, flourishing his sword, galloped forward from behind his troops. He even boasted of a bullet hole in his hat. Charles, wounded in the leg, bareheaded as usual, had been leading his troops from a stretcher. After the battle he somehow managed to escape to Turkey, where he proved himself an awkward guest.

Later Peter himself repeated Charles's mistake. He found himself enticed into enemy territory and surrounded at Pruth by the Turks. All seemed lost. Peter escaped capture and the annihilation of his entire army by resorting to bribery.

The eighteenth century was the time of conquests. Soberly viewed, however, there was little else but good or bad luck in all the much vaunted tactics and maneuvers, taken so seriously, prized so highly, by grown-up adolescents. Peter had put his foot down when Golitsin had staged a triumphal procession to dissimulate a Russian defeat against Turkey. But now, having bribed himself free at Pruth, Peter himself, to cover his shame, simulated a victory by entering Moscow in unashamed triumph.

IV. PETER PAN

IT is always easier to give orders, make plans, than to carry them out. Hence art, in which you do both, is the most difficult of all tasks. Potemkin, an abler man than Peter, had accomplished more with less ado; even though a famous Austrian commander and ally had bitterly condemned his economy in men as "a mistaken regard for human life." Peter, fortified with strong drink, felt equal to anything. The difference between a dictator and your ordinary drunk, who also feels equal to anything, is that the drunk-in-the-street either undertakes nothing till reduced to the shrunken outlook of sobriety, or, if he does, the result of his undertaking shrinks hand in hand with the clarified view of the morrow. But a drunken autocrat bawls out his orders there and then; and he is obeyed.

"Turkey," said Mussolini, "is governed by three drunkards."

This came to the ears of Kemal Atatürk, who called the Italian Ambassador and said: 'Tell Mussolini that he is mistaken. Turkey is governed by *one* drunkard."

So was Russia. It is difficult for me to extract any poetry, to savor any "emotion recollected in tranquillity" from Peter. To Peter himself his life, no doubt, was that of a man much tried and often irritated, who occasionally lost his temper, but meant well. He had the short nose of one habituated to popping up close to the actualities of life. Half his cruelty sprang from the natural irritation of anyone who tries to accomplish anything in the teeth of the obtuse malevolence of mediocrity. Irritation, yes, coupled with the opportunity only permitted to an autocrat, of giving instant bodily expression to righteous anger. Among his engaging qualities must have been his enthusiasm, his spontaneous gratitude when his subordinates fulfilled his expectations.

Russian as well as Western novelists and historians have again and again tried to engage the general reader's attention with the life and character of Peter the Great. In vain! They have been at pains to point out that he, while Tsar of Russia, worked in Saardam as a common ship's carpenter in the endeavor to master the shipbuilding trade; that he transformed Russia in a few years from a medieval State into a modern power; that he "hacked a window through to Europe."

Not a bit of use. The general verdict is: not interested. Writers in search of a Russian theme worthy of Hollywood have again and again presented Peter as a great subject for the screen. He may be great and greater than his self-imposed appellation, "the Great"; but he won't go over. Pushkin, the first among Russia's poets, tried his hand, at the prompting of his emperor, Nicholas I, who recommended the subject to him as eminently worthy of his pen. But even Pushkin's narrative lacks charm.

That was the trouble with Peter. He was impetuous, cruel, revengeful, terrible; he was quite simple and unaffected. But he lacks all charm, because he lacks the elements of humanity. He was the real Peter Pan who never grew up: but the Peter Pan who tears off the wings of flies from an impish, subhuman, mechanical curiosity lacking any trace of imaginative sympathy. As a child he played with toy soldiers and toy guns. He sailed little ships across the lakes near Moscow to where, as a small boy, he had been exiled with his mother. As an adolescent, as an adult, too, he really did nothing more than play with life-size soldiers, full-size vessels, deadly cannon. He merely played his childlike games on a big scale. Instead of the wings of insects, he tore off human limbs. Instead of the box buzzing with pinned flies, the torture chamber.

Goethe speaks somewhere of the indefensible position of Petersburg, which Peter the Great chose in the teeth of the advice of an old Finnish seaman who warned him that the population of Petersburg would drown every seventy years from the overflow of the Neva. Even an old tree was found which bore unmistakable traces of the flood, and Peter the Great was earnestly advised to move the capital, which had not yet been built, a short way inland where the ground was much higher. Peter destroyed the tree which might have borne witness against him. The reason for his obstinacy, says Goethe, is that we love nothing so much as the realization of our youthful dreams. As a young man Peter was so taken with Amsterdam, where he went to acquaint himself with the rudiments of shipbuilding, that he was determined to build a New Amsterdam on the banks of the Neva. Moving the capital up the stream did not suit his imagination, though it would have been quite practicable to do so and leave only the harbor at the mouth of the river. But he was merely doing what so many men who are determined to found their "New Amsterdam" in remote colonies, find themselves doing: trying to realize the promise of an early happiness.

V. PETER'S MORALS AND MANNERS

IN the summer of 1717, that is to say at a time when Peter had rubbed shoulders with reasonably civilized people for two decades, a resident of Spa relates how he often ran across the Tsar, who came there regularly to cure his syphilis by a process of sweating. On one occasion this resident regaled the Russian sovereign with cherries and figs from his own garden, and the Tsar there and then swallowed twelve pounds of figs and six pounds of cherries, though he had just drunk his usual twenty-one glasses of water.

By way of returning hospitality, Peter asked him to dinner.

The table was only big enough for eight, but they managed to squeeze in twelve people. The Tsar, in nightcap and without his neck-cloth, sat at the head. Two soldiers of the Russian garrison each brought in an enormous tureen which, however, only held at the very bottom six wretched bowls of soup. Each man then took a bowl and placed it in front of his plate. Because of their number they all sat so far away from the table that every spoonful of soup was taken at arm's length and spilled in transit. A man brought six bottles of wine. He did not so much put them down as threw them onto the table as though they were dice. The Tsar took a bottle, and, with shaking hand, poured out each guest a glass. By now the table looked a pretty sight! From all the bowls soup was spilled on the tablecloth which, in the end, was soaked through and through with gravy and wine.

Then came the second course. A bewildered soldier carried in a dish which had been thrust into his hands as he was passing by. As he could not remove his cap, he began violently to shake his head, hoping it would fall off onto the floor. But the Tsar motioned to him to come up as he was. This second course consisted of two calves' heads and four young chickens. His Majesty lifted the biggest chicken with his fingers, rubbed it inquiringly under his nose, and, with a meaning wink signifying that it smelt good, threw it onto his guest's plate.

After the dessert the Tsar went up to a window. Here he found a pair of scissors for cutting candle wicks. They were rusty and all covered with tallow. With these he began to clean his nails, and his guest took this opportunity to retire while the going was good.

While on a visit to Berlin, Peter insisted, much to her mortification, that the Queen's own castle, Monbijou, be placed at his disposal. What Bedlam went on there no one can tell. But when he vacated it, it had practically to be built anew. He also fancied an onyx vase costing a fortune, which had to be given to him. In exchange he made a present to the King of Prussia of a company of Russian grenadiers—all giants. He exchanged his plain iron sword, which he had flourished at the battle of Poltava, for the King's gold and diamond-hilted one.

At Magdeburg he fondled the breasts of two Russian women while the head of a learned deputation from the Colleges harangued him with an address of homage. The King of Prussia had ordered that the utmost honors be lavished upon this useful and potentially powerful ally. One can imagine the non-intellectual expression on Peter's face, mingling the frankly salacious with a distant look of satisfaction as he lent an inattentive ear, and never for a moment stopping the fondling, to the academicians high-falutin' him in Latin.

If Peter shocked the courts of Europe, where he was regarded as a rich and rising upstart, they did not know how much more he shocked his own people whose meager treasuries he drained, while debasing the ancient traditions of bearded and dignified Muscovite tsars of the old school.

Like most Russians abroad, he lived on false pretenses. The Russian chest was invariably empty. At home he had to squeeze his nobles, merchants and clergy to yield enough ready money to enable him to carry on at all. He found it difficult to square this sorry fact with the expensive reputation he enjoyed abroad among the German princelings, as of a sovereign of immense, almost bottomless, wealth. If there was wealth in Russia, it was, as ever, potential and untapped, reposing deep down in the Ural Mountains.

VI. NEW RELATIVE: THE DUKE OF MECKLENBURG-SCHWERIN

TO consolidate his power in the Baltic, Peter planned to set foot on the German coast. He was looking for a plausible excuse to meddle in those provinces. Soon after his conquest of Livonia, Peter in 1712 applied to the Court of Vienna for a seat and voice on the council of the German Empire, on the grounds that he was in *de facto* possession of this once German province. For his part, he was ready to contribute 30,000 men for the war with France.

Emperor Charles VI, however, declined both the request and the offer, because the German princes were dead against Russia insinuating herself into Germany by the thin end of the wedge.

Just after Peter's failure to reach his goal, the young Duke of Mecklenburg wooed for the hand of a niece of Peter—to wit, the elder daughter of Tsar Ivan, that half-witted half-brother of his who could barely open his eyes, but had nevertheless apparently produced two daughters buxom enough for their Uncle Peter himself to desire them. For Peter only liked buxom girls. In later years he developed a taste for whipping young girls in their teens.

The idea of sealing the marriage bond with an exchange of Livonia for Mecklenburg so appealed to Peter that when the Duke referred to certain difficulties, such as, for example, that he already had a wife from whom he was not as yet divorced, Peter waived this objection as being immaterial. What did it matter? He had himself set a precedent by marrying a second wife while his first was, by his orders, languishing in a cloister. He foresaw no difficulties in this respect. The marriage contract was celebrated in February 1716, and was followed two months later by the wedding, which took place in Danzig.

The Duke was a young man of singular ideas. When he had insulted anyone, he confessed he felt better for it, having, as he put it, "eased his heart." He was in a state of chronic financial embarrassment. His motto was: "Never pay old debts; and let new debts grow old." As dowry the Duke of Mecklenburg received from Peter the town of Wismar. But as

Wismar was a recent Russian annexation in Germany and was not considered permanently tenable, the Duke was to receive, in the event of Wismar being reconquered by other contesting powers, the sum of 200,000 roubles—that is, £20,000.

On the day of the engagement an eternal alliance was concluded between Peter and his new relative. In those days they were rash to conclude "eternal alliances"—a custom revived by Hitler, who is fond of decreeing laws and arrangements "to all eternity." Peter undertook to defend the bouncing duke against his rebellious subjects and to prevent them, if need be, by force of arms, from launching complaints to the Holy Roman Emperor of the German Nation.

The situation resembled that of today brought about by Hitler's spasmodic lust for protecting minorities. "There is every reason to believe," writes the English Minister, Stanhope, to his colleague Townshend, in October 1716, "that the Duke of Mecklenburg has signed a treaty with the Tsar to give up his country to him in exchange for Livonia, and other tracts of country that way. It is certain that if the Tsar be let alone three years, he will be absolute master in those seas."

Peter duly occupied Mecklenburg with his troops among a chorus of protestations from sundry sovereigns of Europe, the loudest protest coming from George I of England. It was here, at Schwerin, the capital of Mecklenburg, that Peter seduced his niece, the Duke's consort; or at least continued to do so, the first seduction having taken place at Magdeburg. Ivan's eldest daughter, Catherine, now Duchess of Mecklenburg, escorted by her husband, the Duke, had hurried from Schwerin for the purpose of accompanying the Tsar on his visit to Berlin. When Peter saw his niece, he ran towards her, kissed her tenderly and took her into the nearest room where, having pushed her onto a sofa, and without troubling to close the door, and without the slightest regard for those of his suite who lingered in the anteroom, or even his niece's husband, who could not fail to see what was afoot, the Tsar there and then gave unashamed expression to his natural predilection for Ivan's buxom daughter. What of the Duke? Knowing his character, we must assume that he took the rough with the smooth. With his lust for power, territory and money, the Duke proved accommodating in a matter in which, to borrow the language of politics, no vital interests were involved.

Peter was satisfied. If he had raped the Duchess of Mecklenburg, it should be mentioned that he likewise ravished the Duchy of Mecklenburg with his soldiery. The Russian troops were accustomed to treat their own civilian population as enemies; and now they fell upon the Mecklen-burgers as to the manner born. Cries of indignation went up from every corner in Europe; but, again like Hitler, Peter was not slow in repartee.

In Wismar the Petersburg-Schwerin axis found no favor with the local population, who endured the vicissitudes of an unending campaign for the reconquest of their town. They were for peace at any price. Peter and the Duke alone were for prosecuting the campaign with unflagging en-thusiasm. Sometimes they drove out the Allies, and sometimes the Allies drove them out, or drove out each other. When chased out of his terri-tories, the Duke would turn up in Petersburg in the manner of one regarding it as his natural home, sniveling and nosing around for the imperial crown, for which, as the husband of the Tsar's niece, and in view of the receding prospects in Wismar, and even in Mecklenburg and Livonia, he considered himself peculiarly suitable.

In due course the Duke of Mecklenburg-Schwerin was driven out of Wismar, which, he never failed to stress, he had received as his wife's dowry; and he was not slow to call for the 200,000 roubles stipulated in the wedding contract. Peter was extremely unwilling to part with gold pieces and instead suggested having another go at Wismar. In vain! Approached once more for the 200,000 roubles, Peter promised the Duke of Mecklenburg an allowance instead. This he kept up for a time, but soon fell behind and remained chronically in arrears.

CHAPTER XIII

VIOLENT MEN LEAVE NO HEIRS

I. HUSBAND AND WIFE

PETER'S first wife, Eudoxia [Lapukhina], whom in 1698 he consigned to a convent, bore him two sons: Aleksei, born in 1690, and Alexander, who died a year after his birth in 1692. The father's dislike of their mother made him neglect the education of his legitimate heir, who, till he was thirteen, was left in the hands of women and priests. When, at the age of thirteen, Peter provided his son with a foreign tutor, the young prince quickly developed his natural gifts. He showed good judgment, a mild character, ability and humanity, and a commendable zeal for knowledge.

On the other hand, he revealed little taste for his father's tyranny and bestiality, and still less for that which his father treasured most of all, the business of war. Peter, forgetting that his own interest in military and nautical matters was the fruit of his early games of childhood, deplored this defect in his son, brought up in the midst of nuns and priests. He proceeded, as he thought, to inculcate the military spirit in his son and heir by conscripting him into the Army as a humble private: "make him start at the bottom"—the favorite device of domineering fathers who fancy their own achievement. Europe called Aleksei "the illustrious ranker."

It is doubtful whether Peter would have developed such distaste for his legitimate heir had it not been for the "stepmother" with which Aleksei found himself provided in the guise of the future Catherine I, who was born in Garmunnared in Westergothland in 1682 as the daughter of a Swedish regimental quartermaster, Johann Rabe. I have earlier stated that Catherine I was the daughter of a Lithuanian peasant, by name Skavronski. This we have on the authority of Catherine II, who must have got her facts reasonably right. The new details are accounted for in a contribution from the Swedish scholar Rosenhane to a learned work published in Berlin in 1791 in two formidable tomes entitled *Materials Towards A History And Statistics Of The Northern States* by Gadebusch, and are confirmed, if it please you, by another scholar, Oldekop. According to his version, the child, later to become Catherine I, had been handed over to an orphanage in Riga by her needy mother. From there she found her way into the house of a Pastor Glück at Marienburg, in Livonia, where she was employed as a nursemaid and chambermaid and was about to be married to a Swedish corporal in the Royal Bodyguard Cavalry, in 1701, when the news of a Russian invasion of the province caused her bridegroom to slip from the marriage feast into the saddle, never to be seen by her again.

When Marienburg was captured by the Muscovites in September 1702, Catherine, among other inhabitants of the little town, was taken prisoner and just as she was about to be raped by a Russian soldier, was earmarked by Field Marshal Sheremetev and reserved for his personal delectation. But a few months later she was taken away from him by Menshikov, the ex-pieman, who had been promoted by Peter to the rank of general and later Prince of the Russian Empire. Menshikov lived with her only a short time as he found no better means of ingratiating himself with the Tsar than by offering to surrender his pretty mistress who, even more than by her beauty, appealed to men by reason of her uncanny facility for adapting herself to their moods.

Peter and Catherine lived in a little house where the Summer Garden now stands, and she washed his shirts for him. Like D. H. Lawrence, he "had to feel he had a woman at the back of him." He suffered from the most terrifying nightmares. His dreams were troubled by malevolent spirits—probably of the people he had tortured to death, without giving them a thought, and who now impinged themselves on his attention in a sphere in which their relationship was no longer that of subject and autocrat. He was afraid to close his eyes without Catherine "at the back of him"; and when, a quarter of a century later, death came upon him, he died raving and screaming.

On the other side of the Neva, Peter built with his own hands a little one-storied wooden house—the sort of thing you might see at the Ideal Home Exhibition. Today this work of the tsar-carpenter is preserved within protective outer walls of brick and is open to public inspection.

Catherine advanced rapidly, to become the prima donna of Peter's mistresses, chiefly because she was clever enough to ignore all the others and provide the Tsar with new women when he tired of the old; which he did soon and often, for Peter was indefatigably promiscuous. Her continued and ever-growing influence with him was rooted in this easy spirit of accommodation—being a true helpmate to him, as he conceived it. His new luck, which seemed to date from the time he met her, bound him even more closely to Catherine. But chiefly he owed to her his escape from the desperate position in which he found himself at Pruth; and he rewarded her by making her his wife.

When Peter, despite the lesson he might have learned from Charles XII's encirclement at Poltava in 1709, let himself be lured into the interior of what was then Turkey, he awoke to find himself, with his army, entirely surrounded by the Turks. Having given up all hope of escape, resigning himself to an ignominious defeat, to an end of all his ambitions and to rotting away his life in a Turkish prison, Peter listened dourly to Catherine's suggestion. This was to bribe the Turkish vizier with the offer of all her jewels. Oddly enough, this worked: Peter and his army were allowed to escape by a simulated Turkish maneuver which left open a gap for the Russians to pass through. Charles XII, now marooned in Turkey, gnashed his teeth when he heard of it. He had almost had his revenge. That they should let the Tsar escape when he, Charles, was within striking distance! He cursed the Turks, and they began to hint that he was an international nuisance and that they would be glad to see the back of him; while he swore he would not return to Sweden without first regaining glory.

Peter's thankfulness for his delivery took the form of regularizing his relations with Catherine by making her his wife and consort. Secretly, Peter had married her on May 29, 1711, shortly before his fatal Turkish campaign. But he married her officially on March 2, 1712, crowning her with his own hands as his Empress. The awkward circumstance that Peter's first wife, Eudoxia, was still alive and could not, according to the tenets of the Russian Church, be divorced, had long prevented Peter from taking the plunge. Now he apparently possessed two wives. Orthodox Tsarist historians (Voltaire among them, who was commissioned on lucrative terms by the Empress Elizabeth to write her dad's *Life*) declare with an eagerness that does not seem natural that Peter privately married Catherine as far back as 1706 or 1707. Their object, a loyal one, is to plead that the two surviving children of Catherine—Anna, (mother of Karl Peter Ulrich, later Peter III) and the Empress Elizabeth—were not, so considered, bastards.

When Peter placed the imperial crown upon Catherine's head, she went down on her knees and wept with emotion. It was too much, altogether *too* much; it was infinitely more than she could have dreamed.

But human beings soon take their elevation for granted, interpreting good luck as an outward and visible sign of an inward invisible merit. The pride of the Swedish quartermaster's daughter (or, as others say, the daughter of the Lithuanian peasant and serf) was not satisfied with a diadem. She was determined that her own progeny should presently succeed her husband. The Russian people, and especially the foreigners, were still conscious of a social difference between the Tsar and his wife. A Dutch seamen toasted them thus: "Long live His Majesty My Lord Emperor Peter, and ... her Excellency the Empress!" The Empress was clever enough to ignore the slight. As the fertility of her liaison with Peter gave hope that the Empress would finally produce a son and heir, all her energies were bent on frustrating the rightful claims of the timorous youth Aleksei, Peter's first-born by Eudoxia. She strove to widen the gulf between the Tsar and his legitimate heir and successor. As a son was at last born to them in November 1715, Aleksei began to fear the prophecy of those who warned him that as soon as Peter's Swedish wife bore him a son, Aleksei would have to follow his mother to a monastery.

II. FATHER AND SON

AMONG our major blessings may be reckoned that none of us has been born the son of Peter the Great. To look on while a man, in adult years, gives substance to the games of his childhood, and not to be able oneself to share his enthusiasms and be thought an imbecile and a traitor to "the cause," is a bitter fate indeed.

Three months after a son had been born to Catherine, the Tsar "invited" Aleksei to renounce the succession and retire to a monastery, unless he changed radically—that is to say ceased to be Aleksei and became Peter the Great. He was, Peter wrote, most dissatisfied with Aleksei's lack of interest in military matters and was convinced of his inability to rule over Russia.

Aleksei, who knew only too well what his fate would be if he dared for a moment resist his father's invitation, immediately complied with it. With an almost joyous alacrity he renounced his right to the succession, blamed his weak health, declared himself prepared to be a monk, and placed his entire fate at the disposal of his father.

The Tsar was not satisfied with his son's answer and reproached him for making no effort to turn a new leaf.

"You place," he wrote, "at the disposal of my will what was always there." And he showered reproaches upon his unworthy son. "Look at me," he said in effect. "And look at you." Aleksei's ill-disguised relief at the prospect of being let alone by his terrifying father did not please Peter, who wanted him to remain at his beck and call. It irritated him particularly that Aleksei should take no *natural* interest in "war pursuits." Forgetting that he had himself fled, howling with panic, even before the battle of Narva had begun, Peter extolled war as the proper occupation of a man who *was* a *man*. Kipling could not have done it better.

Aleksei, as a child, had played neither with tin nor with live soldiers; nor had he floated large or small sailings boats, and had therefore no natural wish to realize the childish dreams of his father, who had not bothered to provide him with games but had left his son's upbringing to the nuns and every kind of sanctimonious rabble who gathered around the boy's mother, Eudoxia. Peter was no psychologist and did not himself understand the source and origins of his enthusiasms, which is perhaps not surprising. He had not the advantage of reading Dr. Freud.

The Tsarevitch Aleksei pleaded illness, which he thought the most natural and least offensive excuse for not coming up to his father's expectations. Aleksei drank, but not vigorously, like Peter. He could not carry the volume of alcohol his father put away with impunity; a little with Aleksei went a long way. This in itself was, he thought, a weakness, frail health: an excuse which does not carry much weight with ruthless fathers who enjoy robust health.

"The late Tsar," Peter wrote, "enjoyed even worse health than you, yet he took an interest in horses," perhaps referring to Tsar Feodor, because Tsar Ivan was too far gone in idiocy even for that.

If Peter had had for a son, let us say, a chap like Benito Mussolini, who pilots his own bomber, how they would have romped together, how they would have trained their cannon together on moving targets! But Aleksei was more nearly a Count Covadonga; a type of youth who would not of his own accord select a Peter the Great for a parent.

III. THE TRAP

THE Tsar wrote that he had the right to sacrifice even the life of his son if he thought this might benefit the Fatherland, since, he added, he had often enough risked his own life. When he read this, Aleksei began to doubt whether even meekness was the safest attitude to take with a father to whom his son's very existence seemed irksome. Peter and Catherine both knew that even retirement to a monastery was no guarantee that, on Peter's death, the Muscovites who loved the Tsarevitch Aleksei and disliked the foreign adventuress and her offspring, would not send for him, place him on the throne of his fathers and reverse Peter's life-work. It was clear that so long as Aleksei was alive Catherine had little chance of insuring her child's succession.

Peter's "invitation" from Copenhagen for Aleksei to visit him there made the young man very anxious. He was advised that the Tsar was setting a trap for him and would get him discreetly murdered on his journey abroad—a more convenient arrangement than was possible at home, where such a deed would arouse some suspicion and might be traced back to its source.

Aleksei, now really frightened, decided on flight. Instead of traveling as required by his father to Copenhagen, he betook himself in December 1716 to Vienna. The Emperor Charles VI was married to a sister of his wife, and Aleksei thought he could surely count on his brother-in-law protecting him from his terrible father who, he was certain, was intent on destroying him.

It does not seem an altogether unreasonable assumption. The Holy Roman Emperor of the German Nation was a little put out by the request. He decided that it was best to keep Aleksei's whereabouts secret, to deny all knowledge of the Tsarevitch's presence in his realm. He accordingly sent him to the lonely Castle Ehrenberg in Tyrol.

The Tsar was not long in discovering whither his son had fled for protection and reproached Charles VI in a bitter letter in which he complained that the Emperor was depriving him of his parental right to exercise control over his own son, and was, moreover, holding him up to ridicule before all Europe. Though the Holy Roman Emperor was by no means famous for his courage, and the Tsar's veiled threats made him nervous, he yet refused to deliver his docile brother-in-law to an angry father. For greater safety Aleksei was transferred from Tyrol to the Castel San Elmo in Naples, which was then within the Holy Roman Empire.

Peter's spies discovered the whereabouts of the imperial fugitive, and the Russian Ambassador at Vienna, the wily Count Tolstoy, together with Count Rumiantsev, traveled to Naples, obtained admission and persuaded the nervous Tsarevitch to return with them to Russia. This they managed by producing a letter from Peter in which he promised before God and the Last Judgment to his son, if he returned, complete immunity from punishment. Aleksei was won over by his father's envoys, who had bribed the people around him, including the girl Afronsinia with whom he had eloped. There was no lack of persuasion in the one direction—return. What really decided Aleksei was the Viceroy of Naples representing to him that the Emperor Charles did not think it fair that he should be exposed to a war with Russia on the Tsarevitch's account. The prodigal son proceeded meekly with Tolstoy and Rumiantsev back to Russia.

IV. ALEKSEI'S TRIAL AND TORTURE

NO sooner did he arrive in Moscow, on February 11, 1718, than Peter, in the teeth of his solemn oath, instituted proceedings against him for high treason. This action was taken at the instigation of Catherine, who was determined to insure the succession for her own son. Several historians agree that Catherine, coveting the crown for herself and her children, plotted with Tolstoy, who was the chairman of the inquisition which had set out to convict Aleksei of high treason. The case rested on his desertion abroad and his wishes, expressed openly or entertained dumbly, for the early demise of his father. Accomplices were discovered and compelled through prolonged torture to confess their own guilt.

Even Aleksei's mother, Eudoxia, was dragged out of her convent. A plot was discovered, which revealed little more than that she had, since Peter had shut her up, possessed a lover. The man was impaled in the open. It was freezingly cold. To prolong his life he was wrapped in furs. Even then he expressed his utmost contempt for the Tsar, who stood gloating before him. He spat into Peter's face.

Peter flogged his ex-wife Eudoxia himself. For long months terror stalked throughout the land. All who had ever wished well for Aleksei were put to the torture. And there were many who had.

A certain monk approached Peter in the street. From motives of sincerity, he said, he felt it incumbent on himself to inform the Tsar that he often wished for his death and for the Tsarevitch Aleksei to succeed him. Peter had the man seized, tortured three times, and killed. That it should not have occurred to the monk, who must have known he had foresworn his life in advance, to kill Peter first, may perhaps be explained by his devotion to Christian principles of self-effacement. Russians have never killed their worst tyrants, only the nicer men. They assassinated the kindest tsar of all—Alexander II.

The conviction of Aleksei was obtained through false evidence on the part of supposed accomplices, who were compelled by unspeakable tortures to testify against him. The judges were men who called themselves the "Tsar's slaves." Aleksei's own confession was obtained by his father flogging him on and on in his cell till Aleksei "confessed," to put an end to the immediate torment.

V. PETER KILLS HIS SON

THE sentence was signed by the same members of the Senate who, on Peter's suggestion, later called him "Peter the Great." It was a death sentence which nobody, however, was keen to carry out.

There are several versions of the manner in which Aleksei was put to death. On July 6, 1718, on which day sentence of death was passed by the Senate, Peter entered the cell of his first-born and gave him a glass of poison. That is one version. On Aleksei declining to drink it, a certain Marshal Adam Weyde, born in Moscow of German parents and a favorite of Peter's, is said to have chopped off the Tsarevitch's head. To hide all trace, they had removed the planks of the floor to allow the blood to soak into the earth.

Another version is that Peter himself struck off his son's head with the ax—at which business he was no novice. One of the Tsar's mistresses, a Mademoiselle Kramer, had to sew on the head to the body which, with a thick cloth wrapped round the neck, was then exposed for two days to public view to substantiate the official statement that Aleksei died as a result of a stroke when he heard the death sentence. Peter the Great posed as a super Brutus who, for the salvation of his country, had sacrificed the life of the being most dear to him in this world—to wit, his eldest son and heir.

Peter's most ardent admirers find it difficult to justify this deed. They search for extenuating circumstances, but all they seem able to find is that it is unfair to assume that the Tsar killed his son with his own hands. As there is no doubt that Aleksei was killed by the will of his father, it seems of little moment whether he was killed by his father's own hands or his orders. It is almost braver if Peter did kill Aleksei himself; not that for a brute like Peter, who took killing as being all in a day's work, the deed required much pluck.

There is still another version which says that Aleksei died under some refined form of torture inflicted either by Peter or by Menshikov in Peter's presence.

Peter's murder of his son is a blot on the Romanov escutcheon which later murders and later blots have not effaced. Exactly two hundred years since, all Peter's work was undone. The Baltic provinces and Finland, his proudest acquisitions, fell away from Russia; and the dynasty itself dissolved in blood.

VI. THE NETHERLAND RESIDENT

PETER was incensed because the diplomatists in Petersburg did not accept his version of Aleksei's death. Charles VI recalled his ambassador and broke off negotiations with the Russian Court. The ambassador left for Vienna without asking for a farewell audience.

Peter replied by expelling all Jesuits from Russia within four days, as a special insult to the Holy Roman Emperor, their protector. Previously Peter had even played with the idea of changing the religion of Russia, dropping the Greek Church and adopting Roman Catholicism, with a view to assuming eventually the position of Holy Roman Emperor after having displaced the Emperor at Vienna from his hereditary position.

Peter raided the Netherland Residence and threatened the Resident, de Bie, with torture because he had given an authentic account of Aleksei's murder, and his version was reprinted in all Dutch newspapers. The free State of Holland enjoyed in those days the freest press in Europe. The public opinion of half the world was formed at Amsterdam, as Louis XIV had discovered to his cost. The Netherland Resident, questioned by the "Secret Chancellery," the Ogpu of the day, who, in the teeth of elementary extra-territorial rights, had ransacked the Residence, now lost his nerve. Threatened with prison and torture, de Bie agreed, under duress, that he was now prepared to believe that the Prince Aleksei had met a natural death. But, he added, it was yet only too true that the common people thought otherwise.

After that he was pressed to disclose the names of such Russians as had influenced his opinion, and by generalizing—which no doubt was true— the Resident deflected the danger from individuals to the whole community. "All," he said, *"all."*

He was allowed to return to his Residence, on condition that he did not leave it till further notice and did not communicate with a soul outside.

With a sigh of relief, he stepped on an extra-territorial yard of good old Holland, only to find to his dismay that all his archives had been broken into and his papers seized. His wife, who was in the last degrees of pregnancy, was surrounded by armed grenadiers. All remonstrances failed to clear the house. Not content with this imposition, the Tsar forbade all other ambassadors at his court to communicate with their Netherland colleague. At last the Dutch Minister declared to the Tsar's face that he was answerable for his actions to no one except the Republic which had sent him; and he asked his own government to recall him, as is the custom today, "for consultation."

CHAPTER XIV

THE AGGRESSOR

I. A STOCKHOLM–PETERSBURG AXIS?

FOR many years Peter had wished to see Paris. Louis XIV had declined his proposal of a visit. Though Peter was bitterly offended, he recovered and later resumed his efforts towards a closer relationship with France. However, the conclusion of a commercial treaty between the two countries was all that the Tsar succeeded in getting from Louis XIV.

Louis was also a despot, but he was a noble-minded despot who never showed himself more generous than when his brother monarchs were in low water. Louis showed his true metal when France's late ally, Sweden, suffered her greatest defeat. Himself hard-pressed, surrounded with growing troubles, invaded from all sides, Louis XIV yet remained a steadfast friend of Charles XII. As the now tattered hero of the North returned, friendless and abandoned by all, to his country, Louis XIV, in the last months of his own life (he died in April 1715) concluded with Charles XII a three-year alliance, by the terms of which he provided the down-and-out Charles with a yearly subsidy of 60,000 thalers, and paid one-half of the sum in advance.

Charles had made a brief comeback. Catherine, who did not know it was to be brief, got Peter to come to terms with him. Peter was really attached to her, even proud of her; though, by the accounts of a contemporary, a Prussian princess, Catherine was a slatternly woman, short, squat, with a waddle like a duck, her dress, which was neither smart nor clean, ridiculously bedecked with medals, ribbons and flags of patriotic colors. Yet Peter, who, if he loved anyone, loved this second wife of his, seemed oblivious of the slovenly figure she cut. His eyes when they fell on her lighted up with pride and love, as though he thought she was showing those German women how to wear the imperial skirt.

So perhaps Catherine's opinions did weigh with him. Her idea was that, in return for the restoration of bits of Finland to Sweden, Charles XII should guarantee the succession of her own children and oppose by force of arms the claims of Ivan's progeny or Aleksei's son.

To this proposition the Swedish monarch, we are told, was prepared to agree. It formed the basis of the understanding reached between the two late enemies. In May 1718, after several months of conversations on Lofö, one of the Aaland islands, an agreement was concluded. Peter I, who evidently expected to die first, declared himself ready to return to Charles XII all the Russian conquests in Finland and the greater part of Karelia. Peter pledged himself to compensate Charles for his loss of Ingermanland, Livonia and Estonia with territory in Norway, towards the conquest of which the Tsar of Russia was to assist the King of Sweden. That was not all. Both mortal enemies were now united in the passionate desire to revenge themselves on King Frederick IV of Denmark, then the owner of Norway.

At this point, conquest seemed to have gone to their heads. Both Charles and Peter hated George I of England, and agreed not only to deprive him of the duchies of Bremen and Verden, but also of the crown of Great Britain. To that end they formed an agreement with Cardinal Alberoni, also a bitter enemy of the Guelphs, with a view to the restoration of the Stuarts on the throne of Great Britain. For the realization of this old dream of the Jacobites, Peter promised to send in the following spring twelve troops ships to Drontheim and to take on 10,000 Swedes under the personal command of Charles XII and convey them to Scotland.

How earnestly this adventurous project of dethroning the House of Hanover occupied the two monarchs is illustrated by the fact that a representative of the Pretender, the Duke of Ormond, came to Russia with passports made out in Russian and Latin and signed by Peter himself, which are still extant. Ormond came under the name of Brunet in order to arrange for a marriage of the Pretender with a niece of the Tsar, a daughter of the idiot Tsar Ivan—probably Anna, later Duchess of Courland, and still later Empress of Russia.

That was not all. Peter the Great undertook to transfer the Polish crown from the head of Frederick Augustus of Saxony to that of Stanislaus Lesczinski, because Peter had long sickened, as he had sickened of all his other early allies, of Frederick Augustus of the House of Wettin, with whom once upon a time he had competed in twisting silver spoons and gold plate during meals. He was, moreover, prepared to oblige Charles XII, who still hated Frederick Augustus.

It was probably at this meeting that Peter and Charles had a bet as to who was the braver soldier: Russian or Swede. Peter proposed that each sovereign should order one of his soldiers to jump off a four-story building. When Charles XII told a Swedish soldier to jump out of the window, the Swede said, why yes, of course he would, if his sovereign really meant it; though, naturally enough, while having no thought of self, he could not help feeling apprehensive about his family whom he would leave behind and who would mourn his death and never get over the dreadful way it was proposed that he should die.

When Peter told a Russian soldier to jump out of the window, the Russian merely crossed himself, leaped on to the window ledge, and Peter (which was surprisingly considerate of him) just caught the man in the nick of time by the seat of his trousers and pulled him back to safety. Charles XII had to admit that the Russian was the braver man, and he lost his bet. But, as the anecdote is Russian, there may well be a Swedish version which, while conforming in the details of the bet, yet differs in the outcome.

Perhaps the most far-reaching undertaking on which the two ex-enemies had set their hearts was a joint invasion of Germany. To force Frederick William I of Prussia to return Stettin and his other Swedish conquests, in consideration for compensations in Poland or Hanover, as well as to enable the Tsar to annex Mecklenburg, for which he never ceased to lust, Charles and Peter agreed that the one should descend on Prussia with 24,000 Swedes and 38,000 Bavarians, Hessians, and other German hirelings, while the other simultaneously attacked Brandenburg with 80,000 Russians; and then by way of Brandenburg attacked the rest of Germany. While the two monarchs were planning this campaign, the Tsar went on protesting his warm friendship for the unsuspecting King of Prussia.

All these plans were about to be formally ratified and Charles XII had begun, according to schedule, his invasion of Norway when, on the eleventh of December, 1718, this northern Richard Cœur de Lion ended his life at the hands of an assassin.

II. KILLED BY LIGHTNING

THE sudden end of the royal adventurer brought about a complete reversal of Swedish policy. It also changed Peter's own policy towards Sweden. From being an ally, he again became an enemy. A stroke of lightning killed his one remaining son, the child of Catherine, and the need of guaranteeing the succession for Catherine's son was, since she no longer possessed one, obviated.

The boy, barely a year after the murder of Aleksei, was struck by lightning. This happened in the presence of Field Marshal Bruce, who was charged to look after him while the Tsar and Catherine were away at Kronschloss. While the boy was in his room, in the arms of his nurse, the lightning struck him. All his limbs were smashed and paralyzed so that he died a few days afterwards. On the other hand, neither the nurse who held him in her arms nor other people present were touched. Peter and Catherine came back to Petersburg, terrified with what they regarded as the avenging hand of heaven. They commanded, on pain of death, that nothing be divulged to the outside world. A courtier, Baron Shafirov, to ingratiate himself with the Tsar, assumed that the nurse had willfully and maliciously injured the child and began to beat her and threaten her with torture; till the Tsar himself pulled him aside and told him what had happened. Whereupon Shafirov went on abusing the nurse, as though to suggest to the Tsar that this might be the best public interpretation to place on the event.

Peter was now left with only daughters and nieces to succeed him. Russia did not know female sovereigns. Sophia, Peter's own half-sister, had been an exception—of evil memory. Peter grew desperate. He even tried to ignite the spark of life in the womb of a Moldavian hospodar's daughter in the hope of producing a male heir. But, alas! their pious hopes terminated in a miscarriage.

III. ENCIRCLEMENT

ULRIKE ELENORE, Charles XII's sister, who followed him on the throne (which by rights should have gone to Karl Peter Ulrich's father), conscious of the exhausted state of her country, concluded in rapid succession peace with George I of England and Hanover in November 1719; with Frederick Augustus of Poland and Saxony in January 1720; with Frederick William I of Prussia in February 1720. Obviously, with great sacrifices. In those days peace appeared to be concluded by cession of territory to the victor, who partly made up for it to the defeated foe with money payments.

Everyone got something back from Sweden. But, as the territories they got back from Sweden were mostly something Sweden had previously taken from them, or someone else, and as they were also ready to compensate Sweden with ready cash, of which she was greatly in need, the treaties seemed humane when compared with the merciless infliction of wounds with bayonet and bullet directly preceding these suave diplomatic agreements.

They were all good friends again, except Russia. Ulrike Elenore was anxious to come to terms with Peter, who, now that Charles was dead, was all for annihilating Sweden. The European powers, conscious that, in coaxing Russia to combat Sweden's might, they had merely exchanged one bully for another, and a bigger one, combined in an anti-aggression front against Russia. The Emperor Charles VI of Germany, the King of England and the King of Poland formed a defensive alliance in January 1719; which was the forerunner of bilateral and unilateral agreements, pacts, understandings and, finally, a mighty series of alliances among all the principal countries of the earth against the rising menace of Russia.

Peter, incensed by Sweden's tentative leanings towards this new policy of encirclement, attacked Sweden and laid waste her land. Sweden could find no friend to assist her, with the exception of England, who, however, could not help her much. Ulrike Elenore saw herself compelled to pay the enormous price which the Tsar demanded as payment on account of his aspirations. The provinces of Livonia, Estonia, Ingermanland, a part of Karelia and some other less important territories went to Russia, in return for which Peter gave back Finland and some of his other conquests to Sweden.

He also paid her two million thalers. The payment took place because the Tsar was anxious to secure a legal right to the retention of Livonia; since, according to an agreement entered into with Frederick Augustus of Poland at the outset of their joint campaign against Sweden, Peter had contracted himself in the event of annexing Livonia to cede it to Poland. For that reason, and no other, Peter *bought* Livonia from Sweden, who was desperately short of gold. The Swedes were so short of money that they even sold their cannons to the Tsar as scrap iron.

This was the famous Peace of Nystadt, of November 1721, by which Peter gained two of the three Baltic provinces which had once belonged to the Order of Teutonic Knights, had changed hands between Russia, Poland and Sweden, and at the present time enjoy a precarious independence.

CHAPTER XV

PETER'S DEATH AND
POLITICAL TESTAMENT

I. GLORIA MUNDI

IN 1722 the Senate proclaimed the man who had created a hundred thousand orphans, "Father of the Fatherland." He was also promoted in rank. The Senators humbly beseeched the Tsar to accept the title of "Emperor of All the Russias," and to agree to be known as "Peter the Great."

Peter, who had himself launched the idea, accepted his new honors, after the briefest show of resistance. The Senate—that is, eight dotards—shouted: *"Vivat!"* and the thing was done.

The Holy Roman Emperor of the German Nation, because he was an emperor, and King George I of England, because he wasn't, objected to another emperor in Europe, and ignored the appellation. When notified, they flatly refused to recognize the Tsar's new title. Tsar he was, and Tsar he would remain!

The Duke of Mecklenburg, in receipt from Peter of an allowance sadly overdue, and the Duke of Holstein-Gottorp, who had expectations, readily recognized him as Emperor; and so did his uneasy ally, the King of Denmark, and likewise the dethroned Frederick Augustus, hoping for his luck to turn.

The powers ignored his presumption. But as each successive sovereign of Russia continued to call himself Emperor, England and Germany in weary politeness succumbed. All the other countries finally had no choice but to fall into line. Russia had become a great power, whose armies were victorious and whose alliance was eagerly sought. There was no point in ruffling the susceptibilities of monarchs, especially when they were women. For its own part, Europe regretted that so distinctive a title as Tsar should be exchanged for the more banal term of Emperor. But in fact the Russian monarch was *both*: Emperor to underline that Russia was an empire; Tsar when sounding the native note.

It is sometimes assumed that *tsar* (*czar*) is a contraction of *caesar*. But Karamzin, the Russian Macaulay, points out that *czar* is Persian in origin, and is found in the last syllable of many Assyrian and Babylonian names of kings, such as Nabochodnoczar, etc., signifiying the conception of the highest power, the throne. The word, an ancient oriental expression, passed into Russian through the translation of the Bible into Church Slavonic, and was applied currently in reference to Byzantine emperors and foreign kings. There was a Tsar of ancient Bulgaria before there was one in Russia. Until the time of Ivan the Terrible, the Russian rulers styled themselves Great Princes—that is, princes ruling over several domains; and foreign potentates addressed them in official documents as *magnus dux,* or *magnus princeps.* Ivan III, who declined to accept the title of King from the alien hands of the Holy Roman Emperor of Germany, sought to raise himself in his own eyes by calling himself Hospodar —which passed into *gosudar,* a form of "high-and-mighty lord," or monsignor. Ivan the Terrible assumed the title of Tsar; and Peter the Great elevated himself to the rank of Emperor; the result being that the Russian monarchs retained all the three titles, each suited to the requisite occasion and diffusing a subtle flavor of its own.

Since Peter's time, the monarch was usually spoken of as *gosudar,* in the sense of—the sovereign. "Tsar" was used sparingly, and "Emperor" (*imperator*) was how the officers liked best to refer to him. Thus, while for a native of Russia it was natural, when touching on intimate associations or stressing ancient traditions, to speak of his sovereign as the Tsar, the ready foreign use of "tsar" carried the suspicion that the user either fancied himself as a linguist or denied the Russian sovereign his full status. Queen Victoria, well-primed by her Russian relatives on the idiomatic subtleties involved, objected to the appellation "tsar," and positively winced at "czar" and reproved ministers and courtiers by presuming icily that they were probably referring to the Emperor of Russia.

The inevitably inaccurate translation into "Emperor of All the Russias" makes it sound a more resplendent title than in the original Russian, which is more in the sense of "All-England Lawn-Tennis Association." In the original, the compound "All-Russia" is rendered as an adjective following the noun "Self-Upholder." Self-upholder literally means autocrat, but sounds somewhat less aggressive. The words *crat* (power), *dominus,* are the exact equivalents of *derzhava,* except that the Russian word derives from the root "hold"—in the sense of a holding company. It is suggestive of the monarch holding the orb in his hand. It also sounds faintly ridiculous, as though he was determined, in the face of all opposition, to hold this heavy orb, personifying Russia, while everybody else was trying hard to knock it out of his hand.

To terminate this little disquisition on the titles of the Russian mon-

archs, the last of the tsars announced himself at the time of his coronation in the Ouspenski Cathedral:

"We, Nikolai II Aleksandrovitch, by the Will of God, Sovereign, Em-
peror and Self-Upholder of All the Russias, Tsar of Poland, Tsar of
Kazan, Tsar of Astrakhan, Tsar of Siberia, Tsar of Georgia, Grand
Duke of Finland and Lithuania, of Rostov and of Podolsk, Lord of Great
Russia, Little Russia, and White Russia, and Autocrat and Ruler of many
other lands...."

II. DISSOLUTION

HOWEVER that may be, the first Russian emperor enjoyed his new
dignity for little more than two years. On January 16, 1725, he caught
a bad cold; and suddenly he was laid low. Syphilis and drink had aggravated his other complaints. All his ailments, which his iron constitution had hitherto held at bay, now attacked him at once. His bladder
was badly affected; he could not pass water and he yelled aloud from a
cutting pain.

He was also frightened as he felt the approach of the death pangs; and
a religious zeal assailed the dying despot. He ordered a field chapel to
be set up near his bedroom, with two shifts of priests to pray night and
day for his recovery. His condition grew worse. He made his confession and took holy communion. All the doctors in Petersburg gathered
around his bed. They were silent; they saw the hopeless condition he
was in and could do nothing to help him. He was frightened to fall
asleep, and when in sheer weariness he closed his eyes, he awoke screaming horribly; and it may be that the spirits of his victims were gloating
at his passing, waiting for him. We do not know these things....

Six days dragged by. He had no strength to shout and only moaned.
Four dignitaries held watch outside his room. On the twenty-fifth the
whole Senate and Synod, Ministers of State, the high command, staff
officers, and the higher clergy assembled in force at the palace. Crowds
gathered outside. All churches were thrown open for prayer for the
departing emperor.

Catherine now wept, now sighed, now fell into a faint. She would
not leave his bedside. She would not go to bed unless he ordered her.
She was, had lately been, under a cloud. His dying, considered from this
angle, was opportune. Peter, in his recent "purge," had alighted on a
disagreeable discovery: his wife had a lover. He was one Wilhelm Mons,
brother of that genteel Anna Mons whom in the old Moscow days when

he frequented the German Quarter, Peter had made his mistress. "Annchen" had never really loved him, and Peter had discovered from her letter, found on the dead body of the Saxon Envoy, that she had been unfaithful to him, with this very envoy of Frederick Augustus of Poland and Saxony whom he had constantly met in her house. Peter had done nothing to her, beyond ceasing to see her. But he had taken it out of her brother, who paid for all the four. Wilhelm Mons was lingeringly tortured; and, to make a lasting impression on Catherine, Peter had put her lover's severed head in spirit, placing the glass container on his consort's window sill, so that she might behold him both on waking and retiring. Grim jests were Peter's specialty. When his first wife had presumed to petition him on behalf of certain people implicated in a rebellion, Peter had them hanged outside her window, their necks twisted round, heads grinning at her, her petitions stuck between their teeth. There they hung for weeks and months, swaying in the wind.

And now he who had killed and tortured so freely and heedlessly, was himself dying in agony. Lately he had been very strange, brooding somberly, considering his Catherine for long at a time, with a dark, gleeful leer, as though meditating on the fate he was preparing for her. Was she glad the danger was receding, passing with his ebbing strength? Was she sad? Who knows? Perhaps her lamentations were sincere. He had loved her and, despite his discovery, loved her still.

And she? A woman may love a brute who treats her differently, ascribing his brutality to State considerations, some implacable iron necessity inseparable from the hard core in man which women so readily and foolishly accept: yes, and are proud that their baby boy has killed in this or that war so many Frenchmen, oh! such a lot of Germans! Woman has never helped man, except on his natural way to perdition, and will never help him till he learns to help himself.

Though he had pondered deeply on what he might eventually do to her, Peter did not repulse his erring wife from his deathbed; now, if ever, he needed "a woman at the back of him." He would not let his daughters, Anna and Elizabeth, come to him. On the twenty-sixth, Peter decreed that convicts (other than political prisoners and murderers, whom he classed together as beyond the pale) should be set free to pray for the recovery of their sovereign.

The same day, in a moment of relief, he issued a ukase concerning fish and glue, which were monopolies, threatening the most barbarous punishment in case of any failure to comply. Towards evening he felt worse and received extreme unction.

On the twenty-seventh he issued a free pardon to the nobles who had not attended the military rally. "Persons," it runs, "condemned to death for failing to attend, in accordance with the Clause relating to the War Ministry, to be pardoned (with exceptions) that they may pray for the recovery of their sovereign."

Peter then called for pen and paper and scribbled a few illegible words, of which one could decipher only: "give back everything to ..." The quill fell from his hands. He asked that his eldest daughter, the Tsarevna Anna (later the mother of Karl Peter Ulrich) be called to him, so that he might dictate to her. She came in; but he could no longer speak.

Peter did not resume the attempt to nominate a successor. Some two years previously, he had issued a manifesto abolishing the principle of legitimacy and abandoning the throne to hazard. Perhaps, as he strove to gather his sinking wits, a feeling of impotence overcame him when he realized how he had messed up the succession. "Give it all back to ..." suggests poor Aleksei's son; or it may be Ivan's progeny.

The Bishops of Pskov and Tver and the Archimandrite of Tchudov Monastery began to administer the propitiation. Peter revived, made a sign that he be raised and, turning his eyes to heaven, repeated some of the words in a parched, almost inaudible voice.

The administering priest began to speak to him of the infinite mercy of God. Peter repeated several times: "I believe and trust."

The priest, standing over him, recited a prayer. Peter repeated: "I believe, O Lord: help my unbelief"; and was silent.

The people present began to take their leave of him. He greeted them all with a dull look; than said, with an effort: "Later ..." All went out, obeying his will for the last time.

He did not speak again. For fifteen hours he was in agony. He moaned, incessantly pulling with his right hand—the left was already paralyzed. The priest administering absolution did not leave his side. Peter listened to him hopefully and several times tried to cross himself, but could not.

The Archimandrite proposed that he confess again. In acquiescence, Peter slightly raised his hand, and once more received absolution. Till four in the morning he was conscious. Then he began to grow cold and showed little sign of life. The Bishop of Tver continued to speak into his ear, administering the propitiation and reciting prayers for the dying. Peter ceased to moan, stopped breathing. At 6 A.M. on January 28, 1725,

Peter the First, called the Great, died in the arms of his second wife, Catherine.

Menshikov, who had first obtained her from the hands of Sheremetev and passed her on to Peter, now assumed charge of the situation. He took care not to let power slip out of his hands. He had bribed, primed and posted the guards at strategic points round the palace and at the fortress. No sooner had Peter expelled his last breath than Menshikov proclaimed the new Empress and Self-Upholder, Catherine the First.

III. PETER'S "MEIN KAMPF"

PETER the Great left a testament, which opens:

"Summary of the plan for the aggrandizement of Russia and of the subjugation of Europe as sketched by Peter I."

The document makes pretty reading:

(*1*) *Neglect nothing that might give the Russian nation European forms and usages. With this in view, attract the various courts and especially the scholars of Europe, by appealing either to their greed, or their idealism, or any other motive likely to serve the same end.*

(*2*) *Keep the Empire in a perpetual state of war in order to make the soldier war-conscious, and hold the nation always on tiptoe, ready to march at the first signal.*

(*3*) *Expand by every possible means towards the north, along the Baltic, and towards the south.*

(*4*) *Excite the jealousy of England, Denmark and Brandenburg against Sweden, so that the first three powers should close their eyes to the usurpations that we might effect in that country, which we will end by subjugating.*

(*5*) *Interest the house of Austria in the idea of chasing the Turk out of Europe; under that pretext keep a permanent army and build ship-yards on the Black Sea coast, and by advancing continually, expand towards Constantinople.*

(*6*) *Sustain anarchy in Poland: influence the Diets and above all the elections of her kings; decimate her on every possible occasion and end in subjugating her altogether.*

(*7*) *Contract a close alliance with England; entertain with her direct relations by a commercial treaty; even allow her to exercise some kind of monopoly in the interior. This will unnoticeably bring about a useful* contact between our own nationals and the English merchants and sailors, which will of itself provide all the means for improving and enlarging the Russian Navy, with the aid of which one must at once envisage the domination of the Baltic and the Black Sea. This is the crucial point on which the speedy success of the plan depends.

(8) *Intervene at all costs, whether by force or by ruse, in the quarrels of Europe—especially those of Germany.*

(9) *Appear always as the ally of Austria, profit from the smallest ascendancy that we might enjoy over her in order to drag her into ruinous wars, with a view to weakening her by degrees. Even help her occasionally, but never cease secretly to create enemies for her in the interior of her empire by exciting the jealousy of the other princes against her. . . .*

Note: this clause will be the easier to fulfill as the house of Austria has never ceased to delude itself with the project of establishing itself as the universal monarchy, or at least of re-establishing the Western Empire, and to that end Austria must begin with the subjugation of the rest of Germany.

(10) *Always choose among the princesses of Germany possible wives for our Russian princes, and thus, through family relations and relationships of interest, multiply our alliances and, through those, our influence everywhere in that empire.*

(11) *Avail ourselves of the advantages of religion among the Greeks divided and dispersed in Hungary, Turkey, and the North of Poland. Attach them by every ruse, call ourselves their protectors and gain the right of exercising over them a religious hegemony. Under this pretext, and by such means, with Turkey subjugated and Poland defeated, the conquest of Hungary would be child's play. Austria deflected by the promise of compensation in Germany, the rest of Poland no longer able to sustain itself either by its own strength or its political connections, would of its own accord place its head under the yoke.*

(12) *From there on every moment will be precious. In great secrecy, everything must be got ready to strike with a bang, to act with a precision, a foresight and promptitude which would not give Europe the time to collect its wits.* [Peter, like Hitler, is evidently planning a "Blitzkrieg."]

One must begin by proposing separately, very secretly, and with the greatest circumspection, first to the Court of Versailles, next to that of Vienna, the idea of sharing with them the Empire of the World. In drawing their attention to the fact that Russia, in real deed, dominates the whole of the Orient and has nothing more to gain by any formal *recognition, this new proposition on her part will not seem to them suspect. On the contrary, there is no doubt that such a project will not fail to flatter them and to ignite a suicidal war between them: a war which will soon become general on account of the extensive connections and relationships of those two courts who are natural enemies, to say nothing of the individual interests which will induce all the other countries in Europe to take part in this quarrel.*

(13) In the midst of this general carnage, Russia will demand the help, now of this, now of that, belligerent power. Having given them enough time to exhaust themselves and to enable Russia to gather her own forces, she will pretend, after a great deal of vacillation, to decide in favor of the house of Austria; and while Russia lets her line regiments advance to the Rhine, she will release on their heels a swarm of her Asiatic hordes: and as they advance into Germany, two strong fleets will set off, one from the Sea of Azov, the other from the Port of Archangel, crammed full with these same Asiatic hordes, convoyed by the armed fleets of the Black Sea and the Baltic. They will appear unexpectedly in the Mediterranean and on the ocean and pour out all these ferocious nomadic folk, avid for booty, who will flood Italy, Spain and France, where they will kill a part of the inhabitants and drag others away into slavery so as to people the deserts of thinly populated Siberia, while leaving the rest at home in a condition which will prevent them for ever from shaking off the yoke.

The document, with its "sickening technique," would seem to exhibit what Mr. Neville Chamberlain would call a desire to dominate the world by force, or the threat of force, rather than by peaceful methods of negotiation.

The authenticity of this testament of Peter the Great has been doubted, has been denied and again affirmed in turn. It is, especially in its latter conclusions, as idiotic as any dream of world conquest with which the dictators have been coquetting today. It is difficult to imagine the number of ships necessary to convey sufficient savages to flood France, Italy and Spain. Potemkin, a realist, who had been tempted with a morsel of British colonies in return for military assistance in America, said to the English Ambassador: "You will ruin us. Our ships can't even get out of the Baltic without floundering, let alone cross an ocean." It is difficult to imagine Russian shipyards being able to deliver the requisite number of vessels to schedule.

But what strikes one even more forcibly is the moral imbecility of it all. The end in view, the aim, the final result—of populating the icy plains of Siberia with Neapolitans and Andalusians—seems oddly pathetic after the strenuous and sustained preparations of the "plan." It is such an insipid ending to a scheme so grandiose in conception, so insouciant, so "beyond-good-and-evil" Nietzschean in its fearless condonation of crime and ruse to gain some supreme end. That the end justifies the means is the tragic misconception of the conqueror. But—here—what a piffling end to justify an excess of ferocious activity! It is such a pitiable exposure of the dire unimaginativeness of the supreme man of action, who, filled with overmastering ambition, an overriding pride, is determined to "act" at all cost without any clear conception *why*. It all sounds like the overbearing threats of a drunkard ending suddenly in a hiccup. The cunning is that of an inmate in a mental home planning secretly in his bed to set a match to the mattresses of the other inmates, and, in the general panic that he hopes will ensue, to slit the throat of the warder and lead all the other inmates out into the street for the final grand climax of setting the whole town ablaze.

It is the tragedy of mankind that men of action, who possess the faculty for setting other men in motion, have the imagination either of infants or of criminal lunatics; and that the men of thought exercise just the sort of influence which teaches other men of thought to foresee the consequences of the actions of the men of deeds, without directly affecting these consequences. For men of thought cannot teach men of deeds, because men of deeds cannot think and men of thought cannot act. It has always been, still is, as though the philosopher, who has civilized the inward attitude of a whole age, can do no more to stop the outward conflagration than to provide the victim of it with a quiet book of thoughts potent enough to deflect his mind from the distressing mischief caused by the zealous lunatic still prancing on the roof of the world.

CHAPTER XVI

THE WOMAN'S KINGDOM

I. THE WASH OF THE WAVES

WHETHER Peter's political testament is accepted as genuine or is dismissed as a fake, the reader may be interested to trace its application, not only in Peter's own foreign policy, but in that of his successors. It is particularly noticeable during the longer reigns. That intervention in European quarrels, which is so stressed in Peter's testament, is noticeable during the reigns of Anna Ivanovna, Elizabeth, Catherine II, Paul, Alexander I, Nicholas I, Alexander II; and may be said to continue right up to the establishment of the Soviet republic, which has abandoned imperialistic ambitions, reversed the tsarist policy, and is exerting a quasi-salutary influence for a Bolshevik peace.

The moral to be drawn from the despotism of Peter the Great, a moral of special interest in our own day of rampant dictatorship, is that strong men who lay down laws to all eternity cannot decree beyond their own span of life. In a manifesto issued in 1722, Peter laid it down that the old law of primogeniture which had determined the succession was abolished and that, in future, the reigning sovereign was to have the right to appoint his own successor according to his personal predilection, being free apparently to choose an emperor from any stratum at home, or, for that matter, abroad.

Peter, a colossal despot, was despotically democratic in his outlook. Himself by birth a tsar, by inclination a carpenter, the prospect of his blood relations claiming their hereditary right to succeed him to an empire he had put together by swinging the ax, made no appeal to him at all. But in abolishing the principle of legitimacy, Peter only succeeded in sowing uncertainty and confusion without being able to have his decree observed beyond his own lifetime. He provided future sovereigns with a legitimate excuse for overlooking their legitimate heirs in favor of their immediate supporters. They could always justify their whims by an appeal to Peter's decree of 1722. On the other hand, others, who ran their candidates by appealing to the generally accepted principle of primogeniture, could always say: "Peter is dead, and his law with him."

In the last years of his life, Peter, faced with the task of choosing a successor, found himself in a quandary. There was his grandson, Peter (later Peter II), son of the unfortunate Aleksei. He was anathema. There were Peter's own daughters, Anna (later mother of Karl Peter Ulrich, i.e., Peter III); and Elizabeth (later the Empress Elizabeth). On the other hand, there were the daughters of his elder brother Ivan, who, once the principle of primogeniture was allowed to voice itself at all, had a prior claim. The elder daughter was that Catherine whom her uncle Peter had given in marriage to the Duke of Mecklenburg, with Wismar for a dowry. The younger daughter was Anna (later the Empress Anna Ivanovna), whom he had married to the Duke of Courland to keep Courland in the family.

Who was to succeed him? His insistence that he could choose a successor outside the rank of his relatives emboldened many of his newly risen parvenus to think—and no one more so than the ex-pieman Menshikov —that the crown, if they played their cards well, was within reach. Such a prospect pleased Peter, who was a king but kept the common touch, even less than the claims of his relatives. He did not fancy leaving his throne to men who were not kings but would affect the royal touch. Least of all did he want some scion of a family with a suspicion of Rurik blood, like the Dolgorukis, who had been somebodies when the Romanovs were nobodies, to take over a business that for four generations had been kept in the family.

He turned it over in his mind, and decided that, when all was said, it was best for his wife Catherine to have the throne. She had, from his point of view, several advantages. She was a peasant, but she was simple. She was bright, she was his consort and already an empress. She would do. He had definitely fixed his mind on her, when he discovered her in adultery with Wilhelm Mons. Mons was promptly dispatched, if one can say so of a man made to die a lingering death. But the sting remained. Peter was not like the Duke of Mecklenburg, who, once he had insulted a man, felt that he had eased his heart. Peter, after torturing an enemy to death, still felt a grudge against him. If Peter found that he had flogged a man unjustly for an error he had not committed, he flogged him again, this time out of vexation with himself. Having discovered his wife's infidelity, Peter wondered whether she deserved the throne. On his death-bed his thoughts, as the unfinished sentence: "Give everything back to ..." seems to point, turned to ten-year-old Peter, the son of the executed Aleksei, to whom it all rightly belonged. Or it may have been the daughters of his elder brother Ivan that he meant, if his idea was to give it all back to those in the direct line of succession, even though they were daughters.

As it happened, they all had their turn. First Catherine I, who reigned just over two years. Then Aleksei's son, Peter II. Then Ivan's younger daughter, Anna. And, finally, Peter's younger daughter, Elizabeth.

II. MENSHIKOV AND PETER II

Catherine I, from sheer joy, gave herself up to drink. Menshikov, but for whom she would not have met Peter, allowed her to reign in name, while he ruled in fact. Menshikov was the son of a Moscow tradesman who had made a point of flogging his boy out of excessive devotion to the sterner tenets of the Old Testament. He flogged his son continually and unsparingly, trying to live up to the principle of "Spare the rod and spoil the child." The child at last escaped from home and took a job with a pie vendor. Menshikov was indeed a bright lad. He sold pies in the streets of Moscow, in the days when Peter himself was little more than a lad, and he sold them, literally, like hot cakes; which, incidentally, they were. On one occasion he ran after a coach and held on behind, alighting when the coach halted outside a house in the German Quarter. Out of the carriage emerged a famous figure: the Swiss Lefort, Peter's friend and preceptor, the moving spirit of his military games. Lefort, questioning the boy, was so struck with his alertness and quick wits that, there and then, he took him into his service. Peter, on his many visits to Lefort's house, noticed young Menshikov, took a fancy to him, made a companion of him, then a favorite, and so, by degrees, a prince and a field marshal. It was Menshikov, as already related, who, taking Catherine over from Sheremetev, had handed her over to the Tsar, who loved her if he ever loved a human being.

Having got so far, Menshikov thought he had not, at Peter's demise, as yet reached the limit of his ambition. As the ex-lover of Catherine I, whom he had fondled when she was but a servant girl raised to the rank of old Sheremetev's darling; as the dashing officer, the Tsar's favorite, who had laughingly snatched her away from the arms of an older man; as the man whom she loved and obeyed and who had started her on her brilliant career; as, in short, her initial benefactor, surely there was something more for him now than what he had already achieved during Peter's lifetime. Yes, he thought he ought to be emperor.

As this was impossible, he remained Prince Menshikov, the man behind the throne, though very much in the foreground. He was more a tsar than the Tsar, more of a Peter than Peter. Catherine I, as stated, abandoned herself to fathomless drinking, and was glad to have her ex-lover take the burden of empire off her unstable hands. When Peter died, the old families thought that a welcome change was imminent. Here, at last, was a chance to return to the dignified Muscovite traditions of old, to the easygoing rule of the nobles, the slow-witted, long-bearded boyars. Steady murmurs of discontent at what was regarded as her usurpation of the throne were reaching Catherine's ears. Considering the perplexities and vicissitudes of an unlimited monarchy, her own ambitions literally crowned with a self-upholder's diadem, with no male issue left of her own, her elder daughter married happily to the Prince of Holstein-Gottorp and her younger, Elizabeth, still in her teens, Catherine, mellowed with drink, decided that, when all was said, it was best to heed the clamor and honor what did seem to be Peter's dying wish: and she named the boy Peter, son of the executed Aleksei, as her successor.

He reigned after her—but for under three years—as Peter II. He was as he came to the throne scarcely twelve years old; and Menshikov took him severely in hand. The boy's grandmother, the widowed Tsaritsa Eudoxia, who had outlived Peter's second wife, was fished out of her convent and appeared at the court of her grandson. Peter II proved to be a chip off the old block. There was nothing in him of the temerity of his father: he was his grandfather all over. Menshikov, who had bullied the unfortunate Aleksei, now thought he would tame this young stripling. But Peter II sent for him and addressed him in the language and manner of Peter the Great. No doubt Menshikov, if he had the chance, said the boy emperor, would do the same to him as he had done to his father— namely, flog him to death in a prison cell. He said in effect: "You can't do that to *me*."

Menshikov, thwarted of his major ambition, tried the next best thing. Unable to be tsar himself, he attempted to marry his young daughter to the boy tsar. With the help of rival factions, Peter II consigned Menshikov, complete with daughter, to Siberia.

There was no animosity between the younger generation of Peter's two families. Peter II, the grandson of Eudoxia, spent all his days hunting in the company of his fifteen-year-old aunt, Elizabeth, daughter of Catherine. At that time, when they roamed about and galloped together after hares and wolves, she little knew that, twelve years hence, she herself would mount the throne, and stay there, not an odd couple of years but for two decades.

With Menshikov in Siberia, where he died, and the old families having re-established their ascendancy, there now began a tug of war between two rival factions, the Golitsins and the Dolgorukis. Peter II was being pressed to marry a young Dolgoruki girl, when he fell ill with smallpox. Some say he was poisoned by the rival faction. Not to be bilked of their prize, the Dolgorukis, as the boy was dying, rushed the marriage and positively thrust the girl into his bed, in the hope of establishing that coitus had taken place, and that she was the empress. The boy emperor died, and the rival faction would not recognize the marriage. The girl lived on, and Karl Peter Ulrich later flirted with her on occasion, though by that time she was old enough to be his mother.

III. THE EMPRESS ANNA IVANOVNA

ONCE again the throne was vacant. The old noble families put their heads together and decided to retain all power in their own hands. They would have a figurehead responsible to themselves; a constitutional monarch, like the first Romanov, Mihaïl, elected by them on these express conditions.

They looked round for one who might prove amenable to such tutelage. Anna, married to the Duke of Holstein-Gottorp, had just died, after giving birth to a son, Karl Peter Ulrich (later Peter III). The younger sister, Elizabeth, was about and unmarried, and very good-looking she was, but considered to be altogether too wild and immoral. At the age of fifteen she had lovers galore. And, anyway, they had had enough of Peter's brood. They would try Ivan's progeny for a change.

Ivan had been the elder brother, anyhow, and though an idiot, if they were now going to adhere to strict primogeniture, they should go back to Ivan. There were no males left—anywhere. The choice was between Catherine, Duchess of Mecklenburg, and her younger sister, Anna, Duchess of Courland. The elder daughter meant importing to Russia the same Duke of Mecklenburg who, in Peter the Great's lifetime, when done out of Livonia, Wismar and Mecklenburg, had been nosing for the Russian crown; and no one was going to chance *that*. The younger, Anna, was now happily a widow—and, they thought, an excellent choice.

A deputation, headed by a Golitsin, set out for Courland to offer Tsar Ivan's younger daughter the crown on a strictly constitutional basis. That meant she was to be responsible to the nobles, as of old. Like the first Romanov, she could neither make war nor peace, nor promulgate laws except at their bidding. She was to sign a document limiting her powers. She was to be a sort of constitutional monarch, except that she was responsible not to the people (there were no "people" except peasants, who were serfs and had as much voice in the government of their country as Negro slaves in America) but to the aristocracy.

Anna Ivanovna accepted unreservedly, signed the document and came to Moscow for her coronation. She was duly crowned, but her actions were so closely watched, her interviews so jealously controlled, that her position resembled rather that of the Prisoner of Chillon than of an empress. She brought with her from Courland her favorite, Biron, and shortly after her coronation Anna Ivanovna staged a curious little revolution. She declared to a crowd of people assembled outside the palace that the nobles had limited her imperial powers by a ruse; that she had signed a document to that effect under duress. The crowds shouted: "Shame! Down with the nobles!" Anna Ivanovna there and then tore up the document and began to reign as an unlimited monarch, autocrat and Self-Upholder of All the Russias.

It is an odd inversion of the 1917 Revolution. Here was an empress who was almost a constitutional monarch, answerable to the nation—at least to the literate part of the nation, which consisted exclusively of the nobility and gentry. Yet she had but to complain to the common people that the nobles were depriving her of her full sovereignty, for the people to stick up for the autocrat as against the constitution. The reason for this popular response lay in the belief inherent in the common people that the Tsar, like God, was there to protect them from undue oppression; and since oppression could only come from the gentry and nobles, a constitutional monarch, in their view, was bound to be more tyrannical than an absolute one. They wanted God's anointed to rule over them and be responsible, not to the nobles who oppressed them, but to God, whose temporal representative he was.

Anna Ivanovna accordingly reigned unhampered by the wishes of the Russian nobility, or any wishes except her own and those of her favorites. She surrounded herself with adventurers from the Baltic provinces as—perhaps rightly—she did not trust the Russian nobility. The Russians took a violent dislike to these foreign stewards, notably Münnich and Bühren (who transformed his name to the more aristocratic Biron, to suggest that he was in fact a descendant of the French duke of that name). These two favorites, who alternately ruled Russia in the thirties of the eighteenth century, acquired all the defects of the "broad Russian nature," though they were detested for their vices precisely because they were Germans. Practically all the Russian emperors, from Peter III onwards, married German princesses. But these German empresses of Russia never stayed German at heart, but grew to be more Russian than the Russians. It was the Russian princesses (like the two Annas who had married Germans) who became Germanized. Which perhaps shows the superior influence of the male over the female in all conditions and circumstances.

IV. ANNA LEOPOLDOVNA AND JULIA

ANNA IVANOVNA was the first to introduce a certain Western elegance into the manners of her court. She interfered in the wars abroad to deflect the unrest at home. And her policy of interfering in foreign quarrels tallied with the rules laid down in the testament of her uncle, Peter the Great. Before she died, she searched her mind as to whom she might leave the Russian throne. Being herself of the blood of the Tsar Ivan, and not of Peter, she ignored Elizabeth's claim and decreed that the baby son of her own niece, Anna Leopoldovna, should succeed her.

The niece was the daughter of Empress Anna's elder sister, the Duchess of Mecklenburg, and was accordingly on her father's side German. Anna Leopoldovna was married to the Duke of Brunswick, and they had a boy, a babe-in-arms, a suckling, called Ivan VI after his great-grandfather, the weak-minded Tsar Ivan V. Though he was three-quarters German and one-quarter Russian, this baby was proclaimed emperor of Russia, and his mother, Anna Leopoldovna, declared to be regent during her baby son's minority.

Anna Leopoldovna, even more than her aunt, Anna Ivanovna, favored German and Baltic barons. Her own husband, the Duke of Brunswick, she detested, and spent all her time with a lady in waiting—by name, Julia Mengden, from whom she was inseparable. Anna Leopoldovna, Julia Mengden and the baby Tsar Ivan spent all their time in one room, huddled together in one bed; and what went on in Russia from Petersburg to Tobolsk, from Archangel to Astrakhan, troubled them not at all. The country was alternately misruled by Biron and Münnich. As reign succeeded reign, the one exiled the other to Siberia. One was returned to grace just as the other was being dispatched to exile; and as they crossed each other on the Siberian frontier they bowed gravely and raised their hats in salute.

At last, in 1741 the Russian nobility felt they had had enough of foreign rule. The progeny of Ivan had proved a sorry disappointment. They had been chosen because the country had tired of Peter's un-Russian ways and alien innovations; and they had proved themselves to be more German than their uncle.

Back to Peter's brood, then! In the old, approved way, by means of a little palace revolution supported by the Guards, Princess Elizabeth as the only surviving daughter of Peter the Great and Catherine I was now placed on the throne of her father and mother. Anna Leopoldovna, Julia Mengden and the baby Tsar Ivan were displaced early in the morning of November 25 while they were asleep, snuggling together tightly in one bed. Anna Leopoldovna said she did not care so long as she was not separated from Julia. They were all dumped into a sleigh, including the hated husband, and taken to the frontier. But Elizabeth changed her mind and detained them at Riga, where she separated Julia from Anna Leopoldovna; and from that day on they were chivied from one place of detention to another, till, after twenty years of almost solitary confinement in the damp cell of a fortress, the boy was killed in the reign of Catherine II.

Crowding round bonfires lit in the square before the Winter Palace, Guardsmen were drinking vodka to the health of "our little mother the Tsaritsa our colonel." Soon after the *coup d'état* the English Ambassador wrote from Petersburg: "I cannot describe the impudence of the troops, especially those who had taken an active part in this event. They were being coaxed and flattered, as though they were the masters here."

V. BACK TO ELIZABETH, CATHERINE II AND ALEXANDER

AND we are back in the reign of Elizabeth; only three years removed from the time when Figgy will set off with her mother from Zerbst on that mid-winter journey to Russia. We are back in the seventeen-forties, in the days when the Empress Elizabeth would take her nephew, Karl Peter Ulrich, and Figgy about with her on her travels through Russia. Here they are at a picnic, and the Empress is upbraiding Catherine for over-spending her allowance, for the extravagance of her dress. Why, when she herself was a princess she dressed simply and economically and lived strictly within her allowance. And she was an emperor's daughter. She sends a baleful look across the table to where Catherine is sitting. The Empress is in a thoroughly bad humor. The table is set in the open. Dinner is about to be served. But the Empress's temper has not yet vented itself; and she turns on the man in charge of the hunt. "How is it there are no hares about?" The chief huntsman turns pale and stammers excuses. "When I used to hunt here in the old days with Peter II this place was chock full of hares. That was only fifteen years ago. What's happened to the hares?" The Empress, her face flushed red with anger, turns suspiciously on the man. "I dare say, you scoundrel, you, you let the place to the gentry to hunt here while I'm away."

To put the Empress in a better humor, somebody sends for her court fool, who appears with a hat on his head. The hat is obviously giving him trouble. The Empress says: "What's the matter, fool?" He produces the hat, from which a hedgehog shows his head. The Empress, who is terrified of rats, gives a long piercing shriek and runs away to hide in the imperial tent. She sends word that dinner is off, and they all retire to bed, hungry.

Now we are back in the Seven Years' War; and Frederick the Great is writing to his brother Henry—that same Henry with whom Catherine used to dance the minuet in Berlin—complaining of the cruelty of the Empress Elizabeth's troops fighting in Prussia. "I couldn't give you any idea," Frederick writes in his Voltaire-modeled French, "of all the barbarities that these infamous people commit. My hair stands on end. They strangle women and children; they mutilate the private parts of the unfortunates whom they catch; they pillage, they burn; in fine, these are horrors which a sensitive heart cannot support except with the most cruel bitterness."

It was said that Count Fermor, the Russian general in command, could do nothing to prevent the ranks and even the officers under his orders from committing excesses. But the English Envoy with the Prussian Army, Mitchell, in his dispatch to Lord Holdernesse, writes: "Since we have so many Russian generals prisoners, the burnings have ceased— which shows that Fermor had power to prevent them."

Mitchell adds: "Every step one advances moves compassion. Had I not seen it, I never could have believed that it was possible for man to be so much enemy to man, as totally to be divested of every feeling of humanity. I cannot bear these sad scenes much longer; pray send somebody in my place, whose breast is better steeled than mine is."

The Russians were getting conflicting orders from St. Petersburg which sometimes operated to the advantage of the enemy. Mitchell again writes to Lord Holdernesse: "We were upon the very brink of destruction. The Russians fought like devils. Sometimes the Russian generals showed a desire to meet the enemies' wishes on their own initiative. General Palmbach proposed to raise the siege of Kolberg, provided the Prussians would pay him 300,000 crowns. To this the commandant of the town replied that he would not give him 3*d.*, and bid him go on."

Time marches on. Another four years, and we are in the reign of great Catherine. Here she is engaging in intellectual flirtations with Voltaire, who had had dealings of a more mercenary, from his point of view more satisfactory, character with the Empress Elizabeth, whom he had approached with a view to his writing for her own delectation and the glory of her country a fitting *Life* of her father. In this project, which was to diffuse the news of the greatness of the late Father of the Fatherland throughout the wide world, a sum commensurate with the greatness of the author's and his subject's glory was a crucial point in Voltaire's negotiations with the Empress Elizabeth. Elizabeth agreed, but both deferred her payment and when pressed to honor her obligation did not pay in full. But for Voltaire, who fostered the tradition abroad, it is doubtful whether Peter the First would have passed into history as Peter the Great. In his own country the title never caught on. Voltaire was not insensitive to money. But it was not money alone which caused him to see greatness in Peter. Peter's contempt for his Russian nobles was a retrospective solace to Voltaire for the humiliation and acerbations he once suffered in his youth at the hands of French aristocrats who placed their birth above his wits and matched his wit with their insolence.

Talleyrand, an aristocrat, said that nobody who had not experienced life under the old regime in France had known *la douceur de vivre*. Voltaire, a commoner, had lived under the mellow old regime of the Bourbons. His reaction to its sweetness was a passionate admiration of Peter the Great for axing the Russian old families and raising a new aristocracy of merit from the ranks.

Catherine II admired Peter the Great, who admired Ivan the Terrible. "Whenever I thought of introducing some new law," says Catherine, "I invariably ordered that the archives be searched to ascertain whether or not there had been any talk of the project under discussion in the time of Peter I. And it transpired that in nearly all cases the subject had been already considered by him." We are well advanced in Catherine's own reign. Already she throws a retrospective glance down the years. She asks herself wonderingly how it is that she, an obscure German princess from Zerbst, is for a third decade usurping the self-upholder's throne.

Catherine seems to try to justify her occupation of a position rightly belonging to Tsar Ivan's descendants by pouring contempt mixed with pity upon his progeny and inadvertently revealing to us that they were in fact far more numerous than we were led to suppose. She describes them, one and all, as medically unfit. Catherine relates that their great-grandmother, the Tsaritsa Praskovia Feodorovna, consort of the Tsar Ivan Alekseivitch, was morose and *difficile* in character. Her three daughters—Catherine, Duchess of Mecklenburg, the Empress Anna, and a third, Praskovia, who died unmarried—were badly brought up and on the worst terms with their mother and with each other. When the Tsaritsa was approaching her end she was visited with the idea, not of blessing her daughters, as might be conventionally expected, but of sending them one and all her maternal curse.

This curse was apparently taken very seriously by all of them. They appealed to their uncle, Peter the Great, to do his best to induce their mother to take back the curse; but the old lady was obdurate. Peter the Great could do nothing to induce his brother's widow to change her mind. As she was dying, he could not threaten her with death. He could have threatened her with torture. But he evidently entertained some small regard for his sister-in-law. Down he went on his knees and implored her to forgive her daughters.

At last Praskovia relented, but only in the case of her second daughter, who in due course became the Empress Anna. All the rest came to a bad end. Far from removing the curse from the Duchess of Mecklenburg and the third daughter, the Tsaritsa Praskovia Feodorovna cursed them and their houses again, cursed them to all eternity.

The curse had disastrous consequences. The youngest daughter with her illegitimate child was cursed effectively into obscurity. The eldest, the Duchess of Mecklenburg, gave birth to Anna Leopoldovna, whose baby son Ivan came to an unhappy end in the Schlüsselburg fortress. Her other children, who, by right of primogeniture, should have sat in Catherine's place, make medical history. One brother limped, the other was a hunchback, one daughter had melancholia, the other intermittent attacks of insanity. The eldest, Ivan, who was Emperor of All the Russias when still a suckling, deposed as a babe, and shot in the fortress in his twenties, was, Catherine says, like his great-grandfather, weak-minded. "Besides," she adds, "he stuttered."

At the height of her glory, when the idea that a real Romanov might have reigned in her place would have seemed unnatural, some obscure retired officer was introduced to the Empress. "I never knew you before," the Empress said pleasantly.

"And I never knew you, Madam," he answered naïvely.

"I can well believe it," she said. "Who's to know me, poor widow that I am!"

The Empress was now a grandmother taking an interest in her grandson Alexander's education, telling his tutor, the Swiss revolutionary Laharpe: "I don't care about your politics. You are an honest man." Much as the mother of Peter the Great did not care about *his* tutor's drunkenness: "You're an honest man," she used the same words. When the Empress studied the countries of the world on the globe she would send for her grandson—"Monsieur Alexandre," as she used to refer to him—and find that the future emperor was brilliantly ahead of her in everything pertaining to geography. This globe was as large as a room. Several people could dine inside it, and it revolved in such a way as to enable you to walk across seas and continents within it. Peter the Great had it specially made for himself in Germany. As the author of the Testament, he thought he had better know something about the disposition of the world before he attempted to conquer it. The globe was carried partly by hand, partly on sleighs, into Russia. Trees had to be felled to allow of its progress. It took many months to hack a way through the forests. Finally, the globe reposed in the palace of Tsarskoye Selo.

Alexander, when he came to the throne, gravely studied the globe, which seemed in a fair way to being overrun by the hero of the new century. For a descendant of the man who had pushed Charles XII off the map and had left a political testament showing how the thing was to be done, the emergence of Bonaparte in the west when the sun should clearly have risen in the east, was, to say the least of it, vexatious.

BOOK FIVE

BOOK FIVE

CHAPTER XVII

THE DUEL WITH
NAPOLEON BEGINS

I. TWO LUNATICS

ALEXANDER began his reign by making peace with Great Britain and also with Bonaparte. Indeed, with the latter he concluded a secret treaty.

We shall now follow the extraordinary duel between these two men which ended in Alexander, the lesser man, getting the better of the hero of the century. The story, the most astounding chapter in Russian history, reads like a combat between two blind lunatics pursuing each other round and round the ward, being very wily and desperately cunning, as lunatics are; the mortal combat ending in the thin lunatic hiding himself in the cupboard and the fat one, perplexed at such behavior, running away in a panic, to be pursued again by the lean one, who, leaping out of the cupboard, dashes across the ward past his fat brother-inmate floundering in this game of blind-man's buff, there to lock himself up in the other's cupboard; from which, finding there is nothing to do there, he emerges in due course.

But if that combat with Napoleon was a farce, it was a tragic farce involving human carnage for the sake of conflicting loyalties and ideals, very much in the air when compared with the reality of agony and horror of the battlefields. It is, by the futility, the utter hazard and helplessness of all the chief actors involved, a moral story showing plainly that the intelligence of men is of next to no avail in a struggle precipitating to their deaths millions of suffering beings who have no idea what the conflict is about; and that just when the clever leaders think they are pulling strings, it is *they* who obey the movements of an unseen hand dangling them on a thread. "For the wisdom of this world is foolishness with God."

The tragedy notwithstanding, the story is a diverting one. It tells how by continual double-crossing of everyone, himself included, the most charming sovereign of Russia played out the ablest military strategist of the age. With guile and charm, pushed hither and thither, not knowing whether it was Christmas or Easter, Alexander awoke to find, to his own surprise, that he had defeated Napoleon in the last round.

II. EXCURSION INTO EUROPE WITH ALEXANDER

AUSTRIA and Prussia were at that time paying the penalty of their earlier intervention in the internal affairs of France. Bonaparte had resolved not to sign the peace of Lunéville except on the express condition that the Emperor of Austria, in his patriarchal position as Emperor of the Holy Roman Empire of the German Nation, assumed responsibility for all the German States. Francis II agreed under duress, even though he exercised from his throne in Vienna no more than a very nominal influence in German affairs. And Kaiser Franz knew it, too, though he considered himself the first of God's anointed.

Napoleon's idea was simple. He did not pay the Emperor Francis the compliment of imagining that the Roman Emperor, as he still was, had the military strength with which to hold down the new territories France had acquired in Germany. Snatched away by the sword, these German lands could only be kept French by Bonaparte's resting his hand on the hilt of his sword. But Kaiser Franz's acquiescence—"recognition" is the diplomatic term—was useful to him in another respect. By obtaining the sanction of the nominal head of the thirty-six independent German States (which head in those days was the Emperor of Austria and by no means the King of Prussia, proclaimed German Emperor only after the Franco-Prussian War) Napoleon could turn to the rest of the world and say: "If he, the Emperor of the German Roman Empire, as he anachronistically calls himself, says it's all right, who are *you* to say it isn't?"

And, of course, there were to be "considerations." In return for Austria's tacit permission to Napoleon to help himself to territory which was not Austrian—the left bank of the Rhine—Napoleon generously recompensed the Emperor of the moribund German Roman Empire by handing him over lands which did not belong to France—Istria, Dalmatia, and Venice, together with her dependencies in the Adriatic.

Alexander, at the invitation of Bonaparte, took an active part in this reshuffling of German territory. Alexander's qualification for playing umpire lay chiefly in the fact that on his mother's side and through his wife he was closely related to the ruling families of Württemberg, Bavaria and Baden—the States Napoleon plotted to dissociate from the rest of Germany and bring under his own sway.

Thus Alexander had to be consulted. In a German-speaking country of nominally independent States, the middle-sized States would be bound to resent the hegemony of the larger States. One can imagine Alexander's mother, the Empress-Dowager, a Württemberg princess by birth, assuring her distraught German relatives nursing a grievance against Prussia or Austria, assuring them that "my son will never tolerate..." or: "I have asked my son.... My son will see to it.... I'll tell my son...."

This plan of splitting up Germany was to be achieved according to a system of compensations designed to appeal to the singular greediness of the King of Prussia, Frederick William III. He was to be compensated at the expense of a third party. The third party was not to be compensated at all, because the third party was too small and too weak to dare raise its voice.

What was Alexander, the tender idealist brought up on Rousseau, doing in this game of smash-and-grab in Europe at which Napoleon was an adept? What had they in common? If Napoleon be romantically imagined as a kind of Byron in Satanic mood overrunning the visible world, then Alexander is Ariel-Shelley with his idealism come to grief after doing his best at too many points to please too many people. For, while the heads of German States were accepting their new frontiers out of the hands of Bonaparte and Alexander, meekly submitting to these two new masters throwing their weight about in Germany, England and France were quarreling furiously over Malta. While Alexander respected the secrecy of his treaty with Bonaparte, it was by no means a secret in Downing Street. The Tsar, through his ambassador at the Court of Saint James's, emphasized his predilection for England as against France —though Bonaparte fascinated him as a man.

By the terms of the Treaty of Amiens Great Britain was to have evacuated Malta within three months of the ratification of her agreement with France. But the more sincerely the English convinced themselves that in evacuating Malta they would be surrendering their newly won power in the Mediterranean, the less eager were they to comply with so uncongenial a stipulation. Nor was Napoleon at all disposed to waive the point in favor of his rivals. "Malta," he said, "means the domination of the Mediterranean. Does anybody think I am going to hand it over to the English without having measured my strength with them? That would mean I would lose at once the most important sea in the world, as well as the respect of Europe, which believes in my energy and considers it superior to all the dangers."

Hearken to your Mussolini!

British resentment at being asked to vacate Malta expressed itself, as is customary with us, in a leading article which made no mention of Malta. "If," said *The Times,* "Buonaparte be alarmed at the language of truth, a language which is not spoken at the Court of the Tuileries, let him give to the journalists of France the right of exercising fair and free discussion! Let him not, after having raised himself to supreme power, by the sword, still keep that sword suspended by a thread over the heads of those who may dare to think, or speak differently from himself! ... But if he will continue to receive these fulsome adulations, of which a Louis the Fourteenth would, in the height of his power, be ashamed; if he will impudently impose, not only upon thirty millions of Frenchmen, but upon all the inhabitants of the countries which still exist by his permission, a despotism over the *mind,* let him at least endure in silence, if not with patience, the honest and manly expressions of a press whose privileges are secured by a constitution he once had the power but not the wisdom or honesty to imitate!"

Napoleon said he would compel the English to respect the Treaty of Amiens, which expressly provided for British evacuation of Malta.

"Until," said *The Times,* "we have better authority than that of the *Moniteur,* we cannot believe 'that the English who reside at Paris eagerly solicit for themselves and *wives* the honor of being admitted with the society of that capital.' None of our fair countrywomen who know 'how tender reputation is,' could possibly seek admittance at the Court of the Tuileries. An English matron would blush to associate with the discarded mistress of Barras."

The British held onto Malta, and Bonaparte declared war on England by occupying the whole of Hanover, of which George III of England was hereditary elector. Not contenting himself with the acquisition of Hanover, Napoleon spread himself out and in his stride swiped up the lands of the Dukes of Oldenburg and Mecklenburg-Schwerin, both, as we may well guess, relatives of Alexander and enjoying his protection.

This unfriendly action brought Napoleon into open conflict with the Russian Court, where feeling ran high against him. The arrest of the Duc d'Enghien on Baden territory was a further provocation. Alexander's consort, the Empress Elizabeth, was the daughter of the Margrave of Baden. Alexander was willing to overlook the offense. But, as his ambassador in Paris remarked: "The Emperor has his will, but the Russian nation has hers." There was no doubt that the Russian Court was pro-English and anti-Bonaparte. Alexander obeyed the conditions attending

Russian autocracy: which were to do as he was told—on pain of early assassination. He declared war against Bonaparte.

Any lingering republican sympathy he had felt for Bonaparte had evaporated when Napoleon proclaimed himself Emperor. Yet there was a price which, had Napoleon paid it, might have kept Russia out of the war.

The price was a free hand in Turkey. But Napoleon was not willing to pay it. Now the murder of the Duc d'Enghien completed the rupture. They had started on their first round.

III. ALEXANDER'S MULTIFARIOUS LOYALTIES

THE warmth with which Alexander intervened on behalf of the injured States of Germany was not appreciated by the Emperor Francis in Vienna. Alexander's new role as protector of Germany, in which part he seemed gradually to be pushing Kaiser Franz off his Holy Roman throne, did not commend itself to the pride of a Habsburg. Alexander was urging the Austrian Emperor to join a coalition consisting of Russia, England, and possibly Prussia, against Napoleon (with whom the Emperor Francis had only recently concluded a very stiff treaty and whom he was not anxious to provoke again).

The Germans, though sensible of Russia's indignation on account of Germany's injured pride, nevertheless deprecated Alexander's eagerness to take the field on their behalf. In July 1804 representatives of all the German States met reluctantly at Regensburg, where they were harangued by the Russian ambassador. Was the dignity and independence of the Holy Roman Empire of the German Nation worth nothing to them? he demanded threateningly, urging them to take the field. On and on he thundered. Whereupon, fearing to commit their countries, but fearing even more to ruffle the tender sensibilities of the Tsar, the assembled delegates of Germany deserted in a mass.

Lately Alexander's mind had been much occupied with a cherished project, which was to push both Prussia and Austria out of the Holy Roman Empire. He considered the Hohenzollerns and the Habsburgs bad boys—always fighting for supremacy in German affairs. And he rather fancied forming a new Germany centered round the States of his own relatives of Württemberg, Bavaria and Baden. He might pump up the deflated Holy Roman Empire by throwing in Switzerland, Holland and Belgium, to make up the bulk of the new Germany reduced by the expulsion of Prussia and Austria. This new Germany was to be free of the nefarious influence of Austria and Prussia and would enjoy the beneficent influence of Russia and Alexander. And—who knows?— his grateful German relatives might see fit to elect him Holy Roman Emperor of the German Nation, which, in addition to his already being Emperor of the Holy Russian Nation, might assist the hereditary ambition of restoring Byzantium—with himself or his brother Constantine as emperor. The testament of Peter the Great was taking shape—in Alexander's imagination.

But—unfortunately—there was Napoleon. He was in the way. An awkward customer, to say the least. Perhaps Austria and Prussia had better be used before they were discarded.

And there was England—an obvious ally. Even before breaking with Napoleon, Alexander had a secret treaty with Pitt, so profoundly secret that it was not even known to Pitt's colleagues. In alliance with Great Britain and Austria, Russia undertook to resist all further aggrandizement by France. But being an ally of Austria did not hinder Alexander from dreaming of the day when the hegemony of Austria in Germany would pass to Alexander's own relatives who ate out of his hand.

Such was the moral virtuosity of the Tsar that he contrived to plan the ejection of Prussia out of Germany while nourishing a sincere attachment to her king. More than that. Alexander and King Frederick William of Prussia concluded an intimate alliance of a personal character, and Alexander now urged the King to break with Napoleon and to join in with Pitt, Kaiser Franz and himself.

He was not insincere. Alexander's loyalty was on several planes at once. He was multifariously sincere. He always meant well. But he meant well in respect of far too many people, nations, dynasties and interests—meant simultaneously well or in too quick succession and, unavoidably, at the expense of other parties whom he did not want to think ill of him for the momentary accommodation he required in order to fulfill a more pressing pledge elsewhere. And that was not all. If Alexander was double-faced, his government was too, with the result that, putting it at its simplest, Russian diplomacy was quadruple-faced at the best of times and octangular in a crisis and ever at cross-purposes even with itself.

Pitt was of opinion that there was no prospect of winning the King of Prussia over to the Coalition against Napoleon unless they could offer him better terms than Napoleon was disposed to do. Pitt was of opinion that King Frederick William should be offered for his participation the left bank of the Rhine as well as Holland. It is extremely doubtful whether the Prussian king, with his indecent lust for land, would long have resisted so tempting a proposition.

The Tsar, who was entrusted to win the King over, frowned on such unmerited aggrandizement of Prussia. He accordingly confined his offer to the left bank of the Rhine, making up for the rest in personal charm on the one hand, and veiled threats on the other.

Drawn as the King was towards the young Emperor, whose charm was irresistible, he resented the blunt language of the Tsar's envoy, suited to a vassal but hardly to the sovereign of an independent State.

The King thought the envoy must have exceeded his instructions, and he dispatched his own envoy to St. Petersburg, who reported that if the Tsar's emissary in Berlin had been blunt, the Russian Minister for Foreign Affairs, Prince Adam Czartoriski, had seen fit to use language which he could only describe as brutal. The Tsar had, of course, been charming, but he had merely hinted at consequences which Prince Czartoriski had hissed and shouted at him for all to hear. There was no question that if Prussia did not soon declare herself for the Coalition, they would all declare themselves against Prussia.

The Tsar next conceived the ingenious idea of using his friend the King as a decoy. To ensure Napoleon's inactivity until the Allies were able to put half a million men in the field, Alexander wrote Frederick William a letter in which he pretended that Napoleon had been tentatively sounding for peace in London, and that the British Cabinet had requested Russia to make efforts towards a peaceful settlement. Alexander was therefore writing to his friend in Berlin, who was still on fairly good terms with Napoleon, to request the King to procure passports for the Russian envoys about to leave for Paris with a favorable reply to Napoleon. Napoleon, though he sent the passes, strongly suspected this belated move for peace on the part of the Allies who had been arming unremittingly against him. Napoleon rightly suspected it was a trap, but wrongly suspected the Prussian king of being in the know.

The King dallied in his neutrality when in September 1805 he received a communication from the Tsar. From the banks of the Neva, Alexander notified his confrere on the Spree, without requesting his permission, that Russian troops, by way of taking a somewhat shorter cut, would presently have the pleasure of marching across South Prussian territory.

The Prussian monarch's blood was up. Was he Alexander's vassal? Or was he an independent king? He refused point blank the proposed entry into his kingdom of Russian troops. The idea of it! And what would Napoleon think, who already viewed Prussia's role as intermediary with misgiving. *"Cette cour de Prusse,"* he remarked on a later occasion, *"est bien fausse et bien bête."*

It was stupid, yes; but, as yet too nervous of Napoleon to be false, King Frederick William threatened that if a single Russian set his foot on Prussian soil he would send an army corps into Bohemia. A clash between Prussian and Russian troops in East Prussia was imminent, was expected daily, when Napoleon, wrongly suspecting the King of complicity with the Tsar, anticipated Alexander in violating Prussia's neutrality, and by so doing forced the frantic, now entirely bewildered King into the arms of the maddening, though charming, Tsar.

IV. HAIL AND FAREWELL

ALEXANDER was not slow to rise to his opportunities. He was with his troops, who were marching from Poland to South Germany. Leaving them, he hurried to Berlin. Here his charm won everyone over. The Queen in particular was affected. She was the beautiful—at least, it is the custom to say she was beautiful; her portraits make you wish to look the other way—the beautiful Queen Louisa of Prussia, a Mecklenburg princess by birth. Mecklenburg and Russia! Russia and Mecklenburg! The association echoes in our ears; does it not?

The other day, a friend of mine, a young woman, glancing casually over some beauty treatment brochure, remarked to me: "This will interest you."

I read: "Mrs. Parker (*née* Fräulein von Glotz) whose hair restoratives have now enjoyed a reputation of one hundred and twenty years' standing, was for twelve years first chamberwoman to Queen Louise, Consort of Frederick William III of Prussia, the loveliest princess of her time and remarkable for the length and beauty of her hair."

Mrs. Parker in her post acquired—the pamphlet runs on—the knowledge of various preparations for the hair and skin. Among these is "Mrs. Parker's celebrated 'Queen Louise' Emollient Lotion which cleanses the pores"; "Mrs. Parker's 'Crême Louise' especially suited for dry skin"; "Mrs. Parker's celebrated 'Queen Louise' Tonic Lotion acting as a gentle stimulant upon the capillary vessels of the skin"; and "Mrs. Parker's celebrated 'Queen Louise' Astringent Lotion, a very valuable preparation for flabby and relaxed skins."

Now, fortified by the full knowledge of Queen Louisa's acknowledged celebrity, we may return to her and observe that she dominated her husband, the rather helpless King Frederick William of Prussia, whom we have left trying to choose between Napoleon and Alexander—that is, between the devil and the deep sea—and alighting on the latter. Having seen him choose the deep, incalculable sea of a Russian alliance, we are soon to follow him bouncing on the billows of his choice.

The King was at that time thirty-five, and the theory is that Queen Louisa could not love a zany like Frederick William, stubborn, meticulous over small matters, seldom able to make up his mind, and when making it up, acting with a recklessness which made those dependent on his decisions deplore his having a mind to make up.

The three of them had met before at Memel, when Queen Louisa tried her best to vamp the imperial idealist whom she conceived as a romantic lover sent to her by Providence to complete her exalted ambitions and fill the need of her heart. The Queen was vain about her beauty, her dress, her intellect, her powers of seduction, her poise and charm. She had a passion for evoking the admiration of men—the greatest, but if those were absent, then even the least of men. She could not endure emotional neglect. She belonged to that ghastly species of womanhood typified by Princess Dashkov who cannot take a back seat in anything—a type of woman which they themselves as well as other women imagine to be the very wine of life to men; who avoid them like the plague. Queen Louisa lacked romance. She would have liked men to carry everything before them on the crest of their passion for her. "I could not have done this but with you and for you!" Then, as the consummation of every still-untasted vanity in life, she would have liked the hero to take her in love, in passionate acknowledgment of her total indispensability.

She had a long, ample neck, like an ivory tower, reminiscent of those classical warriors who resemble women. She in fact looked not unlike Alexander of Macedon; and she was rapidly growing massive. She encouraged the young Tsar as far as she decently could, arranging during Alexander's stay in Memel for adjoining bedrooms. And the Tsar, to whom sexual pleasures did not appeal unless preceded by emotional commitments, got so scared that he locked his door.

Now that he had something to seek, Alexander confronted her with a kind of chivalrous and respectful attention which could be taken either for simple homage due to her merits, or the restraint hiding a warmer emotion. The Queen interpreted it as restraint. And she identified her passion for Alexander with a passionate hatred of the French, and urged her king and consort to take the field. In a very few days she was already deeply in love with the Emperor, who, she thought, was precluded from openly declaring his feeling for her by his loyalty to her husband.

Not only the Queen, but the whole Court was in rapture about the Tsar of Russia. It was a hundred years since Peter the Great had visited Berlin, insisting that the Queen's private palace, Monbijou, be placed at his disposal and which he treated so well that after his departure it had practically to be built anew.

A hundred years had marked an evolution in the manners of a Tsar of All the Russias. Alexander's charm and flattery won over every person of importance at the Prussian Court. The King remained more cool. He alluded painfully to the blunt language and threats recently used by his imperial guest's envoys and ministers. The Tsar said that such sentiments were wholly alien to his heart. He blamed his Foreign Minister, Czartoriski, who was a Pole; and Poles, the Emperor said, felt sore about Prussia, who had partitioned Poland by a ruse rather than by honest conquest. The Queen agreed in everything with Alexander. The moist look in his eyes, his soft fresh voice, the tender way he took her hand and raised it to his lips. Yes: her husband must place his army at the disposal of Great-heart Alexander. She and he would conquer Bonaparte together.

It was the brother of Kaiser Franz, who, arriving five days later, decided the still-hedging King to take up arms against Napoleon. Very reluctantly and full of misgiving, the King of Prussia agreed to act as armed go-between with Napoleon. It was resolved that Frederick William was to present the Emperor of the French with a basis for peace negotiations which Napoleon was required to accept within four weeks, failing which the King would put a hundred and eighty thousand Prussians into the field against him.

The Tsar thereupon staged a little comedy. He had fixed his departure for the evening of November 4, but so painful was the parting that he put it off till midnight. In the stress of emotion roused by their impending, well-nigh intolerable separation, Alexander expressed the wish before he left them to seal the bond of their hearts in a solemn and memorable way over the coffin of Frederick the Great. The King, though no great lover of the macabre, agreed; but without enthusiasm. He gave orders that the vault in the Garrison Church, which contained the body of his ancestor, should be opened.

If all we hear is true, and Catherine II really was the illegitimate daughter of Frederick the Great, Alexander would now be standing over the coffin of his own great-grandfather.

Alexander kissed it and then extended his hand to his friend, the King, swearing eternal loyalty over the coffin. Unable to contain his emotion, he then embraced the King, then the Queen, and tore himself away, deeply moved and hardly able to restrain his tears. Reaching his carriage, he set out into the night towards the distant field of battle.

CHAPTER XVIII

AUSTERLITZ

I. NAPOLEON IN THE HOLY ROMAN EMPEROR'S BED

LEAVING the King and Queen in Berlin, Alexander in his luxurious traveling coach was galloping towards his headquarters at Olmütz, where Emperor Francis urgently awaited him.

For in the meantime something rather shocking and quite unexpected had happened to the cause of the Allies. While everyone at Vienna anxiously waited for news of Napoleon's widely boomed attempt to land in England, he had instead sent two hundred thousand men against Austria. The Austrians, who excelled at planning campaigns they lacked the capacity to carry out, were at the time, as part of a strategic plan, expecting their allies, the Russians. The Austrian commander, Mack, looking out of the window for the approach of the first Cossack contingent, was surprised to see the French instead. Mack, thoroughly upset in his calculations, capitulated. Practically the whole Austrian Army was taken prisoner. Four weeks later the French entered Vienna and Napoleon galloped astride his white steed into the grounds of the castle of Schönbrunn, sleeping that night in the Holy Roman Emperor's bed.

The Holy Roman Emperor was, of course, no other than Kaiser Franz, five years later to become the father-in-law of the man who now so shamelessly reclined in his bed.

Whatever amazement he may have experienced in his heart of hearts on awakening in the bed of the Holy Roman Emperor, Napoleon, who had crowned himself at Milan with the iron diadem of Charlemagne, must have regarded it all as essentially in the fitness of things. Vulgar as it may seem, the idea of occupying the bed of a conquered sovereign is, after all, merely an attenuation, and in so far as it is an empty bed, a considerable attenuation, of the ancient custom of a conqueror sleeping with the wife of his defeated foe. So rooted in instinct was the tradition of prostration and possession, so fitting in symbol, that King Darius could not believe his ears when he heard that Alexander of Macedon had magnanimously waived his right to tamper with the Queen. As the Queen was then the mother of six adults, Alexander's magnanimity was perhaps to himself in the first place, and to King Darius in the second. The King, however, was so touched by Alexander's self-sacrifice that he appointed his conqueror to become his successor to the throne of Persia; thereby giving Alexander less than he had already won.

In progressive attenuation of the rights of conquest, Herr Hitler in annexing Austria gave the ancient residence of Maria Theresa a wide berth, contenting himself with putting up at the Bristol Hotel—a stronghold inaccessible even in his dreams during the abject years of his youth when he sold picture postcards in the streets of Vienna, and therefore no less a moral assault than the rape of a Queen, as of old, or the seizure of an empty royal bed.

Napoleon, waking in the bedroom of the Emperor Francis, let his mind roam over the past and dwell a little on the present. He experienced sensations not displeasing to an upstart and a traveler. But he was debarred from visualizing the future. Here in this castle of Schönbrunn, twenty-seven years later, his own son, as yet unborn, was to die. He was to die as a captain of the Austrian Army, he who was to have succeeded his father as Emperor of the French and had borne that legendary title, the King of Rome. Napoleon strolled through the rooms of Schönbrunn as he might have strolled through Hampton Court. What did he feel? What you and I would feel, no doubt, if they dumped our bed in the National Gallery and bade us make it our home.

However, hardened by a year of residence at the Tuileries, Napoleon took it as being all in a day's work.

II. "ALARM ... AN UNDERSTATEMENT"

THE day Napoleon galloped to Schönbrunn, Alexander was lingeringly saying good-by to his sister at Weimar, who was married to the local hereditary prince. Before leaving the castle at Weimar he wrote a letter to his dear friends the King and Queen of Prussia: "The situation is rather more alarming than I anticipated while I was with you in Berlin. Every moment is precious. The fate of Europe is in your hands."

The life military, Napoleon was beginning to feel, was a jolly one. A little audacity, a touch of unconventionality in attack, and you had the enemy in your pocket. Everything was yours for the asking, at home and abroad.

Napoleon, having achieved a totalitarian State, was not subject to the initial disadvantages of the Allies, who, though nominally monarchical, were exposed to division both within and amongst themselves—characteristics of democracies at war. Russia was an absolute monarchy, in name. In real fact, she was an oligarchy. She was, more precisely, a State ruled by one man—the emperor—who, in his perpetual fear of being violently displaced, from time to time deflected his own policy to suit now this, now that courtier, relative or general. The "power behind the throne" was not so much the acknowledged leader of a party as the probable head of a possible band of conspirators. He was imperially deferred to according to the pressure he applied by sincerely predicting the Tsar's forthcoming assassination as a sure alternative to his heeding his faithful servant's counsel. He warned—he did not threaten. And others warned the Tsar against *him,* so augmenting the Self-Upholder's apprehension without resolving the confusion in his mind.

It was virtually impossible for the monarch to rid himself of conspirators. He could—to paraphrase Abraham Lincoln—rid himself of some of the conspirators all the time. And he could rid himself of all the conspirators some of the time. But he could not rid himself, try as he would, of *all* of the conspirators *all* the time.

They were always about and around him. They included members of his own family supported by whole regiments of Guards. His brothers, sisters, even his mother—all had an eye on the throne, at one time or another. What made it difficult for the Tsar to take steps against them was that they were potential rather than actual conspirators, and did not become actual conspirators till they were potential assassins and either pounced on the monarch, or else he pounced on them, in a race for instantaneous mutual extermination to the greater glory of the fatherland.

They never ceased to remind the Emperor of what had happened to his father, the ill-fated Emperor Paul; and what had happened to his grandfather, the equally ill-fated Emperor Peter III. Till the Self-Upholder could scarcely keep up his courage, let alone uphold the Russias. One more such scene, and his heart was in his boots.

Having been bullied by one party to go to war, much against his will, with Napoleon, Alexander was now being bullied by another to make peace. The chief protagonist of peace was Alexander's younger brother, Constantine, who objected to war because, he said, it so messed up the uniforms.

Arriving at headquarters in Olmütz, Alexander discovered that the alarm he had expressed in his letter to Frederick William was, if anything, an understatement. Kaiser Franz explained to the Tsar that the

Austrians were not alone to blame for the disaster which had attended the Allied arms. A Russian army corps stationed at Lemberg could have got to Austria before Napoleon, but Kutuzov, the Russian commander in chief, had wasted three weeks in the capital of Galicia, and when at last he made his way out he moved so leisurely that his troops arrived just as Mack, who had not allowed in his calculations for such procrastination on the part of the Russians, capitulated at Ulm.

III. A FOOL IN FULL DRESS

INDEED, shocked by the fate of the Austrian Army, the Russians lost their heads and made no attempt to hold their lines of defense. They made not the slightest attempt to prevent Napoleon from crossing three rivers, much to his surprise. They let him take both Braunau and Linz, fortresses built to withstand a long siege, without firing a shot.

"I have arrived at Braunau today," Napoleon wrote to his brother, Joseph. Napoleon's limitations as a creature hopelessly rooted in time here become pathetically apparent. Endowed with a sixth sense of multi-dimensional time, conveniently opening a view of the future, he could not but have added "...Braunau, Hitler's birthplace."

But he just goes on: "The Russian Army seems greatly horrified by the fate of the Austrian Army. It has left me Braunau, which is one of the keys of Austria. It is a fine fortress and is well provided with munitions of all kinds. We shall see what this Russian Army will do. It has lost its head."

This indeed soon became plain. The Russians made up for their own lack of success by proclaiming a loud contempt for their Austrian allies, whose soldiers they accused of cowardice, their officers of criminal neglect and a pitiful inefficiency. The contempt which the Russians flung in the faces of the Austrians they reserved for the person of His Imperial and Royal, Apostolic Majesty, to be conveyed to him in innuendo. Mack's capitulation was the favorite jibe. The headquarters staff surrounding Alexander regarded the Austrian Emperor as a shipwrecked fellow who should be grateful to his generous rescuers, and who could only redeem to some extent the shameful capitulation of his army by resigning his will and placing himself unreservedly in the hands of Great-heart Alexander.

It was a bitter pill to swallow for Kaiser Franz, who entertained the loftiest conception of his own Holy Roman Apostolic Majesty, who at best admitted merely a nominal difference—as of an *"Erlaucht"* and a

"Durchlaucht"—between himself and the eternal Father in Heaven, whose opposite number, rather than steward, he considered himself to be: lord over all the earth, but whom the Russians nicknamed "a fool in full dress."

IV. WAR: A SCIENCE OR AN ART?

KAISER FRANZ, resplendent in white uniform and accompanied by an archduke, could be seen trotting to and fro between the Austrian and the Russian headquarters in an exceedingly elegant cabriolet. He did not understand the art of war and, thinking it was a science, covered up his ignorance of military tactics by firing off questions in quick succession at his own and the Russian officers whom it was his duty to receive in audience: *how? why? how many? what was the number? exactly at what point? precisely at what time?*—which disconcerted them. He took full advantage of the privilege of a sovereign who questions but is not questioned in return, who disagrees but must in all circumstances be agreed with.

Besides, nobody understands war, and daring men like Napoleon succeed, for a time, by taking advantage of those others who act as though they knew what they were about. During the Battle of Jutland, Admiral Jellicoe signaled a message to Admiral Beatty, which read: "Where is the enemy?"

It is eloquent of that expanding game of blindman's buff we still call war, in which the number of ascertainable facts must be multiplied by an equal number of incalculable factors to get at the correct sum of uncertainty. Kaiser Franz, who imagined he did not understand a science clear to others more gifted than himself, was astonished how his pointed questions put out the officers, Russian as well as his own, reputed to be veritable geniuses at military strategy. War—they might have wished but had not the ready words with which to answer a sovereign desirous of precise information on a subject not clear to himself—war, like art, was conditioned by ineffable inspiration. It was further conditioned by largely unknown laws of psychology. It was, finally, a game of hazard, like roulette, in which red days of victory are succeeded by black days of defeat, no one can tell when or why—a game of hazard of which the law of averages, to include the rise and fall of empires, may be worked out only over a far longer stretch of centuries than this planet has yet achieved.

The officers did not expatiate on this aspect of supreme uncertainty to His Holy Apostolic Majesty, basing their prediction of victory on the more cheerful, at least certain, fact that they were Austrians or Russians, as the case might be. And Kaiser Franz, his bright faith in his own supreme elevation by right divine momentarily dimmed at the sight of his subjects and allies, hoped God would not abandon His Apostle.

V. REVIEW BY TWO EMPERORS

THE two emperors, riding side by side and followed by their suites prancing in elegant array, reviewed the combined armies. Eighty thousand men were drawn up at daybreak and awaited for many hours the arrival of their majesties.

Some troops had that very night arrived from Russia, dead with fatigue after a forced march in the pouring rain. Roused just after midnight on a cold drizzling December morn, an hour after having fallen asleep in their wet clothes, they were told to fall in and then dismissed to smarten themselves up for the review by the two emperors.

There was some confusion about kit—field kit or dress uniforms. Conflicting reports. Cancellation of a previous order and, when officers had changed once more, a last-minute reversal—the confirmation of original instructions. And a great deal of bad blood.

One can imagine the bullying all down the scale. From the commander in chief to the lowest private, in a descending hierarchy of authority, a torrent of faultfinding and abuse would be let loose and roll down the ranks. An orgy of activity would ensue. Eighty thousand men shaving at once. Frantic polishing of leather. Frenzied burnishing of steel. Crazy blanching of white cord. Kicking horses groomed and brushed down till their coats shine like satin and their manes hang like fringe. Meanwhile ample officers of field rank getting their bellies into uniforms tightened in the waist and buttoned up to the chin and dispensing curses to hot-and-bothered batmen. Leisurely generals emerging from their village quarters in dress uniforms blazing with decorations and grunting to subservient red-necked colonels. The latter giving sharp orders to majors and captains, who pass them on with added zest of severity down the line. Wrath, curses, kicks, fists. And hell to pay.

At last all is ready. Banners are flying. Gorgeous trumpeters in embroidered jackets, mounted on grays ambling along to the rhythm of the music, lead the cavalry into position. With a brazen clatter, the shining cannon jolt on their gun carriages, leaving a smell of linstocks behind them. Then comes the infantry, halting at the word of command. The plain is a mass of colored columns. Tolstoy, in *War and Peace,* speaks of a breath of wind stirring the air and fluttering the streamers on the lances, as though the army itself, motionless, as if turned to stone, silently expressed its joy at the approach of the emperors as a party of horsemen is sighted in the distance. The unfolded standards flutter ecstatically against their staves, and a shiver of anticipation passes down the serried ranks. "They're coming! . . . Here they are!"

The command: "Silence!" is rapped out and repeated all along the line. Then silence falls. Nothing can be heard but the tramp of the approaching horses. The trumpeters give out a triumphant flourish and cease. And all hear—they can scarcely believe their ears—the fresh, soft voice of none other than Alexander I, their Emperor, greeting his Army.

Tolstoy depicts the sudden self-oblivion which comes over a young officer as he sets eyes on the handsome young Tsar in his Cavalry Guard's uniform and his cocked hat base forward and tilted at a rakish angle, with his pleasant face beaming with good looks and his resonant though moderate voice. He is bewitched at the sight of his Emperor and a warm gush of love engulfs his being, a proud consciousness of the might of him who is the cause of this triumph, a devotion so ardent that he feels there is no crime, no act of heroism he would not commit at one word from that man. No doubt the Nazis feel thus when they see and hear their Hitler.

The Tsar, pausing, smiles at the Emperor Francis at his side and says a few words in French; and Tolstoy's young officer "smiles in sympathy" and, finding no other available outlet for the loyal passion swelling within him, joins with all the strength of his lungs in a deafening "Hurrah!" A "Hurrah" so deafening, continuous and joyful that each man is awed by the multitude and immensity of the power of which he is himself a component.

For a minute the Tsar seems to hesitate. And here we have a good example of the exacting intolerance of hero worshipers and fans of all kinds. The young officer is disappointed in his hero: "How can he hesitate or doubt?" he asks himself. But the following moment his hero worship overcomes his carping criticism: the Emperor's indecision now seems to him no less enchanting and majestic than his decisive gestures. And at this moment Alexander, touching the flank of his sensitive dark-bay thoroughbred with the heel of his narrow-pointed riding-boot, then fashionable, gathers up his bridle in his white doeskin-gloved hand and rides off, followed by his jostling feathered suite. Farther and farther away he rides, stopping in front of each regiment along the line, till at last only the white plumes of his cocked hat can be seen waving above the heads of his suite.

VI. KUTUZOV AND ALEXANDER

THERE was clearly no enthusiasm among the Russians for Kaiser Franz, though when the review was over the Russian officers, gathering into groups to discuss the distinctions conferred by the two emperors, had something to say about the Austrian uniforms. Tolstoy provides his young hero with the opportunity of riding past his emperor. Spurring his horse he rides forward at a hand gallop. The horse, with his foaming jaw held back against his breast, and his tail in the air, tossing up his heels, his graceful, slender legs, as though flying through the air without touching the ground, seems also conscious of the Emperor's eye upon him. The young man, with his legs pressed back, and an anxious though blissful face, sits bolt upright as if he and his horse were of a piece; they fly past the Emperor in all their gleaming grace and beauty.

Finally, all that his officers seem to ask of their emperor, who has so completely bewitched them that every gesture has been ingrained on their hearts, is to be allowed to advance under their god's command against Bonaparte or anyone else he chooses to name. For with him they were—as Napoleon's grenadiers with *him*—"confident of victory."

Napoleon could count on an even more absolute devotion. His promise to his men might seem comical—and *is* comical—but still shows the depth of affection he evidently inspired among his troops. Wellington, asked what was the least encouraging address he ever heard before a battle, replied it was a speech addressed by a Portuguese commander to his army: "Men! Remember you are Portuguese!" Napoleon's address to his troops strikes me as even more damping: "Soldiers, I myself will direct your movements. I shall keep out of the way of fire if you, with your habitual valor, carry disorder and confusion into the enemy's ranks. But if victory should for one moment hang in doubt, you will see your emperor expose himself to the foremost fire; for victory must not tremble in the balance on a day when the honor of the French infantry is at stake. That honor is essential to the honor of the nation. Do not break your ranks under pretense of rescuing the wounded! Let every soldier be imbued with the thought that we must defeat these hirelings of England, inspired by such hatred of our nation!"

"Up guards and at 'em!" may not be eloquent, but it is to the point. The British military mind lacks the grandiloquence of the French. The difference is typical. A French commander in Egypt during the Great War harangued his troops before a battle, urging them, soldiers of France, to remember the glories of the past, reminding them in strident tones that the Pyramids which had beheld Napoleon were at this moment watching them, that the Sphinx herself was contemplating them and wondering how they would acquit themselves in the face of such a heritage of glory as was linked forever with the name of France. The British commander could not contrive a more inspiring message than: "N.C.O.'s and men will pick up all empty tins and other rubbish before leaving camp."

However that may be, the Russians in 1805 had their Alexander. Before the battle of Wischau he issued forth on his charger, and Tolstoy's young officer had again the satisfaction of overhearing the Tsar ask a question: "The Pavlograd Hussars?"

"The reserve, sire."

There is an impressive scene when the Emperor rides out to meet his troops and the commander in chief, Kutuzov, rides forward to meet his sovereign, dismounts and salutes the Tsar in a manner which seems to say: "I am nought; you are our master." This gesture of the old experienced warlord bowing in submission before his young imperial master was not prompted by sincerity and was not well received by Alexander, who hated Kutuzov. Capable of a show of submission, Kutuzov could answer his sovereign with veiled but studied insolence.

The Emperor, eager for battle, asks Kutuzov when he intends to start the attack, adding testily: "Mihaïl Ilaryonovitch, you know we are not on the parade ground."

Kutuzov performs one of his deep bows denoting complete submission to the overriding will (rather than competence) of his imperial master. He dissents in fact, but, as royal etiquette requires, assents in form: *"Precisely,* sire; we are *not* on the parade ground."

With an expression of one who might say, "If you are in a hurry to be beaten, well and good, we'll start," Kutuzov, whose military philosophy appears to be that a Russian army generally has everything to gain by neglecting to engage the enemy, gives the order to advance.

Alexander, all excitement—it is his first experience of war—rides forward, against the advice of his counselors, who assure him that his first duty is his personal safety.

The young Tsar, who was only twenty-eight, was at the time fired by his hatred of Napoleon, whom he had held up to universal execration over the foul murder of the Duc d'Enghien. But Napoleon, unable to see that two wrongs don't make a right, retorted by giving the widest publicity to a question which Alexander had for five years been trying in vain to forget: "Who killed the Emperor Paul?"

It was quite in the vein of Herr Hitler's retorts. "What about the Jews?" asks President Roosevelt. "What about the Negro lynchings?" answers Hitler. "Yes, what about the Jews?" repeats Mr. Chamberlain. "What about the Indians?" says Hitler. "What about them?" "What about what?"—and the matter dries up. Like the British Press, Alexander considered such raking up of the past as being in rather bad taste: Napoleon was clearly no gentleman.

Inspired by a detached idealism to liberate Europe, but fired by indignation of a very personal kind, Great-heart Alexander left the third column with which he was riding and was about to join the vanguard when he was informed that his brave Russians had routed Napoleon's army. The war was over.

The Tsar was overjoyed. But he was also chagrined. He should have been at the head of his troops. Just his bad luck! And glory had been so near at hand!

He was deploring his fatal dilatoriness when news was brought him that, after the smoke had cleared off, it was found that the French army was still there. The French had neither been defeated, as it was hoped, nor had they retreated, as it was expected. The capture of a troop of horse, the total result of the battle (which turned out to have been not a battle but an abortive engagement between outposts), was admittedly incompatible with the earlier Russian claim of an overwhelming victory shrinking, on further inquiry, to—well, the capture of a troop of horse.

Riding on to the village of Wischau, Alexander, followed by his military and civil suites, caught sight of some dead and wounded soldiers whom nobody had bothered to attend to. A dying man bareheaded and lying in a pool of blood arrested his attention. Reining in his horse, Alexander leaned over in a graceful attitude and observed him through his gold *lorgnon*. He was even then a little shortsighted. Tolstoy's young officer happened to be again on the spot. "The sight of this wounded wretch," Tolstoy tells us, "horrible to behold, so close to the Emperor, appalled and quite sickened Rostov," who—we can only surmise—was indignant with the soldier for his effrontery in appearing in a recumbent position with his blood outside him which he should have decently concealed inside and out of sight of the beloved tender-hearted Emperor, or, alternatively, have sunk through the ground. Rostov "could see the pained look in the Tsar's face and the shudder that ran through his frame; he saw his foot nervously thrust against the ribs of his horse, which was too well trained to stir an inch. An aide-de-camp dismounted and took the man by the shoulder to raise him on a stretcher. The soldier groaned.

" 'Gently, *gently*—can it not be done more gently?' the Emperor uttered in a tone almost betraying keener pain than the dying soldier's; and he rode away. Rostov, who had seen tears filling the Emperor's eyes, heard him say to Czartoriski: *'Quelle terrible chose que la guerre!'* "

VII. THE TENDER HEART

ALEXANDER went to bed and stayed there, having entrenched himself against the onslaught of the brutal world on his emotions. His physician, Sir James Wylie, was sent for. But the Tsar was morally ill. The sight of the dead and wounded had impinged on his tender soul. He was thoroughly upset. The Emperor, it was said, had, on account of his exquisitely sensitive nature, suffered more than the soldiers through his participation in the war. Such excruciating moral pain his army had happily been spared.

A French general arrived early in the morning under shelter of a flag of truce, requesting an audience of His Imperial Majesty. He was conducted past the outposts to the imperial quarters, where he was bidden to wait. The Emperor had just fallen asleep and could on no account be wakened. If there was one thing which the Emperor forbade his courtiers, it was to cause his artificial return to consciousness. He would *not* be torn from Lethe's stream, where he was gently floating, to face his imperial responsibilities and to solve military conundrums. When he awoke of his own repletion, with his nervous batteries recharged, was soon enough for him.

Savary—for the caller was no other than Napoleon's trusted henchman —had to wait. He was the bearer of a letter from Napoleon to Alexander in which Napoleon hoped that Alexander would receive his envoy with courtesy. As all the Russian courtiers knew quite well that Savary was both the kidnaper and executioner of the Duc d'Enghien, the politeness shown to him while the Emperor was asleep was strained.

At noon the Emperor awoke and Savary was admitted. He delivered the letter. Addressing Alexander as "Sire," Napoleon began by congratulating His Majesty on his arrival to take command of his army. He instructed his plenipotentiary to express all the esteem which he, Napoleon, felt for His Majesty the Emperor of Russia, and to assure His Majesty of his desire to find an opportunity of showing how anxious he was to secure His Majesty's friendship. Napoleon concluded his letter with the hope that His Majesty would receive his envoy with the courtesy which His Majesty always showed to everyone, a trait so characteristic of His Majesty; and Napoleon also hoped that His Majesty would believe in his desire to make himself agreeable to His Majesty, whom he prayed God to keep in His holy and worthy protection. The letter was signed: "Napoleon."

Alexander's reply was hardly calculated to mollify the uneasy feelings of a man who, having himself set a crown on his head, was not sure that his brother monarchs regarded him as a sovereign by divine right. Alexander did not address Napoleon as "Your Majesty." He headed his letter: "To the Head of the French Government." He acknowledged, with thanks, the letter which General Savary had delivered to him. His one desire was to see the peace of Europe established on an equitable basis. He added, coldly, almost disgruntledly, that he would be glad, when that was done, to have an opportunity of showing Napoleon some politeness; and he assured him of his distinguished consideration.

Alexander's brother and successor, Nicholas I, provoked the Crimean War by offending the susceptibilities of Napoleon III in replying with "Mon Ami" to a letter addressing him as "Mon Frère." The idea of engaging Sweden in war first occurred to Peter the Great when, on his journey through Sweden, he was ignored by Charles XI as a Muscovite barbarian beneath royal notice. It is true that Peter traveled *incognito,* and one might well assume that the King of Sweden merely respected Peter's wish to be left alone. But Peter's *incognito* was due to a mixture of shyness and pride. He was perpetually susceptible to snubs—potential rather than actual. Actually nobody snubbed him because nobody was specially aware of him. It was sheer lack of interest. Russia was still the ultimate Thule. Unaccustomed as yet to intercourse with his equals abroad, Peter was painfully conscious of his own lack of manners and of the backwardness of his country. But he was also conscious of the tremendous expanse, even then, of Russia. His pride at its size, and his humility in the face of European amenities wholly lacking in his own semibarbarous land, made him extremely self-conscious. Since he could not be a Louis XIV, who ignored him, well and good; he would be the opposite—a tsar traveling across Europe disguised as a man of the people. But that did not mean he wanted Charles XI to assume that no disguise was needed. The German princes knew how to treat him. They cajoled him to reconsider his unkind decision to deprive them of the high privilege of making his acquaintance. They sent their courtiers for him in State coaches and placed palaces at the disposal of the High and Mighty Tsar of Muscovy; and he took offense because the reigning duke had not arrived in person. Stormy scenes took place at the inns and pubs at which Peter put up for the night. Threats and some manhandling from the giant Tsar carousing with his staff and already in his cups; pleadings and cajoleries from abashed Masters of the Horse. Peter would lift a chamberlain or gentleman of the bedchamber by the collar and throw him out, calling after him in a mixture of bad German and seamen's Dutch to go and tell his duke to come and welcome him in person if he wished him to accept his hospitality, and not to come back without him. "Son of a bitch!" he roared through the window amid a chorus of drunken imprecations from his satellites—a fine bunch of hail-fellow-well-mets, alternately soulful and violent when in their cups; grimly suspicious when sober.

The Germans, well-behaved and meticulous in etiquette, would be thrown off their balance by this unaccustomed display of Muscovite "broad nature." But out of the thirty-six or more independent German States there were always two or three who could not overlook the advantage of a Russian alliance whereby another independent German State could be annexed, and another, thus creating those strange compound States like Mecklenburg-Stettin and Mecklenburg-Schwerin and Schleswig-Holstein-Gottorp. The sovereign prince would at length arrive at the pub, nervously poke his nose inside to find most of Peter's boon companions by now unconscious on the floor, but Peter apparently still going strong and none the worse for having emptied his twenty-first bottle. The prince, moving like a marionette, would come forward to greet his tsarish majesty and, taking him by the hand and moving backwards before him, conduct him, suddenly sobered and now extremely self-conscious, to the royal carriage. Peter, on the rebound from arrogance caused by wine and wounded pride, completely swept off his feet by remorse, overwhelmed by the unexpected honor accorded to him on foreign soil, would subside into a guilty humility. The duke, still walking backwards, would lead the Tsar in to supper. With the St. Vitus dance coming upon him in his returning sobriety, a terrible twitching would distort his face into grimaces frightening to their more youthful Highnesses sitting at table with him. With shaking hands he would lift a knife and fork. Utterly incapacitated by his feeling of shyness at showing himself unequal to their expectations, he would wish himself back in Russia.

Still, the Germans at least did the right thing by him and he had earmarked the royal families of Germany as a marriage mart for all the future tsars of Russia. Their manners were good—a thing always valued by people devoid of any themselves. But for Charles XI of Sweden to take him at his word, when his *incognito* was but the shy approach of a man uncertain of how to behave with his equals and afraid he might be laughed at, that was a vastly different matter. It stuck in him like a barb. The wound festered. Ideas of vindicating his importance, revenging the slight, spun in his brain, catching in the web of political considerations. The courts of Vienna and Dresden took advantage of his prepossession. The coming struggle for the Spanish succession was splitting Europe into two camps, with France, Sweden and Turkey ranged against the Holy Roman Empire of the German Nation, Holland and England. And Peter, guided by his hostility to Sweden's king, began to plan the destruction of Sweden, his ambition spreading like wildfire ignited by that spark of resentment which had set all that combustible stuff of war and politics aflame.

For it is an error to imagine that the pangs of snobbery do not assail the hearts of royalty. Where there is still degree, and still pride, a snub is latent, no less real because in abeyance. Insensitive people in advantageous situations deny the suffering occasioned to the pride of people at a disadvantage, or dismiss it as unworthy. Well-fed people may as well deny the existence of hunger, or dismiss it as something "morbid" or "unhealthy." If Thackeray had invented a comic name for hunger— perhaps called aspiring eaters "fullups" and castigated the vice as "fullupery"—and depicted hungry men and women as unpleasant people, who knows, the desire of the needy to eat well might today be regarded by those who take their good meals for granted as the pushfulness of vulgar upstarts ostentatiously aspiring to a standard of cooking appreciable only by palates evolved by centuries of exquisite eating.

And when we say that kings and emperors are subject to the pangs of snobbery, we must bear in mind that snobbery is a crystal with many facets. A mighty emperor of doubtful origin might be snubbed by a petty king of ancient lineage, and vice versa. Alexander himself was later snubbed by a legitimate king of the House of Capet, and was never to forget it.

Do not, therefore, let us pretend that Napoleon did not suffer when he read Alexander's reply to his letter, even though historians tell us that Napoleon's letter was a ruse and that Alexander fell into the trap prepared for him. The theory is that Napoleon wished to dispose of the Russians while the going was good. The idea behind his letter was to make Alexander think that he, Napoleon, was frightened of him, so as to cause the Russian army to attack him quickly before assistance reached it from King Frederick William of Prussia.

But if that were true, what was there to prevent Napoleon from attacking the Russians? They might have retreated; in which case what was to prevent his pursuing them?

It is surely far more likely that Napoleon, who numbered 70,000 men against 80,000 Russians and Austrians, was not averse to detaching the young Emperor, who had been his ally, from Kaiser Franz, and winning him back by flattery, as indeed he later succeeded in doing. In penning his letter, Napoleon had not spared the attribute of majesty, which he hoped Alexander would return and so confirm his own title, which, since it was the zenith of his personal ambition, occupied his thoughts no less than the means by which he planned to extend his dominion. Alexander's letter must have been a real shock to him. One can imagine Napoleon reading this letter with a sudden flush suffusing his cheeks; and Savary, the murderer of the Duc d'Enghien, reflecting, probably inopportunely, on the insensibility of men born in the imperial purple to others, like his master, who have reached the same goal by the sweat of their brow.

VIII. THE BATTLE

ALEXANDER did infer that Napoleon was afraid of him. He dispatched a letter to his friend Frederick William in Berlin, telling him that Napoleon was obviously sounding for peace, but that they were going to let him have it hot and strong without even awaiting the army of Frederick William, who would have to be quick if he wanted to draw any share of glory from the victory. They had already won a provisional victory over Napoleon. True, in the end it had boiled down to the capture of a troop of horse, which nevertheless was significant as a break in their long run of misfortunes, and a turning-point; and, small though it was, it was a symbol which augured greater deeds involving wider issues and broader scope in the battle which was upon them.

It is commonly assumed that the battles of the last century were a reasonable, and even heroic, way of settling national differences. It is thought that only the advent of the airplane, of the submarine, and the extraordinary rapidity of transport has dehumanized warfare. And, of course, the danger to the civil population exposed to aerial bombardment has made war, we say, too horrible to contemplate. But in many ways the wars of the last century were even more fantastic. Imagine the Russian infantry tramping from central Russia across Europe: left, right, left, right, left!— left! for months, with no more gladdening prospect on reaching Bohemia than a bayonet charge: all because the Emperor Alexander, despite his well-known love of peace, resented the personal imputations of the Emperor Napoleon. It may be argued that in his day war was the accepted means of settling national differences. But Alexander himself was the first protagonist of a League of Nations. The sight of wounded men in the engagement of the day before had so upset him that he could neither eat nor sleep. Yet a betrayal of fear which he read into Napoleon's letter was enough for him to scatter all his ideals of peace and good will among men to the winds and issue the order setting 80,000 Russians and Austrians at the throats of 70,000 Frenchmen who had never met and bore each other no grudge.

He had not, like Mr. Neville Chamberlain, the courage of his convictions to make a complete break in a sanguinary tradition grotesquely at variance with the reality of individual lives. Mr. Chamberlain broke the vicious circle: he said that, since there was nothing worse than war, he would at any rate not go to war about it. So, like a solicitor entrusted with the interests of forty million clients desiring to stay alive, he straight away flew over to see the solicitor of the opposing side and talk it over. Alexander refused Napoleon's suggestion for a meeting, but he sent Prince Dolgorukov back with Savary to hear what Napoleon had to suggest in the way of climbing down from the ascendancy he had established for himself in Europe. Prince Dolgorukov—called the captor of Wischau because in the recent engagement he had, after the capture of the troop of horse, retained the village of that name—returned the same evening and was closeted for a long time with the Tsar. The news he brought back was that Napoleon's idea of peace was to hold on to everything he had seized, but to give a share of what he might seize next to Alexander, provided the Tsar forthwith dissociated himself from the Emperor Francis and the rest of the bunch.

These mutual messages between Alexander and Napoleon on the eve of the decisive battle disconcerted Kaiser Franz. Though Alexander assured him that there was nothing in it and that Napoleon's advances merely betrayed how anxious he was to avoid the coming battle, Kaiser Franz could not square this view with Napoleon's attitude to the emissaries which the Austrians had sent him with the earnest request to conclude, here and now if possible, a tolerable peace before another Ulm, Marengo or Hohenlinden. While Napoleon hardly deigned to listen to them and sent them to Vienna to confer with Talleyrand, Kaiser Franz twice came across Savary at the Russian imperial headquarters at Wischau and was surprised to see Alexander receive him with quite conspicuous graciousness.

The Russians considered—and Alexander rather shared this view—that after Mack's shameful capitulation the Austrian Emperor was no longer entitled to pursue his own policy but had to eat out of the hand of the Tsar. And while Kaiser Franz was suspicious of what was going on behind his back between Napoleon and Alexander, the Tsar reproached the Holy Roman Emperor with disloyalty amounting to treachery by sending emissaries to Napoleon to plead for peace when, as Napoleon's own messages to Alexander clearly showed, he was afraid of them and anxious to avoid the coming battle. He would not go on being afraid of them, Alexander argued hotly, if Kaiser Franz went on pleading for peace at any price. Surely a child could see that!

But Kaiser Franz was one of those intellectually modest men who, while they find it difficult to hold their own in argument, do not feel it incumbent on them to believe what they are told. For there were other counselors who told the Emperor of Austria that Napoleon's motive was merely to confuse his enemies. And since the Emperor of the French had all but conquered Austria, while Russia was many leagues away, there was little doubt that if Napoleon favored peace at all it was at the expense of Austria. Kaiser Franz could not forget an article, inspired by Napoleon, that had appeared in the *Moniteur* six months before. It was very foolish in the opinion of the writer of this article (for Napoleon had his "Signor Gayda" of the day) for France and Russia to fight each other. They were not adjoining territories and in no danger from each other. Very much the contrary. They could be extremely useful mutually.

Who could assure His Apostolic Majesty that there were not secret relations between France and Russia *now* before the battle? Who could guarantee that Alexander was not a turncoat like his father, the mad Paul, who had turned overnight from a savage enemy of Napoleon into a passionate admirer? Alexander, only recently Napoleon's ally, had swung over to the opposite pole and become his sworn foe. He might any day complete the circle.

Neither were the Austrians at all satisfied with the way the Russians treated the local Austrian population. "The Russians are greatly disliked in Austria," Napoleon wrote to his brother Joseph. "They pillage, steal and violate everywhere." When the Allies opened fire at the enemy next morning they felt they would far sooner have turned their guns on one another than upon the joint enemy with whom only yesterday they had conducted clandestine negotiations behind one another's backs. Nor did the battle seem to proceed at all according to expectation. Alexander himself was—and was not—in command of the operations. Nobody quite knew. He had appointed to take supreme command under himself, or rather to guide him in the manner of an instructor who takes a learner up for his first flight, a Prussian general who issued his orders to the Russian generals in German which they did not understand. Besides, there was no "double control," so to speak, as in an airplane, and the German general had to adapt his further operations to Alexander's mistakes. More concerned with the Tsar's safety than with the issue of the battle, the Prussian general exercised merely a nominal control over the other commanders, who, not knowing German and loath to take their orders from a Prussian, conducted independent operations on their own. Only Alexander's brother, the Grand Duke Constantine, who hated war, was optimistic. He took one look at the French and bellowed: "Why, to defeat these gents it's enough for us to throw our caps at them!"

It proved to be not quite enough. The Russians were handicapped by lack of food, which was so great that the men had had practically nothing to eat for two days before the battle. Their horses were so starved that they could not draw the guns, which, for that reason, could only be used where they had been planted. For this lack of supplies and fodder the Russians were themselves to blame. They had desolated the Austrian districts far and wide, making a desert of the villages, treating the peasants as their enemies rather than as their allies. So much so that the Austrian peasants looked forward to the arrival of the French. "Better the French for enemies than the Russians for friends," they said.

Kutuzov abandoned the heights of Pratzen, the key position of the battlefield which he was fortunate to hold, in order to attack the right wing of the French where he assumed it to be—but where it wasn't. And Napoleon occupied the heights of Pratzen and, with it, the key position of the battlefield the minute Kutuzov vacated it to look for the right wing of the French army. Though the Russian soldiers fought bravely, as usual, the Russian command was, as usual, abject. The Russian generals put their heads together for something new and daring wherewith to startle the military genius of the century. But, finally, all they could rake up out of their store of military knowledge was a well-worn piece of conventional surprise.

They in fact executed the rudimentary military maneuver of trying to circumvent the right wing of the French in order to take the enemy in the flank. To insure, however, the success of this stale little trick, it is above all else essential that the patient upon whom the operation is being carried out should stand perfectly still and not stir an inch. As the French, however, were in the highest degree mobile, Russian cunning was frustrated in its inception by Murat, who guessed what they were up to. There and then he charged with dropped reins his cavalry reserve through the thin double-ranked line of Russian infantry, to whom it never for a moment occurred to ward off with their bayonets this time-honored classical maneuver.

Murat drove the Russian infantry over the lakes where the thin ice broke under the sudden weight. Even Kaiser Franz, no great tactician at the best of times and who never observed anything till it was over, this time saw plainly what was coming and remarked to Alexander: "They're in for a good drubbing, I can see!"

The tactical and strategic mistakes of the Russians enabled Napoleon with an army of seventy thousand to win, after six hours of the hottest fighting, a smashing victory over the Russians and Austrians, numbering together eighty thousand men. But then Napoleon enjoyed two supreme advantages: he was Napoleon, and he had no allies.

Later, on St. Helena, he was wont to refer to Austerlitz as perhaps his supreme masterpiece—at least tying for first place with Jena. Just as Wagner in his old age might ponder over the rival merits of *Meistersinger* and *Tristan*. Austerlitz was in all respects, Napoleon thought, a beautiful piece of work: masterful in conception, flawless in execution.

The Allied casualties alone were 30,000. The Austrian troops, consisting almost entirely of raw recruits, acquitted themselves well and after the battle blatantly accused the Russians of having been more of a hindrance than a help to them. The Russians blamed the Austrians for lack of good will and accused them of being only too glad to see the Russians beaten so as to make up for their own earlier capitulation.

Czartoriski, abusing the candor which Alexander said he encouraged in his friends, afterwards reminded Alexander that he had been an unmitigated nuisance all through the Austerlitz battle. His Imperial Majesty's presence, he argued, was at no point an advantage, for precisely at whatever point the Tsar happened to be stationed the rout was most immediate and complete. "Your Majesty yourself took part in it and had to flee in haste. Your departure augmented the stampede and the general discouragement."

But *The Times* did not share Czartoriski's view of the usefulness of his sovereign. "The general engagement," it said in its leader under date of December 20, 1805, "which we announced in our paper of Wednesday, as having taken place on the 2nd instant, was not decided on that day. It was renewed on the two subsequent days, with a vigour and obstinacy unparalleled in the annals of modern warfare, and terminated at length in favour of the Allied Army.... Under no man but Buonaparte would the French have made so gallant and determined a resistance; and, brave as the Russians are, the victory would, probably, not have been theirs, but for the enthusiasm which the presence, and the example, and the noble daring of their Sovereign, inspired.... From all accounts, Buonaparte's career is nearly at an end."

The disaster had been complete. Alexander galloped for dear life. For a time he could not make himself jump a wide ditch. There he was skirting alongside while his escort leaped past him. Finally, taking his courage in both his hands, he forced his horse to jump and, sliding off the saddle on the other side, he collapsed under a tree and there, overcome with misery, sobbed into his handkerchief.

IX. MOTHER LOVE

"UNTIL," *The Times* wrote on December 31, "the Hamburgh Mails arrive, it would be idle to observe upon the French account of the battle of the 2nd. If the extent of their successes have equaled their official representations, the war is finished.... But we cannot believe that they have obtained so easy a triumph over the hardy Russians."

Alexander traveled in a chaise, with his friend and foreign minister, Adam Czartoriski, sitting beside him, the horses lunging forward into the night at full speed. There was still danger of being captured by French outposts and they traveled without a stop. He cried freely, while Czartoriski reproached him. Adam was his bosom friend. He had been, perhaps still was, the lover of Alexander's wife Elizabeth—with Alexander's full approval, blessing and encouragement. He had been one of the band of young idealists with whom Alexander had begun his reign. He had been the leader of the "Committee of Public Safety" which had discussed ways and means of introducing their idealism into international relations. They had even planned nothing less than a League of Nations. And this was the sorrowful outcome! Czartoriski now reminded him that not only had Alexander by his interference with military operations carried confusion into his own ranks, but that, ever since the very day of his arrival at headquarters, his flirtation with Napoleon had sown dissension, division and uncertainty among the high command, who before his arrival had been single-minded and united in their opposition to the enemy.

Alexander listened and cried. When, in the good old days of their idealism, one of the young men of the Committee of Public Safety had in the heat of argument with Alexander overstepped the mark and later written him a letter to apologize for his behavior, Alexander had deprecated the need of an apology. "Good God!" he had exclaimed. "What is the point of having friends at all if they cannot tell me frankly what they think of me?" But Czartoriski, as a too candid friend, Alexander felt, perhaps imposed on him by carrying candor further than one was reasonably prepared to let him go on this occasion.

At last, out of reach of pursuit, spending the night at a wayside inn, Alexander sat down to write post-haste to his mother, the Empress Dowager at St. Petersburg, holding up the Austrians to execration, cursing them, root, stem and branch, to all eternity. Try and win a battle with these gentlemen! Oh, the cowards! Oh, the fools! The traitors parleying with Napoleon on the eve of battle! What despicable soldiers! What execrable officers! ... And Kaiser Franz! *Good God!* Kaiser Franz! ...

The defeat of the Allies at Austerlitz was slowly percolating through Europe, and *The Times* admitted what by now was common knowledge: "The Emperor of Russia is, through the signal condescension of Buonaparte, to be permitted to return to his own country, under such conditions as, we believe, a Sovereign, who was four days previously at the head of eighty thousand men, was never before obliged to submit to. ... Incredible as this sudden and unexpected termination of the war is, we are compelled to give it reluctant credit....From the Baltic to the farthest extremity of Italy, there is not a Sovereign or Prince, who at this moment may not be said to hold his power by sufferance from Buonaparte. What this frightful state is to lead to, is in the womb of time. The Victor may be merciful on the Continent, but we, who despise his power, are not to expect peace from his moderation. He pledged himself to his troops that he would make peace at Vienna before Christmas, and in London before Easter. He has redeemed that pledge in the first instance; we are persuaded he will endeavour to do so in the latter."

Seven years later, another hasty traveler was fleeing in a chaise, but in the opposite direction, also with his diplomatic counselor at his side. He was Napoleon.... But we must not anticipate events.

Alexander entered Petersburg by night, to avoid hostile demonstrations, longing to conceal himself from sight—and die.

He was surprised to find the capital illuminated in his honor, his mother having spread the news that Austerlitz, if all were known, was, rightly seen, a victory.

CHAPTER XIX

ALEXANDER LEAVES
KAISER FRANZ IN THE LURCH

I. INTERVIEW WITH NAPOLEON

ALTHOUGH the defeat at Austerlitz was far more Russian than Austrian, Austria having sustained but one-third of the total casualties, yet the major consequences of this joint calamity fell upon the Emperor Francis.

At the conclusion of the battle Kaiser Franz was seized with panic at the thought that the Russian army, no longer held in check by the French army, would turn and rend the Austrian. Kaiser Franz rushed to Napoleon to implore his protection. He was prepared to accept the most ignoble conditions of peace, merely to get rid of his awkward bed-fellows. For the situation of Francis II was by no means as desperate as was generally supposed. What was desperate indeed—enough to send you crazy—was to possess an ally who presumed that you were now completely in his power. Kaiser Franz lost his head. The wear and tear of long months of uncertainty had turned him into a nervous wreck. He could no longer bear the suspense of living cheek by jowl with an ally of whom you could never be sure that he would not overnight become the ally of the enemy and both together attack you next morning.

If the Russians had been contemptuous of the Austrians after Mack's capitulation, now after Austerlitz they were openly derisive. The Austrians—what there were of them—the Russians said, had not pulled their weight; and so the French, if you ignored the Austrians, who did not count, had outnumbered the Russians. Quite simply.

An armistice ensued, during which the famished retreating Russian troops fell like hungry wolves upon the Austrian villages in search of provender.

The Emperor of Austria earnestly solicited the favor of a personal interview with the Emperor of the French. This was accorded on December 4. The interview took place in a little village and lasted two hours. The Holy Roman Emperor pleaded good will among men. Napoleon looked stern. Would they *never* cease fighting the French? This hostility between the two countries—it was the same at the time of

Louis XIV. Would Vienna *never* cease plotting and combining against France? A look of intense puffed-up gravity came over Napoleon's face, which Kaiser Franz watched anxiously. Napoleon pierced the Holy Apostolic Emperor with his two gimlets. *"C'est grave!"* he intoned, lifting a fat warning forefinger. *"Oui ... c'est grave!"* Kaiser Franz echoed in awed propitiative imitation.

So far as the Russians went, their army was now completely in his power. Napoleon tapped the table, and rose, briskly pacing up and down, his hands clasped beneath his coat tails. It was finished! Should he so desire it, not one man could escape him. But he would allow them to go home because he wished to render the Tsar a service.

Allow the Russians to go home? Kaiser Franz heaved a sigh of relief. But render the Tsar a service: why?

Napoleon, with just a flicker of mirth across a still serious mien, assumed that this was not disagreeable to the Emperor of Austria.

Napoleon's conditions so far as the Russians were concerned pleased the Austrian monarch. The Russian troops were to clear out of Austria in prescribed stages. These conditions were humbly complied with by Alexander. Napoleon's assertion that he had the Russians in the hollow of his hand was more true than is generally considered to be the case. For had it not been Napoleon's wish to render the Tsar a good turn by concluding an armistice, it is probable that the remainder of the Russian army would have been settled by Davoust, who was in hot pursuit of the retreating Allies.

An armistice followed, with conversations paving the way for the Treaty of Pressburg, which condemned Kaiser Franz to loss of territory, a heavy indemnity, the recognition of all Napoleon's conquests since the last treaty he had concluded with the Austrian monarch, and, finally, the latter's complete renunciation of the last remnant of influence he exercised in Germany, Switzerland and Italy. The Emperor, who had the year before already assumed the title of Emperor of Austria because his position as Holy Roman Emperor of the German Nation was becoming increasingly untenable, now dropped the ancient title, and the Holy Roman Empire at long last came to an end.

Five years later, married to Marie Louise of Habsburg, Napoleon came into her room while she was writing a letter. "Who are you writing to?" he asked tenderly. He was fond of his wife, and the fact of her being the daughter of Kaiser Franz appealed to his vanity.

"I am writing to Papa," she said.

Napoleon bent over her shoulder as, having folded the letter into an envelope, Marie Louise was penning the address. "To His Imperial and Royal, Apostolic Majesty The Emperor," she wrote in her girlish hand.

Napoleon pondered. *"C'est bien!"* he said. He approved. He approved wholeheartedly. Tradition was a fine thing. It was a grand thing. For the son-in-law of Apostolic Majesty in Vienna there was nothing whatsoever to be said against it.

But this is to look five years ahead. For the present the future father-in-law was a crushed, a hopelessly defeated enemy, whose wounded pride was not salved by the friendly relations which ensued between Napoleon and Alexander's representatives after the armistice. Francis concluded a peace with Napoleon with an alacrity which could only be explained by his urgency to get rid of the Russian troops on his territory. Alexander in treating with Napoleon kept Francis in the dark. The Tsar took not the slightest interest in the peace conditions which Napoleon was imposing on Kaiser Franz. Rather did he take the attitude of one who, out of sheer highmindedness and natural generosity, was releasing his former ally from his contracted obligations.

II. CHANGE PARTNERS

HAVING begun the campaign by announcing to all the world that he was taking up arms for no personal motives or even for the sake of Russia, but was fighting for the salvation of Europe and more especially for the liberation of Austria, Alexander now incurred some criticism in Vienna where, in view of his earlier pledge, they expected him to stick up for them in their hour of need against Napoleon, who was imposing stiff terms on the conquered land. It, however, became increasingly evident that there was little indeed to hope from the Tsar, to whose envoy, Dolgorukov, Napoleon had declared just after the battle of Austerlitz that he had nothing against the idea of the Tsar enlarging his territories at the expense of Austria, should the Tsar by any chance entertain such thoughts. He, Napoleon, had nothing whatever against Alexander's helping himself to as many Austrian provinces as he liked. Prince Dolgorukov was to tell Tsar Alexander that he was to help himself to his heart's content.

When this information percolated through to Vienna, the Austrians understood that their disappointment in the Tsar was complete and that the Austro-Russian alliance had better be written off as a bad debt.

Nor could they remain indifferent in Vienna to the extraordinary generosity Napoleon was showing the Russian prisoners of war. Napoleon made a point of commending various Russian officers of importance for their brave exploits or, in the absence of deeds, for their mere appearance. With characteristic brevity, Napoleon would come out with some such remark as: *"Voilà un brave soldat!"* Drawing himself stiff, the Russian officer would shoot back: "Commendation from the Emperor Napoleon is the highest award a soldier's heart could desire."

A picture of extraordinary inanity is brought to light in these exchanges of civilities. On the one hand, here is this bloated monster beyond the pale of humanity for whose defeat no individual sacrifice of life or limb is deemed to be too great. On the other hand, no greater honor for the loser of a limb than commendation from the said monster. It all reads like a children's game, with some insane nurse in charge of the children, egging them on to bash in each other's heads with a poker, but take it all in good part, above all never cheating and observing all the rules of the game.

Napoleon immediately set free Prince Repnin and other distinguished Russian officers who had fallen into his hands, and all the men in the Guards, without stipulating for an exchange of prisoners. The rest of the Russian captives he took to France, but soon sent them back dressed in new uniforms and free of charge. Alexander, a man of exquisite sensibility, was touched by such attention.

The only hope which Austria had of modifying the severity of the Treaty of Pressburg was to call in Prussia, who, a month earlier, had signed an alliance for mutual defense and whose army was intact. If Prussia were called upon to fulfill her obligations, Austria might succeed in getting better terms from Napoleon and obtain at least an endurable treaty. Kaiser Franz sent a general to Frederick William with the fervent request that the King should assemble his Prussian troops in a military demonstration intended to convince Napoleon that Austria still had allies who could, if need be, take the field in her cause.

At the same time, the Emperor of Russia let it be known officially that he would regard compliance with the Austrian request as a personal favor. He also officially placed his Russian troops, thirty thousand strong, which had now reached Silesia (and were soon to prove as importunate to the Prussians as they had been to the Austrians) at the disposal of the Prussian king. He also sent the Russian troops stationed in Hanover.

But in a private letter in his own hand delivered by Prince Dolgorukov, Alexander earnestly advised his royal friend in Berlin against anything so foolish as a demonstration directed against Napoleon.

CHAPTER XX

ALEXANDER LEADS
FREDERICK WILLIAM A DANCE

I. THREE DOUBLE-CROSSERS

AT this point some historians frankly capitulate. They confess their inability to understand the mind of Alexander. Others dismiss him as a twister, a shameless double-crosser and perjurer. Others, again, credit him with unusual foresight and fortitude. He is taking, you see, the long view. He visualizes, across the years strewn with obstacles and defeats, the vindication of his policy, the eventual destruction of Napoleon. An end which Alexander in fact achieved.

These views are a little naïve in the light of Alexander's volatile changes of enthusiasm. The explanation of his vicissitudes of conduct must rather be sought in his capacity for spotting new facets on old facts, his unswerving loyalty to a mood. Things rarely work out to plan in the life of the individual. How much more rarely in the composite affairs of peoples.

According to the November understanding with Alexander, Frederick William was to inform Napoleon that unless he accepted the Allied peace terms, Prussia would join the Allies against him. But after Austerlitz this mission of mediation by threat ended unexpectedly in a convention between Napoleon and Prussia, by the terms of which Napoleon allowed the Prussian king to annex Hanover in exchange for the county of Ansbach, which was to go to Bavaria in return for the duchy of Berg, which Bavaria was to hand over to France. France was also to get from Frederick William the principality of Neuenburg, the balance of the duchy of Cleve, and the fortress Wesel.

The Prussian king was not pleased with this exchange. On the one hand he was surrendering genuine Prussian territory in return for Hanover, which Napoleon was giving him though it was the hereditary property of the King of England. Without daring to reject the proposal, Frederick William did his best to try to get out of it, to the honest anger of Napoleon, who wrote to brother Joseph: *"Cette cour de Prusse est bien fausse et bien bête."*

By February 1806, Napoleon had decided to break with Prussia, which, he said, combined rapacity with cowardice and broke faith with friend and foe alike. Napoleon, who kept faith so long as it suited him, was sincerely indignant with Frederick William, who had not synchronized his rare intervals of good faith with Napoleon's own. From now on Napoleon did all he could to get Prussia to take the initiative of breaking with him at a moment when all the advantages were on his side. He could not, he said, rely on Prussia. Neither could he rely on Russia. It therefore suited him to utilize for his own end Russia's habit of double-crossing her friends. Russia's friend happened to be Prussia, who had the same habit. Nor was Napoleon immune from this trait.

In addition, of course, factions and parties in Prussia and Russia were double-crossing each other in every direction; and thus the statement which follows is not as improbable as it at first appears. Frederick William, it is the contention, was forced by his friend Alexander, who had a month before sworn eternal loyalty over the coffin of Frederick the Great, to engage the victor of Austerlitz, at this most unpropitious time for Prussia, in a war which suited Russia even if it also suited Napoleon. Count Golz, at that time Prussian ambassador at St. Petersburg, writes in his reminiscences that his king had, in the spring of 1806, signed, behind the back of all his ministers, a treaty with the Tsar, binding himself to engage France in a war as an alternative to an immediate invasion by Russia. The Prussian monarch, in other words, had no choice except that of the lesser (*if* lesser) evil; and, scratching his head, he decided in favor of a war with France.

II. TURKISH INTERMEZZO

WHY should Russia at this or any time force Prussia into a war with France? The reason is plausible, if not entirely convincing. Russia considered this an opportune moment to resume her cherished campaign against Turkey. As France was the only power likely to intervene on behalf of Turkey, Russia, by embroiling France in a war with Prussia, hoped to occupy Napoleon sufficiently in central Europe to divert his attention from the impending Russian conquest in the Near East. That the desired diversion did not last long enough to enable Russia to accomplish her object in Turkey was, of course, something that Alexander or his advisers could not foresee.

Russia's cherished ambition before the Revolution had always been the acquisition of Constantinople and the further expansion of the Russian Empire at the cost of the Sick Man of Europe. Whoever appeared to be helping her towards this objective—whether Germanic Christendom, or Greek enthusiasts, whether a son of Saint Louis, or a Corsican atheist, a royalist or republican, he was equally welcome and deemed a noble ally to a holy cause.

Europe today does not sufficiently realize that Soviet Russia is in fact the only kind of Russia likely to renounce her hereditary ambition to restore Byzantium and repudiate the policy of imperialism and progressive annexation in the spirit of the testament of Peter the Great. Soviet Russia entertains no such imperialist ambitions, though it would welcome an emulation of its system in the entire world. Napoleon was not inclined to let Russia, which he had so easily defeated on the field of battle, help herself to large chunks of Turkey and so increase her power and prestige in Europe.

Russia's designs on Turkey had also attracted the notice of Downing Street, which had not tarried to acquaint the Tsar that the British Government regarded the preservation of the independence and integrity of Turkey as one of its basic principles. "That," Novosiltsov said to Pitt, "is an exceedingly bad opening for the desired alliance between Great Britain and Russia. My illustrious master is the noblest, finest and most generous man in the world. As such, he naturally expects blind confidence in his unshakable integrity and is justified in feeling himself deeply wounded if anyone, with threats or mere innuendos, should presume to step across his path, which might easily result in provoking him to take the very step from which one might wish to deflect him. Moreover, what disadvantage can it be to England if Constantinople is no longer in the hands of the Turkish barbarians but belongs to a cultured people such as the Russians? Isn't British trade in the Black Sea going to gain enormously? Of course, if it were a question of the Orient falling into the hands of rapacious France, that would be another matter. In that case there would be real danger for Great Britain. But in the loyal hands of the Tsar, why, no reasonable person could see any cause of anxiety for England!"

Pitt, who knew no more pressing need than to win Russia's alliance against Napoleon, assured Novosiltsov that, for his own part, he entertained not the slightest anxiety in this respect and foresaw no great danger in Constantinople belonging to the Emperor of Russia. Unfortunately, the opposite view was a deep-rooted prejudice of the British nation, which, alas! it was his business to appease.

Novosiltsov left London with the conviction that his master at St. Petersburg would encounter in his undertaking against the Sultan no serious opposition from the British Government. Turkey was in a sorry state, and the Tsar deemed it an opportune moment to strike hard at her. He was anxious to prevent a diversion of French troops to Turkey from Napoleon, who had an army in Dalmatia and entertained designs in the Near East in opposition to Russia's ambitions. Having deprived Austria of Venetian Dalmatia and the estuaries of Cattaro, Napoleon had acquired facilities hitherto lacking for the execution of his long-cherished plan to pocket the Ottoman empire.

To make Napoleon stay put, Alexander had sent to Paris Pierre Oubril, a Frenchman naturalized in Russia, with powers to conclude peace at any price. The Tsar expected that if he met the French demands in all major respects, Napoleon might be disposed to show himself generous in regard to the minor point which concerned him very little but meant a great deal to Alexander—Russia's ambitions in Turkey.

Napoleon, however, showed himself extraordinarily generous in every other respect but proved unexpectedly sticky on the Turkish question. Here he wouldn't budge an inch. He allowed the Tsar to retain 4,000 troops in the Greek islands, but he neutralized this concession by a clause in the same treaty which bound them both to respect the independence and territorial integrity of the Ottoman empire. An awkward stipulation for the Tsar, who was determined to attack the said empire.

As Alexander had now succeeded in forcing his friend's hand, and Frederick William had nervously proclaimed mobilization against France, the Tsar, who had tarried with the ratification of the treaty Oubril had signed in Paris, now made it known that he considered the treaty incompatible with his own dignity, his obligations to his Allies, the security of his State and the peace of Europe. For these weighty reasons he was, he said, unable to ratify the treaty. Oubril had exceeded his instructions.

Oubril could have easily proved to his sovereign that this accusation was unjust. But he was sensible enough not to do so. Oubril offered himself as a scapegoat, in consideration of which Alexander compensated him for his dismissal and exile from court with the gift of a considerable estate complete with serfs.

III. PRUSSIA'S COLLAPSE

FREDERICK WILLIAM notified the Tsar in his own hand of his fateful decision, and his imperial friend bade him from St. Petersburg not to be nervous on Napoleon's account. He was placing the entire Russian Army as well as the imperial treasury at the disposal of the Prussian monarch. More than that. He, Alexander, would appear himself at the head of his unconquerable army. He was, to tell the truth, on the point of hurrying to the King's assistance.

Notwithstanding these comforting and copious assurances, not a single Russian soldier had set his foot on Prussian soil when, early in October, Napoleon's rolling surges of steel broke over the Prussian State, which, under the impact, collapsed like a house of cards. The Prussian Army, resting on its laurels since the days of Frederick the Great, puffed up with pride but rotten to the core and considered by its high command as invincible, fell to pieces and almost ceased to exist in one day, after a single encounter at Jena and Auerstadt.

"I had," comments a Prussian Junker, "such a high opinion of the Prussian Army that I admit it never occurred to me that we could have been beaten, just like the Austrians. On the contrary, I was convinced, and the whole country shared my error, that should it ever come to that the French would run like rabbits."

Frederick William sent his S O S to St. Petersburg, but no Russian soldier could be seen on the horizon. The Tsar excused his remissness by pointing out that the Prussian request for help arrived in St. Petersburg neither in good time nor in the requisite official form. Alexander felt (and it was vain to hope Berlin would understand him) that he could employ his troops more usefully in Turkey than in assisting his Prussian friend, to whom he paid the handsome compliment that he had credited the King (alas, mistakenly!) with greater powers of resistance than had evidently been the case.

For no sooner had Alexander seen the 25,000 Frenchmen gathered in Dalmatia march off to battle in the direction of Prussia than he dispatched great masses of his own troops by forced marches towards the Turkish frontier. Napoleon had not shared Alexander's high expectations of the Prussian Army's powers of resistance. *"Si l'on ne s'arrange pas,"* he wrote to Joseph, *"les Prussiens soient tellement battus aux premières affaires, que tout soit fini en peu de jours."*

Every age has its Sudeten problem. The British Government at first supported morally the Christian minorities in Turkey until it appeared that the Christian cause was but a hidden plot for Russian aggrandizement; when, abruptly, England sided with the Turkish oppressor. The Sultan had, contrary to treaty, dismissed the hospodars of the Danube principalities bolstered up by Russia. The hospodars and the regent of Wallachia, so Turkey claimed, had entertained treacherous relations with the rebellious Serbs and other minority subjects of the Porte, who were being supported, covertly, by St. Petersburg. Alexander saw in it a pretext for a war with Turkey.

The British Ambassador, Arbuthnot, was instructed to support his Russian colleague, Italinski. A young secretary of the British Embassy, William Wellesley Pole, galloped across the town and presented himself, riding whip in hand and covered with mud, before the Turkish council of ministers, who were pursuing their deliberations, and threatened that a British fleet which had already left Gibraltar would sail through the Dardanelles and bombard Constantinople if the Great Turk did not consent here and now to re-establish the dismissed nominees of Russia.

The Sultan was so frightened that he recalled the dismissed hospodars. But the Tsar did not consider the incident thereby liquidated and sent 80,000 men to occupy the Danube principalities.

Italinski, the Russian Minister of Constantinople, had obtained from the Divan entire satisfaction of all his demands when he learned that a Russian army had invaded the Danube principalities. The Turks asked him: "Why? We have complied with all your wishes." Italinski, in reply, could not insist enough that the fact was impossible, and he would not depart from his refusal to believe it was impossible till the news was brought to him officially.

German papers which were pro-Russian justified this occupation of the Turkish provinces by the assumption that the Emperor Alexander was merely placing his army at the disposal of the Porte with a view to rendering the Sultan any assistance of which he might stand in need. As, however, the Sultan required no assistance, except against the risen Serbs, the German contention did not harmonize with the fact that the Russians after their occupation fortified the position of the leader of the rebellious Serbs, Czerni Georg, formerly a cattle dealer, by appointing him a general in the Russian Army.

The Turks, who had been attacked without a declaration of war, resisted this aggression, but without success. Within a week the Russians took Jassy and both principalities fell into General Michelson's hands, who also defeated the Turks by Gordau and drove them out of Bucharest.

IV. NAPOLEON RAISES HIS PRICE

MEANWHILE, Napoleon informed Frederick William that French peace terms were rising crescendo with every new victory. Every day saw French reserves pouring into Prussia. And still no Russian soldier was visible on the eastern frontier.

It might have been better for Frederick William had he accepted Napoleon's initial offer, grim though it was, before the French emperor acquainted himself with the internal situation in Prussia, which had rapidly deteriorated under the misrule of the Junkers and bureaucrats. The Prussian king might have seen that in existing conditions there was not the faintest hope of getting better terms from Napoleon. All people of influence at the Prussian Court were of opinion that even the hardest terms should be accepted immediately and peace concluded with the French.

But the Tsar did not think so. Nothing worse could befall him at the moment than that Prussia should back out of her fight with France, so that he should find he had this terrible and now much embittered foe on his own back and see his victories against the Turks postponed perhaps indefinitely.

To preclude such a painful eventuality, Alexander threw all his weight into advising his royal friend at Berlin to continue the war. He adjured him not to let himself be discouraged by the reverses and disasters he had suffered. He promised him sacredly that already in the near future 180,000 Russians would be hurrying to his assistance. Alexander further assured the downhearted King that there were well-grounded prospects that once more the Austrians would shortly take up arms against Napoleon.

These eupeptic communications from the Tsar reached the King of Prussia at the very moment when a new prospect presented itself of making peace with Napoleon. Of course, at a far higher cost than before, but nevertheless a prospect . . . not to be despised, seeing that Napoleon advanced like a whirlwind into Prussia and could hardly understand himself how effortlessly he was breaking up into pieces the famous military State of Frederick the Great.

When he stood, as Alexander and Frederick William had once stood, over the coffin of Frederick the Great, somebody told Napoleon that, as conqueror, he was entitled to take Frederick's sword.

"I have my own sword," he replied.

At last an armistice was signed between Prussian and French plenipotentiaries and the document placed before Frederick William for his acceptance. Encouraged, however, by the assurances of the Tsar, urged to patriotic resistance by his Russian relatives, and influenced by his wife's predilection for Russia and the personal charm of her monarch, Frederick William rejected the armistice and resolved to continue the war hand-in-hand with Great-heart Alexander.

At the time of Oubril's negotiations in Paris, the Tsar's envoy had been constantly reminded by the French that if the Emperor of Russia desired to expand his domains in Poland at the expense of Austria and Prussia, France would regard such natural aspirations with a benevolent eye. Could the Tsar really have believed that this offer still held good, and also that Napoleon would at last allow him a free hand in Turkey, Alexander would have abandoned Prussia to its sorry fate. But when it came to his ear that Napoleon, in his conversations with the Prussian monarch, had insisted that Prussia was to join her forces with those of France in ejecting Russian troops from the Turkish provinces to ensure that the Ottoman empire should on no account whatever fall a prey to Russia, the Tsar had no alternative but to rush to the help of his Prussian friend lest Frederick William be forced to march against him.

V. "POLEN IST NOCH NICHT VERLOREN..."

NAPOLEON'S advance into Poland created the liveliest enthusiasm in that unhappy land. It was interesting that precisely in that part of their vanished kingdom which had been ceded to Prussia, the Poles cherished the greatest resentment and hatred, though they had not been nearly so ruthlessly treated by the Prussians as in the other parts ceded to Russia and Austria. They hated the Prussians with a deadly hatred because Frederick William's father, a contemporary of Catherine II, had shamelessly broken his oath after having most solemnly pledged himself to respect Poland's integrity. The Poles could never forget that.

Their joy was great when they learned of the awful judgment which had befallen the son of the thrice-perjured traitor and breaker of oaths at the hands of Napoleon. A Pole named Dombrovski, who had found a new fatherland under the French flag, appealed to his compatriots

under the Prussian heel to rise against the domination of the Hohenzollerns. In a few weeks the Poles were up in arms. The weak detachments of the Prussians were attacked and cut off. Towns and fortresses
fell into the hands of the insurgents, from which Dombrovski, two weeks
after the entry of the French into Posen, formed two regiments which
could unite with the French army. Twelve thousand Lithuanians and
Volynians sprang out of the ground to form themselves into regiments
under Napoleon's colors. No sooner had they entered Warsaw, then
the capital of Prussian Poland, than Murat proclaimed a national government, composed of the noblest scions of Poland, who sounded the
clarion call to all her sons, whether under Prussian, Austrian or Russian
domination, to unite under Napoleon's banners. Had Napoleon cleverly
used his advantage and promised the Poles the complete restoration and
independence of their kingdom, had he boldly crossed the Niemen,
Poland would have risen like one man.

It was chiefly this danger which caused the Tsar to neglect his commitments in Turkey and to rush to the assistance of his Prussian friend.

VI. ALLIES AND GUESTS

BUT, though the Russians came to Prussia in their own interests, they
yet extracted the admiration and gratitude they thought only due to
them and their great-hearted sovereign for their unselfish and heroic
intervention. Here they were, always the old trusted Allies, here they
were, men of their word, come up to scratch! Yes, pouring into Prussia,
ready as usual to help their poor shiftless friends, seemingly in a stew.

Although Prussia's salvation now depended alone on the Russians,
to whom the king and his countrymen were eager to extend every sign
of gratitude and admiration, the Russian commanders and troops did
not make it easy to admire them or to feel grateful to them. The trum-
peted deeds of the heroic Russian commanders took the form of a steady
retreat towards the Russian frontier to cover holy Russian soil beyond.
The last unoccupied province of Prussia, which the Russians had hurried
to Prussia to save, fell into French hands.

It was even more difficult for the monarch and people of Prussia to
feel themselves sincerely indebted to their Allies. All too soon they
were making the discovery that in these helpers and friends who had
come into their land they had encountered even worse guests than in
the enemy. Wherever Russian troops went they turned the land into a

desert. As in Austria, Prussian inhabitants prayed to heaven that they might be relieved of their friends by the enemy. The French, too, marauded and helped themselves to anything they could lay their hands on, boiled, roasted and ate, but said: "Here, peasants, if you're hungry, come and eat with us." The Russians devoured everything like wolves, gave nothing, stored nothing, but threw out the superflux onto the dunghill.

The Russians had no storage system. They took everything as it came, far and near, whatever they set their eyes on. They laid bare regardless of requirement, but without laying by any provision for the morrow. For that reason they could never stay long in one place without feeling a lack of subsistence. They roamed and desolated new villages far around.

The Russian generals had a peculiar way of provisioning themselves. Under the pretext of not wishing to be a burden to the army, they undertook to provision themselves and drew their rations in cash. But, keen on saving their cash, they commanded that Cossacks bring them by force everything they required. The Russian army really was short of provisions, because by some unwritten law highly placed personages claimed the perquisite of competing with the quartermaster-general in marauding the villages. As saviors and allies who were defending Prussian villagers against rapacious Bonaparte, the Russian generals considered that the villagers had, properly speaking, already forfeited their goods and chattels, which, if still their own, were so by force of Russian valor, and, assuming a modicum of gratitude, at Russian disposal. Besides, Russian officers lived by the sweat of their peasants' brows at home. Why not abroad?

Nobody knew better than the Tsar himself the scope and extent of the deep-rooted habit of theft ingrained in the Russian people in all matters which concerned the common weal. He had tried to eradicate this national vice, but with little success. He was in the habit of saying to his intimates that his dear Russians would steal his ships did they but know where to conceal them. Could they pull out his teeth in his sleep without waking him, they would do it.

VII. EYLAU

THE terrible Battle of Eylau in February 1807 would have been another Austerlitz but for a dispatch from Napoleon to Bernadotte intercepted by the Russians. The notorious murderer of the Emperor Paul, General Bennigsen, who had intrigued his way up to the high command and incidentally enriched himself in the process, was a pacifist where Napoleon was concerned. Bennigsen did his best to avoid an encounter, but he was at last compelled by Napoleon to give battle at Eylau.

Though that battle was far more bloody than Austerlitz, it did not result in a rapid decision as Napoleon had hoped. In the very moment when a last thrust from the French would have turned the left wing of the Russians, already breaking and scattering in flight, a small Prussian corps under General Lestocq (a Prussian of French extraction) came to their rescue and prevented the battle from ending decisively for Napoleon.

The Russian chief of the General Staff was in favor of continuing the battle the following day, but the commander in chief, Bennigsen, was very wisely against it. The Russians had lost 30,000 men. They had not a battalion which was not at its last gasp, whereas Napoleon already next day could command considerable reserves of troops in Ney's corps as well as the foot guards.

But Napoleon, too, had suffered terrible losses and he had made the discovery that the Prussian soldiers, if led by capable officers, did not deserve the dour contempt entertained by their allies but not shared by their enemies.

Napoleon resolved to conclude a separate peace with the Prussians to enable him to attend to the Russians, who had not kept faith with him after his generous treatment of them at the conclusion of Austerlitz. Five days after the slaughter at Eylau, Napoleon sent his personal adjutant, Bertrand, to the Prussian monarch to propose peace on much more acceptable terms than before. They exceeded anything that the King could have hoped for only a few weeks ago. They included the restoration of several lost possessions, and even (which shows Napoleon's blindness and cowardice) the return of the Poles to Prussian domination.

This offer, which marked a singular turn of fortune such as Prussia dared hardly have hoped for, was curtly declined by the Prussian monarch, though the whole of his country was pining for peace. As his consort, the high-falutin' Queen Louisa, still deeply in love with the Emperor Alexander, declared, her husband could never have signed a separate peace, for that would have meant his leaving in the lurch a faithful ally and a noble friend.

The conventional morality of individuals, as it exists between friends or members of a family, is out of place between nations employing such questionable means as the slaughter of hundreds of thousands of human beings to achieve an end rooted in "personal" honor, pride, ambition or aggrandizement. Like most of the legitimate monarchs of his time, Frederick William III was full of envy and hatred for the lucky upstart Napoleon, and drawn towards Alexander, whom he valued even more for the size of his army than as a friend. In Napoleon he saw a faithless Corsican, an impudent usurper, but nothing of his cleverness. But in the Tsar he saw a knight without fear and without reproach, whom he believed incapable even of a mental reservation. From the treaty proposed by Napoleon, who, only a few months ago, had treated the Prussian monarch with haughty contempt, Frederick William rashly concluded that Napoleon's position after the Battle of Eylau must be pretty hopeless for him to take the initiative of a *rapprochement*. The day was not far, the Prussian imagined, when he, in alliance with his noble-hearted friend from the Neva, would be in a position to dictate peace terms to the usurper.

Frederick William was afflicted with the hereditary malady of German potentates: a deplorable lack of political insight aggravated by a total absence of political education. He was about as much acquainted with the peculiarities of Russian politics and Russian statesmanship as with the daydreams of the Emperor of Japan. He did not know how little the Autocrat of All the Russias was at any time the master and how much the slave of court cliques. Nor did he understand that Turkey was the real, abiding interest of Russia. Three weeks before Napoleon's peace offer, Frederick William had received a personal intimation from the Winter Palace. While Alexander repeated his promise not to leave Prussia in the lurch, he yet assured the King that it would not displease him if his royal friend and ally should succeed in coming to an understanding with Napoleon.

Anyone but Frederick William III would have understood what that meant. The Tsar, while speciously assuring the King of his support, was evidently not sure whether he would be able to support him any longer. The King, in addition, deluded himself with the hope that Austria might be induced once more to take the field against Napoleon. But Austria could not make up its mind what it liked less: Napoleon swallowing Prussia, or Russia pocketing Turkey.

The dormant lassitude, the continual retreating of the Russians in East Prussia contrasted strangely with the brisk mobility, the rapid advance of the Russian army into the Sultan's domains. Austria did not see her way to joining Prussia merely to relieve Russia of her irksome obligations. Austria was in no mood to do Russia the service of fagging for her in Prussia—a job of which Russia was heartily sick—merely to enable Russia to help herself to bits or all of Turkey, which was rapidly succumbing to the success of Russian arms by land and sea.

The Russians were in fact doing very nicely indeed. They were just about to snatch the key to the Dardenelles, and, having joined up with the Serbs, transfer the war to Bosnia and the adjoining provinces, when Napoleon's Marshal Marmont in Dalamatia, by creating a diversion on the Russian flank, checked their advance.

In London, too, there was little enthusiasm to oblige Tsar Alexander. Russian ambitions in the Near East were the real reason why England during the campaign of 1807 supported Russia so half-heartedly. Nor had Austrian memories of their guests of yore grown dim. Neither did the report of their behavior in Prussia tend to soften Austrian hearts. Prussian officers attached to Russian headquarters in their letters home expressed their opinion that the Russian alliance, even if the Russian army marched forward rather than backward, was of little use to them, since the Russian idea was to make a wasteland of Prussia in order to cover their own retreat with the idea of starving Napoleon out.

"Next day again," writes a Prussian officer, "we were ordered to send out a detachment of twenty horsemen to prevent the marauding by Russians roaming about the villages. The most terrible complaints are reaching us about the atrocities perpetrated by the Russians, and we had orders to shoot at sight and to use our sabers if milder methods should fail to ward them off."

Russian soldiers would commandeer German peasant carts complete with horse and peasant. They would thrash out at the peasant and the horse till the peasant preferred to abandon both horse and cart and stagger home. Nor was there much argument about it. Before a peasant had said two words in protest, down came a Cossack sword, off flew an arm.

General Bennigsen, who, since murdering Paul, was regarded as a man of few words, was for concluding peace with Napoleon, whose military genius he thought was hard to get by. Bennigsen's idea was that Russia should instead bend all her energies to the carrying out of the plan of Peter the Great and Catherine II in the Near East. He accordingly began an agitation for peace among his own troops. A defeatist outlook soon spread and gained the upper hand in the Russian camp. Why should we, asked the Russian officers, fight for the personal friendship of the Emperor with the King of Prussia?

This mood ripened before the Battle of Friedland, which took place on June 14, 1807. At this battle Bennigsen committed such glaring mistakes that it could only be concluded that he was beaten because he wanted to be beaten so as to terminate the war. His whole bearing after the battle strengthened this suspicion. Though he had lost 16,000 men, yet his position was by no means as desperate as he made it out to be in his despatch to the Tsar, to whom he made it clear that nothing but an armistice could save the Russian Army.

This was an exaggeration. Bennigsen, to save his personal prestige as a commander, pretended he was ill and spent the day of the battle in bed. The Emperor's brother, the Grand Duke Constantine, who belonged to the Bennigsen party in Russia, which was in favor of making it up with Napoleon, tried to impress on the Emperor the immediate need of an armistice. Two days before the battle there was a violent scene between the brothers. The sovereign threatened his brother Constantine with Siberia, while Constantine spoke of pushing Alexander off the throne. The scene was so violent that Adjutant General Count Lieven, to prevent an open scandal, withdrew the bodyguards stationed outside the Emperor's room.

The King of Prussia, who had rejected Napoleon's advances for a separate peace after the Battle of Eylau, learned with astonishment that, immediately after the conclusion of an armistice after Friedland, there followed a meeting between Napoleon and Alexander foreshadowing a separate peace at the expense of Prussia.

VIII. TILSIT

THE two emperors met on a raft on the river Niemen at Tilsit on June 21. The tents and rafts displayed the interlaced initials of the two sovereigns. Napoleon on the farther shore paced up and down in front of his Guards. Alexander, grave and pensive, awaited in a tavern the arrival of his future ally. The two monarchs got into boats. Napoleon, who reached the raft first, hastened forward to meet the Tsar with outstretched hand. Then they disappeared into the marquee.

No one else was present at this interview, which was concluded under four eyes. Alexander opened with: "I hate England as much as you do"; after which everything went swimmingly. The two monarchs had no difficulty in coming to an understanding in the course of a couple of hours of the early afternoon. The French emperor knew what the Russian emperor chiefly wanted. Alexander was prepared for any concessions so long as Napoleon met him on the question of Turkey.

Men of strong will who are supposed to know their own minds, in fact rarely know what they want. They want power and more power, and they shift their objective, perjure themselves, let down their friends and make solemn new oaths. Turkey, which had formally declared war on Russia at the instigation of Napoleon, who had solemnly assured her of assistance, was now to be offered up to Russia. When Alexander heard that, his sorrow for the misfortunes of his royal friend and ally, Frederick William of Prussia, was tempered with joy and his tears ceased to flow.

When Napoleon added that he saw no objection if Alexander, to round off his territories in the north, took Finland from King Gustav Adolf of Sweden (who was married to the younger sister of Alexander's consort Elizabeth and was his faithful ally) the conviction assailed Alexander that it was extremely foolish to go on fighting the hero of the century who distinguished so subtly between main and subsidiary objectives.

It went without saying that, in consideration of such generosity at the cost of a third party, Napoleon demanded the equivalent. This was the carving up of Prussia. Further, both emperors were to compel England to accept French conditions of peace, if need be by force of arms. Furthermore, Napoleon required Alexander's strict adherence to the Continental System.

Lastly, Russia must recognize all the territorial rights which the Emperor of the French had gained on the continent of Europe, and would gain in future. He was to exercise in western, southern and central Europe the same unlimited dictatorship as he was going to accord Alexander in the North and the Near East. This, with certain reservations, was the meaning of the Treaty of Tilsit, concluded in July of 1807.

The King of Prussia was not included in these deliberations. While Alexander was closeted with Napoleon on the decorated raft in the middle of the Niemen, the King sat for two hours astride his horse on the bank of the river, and, in his impatience, from time to time forced his steed into the water, as if he thought he might overhear some of their conversation from which he was excluded.

The treaty concluded two days later between Napoleon and Frederick William made a very different story. Napoleon deprived the King of

Prussia of one-half of his kingdom. Even more than the peace itself, the manner in which the treaty was concluded pained the King, who remembered how the Tsar had sworn with tears in his eyes, and repeated before witnesses: "You understand, don't you? Neither of us will fall alone. Either both together or neither."

According to the terms of their agreement, neither the Tsar nor the King was to treat separately with the enemy; and the King in this dark hour not unreasonably expected that his noble ally would honor this stipulation.

In vain. His ever faithful friend did not even deem it necessary to communicate to his ally the names of his plenipotentiaries or their instructions; still less, to keep him informed of the progress of the negotiations with Napoleon. Like an eel, the Russian minister, Budberg, slipped out of every attempt to cross-question him and declined under plausible pretexts even a meeting with his Prussian colleague, Hardenberg. The Prussian minister was *persona ingrata* with Napoleon, who could not stand his manner, in much the same way as Hitler could not abide "that maddening Beneš."

Alexander, at whose express wish Frederick William had appointed Hardenberg to the head of his ministry, now did nothing at all to prevent Napoleon from insisting that the Prussian chancellor be dismissed from his post. It would not have required a great deal of the Tsar's eloquence to spare the King of Prussia the humiliation of having to dismiss his own minister at the dictation of the Emperor of the French. We remember how, in 1912, Delcassé was dismissed at the instance of Kaiser Wilhelm. But the Russian emperor was so delighted with Napoleon for apparently allowing him a free hand in Turkey that he did not consider such trifles justified his intervention.

The two emperors became inseparable. The afternoons were spent in riding together, while the King of Prussia ambled behind on his horse. Sometimes Napoleon would take a malicious pleasure in letting the King almost catch up with them, when suddenly Napoleon and Alexander would gallop off and leave Frederick William a mile behind.

Or just when the King hoped he had at last secured a suitable opportunity to plead with his victor for the return of some of his territories, Napoleon, who had given signs of lending a gracious ear, merely chaffed the pleading King about his archaic uniform. "What's the idea of having so much gold lace? What do you do with all these loops? However do you manage to button up your tunic with so many hidden buttons, eh?"

As he teased the poor King, Napoleon cast side-glances of malicious complicity at Alexander, reading: "We great modern emperors don't wear such frumpery, do we now?" Of affairs of State there was no mention.

Napoleon, pleased to be treated as an equal by a real emperor, who only recently had addressed him as "The Head of the French Government," emphasized the significance of the hereditary character of the Tsardom. He was already thinking of laying the foundations for his own dynasty in France. The Tsar's favorite reply, that he, Alexander, was just a happy accident, astonished Napoleon, who did not realize that Alexander, who suffered from compunction for his complicity in the murder of his father Paul, tended to lighten his conscience by considering the manifest illegality of the entire succession since Peter III. If it came to that, neither his father nor his father's offspring—himself— were legitimate monarchs. It was all a game. Ability was the modern rule. He and Napoleon reigned by sheer personal genius. That was how it struck him.

Napoleon wrote to Josephine that he had found Alexander all he was reputed to be—a fine young man, tall, handsome, graceful in bearing and address—the last word in charm. As for the Prussian king, what a driveling, sniggering, sniveling fellow!

Hardenberg, despairing of his royal master's ever getting anything from Napoleon, suggested that Queen Louisa might be sent for. To the Queen, who was at Memel, this request to meet the bloody tyrant whom she abhorred, in order to plead with him on behalf of her country, was the last straw. When she read the King's letter summoning her to Tilsit, she grew pale, and suddenly fell to the floor in a faint. But she rallied later, and next day she arrived at Tilsit.

Napoleon, calling on the Queen the moment she arrived, opened with that blend of gallantry and mock severity due from a conqueror to a pretty woman: "Madame, how did you dare to make war on me?"

Queen Louisa said: "Sire, the great fame of Frederick the Great blinded us."

Talleyrand afterwards told Napoleon that this was one of the noblest answers he had ever heard, and he went on repeating this to annoy Napoleon, till the Emperor said, irritably: "I don't see at all why you think it's such a noble answer. There's nothing particularly fine about it that I can see!"

Napoleon's emanations of generosity proceeded from a gross and ill-informed sensibility. Queen Louisa had arrived to plead on behalf of her husband, but Napoleon thought that Alexander and the Queen would be glad of an opportunity to cohabit under his benevolent eye. Alexander and Queen Louisa had in fact never had what is called an "affair" because Alexander was not specially attracted by her. But Napoleon had, during the years of war, ridiculed them as lovers. The Goebbels of his day had made malicious propaganda of what was in fact a libel against both. Now, in a spirit of "Let bygones be bygones," Napoleon, as he thought generously, placed them in adjoining apartments. "Give the youngsters a chance." That night Queen Louisa dined with them. She had Napoleon on her right and Alexander on her left. She hated the Corsican, who was small, gross, short-legged and had a protruding belly, whereas she was still in love with Alexander, even though she reproached him bitterly for having betrayed them and their country. Alexander, indeed, found little to say to her. He sat there, very handsome in his smart Preobrazhenski uniform, eating for the most part in silence and looking rather sheepish.

Napoleon, inflamed by wine, still intrigued by the notion that they were lovers, but disappointed by their boring backwardness in rising to the opportunity with which he had so generously provided them—he had imagined this little intimate *diner à trois* as an amusing Rabelaisian affair—decided that he would show himself more game than bashful Alexander. He was fumbling for some not too crude, yet adequate, excuse to show it was now the Emperor of the French who was going to make a bid for the notorious Queen of Prussia. Caesar was no less a man than Antony in wooing Cleopatra. He touched Queen Louisa's garment—she was gorgeously dressed—and said: "What kind of silk is this, Madame? Is it French or Italian?"

"Sire!" she exclaimed, on a note of wailing reproach, "how *can* you talk of fripperies at a time like this?"

Napoleon, as well as Alexander, now ate in silence, with the Queen between them.

At the end of the dinner Napoleon escorted the Queen to her carriage and handed her a rose he had plucked on the way.

She took it with some hesitation and said in a wailing voice: "At least, give me Magdeburg with it!"

"Madame," replied Napoleon, "it is my place to offer, and yours to receive."

IX. ALEXANDER AND NAPOLEON EXCHANGE CIVILITIES

ALEXANDER dropped a remark to his minister, Budberg, that Prussia, compressed to half its size by France, was, all things considered, more amenably useful to Russia than the Prussia of 1806. Neither did he demur when Napoleon explained to him that now that Prussia was no longer dangerous there was no reason why he should spare her. Therefore, he would not keep any of the promises he had made to the Tsar during their earlier meeting. The new Russian policy was foreshadowed by a remark of Budberg's which he let fall during the negotiations at Tilsit, which ended in a formal alliance between France and Russia, that now if Austria, too, were to declare war against France, then Russia and France together would swipe up Austria.

Meanwhile, Napoleon and Alexander exchanged civilities. One day Napoleon gave the password, the next day the Tsar. Yesterday it had been "Napoleon, France and courage." Today it was "Alexander, Russia and glory." Tolstoy tells us of the ceremonial as first a sound of spurs was heard on the steps of Alexander's headquarters and his suite all came down and immediately mounted. An equerry was leading up the Emperor's charger. Presently a slight creaking of riding boots could be heard on the staircase within, and all guessed who was descending. The Emperor wore the uniform of the Preobrazhenski Guards with tightly fitting breeches and high boots. On his breast blazed the Legion of Honor. He held his hat under his arm while he gracefully pulled on his white doeskin gloves. His brilliant glance traveled and seemed to light up everything on which it alighted. He addressed a word or two as he passed to a few privileged beings and, laying his hand on the saddle, turned once again to a general who had petitioned him on behalf of a friend, and said in a sweet, distinct and resonant voice, as though he wished to be heard by all:

"Impossible, General. *Impossible*—because the law is greater than I." He put his foot in the stirrup. The general bowed submissively. The Emperor rode off at a gallop.

Just as the Tsar rode up, and the French Guards with their tall fur caps were presenting arms, another party of horsemen headed by a personage whose seat was not above criticism and easily recognizable as Napoleon, pranced up from the opposite side of the square. Napoleon galloped up on a thoroughbred gray Arab, covered with a purple housing embroidered with gold. He wore his habitual rather small three-cornered hat. Across a dark blue uniform unbuttoned over a podgy white waistcoat was the Russian ribbon of St. Andrew. As he came up with the Tsar he raised his hat. Alexander raised his. The Russian soldiers shouted, "Hurrah!" The French, *"Vive l'Empereur!"* Having exchanged a few words, the newly allied sovereigns dismounted and shook hands. Napoleon's smile was unpleasingly artificial; Alexander's full of natural benevolence.

"Sire," began Napoleon, "I would request your leave to present the Legion of Honor to the bravest soldier in your ranks." He had a clear succinct voice, pronouncing every syllable distinctly. As he spoke he looked up from his low height straight into the tall Russian emperor's eyes; and Alexander, who was a little deaf, listened attentively, smiled and bowed assent.

"To the soldier who displayed the greatest courage in the late war," added Napoleon succinctly; and he looked along the Russian ranks, who had presented arms, but never took their eyes off their own sovereign's angelic face.

"Your Majesty will permit me to consult the colonel?" rejoined Alexander, advancing a few steps towards the officer commanding the battalion. Napoleon, with some difficulty, pulled his glove off his small white hand; it tore, and he threw it away. An aide-de-camp quickly picked it up.

"Who should it be given to?" Alexander whispered in Russian.

"To the soldier Your Majesty may deign to designate."

The Tsar frowned: "I must give him an answer."

The colonel's eye earnestly ran down the ranks. "Lazarev!" he called. The first man in the front rank stepped forward, his face quivering with excitement.

"Where're you going? Stand still!" muttered several voices; and Lazarev, at a loss what to do, stood still in alarm.

Napoleon slightly turned his head and held out his plump little hand as if there and then to take something. The officers of his suite whispered to one another. There was a stir of activity, and a small object quickly passed from person to person, till a page came forward and, with a low bow, placed a cross with a red ribbon in the waiting hand. Napoleon took it without looking and went up to Lazarev, who still stared wide-eyed at his Tsar. With a glance at Alexander, intended to convey that the courtesy was really to him, Napoleon's hand for a moment graciously rested on the private soldier's breast, the cross being immediately pinned into the place where *he* had held it, by eager officers, Russian and French. Lazarev watched the little man's proceeding with gloomy gravity, looking at his sovereign as if to ask him what he was to do.

The emperors remounted and rode away. The Preobrazhenski Guards dispersed, mingled with the French grenadiers, and took their places at the laden tables. Such is war and peace.

X. ALEXANDER LETS DOWN FREDERICK WILLIAM

KING FREDERICK WILLIAM and Queen Louisa felt it to be the last straw that Russia, who had pledged herself to stand by Prussia come what might, should conclude a joint campaign by helping herself as a *douceur* to a slice of Prussian territory. Russian diplomatists met all reproaches with the declaration that but for Russia the Prussian king would not have received even the terms Napoleon had seen fit to grant him, and that if the King of Prussia retained one-half of his kingdom he owed this privilege to Napoleon's regard for the Tsar.

Napoleon himself declared, in his opening address to the legislative body in Paris, that the House of Brandenburg owed it to the sincere friendship which he had wished to testify to the Tsar of Russia, that it reigned at all.

But that was not all. There was the question of contributions which were not mentioned in the Tilsit treaty, and the amount of which depended on Napoleon's pleasure. Until all the contributions were paid, even that part of Prussia which Napoleon generously allowed, on paper at least, to be retained by the Hohenzollerns, remained under French occupation. These troops must be provisioned at the expense of the Prussian provinces, already ruined in competition by French and Prussian soldiers and turned into a desert by Russians.

Like most monarchs deprived of activity in the field of external affairs, the King of Prussia reluctantly turned towards improving internal conditions. He had tried his best to induce Napoleon to withdraw his Army of Occupation, but in vain.

When, however, embarrassed by his commitments in Spain, Napoleon found himself compelled to withdraw some of his Army of Occupation from Prussia, he agreed to do so on the express condition that Frederick William, in consideration for such indulgence, undertake to pay him within forty days 140,000,000 francs. In addition, Napoleon also required the King to place 12,000 men at his disposal for the contemplated war with Austria.

When the King appealed to the Tsar to secure milder terms from Napoleon, Alexander, in forwarding Frederick William's request, supported it, "in order," as he wrote to Napoleon, "to be delivered from the importunities of unhappy people who reproach me for their misfortunes."

Napoleon finally knocked off 20,000,000 francs and allowed for a somewhat longer term in which to pay. But that was all, and he helped himself therewith to another snippet of Prussian soil.

A secret clause in the Treaty of Tilsit stipulated that in the event of Napoleon annexing Hanover to France, Alexander should likewise enlarge his territory with the acquisition of a piece of Prussia. Alexander responded to this friendy offer of Napoleon's with a declaration that he attached no value to the fulfillment of this clause. A declaration of which Napoleon availed himself in order to leave this clause unfulfilled.

At the end of the following year, the King of Prussia succeeded in inducing Napoleon to recall the balance of his troops, which the Emperor agreed to do for a consideration. This took the form of a little present to the Tsar of Russia which comprised another piece of Prussian territory. It was the Province Byalostock, of 480 square miles and a population of about half a million souls, a present at which the Russians scoffed and which the pro-Russian apologists at the Prussian Court described as negligible. A description not quite tallying with the Tsar's own claim in his manifesto to his subjects, in which he rejoiced at the happy termination of the war with the Treaty of Tilsit, "by the terms of which Russia was not only strengthened in her former frontiers, having retained her full integrity, but was in point of fact enlarged by the addition of an adjacent territory providing her with a natural frontier line much to her advantage."

BOOK SIX

BOOK XIX

CHAPTER XXI

ALLY OF NAPOLEON

I. SAVARY AND CAULAINCOURT AT ST. PETERSBURG

NAPOLEON sent as his first envoy to St. Petersburg his executioner in chief, General Savary.

He could not have made a more unhappy choice. Savary was detested in Petersburg as the man who had abducted and executed the Duc d'Enghien, who had been kidnaped on German soil. More precisely, on the territory of Baden, of which Alexander's consort, the Empress Elizabeth, had been a princess. It was more than the Russians could stand. Somebody had even bribed a cabman to bump into Savary's coach and spill him in the snow.

Savary did not hold the rank of ambassador, but of chargé d'affaires. He had none of a diplomatist's qualities. He was a policeman. He was an aristocrat neither by origin nor in bearing. He was perky, vulgar and self-assertive; and Russian society gave him a wide berth. The best houses were closed to him; which meant that all houses were closed to him. They would not sit down to table with a murderer. Nevertheless, they dined continually with other murderers, notably those who had killed the Emperor Paul.

Even the restaurants boycotted Savary. Alexander alone received him. Several times a week Savary dined at the Winter Palace. The general wrote disconsolate letters to Paris, complaining that apart from these dinners with the Emperor he was constrained to dine in solitude with his secretary. The boycott was not extended to other members of the French Embassy, who bore glittering names of the old regime (and were annoyed when the Tsar, as he thought appropriately, addressed them as *"citoyens"*) and made the most of their invitations, leaving their chief to amuse himself as best he could.

The Emperor, too, excused himself as best he could for this attitude of his Court; and at last he said he would put his foot down. "After all, I'm the sovereign and they'll have to obey me!"

Savary endeavored to obtain an audience with the Empress Dowager, which was finally granted, though with the utmost reluctance, and the general was writing to Paris that he seemed to be making headway at last. But when the audience took place it lasted exactly one minute.

Alexander ordered certain families to receive the general, who found himself facing the Dowager Empress across the table. In a manner affecting to be pleasant, she inquired whether it was true or no that he was the son of a Swiss hall porter; which indeed he was. A question which showed up the Dowager Empress as being more common than the General.

He wrote to Paris and begged to be recalled. But the Foreign Minister replied that the General should cultivate another stratum of society. Savary wrote back that there was no other society in St. Petersburg, except serfs. The Tsar, appealed to, replied that Savary must dine with him even more often than he already did.

Finally, Savary was recalled. He was sent to Spain, where he found himself more in his element. He kidnaped the King of Spain, the Queen, and their eldest son, the Prince of the Asturias, and prepared the throne for his master. Napoleon handed it on to his brother Joseph, then, on second thoughts, to Murat.

The new ambassador was the Marquis de Caulaincourt, Napoleon's Master of the Horse, an elegant and generous man who at once set out to reassure the Emperor, himself, and everyone, that he had no responsibility for the kidnaping, still less the murder, of the Duc d'Enghien.

Caulaincourt wrote the Tsar a long letter of explanation and extracted from him a testimonial embodying Alexander's belief in his innocence. Suffering from an uncertain conscience in regard to his own complicity in the murder of his father, Paul, Alexander was glad to give Caulaincourt a testimonial absolving him from every suspicion in the matter of the Duc d'Enghien; and the two men, two Macbeths, Russian and French, became the closest friends, meeting continually to discuss life, women and love, and leaving politics alone.

Caulaincourt in his letter to Alexander had not denied participation in the plot to kidnap and execute the Duc d'Enghien. He merely pleaded that he had no choice in the matter. He had been one of the principal plotters and had been well paid for his services, but—he argued—this was neither here nor there. He had acted under compulsion. Under a totalitarian regime one must obey orders.

Alexander, who preferred to think that his own tentative participation in the plot to assassinate his father had been forced on him by the implacable logic of events, saw Caulaincourt's point of view and readily absolved him from all blame. The Tsar replied that he was bound to recognize from reports he had received from his ministers in Germany how completely innocent Caulaincourt was of any connection whatsoever with the horrible event about which he had written to him.

Napoleon, who had commanded such astonishing loyalty in the army, was less happily served by his diplomatists. Talleyrand, once again Napoleon's Foreign Minister, was already pursuing his own policy independently of his master, and Caulaincourt seemed to be in the secret. Napoleon, despairing of seeing his own point of view adequately represented at St. Petersburg, began to call Caulaincourt "Alexander's Foreign Minister," and he was not far wrong. "What do they want with fate?" he coined the aphorism about this time: "Politics is fate."

Fate was beginning to take a hand in his politics, which were taking a turn not envisaged in his view of politics. Particularly in Spain Alexander was getting restive. He was impatient to see the "great ideas of Tilsit," as he called Napoleon's promises, taking shape. Napoleon dillydallied. His hands were full with trouble in Spain and elsewhere. Russia was getting tired of waiting for his permission to help herself to Turkey. In view of the Spanish rebellion and the early prospect of a break with Austria, Napoleon felt it might be opportune to impress his enemies with Franco-Russian solidarity. For that reason he jumped at Alexander's suggestion of an early meeting.

II. TWO SWINDLERS

THIS meeting took place at Erfurt in the autumn of 1808. It lasted nearly three weeks. The two emperors parted, seemingly very gratified, actually embittered. Both had played the same role: that of two honest men each harboring the same secret intention—thoroughly to cheat each other.

To get the Tsar to recognize French acquisitions in Prussia, Napoleon tempted Alexander with the early prospect of seeing the highest and holiest article of faith known to tsarist politics—the acquisition of Turkey's possessions in Europe—realized at last. Russia had always regarded herself as the heir of the Byzantine empire. Ivan the Third, a Rurik, had married the refugee sister of the last surviving Emperor of Byzantium, from whom he had inherited in trust the double-headed eagle. The Turk had been a lengthy intruder—like the Arab in Palestine—and Russia would not rest till the Orthodox cross blazed again on the gilded cathedral dome of St. Sophia.

Napoleon had signed a stipulation which had led Alexander to believe that he would really grant him this sweet satisfaction. But Napoleon had no such intention, having fixed his own eagle eye on the East. He merely tarried till he had settled the rest of Europe before he turned to that cherished counterpart of his imperial design. He was but concerned to keep the Tsar inactive and to retain his friendship till he himself succeeded in making peace with England. When he had carried out all his major plans, still pending, then he would be in a position to tell Russia where she got off.

Alexander also harbored mental reservations. His idea was to keep Napoleon at bay with smiles and promises, while opportunities for conquering Turkey were so propitious. When he had got what he wanted in Turkey, Alexander was prepared to face Napoleon again.

It was a race between two swindlers, each trying to steal the other's booty and get away with it before the other was on his track. Napoleon had never regarded the Treaty of Tilsit as a durable, or indeed a workable, treaty. When Alexander demanded the carrying out of its provisions which ceded to him Moldavia and Wallachia, Napoleon for his part promptly required the Tsar's consent to his own proposed annexation of Silesia. According to treaty, Napoleon was entitled to help himself to a further chunk in central Europe if Alexander helped himself in the Near East. But what, and where, remained designedly unspecified: the Tsar now began to see why. Napoleon knew that Russia would reject out of hand the idea of a French annexation of a Prussian province situated on the Russian border—that is, of having Napoleon for a neighbor. That was precisely why he demanded Silesia. The realization of the Tilsit treaty was, accordingly, just as Napoleon had in fact intended, indefinitely postponed.

How keen the Tsar was to go ahead with his Turkish project appears from his facile suggestion that instead of Silesia, Napoleon should help himself to Bohemia. There was no Czecho-Slovak problem in those days, Austria having sat on Bohemia as to the manner born. Though the Czechs were brother Slavs, Alexander thought they might just as well exchange their masters: Austrian for French. Like Napoleon, Alexander regarded Europe as a sort of general store where he could shoplift as the fancy took him.

But complications in the Pyrenees for the moment deflected Napoleon's territorial ambitions. The unprovoked French invasion of Spain, the occupation of Madrid, the kidnaping of the Spanish Bourbons to Bayonne, their forced abdication and Joseph Bonaparte's elevation to the throne of Spain—all this the Emperor Alexander found natural, comprehensible, even necessary for the preservation—as the saying was, and still is—of the peace of Europe.

"You see," the Tsar had expressed himself to Caulaincourt, "I am not jealous of your master's growing power. But isn't it only fair that he should entertain the same liberal ideas on my account and let me, too, make some appropriations, which my empire needs no less than his and which would certainly be quite as easy to justify as the latest acquisition of your sovereign?"

Napoleon, anxious to secure Russia's recognition of his annexation of Spain, and to insure Russia's neutrality while France went to war with Austria, took the hint. He understood that he would have to drop Silesia and hand the Tsar without further ado Moldavia and Wallachia if he was to retain his friendship much longer.

With this intention he came to Erfurt. But Alexander came in the earnest hope of carving up Turkey. These two questions were the subject of their earliest deliberations. Alexander soon perceived that Napoleon wished to hear nothing more of the "great ideas of Tilsit"; that he had merely been playing a game with him.

Even if Napoleon had ever been serious about dividing Turkey, he had since thought better of it. For this very conclusive reason: Napoleon had realized, and nowhere more clearly than at Erfurt, that however much he might give Russia of Turkey it would never satisfy Russia for long unless she also got Constantinople and the Dardanelles. Unless he gave her those two things, he in fact gave her nothing. But to give Alexander those two priceless pearls was more than Alexander's friendship or the Russian alliance was worth. As, however, it was essential for Napoleon at this crucial moment to satisfy Russia's appetite, he decided to let Alexander have Wallachia and Moldavia. He was doing so not at his own expense but at that of Austria; moreover, making bad blood between Russia and Austria, which in his forthcoming fight with Austria was at any rate useful.

III. NAPOLEON MEETS GOETHE

ALEXANDER was subtle enough not to show during their meeting at Erfurt any outward sign of displeasure at the bitter disappointment of his hopes. He declared himself willing to forego for the time being the realization of his real wishes, if only Wallachia and Moldavia were handed over to him without further fuss or delay.

The meeting at Erfurt marks the high-water mark of Napoleon's career: already it contains the seeds of his impending dissolution. The rocket had reached its full height and was just bending on its downward course, breaking into the most brilliant of coruscations. Napoleon was nearly forty. He had been Emperor of France three years. He was still married to Josephine, but, dissatisfied with her sterility, was looking for new means to perpetuate his glory. One other emperor, nominally an ally and equal, four kings and thirty-four reigning princes, and as many heirs to the throne, had assembled at the little town of Erfurt to do homage to the upstart suzerain who had summoned his vassals to show the fickle world who was master in Europe. Napoleon left no doubt who was his equal, and who were his servants. The Tsar was the only prince who did not owe his power to the good will of the Emperor of the French. The rest were submissive stewards who had come to ingratiate themselves with their lord. The King of Bavaria, feeling the indecency of that characteristically German inability to preserve a mean between puerile haughtiness and doglike prostration, endeavored to assert a little of his royal dignity by venturing to interject a suitable remark into a conversation confined to Napoleon and Alexander in the midst of thirty-eight respectfully silent reigning princes; which interjection brought forth from Napoleon the snarling injunction: "King of Bavaria, hold your tongue!"

Fresh from the carnage of the battlefields of Europe, Napoleon was provided with a real royal entertainment, and readily relaxed from his more serious labor of killing human beings to the innocent recreation of slaughtering animals. A glorious hunt of deer was provided for the hero in the company of one other emperor, four kings and thirty-four reigning princes, and as many heirs-apparent, all cheerfully agreed that to enhance one's sense of life there was nothing like dealing out death. The site selected for the hunt was, as a charming compliment to the conqueror, the battlefield of Jena, which two years before he had strewn with human corpses.

Next door to Erfurt, in the capital of the pocket state of Weimar, lived Goethe, described by Byron as "for fifty years the undisputed sovereign of European letters." The anomaly of Goethe's position was that he, the greatest name in Germany, was a subject of one of the tiniest of dukes in the German-speaking land. This duke, Carl August, had hitched his wagon to the disastrous star of Frederick William of Prussia, and had incurred Napoleon's wrath. He was awaiting his due punishment. The only thing that could save him and his little country was the propitious circumstance of his son's marriage to a sister of the Tsar Alexander. Napoleon was not going to quarrel with the Tsar, at this stage at any rate. And what Alexander might not feel disposed to ask for the King of Prussia he was willing to do for the wretched father of his own brother-in-law. Goethe, who had been for long accustomed to seek favors from his duke and pay homage to his petty sovereign, now found himself in the more flattering position of being summoned by his duke to Erfurt in the hope that the poet might put in a good word for him with Napoleon.

A deliciously ludicrous situation in fact took place, which German biographers, with that peculiarly portentous stupidity which distinguishes nearly all biographies in German, depict with a funny solemnity which misses the point. Here, if ever, was an exquisitely humorous clash of incompatibilities, of meaning, of idiom, of style, of intention. Napoleon, hearing that Goethe was in Erfurt, summoned him next morning. Goethe, whose early renaissance of German literature was ignored by Frederick the Great, who patronized Voltaire instead, was flattered by the attentions of Napoleon, who knew nothing of his works save his immature early effort, *The Sorrows of Werther*. Napoleon, the swaggering man of action, did not have enough sense to know that a great man of letters would necessarily see through his pose.

The great man of letters, on the other hand, handicapped by Napoleon's inadequate understanding of intellectual processes, and further handicapped by his own imperfect conversational use of the other man's language, did his poor best to be playful in the Gallic style; which effort, delivered as it was with a heavy German accent in stilted French and in the German idiom, Napoleon did not catch. He looked thoughtful and answered cautiously: *"Oui"* and *"C'est bien."* Or he himself made an embarrassingly poor intellectual statement and asked: *"Qu'en dit, Monsieur Göt?"*

He, however, moderated his bombast and, probably sensing an intelligence a cut above "guns and butter," confined his questions to simple matters.

"How old are you?"

"Sixty years old."

"Does it please you here?"

"Very much."

"Are you married? Have you any children?"

The same night Talleyrand procured for Goethe a stall for Voltaire's *Mahomet*. The theater was packed with royalty; and as somebody in the play questioned: "Who has made him king? Who has crowned him?" and was answered: "Victory!" all eyes in the auditorium turned towards the imperial box. And as Omar said on behalf of Mahomet: "To the name of conqueror and hero-triumphant he wishes to add the name of pacifier," Napoleon described from his box a wistful Caesar's gesture indicative of his own identity of purpose, his solidarity in this respect with Mahomet, to the applause of thirty-eight royal vassals and as many crown princes.

Another night, at Weimar, Napoleon was again treated to a play. *Death of Caesar* struck him as an odd choice for the occasion. *"Pièce étrange!"* he complained to his hostess. *"Pièce républicaine!"* It was indeed as though Mussolini on a visit to London had been invited to a gala performance of *Julius Caesar*.

Passing through the ballroom, Napoleon inquired for the names of the more beautiful women, then indulged in a harangue on the subject of classical tragedy with Wieland, who, having prepared his discourse, easily got the better of Napoleon, who broke off with the words: "We'll return to it presently, Monsieur Wieland. I don't consider myself beaten. But enough of it now. Look how beautifully the Emperor Alexander dances the minuet."

Alexander, in effect, danced with a consummate elegance, a simple dignity, a finished grace, with the exquisite charm of one who abandons his heart and soul to the unilateral exercise of art for art's sake. But next morning, with feverish impatience, he was insisting on the immediate incorporation of the Danube principalities, while Napoleon insisted that hurry was a new demand, itself entailing a *quid pro quo,* that they were in effect making a new treaty in which there was room for reciprocal conditions.

The condition was to postpone realization by only a few weeks. In reality, this clause, qualified by another, enabled Napoleon to postpone it for years. Two weeks elapsed before it was possible to agree on a version which remotely satisfied both parties.

Two clauses in the new treaty confirmed the Russo-French dictatorship over Europe. No campaign against the Ottoman empire could be embarked upon except by previous mutual consultation and agreement.

Both emperors pledged themselves to absolute secrecy on the subject of the treaty for the next ten years. The brunt of it all was that, while Napoleon was not disposed to permit Russia a further hand in Turkey, he did not think it wise to rob the Russian emperor of every vestige of hope. This ten-year pact of secrecy indicated that at the expiration of that term each emperor hoped to be able to carry on merrily without the other.

In what mood Alexander left Erfurt can be guessed from his remark to the King of Württemberg, who was the Empress Dowager's brother. "Napoleon," Alexander said to his uncle, "is now too powerful for us to be able to fight him. One must first let him weaken himself. Spain will serve the purpose, or Spain will render good services in this respect. His vanity, which tears him from one undertaking to another, will do the rest. The time will come when I will revenge myself for the part I am playing here in Erfurt."

Nobody gained much from the Erfurt meeting except "Monsieur Göt," who, at the close of the celebrations ending in another gigantic holocaust of deer, was decorated, respectively, with the French Cross of the Legion of Honor and the Russian Star of St. Anne "for services to German literature."

IV. THE PARIS–PETERSBURG AXIS

YET nobody was less entitled than Alexander to complain of Napoleon's duplicity. If he resented the gulf which yawned between Napoleon's expansive assurances at Tilsit and his shrunken promises at Erfurt, Alexander had already double-crossed Napoleon at every turn. While officially in a state of war with England, whose government the Tsar had castigated in no uncertain terms in a manifesto condemning the British naval raid on Copenhagen, voicing Russia's anger, declaring the Baltic closed to English ships, Alexander had sent a confidential agent to London to advise the Cabinet not to take his words to heart. They were meant for the Franco-Russian Axis, not for Great Britain. He congratulated the British statesmen on their prompt perspicacity in carrying out the raid on Copenhagen before the now indignant French had had a chance to do the same, and he invited the English to continue the confidential understanding existing between them, and to remember that if by force of circumstances he was sometimes temporarily compelled to yield to Napoleon's pressure, he was at heart as firmly bent on his destruction now as ever before.

"Never," says Bismarck, "has a human being possessed the art of dissimulation in so rich a measure as Alexander I, who in this respect was an unsurpassed master."

But dissimulation, like patriotism, is not enough. Napoleon learned he had his work cut out in Spain; and Alexander found Finland a handful; and the Turks, discovering that the Corsican had betrayed them to his new friends, the Russians, put up enormous resistance in Wallachia and Moldavia. With English support, the Turks fought the Russians with such energy and for a long time with such luck that Alexander, having wasted 50,000 men and 100,000,000 rubles, could not reach any decisive success till the autumn of 1811.

V. MISLAID LOYALTIES

IN the war which now ensued between Napoleon and Austria, the Russians, though Alexander had pledged himself at Erfurt to provide Napoleon with an army corps against Austria, proved themselves of more assistance to the Austrians than to the French. At Austerlitz, when the Russians had been allies of the Austrians, they seemed to hate them more than their enemies, the French. Now, with Austria for their enemy, the Russians conceived a sincere attachment for her troops. They congratulated them on their victories, and made a thorough nuisance of themselves to the French.

Napoleon's idea was to enlarge the Duchy of Warsaw at the expense of Austria—that is, of Polish territory which Austria had previously taken from Poland. But the Tsar was firmly of opinion that if any Polish territory was to be taken from Austria it was to be handed to Russia and not to the Duchy of Warsaw, which he regarded with aversion.

Poland had been devoured in the previous century by Russia, Prussia and Austria and was entirely swallowed up. The Tsar accordingly regarded Napoleon's creation of a French protectorate, the Duchy of Warsaw, as a dangerous rallying point, as indeed it proved to be. The advent of French troops into Poland roused the Polish national spirit, never long dormant, and their most ardent hopes of re-establishing their ancient kingdom. Old men wept at the sight of national banners. Youth clamored to join the ranks of the liberators. Galicia organized itself overnight into infantry battalions, cavalry squadrons, national guards. Women and girls threw flowers in the path of the conquerors come to free them from the Austrian yoke.

This did not suit the Russians. Nominally allied to France, the Russian army placed itself like a wall between the risen Poles and their joint enemy, the Austrians, but expressly to protect the Austrians against the Poles. Everywhere they got in the way of the French and spoiled their operations. Everywhere they were hindering the Poles, who could hardly understand their attitude. Prince Golitsin, the Russian commander in chief, with his army of 48,000, was everywhere suppressing the Polish insurrection.

VI. ALEXANDER NEGOTIATES ABOUT HIS SISTER

WITH his Duchy of Warsaw, Napoleon fell between two stools. It was far too much for the Russians, and much too little for the Poles. Napoleon had made the King of Saxony the hereditary duke, and the new duchy a dependency of France, a focus for Polish national uprising—in fact, a red rag to Russia.

Alexander had repeatedly told Caulaincourt that if anyone was to cede any Polish territory it was to be to *him*. He had been ignored. In 1809 a certain coolness manifested itself in the conduct of Russia towards France. Napoleon was loath to commit himself before he had settled the war in Spain, and Alexander was reluctant to engage in war with Napoleon before he had settled his own campaign in the Near East.

To calm the Tsar, who lived in dread lest this satanic Napoleonic creation, the Duchy of Warsaw, should swell overnight into the old Poland, Napoleon agreed reluctantly to furnish guarantees in this respect. A treaty was drawn up stipulating that the Duchy of Warsaw was not to be enlarged in future and was to remain solely a Saxon province.

One might well wonder why Napoleon, who was no fool, should sign such a treaty, which raised a wall between him and the hitherto hopeful and devoted Poles, and deprived France of an excellent instrument with which to blackmail Russia whenever she made herself inconvenient. The secret, however, was that in propitiating the Russian emperor Napoleon had a counter-request up his sleeve. It was his projected marriage with a Russian princess, Alexander's young sister.

The idea had attracted him some time back, and the more he thought of it the more strongly it appealed to him on all accounts, though he was a little shy to speak of it. It began to take precedence over the earlier idea of restoring the Kingdom of Poland and giving the crown either to his brother Jerome or to Murat.

Already at Erfurt Napoleon had sounded the Tsar, and Alexander had made it clear that, for his own part, he would be honored to give him his sister Anna, but foresaw difficulties on the part of his mother. This appears to have been a sincere reply. The widow of the Emperor Paul did not get on too well with her eldest son, who had so soon curtailed her glory. Willful and bad-tempered, she had, when her husband was murdered, entertained the idea of following in the footsteps of the Catherines and promptly proclaiming herself Empress and Autocrat. Bilked of the scepter, she jealously retained her prerogatives in the family. Nor did she regard Napoleon as anything but an upstart, a vulgar usurper, and considered her Anna, the daughter of proud Paul (bastard and insane though he had been) as much too good for the Corsican miscreant.

Napoleon, in proposing the treaty limiting for all eternity the Duchy of Warsaw to its present size, thought fit to press forward simultaneously, but in the greatest secrecy, the tender request for the hand of the youthful Grand Duchess. Alexander signed the treaty with alacrity, but tarried on the subject of his sister. His communications were friendly, even excessively frank. He stressed the extreme youth of his sister, commented on her physical charms, said her breasts were developing and it was thought that she would soon attain a condition enabling her to undergo a state of marriage. But the time was not quite at hand; they could not hurry Nature, nor was his mother as yet of a like mind with himself. Patience was necessary. In the meantime he hoped the Emperor would proceed with the ratification of the treaty to which he had laid his hand.

Napoleon, who meanwhile was entertaining the rival idea of espousing the buxom young daughter of Kaiser Franz of Austria, tarried with the ratification. Alexander, unnerved by Napoleon's procrastination, complained to Caulaincourt of the incompatibility of his master's conduct with accepted standards in combining two questions which, the Tsar urged, had nothing to do with each other. At the same time Alexander implied that Napoleon would not obtain the hand of his sister till the treaty limiting the Duchy of Warsaw was ratified.

Napoleon, who agreed that the two questions were strictly separate, yet stressed that he could not wait indefinitely for the Tsar's sister. No wife, no ratification, he meant.

In February 1810, the consent of the Tsar, his mother and sister reached Paris: too late, however. The Emperor of the French discovered that, without sacrificing his political credo either in Poland or Turkey, he could obtain for the asking the daughter of the proudest and most ancient house in Europe—a Habsburg. While Alexander tarried and waited, news reached him of Napoleon's engagement to Marie Louise of Austria. Alexander, who had not been very keen on the idea of marrying his youthful sister to the gross and crafty Corsican, now declared himself injured in his deepest feelings and pressed with the energy of despair for the immediate ratification of the treaty guaranteeing the limitations of the Duchy of Warsaw. Napoleon implied that his mind at the present time was too distracted with family questions to enable him to devote sufficient thought to the matter; and the treaty safely limiting the Duchy of Warsaw remained unratified.

The Times under date March 9, 1810, wrote in its leader:

It is now certain that a Princess of the House of Austria, the Archduchess Marie Louisa, is to be elevated, if we may use the term, to the throne of France. We sincerely compassionate the sorrows of the father, who is thus constrained, for the safety of his throne, to surrender his daughter to the embraces of a sanguinary Tyrant, of whom the dread is so great, that it has smothered the feelings of nature....The political consequences likely to result from this new contract are most important. Those which more immediately stare us in the face are very painful ones. Our inveterate enemy may be at last considered as having secured the acquiescence of Austria in his designs upon other nations: the poor Tyrolese, it may be feared, are abandoned, and all hopes of further insurrection upon the Continent extinguished as the only support upon which the insurgents could lean is withdrawn; Russia...being both too much distracted in her internal councils, and too remote to afford them assistance.

...Such are the immediate consequences of this odious marriage; and does it not then behove us, above all things, by frugality, and the evidently practicable curtailment of our expenditure, to hoard up our means of defence and self-support, for a contest so alarming, and that must clearly be of so protracted a nature?

Napoleon, impatient to meet his bride, rode out to meet her coach at the frontier. He got in, the fat man, and the springs of the coach creaked and sagged under him. Tested too long by the Orthodox Tsar, racked by suspense, the podgy Corsican adventurer was now getting his own back from the rosy-cheeked, plumpish virgin daughter of His Apostolic Catholic Majesty of Austria. On the frontier. In a coach, too, tired and dusty, with no washing accommodation to speak of. Just to satisfy his self-respect by unwedded pleasure with a pure-blooded princess.

When it was all over, Napoleon looked before him with an expression of critical thoughtfulness. Marie Louise, recovering from her shyness, ventured to ask him what he was thinking. He could not tell her. But it was then that the aphorism he later applied to his situation in Moscow occurred to him: "From the sublime to the ridiculous is but one step."

Marie Louise was silent at his side for the rest of the journey, and she could have hardly said that Napoleon was fluent either.

But when she got to Paris...there was her own little doggie from Vienna already awaiting her, and she cheered up at once.

On April 11, 1810, they were married.

The Times, its unfailing felicity and good grace strained by the spectacle of Bonaparte still at large and now a bridegroom, commented as follows:

...The Imperial Pair then resumed their seats on the throne, and went through the forms of kissing the Gospels....High Mass was then performed, during which the happy couple took the Sacrament, and were repeatedly perfumed with incense, and sprinkled with holy water. During the Propitiare, *the Emperor and Empress kneeled on the cushions placed for them at the foot of the altar....The Imperial Ruffian and hisq spouse again knelt at the* Ite missa est....*And thus terminated one of the most abominable profanations of the solemn offices of Christianity recorded in modern history.*

ENEMIES AGAIN

I. THE ROYAL VISIT TO PETERSBURG

SOON after Erfurt, as a gentle remonstration to Napoleon and a gesture to the King of Prussia, Alexander had invited Frederick William and his Queen to Petersburg, where they were lavishly entertained. Since the three nations were allies, Napoleon could not object to the invitation, even though he knew that his disgruntled partners had met to sulk together.

A separate palace had been assigned and prepared for the royal visitors, all the rarest furniture having been transferred for their use, as for our own King and Queen's visit to Paris in 1938. Alexander rather overdid the presents for Queen Louisa, who had been denuded of all her possessions. He gave her dresses and jewelry and a golden toilet set. People whispered: Queen Louisa was being compromised. She was still good-looking, but had grown flabby. The Empress Elizabeth wrote to her mother at Baden that Louisa certainly had beauty, but she *must not* grow any fatter, particularly about her neck.

Indeed, Queen Louisa was looking more and more like Alexander of Macedon.

Everyone wanted to see what the famous Prussian beauty was like. But Alexander's mistress, Marie Narishkin, affecting simplicity of dress in contrast to the heavily ornamented Queen, with but a bunch of forget-me-nots in her hair, won the day. With a meaning look, Alexander himself made it clear to her. Even Alexander's consort Elizabeth, many said, looked more attractive than the bloated beauty from Berlin. Queen Louisa had been a Mecklenburg princess by birth and a great beauty in her day. Now she had toothache, her health was crumbling, she had grown fat about the shoulders; but she made a desperate attempt to live up to her reputation. Alexander, though charming to her, did not fall for her fascinations. Though she flaunted a low-cut dress designed to display her attractions to the confusion and undoing of the Emperor, whom she believed to be deeply in love with her, his inveterate chastity where she was concerned (which she explained to herself by his sentimental respect for her rooted in a super-sensuous idealism) easily withstood the assault.

The Queen was in the first stages of pregnancy, which made her suffer and gave her otherwise lustrous eyes a dull look. Besides, she could not sleep, she had fever, toothache and was sick; she was dead with fatigue and hoped she might be buried in the Alexander Nevski cemetery. She was dog-tired, she had a chill on the liver and another on the chest, and a running cold. Yet she would not give in.

All these ailments she noted day by day in her diary. Her visit lasted several weeks. Queen Louisa was desperately in love with Alexander. The Empress knew it. But she also knew that Alexander was not in love with Louisa; she could therefore appear magnanimous. Elizabeth showered favors on the beggared Queen of Prussia and pitied her without reserve. The Empress had long been jealous of Marie Narishkin, and was still jealous of her. It therefore pleased her to think that Marie Narishkin might be jealous of the Prussian queen. But both the Empress and the Queen were only German women, and what could they do against the charm of a Pole? For Madame Narishkin was born a Princess Tchetvertinski; and had not the Empress herself fallen in love with Prince Czartoriski, likewise a Pole? Louisa communicated her innermost thoughts on the subject of her feeling for Alexander to her brother, adjuring him "by the bowels of Christ" to keep her letters secret. After weeks of brilliant receptions, banquets and command performances in the Russian capital, the King and Queen returned to their penurious life in a small wooden house at Memel, the farthest corner of what remained of their domain.

II. WAR IS COMING

WHEN, in July 1810, Napoleon declared once and for all that he would *not* ratify the treaty concerning the Duchy of Warsaw on *any* conditions (adding: "At least not in its original form"), negotiations were brusquely broken off by Russia. And when Napoleon swiped up the Duchy of Oldenburg, belonging (as we surely know) to a relative of the Tsar, Alexander retaliated by breaking his agreement over the Continental System. He authorized the importation of British goods into Russia on neutral vessels, and prohibited the introduction of certain French cosmetics and luxury products, and put a prohibitive duty on others.

The world concluded that "the great ideas of Tilsit" were indeed at an end and that war between France and Russia was imminent.

Nobody was so alarmed at the prospect as our old friend Frederick William of Prussia. From Memel he sounded his old ally at St. Petersburg. What was he to do? Napoleon would not let him stay neutral. On the other hand, it would pain both him and Louisa to take the field against his dear ally and friend.

Alexander replied coolly and noncommittally. But he sent the King a private message by word of mouth. He would place, on the first demand from the King, the entire Russian Army at Prussia's disposal. That was the secret message.

The surreptitious arming of Prussia in the summer of 1811 did not escape the notice of Napoleon, who threatened that he would deprive the King of the other half of his kingdom, indeed liquidate the Hohenzollerns as a dynasty. To lend weight to his assertion Napoleon moved troops into Prussia; whereupon the King sent a panicky message to St. Petersburg imploring the Tsar to state in writing, and without equivocation, that Prussia in resisting Napoleon could count on Russian support.

But the Tsar had changed his mind. In a number of postscripts he advised his royal friend against any open defiance of Napoleon and urged him to possess his soul in patience. The Tsar stressed how hard it would be for him to stand aside if dear, valiant Prussia were again to come to grief, meet with complete and final calamity under the hammer blows of Napoleon's big battalions.

The King, feeling helpless and abandoned, submitted to Napoleon's dictation. He signed a treaty which subjected him to Napoleon's will and placed the Prussian Army at the disposal of France.

Alexander was not prepared to face Napoleon till he had settled with Turkey. This he did, thanks to a number of happy coincidences, which included a forged letter purporting to come from Napoleon and proposing a partition of Turkey—a successful fabrication which completely destroyed any lingering confidence the Turks reposed in the Corsican who had several times, abortively, betrayed them.

Alexander's success was, however, mainly due to the time-honored method by which Peter the Great got out of a jam at Pruth in the previous century: the bribing by Russians, expert in the craft, of the proverbially corrupt Turkish diplomacy. Alexander annexed Moldavia and Wallachia by making it a "Sudeten" question. He was to save a

Christian and Slavonic minority from their Ottoman oppressors. His troops did indeed save them, with such general results that the Tsar himself exclaimed before Admiral Tchitchagov: "The excesses of our troops in Moldavia and Wallachia have exasperated the inhabitants. I cannot suffer such horrors any longer!" The Admiral in his memoirs admits that he has found the complaints of the inhabitants only too justified, but that to all representations Kutuzov merely replied: "I shall leave them their eyes to weep with."

The world was greatly astonished at this puzzling Treaty of Bucharest. It was known that France and Austria had previously signed an alliance providing for the integrity of the Ottoman empire, mutually guaranteed by Napoleon and his new father-in-law, Kaiser Franz. At the very moment when Russia was prepared to cut her losses and retire gracefully from a situation become untenable, Turkey bought the peace by sacrificing more than even Catherine the Great had obtained through long and bloody wars. And fortune further favored Alexander in securing for him, as a new ally against France, his country's historic enemy, Sweden. So favored and fortified, Russia could now prepare to meet the coming storm.

III. 1812

THERE were rumors of war. The tone among the fashionable set of Russian society was frivolous, or what today is called "sophisticated" or "hard-boiled." They were consciously imitating the petulant cynicism of the time of Louis XV. Love of one's country was regarded as pedantry. The clever young people hailed Napoleon with an enthusiasm amounting to fanaticism and joked over their own defeats. The patriots were over-simple and were being laughed at. They had no influence left. Their patriotism took the form of condemning the use of French in society. The young fops spoke of everything Russian with contempt or boredom and laughingly predicted for Russia the fate of the Confederation of the Rhine. Contemporary society, growled the old fogeys, was pretty foul and degenerate!

Suddenly news of Napoleon's invasion of Russia, of the Tsar's urgent appeal to his countrymen, struck them like a thunderbolt from the sky. Moscow got scared. Propaganda leaflets issued by her energetic governor general, Count Rostopstchin, appealing to the populace to defend the old capital against foreign hordes, were being distributed in the streets and posted on the walls. The clever young got cold feet and lay low. The abolitionists of the French language raised their voices in Moscow's clubs; the cynics began to eat humble pie. Ladies thoroughly got the wind up and began to pack up. The drawing rooms filled with patriots. They shook out French tobacco from their snuff-boxes and filled them with home brands. Some burned their French libraries, others ceased drinking French wines and took to *kvas*. As though by a signal, all stopped speaking French, cited Minin and Pozharski, Alexander Nevski, and any other home-grown hero they could find in history, and meanwhile got ready to slink off to their distant country estates situated at the opposite pole from the frontier.

The arrival of the Tsar in Moscow fanned popular excitement. A warm wave of patriotism rose and engulfed even the cynics. Subscription to the Tsar's Patriotic Fund was the order of the day. Young Count Mamonov, carried away by his own eloquence, subscribed the whole of his estate. His noble speech was recited in all the drawing rooms. Young debutantes swooned with love for him, though their mothers no longer considered him eligible. The Tsar slunk off back to Petersburg, where he immured himself in the Winter Palace for the duration of the war.

Napoleon steadily advanced on Moscow, and the Russian troops as steadily retreated before him; while Moscow families who could afford to hire carts and horses cleared out one by one. The idea was to save themselves and their movable property. They rightly reasoned that Napoleon could not remove their immovables. To cover their shame at fleeing thus before the enemy, they advanced the plausible theory that their flight was part of a plan to frustrate Napoleon by leaving him an empty capital to starve in. The poor, who could not thus assist their country, because they had no carts on which to take away their belongings, were urged to burn what they had and stay behind to molest the enemy.

The Tsar had only 200,000 troops commanded by indifferent generals as against Napoleon's Grand Army of 600,000 led by himself and his brilliant marshals. This initial inferiority, and no native cunning, was responsible for the decision to wage a defensive war. The Russians had no ready plan of defense. The initiative was Napoleon's. The Russian high command, sensible of their own inferior strength, were inspired by the one idea that their two armies should join forces before meeting Napoleon's onslaught. As Napoleon rapidly advanced into the interior of Russia, the two native armies had no choice but to postpone until farther and farther afield the realization of their cherished idea of joining forces.

Charles XII of Sweden had committed the same error of advancing too far into Russia before the retreating Peter I, who had lured him into the hinterland, through no cunning strategy, but of sheer necessity. That Peter had learned nothing by this defeat which, through no virtue of his own, had turned into victory, was proved by his emulating Charles himself, and coming to grief at Pruth by advancing heedlessly into Turkey.

No more now than then, despite two calamitous historic examples, did it occur to the Russians to embark on the retreat as a deliberate plan to confound the enemy. They did so, against their own wishes and in the teeth of repeated imperial commands to make a stand against the enemy, who was desecrating holy Russian soil. All manner of patriots, including Alexander's own mother and favorite sister, Catherine, threatened to unseat him if he did not make a stand. And it may be added that Napoleon, who had in his youth carefully studied the campaigns of Charles XII, had in this respect also learned but one thing— how to repeat his master's mistake. Napoleon pushed the Russians before him; and all their attempts to halt him at Vilna, Smolensk, Borodino, and Moscow were of no avail.

War is not lawn tennis, and Napoleon too had suffered cruel losses at Borodino (regarded as a Russian victory in Russia). But he recovered and advanced—while the Russians backed—towards Moscow. When we say, "Napoleon had suffered cruel losses," it only means that he cheerfully suffered other men to suffer loss of life and limb, and would not let such trifles hold him back. If, for example, he had had half his own jaw blown off in the engagement, he would have turned back post haste to Paris, feeling that the war was more than he could bear.

But supreme detachment distinguishes artists of action. The sight of burning Smolensk, Napoleon confessed to his companion, Caulaincourt, who shared his coach with him, was a beautiful sight. Napoleonic lore, which reveres him as a general, a statesman and a lawgiver, neglects Napoleon the aesthete.

The enormous distances, the climate, scarce cultivation and the thin population were the natural allies of the defenders. The Russian command was characterized both by the Tsar and by a leading Russian general, Buturlin, as abject. "The Russian Army," Buturlin comments, "fought excellently in particular instances. The leadership of its generals, however, was beneath contempt. Later they pretended to have done of their own free will and design that which Napoleon had compelled them to do. Alexander delayed him with negotiations till the bad weather set in; and then broke them off. Napoleon, thinking he would starve, began the two-hundred-mile retreat. His troops froze and starved but a small residue escaped, which would have been impossible if the Russians had not operated as abjectly as they had done when he advanced."

Napoleon's greatest error, a fundamental error inherent in his assumption of the crown (which made Beethoven cancel his dedication of the *Eroica*), the fatal error which proved his undoing was his refusal to enlist the sympathy of the Poles and the serfs. It seemed to go against the grain of one who had turned his back on his own foster mother, the French Revolution which had reared him. Had he, on entering Vilna, promised the Poles the complete restoration of their country; had he proclaimed far and wide the abolition of serfdom, he would have been supported by the revolted peasantry, and Poland would have marched with him to a man. The Russian rebel Cossack chief Pugatchòv nearly succeeded in unseating Catherine. All the common people, angered against their landowners, had risen with him, and the rebellion was only quelled after the outcome had swayed in the balance.

Napoleon had the big battalions, too: all he lacked was a popular mood he could so easily have harnessed to his end. The Diet in Warsaw had formally proclaimed the restoration of Poland as a nation. Many Russian peasants, too, believed that Bonaparte was bringing them their freedom. Nor was there the slightest opposition to be feared from Austria. In the treaty which Napoleon had concluded with Marie Louise's father, Kaiser Franz forfeited his share of Poland if Napoleon thought fit to restore the ancient kingdom within its former frontiers. Russia in a state of war would not be asked. And Frederick William had to do as he was told.

What prevented Napoleon from availing himself of these two obvious remedies to turn defeat into victory? The answer is habit—the habit of complete totalitarianism with himself the sole authoritarian, and the consequent dislike of popular franchise. Napoleon had turned his back on the Revolution and was now an absolute monarch married to the daughter of His Most Catholic Majesty. Revolution, which in the early days was an opportunity for power, had turned into fear and anathema. A despot does not readily embrace revolutions. Hitler, once raised to power, proclaimed the object of the revolution as achieved: "The Revolution is ended," he said. Napoleon, in fanning a Polish revolution against Russia, feared that it might raise its head against him in Germany; perhaps at home in France. He was at that time still fighting a national uprising in Spain. He did not want to start a conflagration which he might find hard to quench.

The Polish Diet had transformed itself into a "General Confederation of the Kingdom of Poland" and only awaited a signal from Napoleon to unleash against the hated enemy. One word of encouragement would have been enough.

Napoleon's proud reply was that he relied entirely on his army and that a national uprising was to him neither necessary nor, indeed, desirable.

This answer would have been as cold rain on any national enthusiasm. It was like ice dropped on a red-hot plate when we recall that the enthusiasm was Polish. And almost quicker than it arose was Polish enthusiasm for Napoleon dead.

Historians are apt to underrate the force of the movement which broke out among the peasants on hearing of the advance of Napoleon's armies. The news spread from the bordering Lithuania that Napoleon's arrival meant freedom for all serfs; an exchange of positions, making masters of serfs and serfs of their former masters. Peasants rose in country estates, smashed wine cellars, broke mirrors and generally behaved with the unco-ordinated enthusiasm of risen slaves. Even in the interior and the vicinity of the capital, the news spread that Bonaparte was no enemy but a liberator, and no sooner had his army passed Vitebsk than serfs pressed forward to the foreposts to deliver their masters into the hands of the new champion. Thus Abyssinian slaves must have felt at the advent of Mussolini's Fascists.

After he had fled to Paris, Napoleon replied eupeptically to an address from the Senate, delivered on December 20, 1812, that he could easily have set one part of the population against the other if he had availed himself of the suggestion to proclaim the emancipation of the serfs, which deputations from many villages had urged him to do. Several independent witnesses, including General Sir Robert Wilson, attached throughout the campaign to Russian headquarters, bear this out. During Napoleon's stay in Vitebsk in August 1812, he was urged to enlist the services of the Russian clergy by distinguishing them individually and by addressing them collectively in a manifesto, and he was informed that arrangements had already been made for him to seize Tula with its munition works.

During his too long and fatal stay in Moscow, Napoleon was called upon by a deputation, addressed by their spokesman in French and advised that his army was still strong enough to withstand the winter and only needed food, forage and horses, which they would provide, also 100,000 well-armed peasants, as soon as he had issued a proclamation calling on the Russian serfs to rally round him for liberty, and won the Russian clergy over to his side.

After Napoleon had heard the speaker in French, he sent for an interpreter and questioned the other three deputies who could not speak French and got the interpreter to translate to him their replies word for word. With a sigh, and saying it was now too late, he ended the interview. The last to leave the room, the man who knew French, heard Napoleon blow up his chest, expel the air and groan as one who despairs of finding pure natures in a world so corrupt with strife: "Rebels everywhere! ... Everywhere rebels!"

What proved disastrous for the Corsican was the way Alexander turned the hatred of tyranny which the peasants reserved for their landlords into hatred of the foreign invader; and the love of that liberty which they hoped to obtain for themselves into a passion for the liberation of their country from a profane and sanguinary tyrant. Their initial enthusiasm, fanned by Napoleon's advance, but now balked by his refusal to harness it to his end, turned against him.

It may be that, face to face with them, he feared releasing these incalculable forces, so difficult to check once let loose. He was in an alien and barbarous land, where only the landlords spoke his language. It was dangerous to trust himself to the dumb savage masses who hardly knew what they wanted, and whom Alexander, as indeed he did, could so easily turn to his side. He was their sovereign; his Church was their Church. The Tsar proclaimed a holy war against the infidel who was desecrating their temples and altars, the despot, the Antichrist, the oppressor; and the peasants rose in a mass against the ragged remnants of the once resplendent Grand Army, now shrunk to sparse bands of hungry and frostbitten Frenchmen and levies from central Europe, and fell on the gaunt and haggard figures staggering in the snow. It suddenly seemed to them—as, no doubt, it seemed in 1914 to many a laborer in England and France, that if only Kaiser Bill were downed and the war won for democracy, they would get a square deal—it seemed to the Russian serfs that with every foreigner safely outside the Russian frontiers, Russian peasants would have land and liberty at home; and they made common cause with their masters.

But it was the burning of Moscow which was the match kindling a great mass of combustible patriotism. Napoleon, the Russian authorities urged, had outraged their finest, their most sacred feelings: he was burning the holy citadel, the white-stoned city of a thousand churches, the golden-domed Moscow. The illiterate peasants could not know that it was on the Tsar's express instructions to Governor General Rostopschin that the ancient capital was set on fire. For Alexander—like Hitler, who saw the hand of God in the burning of the Reichstag—knew the value of propaganda.

The effect was complete, ending in Napoleon and Caulaincourt chasing in a peasant sleigh in the opposite direction to that in which they had come: the one in which Alexander and Czartoriski, seven years before, had been laying distance between themselves and Austerlitz. Here, now, was the unbeatable hero, sublime leader of the Grand Army, making a dash for it across the river Berizina, and narrowly escaping capture; then rushing on with relays of fresh horses across Germany to reassure abashed, astonished Paris. One cold December night, as they were changing horses at a post station, Napoleon casually inquired where he was. They informed him. The little town was Weimar.

"Ah!" And he sent word to be remembered to "Monsieur Göt."

CHAPTER XXIII

"OUR ALEXANDER"

I. HITLER'S PRECURSOR

IT is true that Russia was the first to cause Napoleon's power in Europe a severe shock. But it is also true that the shock was not decisive. Already by April 1813 Napoleon had gathered a new army which, together with the residue of his Grand Army and various garrisons in Germany, comprised no less than 300,000 men. If one remembers that it required the concerted efforts of the rest of Europe to bring him to heel; and not at one go but in stages; and that the issue even at Waterloo hung in the balance, then it will be seen that what Alexander had achieved was not a victory, but a substantial contribution towards liquidating that sanguinary if spectaclar nuisance, Napoleon Bonaparte. He had won the second set.

Russia's exhaustion after 1812 was even more marked than Napoleon's. War is not ping-pong, and Russia's casualties equaled the size of the whole of her army originally raised to meet Napoleon's invasion: that is, 200,000 men. It was easier for Napoleon to create a new army than it was for Russia. He had a well-organized system of government, a dense population, intelligent men to deal with, well-stocked arsenals and considerable financial resources.

Alexander had none of these things. Before the war was over he had appealed to Great Britain to supply him with arms and munitions on credit; and now, victorious, he was desperately short of cash.

Napoleon in 1812 had required the King of Prussia to place an army corps at his disposal; and it was this army corps which gave the signal for the Prussian rising when Napoleon turned tail in Russia. The Prussian corps had fought for the French with more vigor and gallantry than when they had fought against them. Badly beaten by the French, the Prussians were anxious to prove their metal to them. The commander of the Prussian Corps, General York (a Prussian of English extraction), after an unsuccessful encounter with General Diebitsch (a Russian of Prussian extraction), came to a friendly understanding with the enemy. He proposed to detach his troops from the French army and declare himself neutral, pending instructions from Berlin. The document was called "The Convention of Tovrog."

By this decision, taken on his own initiative, York eventually forced the hand of his King, who, twice chastized by Napoleon, would never have dared to cross him again. Constantly left in the lurch by Alexander, the King had accepted Napoleon as the lesser of two evils; and the news of York's defection, however gratifying to sentiment, filled him with dread of Napoleon and new punishment to come. Jubilantly they told him that York had revenged Prussian honor, that the whole country stood solidly behind him. The King rubbed his face, walked up and down, and stopped in perplexity. "It's enough to give a fellow a stroke!" he groaned.

He could hardly show himself lagging behind the patriotic upwelling of his own people. Trembling in his shoes, and vexed with York, the King declared himself as highly delighted.

As it was doubtful at first whether Frederick William really would back up his commander, the Russians hastened to force his hand. The King, they urged, must join them *now:* otherwise, as Napoleon's ally, he was an enemy of Russia, who would confiscate all his lands east of the Vistula.

A fiery Prussian patriot, Stein, who had been to St. Petersburg, now made his appearance in Königsberg, armed with a document from Alexander describing Stein as the Tsar's plenipotentiary, and East Prussia as a Russian province by right of conquest. At this point it became known that the King of Prussia had, after much vacillation and understandable searching of heart, rejected the Convention of Tovrog, signed by York, he urged cantankerously, without authority, and confirmed his loyalty to his ally Napoleon.

In return for his loyalty in the face of such temptation, the King solicited certain concessions as testimony of Napoleon's "sincere friendship." Napoleon, who did not think it politic at this crucial time to appear weak in the eyes of the world, rejected the proffered hand of friendship. What seemed even more rude, he repulsed the King's offer to cement their alliance through family ties, and refused out of hand all concessions.

The King, staggered by Napoleon's ungraciousness, was wondering what to do. Meanwhile, Alexander, using Stein as his tool, resolved to deprive, under the cloak of restoring Prussia's national freedom, his ex-friend Frederick William of the best parts of what remained to him of his kingdom, and cut him off from his sources of men and material.

The situation, already tortuous, was further complicated by men and factions pursuing different ends by similar means, and similar ends by different means, all with the best of intentions. Alexander resorted readily to the use of a revolutionary uprising in Germany, which Napoleon had disdained to make use of in Poland and Russia. Stein, in his fanatical Francophobia, did not disdain any means that would achieve his end of freeing Prussia of the French yoke. Alexander, a Russian, seemed to him a more effective instrument than his proper King of Prussia, sickeningly slow to make up his mind, even after he had been snubbed by Napoleon.

As Alexander's plenipotentiary, Stein took over the till at Königsberg and legalized Russian paper money, much to the annoyance of the Prussian governor, who took his orders from his King in Berlin. Stein commanded everyone to obey the fine and fervent Tsar of Russia, "Our Alexander," now fired with the noble ideal of a free Germany. A National Assembly had sprung up, composed of patriotic citizens imbued with the idea of German liberation. They were nervous. They wondered whether, if Frederick William had definitely rejected General York's convention, they might not be regarded as traitors to their King and country. Nor were they sure that in supporting Stein they were not exchanging the French yoke for a Russian one.

Pooling their wisdom, they resolved that they might assume, without prejudice to the sovereign rights of their monarch, that if he had not declared himself for the national cause, it was because he was by circumstances constrained from declaring his free will. This assumption was their legal instrument for doing his thinking for him.

All the leaders were at cross-purposes and accusing one another of muddle-headedness. Alexander, an absolute monarch at home, was all for letting loose the revolutionary forces in Prussia, for making the voice of the people heard so that they might force the hand of their King. Schön, a bosom friend and colleague of Stein's, turned against his pal and threatened to unleash the German national rising against the Russians. It was for the King of Prussia, he said, to lead the movement of Prussia's liberation.

York, threatened by the King with court-martial, stormed at Stein, calling him a hothead who turned everyone against them and was about to ruin the valiant beginning he, York, had made at Tovrog. Stein shouted at the General that he had made a good start with his convention of Tovrog, but did not know what to do next. Stein threatened

York that he would set Russian troops against him. A threat which the General met with: "All right! I'll march away with my troops now, and you'll be left with your Russians, of whom I wish you joy!" And the population once again was beginning to murmur: "Better the French as enemies than the Russians as friends."

Frederick William still dallied. He could not decide which of two courses offered a more cheerless prospect: to resist Prussian patriotism fanned by Russia and be pushed off the throne by the Tsar, or to obey the Tsar and be pushed off the throne by Napoleon.

Alexander helped him to make up his mind by informing him through Stein that, if he still clung to his alliance with Napoleon, Russia would relieve him forthwith of all Prussian territories up to the Vistula.

The King still sat on the fence.

At last, the People's Assembly of East Prussia, meeting at Königsberg and whipped up to a frenzy of patriotic excitement against Napoleon and France, sent a deputation to Alexander to present him with this, then the most important, province of Frederick William. And Stein, on the instruction of Alexander, earnestly asked the King whether he wished to see the *whole* of Prussia going over to Russia, or whether he would act as his people wished him to do.

The King then decided to act. The alliance which he concluded reluctantly with the Tsar at Kalish showed that the King had no choice in the matter. The conditions of that treaty were wholly unfavorable for the King. In return for the plunge which might cost Frederick William his crown and indeed his dynasty, Alexander, without offering guarantees, promised that he would not sheath the sword till the King's domains were restored to the position and condition they had enjoyed before Napoleon's aggression. In return, Alexander stipulated that the King was to turn over to him anything and everything he had ever owned of Poland, and content himself with suitable compensation in northern Germany. The Tsar had in mind territory belonging to some other German prince—anyone except the English House of Hanover.

In a confession written ten years later, Stein says: "Prussia's siding in the struggle begun by Russia was daring. Her own forces were limited and undeveloped, and those of the Russians still weak. There were less than 40,000 men between the Oder and the Elbe. Facing them was Napoleon with all the forces of France, Italy and the Confederation of the Rhine."

But more energetically worded than the Treaty of Kalish was the Russian commander, Kutuzov's, proclamation entitled: "Appeal to the Germans." In the joint names of the Tsar of Russia and the King of Prussia, the proclamation informed the German Nation that German liberation from the French yoke was the one purpose of the two powers in calling Germany's princes and peoples to join the cause, and that those of her sovereign princes who would not answer the call within a stipulated period would be punished by the confiscation of their States.

As, however, the prospect of getting rid of their lords and overlords, tempting though it must have seemed, was not deemed adequate to cause a general conflagration of patriotic enthusiasm among the placid race of Germans, the somewhat formal opening of the proclamation conceived in official Prusso-Russian style lapsed abruptly into emotional hysteria in the concluding passages. Turning to the people, it promised them the renaissance of their lost liberties and unity; promised them their rejuvenation and restoration to that place among the Nations which was their birthright; promised the people that they themselves should cooperate in the coming task of reorganizing the Fatherland. This last sounded almost like franchise.

Alexander, increasingly the autocrat at home, was the fervent revolutionary abroad, a fit pupil of Laharpe. "Terror restrains your governments," he wrote in his proclamation to the German people. "Do not let that hold you back! If your sovereigns, under the influence of cowardice and servility, do nothing, then the voice of their subjects must be heard and must compel the rulers who are leading their peoples into slavery and misery to lead them into freedom and honor."

A Russian general issued a proclamation in Saxony, urging the people, against the declared intention of their King (who by Napoleon's grace was also Duke of Warsaw) to take up arms for the "great holy cause" and not allow themselves to be condemned by order of their monarch to a shameful repose. "Freedom or Death is the solution!" said another Russian proclamation. "Saxony! Germans! Forward! Heil!" Alternatively, this proclamation, signed by a Cossack colonel, informed the public that the Tsar had commanded that every German who was caught fighting on the other side was to be sent to Siberia.

II. ALEXANDER GETS IN THE WAY

IN the first campaign of the newly allied Majesties of Russia and Prussia, which now took place against Napoleon, it looked as though their high-sounding words would not be crowned with success. The first of the battles, at Lützen, ended to the eminent disadvantage of the Tsar and the King, despite the bravery shown by the Prussians. The Russians supported their allies but tentatively and had no idea of how to employ to advantage their superiority in cavalry. The campaign, brilliantly planned by the Prussian general, was not followed out by the Russians, because the Tsar by his interference caused the utmost confusion among the supreme command. Everywhere he got in the way.

All through the anxious days of 1812 when Napoleon's Grand Army rolled into Russia, Alexander had been hiding in the Winter Palace in Petersburg. Now, at the turn of the tide, he was anxious to display his courage. At Austerlitz he had contributed to the general panic and stampede of his own troops and was among the first to flee before the charging enemy. Now he rushed suddenly without any necessity into the keenest fire, so that the Russian commander in chief, instead of attending to the campaign was only exercised with the problem of extricating his Emperor. For this purpose no sacrifice of troops, Russian or Prussian, was deemed too great. As a result of this commotion, nobody was in command, or rather everybody: the Emperor, d'Auvray, Diebitsch, Blücher, Scharnhorst, even the aides-de-camp of the Emperor. But certainly not the commander-in-chief, Wittgenstein, who did not even know where the brigades and regiments were.

The general retreat which this battle necessitated at its conclusion gave rise to a very unpleasant discussion between Alexander I and Frederick William III. As the Tsar was explaining to the King the painful necessities of a situation imposed on them by existing conditions, the King retorted with some vehemence: "I know all that! Once we start to retreat, we shan't stop at the Elbe but will cross the Vistula; and before I know where I am I shall find myself back again in Memel."

The Tsar's attempts to soothe the King of Prussia, whom he surprised in bed, only irritated Frederick William, who wanted to get up. For loss of ready repartee, the King suddenly pushed back his bedclothes and, remarking shortly: "I present to you my compliments: I must get up!" jumped out of bed, causing the Tsar to beat a hasty retreat. In his nightgown and bare feet, Frederick William ran to the open window and there, beholding what he did, wailed aloud: "The old, old story! Auerstadt all over again."

The second battle, near Bautzen, also ended in defeat and retreat for the Allies, and for similar reasons: the extraordinary mania of Alexander, devoid of all military talent, to override words of command at decisive points.

Napoleon with his raw recruits but brilliant command got the better of the seasoned Russian and Prussian troops abjectly directed. Alexander and Frederick William began to wish they had never begun. When they came to Dresden they both appeared on the balcony of the castle and impersonated before the crowds assembled below the triumph of an Allied victory. Meanwhile long trains of wounded were coming up, and the people began to wonder whether victory had really been as complete as claimed by the two sovereigns, who, to allay any further doubts, ordered a thanksgiving service.

As defeat succeeded defeat, the monarchs found it more and more difficult to bolster up the spirit of the people, who had been led to expect a great battle at the source of the Spree, where the enemy was to have met with the fate prepared for him in Russia. Whenever a battle was lost, the public was now being told that the Allies had "broken off" the battle—a new expression which suggested that they had done so of their own free will because they could see no immediate advantage in going on with it. The truth was that Blücher postponed his retreat till he was positively compelled to flee before the enemy. Another quarter of an hour's delay, and nothing would have been left of him.

III. A COOLING OFF OF RELATIONS

HISTORIANS at this point testify to a regrettable cooling off of relations between the two sovereigns; and an increasing chilliness as Alexander, in proportion to an accumulation of defeats largely due to his own meddling, pressed the necessity of a single command—Russian—over the Allied forces.

In this he succeeded, to a point. The new commander in chief, Barclay de Tolly (a Russian of English extraction), while commending in his orders of the day Blücher's dashing cavalry charge at Heinau (which had so raised the spirit of the troops, sadly in need of encouragement) was yet careful to point out that enterprises of that kind which decimated forces that should be spared for the greater ends of the combined armies must not be attempted in future. This censure from a Russian so depressed the Prussian high command that they were on the point of negotiating a separate peace with Napoleon. Even Frederick William, in an assembly of Prussian and Russian generals, spoke violently against

York, whom he accused of having started all the trouble through his confounded Convention of Tovrog.

Scarcely less than the depression of Prussia was the pessimism in Russia. The Tsar himself compared his position to that of Peter the Great at Pruth, in 1711, and said: "Now Napoleon has got his revenge."

Most of the Russian generals were of opinion that one should end the fighting, contenting oneself with bagging the Duchy of Warsaw, and also trying to take all Frederick William's territory east of the Vistula. This, they argued, was surely more sensible than to go on sacrificing oneself for Germans who should fend for themselves. Still less could the Russian private soldier, who felt homesick after legging it across these hazy distances, understand why his Tsar was so keen on liberating another nation while his own was in chains.

Yet Napoleon's evil star apparently required that he should know nothing of this defeatist mood among his enemies. He considered, on the contrary, that it was he who had good grounds to wish for an armistice.

Such an armistice was concluded on June 4, to last till July 20. It was the biggest mistake which Napoleon had committed. All Russians agree that the most fatal error Napoleon made throughout his military career was to consent to an armistice after the battles of Lützen and of Bautzen, just when his conspicuous successes had restored the spirit of his troops, badly shaken in the Russian campaign. "This suspension of hostilities," Napoleon himself confessed in the memoirs he wrote in exile at St. Helena, "was fatal for me. Had I pursued the enemy, I should have dictated the peace on the banks of the Niemen."

It should not have been unduly difficult for him to dispense with the armistice, since his troops outnumbered those of the Allies.

IV. KAISER FRANZ JOINS IN

IN the first months after Napoleon's *débâcle* in Russia, Austria betrayed a lively wish to join the Allies against him. Napoleon had in the past played such havoc with Kaiser Franz that the mere fact of his now being his son-in-law did not weigh appreciably with His Most Catholic Majesty, still less with his minister, Metternich. What held them back was the uncertainty whether, and to what extent, it was wise to exchange a French for a Russian bully.

Kaiser Franz was shocked and horrified at the revolutionary principles which Frederick William and Alexander together had introduced into their proclamations in urging the subjects of the Rhine Confederation against their legitimate rulers; which seemed to him a greater evil than any conceivable on this earth. Stein, York, Blücher, seemed to him little better than Jacobins. Kaiser Franz said aloud for all to hear that he sadly feared Frederick William was not the man he had been. He was no longer—that was it—at the helm of his State, but merely, as it were, walked beside it!

Nor did the repeated failures of the Allied armies dispose the Emperor of Austria to take up arms against his daughter's husband. He would certainly have remained neutral if only his son-in-law had taken the hint and settled the account still outstanding between them.

For Kaiser Franz pined for the return of Illyria, of which his son-in-law had so cruelly deprived him in the past. But Napoleon's evil star blinded him again. Austrians in the pay of Russia aroused suspicions as to Vienna's purity of motive. Napoleon dallied, and when he at last consented to meet the demands of his father-in-law, it was too late. Kaiser Franz, by force of circumstances and with genuine regret, had already joined the ranks of his enemies.

It was the coming-in of Austria which brought the scale down against Napoleon. The Prussians and Russians would have fought on till doomsday without ever succeeding in bringing Napoleon to heel. But the addition of Austria decided the issue.

This can be seen in the change of fortunes which followed the combined forces of Prussia, Austria and Russia. The battle which ensued was won by the Allies under the leadership of Blücher, in spite of his being handicapped by the unruly interference of the Russian generals. Blücher not only defeated Napoleon's plan to march through Silesia to Poland and strike the Tsar in the rear; he also neutralized the dangerous consequences of the simultaneous defeat of the Allies at Dresden, brought about by the unfortunate passion of the Russian Self-Upholder to play the generalissimo while being shortsighted and rather deaf into the bargain. That habit of throwing himself between the commanders created such a depressing effect on the Allies that, had it not been for Blücher's victory at Katzbach and another at Kulm, it was a near certainty that the alliance would have dissolved in recrimination. Frederick William as good as considered the Coalition at an end. Metternich was so panic-stricken that he dispatched a secret agent to Dresden to discuss with Napoleon ways and means of terminating the slaughter.

The Russians retaliated by fighting with such bitterness over any spoils after the battle that, in the confusion which ensued after a victory, they even got away with Prussian guns, swearing to God they had captured them from the enemy. They even picked the pockets of their wounded allies.

Blücher succeeded, against Russian opposition, in crossing the Elbe and insuring the simultaneous arrival of the three Allied armies near Leipzig. A tricky operation. Though the Russians did not specially distinguish themselves in the fighting, yet the Emperor Alexander assumed the position of supreme overlord, and in all political decisions Russian diplomatists had the decisive word.

Goethe did not warm at the uprising of the German national spirit. Neglected as a writer since his two early successes forty-five years before, he entertained a smoldering contempt for the German people. Napoleon had flattered him. Napoleon was his supernational hero. "Pull at your chains," Goethe cried to the young poet Körner, going to the wars, "you won't break them! The man's too big for you."

He declined the invitation to write stirring patriotic verse. "Were I," said Goethe, "a young man billetted in a tent, warming before a camp-fire within sound of the trumpet, the neighing of chargers and the beating of drums, there might have been something—though not much—in writing war poems. But as an old man, sitting in dressing gown and slippers by my big stove—no! It's not my affair!"

That Germany had merely exchanged one bully for another became increasingly evident to them after the Battle of Leipzig. The despotism and caprice with which Alexander chivied the German princes left Napoleon in the shade. Some legitimate sovereign princes were deprived of their States, others threatened with confiscation, merely because they had previously bowed to necessity, though no more than Alexander himself had done while he had been in fact an ally of Napoleon. That neither Austria nor Prussia dared to intervene on their behalf showed to what extent they had subjected themselves to his will.

The small and middle-sized States of Germany were even more blameless for finding themselves under the weather than the bigger States which had some means of defending themselves. "Napoleon, the world conqueror," Bismarck writes, "has never dared to go quite the length Alexander, the world liberator, has traveled."

It is possible that Alexander might have swiped up most of the reigning dynasties if he had not had an ulterior purpose in desiring their continuation. Stein, a precursor of Hitler, suggested to Alexander to make an end of the German small sovereignties, wherein he saw the source of German disunion and weakness. But Alexander objected. If only for the sake of providing his numerous grand dukes and grand duchesses with adequate consorts, he could not wish, he said, the destruction of such a valuable royal marriage market. Stein replied: "That your Majesty desires to make a Russian stud out of Germany is, I own, a consideration which has not occurred to me!"

And a Russian stud Germany certainly was; without, however, the slightest benefit to Germany. Nearly all Russian sovereigns and grand dukes since Peter the Great provided themselves with German wives. And the result was invariably that these German women on assuming the Russian crown threw themselves into orthodoxy and pan-Slavism with a fervor and lustiness ridiculous even in a native.

Alexander entrusted Stein with the management of the central commission in charge of the confiscated German States. This commission had an essentially Russian character. Saxony got the worst of it for her failure to comply with the policy advocated in the Russian proclamations —to overthrow her legitimate sovereign and join the German national rising. The King of Saxony's crime was aggravated by his being Napoleon's nominee in the Duchy of Warsaw. His ancestors on and off had been Kings of Poland, and Napoleon had, not unnaturally, made him Duke of Warsaw. Now he had to pay for it. He was sacked from both thrones.

The new governor general in Saxony, the Russian Prince Repnin, gave one brilliant feast after another, while the population starved. Russian soldiery committed excesses. Despite severe punishment threatened in the Russian orders of the day, Russian soldiers indulged in robbery in the streets in broad daylight. They even robbed Protestant churches. Their passion for alcohol led them to break into the Natural History Museum at Dresden, where they smashed the glass containers preserving anatomical parts and drained the alcohol as the nearest thing to vodka.

Metternich, to bring an end to increasing Russian domination, proposed a rapid peace with Napoleon. As Russia and Prussia were both sadly dependent on British financial support, Downing Street, in pursuance of its new policy of appeasement, secured the adhesion of all the Allies to peace negotiations with Napoleon. The conditions proved so unexpectedly favorable to France that but for pressure from Great Britain and Austria it would be difficult to account for them. The Emperor of the

French was to retain the territories possessed by him at the time of his assumption of the imperial crown. He was to retain Belgium, the whole of the left bank of the Rhine, the Duchy of Savoy, and a good slice of Italy.

But Napoleon's blindness prevented him from accepting these favorable conditions. Instead, he proposed counter offers containing conditions, in the circumstances most vexatious, which struck directly at the maritime interests of Great Britain. These conditions were veiled in mental reservations which the Emperor Alexander delighted in exposing to the British Envoy, Lord Aberdeen, all the more so since he had only begun peace negotiations against his own will at the prompting of his English creditors. Alexander convinced Lord Aberdeen of the insincerity of Napoleon, whose simultaneous rearming did much to strengthen the Russian case against him. Metternich, in a postscript to his letter, implored Napoleon not to tarry a single day in accepting the Allied offer.

Napoleon, who was bluffing the Allies with a show of force he deemed favorable to his own cause, at last fell in with Metternich's request. But it was too late. The day before his acceptance the Allies, assembled at Frankfurt, had decided on continuing the war.

CHAPTER XXIV

ALEXANDER IN PARIS

I. THE GREATEST DAY OF HIS LIFE

FOUR months later, on March 30, 1814, was fought the battle before Paris which laid the capital, and the whole of France, defenseless before the Allies, and on April 11 the greatest military adventurer of the century renounced for himself and his descendants the throne of France.

It may be taken as proved by innumerable case histories of fateful characters that their future is likely to conform to the view which Providence may take of their continued usefulness on earth. If his mission in life is not yet over, no blow will assail him other than that meant specially to accelerate the work expected of him. Secure in the arbor of his fruitful mission, he may take risks in pursuance of his duties, though not indulge in senseless heroics; and no harm will befall him. But once he has accomplished his task, once his destiny is fulfilled, Providence withdraws the protective cloak it has cast over his shoulders; and, as if to spite him for the privileges he has enjoyed, all the guttersnipes of lower nature put out one foot after another for him to trip over; till, thoroughly humbled, reduced indeed from the sublime to the ridiculous, with unseemly haste, he is kicked out of this world.

So it was with Napoleon. A scramble ensued between the Allies to reach Paris first—precedence which the Emperor of Austria, as His Most Catholic Majesty, ex-Holy Roman Emperor, deemed to be due to his station. But Alexander made haste to get there first. This was just before the Battle of Paris. It was not a question of fighting his way there. Alexander seems to have pushed his way past Napoleon, who was floundering somewhere away with the idea of cutting off the Allied army from its base. Anyhow, Alexander reached Paris in advance of both Kaiser Franz and King Frederick William; and it was a situation which suited him down to the ground. It was, in the words traditionally employed by actresses taking a curtain on a London first night, the greatest day of his life.

On the top of a hill overlooking Paris, Alexander paused and surveyed the twinkling lights of the prostrate capital, as Napoleon, eighteen months before, had contemplated Moscow from a window in the Kremlin. It must have occurred to Alexander that he had beaten the Little Corporal at his own game. More than ever before he could take lightly his scepter and his crown—he who, even if born to the purple as the result of an accident, was born nevertheless a military genius.

Then he drove through the streets of Paris to the acclamation of the crowds who shouted, *"Vive l'Empereur Alexandre!"* He regarded himself, and what was perhaps more remarkable, he was regarded by others, as the liberator of Europe. And what was more than remarkable was that he was regarded as the liberator of France by the French, as he had been called "Our Alexander" by the Germans.

Perhaps after all it is not remarkable. Napoleon's tenacity, his "courage" and determination to fight to the last Frenchman in the interests of preserving his personal glory at no special danger to his own person had, after twenty-five years of glorious slaughter, struck the French man-in-the-street as perhaps being more than Napoleon was worth.

On the Place de la République Alexander surveyed with a benignant smile Frenchwomen hanging to the saddles of his Cossacks, and remarked: "I hope my Cossacks won't rape these modern Sabines."

Then he awaited impatiently the arrival of Louis.

II. ALEXANDER MEETS LOUIS XVIII

LOUIS XVIII was still in England. He was over eighty, gouty, obese and not otherwise in good health. His brother, the Comte d'Artois, now promoted to "Monsieur," customary title of brother to the King of France, deputized in his absence. The King was urgently awaited, but an attack of gout kept him in England. Alexander rehearsed before the mirror the impassioned speech he was going to deliver before this last, decrepit and, in both senses, ancient son of Saint Louis.

Political motives intermingled with private inclinations. Never his own master, ever the instrument of power factions of the Court of St. Petersburg, which reminded him at short intervals that the Russian throne was "occupative" and not strictly hereditary, Alexander proceeded with zest to trace a new policy for France which he thought it was his privilege and his pleasure to impose on a defeated foe. Napoleon had been the enemy who had humbled Russia. Napoleon was destroyed. But England and Austria were opposing Russian domination in Europe and the Near

East. With Prussia alone for his ally, Alexander was not equal to Anglo-Austrian opposition. Where could he seek an additional ally?

The question answered itself: France. Who in France would have the greatest cause to be grateful to him? The answer read: a Bourbon. Little sympathy as he felt for that unteachable dynasty, he could not resist the pleasure of acting preceptor to a son of Saint Louis. Alexander loved to strike generous attitudes, and here, before the mirror, he was rehearsing what he would say to Louis XVIII.

At last Louis had crossed the Channel and was on the sacred soil of France. Once again France had a king.

"This," said *The Times* in a leading article, "is how London received the news. The heartfelt and universal joy which pervades this great metropolis was last night testified by the most brilliant illumination we have ever witnessed ... the discharge of cannon,—the splendor of emblematic transparencies,—the display of the White Cockade,—the shouts of *the Bourbons for ever! Louis XVIII and Peace!* These and a thousand similar demonstrations unequivocally evinced the sentiments of all ranks of people to be those of unfeigned delight at the occurrences which have restored tranquillity to Europe."

On the eve of their meeting Alexander wrote Louis a long and impassioned letter in which he besought him not to forget that France had grown accustomed to twenty-five years of glory, and he begged "Your Majesty, my Brother," to think well and think earnestly how he was going to rule the country restored to him by the victorious Coalition, of which he, Alexander, was the natural spokesman. In particular he warned Louis to be guided by his, Alexander's, long experience in politics and affairs and lighten his touch in dealing with contemporary realities. He abjured the King from introducing reactionary measures or from punishing the people who had been loyal to the previous regime. More and more he wrote in the same strain, and the more he wrote the more he was seized with uplift. He felt he was perhaps being too copious, that his pen was running away with him, but he could not contain himself and wrote, wrote, wrote....

He could hardly bear to wait till next day; he could imagine the old King at his approach dissolving in tears of gratitude, weeping on his neck.

The King briefly and formally acknowledged the Tsar's letter, without, however, commenting upon it. Next day Alexander drove down to

Compiègne. He was ushered into the presence of the King of France, who, without leaving his seat where he reclined comfortably upon cushions, motioned his visitor to a hard narrow chair with a stiff back. Alexander indulged in his speech which he had prepared before the looking glass, and called on the King to prove himself worthy of the crown entrusted to him.

The King listened with coy politeness, and when Alexander had concluded, made a few formal remarks having no bearing on the points raised by the Tsar. Louis XVIII expatiated on the satisfaction which all Europe must feel at his having ascended the throne of his forefathers. It was plain to the Tsar that, far from appreciating the sacrifices which Russia had made in restoring the throne to the decrepit parcel of gout who lolled before him while he sat bolt upright like a schoolboy, this Bourbon in fact assumed it as perfectly natural that the peoples of Europe should have been glad to shed their blood to restore him to his rightful place as the occupant of the proudest throne on earth.

After this cool if polished exchange of civilities the King turned to his visitor, proposing that he now retire to the apartments prepared for him: they would meet again at dinner.

The Emperor of All the Russias was then conducted across the King's bedroom and along a phalanx of royal anterooms draped with pomp and majesty; through the gorgeous apartments occupied by the King's brother, the Comte d'Artois, now "Monsieur"; then through a succession of noble rooms reserved for the King's relatives: the luxurious drawing rooms of the Duc d'Angoulême; the opulent suite of the Duc du Berry; finally down a dark and smelly corridor into the surprisingly humble—really quite abject—apartments situated in the servants' quarters ordinarily occupied by the steward of the palace, now vacated and placed at the disposal of His Imperial Majesty the Tsar of Russia.

When dinner was served the Most Christian King preceded his imperial guest to the dining hall. The majordomo, about to serve the first course and hesitating an instant, the King quickly disabused him of any lingering doubts on the score of precedence, calling out in a loud, rather irritable voice:

"Me first!"

The Emperor Alexander, who for thirty-five years had known nothing but adulation, who had been so fond of saying he was no emperor but a happy accident, was shocked to the marrow of his being by the gross incivility of this king of two weeks' standing and refugee of a third of a century whom he had restored—he began to think, inadvisedly—to a throne better graced by the Corsican upstart.

The Corsican upstart, not famous for his sense of humor, had indeed expressed loud merriment at the news of the royal procession setting out from the port of disembarkation in a cortège of cabs trailing their sorry chattels of boxes and parcels tied up with bits of string and all manner of junk accumulated during long years of exile in England. Alexander began to think he should have left Napoleon on the throne of France instead of resurrecting this ungrateful *cadavre*. He flatly refused to stay the night in the shabby apartments with the dingy bedroom allotted to him. Dinner over, he at once sent for his carriage.

In the days which followed he consorted demonstratively with Napoleon's relatives. He visited Marie Louise at Rambouillet and Josephine at Malmaison, and Queen Hortense, who lived at the Hôtel Terutti. He became their daily visitor, "carrying on" against Louis XVIII, telling them how much he liked them all and how chagrined he was, how sincerely sorry, to have deposed their beloved Napoleon. He spent hour upon hour expatiating on the backwardness, narrowness, insipidity, the black ingratitude of the Bourbons, of whom it was truly said that they had learned nothing and forgotten nothing.

Madame de Staël, who had been on a visit to Russia, gave a party for him. The guests included Madame Recamier, La Fayette, Talleyrand, Caulaincourt, and the brothers Humboldt. Alexander, who could speak of nothing else, carried on like this for three hours: "None of them is capable of understanding me. Obsolete prejudices. Intolerable narrowmindedness. Comical preoccupation with precedence. Empty dynastic conceit! But what ingratitude! *No:* can you understand it, can you *explain* to me such black ingratitude?"

Madame de Staël at length tried tactfully to deflect his conversation to a happier topic, but again and again he returned to it; and when he left they raised their tired eyes to heaven and someone murmured: "God! What a bore!"

Queen Hortense was then in her early thirties, and game. Alexander is said to have had an affair with her. As a slight and graceful return, he undertook to extract—and it was like extracting a bad tooth—from Louis XVIII a royal brevet, making the ex-Queen the Duchesse de Saint-Leu.

The Tsar is also—which is less credible—said to have had an affair with Hortense's mother, Josephine. From the same source—French—we learn that Alexander had also had an intermittent affair with his sister Catherine. He sends her constant greetings, couched in such terms as "I kiss your beautiful breasts..." But, though not absolutely impossible, a love affair between brother and sister, such as was consecrated by dynastic usage among the Pharaohs of Egypt, seems as improbable as Alexander's affair with Josephine.

Josephine had now reached an age when pretty women, though ceasing to be pretty to the general eye, have not themselves, by reason of constant resort to the mirror, grown aware of any appreciable change for the worse; and in wishing to produce on the newly encountered male the effect of lightheartedness, produce instead the effect of being light in the head. She was fifty-five.

Josephine now made a bee-line for Alexander. It was her last conquest. Who indeed could have been a more welcome visitor than he who had dethroned the man who had uncrowned her? She tried to charm him with her withering attractions, while he poured out his heart to her. He, once so careless of his diadem, was indeed in danger of becoming a dynastic snob. The snub administered by the great-great-grandson of the *Roi-Soleil* forced him willy-nilly to examine his Romanov credentials in the light of the none too illustrious, or even certain, Romanov family tree. Besides, Talleyrand was going about spreading rumors—and he had told his king—that the Romanovs were nobodies. Not fit to lace the boots of a Capet. Josephine did not seem to understand. He was Tsar, wasn't he? And conqueror—certainly! He had charm, hadn't he? What then was he worrying about? She gave him a playful whack on the arm with her folded fan.

Josephine gave a party for Alexander and she went for a moonlight walk with him, caught a chill and died a few days later. Alexander sent a detachment of his troops to the funeral.

III. ALEXANDER IN LONDON

THE Peace of Paris, inspired by Great-heart Alexander, provided for no indemnities or contributions. There was no mention even of any return of art treasures that Napoleon had bagged from the capital cities of Europe. The treaty provided for the reinstatement of France within her own natural borders—no longer, of course, Napoleonic frontiers, but the frontiers of the old monarchy. Alexander insisted, with some eloquence, that France should remain great and strong "for the salvation of

Europe." The settlement of details was left over for the Congress of
Vienna, to take place in November.

From Paris, Alexander took a trip to London, where he put up at a
hotel in Piccadilly. "The Agamemnon of Kings," as Europe fulsomely
called him, though at the height of his glory, was not a success in London.

It was the first time since Peter the Great that a Russian sovereign had
paid a visit to England. Catherine I, Peter II, the two Annas, Elizabeth,
Peter III, Catherine II and Paul could not vacate a throne that was
"occupative" rather than hereditary without the risk of its being occupied
in their absence by a relative, a connection, a consort or even a favorite.
Alexander had nothing of the uncouth awkwardness of Peter, nor
indeed of Peter's innate modesty when confronted with superior techni-
cal achievements, or of Peter's wish to sit at the feet of a master and
learn in humility the rudiments of his craft. Alexander was a man of the
world—and yet in London he proved himself oddly deficient as a
worldling.

Was it that Louis XVIII had shaken his confidence in himself? Was it
that the mantle of the conqueror had too suddenly descended from the
Corsican's podgy shoulders on Alexander's high shoulder blades? Had
Napoleon's baleful example of strutting upon Europe like a cock on a
dunghill contaminated the victorious Tsar? Alexander could not keep
an even keel. He was arrogant where English custom expected a gracious
modesty; hail-fellow-well-met just where tradition required a royal reserve. He expressed republican sentiments when exhibited as an example
of absolute monarchy. He was stiffly the autocrat just when expected to
unbend himself.

He made people sit down with him in the presence of the Prince Regent
when they felt they should stand; and he caused everyone to jump up just as
they had comfortably seated themselves at some informal concert by making an entry with a flourish as though he had arrived for his own coronation. Or he would slip in unnoticed through a side entrance when scheduled as the very climax of pomp and circumstance at a ceremonial of
official welcome.

His sister Catherine (whose breasts he lovingly kissed in his letters)
had preceded him and had made herself unpopular at the English Court
by her blatant advances to the Duke of Edinburgh, whom she wanted
to marry, and by openly consorting with Whig politicians. She had
advised Alexander with a view to winning the heart of the English

populace, who hated the Prince Regent, to be rude to him and cultivate the friendship of Whig politicians, who also hated him. Alexander arrived two hours late at the gala performance given in his honor at Covent Garden and explained to the Prince Regent that he had been carried away by a *most* interesting discussion he had had with a Radical. Then, inopportunely, he created a diversion from the Royal box by leading three cheers for the Prince Regent's consort, the Princess Charlotte, whom the future George IV loathed with all his heart.

The explanation of Alexander's behavior may be found in the circumstance that he had never had any experience of how to treat an equal. In Russia he had been Catherine's "very humble and obedient grandson Alexander," and a madman's will-less son and heir. Napoleon had been a self-made emperor, and Kaiser Franz and King Frederick William were always either junior partners in urgent need of military assistance, or nominal enemies subject to his pleasure. Louis XVIII was a painful anachronism who imbued him with a dynastic "inferiority complex." And the Prince Regent of England was not yet a fully fledged king.

Moreover, Alexander's behavior reflected precisely the Russian attitude to England—that of a large and compact continental mass with a weak and loosley knit economy to a small island with a compact and powerful economy pulling the strings of a far-flung net of loosely strung appendages. Alexander's attitude was: French ways, German blood, and Russian sincerity will let no man down. Anyway, why should the English, whose manners are derivative, too, consider themselves a criterion? That was how he felt and reasoned.

The Prince Regent no doubt lamented how far, how *very* far, Alexander was removed from the conception of an English gentleman. Princess Lieven, the Anglophile wife of the Russian Ambassador, entreated her sovereign to be nice to Lady Hertford, the Prince Regent's mistress. "What! That old hag!" he exclaimed. Turning his back on Lady Hertford, he conversed with eager animation with a pretty young woman.

From London he went to Baden, where his wife was staying with her mother, the Margravin, and then he returned home to Petersburg. The Dowager Empress organized a reception for her son who had achieved European fame.

Then Alexander sank into gloom. After so much adulation abroad he felt dull at home. From too much self-satisfaction he experienced a restless reaction. Like Hannibal after his victories, he spent days in prolonged basking self-contemplation. Russia bored him. The Agamemnon of Kings longed again for the limelight of Europe, and counted the days which divided him from the coming Congress at Vienna.

BOOK SEVEN

CHAPTER XXV

VIENNA CONGRESS

I. ALEXANDER AT THE CONFERENCE TABLE

THE Allies had divided themselves into two factions: Russia and Prussia against England, Austria and France. It didn't seem to matter whether the French had been beaten or otherwise: they wrangled as furiously as if nothing had previously taken place. Alexander had determined to bag the Duchy of Warsaw with himself as King of Poland. He would have granted the Poles their independence, but, he said, their flirtation with Napoleon made this difficult without straining his conscience. At Warsaw Alexander danced with a delightful Polish young lady, to whom he all but lost his heart. They were enchanting, these Polish women. He freely acknowledged it. He was benevolent; he wished them well; everywhere he kissed the hands of Polish ladies; but he could not commit himself to more.

At the Congress of Vienna Alexander ranged himself with Frederick William of Prussia against the other powers, with a view to keeping the Duchy of Warsaw and appropriating, in addition, all of Prussian Poland, while proposing that Prussia should compensate herself by annexing Saxony. Austria, jealous, attempted to resist Prussia's aggrandizement at the expense of another German State. Kaiser Franz still considered himself hereditary protector of the German princes and he thought that Prussia's liberty-and-self-determination uplift ill accorded with these rapacious designs on Saxony.

King Frederick Augustus of Saxony had been given the Duchy of Warsaw by Napoleon, and was now singled out for punishment at the hands of Alexander and Frederick William. The Russians privately condoled with Saxony, blaming the rapacity of Prussia, yet insisted on their claim to Prussian Poland. Saxony had been singled out as the sole culprit. She was clearly a scapegoat. The kings of Bavaria and Württemberg had also stuck to Napoleon. Yet these two kings were spared. The King of Württemberg was Alexander's uncle. The King of Bavaria had been shouted at by Napoleon at Erfurt: "King of Bavaria, hold your tongue!" and, cowed and frightened, he had held on to Napoleon till the very last.

Talleyrand remarked to the Tsar that he doubted whether Frederick Augustus of Saxony would agree to having his country taken from him, and Alexander replied: "In that case the king will perish in Russia. He won't be the first Polish king to die there. Stanislaus Augustus had the same fate."

Lord Castlereagh was prepared to throw Saxony to the wolves and to pardon the remaining princes of the Rhine Confederation who had offended through consorting with Napoleon. But English opinion in Press and Parliament rose against such flagrant injustice. The Prince Regent himself enjoined Castlereagh, in a letter, not to behave in *sansculotte* monarchical fashion, but to preserve the dynastic principle and resist any new-fangled revolutionary ideas attempting to dispose of a legitimate dynasty.

Thereupon Castlereagh changed his whole attitude. Metternich, too, displayed a fresh spurt of activity on behalf of the Wettin dynasty, about to be axed. Despite considerable sums paid to him by the monarch of Saxony, Metternich was becoming tepid in his support of the head of the House of Wettin. But now, encouraged by Castlereagh, he was prepared to view the proposed annexation of Saxony with far more concern.

Alexander, on his side, attempted to drag in Stein, the hysterical liberator of Germany. A useful voice at the conference table. Metternich flatly opposed. Alexander was called the King of the Congress. He raised his voice, banged the table, his eyes darted fire. Wrath and contention penetrated into the lobby from behind the closed doors of the conference chamber.

Talleyrand attempted to repair the broken international prestige of France by sticking up for Saxony. In doing so he had the satisfaction of feeling that he was earning the 3,000,000 francs paid to him by Frederick Augustus for the support of his cause.

As Alexander would not consider returning Prussian Poland to Frederick William, the fate of Saxony became the apple of contention between Russia and Prussia ranged against Austria, England and France. Talleyrand, softened into benevolence by his 3,000,000 francs, became the spokesman of humanitarianism. The annexation of Saxony, he contended, was based on the pernicious principle of "Might is Right," a principle they all hoped Europe had recently outgrown. The moral judges of the King of Saxony, Talleyrand pointed out with his customary suavity, were the very men who wanted to rob him. Was that fair? The confiscation of property, a measure removed from the law books of all civilized nations, was still to be applied, it seemed, in international law. Human beings were not to be allowed—if he understood the Tsar and King aright—any liberty in their own right apart from the fate which might overtake their princes. They were no better than cattle changing hands with the sale of a farm. There was another consideration. What would the powers have to say to it, Talleyrand asked, with a cunning which was second nature to him, if, as seemed probable, in return for her support of Prussia's designs on Saxony, Russia obtained the promise of Prussia's help in furthering her ambitions in Turkey?

During the Congress of Vienna Alexander came up a great deal both against Talleyrand and Metternich. Of these two statesmen he hated Talleyrand even more than Metternich. Talleyrand had soon after Erfurt ingratiated himself in too transparent a form. In a letter to Alexander which declared his warmest admiration and sincere affection for the Russian sovereign, Talleyrand had hinted that these sentiments deserved a reward.

When Talleyrand developed his suave theories about the rights of man and the patent injustice in bartering human beings as though they were cattle, Alexander hotly retorted: "Justice is just what happens to suit one!"

Alexander was not unaware that Talleyrand went about telling everyone, and in Paris was rubbing it into Louis XVIII, who was haughty enough as it was, that the Romanovs were less than nothing. Compared with the House of Capet or even his own, the Périgord, they were nobodies. The first of the Périgords, Adalbert, when asked by Hugh Capet: "Who made you a count?" had said: "Who made you a king?"

Alexander, the "happy accident," did not feel too happy at these uncalled-for excursions into family trees. They showed up only too plainly the "occupative" nature of the Russian throne on which he had alighted by the accident of murders and usurpations which made him a Romanov when he was either a Saltikov or the progeny of a lover of Elizabeth's—name unknown.

In insisting that Prussia swallow up her sister State, Saxony, Alexander incurred the determined opposition of the Most Christian King, who was affronted by such piracy. Frederick Augustus was in fact his cousin-german, for Louis XVIII's mother had been the daughter of Augustus III, Elector of Saxony and King of Poland. Louis resented the fact that the present monarch of Saxony should be a prisoner in Berlin and declared that he would not hesitate for a moment to take up arms in his cousin's defense. True, Frederick Augustus had sinned grievously in remaining to the last an ally of Napoleon; but this, in the eyes of a Bourbon, was no excuse for penalizing a sovereign prince raised high above other rulers of the earth by being a relative of himself.

II. MYSTICISM, EROTICISM, DIPLOMACY

WITH Metternich, Alexander's relations were further acerbated by the handsome Austrian minister presuming to compete in affairs of the heart with the Self-Upholder of All the Russias. At a conference Alexander suddenly attacked Metternich in words which—so somebody said—"one would not use to a servant."

He did more. He nearly threw Metternich out of the window. Having stopped short of ejecting the Austrian statesman by violence, Alexander challenged him to a duel, much to the horror of His Apostolic Majesty, who exclaimed: "What! A ruler by Divine Right to fight a common or garden nobleman descended of mere barons or counts of the Holy Roman Empire, a man who was raised to the rank of a prince only a year before! Good God! What times we live in! ..."

Kaiser Franz regarded himself as a being just a little below his own Maker; and though he considered Alexander as a sovereign of inferior vintage (the Romanov line was at that time one-third as long as that of the Habsburgs), he was yet of opinion that between a sovereign and a nobleman there was as much difference as between a human being and an orangutan. He begged the Tsar not to disgrace the race of sovereigns. It was therefore arranged, much to the relief of Alexander that, upon an aide-de-camp of the Tsar calling on Prince Metternich, who supplied evasive explanations and conventional regrets, the matter should be liquidated. In later years, when Metternich was in the pay of the Russian Emperor, he gained and retained Alexander's complete confidence and esteem.

In the erotic atmosphere of Vienna Alexander abandoned himself to mixed delights, mystic and sexual. Every day he would trudge up the staircase of the Hofburg to the fourth floor where, in a modest room, Roxandre Stourdza, a lady in waiting to his wife, was lodged; and with her he communed. For many hours of the night they united in the spirit.

At other hours he united himself, in the flesh, with such conspicuous lovelies as the Duchess of Sagan, the Princess Bagration, nicknamed "the beautiful nude angel." She was the wife of one of Alexander's own generals; or perhaps at this time she was already the widow.

It would not have mattered either way. Metternich, who was attached to the Duchess of Sagan and combined love with diplomacy, pumped her unsparingly for information on the subject of Alexander's intentions as soon as the Emperor had left her. But Metternich shortly switched over to Countess Julia Zichy, whom he declared to be his ideal.

Alexander varied these visits with others which included four lovely countesses and a beautiful princess. Nor were these his only affairs in Vienna. His attachments, however temporary, were interspersed with a number of intrigues with several pretty girls, natives of Vienna, who helped him "to forget"—whatever it was he wished to consign to oblivion.

The intoxicating air of Vienna sent everyone into convulsions of love. Alexander's wife, the Empress Elizabeth, tolerably good-looking, but cursed with a bad skin full of pimples, rejoined the Tsar after two years of strained separation. Returning from Baden where she had been staying with her mother, the Margravin, to Vienna, she was put up at the Hofburg, and promptly succumbed to her old lover, Czartoriski. Receiving no encouragement, she flew abruptly into the arms of the Austrian Empress, and the consorts of Alexander and Kaiser Franz consoled themselves in a well of imperial loneliness.

Nor did Talleyrand remain unattached. He fell in love with the young Dorothée of Courland, Countess of Périgord, who later became the Duchess of Dino. She was then twenty-one and at the height of her beauty, and her old Uncle Talleyrand, who had betrayed king, republic and emperor, was prepared if need be to betray them again in the opposite order for this ravishing niece who adored him.

III. NAPOLEON'S COMEBACK

WHILE sovereigns and statesmen alike were indulging in love and power politics at Vienna, Napoleon, according to the Prince of Ligne, was playing at Robinson Crusoe on Elba.

Frederick William declared that he would regard any further opposition to the incorporation of Saxony into Prussia as tantamount to a declaration of war. Russia concurrently handed in a note laying down that the annexation of Saxony by Prussia was one of the cardinal principles of the new Europe. England, Austria and France replied by concluding a triple alliance to resist, if necessary by force of arms, the aspirations of the Petersburg–Berlin axis. This alliance, in fact, already existed but was not known.

Metternich threatened at the conference table: "We have 70,000 bayonets to lend force to our demands."

Alexander jumped up, ears glowing purple, eyes darting fire. Banging the table with his fist, he shouted:

"And I have 80,000 bayonets!"

Kaiser Franz declared: "The King of Saxony has his country returned to him or I shoot. And I can count on the peoples of Germany."

And he moved troops to cover Vienna. Sixty thousand Bavarians marched towards Saxony. British-Hanoverian troops took up positions to cut off stray Prussians on the Rhine and in Westphalia. Russian troops moved against Bohemia and Galicia, and French and Prussians set in motion respectively against the Rhine and the Elbe.

Not unlike boxers before a fight, both sides boasted loudly that they were absolutely certain of victory. The Russians, still guests of Kaiser Franz in the Hofburg, declared: "In a few weeks we shall be telling you how to receive us here as conquerors!"

A new war nearly broke out, when Alexander and Frederick William decided to give in. But that was because, while they were contending and disputing among themselves, the Allies received disconcerting news: Napoleon had escaped from Elba. Harmony was restored among the wrangling powers. Metternich took the initiative, and the Allies all quickly agreed: first Kaiser Franz on whom Metternich called within half an hour of receiving the news early in the morning; then Alexander; and finally Frederick William, on whom Metternich called last and who never gave in unless others forced him. Napoleon was advancing on Paris, and Louis XVIII had fled to Belgium.

In his anthology, *What They Said At The Time,* Hugh Kingsmill quotes the Press of the period. This is how *The Times* described Napoleon's comeback:

Early yesterday morning we received by express, from Dover, the important but lamentable intelligence of a civil war having been again kindled in France, by that wretch Buonaparte, whose life was so impolitically spared by the Allied Sovereigns. It now appears that the hypocritical villain, who, at the time of his cowardly abdication, affected an aversion to the shedding of blood in a civil warfare, has been employed during the whole time of his residence at Elba, in carrying on secret and treasonable intrigues with the tools of his former crimes in France. At length, when his plots were ripe, he sailed from Elba, with all his guards, between

1200 and 1300 in number, on the night of the 28th ult. and landed near Fréjus, in France, on the 3rd instant.

...When the intelligence reached Paris, the King immediately took the most decisive steps for quelling the insurrection. He issued a Proclamation, declaring Buonaparte and all his adherents traitors and rebels, and authorising any person to seize and hand them over to justice.... This virtuous and excellent Monarch, who, since his accession, has done so much good to the country blessed with his government, may boldly appeal to the nation, and its representatives for support. If they can be insensible to the blessings of a constitutional and liberal government, if they can be ungrateful to a truly paternal Monarch, if they do not with abhorrence shake from them this Viper of Corsica, their former stain, their scourge, and their disgrace, they are not worthy to be reckoned among mankind.

Two days later *The Times* struck a more eupeptic note:

The advices of yesterday from France are exceedingly satisfactory.... A careful perusal of the different accounts, both public and private, which reached us in the course of yesterday, convince us that we had given this Impostor more credit for policy and prudence than he deserves.... The blessings and benefits of a peaceful reign have made themselves felt, during the last ten months, in every part of France; and the news of the Corsican Usurper's temerity has very generally called forth expressions of attachment to Louis *the* Desired.

The Radical Press of Great Britain (unlike the Radical Press of today, which abhors Hitler and Mussolini) was favorably disposed towards Napoleon. The *Morning Chronicle,* the Whig organ, waxed sarcastic at the Tory attitude:

Louis XVIII after reigning peaceably for eleven months, has been dethroned and expelled—ergo, he is universally beloved by his late subjects.

Louis XVIII was unable to muster a single regiment, nor was a musket fired in defence of his cause—ergo, we may calculate on a strong royalist diversion in the interior of France.

Napoleon Buonaparte, landing without any military force, has been at once replaced on the Imperial Throne—ergo, he is universally hated by all ranks of Frenchmen.

With furrowed brow, a face screwed up with cumulative concern, with painful optimism *The Times* had reported the inexorable march of events.

[*March 14*] ... *The news of yesterday has revived the first impressions of alarm.... We trust that by this time the Duke of Wellington is on his way from Vienna to put himself at the head of the powerful army in the Netherlands, prepared to march at a moment's warning in support of our well-deserving ally, King Louis XVIII.*

[*March 16*] ... *It may prove, and we fervently hope it will, that none but an unorganized, though perhaps numerous rabble of deserters, the scum and disgrace of the French Army, will join the rebel standard.*

[*March 20*] *The Marshal is marching at the head of a corps of about 10,000 troops of the line and national guards ...these troops are animated with an excellent spirit, and with that energy and courage which Marshal Ney never fails to inspire.... This Marshal has offered, out of his private purse, three millions of livres, or £126,000, to whatever regiment shall bring in Buonaparte to him, dead or alive.*

[*March 22*] *There is no doubt of the loyalty of such men as Ney....*

[*March 27*] *The hypocrite Ney, who, at parting from the King, kissed his Majesty's hand with fervour, and swore he would bring Buonaparte back to Paris, has jesuitically performed his promise. Is this like a soldier?*

[*April 4*] *We know well enough what is to be expected from such a Monster as Buonaparte, at the head of a gang of Neys and Caulaincourts, and Fouchés and Carnots. If we could suffer these wretches to triumph, to trample under their feet all that is respectable in France, to begin with treason and robbery, and proscription at home, we know how lightly they would overleap all the barriers that separate them from other objects of their cupidity: and we know that neither their passion nor their malice would be satiated until they had laid waste the cultivated fields, and burnt the commercial cities, of England.... We know our man. We have already suffered enough by his arts: and are now proof against him, though he assume the cry of the hyena, or the tears of the crocodile.*

There is something splendid in the complete liberty now, as then, with which opinion can voice itself in England in the face of a world crisis.

The Whig *Morning Chronicle,* favorable to Napoleonic totalitarianism, laid out its views, thus:

[June 7th] It is manifest that the whole people of France believe that it is not so much against the person of Buonaparte as against the spirit of liberty that the Potentates of the Continent are armed. And that in fact it is more for the re-establishment of feudality, of tythes, of the privileged orders, than of the Bourbon family, that they threaten to invade the territory of France. With this conviction on their minds—with more than six millions of men, individually interested in the preservation of their estates —with fourteen fortresses on their frontier fully garrisoned, and with 600,000 armed soldiers, led by experienced Generals in the field, can it be believed that France will be overwhelmed in one campaign—that if not in one campaign, what will be the fate of Europe?

The harmony between the Allies during the Hundred Days—the term allotted to Napoleon's "comeback"—was assisted by the Tsar's climbing down on the question of Saxony and Poland. It transpired—who could have thought it!—that, of all unexpected men, the King of Prussia himself was not too keen on being given Saxony. A general revulsion of feeling had gathered force in Prussia at the unpalatable idea of swallowing a German sister State. "I've *always* thought and *always* said it's a premature step," declared Frederick William. "But they all wanted to be clever. And that's what happens! No sooner have we settled in than we've got to clear out again. There's nothing clever about *that,* that *I* can see, is there?"

Hardenberg could not get a word in edgeways, and Blücher and others who urged the necessity of "living space" for Prussia by annexing Saxony could not get their king to agree.

The result of it all was that the Tsar had to return to Frederick William a good slice of Poland—the territory known as Posen. Frederick Augustus was to keep his Saxony. So at any rate it seemed at first. When it came down to a final settlement, Frederick Augustus had to part with more than half his kingdom to Prussia.

For the time being, however, the Allies had ceased to be enemies and formed a common front against the escaped prisoner of Elba. *The Times* took up the "hang the Kaiser" cry. In a leading article of April 25, 1815, it gave expression to a view at once ludicrous and reasonable:

We have the satisfaction to lay before our readers an accurate copy of the Treaty of Vienna, concluded on the 25th ult., by which the principal powers of Europe are united with us in one grand and sacred Alliance.... Adhering to the firm and resolute policy which dictated the declaration that Napoleon Buonaparte was without the pale of civil and social relations, and viewing him only in his true light as a criminal, *this treaty pledges the Contracting Powers to use all their efforts to bring him and his deluded adherents to justice....*

Is not Buonaparte a poisoner? He confesses it. Is he not an assassin? He would in vain deny it. Is he not profoundly, nay, ostentatiously, an incendiary? Moscow proves it; and but for the resolution of Marshal Marmont, Paris herself would have furnished a corroborative testimony. Then, any or all the Allied Powers might bring him to justice, as an hostis humani generis. *In England, for example, he might be tried specially for the murder of our brave countryman Captain Wright.... It appears that some public-spirited individuals in this country have conceived it possible that he may be seized and brought to trial for that crime, and with such view they have offered a reward of £1,000 for his apprehension, as they would for that of any other thief or murderer. It is very natural that the* Morning Chronicle *should be exceedingly angry at this. It is very natural that the writers in that paper should be insensible to the atrocity of torturing a brave British Captain to death, for the faithful discharge of his duty to his King and country; but we only wish that the reward were fairly earned.... There is not a street in London in which at least ten individuals would not joyfully pay their hundred pounds each, to see this monster hanged.*

The monster during the Hundred Days tried hard to ingratiate himself with Alexander. But his medium—Hortense—was a poor choice. Alexander had completely forgotten her. After the assortment of glamorous women he had sampled at Vienna, Hortense was small beer.

Napoleon, the outcast, was all for making friends with the man of charm, Alexander. He sent the Tsar a message of good will and a wealth of good wishes through Hortense. Never, but *never!* never again would he bait or worry or rub Alexander up the wrong way over Turkey. He could have all he wanted in Turkey—"only let's be friends!"

Alexander, though delighted at the flight of haughty Louis, was not keen on resuming relations with a Napoleon "without the pale of civil and social relations. " Besides, the Tsar had a new protégé whom he was anxious to push on to the vacant throne of France the moment the enemy of the human species was liquidated. That this would happen they all took for granted—rightly as it happened, though it was touch and go.

Men are limited in good will by their disabilities. A man wounded in the leg will still try and march as well as he can in the cause of his King and country. A man wounded in the heart will endeavor not to allow the wound to prejudice him in his benevolence for the man who struck the blow—so far as he can: which will not be far. Alexander voted against giving dynastic old Louis another chance and proposed the Duke of Orleans, whose democratic convictions he thought made him eminently acceptable for the times in which they were living. But Alexander had yet to learn that with England and Prussia having taken hold of the campaign, and his own troops far away, he could no longer carry decisions at the conference table.

Napoleon sent Alexander a dispatch which a royalist diplomatist had left in his desk while hurriedly vacating the Ministry of Foreign Affairs before the return of the conquering Napoleon. This was the secret treaty concluded between Louis XVIII, England and Austria long before the Vienna Congress, pledging themselves to resist the joint aspirations of Russia and Prussia. Alexander was furious. But, mastering his emotions, he produced the document before the Allied statesmen sitting in council. "Have any of you, Gentlemen, ever seen this document before?" he said with inquiring charm. Metternich, Talleyrand and Castlereagh lowered their eyes and traced "doodles" on their pads.

But he adjured them to waste no time harboring recriminations. They must all be united to put an end to that international nuisance, Napoleon.

The Whig newspaper, the *Morning Chronicle,* though sarcastic at the expense of *The Times,* proved no more successful than the Tory organ in forecasting the issue of events. *"The Times* and *Courier,"* complained the *Morning Chronicle* on the day after the battle of Waterloo, but before news of victory had reached England, "will not give Buonaparte credit either for preparation or military skill. All accounts of the French force are derided as false. But we shall presently see another description. As soon as a battle shall take place, we shall hear of the superior numbers of the French, of the overwhelming majority of Napoleon's army, and that he never contrives to attack without having double the force opposed to him. This always was the language of the war faction; they diminish the force of the French to draw us on to the sacrifice, and aggravate the amount to reconcile us to the calamity!"

But on June 23 the *Morning Chronicle* changed its tune from a negative criticism to one of wholehearted if prudent patriotic approval. "...The glorious victory gained by the Duke of Wellington over Buonaparte.... The whole brunt of the day was borne by the British. The Prussians came on *fresh* at night to assist in the pursuit; but we do not hear of their active co-operation during the day.

"...We have seen the devotion, bravery and zeal with which the French army in the battles maintained the cause for which they fought; and if the whole nation be animated with the same spirit, there is yet an arduous task to be undertaken by the Allies."

On July 22: "The voluntary surrender of Buonaparte into the hands of the Prince Regent of Great Britain, as prisoner of war, decides all questions as to his treatment. It is only now to be inquired where he is to be kept...."

The Battle of Waterloo was won on June 19, 1815, and—what took the wind out of Alexander's sails—the "Agamemnon of Kings" had no hand in it.

CHAPTER XXVI

A FULL LIFE

I. GUIDANCE AT WORK

ALEXANDER now did a contradictory thing. On the one hand he proclaimed the restoration of the ancient kingdom of Poland—to the immense joy of the entire Polish population. On the other hand he let it be known that the King of Poland was to be no other than His Imperial Majesty Emperor Alexander I of Russia—to the bitter mortification of Polish patriotic sentiment.

Alexander was lavishly entertained in Warsaw. He avoided Adam Czartoriski, who might have something biting to say about such a "restoration" of Poland. Everywhere Alexander made agreeable non-committal speeches. He kissed incessantly the hands of pretty Polish ladies and danced a good deal. He was, he said, absolutely delighted with Poland. On his choice of himself as their king he neither expressed nor sought an opinion; he assumed the choice was a happy one. His heart bled, he said, that not all Poles as yet had been united under the same scepter, and he promised that it would be his endeavor to alleviate to the utmost of his power the hardships of separation and obtain for them everywhere the full enjoyment of their nationality.

A man of many parts, Alexander enjoyed partial fulfillment of his youthful idealism in conferring on this alien people the benefit of those liberal ideas which his tutor, the Swiss revolutionary, Laharpe, had infused into him during his childhood. Simultaneously, and without experiencing the least discomfort, Alexander stamped upon his native land with the heavy tread of reaction. It seemed to him reasonable that while the Poles enjoyed liberal ideas in return for enduring an alien for their king, his own people, enjoying a native tsar for an autocrat, should content themselves with a reactionary regime. It seemed to him natural that in uniting under his own scepter two incompatible peoples, he had made everyone happy.

After the Battle of Waterloo Napoleon enjoyed—if "enjoyed" is the word—another lease of six years of life on St. Helena; Alexander, ten years at large. But life had made heavy inroads into his health and looks.

At thirty-eight Alexander looked prematurely old. He had grown very bald. His carriage had lost its spring; he stooped. His increasing deafness and short-sightedness made him feel awkward and suspicious in public. He tried to guess what people said to him, and suspected that it made him look foolish, that people inwardly made merry at his expense. His expression as a result was a furtive change-over from shyness to sternness—from a doubtful sternness to an apologetic shyness.

At thirty-eight Alexander could claim to have lived a full life. That it was the English who had put paid to Napoleon when he thought *he* had liquidated him and written *finis* to that chapter with his triumphant entry into Paris, had tarnished his glory. Alexander was disgusted with glory and sought compensation in mysticism. Baroness Krüdener, a professional mystic with an overheated imagination and little self-criticism, a type familiar today, had no difficulty in inducing the disappointed Tsar to regard himself as the tool of Providence. Obeying his own vanity, heeding the voice of his own ambitions, Alexander acknowledged to her that he felt the hand of Providence.

In all subsequent transactions of State his subjects and Allies discovered, to their cost, the guidance of Alexander's Maker. When Alexander explained to Castlereagh in the presence of Wellington the principles of the new Holy Alliance concluded in the name of the Most Sacred and Holy Trinity, Castlereagh afterwards confessed that he thought Alexander was mad.

The Tsar staged an enormous military review of his troops in France in conjunction with Baroness Krüdener, who attended to the mystic nature of the ceremony and beside whom he knelt in the midst of his soldiers.

Back in Russia, he threw himself with a vehemence into religiosity, this time of the orthodox brand. Father Froty, a precursor of Rasputin, for a time constituted himself the Tsar's spiritual director. He pronounced himself against the Krüdener woman, and indeed Alexander himself had grown bored with her and no longer replied to her long letters. She had called Alexander "the white angel" in distinction to Napoleon, "the black angel." But the black angel was now pouring a stream of self-pity into a book of memoirs and, as a relaxation, shooting birds on St. Helena. And the white angel, when he was not kneeling in prayer, was chasing across and athwart his empire in a post-chaise in an attempt to work off his growing restlessness. He prayed all the time. Alexander, through incessant kneeling on the stone floors of churches and monasteries, had contracted housemaid's knee.

In a suburb of Moscow lived an old maid who had renounced the world and, on the advice of her spiritual father, the same Froty, had handed her enormous wealth in land and jewels back to the monasteries and the crown to which they had belonged before Catherine II had given them to her father for services rendered to herself. She was that Anna who had danced before Princess Dashkov when her father, Aleksei Orlov, celebrated their reconciliation. She could not forget that her father had murdered Peter III and she thought that by renouncing his ill-gotten wealth she was in some way assisting his soul in purgatory. Day and night she prayed for him under the direction of Froty, who exploited her. A great part of her wealth she had, on his instructions, returned to Alexander. The rest went to the monastery where her empty coffin, at the side of her father's sarcophagus, reposed in a vault. A lamp burned forever, as if to ward off evil if congenial spirits. His daughter, the tender Annushka, had declined all illustrious offers of marriage, had renounced all her dreams of happiness, to bribe the Heavenly Judge with her fortune transformed into pearls, diamonds, sapphires, emeralds and rubies which, in the church twilight, glittered mournfully in the miters of bishops and archimandrites, and in the settings of a thousand ikons.

Two ministers, Speranski and Araktcheyev, stood (according to Pushkin) at the opposite poles, as the white and black angels of Alexander's reign. When the liberal mood of Alexander gave way to reaction, Speranski was exiled to Siberia. At a roadhouse there was some trouble about changing horses, and Speranski's warders appealed to their prisoner to intervene on their behalf with the superintendent. "Your Excellency!" they complained, "that scoundrel won't give us any fresh horses. Be so kind, your Excellency, and use your influence."

Araktcheyev soon became the real autocrat of Russia and had no hesitation in countermanding imperial commands. Army orders and honors lists announced promotions in these terms: "Whereas his Imperial Majesty the Emperor has decreed that Colonel Ivanov be promoted to the rank of Major General, I, General Araktcheyev, command that Colonel Ivanov remain in his present rank on account of his inefficiency." The Tsar's submission to Araktcheyev's dictatorship is explained by his growing weariness of the world and because in the last years of his reign Alexander lived in fear of attempts on his life. Araktcheyev, at once a pillar of reaction and legitimacy, inspired the weary Emperor with confidence as the natural protector of the Tsar's person. Araktcheyev in his strangle-hold on Russia was another Potemkin, but with none of Potemkin's genius and geniality. Araktcheyev was the arch-policeman. Though he disregarded his Emperor's orders, Alexander felt he could rely on him for protection. In the village church on his estate Araktcheyev flaunted an inscription on the portrait of the Emperor Paul, which read: "I had no hand in your death." Whatever else Araktcheyev was, he was not, Alexander felt, a regicide.

All over the country Araktcheyev was setting up military settlements, turning the villages into barracks, forcing the soldiers to plow and the peasants to drill and conscripting even their children and wives, flogging everyone unmercifully at the least sign of insubordination.

Araktcheyev certainly had sadistic tendencies. There is a well-known story of how, displeased with a girl of sixteen who had failed to sweep the garden path to his satisfaction, he ordered her to be flogged to death. Her companions were told to be present at the execution and forced to sing a funeral dirge while the girl was being flogged.

In 1825, the Prince of Orange, married to Alexander's youngest sister, that Grand Duchess Anna who was to have married Napoleon, arrived in St. Petersburg and Alexander informed him that he wished to abdicate the throne. He spoke of his wish to live in the Crimea as a private individual. Alexander was still under fifty. Like the Duke of Windsor, he had served his country for twenty-five years. Soldiers, he said, were allowed to retire after that term of service. He had had enough.

He was tired. Napoleon had died in 1821. The eighteen-twenties corresponded to our own postwar period a hundred years later. There was the same disillusionment and disenchantment. Alexander's life and character represented the whole scale and gamut of experience which linked Catherine's age of innocence with his own, starting with a lofty idealism and closing in worldly cynicism coupled with a facile mystic religiosity.

"When I was seventeen," Goethe said, "Germany was also seventeen, and it was easy then to make an impression. I would not like to be a young man starting on his literary debut today." That was said by him in the eighteen-twenties, at the close of Alexander's reign. The high-water mark of Germany's literary achievement coincided with the blossoming of Russian literature. When Pushkin was eighteen, Russia, it may be repeated, was also eighteen in development. He had virgin ground to explore. His predecessors had merely scratched the surface of poetry. As Russian literature was bursting into flower, Alexander was shutting up shop.

Like Byron, he was unhappy; and like Byron, who was a beautiful lordling, Alexander, who was a handsome tsar, was sincerely pitied; as though the rest of mortals had never been burdened with anything but joy. "He is unhappy," they whispered in the palace, and hung their heads, and sighed.

"Here comes the hearse with the remains of Lord Byron," bystanders had whispered as Byron's funeral procession came up the Tottenham Court Road. "He was a great poet. But," they added, heaving a sigh, "he was unhappy."

Byron had said that Napoleon had robbed him of first place in Europe, apparently ignoring the claim of "bald-pate" Alexander, as he called him. Whatever the reason of Byron's much-advertised melancholy, Alexander had good cause to be unhappy, having stepped on to the throne over his father's corpse. His complex character is explained by his remorse. His wars and occasional brutality are explained by fear of murderous plotters who might do to him what they had done to his father if they fell foul of his policy at home or abroad. His occasional bravery, when he galloped in front of his troops, is the reaction from insult levied on him for his prolonged timidity. His humanitarian ideas were part of an innate idealism, emanations of a tender heart. His despotism must be attributed to his disappointments in the world, his country and the material he had to deal with. His brilliance and occasional success in the diplomatic field sprang from the encouragement which came to him at the turn of the tide.

It all seemed more than it really was because the average intelligence among sovereign heads is necessarily below the average. The proportion of brilliant men in the wide world is meager enough. How much less are the chances of a small, closely intermarried race of monarchs throwing up a remarkable man? Alexander had a facility for couching commonplace remarks in impressive phrases, such as: "The law is greater than I," or "Providence is mightier than the will of tsars"—a remark he addressed to his suite as, surrounded by courtiers and generals, he stepped out onto the balcony of the Winter Palace to behold the damage caused by the flood when the Neva broke its banks. The courtiers and generals received the pregnant remark of their sovereign with bowed heads. Here was another Solon. The Emperor, encouraged by their reception of his apothegm, capped it with: "Even the power of the tsars avails but naught against the fury of the elements."

II. THE PILGRIM

ALEXANDER'S end is wrapped in mystery. For many years he had been estranged from his wife, Elizabeth of Baden. Suddenly he was seized with the urgent idea of reconciliation. The Empress was delighted, and she noted down her delight in her diary, an entry only to be followed by another in which she expresses her disappointment. These entries support the view that after Alexander had indicated his wish to be reconciled to his wife, and the Empress had begun to look forward to a conjugal life hitherto denied her, Alexander had taken her into his confidence and led her to understand that the proposed reconciliation was merely a means to an end.

He had schemed a traceless disappearance and she was to aid him in the deception. His choice of place would be difficult to justify on normal grounds. Alexander and his consort traveled to Tagonrog, then an obscure provincial port on the Black Sea. The Empress was in poor health and the long journey by relays of horses knocked her up.

There are several versions, each with its set of hypotheses, of Alexander's disappearance, natural death being one of them. He did, in fact, contract a fever; but the circumstances of his official death are suspicious. The theory that the corpse of a soldier was procured from the local hospital to impersonate the dead emperor acquires plausibility when a number of other coincidences, otherwise difficult to explain, are put together to construe the generally accepted legend that Alexander finished his days as a wandering monk in Siberia.

The story is that a hermit having the bearded features you might have expected Alexander I to have had as an old man was many years later, already in the reign of his nephew Alexander II, arrested and even flogged by an obscure police inspector in a district town in Siberia; that a courtier and later a grand duke recognized the hermit as Alexander I and paid obeisance to him. It is said that the hermit, though living the simple life, bore unmistakable traces of refinement; was scrupulously clean in his person, and sometimes, lapsing into reminiscences, "talked big." Personal details of the Vienna Congress, of interviews with Napoleon, with Kaiser Franz, with Frederick William III percolated strangely into the hermit's otherwise pious reflections, and the legend gained credence and in fact never died.

Another version is that an English peer, by arrangement with Alexander, carried him off in his yacht moored off the beach of Tagonrog, and that Alexander ended his days as a pilgrim in Palestine. Whatever the truth might be, the official version of his death at Tagonrog seems, when the conduct of all the people concerned is weighed and the circumstances are examined, the least likely alternative.

For one thing, the few people who saw the corpse could not recognize the features of the Emperor. Alexander's private physician, Sir James Wylie, plainly perjured himself in the autopsy, which does not tally with facts vouched for by other physicians who were made to alter their statements to render the story more plausible. Alexander's coffin, contrary to religious custom, was sealed to prevent anyone from seeing him. The Empress Dowager at St. Petersburg was warned in time. The rumor that the Emperor was alive and the corpse of a soldier reposed in the imperial coffin, now on its long trail to St. Petersburg, was spreading all over the country. These reports were endangering the position of the new Tsar, Alexander's younger brother, Nicholas I, who had stepped on to the throne over the head of his elder brother Constantine. The Dowager Empress was required to discourage these rumors. On the arrival of the corpse in the capital she ordered the coffin to be opened and declared in public: "Yes, this is my son. Yes, this is the body of my dear son Alexander."

But no one else was allowed to see the corpse. The coffin lid was quickly screwed down again and the body was buried alongside the other Petersburg monarchs in the Fortress of Peter and Paul.

Most significant of all, when, in the reign of Alexander II, and again in the last reign, the coffin was opened by order of the reigning tsar, it was found to be empty.

Another legend is that Alexander I finished his days as a hermit in the wilds of Finland; that once a year, in deep winter, the reigning monarch Nicholas I in the greatest of secrecy would be driven to an abandoned spot; and from there, ordering his attendants to withdraw, the new Tsar would wind his way through deep snow, in between heavily laden pines, towards a lonely hut. A tall, gaunt old hermit with a long white beard and a snow-white surplice would step out. The reigning Tsar would advance a few steps and then throw himself down on his knees before the hermit, who would gently raise him to his feet.

The two brothers would retire into the hut and there converse. A few hours later Nicholas would grope his way to the place where he had left his attendants and be driven back to Petersburg, the Winter Palace and his imperial cares.

III. "NICHOLAS THE STICK"

BRUTAL Peter, bloated Elizabeth, adroit Catherine and charming Alexander are the four romantic sovereigns of the new dynasty. The last four emperors, Nicholas I, Alexander II, Alexander III and Nicholas II are respectable and increasingly correct. Nicholas I had a passion for other men's wives. He expressed his satisfaction with the wives by promoting their husbands. The wives liked it; the husbands liked it; and the Emperor liked it. It seemed pure gain all round.

There were, of course, exceptions, when the husbands resented it. In one instance, a certain colonel coming home discovered his wife in a situation which admitted of no doubt, with an officer whom he did not recognize as the Emperor and whom he assailed with rich abuse before his wife could whisper to him: "It's the Emperor!" He was not promoted.

The Emperor's passion for the wives of his subjects had the most tragic results in the case of Pushkin, Russia's greatest poet, whose wife Nicholas fancied more than his poetry. The Emperor simply did not understand poetry. He had been told that Pushkin was an excellent poet with a revolutionary bent, who had got into trouble in the closing years of his brother's reign; and in the simplicity of his heart Nicholas said that he would win the poet from his subversive tendencies to patriotic uses.

He constituted himself Pushkin's sole censor. He gave him the sort of advice which does not profit a poet. "I shall give you work," he said, "which will enable you to be of use to the Fatherland." He required the poet to prepare a comprehensive report incorporating Pushkin's ideas on national education. Pushkin wrote the report, not without transparent and rather pitiful attempts to ingratiate himself with the monarch, whose reactionary views were well known: adding, however, at the foot of the paper a most humble and loyal hope that the Emperor would see fit to entrust him with more congenial work in the future.

Nicholas then enjoined him to write a history of Peter the Great. As the Tsar provided Pushkin, who was hopelessly in debt, with money with which to publish this otherwise rather dry and uncongenial work, this proposal was more acceptable. Thereafter, feeling himself to be Pushkin's benefactor, and, moreover, appointing him to a junior position at court which cramped the poet's leisure and irritated him, the Tsar began to feel that his kindness to Pushkin called for reciprocity; and seduced the poet's wife.

Pushkin, greatly harassed and bothered in every way, with an ardent nostalgia for peaceful leisure and the opportunity for poetic work, jealous and in love with his wife, was at the end of his wits and his tether. Anonymous letters were reaching him by every post, hinting that his wife was deceiving him in the highest quarters. A dashing guardsman, Baron D'Anthes, the adopted son of the Netherlands minister, was also known to be flirting with Pushkin's wife, and he was being teased about that, too. This young guardsman was said in some way to be screening the Tsar.

Provoked, Pushkin challenged D'Anthes to a duel. The Netherlands minister, however, intervened on his adopted son's behalf, begging Pushkin to postpone the duel for a fortnight; during which period D'Anthes married the sister of Pushkin's wife, and the duel was canceled. D'Anthes, however, did not cease to make love to the poet's wife, and it became more and more apparent to everyone that he was doing so to deflect attention from the Emperor, who wished to silence rumor on his own account. Pushkin, unable to touch the Tsar, gave vent to his feelings in a letter to D'Anthes, and another to the Netherlands minister. D'Anthes thereupon challenged Pushkin to a duel, in which the poet was killed.

He was but thirty-six, having reached the first stage of his seasoned powers. He had done magnificent work. Fine and varied as it is, it is nothing to what he could have done if allowed his full span of life. The duel took place in mid-winter on the snowy outskirts of Petersburg. A stretch of snow-covered fields facing the Finnish Bay, called the Islands. The poet fired first, but missed. D'Anthes took long aim. His bullet hit Pushkin in the stomach. He fell, but, gathering his strength, aimed at D'Anthes, who stood sideways and erect. He missed again and was hurried home, where he died after enduring forty-eight hours of agony.

Lermontov, the second greatest Russian poet, wrote an impassioned poem in which he violently attacked the murderers of Russia's brightest genius and spoke of "viceroys of vice," the hint of which was not lost in high quarters. Lermontov was duly exiled.

Nicholas's dull reign produced three outstanding figures of Russian literature: Pushkin, Gogol and Lermontov.

Nicholas I was a handsomer man than his elder brother, Alexander I. He had an even better carriage and more regular features, but nothing like his elder brother's charm or versatile fluency. Alexander had married him off to the daughter of ——. But let this stay a secret for a few pages. Together they produced an extremely handsome young officer, who succeeded his father as Alexander II. Nicholas I, encouraged by his elder brother's European reputation, acquired a taste for visiting Europe. Every year he paid visits to Germany, appearing on the balconies of all the royal residences in the various German capitals, together with his wife, as an example of conjugal felicity. As the Emperor of Russia on a visit to his poor German relations, he squandered so much money that within a few years he emptied the treasury, and the finance ministers at home begged him to desist.

On his accession Nicholas experienced a few anxious hours. Some uncertainty as to the right of succession gave rise to a revolt of a revolutionary character. The event took place in December, and the participants, who suffered execution and exile, became known as the Decembrists.

One of their leaders, Colonel Muraviev, was brought in chains into the presence of the Tsar, who questioned him and promised him his pardon on condition that Muraviev disclose the names of his accomplices. "I, your Emperor," said Nicholas, "solemnly promise you my pardon . . ."

"You're not my Emperor," Muraviev shouted. "You're no emperor at all. You're not a Romanov. You're the son of the bastard Paul, that's all you are!"

It is said that Nicholas was so angry that he began to kick the colonel, who had been made to kneel before him, in the stomach. Perhaps he was angry because he could not explain that his father Paul, as the child of Elizabeth, and not of Catherine, *was* a Romanov, if still a bastard. The scene was so disgusting that Count Benckendorf and the Chamberlain, who were concealed behind a screen to take down the prisoner's evidence, came forward to separate the kicking Emperor from his victim.

Alexander had never liked Nicholas, and wanted his second brother

Constantine to succeed him. Constantine, preferring marriage to an enchanting Polish woman, lingered in Warsaw as Viceroy of Poland. She was a Princess Tchetvertinski, sister of Alexander's mistress, Marie Narishkin. Constantine did not know what he wanted. He was a man of a sweetly docile character who, at the least provocation, flew into mad rages when he surpassed the most cruel of tyrants, ordering men to be cudgeled to death. He had on several occasions resigned his right of succession to the throne, whether in a temper or in sober mood, no one quite knew. No one seemed to know whether Alexander had accepted these resignations, or whether he hoped that when the time came Constantine would change his mind. One thing admitted of no doubt. Nicholas desired passionately to be Emperor. No sooner had the news of Alexander's supposed death reached St. Petersburg than Nicholas leaped on to the throne.

While Constantine's liberalism tempered by autocratic fits was accepted as belonging to a character essentially congenial to democratic feeling, Nicholas, even-tempered, was known as an arch disciplinarian and reactionary. Hence the outbreak in favor of Constantine, who, it was thought, was being unjustly deprived of his right to the throne and taken advantage of on account of his absence in Warsaw.

The Guards, however, leaped into the breach after an awkward half-hour in front of the Winter Palace, and Nicholas was saved. Russia endured almost one-third of a century of what he called a paternal form of government. That dead weight of militarism and reaction was borne for the next thirty years, till his son, Alexander II, lifted the oppression which had smothered and parched every living impulse in the country. Not for nothing was Nicholas the son of Paul.

He knew he was not loved, and as his realm was kept from falling to pieces merely by a vast network of gendarmerie, rising from the lowest policeman to the gendarme in chief, himself, Nicholas could do nothing but proclaim aloud that the growth of the autocrat's power was an end in itself. Peter the Great had begun an anti-national revolution whose aim had been to westernize Russia; and while that revolution continued, the government, however crudely and brutally, played the part of an enlightened ruler. Enlightenment was the excuse for abandoning the old traditions to force westernization down the throats of reluctant subjects. But when, as a consequence of Alexander's excursions in Europe, revolutionary ideas had begun to percolate into Holy Russia, Nicholas abruptly turned the clock back to orthodoxy and nationalism, without yet surrendering a jot of the Caesarean power whose character had been essentially progressive and the whole gist of which had lain in the secularization of the throne and the diffusion of European culture.

Peter the Great had been a progressive despot, but not really a monarch. Nicholas I, a dull-witted dictator, wanted to be at once a Napoleon and a *Roi-Soleil*. Peter had left vacant the post of the Most Holy Patriarch, prohibited the display of sacred relics, and outraged every propriety and convention. Nicholas I contrived to make the best of both conventions. He was Pope and Caesar in one. He exploited Peter's revolutionary license which allowed him to trample on Russia for the sake of Russia, who, Peter said, as he gave her a kick in the stomach, mattered more than Peter. But Nicholas also exploited the ancient superstition which venerated the person of the Orthodox Tsar as the menacing avenger of the common people, their traditional protector against oppression and injustice from whatever quarter. As his instinct was to conserve existing exploitation of the masses, he "protected" the exploited serfs from the liberal elements who would fain enlighten them and ease their lot.

He seized the brilliant revolutionary Bakunin, who had escaped to Dresden and was handed over by Saxony to Austria and by Austria to Nicholas, who clapped him in the icy Schlüsselburg fortress, where once the baby Tsar Ivan was kept caged for twenty years like a wild beast. From his prison cell Bakunin wrote the Tsar a long dissertation. The Tsar was rather fond of reports of all kinds which he annotated with marginal notes. Bakunin pointed out that tsardom automatically ceased to be strong as soon as it became conservative; that, as Russia had long since outgrown the cramped conditions of the past (imposed on her by a series of tyrants who had retarded her natural growth by two hundred years) and felt the need to stretch her limbs, it was only by going forward, in advance of the people, that tsardom could maintain itself. Until now, in fact, the government had always been in advance of the people. If the Tsar would avoid breeding revolutionaries, he need only outdistance them to leave them hobbling far behind him. That was the gist of his argument.

Nicholas, who, to remain an autocrat, had turned the clock back, was struck by the paradox that he could be every bit as much the autocrat by turning it forward. He had, to keep the ship of State on an even keel, to use force and more force. And he was beginning to learn that force was weak-kneed. "True... Perfectly true..." he annotated Bakunin's report. It appeared to him there might be something in it. And yet—he wondered! . . .

Never was there a man who more enjoyed being emperor, tsar, head of his Church, the fount of his country's laws, and the all-highest lord of his fighting and civil services. He prided himself on his good looks, his stature, his bearing, his turn-out. He said that *he,* and not George IV of England, was the first gentleman of Europe. Despite his easily satisfied predilections for the wives of other men, he prided himself on being a model husband. He preened himself as a model Christian, a model patriot. He encouraged, as he thought, even native literature, so long as its influence was "healthy"—that is, reactionary—and not "subversive." He had a heavy touch. He loved Russia, he said, as though referring to an idiosyncrasy of his incomprehensible to others. He must have loved the scenery and the buildings, because he treated the people as though they were his deadly enemies. He made a barrack of Russia. He pulled a curtain over the window which Peter had previously hacked through to Europe. Western influences were baleful, said the Tsar, baleful to the essentially Russian ideal of autocracy. He forgot that autocracy was not a Russian but a Prussian ideal.

The country began to feel the dead weight of his hand. Princess Lieven, forcibly recalled to Petersburg by her new sovereign, after queening it for many years as ambassadress in London, chilled alike by the rigors of climate, emperor and husband, gave vent to her feelings. *"Quel pays!"* she exclaims. *"Quel maître! Quel père!"*

Like his father Paul, Nicholas was authoritarian and disciplinarian —and both unsparingly. Already in his brother Alexander's reign he had itched to take a more active part in meting out punishment to delinquents than was compatible with the dignity of his position of Grand Duke and President of the Court Martial. When the Seménovski Guards revolted and Alexander, trembling in his shoes, passed hysteric sentences from Vienna which meant that the soldiers were virtually to be flogged to death, the generals had on their own authority modified the severity of the sentences, since they discovered that the revolt was a trivial one, directed against one pernickety German commander who had proved himself unpopular with everyone. Alexander had flown into a fury when he heard that his sentences had been modified. He insisted that they should be carried out; and Nicholas, that there should be no mistake about the number of blows dealt out individually, called for chalk and wrote clearly with his own grand-ducal hand on the trouser seat of each recruit the allotted figure. When Nicholas came to the throne he was called Nikolai Palkin—"Nicholas the Stick."

Though he could not come to terms with any human idea, the new Tsar was not entirely without charm or even a certain humor. A Colonel Boldirev, whose promotion was long overdue because the Emperor disapproved of his gambling propensities, was one Sunday morning stopped by Nicholas on his way to church. "Boldirev," said the Emperor, "I congratulate you." Since this was the formula in which the sovereign announced promotions, Boldirev concluded that he had been promoted to the rank of major general; and all courtiers in the Tsar's train hurried forward to congratulate the new favorite. On his way back from church the Tsar, passing Boldirev again, stopped and said: "I congratulate you. I hear you won some money last night."

IV. *"QUEL POUCHKINE...?"*

GREAT events do not harbor the living essence. It is *being*, not *doing*, which absorbs and holds the light. A trivial moment may secrete the indestructible savor. One July morning, six months after his accession, Nicholas the First stood at the edge of the pond in Tsarskoye Selo and threw his handkerchief into the water for his dog to fetch. A servant came running towards him and whispered something in his ear. The Tsar left the dog and the handkerchief and ran back to the palace. The dog, having swum back and not found his master, dropped the handkerchief and ran after him. A maid of honor, who was in love with the handsome Tsar, picked up the handkerchief as a memento.

In this entry, jotted down in Pushkin's diary, there is more of Nicholas than in a psychological examination of his mentality.

Another entry made in Easter week of 1834 records celebrations in honor of the coming of age of the Grand Duke and Tsarevitch Alexander Nikolaievitch; who is none other than the future Alexander II, who has a lease of another forty-seven years of life before he is to be killed by an assassin's bomb. Nicholas has now sat on the throne eight years, and is to sit on it for another twenty-three. Pushkin writes: "The celebrations were at once of a State and a family character. All were in ecstasy from the extraordinary spectacle. Many wept, and those who did not weep wiped their dry eyes, forcing themselves to squeeze out a few tears."

Pushkin notes that they are keeping back from the heir to the throne the news of his tutor's death so as not to mar this great day for him. "He will be told after the ball on the 28th. Araktcheyev is also dead, but the death of this despot has produced no impression."

Araktcheyev died on his estate where he indulged in sadistic excesses, and his death must have been a relief to his serfs.

Pushkin at that time did not yet suspect that Nicholas was, among other men's wives, "carrying on" with his own. Another entry reads: "28th February. The past month has been rather crowded. Many balls, banquets, etc. Carnival week. I attended the Levée. The Emperor permitted me to publish my *Pugatchòv*. My manuscript was returned to me with his comments (very pertinent ones). On Sunday, at the ball in the music room, the sovereign talked to me for a long time. He speaks very well, without mixing the two languages or making the usual mistakes, and he employs natural expressions."

Russian education was at that time cultivated rather than home grown. French was instilled into the young by tutors and governesses imported from Paris, and the people at court expressed themselves at that period more fluently in that language than in their own. Russian was still a comparatively uncouth tongue, ill adapted to verbal subtleties; and it was this same Pushkin who was shaping the language into the supple and flexible instrument it was now becoming in his hands; and all without receiving the slightest thanks or recognition from his sovereign, who, hearing that Pushkin was a poet not without talent, saddled him with the nominal duties of a gentleman of the bedchamber and with uncongenial historical work. In the same way, young Goethe, who had been shaping the German language into a decent instrument capable of poetic use, had been doing so while Frederick the Great, despising his native tongue, glibly exercised himself in French. There had been Russian poets before Pushkin, as there had been German ones before Goethe: but they were small beer compared with this new and potent wine.

Pushkin hated his junior court appointment of *Kammerjunker,* which made him, a man of thirty-five, appear in the company of youths of eighteen. In his diary he notes: "Last Tuesday I was commanded to the Anitchkov Palace. I arrived in uniform. They told me that all the guests were in evening dress. I drove away, leaving my wife behind, but having changed my clothes I spent the evening instead at Sergei Saltikov's, who was having a party. The Emperor was annoyed and kept bringing it up. *'Il aurait pu se donner la peine d'aller mettre un frac et de revenir. Faites-lui des reproches.'*

"On Thursday a ball at Prince Troubetskoy's. The Emperor arrived unexpectedly and stayed half an hour. He said to my wife: *'Est-ce à propos de bottes ou de boutons que votre mari n'est pas venu dernière-ment?'* "

Pushkin relates how the Tsar said to him about his *Pugatchòv:* "What a pity I didn't know you were writing about him. I would have introduced you to his sister, who died three weeks ago in the fortress." That meant she had been there since 1774, and it was now 1834. Another entry reads: "The Tsar lent me 20,000 roubles (£2,000) for the publication of my *Pugatchòv.* Thanks!"

"8th April," is another entry: "Am now driving to the Palace to be presented to the Tsaritsa." Here is a typical example, true to pattern, of the woman of the world turning on her charm, and turning it off just as the innocent, encouraged by her delightful effusions, is venturing to expand responsively: if he did she would freeze him stiff.

"Two o'clock. Presented. We waited for the Tsaritsa about three hours. There were twenty of us; I was the last on the list. The Tsaritsa came up to me, laughing: *'Non, c'est unique! Je mecreusais la tête pour savoir quel Pouchkine me sera présenté. Il se trouve que c'est vous! ... Comment va votre femme? Sa tante est bien impatiente de la voir en bonne santé, la fille de son coeur, sa fille d'adoption ...'* and she turned away. I love the Empress terribly, despite the fact that she is already thirty-five or even thirty-six."

How drastically posterity transforms current values! We have no need to split our heads to know *"quel Pouchkine"* she means. But we may well wonder who is the empress; and we shall be surprised, perhaps delighted, to learn that she is none other than the eldest daughter of our old friend King Frederick William III of Prussia and his consort, the idealistic Queen Louisa, notorious for her cosmetics and beauty. She, who had been so in love with Alexander, must have said to herself and to Frederick William: "St. Petersburg is not to be sneezed at." And here she is, her own daughter, queening it on the banks of the Neva!

The aunt of Pushkin's wife, who had adopted her, regaled the gifted husband of *"la fille de son coeur, sa fille d'adoption"* from the rich store of her memories. A daughter of Count Razumovski, she had as a little girl been taken by her parents to Peterhof, and it turned out to be the very day that Peter III was pushed off his throne. The Emperor, striding up and down, his hat at a rakish angle, she said, looked first terribly angry, next very pitiable. With the other ladies she boarded with him the galley for Kronstadt and they returned to Oranienbaum in ignominy. She had been a friend of Potemkin's. She had known Catherine. She said that during the whole of Catherine's reign she had only twice seen her angry. Both times it was with Princess Dashkov.

Another of Pushkin's entries flares up suddenly like an arc lamp in the wind with a flash of augmented interest: one man of genius is here casually referring to another: "Last night Gogol read me his tale, *How Ivan Ivanovitch Quarreled With Ivan Nikiforovitch*. Very original and extremely funny. Gogol, on my advice, has begun a history of Russian criticism."

During the time of Nicholas, when the spirit had gone out of everything and the irregularities of the administration had become a complacently accepted scandal, Gogol, to clear the air and vent his genius, wrote his famous satiric comedy, *The Inspector-General*. The theme was given him by Pushkin, who, on his journeys in the provinces, had been mistaken for an inspector-general sent from Petersburg to sniff out irregularities in provincial administration and was accordingly received with nervous deference. What a chance, Pushkin thought, for an unscrupulous ne'er-do-well to impose on all manner of people. Gogol, with his satirical genius, made brilliant use of Pushkin's plot. *The Inspector-General* was the talk of the country. It made Gogol. It made literary history. It caused a social cataclysm. The comedy was so poignantly witty that, though it hit unsparingly the whole of Russia's hopelessly corrupt administration, no one could be really angry because it was at once hilariously typical and sadly true. Nicholas went to see it. He looked grave, and when the courtiers thought this forebode disgrace for the author, they suddenly saw the Emperor roaring with laughter. He said at the end of it, looking serious: "We have all got it in the neck; *all* of us; but I more than anyone!"

Nicholas could be sincere, and he always went straight to the point. When it had been decided to build the first railway in Russia, the Tsar took a ruler and drew a determined straight line between Moscow and Petersburg. That's how the railway would run, and he cared not whose country estate or natural precipice it was to cross through, under, or over.

V. WAR

OF course, there were wars. But I refuse to be interested in more wars. I refuse to be interested in the Crimean War. I have been patient over the Napoleonic Wars. I have written of earlier wars in the time of Peter, of Elizabeth, of Catherine, even of the wars of the old boys of the previous dynasty. It is time to call a halt. There is nothing new in this line. A redistribution of partners is all that may be said ever to occur; and at it again! A change of technique perhaps. But ... *plus ça change, plust c'est la même chose.* Enough! I feel like screaming: *"Enfin, c'est* fini. *Vous comprenez? C'est* fini!"

But, insensitive of the monotony to which they were exposing the future historian, they went on with them. It was like this. To keep up his Caesarean power at home the Tsar must be armed to the teeth; and once he possessed a huge army it seemed uneconomic not to give them something to poke at with their bayonets. Failing other fields of diversion, there was always Turkey.

Besides, they were, despite Napoleon's carnage, still hopelessly unrealistic about what a war really was like. Even Pushkin, admittedly not a fool, hailed Nicholas in a poem whose pure motive is suspect. Enumerating the new monarch's virtues, he proclaims: "He enlivened us with a war."

But now Nicholas, for once going too far, brought both England, who likes to have a finger in every pie, and France on his track. One imagines sovereigns soaring above feelings of snobbishness to which mere commoners are subject. But if one needs any assurance that sovereigns are just men, meet a dethroned sovereign. Why Nicholas did it we do not know. Perhaps he remembered his brother Alexander's snub to Napoleon in that letter on the eve of Austerlitz, addressing the Emperor of the French as "The Head of the French Government," and thought that what was good enough for Napoleon I was good enough for his nephew Napoleon III. Perhaps he remembered Louis XVIII's snub to Alexander. They thought, these Frenchmen, a Romanov a nobody! They did! Less than nobody. Did they? To a letter received from Napoleon III, addressing the Tsar as *"Mon Frère!"* Nicholas answered with *Mon Ami!"*

It thoroughly upset the Frenchman. It stung him, it prevented him from enjoying his imperial dignity. When the time came he relieved his injured feelings by throwing his army into the scale against Nicholas.

And now, in the aftermath of this war which was exhausting his resources, the Tsar's spirit was leaving the body that had been mortally affected by some poison, either through eating something that had not agreed with him, or, as some say, something deliberately inserted into his food by some agent of the enemy within the gate. And he had made enemies enough. He had crushed Poland, stamped out its national spirit; he had suppressed every vestige of free thought in Russia. Nicholas the Stick had but the stick with which to share his final isolation.

Whenever one nation sends out men with cold and molten steel to tear the flesh of men of other nations, these men go out picturing a young girl at home, a girl like no other, and who is presumably worth all this fighting and bloodshed. While the British and French were decimating on behalf of Turkey Russian fathers and brothers on the far Crimean shore, the Russians showed up pretty rough in another sector, and some Russian lieutenant, having decapitated a French brother or an English husband and father, was thinking of a girl in Moscow, with light chestnut hair and those frank and melancholy eyes which only the openness, the boundless sincerity, of Russian nature could produce, and for whom he was so nobly risking his life. But these men in the busbies, and those others in the Light Brigade, were thinking that love and maidenhead were English prerogatives not obtainable at Balaclava; and some young Frenchman dreamed wistfully of that unforgettable hour when "... *nous étions seuls, Ninon et moi....*"

When Nicholas was dying, the disasters of the Crimean War were relieved by a brief success for Russian arms; and the Emperor, who took the defeats to heart as personal humiliations, a stain on his honor, a trial visited on him by Providence in order to test the valor of his faith, heaved a sigh of deliverance before he breathed his last. The dying Tsar remembered the "bad quarter of an hour" he had spent on his accession, thirty-one years before, when the Winter Palace was being defended against the Decembrists. From his deathbed he sent his thanks to the Guards. As the end came, he was lifted on his pillows to hear the news of the spurious victory. But he was not deceived in imagining that this meant the end either of the war or of Russia's troubles. To his mistress, Madame Nelidov (who bore the identical name of his father Paul's mistress) he sighed: "Oh, what a heavy inheritance I am leaving my poor son!"

His dying lamentation echoes another: "O God! Horatio, what a wounded name, things standing thus unknown, shall live behind me!"

CHAPTER XXVII

UNLIKE FATHER, UNLIKE SON

I. "THE ROOSHIANS SHALL NOT 'AVE CONSTANTINOPLE"

ALEXANDER II inherited the Crimean War as a running concern, but a concern in such bad running order that he promptly wound it up. Later he had a war of his own.

Every Russian sovereign automatically went to war, usually more than once, during his reign. He either had a war bequeathed to him by his predecessor, or he declared war or had war declared on him, which amounted to the same thing. War on accession, or soon after accession, seemed the routine. War was declared by the sovereign to be necessary for Russia's honor—that is what the sovereign seemed to be for: to stand no affront. Not that the Tsar was especially blood-thirsty. Quite the contrary. It usually happened like this: A minister thought Russia's policy of aggrandizement could not brook this or that. The Army—that is to say, the Officers' Mess—spoke of the honor of the Russian flag involved in some frontier or other incident; and the sovereign as the nominal head of the Army could not, out of kindness and consideration for the patriotic susceptibilities of Russian officers, of whom he was one, declare himself truant to their ideals of military honor. What invariably was lost sight of was that mismanagement and corruption in the Russian Army was almost a tradition.

It was not otherwise when women, who like to think that men are brave, much in the same way as men like to think that women are beautiful and good, reigned in Russia. As colonels of this or that regiment, women took a romantic pride in testing the willingness of men to face mutilation and death for them.

What has been said in previous chapters of the success of Russian arms against the Turks in the cause of Christian minorities in the Balkans does not cease, nor indeed abate, with the end of Nicholas's reign.

When Alexander II declared war on Turkey in 1877 he took the precaution, which he judged to be sufficient, of dispatching to London the delightful General Ignatiev, assisted by a lovely wife all covered with jewels, whose instructions were to charm London society into a state of neutrality, while Russia bagged Constantinople. The Ignatievs took London by storm, and society keenly debated as to who had the best jewels: Lady Londonderry or Madame Ignatiev. Lord Beaconsfield readily promised neutrality—on conditions: No Constantinople for Russia.

We have seen in previous chapters how hard the poor dears have been trying to get Constantinople. They have been at it for at least two centuries. Even the old Rurik boys, as early as the ninth century, would intermittently have a go at it: knock hard at the gates. Tsargrad, they called it, meaning the city of the Byzantine tsars. Olga, on a visit of good will, had been right within the walls of the sacred city and left a notice board nailed on the gate to say the place was reserved—to be called for later. We well remember that Ivan III, a Rurik, had married the sister and heir of the last Emperors of Byantium and had adopted the Byzantine double eagle as the crest of his empire. The early Romanovs, Sophia with her lover Golitsin, Peter, Catherine, Alexander I, Nicholas, all had had a go at it one time or another.

Alas, in vain! First one, then another, had always stood in the way. Napoleon and Downing Street alternately blocked the passage for Alexander I; Queen Victoria and Napoleon III, conjointly, for Nicholas I; now Queen Victoria, again, for Alexander II. From her island the size of a pea, holding the ends of the threads binding one-fifth of the habitable globe, she sent baleful glances at the Russian bear who had but to roll himself over once to cover three continents.

No Constantinople for Russia, was Disraeli's condition. No Dardanelles. And hands off Suez.

As Constantinople was at once the apex of Russia's ambitions and the compensation for pouring out Russian blood in defense of her brother Slavs in the Balkans, the Russian Government agreed to the English conditions in the hope that when the time came to take Constantinople, public opinion in England would oppose a war. It would take some doing to dislodge the Russians from Constantinople, war or no war; whereas failure to placate the English into a state of accommodating neutrality *now* would prevent the Russians from ever getting near Constantinople.

So thought the Russian Chancellor, Gortchakov. His formula, designed to harmonize with the British conditions, was buried in a specious mental reservation, which read: Russia recognizes that the question of Constantinople can only be solved by agreement..." (meaning with Russia's point of view).

The British Foreign Secretary, the young Lord Derby, did not want a war with Russia. He possessed that rare gift, an immeasurable asset in foreign politics—unimaginativeness. He saw no point in unleashing immediate and certain evil in order to avoid an uncertain future evil. He did not admit that even if the Russians got Constantinople the British Empire was doomed to extinction. But Queen Victoria, who hated the Russians, was vitriolic. A small old lady, she was intent on going to the wars and would have girded the sword if her Cabinet had allowed her. *"Really,"* she wrote to her Prime Minister, Disraeli, "the Queen has never *seen* such a Foreign Secretary!!!" To her it was a clear question of Russian *or* British supremacy in the world.

The Queen's mood was reflected in her relatives. Lord Beaconsfield, who tried to keep an even keel, was questioned by Princess Mary of Cambridge, his immediate neighbor at a public dinner. "I cannot think what you are waiting for!" she said. "At the moment, Madam, for the potatoes," he answered.

The Queen wrote incessantly to Lord Beaconsfield to complain that *nothing* was being *done.* "And the *language,* the *insulting* language the Russians use against us!!! It makes the Queen's blood *boil,"* she wrote.

The Russians, whose early hopes of fixing the cross of the Russian Christ over the cathedral dome of St. Sophia were being checked by the unexpected counter-enthusiasm of the devotees of Islam, did not warm at the English failure to wish them Godspeed in this their belated holy crusade against the modern Saracen. Their language accordingly was not unreminiscent of that of Herr Goebbels' department at a low ebb of National Socialist fortunes.

When Russia threw away 80,000 lives without taking Plevna, the British voice rose more confidently. "We don't want to fight," the music halls sang, and the London errand boy, conscious that he, too, was of a conquering race, echoed on his rounds: "But, by Jingo, if we do. We got the ships, we got the men, we got the munn-aye too!" The club-chair strategists in St. James's considered the Russians as good as finished, when Skobolev took Plevna and reached the heights dominating Constantinople.

The British public, discovering that they had committed themselves in song to the political tenet that "the Rooshians shall not 'ave Con-stan-to-no...ple," were alarmed. Something might really have to be done now;

and some people, more impatiently active than others, threw stones at Gladstone's windows. The Grand Old Man's astonishment at this domestic development of his essentially Christian conception of the unspeakable Turk must have been great. The Queen pointed out that Albert had always said the *Russians* were our natural enemies; and where was Lord Beaconsfield now? And did he, or didn't he—she wanted to have this straight—say that he would declare war if they took Constantinople? What was he waiting for *now?* He was in fact no better than the rest of them. All men were cowards! She, but a poor and lonely woman, alas, with no Albert to help her, must attend to everything herself and wage war almost single-handed.

To which he replied: "Lord Beaconsfield hopes that Your Majesty remembers her gracious promise not to write at night or, at any rate, not so much. He lives but for her, works but for her. Without her, all is lost."

A kind of Munich took place at Berlin with Disraeli playing the role of a Hitler, threatening to pull the trigger unless his demands were acceded to, issuing his ultimatum, ordering his train as an indication that he was breaking up the conference and returning to London. Bismarck, with his habit of saying the most brutal "blood-and-iron" things in a small cooing voice, presided, playing, as he said himself, the honest broker. As a check on Russian domination, Lord Beaconsfield, in a heart-to-heart talk with Prince Bismarck, drew the Chancellor's attention to the Balkans as a possible German colony in Europe—an idea of the then British Prime Minister which we are today mentally invoking the intervention of Russia to prevent the present German Chancellor from putting into force.

There would seem to be no need of statesmen but for their counterparts elsewhere. Gortchakov, the Russian Chancellor and plenipotentiary, wrangling fussily over the delineation of the new frontier, could not find Batoum on the map. Beaconsfield, according to Lord Salisbury, had never seen a map of Asia Minor and was completely at sea. Together they wrangled for "principles" and "interests" for which one of them had sacrificed untold lives, and the other was prepared to do the same—for "honor."

Russia had at long last succeeded in liberating the oppressed Slavonic minorities from the Turkish yoke and as good as chased the Sick Man of Europe back into Asia, his natural home. But Russia was the bogey. Russia was the aggressor State. And it would have been odd if England, on Russia's own confession in the Testament of Peter the Great, considered her as anything else.

History bristles with tragic ironies. In the earliest Russian attempts to help herself to chunks of Turkey by making it a "Sudeten" question, England had readily sided with Russia against Turkey. But now that, as a result of Russia's earlier intervention on behalf of the Christian minorities in the Balkans, the Turks really did indulge in the most frightful atrocities, and Russia, with greater sincerity than before, had taken up the victims' cause and emerged from a long and costly war completely victorious, England said *No*.

Lord Beaconsfield, by threat of immediate war on Russia, compelled the nicest of Russian Tsars, Alexander II, who had lost 100,000 men and 100,000,000 roubles and had no fleet to speak of, to return to the Turks one-half of Bulgaria and practically the whole of Armenia with their persecuted Christian populations, who were handed back against their wishes and entreaties to Turkish vengeance. Of a Russian Constantinople and Dardanelles there was no mention. The Russians dared not even suggest it.

Among the most presumptuously foolish and, in the result, mischievous prognostications of which human beings are capable is "the long view" in foreign politics. In pursuance of such a reading of the future, Disraeli had been the cause of Russia's foregoing the fruits of her victory and restoring the Dardanelles to the Turks; with the tragic result that in the Great War we fought vainly in Gallipoli for an opening into the Black Sea, which, but for the mistaken belief that Russia was Britain's natural enemy, would have been at our disposal from the very beginning. In consideration of his services to the Turks, Beaconsfield pocketed Cyprus, which has proved of no use to us whatever, and returned from the conference at Berlin with the boast delivered to a wildly cheering crowd from the balcony of No. 10: "We have brought back to you, I think, peace with honor."

It was a peace, never in danger except from himself, for the honor of which we paid with 500,000 casualties in Gallipoli. The moral to be drawn might be embodied in a maxim for statesmen. Avoid doing anything now to avoid a hypothetical danger in the future. Consign present action on behalf of the future to the perpetual future. Let the hypothetical future bury its own hypothetical dead. History is the sum total of futile calamities strewn over a perpetual present anxious to accommodate a future as fussily foolish as itself.

The British Commonwealth is largely the natural fruit of an admirably unpremeditated absence of foresight in a world of inconceivable combinations of forces and circumstances, in respect of which speculation is vain and premeditated action a sin against the natural crystallization of human conditions. Disraeli's Jewish cunning proved what in fact it was: agreeable to contemporary vanity; disastrous to that very posterity he wished to safeguard.

II. ASSASSINATION OF ALEXANDER II

WAR in those days was still a thing of glamour, though books were already appearing, such as Tolstoy's *Sevastopol,* which strove to give a realistic view. After the Franco-Prussian War a German woman positively assumed that, as a result of her novel which depicted fearlessly the horror and uselessness of war, no ruler in future would attempt to settle his differences with other States except by arbitration.

Alexander II was now very weary. When the German Emperor William I, who was considerably older, and the Tsar met, the Kaiser looked conspicuously the younger of the two. Alexander was tired—very tired. He had been saddled with a war bequeathed to him by his father, and then with a war of his own. He was saddled with cares and saw no hope of relief. Repeated attempts on his life, which he had braved long enough, were beginning to tell on him. His mood, a peculiarly Petersburg mood, was not unlike that of the last bars of Tchaikovsky's Sixth (Pathetic) Symphony. Everything was black, hopeless; there was animation only in despair.

When his father, Nicholas I, had said to him on his deathbed: "I'm afraid, my son, I'm leaving you a heavy burden," Alexander II might have replied: "I'm afraid you are." Before his father's body had grown cold, Alexander, with a stroke of the pen, reversed his parent's policy. Liberalism was the order of the day. The country beheld an interesting transformation. Nicholas I, an inveterate conservative not on the best of terms with his son and heir, Alexander II, had given place to the liberal-minded Alexander II, not on the best of terms with his conservative son and heir, Alexander III.

He had started on his reign with a buoyant, almost despotic, tolerance; and the frozen arteries of Russian life began to flow once more. His great *coup* was to liberate the serfs. A Russian revolutionary writer, an early believer in communism as the rational structure for Russia,

Alexander Herzen, then a political exile in London, hailed the news with undisguised warmth. To celebrate the event Herzen decked out his house in Putney with flags and bunting, hung Chinese lanterns in the garden and gave a great dinner at home to which he invited not only all Russian political exiles but also Polish revolutionary nationalists. Just as, at the apex of celebrations, Herzen began his great speech, announcing amid tears of joy that they had lived to see the day, that their long struggle in exile was over, ideals for which they had fought—ideals of liberty, fraternity and equality—had won the day and there was to be freedom for all—freedom of conscience, of the Press, of nationality—an end to the anachronistic ignominy of subject races, news reached the banquet of Russian excesses in suppressing a Nationalist insurrection in Warsaw. Nothing had changed. Nicholas the Stick might still be sitting astride his throne. The Polish National rising, lit by the purest flame of racial patriotism, was brutally crushed; and—"Order again reigned in Warsaw." Herzen now beseeched his Polish guests, who demurred audibly and refused to go on with the celebrations, not to lose all faith in the new Russia, but to take the rough with the smooth.

Indeed, Alexander II had reversed the policy of his uncle, Alexander I, whose idea had been a liberal government for the Poles, but a reactionary regime in Russia. Alexander II decided to give the idea of the Tsar outdistancing the revolutionaries at home a trial, but to keep the Poles under a paternal form of government in the hope that, by an intensive system of Russification, the Poles as new generations grew up would eventually cease to be Poles and become good Russians.

But the Poles, under continual provocation from the Russians, became more and more Polish and taught their children never to forget that they were Poles; whereas the Tsar's full-speed-ahead policy for Russia alarmed Russian landowners who unconsciously pooled their general dissatisfaction with the times with the Nihilists, who were dissatisfied because they thought the Tsar was not moving with the times. One no longer knew whose were the bombs that went off: Nihilist or reactionary: who was the hiding assassin: a reactionary *provocateur* posing as a Nihilist, or a Nihilist neatly disguised as a rebellious absolutist.

As the years went by Alexander II's initial enthusiasm for government by the people began to cool off. He discovered progressively that it was inconsistent with his personal safety to introduce any appreciable measure of freedom; and equally, *not* to introduce any appreciable measure of freedom. He understood that the revolt begun in the previous reigns against the principle of autocracy had grown too deep to be satisfied with half-measures of liberty; but that the autocratic power could not satisfy the demands in full measure without abdicating its autocracy. He began to hang fire.

As his reign progressed, attempts on the Emperor's life became more frequent. Alexander II was a man of great personal courage. Though his life was in continual danger, more so than the life of any previous or future sovereign, he went about freely, with hardly an escort. He was the best, the mildest and the kindest of all the tsars; and the most threatened. The Russians had never plotted to kill their most savage and tyrannical monarchs. No attempt had been made to liquidate the existence of either Peter or Ivan the Terrible. But the attempts on the life of Alexander II never ceased, till they "got" him. He was shot at while walking along on his customary stroll along the red granite bank of the Neva. A student shot at him near the Summer Garden. The bullet grazed him. Bombs were discovered in the room just beneath the Emperor's dining room, bombs timed to go off during dinner. Bombs were found in a room above his bedroom. The Emperor took no heed of the warnings and lived, drove, rode and walked about his capital as though protected by a charm.

He was a chain-smoker and a man of nervous temperament who was easily elated and easily depressed. His German consort had been a very frail woman who had, however, borne him giant sons. Alexander II was an extremely handsome man. He was a man who liked the girls, but had a single major passion, which was returned. While she was still a girl in the famous convent school, the Smolni Institut, Princess Catherine Dolgoruki fell in love with the Emperor. On a spring night, in the first months of their courtship, Alexander would drive secretly to the ground of the convent school. He would send her word and conceal himself behind a tree. What a distance he had traveled from Peter the Great, who did not care who saw what he did to his niece, the Duchess of Mecklenburg. Alexander greatly admired Princess Dolgoruki's hair, which was abundant and reached down to her heels. She became his wife, first in the eyes of God, then, when his consort died, morganatically. She received the name of Princess Yurevskaya.

On March 13, 1881, Alexander II, escorted by six Cossacks, was returning in an open carriage from a Sunday parade. It was just three o'clock when the sound of an explosion rent the air. As he was passing through a narrow street towards the Ekaterinski Canal, a pedestrian hurled a bomb in front of the carriage, which killed two Cossacks and an errand boy. The Emperor was advised to return at once to the Palace, but he got out of the carriage to see who had been wounded. At that moment a bystander approached the Emperor and inquired sympathetically whether he was hurt. "No, thank God, *I'm* not hurt." The man who had thrown the bomb and was caught and held down by the police, jeered at the Emperor's words and called out to him not to praise the day before the evening. Just then a girl, standing on the opposite pavement, flung a bomb right at the feet of the Emperor which tore off one of his legs and twisted and shattered the other.

Bernard Shaw, commending Frank Harris's absurdly romanticized story of the girl assassin, Sofia Perovskaya, reinforces Harris's view that the people who were hurling bombs at the Emperor were more noble than their victim. A contention which might have had more force behind it if the victim had been Peter the Great or Ivan the Terrible, and not Alexander II, who had freed the serfs and at this very moment had a document on his desk awaiting his final perusal and signature, a ukase granting Russia a constitution—or thereabouts.

The Emperor, bleeding profusely, murmured: "Back to the Palace. Quick! Let me die at home."

He was raised into his carriage and at full speed they brought him back to the Winter Palace. As he was being carried upstairs to his room, blood gushed from his wounds all down the great white-marble staircase. He was lowered on his bed, which at once was soaked through with blood. One side of him was paralyzed. He could no longer speak, and he looked out with an agonizing look in one eye; the other was closed.

As he was dying, the room filled with grand dukes and grand duchesses. Looming over the deathbed was the great bulk of the son and successor, who was to follow his father on the dangerous road as Alexander III. Beside this square colossus stood *his* son, a diminutive boy of thirteen, the future Nicholas II, the last of the Tsars. There was a piercing scream, and Princess Yurevskaya, the morganatic wife of the dying Emperor, rushed into the room, fell across his body, weeping and kissing his bleeding face. His life could not be saved. Nor could he die at once. He moaned and groaned in an agony that would not end. But at last the spirit left the mangled trunk of nerves, and the struggle was over.

Before he was buried Princess Yurevskaya cut off her long plait of hair, which he so loved, and placed it in his coffin, with a note: "From your Katya."

III. "THE KNOUT WITHOUT PETER THE GREAT"

ALEXANDER III believed that every man should remain in the station to which it had pleased God to call him. If his reign of thirteen years proves anything, it is that any strong policy, however shortsighted and misguided, may be shown to work for a time. Far from advancing the cause of the peasants, Alexander III curtailed their liberties by all but nullifying his father's reforms. He believed that once a peasant, always a peasant; that the lower classes were better off without education. He himself, even with a staff of tutors at his disposal, had absorbed no education to speak of; and he managed to be Tsar quite well without it, thank you!

In one respect, however, Alexander III's reign was beneficial. When Europe breathlessly awaited Russia's decision in some conflict which might involve Europe in war, Alexander III commanded the diplomatic corps to wait on him at his residence in Gatchina where he would make an important pronouncement. But when the diplomats assembled at the Palace, the Tsar could not be found. Pages and couriers were sent out to find him. They discovered him on a river bank. He was fishing. His Foreign Minister came running up, puffing and sweating. He implored His Majesty to return to the Palace where all Europe was waiting for him. "Europe," growled the big man, "can wait if the Tsar of Russia feels like going on fishing."

When, having put away his fishing tackle, he at last appeared before the waiting ambassadors, Alexander III made his promised pronouncement. "As long as I live there will be no war in Europe," he said.

And that was all he said.

And as long as he lived there was no war in Europe. It is a pity he is not alive today.

The Tsar was a strong man and a limited man. A not too benevolent despot, he was described by one minister as "Just another Peter the Great with his knout"; and by another as "Just the knout without Peter the Great." The Tsar was ignorant, arrogant and undereducated. But he was a rock of honest simplicity and his word could be trusted. His ignorance made him disdain everything foreign; his arrogance admire everything Russian. As everyone knows, the shortest way to the hearts of the people is for a sovereign to extol the one thing he shares with his subjects—a common nationality. For five generations now the Russian sovereigns had married German consorts. This could only mean that each successive sovereign was more and more German and less and less Russian in blood. They all had blue eyes. Paul had been some horrid miscarriage that had somehow retained life and even managed to crawl to the throne. But his consort, the Württemberg princess, had an imperious stature, and all her sons, and their sons, and their sons, were giants, till the dynasty, like a riotous musical piece ending pianissimo, fizzled out in the diminutive Nicholas the last. Alexander III was the biggest, tallest, broadest Romanov since Peter the Great. Here was the traditional Russian giant with a ruddy spade beard. He broke the custom of marrying into German houses, and espoused a Dane.

Maria Feodorovna, first engaged to her husband's elder brother, who died, then betrothed to the second brother, the future Alexander III, was a sister of Queen Alexandra. She was so small that she hardly came up to his hip, and he lifted her up on one hand. Alexander III's reaction to his father's much-vaunted public life, which had ended in assassination, took the form of marooning himself with his family in the most God-forsaken of imperial residences. He immured himself from the world at Gatchina, where Paul had drilled his soldiers till they dropped. Alexander hated ceremonials and circumspection. But even more than pomp and ceremonials he hated relations, especially foreign ones. His attitude was that he would not be pestered. People are often irritated by relations, in whom they see a sort of caricature of themselves. Persons in high positions, especially sovereigns, who are in universal demand, readily acquire a distaste for their relatives who wish to share with them something of their glory and their power. The disinclination of sovereigns for the society of their relatives and connections is understandable on more than one ground. People who are interested in you make the mistake of thinking that, through the same channel of interest, you must be interested in them; and on making your acquaintance, supposedly because they are interested to hear you, immediately begin to push their own views down your throat, and expect that this can give you nothing but pleasure.

Alexander III entertained contempt for constitutional monarchs, whose position he considered as comically undignified. He called Queen Victoria a gossiping old hag; the King of Serbia an ass; the Shah of Persia a beast; and Kaiser Wilhelm II a lunatic. The Tsar even objected to his Government being described as the "Imperial Government." He said there was no Government in Russia: there was himself and his servants who executed his orders.

Yet with everything at his command, with the possibility present to satisfy every wish of his own, the Tsar had no appetite that could not be satisfied by a married man of limited means. No woman save his wife had the slightest attraction for him; he therefore considered that intercourse between the sexes not consecrated by wedlock was inexcusable. He enforced the most rigid observance of the principle of chastity on his own family and his court and the officers of his army, who were by habit promiscuous. But, as the Tsar was fond of drink, he regarded this habit as essentially Russian and human and made no secret that he approved of it as a commendable relaxation. As a result of the well-known views of the Self-Upholder of All the Russias, the officers tried to make up for an unnaturally restricted sexual life by going all the way in the matter of drink. They indulged in the pleasures of alcohol sanctioned by their master to such an extent that on occasion they turned into animals, and a certain colonel sat on the roof of the barracks and bayed at the moon.

Alexander III, who believed that character was more than intellect, yet displayed a certain boorish humility when confronted by intellectual eminence. His able finance minister, Witte, presented him with a detailed project which the Tsar confessed he was unable to understand but yet empowered Witte to put into force because, he said, he understood just enough of it to assume that Witte knew what he was talking about. Alexander III, who knew his son and heir was not very bright, believed that when anointed with the oil itself divine grace would descend on him.

Nicholas, who was very small though sound in wind and limb, was shy of his giant father and cut an even more modest figure than normally because he knew that his father, who held no store by intellect, even so was surprised at the modesty of his heir's mental endowment. Nicholas was always extremely polite. He did all the things he was supposed to do, never did a wrong thing, but executed all his duties and said all the things he had to say with the strange look and motions of a robot. When a minister suggested that the Grand Duke and heir to the throne might preside over the committee which was to inaugurate the Trans-Siberian railway, the Tsar scanned the minister's face and inquired whether he had ever conversed with his Imperial Highness. "Don't tell me," he said, "you haven't noticed that my son is a complete nitwit."

Alexander's reign resulted in a number of contradictions. A man of extremely modest intelligence himself, he placed Russia in his short reign in an unassailable financial and military position. Entertaining the utmost contempt for foreigners, he was the one Russian monarch who preserved international peace and good will. A giant of strength, his constitution crumbled after a mere thirteen years at the helm.

His death was precipitated by a railway accident in which the dining coach rolled down a bank in a collision and the roof fell in and would have crushed his family had not the Tsar held it up with his giant frame. To the man who tied iron rods into loops the task of holding up the roof of a coach proved, however, just a trifle too much even for his strength. He ruptured himself. After that railway accident he began to suffer from internal complications. In the end even his lungs were affected, and he died in his new palace at Livadia on the Caspian Sea coast, his relatives administering oxygen to prolong, alas, unsuccessfully, the life of the crushed colossus.

THE LAST BUT ONE

I. THE YELLOW MONKEY

WHEN Alexander III, who abhorred all manner of fuss, felt that death was upon him, he muttered a hurried prayer, took leave of his wife, and was gone. His son, who had tears in his eyes, was taken aback by the celerity with which his broad-shouldered father, on whom they all leaned for support, slipped off his burden and let it fall on his own slender frame. The mantle of Peter the Great descended on a small well-meaning young man of twenty-five with beautiful gray-blue eyes who hardly knew whether it was Christmas or Easter. "I don't even know how to talk to ministers. Sandro: what *am* I to do?" he wailed on the shoulder of the playmate of his childhood, his cousin Alexander.

His father, like all men who are pillars of strength in the State while they live, had given little thought to the succession. At one time it seemed just possible that Nicky's younger brother, George, might reign instead of him. Nicky's complacent indifference to *everything* was a little disconcerting even to his parents. Young Georgie, on the other hand, was a charming boy, full of life, and of an exquisite sensibility. But he was frail. No one would have been more glad than Nicky if his younger brother had relieved him of the boring necessity to assume the supreme power.

But, as it happened, Nicholas was inadvertently the cause of his brother's death. During a cruise which took them to India and the Far East, the two brothers, to while away the tedium of the voyage, wrestled on board the Russian cruiser, *Memory of Azov;* and Nicky, unaware of what he was doing, pushed his delicate young brother down the hatch. As a result of the fall, Georgie injured a lung, developed tuberculosis and soon pined away.

This cruise had been decided on to deflect the young Tsarevitch's attention from the ballet dancer Kshesinskaya, in whom he showed a precocious interest. His father, who did not believe in sexual relations out of wedlock and could not encourage wedlock with a ballet dancer, thought a long cruise would deflect the mind of the Tsarevitch. Nicholas himself did not much believe in "affairs," and he induced his fellow officers to marry their mistresses. If the mistresses were not acceptable as "regimental ladies," then he transferred their husbands to civilian grades and found jobs for them in the provinces. His father had bellowed at him for his one and only escapade, when Nicky at the end of a gay supper in the company of his fellow officers and Kshesinskaya had ragged the military governor of Petersburg, who had officiously interfered with their pleasures. Nicky had gone so far as to plant the contents of a dish of caviar on the general's head, declaring that his hair now looked remarkably like a Negro's.

The general had complained. The cruise was the result. What distinguished Nicky from others visiting Egypt, India, China, Japan, was a striking, a quite exceptional, lack of interest in what he saw. It was more than a lack of interest: it was a very positive indifference to his surroundings. The less he was shown, the more he was pleased. He wrote letters home to his mother—simply worded, well-written letters giving the routine of their sightseeing; betraying a slight enthusiasm when he reported that they got away early, or that somebody had left them in peace. The Japanese, Nicky wrote, were just ridiculous yellow monkeys aping European ways.

His astonishment was the more acute when one of these yellow monkeys—a guardian of the law at that—bashed him on the head with his tin sword. The party was being shown round a Buddhist temple whose sacred ground no alien foot had ever desecrated before. The special dispensation was intended as a compliment from the Mikado to the Russian reigning house. The Japanese policeman was there to prevent any hostile demonstration. Suddenly, overcome with religious indignation, the policeman himself struck Nicholas on the head with the very sword intended to protect him. Yes, the Grand Duke and Successor, Nikolai Aleksandrovitch, whilst on an educational visit to Japan.

At Petersburg, Nicky's parents, anxiously awaiting news of their son's condition, prayed that his life might be saved. A telegram arrived from Nicky himself. "Have been grievously insulted by Japanese policeman," it read.

The parents at home heaved a sigh of relief. Later details made it clear that Nicky had not been seriously hurt. The young Prince George of Greece, who accompanied the two brothers on their cruise, had deftly parried the blow with his arm, deadening the impact. Alexander III accepted the profuse apologies of Tokio, but suggested that the return visit to Petersburg of a Japanese prince should be politely but pointedly declined.

II. MARRIAGE OF NICHOLAS II

MEN of unbending will, like Alexander III, often exhaust their despotism in so many small matters that they weakly give way on some important point. Neither Alexander III nor his consort Maria Feodorovna liked Alice of Hesse-Darmstadt. She combined all the qualities least pleasing in an empress. She was shy, proud, gauche, hysterical, high-falutin' shrill, superstitious, sanctimonious, vain and self-willed. Both Nicky's mother, who as a Dane hated all Germans, and Alexander III, who hated all foreigners indiscriminately, frowned on Nicky's choice, but did nothing to stop him. He was so weak and amenable, so easily deflected from his choice, that they felt it would not be fair to interfere unduly with his happiness.

As a very young girl, Alix, as she was called at home, had come on a visit to Russia, where her elder sister was married to Nicky's uncle, the Grand Duke Sergei. The Russians surmised that she had come in search of a husband. She was dubbed "The Hessian Fly." Nobody at the Court of St. Petersburg liked her—save one being. He was the heir to the throne.

Queen Victoria, a royal matchmaker, inquired, with coy and playful slyness, whether all she heard was true and that a Russian Grand Duke was interested in marrying her granddaughter. Alexander III replied somewhat churlishly that if she meant his son Nicholas, he was far too young to think of marriage but was about to join the army.

Nicky seems to have fallen in love with Alix at first sight, and, apart from Kshesinskaya, for whom he entertained a vicarious carnal partiality, he never cared for anyone else. His mother tried to tempt him with a daughter of the Duke of Orleans. With disarming meekness implying that he would readily sacrifice his dearest wish in life to please his parents, Nicky got his own way. With a sigh they bade him go and propose to his Alix of Hesse-Darmstadt.

At Coburg there was a conclave of royalty gathered for the wedding of Alix's brother, the Grand Duke Ferdinand of Hesse and a daughter of the Duke of Edinburgh and Saxe-Gotha, who was no other than the future Queen Marie of Rumania, her husband having been earmarked in the way these things are done in the family for the throne of a foreign country. The future Queen Marie's mother was a Russian Grand

Duchess, her father an English Royal Duke, her husband a German and a Hesse. Though Hesse itself was but an insignificant duchy, nearly all the royalty in the world were Hesses by blood. It would indeed be difficult to find a royal person dead or alive who had not had a Hesse or a Coburg ancestor, or in fact a Coburg who was not a Hesse. Queen Victoria, whose relations they all seemed to be, and were, presided over the gathering; and Kaiser Wilhelm II, whom Nicky dutifully met at the station wearing Prussian uniform, was conspicuously at home at this numerous family conclave. Nicky, who represented his ailing father, never took his eyes off Alix, but was too shy to propose to her, despite Queen Victoria's and Kaiser Wilhelm's encouragement. William II and Alix were first cousins.

At last the Kaiser's patience gave out. He strode into Nicky's room. "Here, buckle on your sword. Now put on your cap," he commanded. "Right about turn!" He pressed a bunch of roses into Nicky's hands. "Now go and propose to Alix. Quick march!"

That evening Nicky wrote in his diary that he was the happiest man in the world.

Though his father's condition was steadily getting worse, Nicky, in his quiet way, got round his mother and wheedled permission to join his fiancée in England. Queen Victoria took their romance to heart. To her it might be Albert and herself, young and in love. . . . The Hesse-Coburg was not the only link. Nicky's mother being a sister of Queen Alexandra, the Prince of Wales was his uncle by marriage. Uncle Bertie took him in hand. No doubt he thought Nicky, when not in uniform, was execrably dressed. He at once, without even consulting his nephew, sent him his tailor, his hatter, his bootmaker. Nicky was fitted out as behoves a fiancé.

After their marriage in Petersburg, the couple, now Emperor and Empress of Russia, paid a State visit to England and a private visit to Windsor. "And there," the Tsar writes home to his mother, "was dear Grannie, waiting for us on the steps."

But that was not yet. After a stay at Windsor with his fiancée, who (like Figgy in her time) was undergoing instruction at the hands of a Russian priest hurriedly dispatched to London to prepare Princess Alice for her impending conversion into the Greek Orthodox Church, the couple parted. He was to return to the sickbed of his father; she to Hesse-Darmstadt to pack her belongings.

When Nicholas got back to Russia, Alexander III was giving up the ghost. Alix was sent for. Alix had been as unlucky as Nicky. He had inadvertently killed his brother; she had killed hers, who was a babe in arms, by dropping him off a balcony in sheer inadvertency. She had been dubbed *"Pechvogel"*—bird of ill-omen—and when she left her native Darmstadt to marry another bird of ill-omen, a woman, as the train drew out, called after her: *"Pechvogel, nimm dein Pech mit!"*

This she appears to have done.

In the confusion caused by the Emperor's approaching dissolution, no arrangements had been made for a fitting entry of the future Empress of Russia into the domain of which, within a few days, she was to become the first lady. She traveled as an ordinary passenger, had to make her own connections, find her way as best she could to Livadia where Alexander's gasping for breath was being relieved with cylinders of oxygen. Nobody took any notice of her. When shortly afterwards the marriage took place, Alix of Hesse-Darmstadt—"Alica Darmstatskaya," as she was sneeringly called in Russia—had her wedding ceremony, which seemed but a continuation of a string of other ceremonies, funeral processions and dirges, linked up with a coronation in which a huge crowd of merrymakers was by accident crushed and trampled to death, and which seemed to augur no good. And throughout it all it was raining, raining....

III. CHEKHOV ON THE RIGHTS OF THE INDIVIDUAL

ON the advice of his English relatives Nicholas began his reign with the intention of showing himself to his subjects, of being *seen*. He inaugurated his new resolution by venturing one fine morning across the Nevski Prospekt to a little French shop where he bought himself a pair of gloves. This daring escapade so alarmed the police and his relatives that pressure was brought to bear on the Emperor. Well, yes, he had taken the bull by the horns. He had been lucky this time. But he must not do it again. He had tempted Providence enough: now he must immure himself from his subjects; then he would die a natural death like dear Papa.

Nicky, who did not need to be influenced in the direction of autocracy, since his own inclination, that of a weakly obstinate nature, ran that way, was exposed to two "opposing" female influences, his mother and his wife, who, counseling sufficiently the same thing—one, that he should emulate his father; the other, Peter the Great—accused each other of ruining his life.

In the popular consciousness the Romanovs had never been kings, in the sense in which the Merovingians, the Capets, the Plantagenets were a breed removed from the lesser race of men. Neither were they representatively human, as our English royal family is today. To the peasants, who could not tell one tsar from another and hardly knew his name, the Tsar was a kind of holy lama who either lived perpetually or, by a Methusalean standard of longevity enjoyed by tsars, was always too young to have imbibed sufficient wisdom or knowledge of affairs, and for whom, bless his heart, allowance must be made on account of his youth and inexperience. Besides, it paid the courtiers to keep the Tsar in the dark: hence his strange indifference to the hard lot of the peasant. To the rest of the population, the Tsar was a mental deficient who, heaven knows why, insisted on saddling himself with the avowedly uncongenial job of ordering the lives of 150,000,000 human beings, to whom he denied the right of opinion but whose prerogatives were, he contended, by their own unexpressed wish vested in himself.

For lack of a recognized opposition, the Tsars were not used to well-marshaled arguments. Their very faculty of logic had atrophied from long disuse. Tsars never *argued*. Peter the Great turned free peasants into serfs who could be sold by their masters as recruits, but, in all sincerity, abolished the very word "slave." Peter's idea was complete subordination of the individual to the State—which, as in the case of Hitler, merely meant to his own idea of the State. It was always on pain of the most atrocious death that the individual was invited to participate of his own free will in the life of the State. Peter was nothing illogical in that either. The exasperation of educated people who could not make the Self-Upholder see the absurdity of maintaining an untenable position he not only deemed tenable but positively beneficial to them, bred revolutionaries. They had the advantage of intellectual attack on a tsar who possessed no intellect, whilst he enjoyed the advantage of not understanding their intellectual attack.

Chekhov, writing in 1899 to Suvorin, the conservative newspaper proprietor who had been defending the absolute power of the State, rejoins in a few lines which are worth quoting.

Letters from Petersburg are coming in; the mood is in favour of the students. Your letters [to the Press] *about the disorders did not satisfy me—which is natural, because you cannot judge in print about the disorders when you are not allowed to touch upon the factual side of things. The State has forbidden you to write, it forbids you to tell the truth, this is an arbitrary act, but you speak lightheartedly, as to this arbitrary act, of the rights and prerogatives of the State—and this somehow does not settle down in one's consciousness. You speak of the right of the State, but yours is not the point of view of right. Right and justice for the State are the same as for every legal person. If the State unlawfully deprives me of a piece of my land, I go to law and the court restores my right; then should it not be the same when the State beats me with a nagaika* [the reference here is to Cossacks dispersing student crowds with their terrible flails], *mayn't I in the case of violence from the State complain of the violation of my rights? The conception of the State must be founded on definite legal relations; otherwise the State is but a shell, an empty sound which frightens the imagination.*

Chekhov in fact puts his finger on what is primarily wrong about all "totalitarian" States. The legal integrity of the individual is the inestimable advantage of a democratic form of government; and the absence of it in totalitarian countries is the germ of their impending dissolution. It is not, as Bernard Shaw pointed out long ago in one of his prefaces, a question of a less or more efficient rule. An enlightened and disinterested dictator might make a better job of it than a fumbling democracy, which is often nothing but a glorified plutocracy. That is not the point. It is also doubtful whether my vote in a General Election is more than a sop to my vanity, an illusion of having a voice in the government of the country. That also is not the point. What matters is the principle, and the consequent self-respect, which allows us to feel and to think that we are our own masters and not the slaves of some tyrant who has by ruse set himself above us and forbids us to have an opinion of our own—that degrading brand-mark of servitude rampant now as ever in so-called totalitarian lands.

But Nicholas II, whom affairs of State bored to distraction, would not surrender the mono-rule because he felt it was a duty he owed to his people. He really felt the indignity of subjecting his trusting subjects to their own control. Why, it would be debasing their standards to pollute them with the untried multiplicity of their own counsel. "I have sworn to them," he said repeatedly and looking the picture of honesty, "at the Ouspenski Cathedral, at the time of my coronation, to preserve the autocracy unabridged and to hand it *intact* to my son, and I will not break my oath."

IV. 1613-1913

IT is facilely assumed by old ladies residing in Knightsbridge and Kensington that the Russian peasant, even now, dearly loves a tsar and cannot conceive of life without one. But that the tsar had, in the course of a year or so, been discredited and is now forgotten, shows that custom bound up with ignorance is not fundamental. Whereas if there was anything at all fundamental in the peasants it is the much more ancient system of the *obstchina*—an old form of commune, now revived on a modern scale. Among warehouse clerks and cashiers there was the *artyel*—a system of communal responsibility assumed by the society of *artyelstchiks* for each of its defaulting members. This sense of communism was something rooted in the Russian consciousness and has probably come to stay.

It is also generally assumed by people in free and comfortable circumstances that someone else, somewhere else, in some remote picturesque part of the map, enjoys being bullied. But it is the fundamental individual law—that nobody does—which is the mainspring of change in all lands and through all ages and which ensures that no tyranny shall last too long without at least changing its face.

Nicholas II little realized that it had fallen to his lot to wind up the dynasty. In manuals of Russian history prepared for school consumption throughout the realm, the last pages wound up a recital of native triumphs with Alexander III, who, the manual said, was succeeded on his death by "the now satisfactorily reigning Sovereign-Emperor Nickolai II Aleksandrovitch." In 1913 the Empire celebrated the tercentenary of the reign of the House of Romanov. Nobody yet suspected it was the journey's end. School certificates in that year were embellished with the portraits of the first and the last of the Romanovs. Separated by three hundred years and a countless number of German consorts, the two monarchs at the beginning and the end of the line looked alike as two peas. The beard gives them both an essentially Russian appearance, and their eyes express the same meek and mild resolution to shoulder the burdens so unaccountably allotted to them, together with the maximum earthly glory which has, much to their surprise, descended upon them.

Tsar Mihaïl's great calf's eyes expressed wonderment and hopeless resignation; the eyes of Nicholas, the melancholy of a spring sky. Melancholy indeed runs through all the clan. Despite buckets of German blood poured into them in every generation, they have all hatched in the Russian mold.

General Krassnov in his novel *From Double Eagle to Red Flag* gives a sufficiently authentic example of the Emperor's rather vaporous attempts at self-expression.

"The summer and the golden autumn have passed," the Emperor said in a low voice—"the winter has come. I love our Russian winter,—the snow, the frost, the drives in sledges and the hunting. All of it is so nice. The snow is so pure and so honest. Isn't it, Sablin? ... Why can't men be pure and honest? ...I am an autocrat, Sablin, and the day shall come when I will prove it! ...

"You may think that all of this is dear to me? No, Sablin, I would have given much to be an ordinary, simple man and to have only the land, flowers, a garden and fruit around me. And a quiet sky overhead, and God. No one else. No intrigues and no strife....It is time to go?—I know. An Emperor hasn't the right to be late. One has to hurry always, to receive someone and speak or answer questions. The freedom of sovereigns?—it does not exist!"

V. MOTHER AND WIFE

NICHOLAS was not assisted by his wife to gain popularity. Alexandra Feodorovna, having attained her ambition of being Empress of Russia, now only craved for a private life, much to the disgust of the Empress Dowager Maria Feodorovna, who in her time had been fussily useful. Alexandra Feodorovna would not inconvenience herself for anybody. She would not come to Petersburg on presentation days, as the Dowager Empress had done, to save the young debutantes and their mothers a midwinter train journey in their ball dresses to Tsarskoye Selo.

She was not gracious. Neither had she charm. She was beautiful in a drawn, thin-lipped fashion. But she was awkward; and she blushed too easily. When the Empress was annoyed or put out, the color rose not merely to her face, but her neck, arms, shoulders all flushed a deep red. She dressed without taste. Alexandra Feodorovna knew that the Russian aristocracy rather despised her, and she piqued them in return by ignoring them in favor of the upper middle class, the higher bourgeoisie. An aristocracy prides itself on being but a step removed from the throne; whereas, by the same standard of exclusiveness which abhors approximation, sovereigns distinguish only between two kinds of human species: monarchs and non-monarchs.

The Empress found her women friends among bourgeois high officialdom, from which stratum she also prevailed on her husband to recruit his ministers. She had odd female friends who *adored* her demonstratively, and before whom she posed as a woman of an exceptionally elevated spiritual nature. As a girl, Alix had studied medicine and taken a degree in philosophy. All of which did not prevent her from being an exceptionally foolish woman—though admittedly brilliant compared with her husband.

As Bernard Shaw once observed somewhere—how are you to know that you are not a fool? In his letters to his mother the Emperor always wrote tersely of So-and-so being an ass, So-and-so a bore or a blockhead. The idea of intelligence being dominated everywhere by stupidity which considers itself as intelligence might be developed in another tome, with world history as illustration. The Emperor wrote simply and well, and in a limited—very limited—field he seemed sensible enough. His Danish mother, a trying, bad-tempered but well-meaning woman who wrote him angelic letters in French interspersed with faulty Russian, had this time gone almost so far as to reproach her dear sweet Nicky. Why had he given orders to down Finnish nationalism, which had never given them trouble before? Now—why?—why a heavy hand in Finland which dear Papa had always ridden with a light rein? She heard—she could hardly believe it was true—that Nicky had forbidden the Finns to sing their national anthem.

Her son replies in that clear simple Russian style betraying the writer as a man translucent with good sense. He did not forbid them to sing their Finnish national anthem. He merely forbade them singing it in their low taverns, when drunk; in which place and condition he would also forbid them even singing the Russian national anthem.

In another letter Maria Feodorovna solicits a favor. The Empress Dowager, oblivious of the fact that her late husband had bilked the peasants of their recent privileges in favor of the landowners, asks on behalf of a family of landed proprietors to whom Alexander III had lent 1,000,000 roubles for a term of fifteen years, to defer repayment for another fifteen years and—incidentally—lend them another 1,000,000. "I feel strongly," she writes, "that the landed nobility should be assisted by the government."

Nicky agreed to the delay in repaying the first 1,000,000, but balked at handing out another. The treasury could not be ladling out millions to oblige needy landowners. The very idea of it would horrify his finance minister. "I should like to know what Witte would think of me if I handed out a million here and there while he was away on holiday?"

Witte, a brilliant but overbearing statesman, at no time thought much of him. While revering the throne, he treated the person who sat on it with thinly disguised contempt.

Alexandra Feodorovna played the invalid. "Oh, when, *when* shall we be able to lead a decent *ordinary* life!" she sighed incessantly; at the same time she tightened her hold on the realm. She wanted to be his sole—but could not have been a worse—guide. In her letters she urged her dear Nicky to be always the autocrat, to make people feel *who* was the boss, to put ministers in their place, to speak angrily, raise his voice at them, even shout. But he replied, with good sense, that it was quite easy by a word or tone to keep his distance in a quiet way, without throwing his weight about. She wrote a queer ungrammatical English interspersed with the wrong slang in the right place, which suggested that she was a woman without a language of her own, and that English was to her, as Queen Victoria's granddaughter, perhaps the least unnatural mode of expression, never quite at hand when she wanted it, yet with nothing better to take its place.

Alexandra Feodorovna wanted to be spared the routine duties of an empress; at the same time to run the whole empire herself. The parallel with Figgy and Peter III could not escape her. How was she any less capable or any less eligible than the Princess Sophie of Anhalt-Zerbst, who had reigned in her self-assumed right as Catherine the Great? Only she herself was much too fond of her Nicky to do anything that might hurt him. She loved him—and she loved Russia. Her reiterated love of Russia, though for a neglected waif of Hesse-Darmstadt no doubt sincere, was sickening, almost hysterical. The Emperor, too, in all his decisions stressed how deeply he loved Russia. Seeing that he was a Russian and virtually owned the place, what did he think he was expected to love: Japan?

He, with his small supply of mental energy, was the most hardworked of them all. But he did not enjoy it. Replying to his mother's detailed description of the coronation of King George V and Queen Mary, Nicholas's own reaction to an account of splendid ceremonial is one of acute commiseration. "I even felt quite tired merely reading of what poor Geordie and May had to do," he writes. He heaves a sigh of relief that for him and Alix such an ordeal is long since past.

The Russian grand dukes had an easy time of it compared with our own Royalty, who are kept with their noses to the Charity grindstone. Few are they who envy them their dreary rounds. But the Russian grand dukes took it easy. Their duties were those of colonels of crack regiments. When they did not lead private lives they sought distraction at official court functions as a welcome change from over-indulging whim and caprice. They were, with few exceptions, a good-looking lot. Queen Marie of Rumania writes of her Romanov uncles as tall, fine-looking and smelling of expensive scent, who when she was a young girl ragged her unmercifully and laughed loudly and heartily.

That is the common type of the Romanov brood of uncles, cousins and brothers. The reigning sovereign is habitually subdued. There is a gravity, an earnestness about him. Care sits on his brow from which his uncles are as a rule reasonably immune: the whole of the rebellious intelligentsia leaving them be for the moment, because concentrating on the laying of bombs under the chair or bed of the head of the family. One autocrat attracts *all* the bombs.

VI. THE TSAR PLAYS LAWN TENNIS

IN due course Russia drifted into war with Japan. Port Arthur fell. The *Daily News,* which today deplores Japanese fascism, burst into a panegyric. "Nothing is more startling than the lesson which the uprising of this wonderful people is setting before civilized Europe." And *The Times,* attributing the Japanese victory to "the whole training of the Japanese in the great fundamental principles of human conduct," asked whether Japan's moral precept "may not well give this country pause and set us considering whether there were not greater ideals than buying in the cheapest market and obtaining the greatest average return upon capital."

The *Daily News* announced Admiral Togo's victory at Shushima as "complete, overwhelming, almost unexampled." "His victory," said the leader, "recalls the noonday of British naval triumph, and challenges the greatest deeds of Nelson himself. . . . The balance of naval power is suddenly shifted to an extent which we can hardly appreciate. . . . By the battle of Shushima Russia has ceased to count, and instead we have the Far Eastern seas once and for all controlled by a Far Eastern navy."

The Times did not lag behind in enthusiasm. " 'The Russian fleet is practically annihilated' was the first message of the great Admiral, and all that subsequent information can do is to eliminate the qualifying adverb."

How did the author know or learn this?

Nicholas II at the moment was playing tennis at Peterhof. When the Emperor was handed a telegram he had two tennis balls in his left hand, the racket raised, ready to serve, in his right. He took the telegram with the right hand, raising racket and telegram to his eyes, reading: "RUSSIAN FLEET ANNIHILATED AT SHUSHIMA STOP NEARLY ALL OUR SHIPS SUNK." The Tsar shoved the telegram into his trouser pocket. "Thirty-fifteen," he said, and served.

President Theodore Roosevelt offered mediation, and the Tsar empowered Witte to go to the Peace Conference at Portsmouth on condition that he surrendered nothing to the Japanese. Witte put up a big bluff. He stuck to his guns. He would not budge an inch. Roosevelt, despairing of success, appealed to the Tsar over Witte's head to accept Japan's minimum terms. The American Ambassador called on the Emperor, who was again playing tennis. Without terminating the game, Nicholas accepted everything and gave way on all points.

VII. BLACK SUNDAY

THE corruption in high quarters revealed by the disasters of the Russo-Japanese War unleashed the first Revolution. There was an unfocused dissatisfaction with things in general, but no very definite alternative advanced to take the place of a discredited administration. The popular feeling was not exactly anti-Tsar. All that the broad masses of working people appeared to ask of the throne was some small token of sympathetic understanding of their difficulties in place of what seemed rigid aloofness. A priest called Father Gapon, popular with the work people, voiced that sentiment exactly. The Okhrana, the secret police, watched him for some time, listened to his impassioned, yet strangely loyal, harangues.

They came to an interesting conclusion. Father Gapon's essentially loyal sentiments and his growing influence with the workers and students might be canalized into government channels. The Tsar was all right, but prevented by the government from coming close to his people. That was his tenet. Supposing he was bribed to extend his philosophy to read: the government too was all right, but prevented from coming close to the people by some ... well, unspecified evil agency—say, the revolutionaries?

The holy father was bribed. He was told that *he* was all right. Carried away by his own eloquence, encouraged by police support, enriched by government gold, he lost his head, feeling that they, too, that *everything* now was all right. Gathering an enormous crowd of supporters, he organized a march to the Winter Palace to tell the Tsar that he and everyone was all right, that all was in fact well in this best of all possible worlds *if only* the Tsar would join with them in their general elation.

The police supplied Father Gapon with loyal banners bearing the image of the Tsar. Holding the Russian cross before him and followed by immense multitudes bearing ikons and singing hymns, broken with love and pity, pierced with holy ecstasy at the thought of seeing the Tsar, Father Gapon, exhilarated by the humble grandeur of his mission to gather the common people into the fold of their Tsar, led the procession. But crowds attract other crowds. Swelling their ranks as they marched on, and now approaching the Winter Palace, were other elements, who did not think the Tsar, the government, the world, or in fact anything was all right—but all wrong and not to be tolerated for another minute. The police got frightened of the dimensions and multiple political complexion of the crowds, and ordered them to disperse. They protested that they had come to petition the Tsar to hear them, to assist them against injustice and exploitation by the rich and strong. They had come to protest, others urged, to lay their grievances before him.

This sounded ominous to the officers commanding the regiments detailed to patrol the streets. "Back!" they ordered. "Disperse!"

The crowds imbued with a holy love for the Tsar were abashed. They had been told by Father Gapon that it was only the government of the rich, the high and corrupt, who kept them apart from their meek-eyed Tsar whose portrait fluttered on their banners and whose beautiful face spoke for itself. They were humiliated as much on their own account as on behalf of the Tsar, who, if they were prevented from going to him, was also prevented by these same officers and police from coming out to them. The more fiery spirits protested their indignation. They pressed forward, and the crowds behind them. They jeered at the soldiers. "You couldn't manage the Japs, but you'd shoot disarmed workers! Cowards!"

"Stand back!" shouted the officers. "Back! Or we shoot!"

The crowd, egged on from behind, pressed on. A sharp volley, and another, rang through the tense winter air, and mowed down the front ranks. The crowds, dropping the banners with the portrait of the Tsar, began to run. They were trampled down as they ran, were cut by the ready flails of the Cossacks hastening to do their job.

The Tsar at the time was away in Peterhof and knew nothing of what had occurred. But the people now hated him bitterly for having so cruelly repulsed their pure-hearted impulse to come to him with their troubles. Father Gapon, outraged in his deepest feelings, sorely disappointed in the Tsar, and more in the police, went over heart and soul to the revolutionaries, who, when they discovered that he had been in the pay of the police, murdered him, believing him to be a genuine *agent provocateur*.

VIII. WITTE

IN the autumn of 1905 the people, incited by students and skillfully directed by seasoned revolutionaries nurtured on Marx and Engels, sprang a revolution on a bewildered sovereign who had just begun to hope that, with the Japanese War behind him, he was in for a quiet life.

The weak Tsar voted for a strong hand. The strong Witte, who fancied the Tsar did not know what he had let himself in for and should be taught a lesson, was all for a statesmanlike compromise. Besides, he had a reputation as a skillful negotiator abroad, which he was now eager to try out at home.

On his way home from the Peace Conference in America, Witte passed through Berlin, and Kaiser Wilhelm II made a big fuss of him, acclaiming him as one of the greatest—if not *the* greatest—negotiators of his time. Wilhelm thought that by conferring honors on the Russian statesman he was pleasing Nicky. But Nicholas, who hated Witte, was annoyed by all this artificial praise and adulation showered on his already overbearing minister which forced the Tsar to distinguish his servant on pain of incurring a charge of imperial ingratitude. He made Witte a count, but sacked him at the first available opportunity.

The opportunity was to come soon. Witte had served under Alexander III as his minister of finance, and Nicholas II accordingly seemed to him very small beer. Witte was like a spirited horse gleefully aware that the man who was now riding him was not his old master. Nicholas knew that Witte knew, yes, and shared, Alexander III's opinion of his son and successor; indeed, barely troubled to conceal his contempt from the man from whom he was now condescendingly taking his orders. Witte delighted in presenting his sovereign with catastrophic situations traceable to the Emperor's own misguided decisions. What was going to happen *now?* How were they going to get out of this jam? Witte regarded his master with ill-concealed glee.

The Emperor in his confusion, and to avoid Witte's eyes, looked out of the window and with his fingers drummed on the pane of glass. After a long silence, pregnant with reproach and frustration, Witte offered to extricate the Tsar from an impossible situation—on Witte's own conditions. He demanded a free hand. Nicholas agreed, tentatively, only later to disown Witte's pledge on his behalf.

Witte considered—and no doubt he was right—that the time had come for the Tsar to grant the country a constitution. Leo Tolstoy had urged as much; but when the Emperor had expressed his willingness to receive the "great writer of the Russian soil," Tolstoy had pleaded old age and sent his son instead. The son conveyed the substance of his father's argument, by no means new to Nicholas; and the Tsar reiterated the pledge he had uttered at the Ouspenski Cathedral at the time of his coronation to preserve intact the autocracy for his son. Both men had parted much in the spirit in which Goethe once wrote to a correspondent: "Dear Sir, by all means retain your opinion since it evidently gives you pleasure."

The Tsar accordingly listened to Witte without enthusiasm. The Tsar had an added reason for not wishing to comply with Witte's suggestion: he hated Witte, hated him as much, he admitted to Princess Golitsin, as Witte hated him. Witte liked to imply that all was lost, that the Tsar had but one asset left him—Witte. All was lost but for Witte reluctantly exercising his prodigious talents on behalf of a monarch who he was by no means sure deserved such exertion and by *such* a man!

He could not, Witte said, guarantee the continuance of monarchy in Russia without the immediate and unconditional grant of a constitution. The Tsar listened politely and wondered about his pledge at the Ouspenski Cathedral.

Of all strange allies, Witte secured an arch-monarchist, a hundred per cent absolutist, whose views had been abruptly modified by a message from the spirit world. He was the tall and spare Grand Duke Nikolai Nikolaievitch, an uncle of the Tsar, a man to figure prominently in the Great War as Commander in Chief of the Russian Army. Nikolai Nikolaievitch had married a daughter of the King of Montenegro, who indulged with him in spiritist séances, in which she was literally the moving spirit. They ordered their lives according to advice tapped out beyond the veil. Nikolai Nikolaievitch lent a willing ear to the voices of his ancestors. They had recently had an evening, as they say, crowded with phenomena. There appeared first the Grand Duke's mother-in-law, then Peter the Great, then Alexander III, whose blunt message was

what a nonsense

spelled out to read: "Give money—a lot of money—to the King of Montenegro."

Significant! They had another sitting. They again consulted the oracle, which this time tapped out: "Nicky should grant a constitution."

Overnight the despotic Grand Duke became an eager convert to a responsible form of government, of the people, by the people, for the people. He rushed to see his quiet nephew and bellowed at him, which was this uncle's way of speaking quietly, that he must obey the Voice. Together with Witte, he set upon the Emperor, making hay of his pledge at the Ouspenski Cathedral. After all, he urged, *they* in the Great Beyond knew best.

Overruled, Nicholas meekly agreed. But he was not happy about it. He consulted another uncle, the Grand Duke Sergei, an out-and-out absolutist unmoved by any voice from the Beyond. He was reputed to be the Tsar's favorite uncle. Grand Duke Sergei, who had staring mad eyes and believed in nothing but violence, brooded darkly. He was married to Alix's elder sister, and as such had been the reason for Alix coming on her first fateful visit to Russia. Sergei took long thought— and came out with a solution. If they were intent on having their parliament, their *Duma,* well and good. But let it be the ancient Muscovite *Tsar's Duma,* where the long-bearded boyars assembled to listen to the will of their sovereign and dared not breathe either yea or nay.

Nicholas, relieved, conveyed this happy solution to Witte, who all but wailed aloud in despair. Really he did not know whether to laugh or to cry! Here was the Ship of State foundering in the heavy sea of Revolution. It was now hardly a question of sparing the Tsar, but of saving the *dynasty.* He, Witte, as a condition of taking on this thankless job, had asked to be able to offer the nation some remotely real thing—a representative Duma, a legislative assembly which, if it did not control the government, at least passed or vetoed new laws. And the Tsar was trying to fob them off with this pathetic museum piece of the Middle Ages! A ludicrous anachronistic simulacrum! How *could* he save the Tsar? How save the dynasty with such nonsense?

Nicholas, who had remained quiet during this outburst, then proffered another idea. It was no use these days being pigheaded, he said. One must move with the times. He did not object to the Liberals joining the government if that would pacify a country in an uproar, provided they were, as before, answerable to the autocrat.

But no Liberals could be induced to join, knowing full well that they would not be allowed to do anything in the least liberal.

The Tsar, then, writhing with pain and disgust, screwed himself up to write "Nikolai" at the foot of Witte's manifesto. There—it was terrible, awful—he had done it now. Adieu to the pledge in the Ouspenski Cathedral!

The elected Duma returned, to the sincere chagrin of Witte, an overwhelming Radical majority. They were received by the Tsar at the Winter Palace and bidden to proceed to the Tavrida Palace (once the home of Potemkin) and take up their legislative duties of endorsing the decisions of the Monarch for the good of the Fatherland.

It would be hard to imagine what else the Duma could do (since it was not allowed to do anything) except do what it did: that is, give voice in spirited, sometimes abusive terms to continual protests. Ministers, responsible solely to the Tsar, communicated to the Duma various official decisions which the Duma members were allowed to approve but had no power to reject. Their function, if they could be said to have one, was "consultative," and they exercised their right by shouting down every minister who rose to speak with vehement cries of: "Resign! Resign!"

The Tsar hastened to put an end to this, he said, baleful example of mass self-expression by dissolving the Duma. He went further. He considered that the promise of a constitution was given by him under duress and as such was invalid, now that the military again had the situation pretty well in hand. For the same reason he broke his promise of a political amnesty and reverted to what is known as a paternal form of government with a vengeance.

The Tsar had no compunction in breaking his oath. He broke a later oath to keep a prior oath. All subsequent oaths automatically broke on the rock of that first oath at the Ouspenski Cathedral.

As for Witte, who had, the Tsar thought, made a pretty good mess of things, everything considered, after throwing his weight about and browbeating him the way he had done—well, he deserved his reward.

"He embraced me warmly," Witte notes in his diary, "praised my work highly, thanked me for what I had done for him and the Fatherland; and when I got home I found he had sacked me. Our Tsar," concludes Count Witte, a Russian of Baltic extraction, "is an Oriental."

IX. BETWEEN TWO WARS

THE Russians are in many ways more shrewd and realistic and less blinded by their idols than the English and the Germans. Their reply to the paternal form of government instituted in the place of the promised constitution was a sustained and comprehensive program of assassinations in high quarters. The signal for such a *riposte* had been given, some time before, when the Tsar had appointed the mad-eyed Grand Duke Sergei, who believed in naught but violence, to keep the peace of Moscow; which indeed he did, till it was broken by a bomb thrown under his wheels, and he died according to the principle by which he lived.

The Tsar's associates did not know how to tell him of this awful death of his favorite uncle and brother-in-law. Foreign royal guests staying in the Palace discreetly assumed that the official banquet was canceled. Presently they learned that the Empress Dowager had braved it. She had broken the news to her son. The foreign guests were rehearsing suitable phrases of condolence. "Irreparable loss ... unforgettable ... a national calamity...."

They were astonished, on entering the imperial quarters, to find the Tsar and his cousin and childhood friend, "Sandro," nudging each other playfully and trying to push each other off the sofa, laughing heartily as they did so.

Nicky was a puzzle to his own mother, whose rough temper at close range was transformed at a distance into those nice smooth letters in which she gave him news of "amama" and "apapa" in Denmark, or told him of the splendor and comfort of Windsor where she went to stay with her sister, Queen Alexandra. He, writing from the very bourgeois surroundings which were Alix's idea of a home, did not respond to his mother's enthusiasm about the beauty, comfort, luxury and good taste in the furnishing and decorations at Windsor. Perhaps he sensed in his mother's commendations a hidden barb for his Alix, whose idea of decorating their "ordinary decent life" was a suburban English villa with furniture which might have come—and perhaps did come—from the Tottenham Court Road.

The Russian Court functions, the scale of refreshments and suppers, the size of the halls and the ballrooms, were grand enough, without a doubt, but not so well organized as the English. The Tsar, according to an old Russian custom, went round wishing his guests a good appetite. But the guests surreptitiously stuffed their pockets full of pears, peaches and sweets—souvenirs to take home to their children; at the same time complaining loudly that the food was not good: the contractors were raking in money and doing the Tsar, who had ordered that everything should be of the best. The Emperor at these functions appeared with his mother on his arm, while his wife came in their wake on the arm of some officer who happened to be around. Maria Feodorovna evidently found it hard to cease being the first lady of the land.

Not that Alexandra Feodorovna was at all self-effacing. She had dearly wished to gallop at the head of her regiment of hussars, as Nicky's sister, Olga, could do, who reined in her steed two yards from where the Emperor stood on parade and saluted jauntily with a dexterous flash of the saber. Alexandra Feodorovna could not ride a spirited horse when she visted her own regiment. Knowing her predicament, they had given her a quiet old hack. The nag was so ancient and ugly that she could have cried for shame as she sat on him, all eyes upon her.

The Empress Mother, writing from Buckingham Palace, mentions how one afternoon she had a shock: she thought it was her Nicky who had entered the room and it was Geordie (the future King George V), and even Aunt Alix remarked how alike the two cousins looked. Then Geordie's children came in, she says, very *noisily*.

Nicky, sparing in comment, mentions *his* difficulties. He had foxy Ferdie of Bulgaria staying with him at Ferdie's own wish; which was a nuisance. They had to give a banquet in his honor, all in the recognized way as though he were a real sovereign. All of which was rather trying and not a little absurd. Kaiser Wilhelm had also squashed Ferdie, who needed squashing apparently, at the time of King Edward's funeral in London.

But the Tsar was facing more acute vexations than the snobbism of mushroom monarchs. His Prime Minister, Stolipin, had started on a new and brilliant idea of his own, which was to uphold the Self-Upholder. Russia must be split up into a vast number of independent farmers, whose instinctive interest would be to uphold the monarchy and combat revolution. This would automatically take place if all available crown land were divided among the shrewd go-ahead peasants who would get the weak and simple to do their work for them. An absolute monarchy of well-to-do smallholders was the solution. A Kulak empire. That was the idea.

Nicholas was so keen on it that he gave away his own private as well as crown lands with both hands. He was generous that way.

And, indeed, it worked—amazingly. It was based on a time-honored principle: immemorial exploitation of man through his fellow man—which has never failed—and was succeeding now with extraordinary rapidity. Russia indeed would have ended as a bigger modern France, and a veritable bastion of absolute monarchy, if the landowning gentry, deprived of cheap labor, did not—damn them! Stolipin swore—go and make common cause with revolutionaries who objected to the said immemorial exploitation of man by his fellow man.

Stolipin was shot in a stall at a theater by, it was said, a man who swore he was put up to the job by the police. The author of the scheme "land for the crafty" died making the sign of the cross in the air at his sovereign who, with his daughters, saw the shooting from the imperial box, while attending the performance of Glinka's standard opera, *A Life for the Tsar.* So ended this interesting attempt to solve the problem: *Whither Russia?* and with it the corollary: *Whither Nicholas?*

X. RASPUTIN

IN due course Russia drifted into war on behalf of Serbia. As it grew more bloody, Russia said she was fighting the battles of England and France. We must go to General Krassnov for a telling epilogue to a cavalry charge, which speaks for itself.

Whilst the remnants of the command were being formed in platoons, Prince Repnin came trotting across the field. His face was calmly majestic. His horse looked nervously askance at the bodies of the men and horses lying scattered about.

"I thank you, my good fellows, for your gallant charge. I congratulate you with your glorious dead....Give me the report-book, Count," he went on, "we must send a cable to His Majesty informing him of the famous and glorious victory."

Prince Repnin gazed at the field on which carts and hospital-cars were driving to and fro and sanitary assistants were picking up the wounded.

"A brilliant deed," he muttered, "a brilliant deed. How many lives of the pick of young Russia it has cost! May Russia, may the whole world know that our nation is united, that our officers are capable of dying together with and ahead of their soldiers. The solemn hour of liquidation has struck, when we must atone in the eyes of the people by paying in full for our privileged position, for our wealth, our landed estates, our luxurious and gay life in time of peace. May the Emperor and the whole

of Russia realize that fathers have sacrificed their sons on the altar of their mother-country and have themselves fallen at their side."

The commander rattles on in this strain, oblivious of the yells and groans of the wounded scattered on the battlefield and imploring for help.

"Poor Sablin! Does he know how tragically his son, that fine youth, met with his death and how mutilated he was? What a merciless fate seems to pursue him! Only a month ago he lost his wife under most tragical circumstances and now he is deprived of his son. Would it not perhaps be better for him to die likewise? What is he to live for now?"

"Fame," exclaimed Count Valersky in a voice full of pride and solemnity, which sounded unusually clear in the stillness of the air. Corpses lay on the field. The wounded moaned and yelled, endeavoring to attract the attention of the hospital corps. The earth had not yet absorbed the pools of blood, the fallen horses lay about with hideously swollen bellies. But that great word seemed to chase away the doleful picture of the field of death.

"The glory of his valiant deed is left to Sablin," the adjutant went on. "Whether he dies or is spared, this date, on which the cavalry charge led by him has ended in our brilliant victory, will forever shine with an inextinguishable brightness."

Well! I *ask* you!

Something might be said in favor of the changed conception of war brought about by the Revolution in 1917. An attack on the Germans was planned, we are told; the officers appeared, *but not one soldier.* "They did not consider the attack necessary."

At no time had Rasputin considered the war necessary. Whether he really was in German pay is difficult to say with certainty; but even if he were, his abhorrence of war might not be any the less sincere for being a German agent. Rasputin was not, like the Emperor, bound by any promises to us not to make a separate peace; an oath the Tsar regarded as second to none; yea, not even to that made in the Ouspenski Cathedral! Nicholas considered himself bound by promises he had made to God and foreigners, but that his word of honor given solemnly to his own subjects should be taken with a pinch of salt.

I once had the occasion to question closely a Luthern pastor on a holiday in Tyrol as to the criminal culpability of the ex-Kaiser in engineering the late war. *"Ach! Herrgott!"* he sighed. "The poor man! he didn't know what he was about!"

"But," I objected, "he took the decision. Had he said no, there wouldn't have been a Great War."

"Ach! Herrgott! He had meant it well enough!"

I feel a similar good-natured tolerance in regard to that other poor bogey, the much-abused Rasputin. *"Ach, Herrgott!* he meant it well enough!"* I inquired from a number of people who had personally known Rasputin what he was like. He was, they said, perfectly charming! couldn't be nicer!

But, of course, there is no blinking at the fact—the saint was oversexed. The irony of the situation is that Rasputin entered the inner circles of the Winter Palace equipped with the highest ecclesiastical credentials. Bishop Hermogen, Archimandrite Theophan, and the priest Illiodor, all highly reputable pillars of reaction, examined Rasputin and declared him to be a man of God. For some time now the Empress, increasingly unpopular with Russian patriots, sought relief for her injured feelings in being more Orthodox than the Orthodox. A convert to the Russian Church, she explored the wonder-working mysteries and miracles with that naïve, over-earnest and humorless intentness which characterizes the alien newcomer.

She threw herself into every available superstition. In imitation of the early tsars and tsaritsas, she applied for the intercession of all manner of holy rabble—the sort that Peter the Great would have swept away with a broom. She invoked the blessing of inspired epileptics, babbling monks, village idiots, wandering nuns, natural imbeciles writhing in convulsions, and cripples foaming at the mouth, on whom, she judged, divine grace descended more abundantly than on those other more formal members of the Church of Christ too slick in putting God's truth into words.

There was, at first, no jealousy on the part of the accredited exponents of the Gospel. They produced Rasputin, *starets,* wanderer and man of God, in all innocence. It was like providing a pony which the Tsaritsa had expressed the wish to own. Certainly, Your Majesty! With the greatest of pleasure! Only too pleased to oblige. But when the Siberian tramp had got ahead of them and become the most intimate associate of the Supreme Power, then Bishop Hermogen and the priest Illiodor had a scuffle with him, abused him roundly and—Rasputin complained to the Tsar—tried to emasculate him.

The Tsar was horrified. He said he could not think of a more serious offense than for a man to raise his hand against his fellow man for the purpose of emasculating him. It was horrible beyond words. The Emperor, with the warm approval of his consort, consigned the bishop and the priest to outlying monasteries. But word reached him that Rasputin, to celebrate his triumph, had stripped himself and danced naked at a public restaurant in Moscow. He had accosted respectable women and, when repulsed in his advances, boasted that he had been more successful at the Winter Palace and flourished his shirt, for all to see, embroidered for him, he said, by the Tsaritsa herself.

The Tsar then sent for Rasputin, asked him, as sternly as he was able, what he had been doing in Moscow, and then, looking straight into the saint's eyes, uttered one word—"Out!"

The *starets,* really intimidated this time, went away crestfallen, but soon found his way back into the fold. They could not do without him.

Rasputin always greeted the Emperor, the Empress and their four daughters and son by kissing them familiarly three times on alternate cheeks—a custom ordinarily confined to Easter Sunday. Rumors quickly spread through Russia, and percolated abroad, that Rasputin had not only seduced the Empress but had deflowered her daughters, too, and that there was not a virgin left within a ten-mile radius of the Winter Palace. These assertions, in all their parts, probably lack foundation, though the wandering monk took his toll of the ladies of the inner circle. The Empress, already unpopular on all other grounds, now added to her reputation of haughty, meddlesome aloofness, the name of a German spy and a wanton. When she traveled to the front to see her husband and son, the generals complained that her train was holding up much-needed supplies, and that she was doing so to assist the enemy. She was, they said, in league with Rasputin, who was a German spy, and worked for a separate peace. In reality, though German on her father's side, she detested the Prussians and the Kaiser in particular, but wanted to stop the bloodshed on religious and humanitarian grounds.

She was much blamed for dragging the name of the dynasty into the mud by her associations with so obscene a saint as Gregori Rasputin. But, *ach! Herrgott!* she believed implicitly in his power to save her little boy. The Tsarevitch Aleksei suffered from hereditary haemophilia. Every accident, a knock or a scratch, might cause him to bleed to death. The successor to the throne was born after all the holy powers had been invoked to grant the Empress a son. The Tsar had, with that end in view, agreed on the representations of the bishops and archimandrites to canonize a

This is a lie!

recently deceased monk in the belief that he would see them through. Yet, despite all these big efforts at intercession, four lovely daughters preceded the birth of a really beautiful but sadly frail son. He might be made of eggshell. An awkward gesture—and good-by to Russia's young hopeful! And there was not a chance of any of the Tsar's four daughters assuming the crown. The bastard Emperor Paul, sorely vexed at his mother Catherine the Great doing his father in, only to do both of them out, had decreed that the female succession was to be barred for all time to come.

No wonder the little Tsarevitch was more precious than all his sisters together. When he fell and hurt himself and the doctors had given him up for lost, Rasputin was sent for, and the boy recovered. True, one of the four doctors had just applied a drastic but dangerous remedy on his own responsibility, without admitting that he had done so, and the Tsarevitch's sudden recovery, coincident with Rasputin's arrival, might have been caused by this natural remedy. At all events Rasputin took the credit. The frail boy seemed to revive in the saint's presence, as though by magic. Rasputin, according to the two spiritist daughters of the King of Montenegro, was a natural medium.

He certainly exercised hypnotic powers. He excelled at reading people's thoughts. Take it at its lowest, a man of such tremendous magnetic virility who, when assassinated, proved to have nine lives, could not help but give out a potent physical energy to sustain the delicate child. He was, doubtless, a spirit healer of exceptional magnetic power.

That he deliberately administered drugs to worsen the Tsarevitch's condition in order to claim credit for the improvement following on abstention, is a conjecture which, in the absence of positive evidence, cannot be sustained. Kokovtsov, the Russian Premier and Finance Minister in those years, a man by nature and training skeptical of anything remotely savoring of the occult or even the untapped physical powers latent in the human organisms, was convinced that Rasputin drugged the Tsar.

This is not so!

The story of Rasputin's murder is too well known to need recounting here. Whatever one's views, one cannot but admire the astounding physical tenacity of this man who was poisoned, shot, clubbed, shot again, and still howled, growled and crawled upstairs on all fours out of the cellar into the yard. Even when his body was pushed under the ice, he was alive, for his lungs filled with water, and he died from drowning.

XI. THE STORM

THE Tsar was besieged by people protesting their sincerity when proffering unsolicited advice; which is always offensive. It costs nothing to give advice, yet implies superior competence on the part of the intruder who deems the recipient sadly in need of it. Nicholas must have thought people wishing to tender advice were holy nuisances. The Tsar, he said, like any creature of God, had a right to a measure of private life. Nicholas, who was as easily intimidated by people of a forceful character as he was obstinate once he was again alone, took away with one hand what he gave with the other. His uncle, the Grand Duke Nikolai Nikolaievitch, was a forceful character and, as such, a pain in the neck to his weakly obdurate nephew who held the reins of government.

The Grand Duke was dismissed from his post as Commander in Chief of the Eastern Front and transferred to a sideshow in the Caucasus. The Tsar himself, egged on by his wife, who based her arguments on the clairvoyant authority of Rasputin, assumed the supreme command of his armies. Nikolai Nikolaievitch, deeply humiliated, professed himself delighted with the change of appointment. Just, however, before his train was due to leave headquarters he asked his nephew, who had arrived to see him off, to come for a chat into his private compartment. There, shutting the door and the windows, the offended Grand Duke shouted the roof off at the thoroughly intimidated Tsar, who bolted out onto the platform. Then, standing rigidly to attention on the step of the already moving coach, with an expression of supreme devotion in his eyes, an attitude of punctilious respect in his tall frame, the Grand Duke saluted his sovereign as the train went past him.

When the prestige of Nicholas II had reached its lowest ebb and the revolution was being freely predicted, and there were also rumors of a palace *coup d'état* designed to forestall a national uprising, Sir George Buchanan, the British Ambassador, at last obtained an audience of the Emperor. Sir George, on behalf of his Government, urged the Tsar to give some small token of good will in relaxing the hated autocracy in order to gain the confidence of the people. Nicholas pretended not to understand. Surely the boot was on the other foot. It was for his people to do something to merit *his* confidence in *them*.

The *Roi-Soleil* himself could not have spoken more haughtily. To see little Nicholas II kicking thus against the pricks almost reminds one of that horrible scene in Dostoevski when drunken peasants are belaboring a miserable little horse which, tried beyond endurance, begins to kick back and sends the crowd of peasants lashing away at it into an uproar of merriment: such a miserable little horse and it dares to kick back!

When the storm came, and even the Empress herself, surrounded by the soldiery and the proletariat howling for her blood outside the Palace at Tsarskoye Selo, had telegraphed to him that "Concessions are necessary," the Tsar, who had been told on his train that the Revolution had won the day and even the progressive Duma members had now thrown up the sponge, still showed defiance. To the men in power who had decided they did not want him at any price, he telegraphed reluctant consent to the formation of a government responsibile to the people, but added: "Reserve nomination of Ministers of War and Interior."

When they boarded his train and told him that all was up and he must go, he stood there as though in a dream, then turned away to the window. Never was a human being more cornered, though he did not spring on them like a rat, but turning back to them spoke quietly.

The sequel is known from the opening chapter of this narrative, and it only remains to tell of the final pilgrimage to Siberia and the end.

CHAPTER XXIX

THE MOST PATHETIC IN RUSSIAN HISTORY

I. THE PATIENT SUFFERER JOB

THE three conspicuously ill-fated monarchs, Charles I, Louis XVI, and Nicholas II, were not the worst of men; yet all three, who bore a curious resemblance in their characters, came at a time when the leaders of the people had tired of the principle of monarchy by divine right. All three were feebly pigheaded, very conscious of their divine prerogatives of kingship, very sensible of their personal honor, yet curiously shifty in their dealings with the spokesmen of the people, whom they regarded as self-appointed middlemen thrusting themselves between the sovereign and his subjects whose relations without these meddlesome intermediaries would have remained those of mutual love and unspecified good will.

Their attitude recalls that of the old-world publisher who resented the advent of the literary agent—a newcomer shoving himself between the publisher and his author, whose relations should be one of mutual trust without regard to terms, which the publisher in his paternal wisdom laid down himself and communicated to his charge, whose welfare, he stressed, was the constant concern of his heart. *not Louis XVI !*

These three mild-mannered monarchs—all undersized—paid with their lives for the misdeeds of a long line of fiercer ancestors, because in an age of criticism they defended principles rooted in tyranny without being tyrants enough to enforce their opinions. To survive, they should have been either very elastic, or very strong. As they were advised to be both, and proved to be neither, all three had cause to complain of a sufficiently similar situation resulting in prompt disintegration of the State. "Pity me," writes Charles I to his friend George Radcliffe, "for never came any man to so lost a business. The army altogether unexercised and unprovided of necessaries . . . Our horse all cowardly, the country from Berwick to York in the power of the Scots, a universal affright in all, a general disaffection to the King's service, none sensible to his dishonour. In one word, here alone to fight with all these evils, without anyone to help. God of his goodness deliver me out of this, the greatest evil of my life. Fare you well."

So lost a business, too, was that of Nicholas II that, with himself definitely out of it, he regarded Kerenski, whom Alix had often exhorted him to hang, as now the best man for the job.

It is easy enough to blame Nicholas II. But how is he to blame? His policy, even apart from his character, which was molded by events, was preordained by his ancestors. The assassination of his grandfather Alexander II, when Nicky was but a boy, and the consequent marooning of the family at Gatchina, had implanted in young Nicholas the idea that there was safety within—murder without. His great-grandfather Nicholas I intensified the reaction already inaugurated, as a baleful aftermath to a liberal regime, by his brother Alexander I. Alexander II, who followed, reaped where his father had sown and fell a practical victim of the intellectual's theoretical hatred of tyranny in his very attempt to relax it. His son, Alexander III, who mistrusted his father's flirtations with constitutions and franchise, vindicated his reversion to complete watertight autocracy with "I told you so"; and Nicholas II, utterly bewildered, continued "papa's policy" which during the short time of "papa's" reign had proved successful enough. How, with his experience and the small store of intellect at his command, was he to think otherwise?

Were Peter the Great to arise today from his grave and behold a Russia plowing with motor tractors and learn that the power had passed out of the family's hands to the Soviets, would he be mortified? Not he! "Good riddance!" is a more likely expletive on the part of one who in his battle orders—just before he fled for dear life at the sight of the enemy— scribbled down with emotion: "As for Peter, don't give a thought to him, if only Russia survive!" With the same commendable uplift, Peter, the foremost of Russian revolutionaries, beholding today the Union of Soviet Socialist Republics, would have cried: "More power to their elbows! ... glad myself to have done any little bit towards it—pray, don't mention it!"

Nor would the strait jacket of totalitarianism, the "purges," the intermittent terror, the lack of free speech, or the dreaded Ogpu discomfit Peter's perfect sensibility. The Oprichina of Ivan the Terrible, the Secret Chancery of Peter and Elizabeth, abolished by Peter III and reintroduced under the new name of the Secret Expedition by Catherine II, the Okhrana of the last Tsars, the Cheka, the Ogpu, or for that matter Herr Himmler's Gestapo: by any other name his Secret Chancery would smell to him as sweet!

Nicholas II was soon reconciled to the new—prophetically named— *Temporary* Government. He thought the eloquent Alexander Feodorovitch Kerenski absolutely first-rate. Incorrigible mono-holder to the last, Nicholas opined that Kerenski should have *all* the power: the more the better. And indeed for the few months which divided him from Lenin, Kerenski was increasingly the Self-Upholder—to the extent to which he could precariously uphold his own balance between the reddening Soviets and the Napoleonic General Kornilov already marching on Petrograd to set up a "Directorate."

Kerenski often called on the ex-Emperor and had a nice quiet chat with him. A sincere mutual regard sprang up between the hitherto political miscreant, now luxuriously occupying the imperial suite at the Winter Palace, and the previous hierarchic owner, "Nicholas the Bloody," now a model prisoner in his own accustomed residence at Tsarskoye Selo. They discussed the experience they shared in common—power and how to use it—and the retired ruler gave the younger man a few tips out of his not inconsiderable store of first-hand knowledge.

Kerenski took to the quiet, disarmingly well-mannered ex-Tsar, though, in the interests of the prisoners, he sometimes adopted a peremptory tone to impress on any hostile revolutionary who happened to be about that he was putting Citizen Nikolai Romanov through the mill. The ex-Emperor did not tumble to it till Kerenski explained the precarious nature of his own position in being suspected by the extreme elements of pampering the dynastic captives of the Revolution.

He went so far as to shout at the Tsar in the presence of some very recalcitrant elements who thought that Nicholas was having far too easy a time; then, when they were alone, said softly: "Your Majesty, tell me; have you confidence in me?"

The Tsar, having just had his ears blown off, did not know what to say and remained silent for several minutes; then answered, doubtfully: "Yes."

Nicholas II had been often heard to remark that he was born on the day of the patient sufferer Job and so knew what to expect. His scroll of life, as it unrolled, in this respect confirmed his worst suspicions. He made up in fortitude what he lacked in sense. Divine Providence, he thought, seemed to require from him some great sacrifice. He must redeem in suffering and humiliation some long-standing wrong rooted in the forgotten, perhaps dynastic, past. He must be destroyed to save Russia.

When he read that the Provisional Government had abolished capital punishment, Nicholas assumed that they had done so to spare his life, as there was talk of bringing him before a military tribunal. He wrote to the Government to protest against such mistaken consideration which had the baleful effect of destroying discipline in the army and thus involved the ruin of Russia; whereas he would gladly die to save the fatherland.

Heroic as this sounds, he did not appreciate that his self-centered request for the restoration of the death penalty implied that, besides himself, who was prepared to die for Russia, other men, who were not, would have to die too; whereas they would rather live or, if die they must, die for another kind of Russia—a Russia that did not take for granted their willingness to die for convictions not necessarily shared by themselves.

When the Tsar's cousin King George V offered the family an asylum in England, Nicholas accepted with but little enthusiasm. Since humiliation was evidently his appointed lot, it was more fitting that the Russian Tsar should climb his Golgotha on native soil rather than suffer the more elegant humiliations in store for him at the hands of over-kind relatives at the immaculate Court of St. James's. For the sake of his wife and children he was not averse from embarking for England; but, for their sake also, shrank from exposing them to the same ordeal and so increasing the field of his own. He could imagine the pitying glances of royal relatives striving hard to conceal their inner thoughts. Here he was, their misguided cousin who, because he had flouted their oft-repeated warning, had come to a demonstrably bad end; and there was the bright British throne, resting like a rock on that very Constitution which gloriously deprived it of all absolute power, and that now was taking him, a refugee from his own people, under its wing.   *nonsense*

The fate of the patient sufferer Job would have it that the children should be down with measles while the British invitation stood open— the short interval which coincided with the Provisional Government's permission to leave the country. The German Government, approached through neutral channels, was willing to instruct the U-boat commanders to give the vessel about to carry the Romanov family to England a wide berth.

While the measles were running their course, the authority of the Provisional Government was severely undermined by the Workers' and Soldiers' Soviets, who were all for trying the Emperor for high treason to the people. The Empress had voted for Denmark instead of England, and the Provisional Government was a little afraid lest the emigration of Alexandra Feodorovna, German by birth, to a neutral country might not lead to leakage of military information. In the meantime, Mr. Lloyd George not unnaturally reasoned that the spectacle of Englishmen dispensing hospitality to the discredited Russian monarch at a time when England was urging Russia to make a last stand to save their common democracies, was not politic, to say the least of it. The British Ambassador had the painful duty to inform the Russian Foreign Minister that the invitation was off.

It was because Petrograd was becoming rampantly revolutionary that Kerenski decided for their safety to dispatch the imperial family, who were attracting jeering crowds outside the palace railings at Tsarskoye Selo, into the quiet depths of Siberia, where he presumed they might be forgotten.

There had been at least one abortive attempt on the part of two over-zealous loyal officers to "save" the Tsar and his son. A motorcar drew up in full daylight before Nicholas and the twelve-year-old Aleksei, who sat on a bench near the drive. The two officers who contrived this feather-brain scheme were aged eighteen and nineteen. They were sons of famous generals, pillars of the old regime, and had only just passed out of their respective cadet schools. Their idea had been to motor the Tsar to Siberia, shave off his beard and mustache and hide him in some monastery. When the chauffeur explained that he had neither petrol enough to get from Tsarskoye Selo to Siberia, nor did he know the condition of the roads, nor indeed the way, the initial idea shrank to taking the Tsar to the chauffeur's mother, a peasant woman who lived in a village near Novgorod.

As the car pulled up in the drive and one of the youths sprang out and, running towards the Tsar, shouted excitedly: "Your Majesty!" Nicholas rose apprehensively from the bench on which he had been sitting and stood up, supporting with his arm the ailing Tsarevitch. "Your Majesty!" cried the youth, "jump in, we're going to save you. Jump in with the Tsarevitch!"

The Tsar shook his head.

"Your Majesty, vow to God, we're real Russian people, none of your revolutionary skunks! We are officers of the old school, cross my heart." He made the sign of the Cross. "Jump in, Your Majesty!"

The Emperor, neither reassured by the youth's impulsiveness, nor yet able to see what use it was his trying to get away with his son while leaving in pawn his wife and four daughters, again shook his head. "It does not behove," he said sadly, "a Russian Tsar to flee from his own country. The Russian people will not harm me, for I have never wished them ill."

"Your Majesty! Get in. Hesitation is fatal. We'll come again for the Empress and the Tsarevnas. Only get in."

The Emperor still shook his head. He was deterred by too many doubts. He did not know how far they would get. He may have recalled Louis XVI at Varennes. He thought the whole thing might be an attempt to compromise them—perhaps to get them shot "while attempting to escape." There was the precedent of Tsar Ivan in the Schüsselburg fortress. Or perhaps they were simply to be "taken for a ride and bumped off."

He refused.

The other loyal youth in the car, at last despairing of his pal's intellectual powers of persuasion, poked out his head and shouted: "Take him by force—because Russia sadly needs a Tsar again."

At this the Tsarevitch began to whimper and his father half-turned, as if for protection, to the approaching revolutionary guard. At which the young officer sprang back into the car and they made their escape through the open gate of the park before anyone tumbled to it to stop them.

So ended the abortive attempt on the part of loyalist Russia to save their beloved sovereign.

II. TO SIBERIA

THERE had been a great hurry and flurry in getting away and leaving the home in which they had spent nearly twenty-five years of their lives. It might have been the parting scene from *The Cherry Orchard*. As they were leaving, the Emperor approached uncertainly the colonel in charge of the guard. On a previous occasion he had been snubbed by a revolutionary officer who would not take his proffered hand and, when the Tsar had asked sadly why not, had answered: "You in your time didn't take Russia's proffered hand of friendship; now I, in mine, don't want to take yours."

But this colonel turned out to be an old-timer. The Emperor, before extending his hand to him, said shyly: "Good-by, Colonel. Perhaps it is dangerous for you to shake hands with me."

"No, Your Majesty."

"Well—good-by, good luck—and thank you for everything." A beautiful fair-bearded real Russian face with gray-blue eyes as honest as day looked into his own, says the Colonel, and he felt a lump in his throat.

As they reached the train on a siding some distance from the station of Tsarskoye Selo, they met with ill omen. The Empress in climbing the raised steps of the railway coach fell over on the floor and hurt herself. The train was scheduled for an early hour so as to avoid hostile demonstrations. To see them off was their new friend, the Prime Minister, Alexander Feodorovitch Kerenski. There were delays, but at last the train started on its long trail for Siberia, that very trek taken in the days of the monarchy by the Tsar's political prisoners.

Yet even now Nicholas could not get used to his altered status. He had been guarded too long to notice any appreciable difference in the internal enemy from whom now, as then, he was being protected by detachments of Russian soldiers with drawn bayonets. He still loved Russia; was still devoutly interested in the progress of the war; still wore a simple tunic shirt with a colonel's shoulder straps.

On the long railway journey he is, as always, making daily entries in his diary. His comments have the curiously *uninterested* ring of a diarist who has in childhood acquired the habit of setting down a few random observations each day to please teacher, who thinks it good exercise. He sets down the time the train stood at this or that station; sometimes adds a comment as though for the benefit of the railway or the general public. He reports the walks they took at this or that siding, mentions who came along, who stayed behind; tells of what they had for lunch, but that Alix had a headache and refused the second course.

In this way, as though traveling for their own delectation, they arrived at Tobolsk, and were led under guard, walking like convicts down the middle of the cobbled street: Emperor, Empress, four daughters, one son: to the governor's residence, where they were installed behind a high wooden fence. Nothing could detract from their dignity, of which they were unconscious; nothing humiliate them, as they were not aware of having done anyone any harm. The whole of Russia was still their garden; the whole people, apart from some misinformed spirits, must, they felt, still love them. Owning everything and nothing, reared in a simplicity derived from a position too exalted to appreciate social differences, they were invulnerable to insult. They could be sad, but not ashamed.

From the time the family arrived in Tobolsk, in August 1917, they had another eleven months to live. Until the Bolshevik Revolution in November of the same year, they lived a simple, rather indigent but tolerably peaceful life. The Empress mended the Emperor's trousers, over and over again; and darned the girls' stockings and turned their coats. But they still had their own palace chef with them, their family physician, their French-Swiss tutor, an aide-de-camp, Prince Dolgorukov, and a few attendants. Local nuns and merchants' wives brought them all kinds of delicacies to sweeten their exile.

At first the soldiers detailed to guard them were surly, but on getting to know them could not resist the simple charm of their exalted prisoners now down on their luck. In the garden, sentries waited to congratulate the Emperor on his name day; he in his turn congratulated them on their regimental feast day. The ex-Tsar was discovered sitting in the guard room, playing draughts with the soldiers. He worried a lot about Russian reverses in the field and rejoiced with all his heart at the news of any spurious victory. He spent the mornings with his son, teaching him Russian history, and notes in his diary that they had just finished doing Peter the Great.

As the winter months approached, the girls staged little comedies, and the Tsar sets down in his diary that he is copying out their parts for his daughters Olga and Maria from Chekhov's one-act farce, *The Bear*. Chekhov had been dead thirteen years and could never have guessed that one day the inaccessible Self-Upholder would turn copyist and transcribe with that small hand of his, which had signed not a few death-warrants, the lines of one of his most trivial pieces.

With the Bolshevik Revolution in November, the family began to feel the pinch. Food became scarce. Their liberties were severely curtailed, the friendly sentries were changed, and the inmates were shorn of most of their staff. The Tsar chopped wood in the yard, to the derision of the sentries. The family took their accustomed walk together within the high wooden fence. The new guards did not let them out of their sight, got drunk and offensive. But, like the former lot, they all ended by taking a liking to their prisoners, relaxed the new irksome rules and grew friendly.

Then came disconcerting news. They were to be moved again: rumor had it—to Moscow. The Tsar felt uneasy. The Tsaritsa shared his anxiety. Nicky, Alix said, was required in Moscow to put his signature to the Treaty of Brest-Litovsk. Without his signature the treaty was obviously invalid. That is how it struck them. Lenin and Trotski, said the Tsar, found themselves in this respect in a quandary, and would use all their wiles to get round him. He would of course refuse to put his hand to so shameful a document, having pledged himself to the Allies not to conclude a separate peace. Now that the first oath he made at the Ouspenski Cathedral not to renounce the autocracy had unfortunately gone by the board, *this* was without doubt the most binding of his oaths. Besides, had he not—though that did not perhaps greatly matter, since they were but his subjects—pledged himself before his people not to make peace while there was a single German soldier left on Russian soil? And now there seemed *millions*. He would, in short, have nothing to do with this treaty.

But if he refused to comply with their wishes, the Soviet might retaliate by penalizing his family; and what could he do then?

He was very worried. When his aide-de-camp, General Prince Dolgorukov, suggested that it might be Kaiser Wilhelm who had insisted, as the first condition of granting an armistice, that the Tsar be handed over to him, Nicholas was painfully struck with this idea. He was quite sure, he said, looking very grave, that this was in order to humiliate him.

When Dolgorukov explained he meant the Kaiser was trying to save the Tsar and his family, Nicholas said that this was worse still: it was an insult.

They had never, any of them, liked the Kaiser, a man of overbearing good will, demanding nothing but mutual love—but *demanding* it! On his own terms: when nobody would have his love at any price. William II, who loved George V and loved Nicholas II, was loved neither by Nicholas II nor by George V. The Kaiser's attitude to his crowned relatives was curiously like that of Prussia itself to the rest of Germany—upstart and overbearing. He had been sincerely desirous of uniting Europe in the face of the Yellow Peril, but his relatives evidently preferred the Yellow Peril to the Kaiser. He was perhaps cleverer than they who, by dint of a becoming modesty, hard work and a disdain of histrionics, attracted more sympathy. Besides, the Kaiser's cleverness was so feeble that it would have passed unnoticed in any but a royal person. He was opinionated, not privately, like George V, or secretly, like Nicholas II, but publicly; and he had nothing of George V's admirable monarchical discretion which appeared to reconcile *all* his subjects' opinions instead of, like Wilhelm, merely betraying his own.

Wilhelm had done such strange things. While a guest on the Tsar's new steam yacht, the Kaiser had expressed to him the wish to be given it *as a present*. Another day he practically demanded to be made Colonel of the Grodno Hussars—to the complete mortification of the Empress Mother, who bitterly disliked the Kaiser and wrote to Nicky that "papa" had cherished that regiment and she was heartbroken. During a fire which had devastated a Polish village on the Russian side of the frontier, the

Kaiser took the Tsar by surprise with the awkward request to be allowed to go and distribute personally 10,000 roubles to the villagers, and, receiving the Tsar's polite consent, actually asked him to give him the money. Nicholas complied with amazement.

On the other hand, the Kaiser was strangely lachrymose. Boarding the Russian yacht to conclude with Nicky a treaty of alliance, annulled overnight by their respective Foreign Ministers, Willy, reversing the position of Frederick William III and Alexander I over the coffin of Frederick the Great, was seized with emotion and cried on Nicky's shoulder from an excess of beatitude. "The Admiral of the Atlantic," he signaled from his own yacht, on departure, "salutes the Admiral of the Pacific." Nicholas, who did not want to offend the susceptibilities of his cousin George V, signaled back: "Greetings. Farewell."

Nicholas and Alexandra had also resented how, on the occasion of their official visit to Berlin, the German Empress took leave of the Russian at the palace instead of seeing her off at the station. These crowned heads were, on their own level, as sensitive to snubs as any of their subjects.

No, he had never liked Wilhelm, and all through the war considered that the break was final. When the Tsar's Minister of the Court, Count Frederiks, brought him a letter he had received from his opposite number in Germany, a flowery letter sounding for a reconciliation between the two houses and a separate peace between the two countries, Nicholas told him to read the letter aloud; but at once interrupted him. "Translate into Russian," he ordered. "I don't understand the German language any more." At a reference to the ties of blood and friendship that had united the two dynasties for a couple of centuries, Nicholas had remarked: "All that is dead and buried now."

His reluctance at this lowest ebb in his fortunes to be saved by one whom he had never liked even in the days of equality, becomes understandable. Wilhelm was clearly one of those relatives that we would rather die than be saved by—relatives who may yet entertain the best of intentions towards us, but who combine with a heart of gold a manner that betrays a limited sensibility. The Kaiser's solicitude on his behalf, at a moment when Russia lay prostrate at the feet of Germany, could not appeal to the Tsar, who preferred to remain a prisoner of his own people.

As rumored, a mysterious agent—a Commissar by name Yakovlev—had arrived from Moscow with orders to remove the Tsar and his family. As the Tsarevitch was too ill to travel, it was decided that the Empress and her third daughter, Maria, should accompany the Tsar, and the rest of the family await the Tsarevitch's recovery.

This Yakovlev proved to be a man endowed with a quick brain and suave manners, who deferred to the imperial family. Though he would not disclose on whose instructions he was acting, or where he was taking them, his chief anxiety seemed to be to get his charges past the obstructing local authorities, who queried his instructions and tried to intercept their passage at every point on the journey. They traveled in peasant carts, narrowly escaping drowning when in fording a river their front axle suddenly broke. Their escort struck with their swords at the horses, which, brutally urged forward, just managed to pull the cart ashore.

At Tiumen they boarded the train for Moscow, but were stopped at Ekaterinburg by the local Soviet, who would not let the Tsar out of their custody. They never got to Moscow.

III.   EKATERINBURG

A PLAUSIBLE theory, in a morass of conjecture of which all the threads seem to have been purposely buried, is that the German Imperial Government which, in those early months of 1918, had the Soviet Government pretty well in their power, had insisted on the extradition of the Russian imperial family. If one places oneself without prejudice in the position of a weak Soviet Government, harried on all sides by White Guards supported by the various Allied Governments, pressed into capitulation by an implacable German Government, whose demands they dare not resist for all that they realize only too clearly that in surrendering the Tsar and his family to the enemy they are throwing away the precariously established Workers' and Soldiers' Republic and giving the dynasty a new lease of life—then one begins to see that what in fact they did was, from their own point of view, an expedient measure.

On the one hand, they were instructing Commissar Yakovlev to bring the Tsar to Moscow in order to hand him over to the German Government, at the special request of goodhearted Kaiser Wilhelm, naturally anxious to save the lives of his relatives. On the other hand, to save their faces, they were going to make it appear that the local Soviet at Ekaterinburg had disobeyed orders and "liquidated" the family. They were sorry, but couldn't do anything more about it.

The Kaiser does nowhere, to my knowledge, speak of his efforts to save the Tsar and his family. There may be reasons for such reticence.

The man who fired the first shot at the Emperor began by reading him the order of the Ural Soviets. "Your relatives tried to save you," he said, "but they have failed."

The Tsar's English relatives had long since given up the attempt. His own Russian relatives were for the most part in prison, and the reference points to the German relatives, the only relatives who at the time were in a position to apply any pressure to the Soviet Government.

Attenuating this conjecture of disobeyed orders, there is the possibility of the local Soviet detaining on their own initiative the dynastic travelers because they suspected Yakovlev of being an agent of a foreign power trying to smuggle the Romanovs out of Russia. A step dangerous to the communist-international, because favorable to the international-monarchist, ideology.

In tracing motives one is apt to overstate the force of intentions. The Moscow Central Executive may at first have only intended that the Ural Soviet should resist the extradition. The German request may have been a pious hope that the Soviet Government would "see their way clear to releasing, etc." The decision to execute the family may not have been taken till the very eve of the fall of Ekaterinburg to the Czech legionaries who were fighting the Bolsheviks all along the railway. Even then the Ekaterinburg Soviet may have acted without reference to Moscow. The documents available are not conclusive.

However that may be, Ekaterinburg, where they arrived in the last days of April, is the journey's end. They were taken to a house requisitioned from a merchant—by name Ipatiev, and the Commissar in charge, Avdeyev, signed a receipt for them which reads like a bill of lading:

> Received as follows:—
> 1 ex-tsar Nikolai Romanov and
> wife Alexandra Feodorovna
> 1 daughter Maria Nikolaievna.

In saying "tsar," not sovereign or emperor, he was unconsciously giving expression to the popular feeling that they had uprooted something more parasitical, more deeply embedded in Russian life than Peter's innovation of 1772.

Ipatiev House, the last residence of the dynasty, is a strange coincidence with Ipatiev Monastery in Moscow where Mihaïl, the first Romanov, 305 years previously, was taking refuge from the Poles who intended to kill

This is interesting and True coincidence

him to prevent his ascending the Russian throne, already on offer to the Polish crown.

Presently the rest of the family, with the Tsarevitch, joined them, at which reunion there was much rejoicing. The Emperor and Empress were relieved that they were not going to Moscow to sign any treaty, nor to be handed over to Germany, which would have branded them as traitors and confirmed the unfounded suspicions current during the closing months of the war that the Empress was a German spy in league with Rasputin.

The Emperor and Empress, as they had never done in their days of supreme power, now, in those closing weeks, enter the tender realm of the imagination. Between the first days of May 1918, when they were installed in Ipatiev House, known officially as "The House of Special Purpose," and the middle of July, when they met their fate, their life radiates a fitful glow of beauty, tapped at those dolorous springs of light, never far to seek for the divining heart, which whisper that the meek shall inherit the earth.

Their pathos is that of two people who had never done anything right, who had flouted a wealth of good advice and come to the bad end predicted by their wise counselors but who, rather than be saved by them and exposed to justifiable homilies, preferred death to dishonor. These two incorrigible innocents, these two babes-in-the-wood, now that night was upon them, turned tearfully to each other and said they did not mind: it was better so, though very fearful it was, better to perish in the wood than to be found and chided by unfeeling grown-ups who did not understand. "Better die in Russia than be humiliated abroad," was what they said to each other.

They were now being exposed to every indignity they had been spared before. Avdeyev, the house superintendent, avoided no opportunity of exerting his irksome authority. Their private belongings were searched over and over again, after which jewelry and valuables were found to be missing. There was a constant guard of ten soldiers inside the house spying on all their movements. The Red guards would get drunk, sing ribald songs. Obscene descriptions appeared on the walls of the bedroom occupied by the Tsar's four young daughters. The men insisted that they had instructions not to let the prisoners out of their sight. Even the lavatory door was ordered to be left open, and the soldiers made caustic remarks.

The Tsar bore everything without complaint. Only once, provoked beyond endurance, he muttered: "Till recently we had to deal with gentlemen. But now—the devil knows what . . ."

He was warned that he was not an autocrat any more, but a prisoner of the people, and if he said another word they would separate him from his family.

The Emperor, a model of patience, notes in his diary that they are living as in prison now. With that characteristic touch of his, as of a simple man assured of his own common sense (as, in 1910, he had commented that people were making far too much fuss over the death of Tolstoy), he now notes that, after two weeks' deliberations and innumerable visits of inspection, six Soviet officials have at last decided which window the family may keep open.

Every evening before going to bed they played dominoes. The Emperor read a great deal. He notes in his diary that he is reading a *Life of the Emperor Paul*. "*Most* interesting!" he finds it.

The four daughters, between the ages of twenty-two and fifteen, slept all in one room on the floor. Sometimes in the middle of the night drunken guards would stagger into their bedroom, wake them up and make them play the piano and sing with them, changing the words of the song to give it a ribald meaning.

The Tsarevitch, now thirteen, was intermittently confined to bed. He had a treasured miracle-working ikon hanging over his head on a thin golden chain, which Avdeyev in a vicious mood snapped and chucked aside. Ever since he was little the Tsarevitch had a sailor, by name Nagorni, assigned to him as his orderly—a sort of male nurse who looked after him and carried him when the boy was unable to walk. This sailor had followed them voluntarily into exile. Shocked by Avdeyev's brutality in tearing down the ikon, the sailor gave vent to his feelings.

The same day he disappeared. One by one all their staff was taken away from them. There remained only their house surgeon, Dr. Botkin, two menservants and the maid Demidova. Food was now brought from a workers' soup kitchen. The house superintendent sat down with them, helping himself to the largest chunks of meat floating in the stew. Once, as if inadvertently, Avdeyev at table struck the Emperor in the face with his elbow.

The Tsar lapsed into a state outwardly bordering on apathy, described by Avdeyev as "idiotic indifference," inwardly transfigured by a religious quiescence. He sat for hours in a chair without moving. His reading was often a pretext for being left alone for meditation. So the weeks went by, and they had reached mid-summer.

But as twice before at Tobolsk, here again the guards were disarmed by the meek simplicity of their prisoners. They recoiled with compunction from their own acts, relaxed their vigilance, in the end even strove to make themselves useful. Strangest of all, Avdeyev himself succumbed to the disarming resignation, the complete "non-resistance to evil" of his captives, whom in the past he had tried, yet in vain, to provoke. He became so friendly that the Ural Soviet displaced him from his post for fear that he might connive at the escape of his charges.

IV. THE END

TWELVE days before the end, Ipatiev House was taken over by the local Cheka. Avdeyev and the Russian soldiers were replaced by a detachment of Letts speaking an incomprehensible tongue and impervious to the winning charm of the Russian imperial family.

The man now in charge of the house was one Yurovski, head of the local Cheka, a man who before he became the Tsar's executioner had been a dentist, a watchmaker and a male nurse.

Of the incomplete and contradictory versions of the end of the family, versions which have been pieced together from circumstantial evidence, that of the official pre-revolutionary investigator Sokolov seems the most convincing. It must be borne in mind that, only a few weeks after the assassination of the family, Ekaterinburg fell into the hands of the Whites, before which day all the Reds who had taken part in the execution had disappeared. Moreover, Sokolov could barely get going with his investigation before the town fell back into the hands of the Reds.

His reconstruction of the scene is largely based on the evidence of intimidated witnesses giving a third-hand account of what they had been told by others. On the other hand, a paper purporting to be a description of the scene by one of the executioners no longer alive and found on another man after he had been executed by the Whites, though even more brutal and gruesome, bears traces of fabrication.

The last two weeks of the family are of the stuff of expiation, of redemption from sin in suffering, almost a break with life in Time, the preparation of half-transfigured souls for the life eternal. They are moving, as though unaware of space, in a mystic light, sustained from a remote and unknown source. They seem no longer of this world, but to be conscious, as those not far removed from their end are conscious, of the future life hovering about them and ready to receive them. They forgave all their tormentors. They embraced all the promises and consolations inherent in the Christian faith. With no less a sincerity than the virgins of old, the four girls, cut off in their prime from the visible world which had beguiled their dawn, only to turn mercilessly upon them, embroidered all their hopes of sweetness and purity into a dreamy pattern of the life to come. Olga, the eldest, copied religious poems. Tatiana yearned for a quiet nunnery in which to end her days. The Tsaritsa and the younger girls sang psalms and said their prayers together.

It does not appear from what we know that they were told of their impending execution, which in any case may have been conditional upon whether or not the Czechs succeeded in taking the town. Their knowledge of their near end seems to have been an inner knowledge. Three days before the night which ended their existence, a priest and deacon of the Orthodox Church were called in to celebrate Mass. In the course of the liturgy recur the beautiful words from the funeral service: "Lay to rest with the saints." The deacon, to the consternation of the priest, began to chant these words, which he should have slurred over. An extraordinary thing then happened. The whole family with their attendants, eleven people in all, as though by a sign, fell on their knees, praying fervently.

They all looked wan, their faces thin and transparent, and the Tsar's blond beard of late showed streaks of gray.

On the night of July 16, soon after midnight, they were awakened and told to get ready. There were disorders in the town. An anarchist rising was expected. So they were told. They were to be conveyed to a place of safety.

They dressed hurriedly and gulped down their tea. There was some rattling noise outside, as though of a lorry backfiring. Then the tramp of soldiers entering a first-floor room at the back, the sound of the butts of rifles coming down heavily on the wooden floor at the "Order Arms."

Ipatiev House was built on a slope, the front of the first floor being level with the street, while at the back the ground floor opened on to a yard. The back room is therefore sometimes described as a cellar.

Dressed and ready to start on their journey preparatory to entering on another stage of their exile, the family filed into this room in which chairs had been placed alongside the wall. One can see them entering in a row. The Emperor and Empress sit down. He has his invalid son of thirteen on his knee. The maid Demidova places a cushion at the back of the Empress's chair. She also holds a pillow in which are hidden some of the most treasured family jewels. Olga, the eldest, is now twenty-two, a young girl of a pronounced Slavonic type of features with a contralto voice. Tatiana is just twenty, a dreamy, romantic girl who, if things had gone differently, might easily have married her second cousin, the Prince of Wales, and been Queen of England. During the war she helped her mother to run a hospital at Tsarskoye Selo. The nurses took care to admit only the most presentable officers. Anybody who was disfigured was sent elsewhere. Repulsive cases were barred for fear of offending the susceptibilities of the youthful Grand Duchesses. A reasonable wound in the leg or the arm sustained by a romantic-looking youth was a clear case for Her Imperial Majesty's Hospital at Tsarskoye Selo. The Princesses would assist their mother, who would herself dress the wound.

After all, she had studied medicine as a girl. The Empress, to complete her vision of herself as a sister of mercy whose quality was not strained, dispensed with rank and titles and ordered her patients to call her "Sister Alexandra." Her daughters were called Sister Olga and Sister Tatiana. Whenever the patient looked particularly handsome and lovable, the head nurse would say: "Sister Alexandra, I think this case needs your attention." The Empress, assisted by Sister Tatiana, would perform a small operation; and afterwards the handsome young patient, recovering consciousness, would see Sister Tatiana sitting at his bedside and hear her inquiring how he felt. It would all seem a dream; the white nurse's apparel hiding her sacred loveliness... and he was in love. When he was better he joined the throng of convalescents who, sitting round a table with the youthful Grand Duchesses, their hands linked, were playing a game called "rouble." The young officer, now hopelessly in love, would sit beside Tatiana. A sense of sweet conspiracy would unite them. She would pass the silver rouble warmed by her divine hands into his own. When his wound healed, he would go out again to the front, ready to die for her; she would perhaps press a parting kiss on his forehead with her exquisite lips....

Maria, the Tsar's third daughter, is now seventeen, and is the beauty of the family. She has that slight plumpness which, when it wears off, will leave her a perfect beauty in face and limb. She is also the most healthy and level-headed of the four sisters. The last, Anastasia, named in honor of the first Anastasia Romanov who married Ivan the Terrible and started the Romanovs on their royal trail, is a little frail and mischievous and given to practical jokes. During a railway journey she once concealed herself on the rack and from there poured water on the head of a resplendent adjutant general seated beneath.

There they stood and sat as though in a waiting room, when Yurovski came in and informed the Tsar that he would now bring in the escort to accompany them on the journey. In marched eleven Lett soldiers armed with revolvers, rifles and fixed bayonets who ranged themselves along the opposite wall. Presently Voikov, of the Ekaterinburg Soviet, came in with a paper in his hand. Facing the Tsar he began to read in a solemn voice a declaration signed by the local Soviet to the effect that the Tsar and his family had been condemned to death. Before, however, he managed to come to the crucial sentence, Yurovski impatiently snatched the paper out of his hand and said, addressing the Tsar:

"Nikolai Aleksandrovitch, your relatives abroad have been trying to save you, but they have failed, and I have orders from the Ekaterinburg Soviet to shoot you and your family."

The Emperor, who stood up, supporting his son with one hand, was visibly taken aback. "What?" he asked. The Tsar was obviously more horrified on his family's account than on his own. The same moment Yurovski raised his revolver to the Tsar's forehead at close range and fired. The Tsar fell to the floor.

This was the signal for the carnage which followed. The eleven Lett soldiers, ranged along the opposite wall, each took aim at one of the eleven prisoners. Apart from the seven members of the family, Dr. Botkin, the two menservants and the maid Demidova were included in the execution. Evidently the Revolution was no respecter of persons. The Empress fell down, clutching as she writhed in convulsions at the feet of her invalid boy who, though the most delicate of them all and addicted to haemophilia, took longest to die. The maid Demidova, who held the pillow with the jewels inside, ran screaming hither and thither along the wall, avoiding the bullets fired at her and screening herself with the pillow as though it were a shield. They rushed at her with their bayonets, and she fell to the floor. Olga, Tatiana and Maria lay dead. Anastasia, the youngest, barely fifteen, had fallen in a swoon, and when she recovered she saw ten bodies lying around her. She began to scream and was killed. Her little dog stood yapping over her body, till they finished him, too.

It is vain to ask why such things are done. It is vain to blame the form of government. The Whites executed Yurovski's whole family and everyone else they could get hold of, their sisters and mothers and daughters, as innocent and as afraid to die as any mortal. It is vain to plead "historical necessity." It is these historical necessities which, by placing distant objectives above the suffering unit, are to blame for the long and heartless tomfoolery of history. It is indeed not they who see nothing in history to justify the crime against the individual who lack "seriousness of purpose," but rather they who, intoxicated by political abstractions, condone these things. For the "seriousness" lies not in the capacity for taking "the long view," to which the future forever gives the lie, but in gentleness, in mercy, in not harming the human being, in not executing four innocent young girls, since, though "ideologies" may be argued about, one need only to have seen the four girls alive before seeing them dead to be convinced, without any recourse to metaphysics, that it cannot be right.

These things do not square with the sense of life that we carrry about with us. They do not make sense on a rational, moral or any other showing; and the irretrievable fool is he who attempts to justify these things on a basis of tit for tat, of criminal reciprocity: who attempts to justify Peter the Great on expansionist grounds, or to justify lunatic savagery on any grounds whatsoever. They who would justify things like these for the sake of problematic liberty in the abstract, and in the future at that, are lunatics, mental deficients. They see no connection in crime. They think time a reality which washes away all bloody stains. They are mistaken. It is all connected: innocence paying in its own blood and the blood lapping back to the mystic principle which will not be flouted, the principle which requires the Many to love one another where all are One, and any judgment other than this a blasphemy, a dolorous dislocation of motive traceable all down the reeking pages of history.

"Judge not, that ye be not judged," is a tenet which gives the measure of the super-sensible life on which this world is trying vainly to model itself. *Judge not:* and if it is wrong to judge, how much more so to reinforce one's judgment by thrusting hard steel into the delicate and complicated human organism, for the sake of solidarity of opinion as to the mere machinery of the political future. Christ's tenet sets the mark on the whole failure of man to build a workable kingdom. Simply stated, it is a premonition of a law that is of another world, a world in which idiotic battles of Austerlitz are not considered historical necessities, to be seriously written about by professors. The flouting of this tenet in our

world, while we try to set up as our model a caricature of the next, does not end with the earlier Romanovs; nor indeed with Napoleon wondering in exile which of his was the finer piece, Jena or Austerlitz; nor yet with Mussolini, who considers the absence of slaughter detrimental to culture; nor certainly with Hitler, who confesses to feel nothing for the individual, only for masses and "ideologies." That new-fangled word which, as somebody has said, is neither a religion nor a philosophy, being too worldly to be a religion and too foolish to be a philosophy. And, indeed, they are not the last; you will see many more such sorry fools: the brutal absurdity of the 1,000 years here briefly sketched in cannot end abruptly.

Was it worth while?

It was not worth a single soldier's elbow grease in polishing a leather strap, let alone having his intestines gouged out by another's bayonet on the field of this or that battle, whose nature and whose purpose I have had my work cut out to unravel and whose result on all counts is *nil*. There is no hope for man unless he ceases to think of the good of Man. There is no hope unless he stops doing evident tangible and immediate evil for the deferred hypothetical general good. The curse of history! The repercussion will not cease. It were better for him, cynic that he is, if he planned deferred universal perdition and on the quiet did only good. With no "ideologies," no mistaken love of Russia, Nicholas I would not have called the poet Rileyev to the Winter Palace and said to him: "I am sending you from here straight to the gallows." And the sight of eleven people breathing and speaking in a house at Ekaterinburg would have deterred others from doing what, to the unsophisticated mind unable to appreciate that he who sticks a blade through you is merely taking "the long view," is still inconceivable, difficult to believe.

The profound thinker in all ages recognizes that this half-world offers no solution to our problems. All the solutions are vested in another world, which is whole; and only in so far as our deeds and thoughts here reflect that other life, of which they are the true denizens, do we touch reality and for a space are lifted over the quagmires and the shifting sands of this sad, queer twilight of existence.

INDEX

INDEX